Human Resources Administration

Human Resources Administration

Personnel Issues and Needs in Education

L. Dean Webb
Arizona State University

M. Scott Norton
Arizona State University

Merrill
Prentice Hall

Upper Saddle River, New Jersey
Columbus, Ohio

Library of Congress Cataloging-in-Publication Data
Webb, L. Dean.
   Human resources administration: personnel issues and needs in education / L. Dean
Webb, M. Scott Norton.—4th ed.
     p. cm.
  Includes bibliographical references and indexes.
  ISBN 0-13-042325-4
    1. School personnel management—United States. I. Norton, M. Scott. II. Title.

LB 2831.58 .W43 2003
371.2′01′0973—dc21   2002023514

Vice President and Publisher: Jeffery W. Johnston
Executive Editor: Debra A. Stollenwerk
Editorial Assistant: Mary Morrill
Associate Editor: Jessica Crouch
Production Editor: Linda Hillis Bayma
Production Coordination: WordCrafters Editorial Services, Inc.
Design Coordinator: Diane C. Lorenzo
Cover Designer: Jason Moore
Production Manager: Pamela D. Bennett
Director of Marketing: Ann Castel Davis
Marketing Manager: Krista Groshong
Marketing Cordinator: Tyra Cooper

This book was set in Zapf International by Carlisle Communications, Ltd. It was printed and
bound by R.R. Donnelley & Sons Company. The cover was printed by Phoenix Color Corp.

Pearson Education Ltd.
Pearson Education Australia Pty. Limited
Pearson Education Singapore Pte. Ltd.
Pearson Education North Asia Ltd.
Pearson Education Canada, Ltd.
Pearson Educación de Mexico, S.A. de C.V.
Pearson Education—Japan
Pearson Education Malaysia Pte. Ltd.
Pearson Education, *Upper Saddle River, New Jersey*

10 9 8 7 6 5 4 3 2 1
ISBN 0-13-042325-4

Dedicated to
Brian, Gregory, Randall, and Pamela,
the children of Scott Norton,
and to
Madeline K. McDaniel

Preface

Public education in the United States is a labor-intensive enterprise. Personnel costs make up 75% to 85% of the typical school district budget. Because personnel are so important to the achievement of the goals and objectives of an educational system, human resources administration is of central importance. How individuals are recruited, selected, evaluated, motivated, compensated, and aided in their development is a factor in determining their personal and professional satisfaction and performance.

Human resources administrators can be successful if they have not only gained an adequate knowledge of specifics, such as relevant laws and policies, the application of computer technology, or successful collective negotiation strategies, but also have developed and integrated planning processes and communication systems and, perhaps most important, fostered a relationship of mutual respect and cooperation among the staff, administration, and school board.

TEXT ORGANIZATION

The text consists of 14 chapters that address all the traditional topics in human resources administration, along with the most current concerns in the field. The two chapters in Part One describe the development of human resources administration and explore its present functioning in the organizational context of the school system. The five chapters that make up Part Two deal with the various environmental and contextual factors within which the human resources function. The six chapters in Part Three discuss the various human resources tasks and processes. The final chapter, included in Part Four, discusses the projected role of the human resources function in the coming decade.

Each chapter begins with a list of learning objectives, which serves as an advance organizer for the chapter. Discussion questions at the end of each chapter address the topics discussed in the chapter and are designed to allow students the opportunity to demonstrate their understanding of the material presented in the chapter and to apply it to real-life situations. Case studies in each chapter not only provide students the opportunity to apply chapter concepts to realistic situations in the workplace, but also provide the stimulus for discussion of complex and controversial issues. Finally, the text contains numerous charts, figures, and tables that serve both as visual organizers and to enrich and illustrate chapter content.

Human Resources Administration is intended for students, human resources administrators, educational administrators, professional educators, policymakers, social scientists, and the interested public. The material in each chapter reflects the most accepted concepts found in the research and literature on that chapter's topic. In addition to establishing a strong research base, consideration has been given to presenting principles that are relevant across all school systems and all states. Where appropriate, actual illustrations and examples from school districts are included.

NEW TO THIS EDITION

This edition of *Human Resources Administration* represents a major revision of the previous edition. Important new material has been included in a new chapter that addresses future issues in human resources administration. At the same time, following the suggestion of reviewers, the chapter on historical aspects has been reduced and the chapter on performance appraisal expanded to more fully address administrator appraisal. Also at the suggestion of reviewers, the law and policy chapters have been placed together and the content more fully integrated. Throughout this text, all material included in the previous edition has been revised, and, as appropriate, the application of technology to the human resources function being addressed is discussed. In addition, new tables and figures have been added, which serve as visual organizers for chapter content and add to the text's visual appeal. Finally, new to this edition is a glossary, which will help students to better understand key concepts.

ACKNOWLEDGMENTS

We wish to express appreciation to the many people who contributed to the publication of this book. We would like to thank our reviewers for their helpful suggestions: Richard Bartholome, Whittier College; Christina M. Dawson, Virginia Tech; Robert Decker, University of Northern Iowa; Randy J. Dunn, Southern Illinois University; Catherine H. Glascock, Ohio University; and Louis Wildman, California State University, Bakersfield.

Finally, we wish to acknowledge our editor, Debbie Stollenwerk, for her support and assistance in the completion of the project.

L. Dean Webb
M. Scott Norton
Tempe, Arizona

Brief Contents

Contents

7 Collective Bargaining and the Human Resources Function: Working with Employee Groups   206

12 The Compensation Process 396

13 The Support Personnel Program 436

Human Resources Administration

Past, Present, and Future

1 Human Resources Administration

Past to Present

Learning
Objectives

After reading this chapter, you will be able to:

■ Compare human resources administration prior to 1900 with personnel administration after 1900.

■ Identify the major principles of the scientific management movement.

■ List some of the key themes associated with the human relations movement.

■ Describe the major contributions of Frederick Herzberg and Douglas McGregor to the behavioral science movement.

■ Explain some of the major core concepts of the postmodern deconstructionist movement.

E ducation is inextricably related to the social, political, and economic influences of its time; its human resources function is no exception. The progress realized in the development of human resources administration is in part a history of education. This chapter presents a historical perspective of human resources administration and discusses some of the concepts and people that have influenced contemporary personnel practices. First, however, we will answer a question: What is human resources administration?

HUMAN RESOURCES ADMINISTRATION DEFINED

One of the earliest definitions of personnel administration was given by Tead and Metcalf (1920), who defined personnel administration as "the direction and coordination of the human relations of any organization with a view to getting the maximum necessary production with a minimum of effort and friction, and with proper regard for the genuine well being of the workers" (p. 2). Tead and Metcalf's text, *Personnel Administration, Its Principles and Practices*, was one of the first works devoted exclusively to personnel. Its publication in 1920 came at a time when the scientific management movement discussed later in this chapter was waning.

Almost half a century later, Stahl (1962) succinctly described personnel administration as "the totality of concern with the human resources of the organization" (p. 15). At about the same time Van Zwoll (1964) defined personnel administration as "the complex of specific activities distinctly engaged in by the employing agency (school district, other unit of government, or business enterprise) to make a pointed effort to secure the greatest possible worker effectiveness consistent with the agency's objectives" (p. 3).

More contemporary definitions of the human resources function are those set forth by Rebore (2001) and Castetter and Young (2000), whose definitions are framed in terms of the goals and purposes of human resources administration. According to Rebore (2001), the goals of the personnel function are "basically the same in all school systems—to hire, retain, develop, and motivate personnel in order to achieve the objectives of the school district, to assist individual members of the staff to reach the highest possible levels of achievement, and to maximize the career development of personnel" (p. 11).

Castetter and Young's (2000) definition closely resembles that of Rebore; that is, the goals of the human resources function are to attract, develop, retain, and motivate personnel in order to (a) achieve the system's mission; (b) assist members to achieve position and work unit standards of performance; (c) maximize the career development of every employee; and (d) reconcile individual and organizational objectives.

All these definitions of human resources administration express the comprehensiveness of the human resources function in education, as well as the basic concept that "schools are people." People, therefore, are a primary concern of human resources administration.

For the purposes of this text, **human resources administration** is defined as those processes that are planned and implemented in the organization to establish an effective system of human resources and to foster an organizational climate that enhances the accomplishment of educational goals. This view emphasizes human resources administration as a foundational function for an effective educational program. The primary elements of the human resources processes, implied in the definition, are recruiting, selecting, and developing staff, as well as establishing a harmonious working relationship among personnel. Although this definition emphasizes the human element, it also states that the focus of human resources administration is on achieving the goals and objectives of the system. This focus includes a major concern for developing a healthy organizational climate that promotes the accomplishment of school goals and the meeting of the personnel needs of school employees.

HUMAN RESOURCES ADMINISTRATION PRIOR TO 1900

Human resources administration as we know it today did not exist prior to 1900. Prior to 1900, employers assumed responsibility for personnel matters in the business and industrial sectors, in most cases delegating some of this function to frontline supervisors or foremen. The *line boss* generally took charge of such personnel activities as hiring, rating, on-the-job training, and firing. No professional group existed that was concerned with the practice of management.

In the educational arena, select lay committees assumed responsibility for personnel duties in the school. Parents and religious groups were reluctant to trust the proper education of their children to persons outside the home or church. The title *selectmen* was commonly bestowed on these early control groups, which consisted largely of local influential and religious officers (Lucio & McNeil, 1969). Selectmen exercised tight control over the policies of the school, the supervision of the subjects taught, and the personal habits of the teacher. Although they knew little about education, these select committees were not reticent to criticize, make suggestions, or recommend the dismissal of an "incompetent" teacher.

The slow development of professional leadership in education before the turn of the 19th century contributed to the administrative authority of the select committees. The first city superintendent was not appointed until 1837. Even as late as 1870, only 29 districts in the country had appointed superintendents of schools. Initially, these individuals were vested with responsibility for the curriculum and given limited authority for personnel. In 1870, the National Association of School Superintendents, which had been formed in 1866, merged with the National Teachers' Association and the American Normal School Association to form the National Education Association (NEA) (Fenner, 1945).

While the city or district superintendent had limited authority in matters affecting personnel during this period, the county superintendency had a great deal of influence on personnel activities, both before 1900 and for some time afterward. This was a significant office in most states from 1850 to 1925. Delaware is credited with having the first recorded county superintendent, as early as 1829 (AASA, 1952). By 1879, 34 of the 38 states plus four territories had created the office of county superintendent (Newsom, 1932).

Teaching staffs in the 19th century, and for some years after, were marginally prepared for their tasks. Many elementary school teachers had only a high school education, with no formal teacher training. Although the 2-year normal school was well established in the last quarter of the 19th century, much of the teacher training was accomplished through other means, primarily the **teacher institutes** operated by the county superintendent. In fact, part of the importance of the county superintendency comes from the fact that the teacher institutes were operated by this office. The county teacher institute provided the majority of in-service training for teachers.

However, toward the end of the 19th century, as urban populations increased and public high schools evolved in greater numbers, the work of the county superintendent was gradually assumed by local supervisors, and the growing number of teacher training programs assumed greater responsibility for the initial and in-service training of teachers. Nonetheless, the county superintendent continued to serve many of the smaller school districts and maintained limited responsibilities for larger districts for several years after 1900.

PERSONNEL ADMINISTRATION AFTER 1900: PERSONNEL DUTIES BECOME MORE CENTRALIZED

During the latter part of the 19th century, various forms of personnel departments began to emerge in business and industry. Such duties as record keeping, preparing salary schedules and rating reports, and other clerical tasks were assigned to one individual (McCoy, Gips, & Evans, 1983). Later, one person became responsible for other, more specialized personnel tasks, such as selecting and assigning the needed personnel.

Prior to 1900, there was little evidence of an organized central personnel office in school systems. However, educational institutions began to initiate personnel practices similar to those in business and industry. One common practice was to delegate certain activities, such as compensation and personnel matters, to the business administrator. With the emergence of assistant superintendent positions, more personnel activities related to the professional teaching staff were assumed by these administrators. Building principals did perform some personnel duties, but many were only part-time administrators and had teaching responsibilities as well.

After 1900 and during much of the first half of the 20th century, personnel administration began to emerge. Moore (1966) points out that "personnel administration as the term is commonly understood, began with World War I. The recruiting, training, and paying of masses of workers in war production forced assignment of such responsibilities to specialized personnel" (p. 5). In education, the establishment of personnel departments was encouraged by school surveys conducted by management consultants and universities, especially in the 1940s and later, which recommended the establishment of positions charged with the management of personnel (Moore, 1966). As a result, the establishment of central offices to coordinate the personnel function increased significantly during the 1950s and 1960s. And by 1966, Moore was able to report that approximately 250 personnel administrators were operating in the public schools.

THE SCIENTIFIC MANAGEMENT MOVEMENT

The scientific management movement, which became extremely popular in the early 1900s, had a major impact on the human resources function in business and industry, as well as on education. Scientific management grew out of the work of Frederick W. Taylor (1856–1915). As chief engineer of a Pennsylvania steel company, Taylor had the opportunity to implement his management concepts in industry. His critical attention to worker efficiency and productivity earned him the title Father of Scientific Management. Today, Taylor's methods are considered by most to be insensitive and authoritarian. Yet his work, along with that of others who contributed to the scientific management movement, did much to focus attention on the important relationships between task achievement and human activity. Many of the concepts that evolved from this era continue to be foundational to many contemporary practices in human resources administration.

Taylor's management methods required managers to plan in advance the daily tasks of each worker and detail the specific procedures for completing them. The manager also was to enforce the standards for completing the task and arrange the necessary relationships and cooperation for accomplishing each task *efficiently*. The art of management, according to Taylor (1911), was "knowing exactly what you want men to do, and then seeing they do it in the best and cheapest way" (p. 21).

Taylor's (1911) management concepts, which he identified as the *task system*, claimed that efficiency and production were conditioned primarily by the following methods:

1. *Identification of tasks.* Scientific methods should be used by managers to discover the most efficient ways to perform minute aspects of every task.
2. *Setting of controlled conditions and specified equipment for completing each task.* The procedures for doing the task and the time specifications for completion must be stated and enforced.
3. *Incentive system that awards efficiency and high production.* A piecework pay system rewards the worker for high productivity. Merit pay and job incentives are essential in the compensation process; punishment or personal loss in case of failure also is to be considered.
4. *Management's responsibility to plan work and control its accomplishment.* Workers are to be hired and trained to carry out the plans under close supervision.

Scientific management served to replace the more arbitrary management procedures with a scientific approach for each job task. Workers were selected and assigned based on the specific job requirements and personal qualifications. Foremen and/or line managers supervised workers by the implementation of the scientific procedures determined for each task. Finally, the method made clear the division of labor between management and workers. Management was to plan and organize the work to be done; workers were to complete each task according to these predetermined procedures.

Taylor's management approaches gained both national and international attention for two reasons. First, management was in dire need of definition. The question of what managers do to assure efficient employee productivity was foremost at the time. Management methods in general in the early 1900s were largely pragmatic and in need of *professional bearing*. Second, the methods of scientific management proved extraordinarily effective in terms of the production outcomes.

Taylor is credited by some writers as being the person most responsible for planting the seeds for the first industrial personnel department in the United States. His in-depth studies and implementation of such personnel practices as selection, training, and compensation served as a forerunner for specialized personnel activities within organizations.

Many other individuals contributed to the scientific management movement, including Henry L. Gantt (1861–1919), Lillian Gilbreth (1878–1972), and Frank Gilbreth (1868–1924). Gantt was an industrial engineer who became acquainted with Frederick Taylor at the Midvale Steel Works in

Pennsylvania. Gantt's ideas on scientific management included the consideration of such topics as motion and time study, record keeping, cost accounting, planning and control, task and bonus, and task setting. Speaking of the relationship between task and bonus, Gantt (1961) held that "the ideal industrial community would be one in which every member should have his proper daily task and receive a corresponding reward" (p. 77). Gantt devised charts that remain in use in the industrial sector, charts for recording a wide variety of worker behaviors, including progress charts, order charts, machine record charts, idleness expense charts, production charts, and others.

Frank and Lillian Gilbreth often are remembered because their work and concern for efficiency were portrayed in the popular movie *Cheaper by the Dozen*. As industrial engineers, they worked as a husband and wife team to improve worker efficiency through such techniques as time and motion studies and were much concerned with job simplification. Both were fascinated with the development of approaches for eliminating inefficiency. In one instance, Frank Gilbreth observed bricklayers on the job and devised standards and techniques for assigning workers, designing work materials and equipment, and positioning the bricks and bricklayers so that physical movements were optimally efficient. Reportedly, he reduced the number of physical movements of the workers from 18 to 5 and increased work productivity by an estimated 200% (Griffin, 1987).

Scientific Management in Education

The concepts of scientific management were accepted enthusiastically by practitioners in educational administration. Taylorism in education was far-reaching and was evident in both administrative practices and terminology in the early 1900s. *Educational engineering*, *scientific education*, the *chief executive*, and *administrative management* became part of the new vocabulary in education. In order to be efficient, it was said that schools had to exemplify the principles of scientific management and emulate the practices of a successful business. In 1918, James L. McConaughy of Dartmouth University stated that "this is an age of efficiency. In the eyes of the public no indictment of a school can be more severe than to say it is inefficient" (pp. 191–192). Elwood P. Cubberly, a school superintendent and later university professor, wrote in 1916 that

> our schools are, in a sense, factories in which raw products (children) are to be shaped and fashioned into products to meet the various demands of life. The specifications for manufacturing come from the demands of life. The specifications for manufacturing come from the demands of twentieth century civilization, and it is the business of the school to build its pupils according to the specifications laid down. (p. 325)

Personnel development in education also was influenced by the work of other scientific management proponents such as Henri Fayol, Luther Gulick, Lyndall Urwick, and Max Weber. Fayol (1841–1925) set forth five basic elements for all administrative activities: to plan, to organize, to command, to coordinate, and to control. The implications of these principles for personnel management were clear. Administrative personnel, according to Fayol (1916/1949), were responsible for the following:

1. Determining those activities necessary to meet the needs of the future
2. Organizing the required physical and human resources
3. Overseeing the work of employees through leadership and direction
4. Coordinating the efforts in the organization through relating harmonious activities and units
5. Controlling all the procedures and methods that have been determined and outlined by the principles and rules of the organization

Many of Fayol's (1916/1949) management concepts remain in practice today. These include such principles as *division of labor* (the more people specialize, the more efficiently they can perform their work); *unity of command* (each employee must receive instructions about a particular operation from only one person to avoid conflicting instructions and resulting confusion); *unity of direction* (the efforts of employees working on a particular project should be coordinated and directed by only one manager); and *scalar chain* (a single uninterrupted line of authority should run in order by rank from top management to the lowest-level position in the company).

Gulick (1892–1993) extended Fayol's five responsibilities for personnel management to include reporting and budgeting responsibilities and extended the personnel consideration under the responsibility of staffing. Thus Gulick's now renowned POSDCoRB paradigm (*P*lanning, *O*rganizing, *S*taffing, *D*irecting, *Co*ordinating, *R*eporting, and *B*udgeting) gave new emphasis to the process of staffing by considering it a separate entity, rather than a subsidiary of organizing. Gulick's management concept of *specialization* proved to be of particular importance to administrative organization. This concept stipulated that workers are more effective when tasks are divided into specific parts. The task parts included both the content and methods for completing the work. According to the specialization concept, all tasks are to be considered jobs, and all jobs are to be assigned appropriately to departments. Not only did the concept tend to reinforce the idea of departmentalization, but it also emphasized the need for such personnel activities as the development of job descriptions and the completion of scientific, in-depth job analyses (Urwick & Gulick, 1937). Specialization supported the hierarchical supervisory structure commonly utilized in organizational administration today.

Gulick's colleague and coauthor, Luther Urwick (1891–1983) articulated seven universal principles of organization that held significant implications for the human resources function. The principles of assignment of duties, definition, and organization effectiveness are especially noteworthy. Urwick's principle of *assignment of duties* stated that the duties of every person in an organization should be confined as far as possible to performing a single function. This idea of specialization ultimately permeated educational practice at both the management and professional teaching levels. The principle of *definition* stipulated that the duties, authority, responsibilities, and relations of everyone in the organizational structure should be clearly and completely defined in writing. Thus, as noted previously, job analyses and job descriptions became essential parts of the personnel activity. According to Urwick's principle of *organization effectiveness*, the final test of an industrial organization is the smoothness of its operation. Such a test was considered more in terms of the ways that departments were grouped and related than in terms of the human relationships in the organization.

Sociologist Max Weber's (1864–1920) early work in social and economic organizational theory provided a foundation for the study of a bureaucracy that he viewed as the ideal organizational structure (Weber, 1910/1947). His work proved instrumental in the implementation of many later investigations by behavioral scientists. Weber conceived the ideal organization as having (1) a *hierarchical structure*, with a well-defined hierarchy of authority; (2) a functional specialization, exemplified by a *division of labor* based on the ability to perform a certain task; (3) *rules of behavior* that prevent the unpredictability of the individual employee; (4) *impersonal relationships* that are free of strong personal and emotional relationships that tend to result in irrational decisions; and (5) *career orientation* based on prescribed competence that focuses on certification of abilities. Promotion must be tied to job-related performance. Security for the worker through protection from unfair dismissal, voluntary resignation, and provisions for retirement contribute to loyalty and career orientation. Weber contended that such ideal bureaucracies were more impartial, more predictable, and more rational than the norm. In Weber's view, these factors allow workers to function with a minimum of friction and confusion.

Weber's concept of rationality in organizations was further illustrated in his taxonomy of domination (1910/1947). The taxonomy describes the three types of authority in organizations as charismatic, traditional, and legal. *Charismatic authority* is power based on the charismatic attraction of the leader that results in an emotional form of follower–leader relationship. *Traditional authority* is based on the dominance inherent to a position or role. That is, the position itself legitimizes certain authority and accompanying privileges exercised by the position holder. *Legal authority* is based on a body of principles, rules, and laws that provides the authority for the position. Weber considered legal authority to be best for forming the foundation of an ideal bureaucratic organization.

Weber's concepts have had much influence on practices in educational administration and, in turn, on the human resources function. His ideas of hierarchical authority, division of labor, files and records, and rules for behavior and his concepts of authority can be identified with many contemporary practices in human resources administration.

Emphasis on accountability, teacher evaluation, merit pay, teacher selection, scientific supervision, on-the-job training, and job analyses were among the personnel outcomes of the scientific management era. In education, teaching personnel learned how to set goals and accomplish them. The personnel performance evaluation practices that had been introduced into business and industry soon were incorporated into the personnel process in education as well. And incentive pay plans advocated in the early 1900s by both supporters and critics of education have gained renewed support in today's climate in which focus has again turned to accountability and performance outcomes.

THE HUMAN RELATIONS MOVEMENT

As early as 1920, the scientific management approach was being brought into question. The scientific management philosophy, which tended to view workers as machines, was considered inhumane and evoked the concern of a number of writers. Mary Parker Follett (1868–1933) was among the first to recognize the importance of human factors in an organization. In a series of papers and in her book *Creative Experience* (1924), she emphasized the need to consider the human element and social ethic in administration. Follett's fundamental premise was that the primary concern of any organization is the building and maintenance of dynamic, yet harmonious, human relations. She stressed that one of management's primary responsibilities was to establish positive working relationships with workers. Her concept of *coordination* was instrumental in refocusing methods of supervisory and personnel practices toward the goal of organizational harmony. According to Follett (1940), coordination in organizations involves the following:

1. *Coordination by direct contact.* The persons responsible for work must be in direct contact regardless of their position in the organization. To achieve coordination, horizontal communication is just as necessary as vertical communication in the organizational hierarchy.
2. *Coordination in the early stages.* The persons responsible must be involved in the policy decisions as these considerations are being formulated, not merely informed about the decisions after the fact. As a result, motivation and morale will increase.
3. *Coordination as the reciprocal relationship of all factors in a situation.* All factors surrounding a situation must be related to one another, and these existing relationships must be carefully weighed and considered.
4. *Coordination as a continuing process.* Participative involvement, ongoing relationships, internal communication, and other such factors of coordination must be viewed as continuing responsibilities of the administrator.

Follett believed that cooperative responsibility must be established to assure an organizational unity—in which each person accepts responsibility for a unique role played in the enterprise and, in turn, is given full recognition for the contributions realized. She stated that "an executive decision is only a moment in the process. The growth of a decision, the accumulation of responsibility, not the final step, is what we need most to study" (1940, p. 146).

Follett's views concerning the resolution of conflict through *integration* were revolutionary. Rather than attempting to resolve conflicts through the use of authoritative measures or by compromise, which often leads to a less than ideal result, Follett suggested that an integration approach was best for all parties. In brief, integration elicits the talents of the parties in conflict and, through discussion, leads both parties toward a solution that serves the best interests of all concerned.

Elton Mayo (1880–1949), Fritz Roethlisberger (1898–1974), and many others were influenced by the concepts of Follett. The now classic Hawthorne studies, conducted at the Hawthorne plant of the Western Electric Company near Chicago primarily by Mayo and Roethlisberger over a 5-year period from 1927 to 1932, were to gain national attention in the fields of business, industry, and education. Through the introduction of such variables as illumination into the work setting, the investigators observed the effects on workers and productivity (MAYO, 1933). The principal finding was that the physical condition of room lighting was not a significant factor on worker efficiency and work production. This led the researchers to conclude that mere observation and interest in the workers were more important to productivity than the physical conditions of the job or workplace. This observation has become known as the **Hawthorne effect**. The studies gave support to the concept that factors other than salary are also important in motivating employees. The implications for human resources administration were clear: human motivation, morale, employee satisfaction, and social relationships were factors of paramount importance. The physical makeup and structure of an organization were secondary to the need for attention to the human element. The Hawthorne studies not only served to refute many of the principles of scientific management proponents, but also set the stage for new inquiry into the dimensions of organizations as human entities.

Kurt Lewin, Ronald Lippitt, and Ralph White were among other individuals who contributed to human relations theory. Their research provided new insights into leadership approaches and the resulting human behavior (Lewin, Lippitt, & White, 1939). Their studies described leadership as democratic, authoritarian, or laissez-faire. *Democratic leadership* is characterized by a structured but cooperative approach to decision making. It focuses on group relationships and sensitivity to the people in the organization. *Authoritarian leadership* utilizes autocratic methods in arriving at decisions and is structured so that authority is vested in the upper hierarchy of the organization. Employee behavior is closely controlled through such means as punishment, reward, arbitrary rules, and task orientation. *Laissez-faire leadership* is characterized by a free-rein approach. Having little structure, this passive style provides great latitude for personal worker initiative. Few restrictions are placed on the employee concerning choices and procedures for accomplishing job tasks.

A 1938 study by Lewin (1890–1947) and his colleagues examined the responses of young children to these various leadership styles. Without using value judgments as to the "rightness" or "wrongness" of the leadership style, the investigators concluded that different leadership styles do indeed produce different behaviors (White & Lippitt, 1960). For example, the children supervised under the democratic style tended to exhibit superior morale, cooperation, work quality, unity, and self-direction. Authoritarian leadership resulted in a higher level of production, but also was associated with a higher level of frustration and lower levels of morale, cooperation, and self-direction. The laissez-faire style resulted in inferior work quality, less productivity, and higher degrees of dissatisfaction. These results had far-reaching effects on the approach in working with personnel in organizations. The study's findings soon were interpreted in terms of "good" administration, and the terms *democratic administration, democratic supervision, democratic teaching,* and *democratic personnel* practices became a part of the terminology of the human relations movement.

The human relations movement had a strong impact on personnel practices in education. During the 1930s and 1940s, it advanced the concept that teachers were people with attitudes, emotions, and needs that had to be considered for positive motivation. Although administrative strategies often were manipulative and based on preconceived goals, the humane processes of cooperation in planning, work completion, and decision making became common procedures during this era. Administrative titles such as *supervisor* frequently gave way to less threatening ones such as *coordinator, consultant,* and *resource teacher.* In addition, staff development as a human resources process was approached through democratic supervision, as opposed to a critical focus on the individual teacher. Staff improvement was considered to be a system goal, whereby each unit was viewed as having influence on the success of other units and on the system as a whole.

The new emphasis on the human element in organizations served to support the growth of human resources services in school districts. Centralization of personnel services, which began as early as 1919, continued at an increasing rate during the 1930s and 1940s. The organization of personnel administrators was evidenced as well. The organization of personnel administrators evolved from a conference of teacher examiners that took place in 1935 (Gibson & Hunt, 1965). In 1951, the group became the American Association of Examiners and Administrators of Educational Personnel and remained such until 1959, when the present title of American Association of School Personnel Administrators was adopted.

THE BEHAVIORAL SCIENCE MOVEMENT

The behavioral science movement also affected the development of human resources practices in education. According to the behavioral scientist, an organization has a structural or institutional element and a human element that are always interacting. How these two elements relate to influence the human behaviors needed to achieve organizational goals is of major interest to the behavioral scientist.

Chester Barnard (1866–1961) is generally recognized as the first theorist to relate the behavioral sciences to administration. His work, *The Functions of the Executive* (1938), is a classic in educational administration literature. Although Barnard's work was concerned with administration generally, it influenced human resources administration throughout the 1940s and continues to influence contemporary practices. Barnard, like Follett, believed that cooperation was essential for individuals in an organization (1938). Because most individuals in organizations have limited powers of choice, cooperation is seen as the most effective way to offset these limitations. Cooperation necessitates the subordination of personal goals and a commitment to a group goal. And an individual's degree of cooperation depends on the level of satisfaction realized, which is based on subjective personal judgments.

Barnard (1938) maintained that the mere existence of an organizational purpose does not assure cooperation. It is acceptance of the organizational purpose that is essential. Therefore, he believed that an essential function of every executive is to instill acceptance of a common purpose in the minds of all organizational members. Another essential function, according to Barnard, is communication: the linking of common purpose with members who are willing to cooperate. Such communication must consider both the formal and informal organizational structures that influence members' attitudes and commitment.

According to Barnard, *effectiveness* is the extent to which organizational goals are met and realized, while *efficiency* is the extent to which a cooperative system remains viable through its satisfaction of individual desires and interests. Barnard termed this phenomenon the organization's *capacity of equilibrium*. This new concept directly considered the human element and its relationship to the achievement of organizational goals. Figure 1.1 illustrates several contemporary human resources practices in education

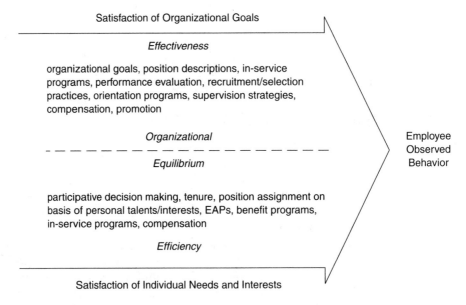

Satisfaction of Organizational Goals

Effectiveness

organizational goals, position descriptions, in-service programs, performance evaluation, recruitment/selection practices, orientation programs, supervision strategies, compensation, promotion

Organizational

Equilibrium

participative decision making, tenure, position assignment on basis of personal talents/interests, EAPs, benefit programs, in-service programs, compensation

Efficiency

Satisfaction of Individual Needs and Interests

Employee Observed Behavior

FIGURE 1.1
Barnard's Concepts of Effectiveness and Efficiency

that are implemented toward the goal of realizing organizational equilibrium in school systems. Barnard's analysis put into perspective the scientific management concepts advanced by Taylor and others and the human relations views of Follett, Mayo, and others.

Work satisfaction and human motivation were primary topics of research and inquiry for behavioral scientists during the 1950s and 1960s. During this period, Frederick Herzberg and Douglas McGregor published their now well-known theories of human behavior in organizations. Both theories held significant implications for human resources administration. Herzberg (1923–) hypothesized that the factors leading to positive attitudes toward work and those leading to negative attitudes are different. His two-factor theory of motivation, published in *The Motivation to Work* (Herzberg, Manser, & Snyderman, 1959), questioned whether different kinds of factors were responsible for bringing about job satisfaction and dissatisfaction.

Herzberg maintained that the most important factors in increasing job satisfaction were: (1) achievement on the job, (2) recognition in the job, (3) the work itself, (4) job responsibilities, and (5) job advancement. These five factors were closely related in that, in contrast with the other factors, they focused on the *job itself.* Therefore, Herzberg called these factors **motivators**.

The factors Herzberg identified with negative attitudes and job dissatisfaction included (1) company policy and administration, (2) supervision, (3) salary, (4) interpersonal relations, and (5) working conditions. Each factor is related to the environment in which the job takes place: the factors surrounding the job itself. Thus these factors Herzberg termed **hygienes**.

According to Herzberg's theory, if a worker had neither a positive or a negative attitude toward the job, the presence of positive factors would increase job satisfaction. However, the absence of the same factors does not, in itself, result in negative attitudes and dissatisfaction. Rather, such absence would result in a return to a neutral position. In a similar manner, if a worker were neither positive nor negative about the job, dissatisfaction would result if such factors as company policy and administration or the technical aspects of supervision were negatively altered. Thus the administrator must focus on the positive existence of hygiene factors in order to resolve worker dissatisfaction and then address the factors that serve to promote worker satisfaction and personal motivation.

While disagreement exists as to the viability of Herzberg's theory, it has had significant impact on approaches to motivation in human resources practices. Certainly, Herzberg's work has emphasized the importance of employee motivation and has provided a basis for new inquiry into morale and organizational climate.

As discussed previously, traditional concepts, illustrated by Taylor's scientific management approach, tended to view the worker as an individual with no ambition, initiative, or intelligence and one opposed to change. Douglas McGregor (1906–1964) challenged these views in his **Theory Y**, explained in *The Human Side of Enterprise* (1960). McGregor called Taylor's views of the worker **Theory X** beliefs.

McGregor's (1960) concepts of Theory Y behavior are summarized as follows:

- ☐ The expenditure of physical and mental effort in work is as natural as play or rest.
- ☐ External control and the threat of punishment are not the only means for bringing about effort toward organizational objectives. People will exercise self-direction and self-control in the service of objectives to which they are committed.
- ☐ Commitment to objectives is a function of the rewards associated with their achievement.
- ☐ The average human being learns, under proper conditions, not only to accept but to seek responsibility.
- ☐ The capacity to exercise a relatively high degree of imagination, ingenuity, and creativity in the solution of organizational problems is widely, not narrowly, distributed in the population.
- ☐ Under the conditions of modern industrial life, the intellectual potentials of the average human being are only partially utilized. (pp. 47–48)

McGregor's Theory Y was revolutionary because it emphasized fostering individual self-direction and full potential, exceeding the mere satisfaction of personal needs. Although it has received criticism as being an oversimplification of reality, McGregor's concepts have encouraged several human resources activities. Perhaps the principal activity deriving from this theory is a "decentralization of activities and a delegation of authority by giving subordinates a larger measure of control, participation, and responsibility in organizational events" (Hanson, 1979, pp. 85–86). Generally, human resources administration was influenced by McGregor's Theory Y to achieve the following:

1. Place new emphasis on the importance of the human dimension in organizations and give a new meaning to the utilization of human resources
2. Emphasize the positiveness of employees' potential to contribute in intellectual and meaningful ways to organizational effectiveness
3. Underline the fallacy of total centralization of administrative actions and emphasize the values of employee participation on a broad scale throughout the organization
4. Present a new view of expectancy motivation and human behavior in that, when management concepts allow for high-level performance expectations, employees tend to respond

Abraham Maslow (1908–1970) proposed a different type of motivation model that encompassed a hierarchy of five fundamental needs: *physiological, safety, belonging, esteem,* and *self-actualization.* According to Maslow (1954), all behavior is motivated by the fulfillment of these needs. However, lower-order needs (physiological, safety, and belonging) must be satisfied before higher-order needs (esteem and self-actualization) can act as motivators. A more detailed account of Maslow's human motivation theory can be found in Chapter 10.

Through the influence of Maslow and Herzberg's theories, Victor Vroom postulated a theory that viewed the interrelationship between work role and motivation. Vroom (1964) concentrated on the following phenomena:

1. The choices made by persons among work roles.
2. The extent of their satisfaction with their chosen work roles.
3. The level of their performance and effectiveness in their chosen work roles. (p. 7)

According to Vroom, the individual's values regarding effort and reward will influence his or her initial work effort, which in turn will influence their future performance (Kempton, 1995; Petrick & Furr, 1995). A more detailed treatment of Vroom's motivation theory can be found in the discussion of his *expectancy theory* found in Chapter 10.

Systems theory was also identified with the behavioral science movement. Eric Trist (1963) developed a systems theory that viewed the organization in a holistic manner. According to Trist, the organization is a *sociotechnical system* that includes both social (individuals) and technical elements, which need to be in balance. The systems approach focuses on the entire organization and assumes that change in one part of the organization will ultimately affect other parts of the organization (Kempton, 1995). As stated by Haimann and Scott (1970), "they [systems] are sets of interrelated, interdependent parts in which the function of any one part fully depends on the other parts which, in turn, rely on the part initially singled out" (p. 3). An open-systems approach to problem solving includes a thorough analysis of the interrelationships of a system's inputs, transformation process, and outputs, as illustrated in Figure 1.2. In brief, *environmental inputs* are represented by the available human, physical, financial, and information resources. Inputs in a school system are represented by financial resources, students, teachers, school objectives, material resources, and communication technology. The *transformation process* is exemplified by the tools and technologies that are applied to inputs to gain the desired outputs. Transformation processes in the school system include such tools and technologies as the organizational administrative, teaching, and support personnel systems; instructional

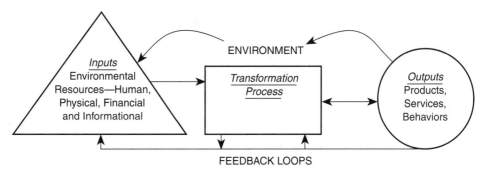

FIGURE 1.2
Systems Model

technologies; reward systems; supervisory strategies; and many other tools and processes. *Outputs* represent the results of the transformation process on the inputs originally introduced into the system. Output in a school system is represented by competent students who possess desired scholarly and behavioral qualities (Saxe, 1980). *Feedback* represents various reports, analyses, diagnoses, and "learning" concerning the system's effectiveness. In a school setting, feedback is exemplified by such information as graduation rate, program evaluation reports, student dropout statistics, student promotion and retention data, student attendance data, financial reports, and reports of the numbers of students entering college or realizing gainful employment upon graduation.

Systems theory holds several benefits for human resources administration.

1. Establishing interpersonal and interdepartmental work patterns that enhance organizational communication and understanding.
2. Gaining insight into system functions that can lead to the identification of organizational strengths and weaknesses.
3. Helping the entire organization to focus on its primary goals and objectives.
4. Helping human resources personnel to utilize human resources in ways that enhance the possibility of more productive outputs in relation to the related costs of inputs and transformation process expenditures.

The concepts behind systems theory have been extended to recognize certain *contingency variables:* the organization's external environment, technology, and people. The resultant **contingency leadership theory** holds that the specific leadership style utilized in a specific situation, to be effective, must consider the nature of the task to be performed, the power position of the leader in the situation, and the existing relationships between the leader and individuals involved in the situation (Fiedler & Chemers, 1974). In brief, Fiedler's contingency leadership theory contends that in some situations a *task-motivated leadership* style is most effective, but in other situations a *relationship-motivated leadership* style serves best. Task-motivated leaders emphasize structure and tend to gain satisfaction through the efficient accomplishment of tasks. Relationship-motivated leaders, on the other hand, emphasize positive interpersonal relationships that are exemplified by subordinate or staff support and approval.

Fiedler (Fiedler & Chemers, 1974) summarized his research by noting that task-motivated leaders generally perform best in situations that are clearly favorable or unfavorable. Relationship-oriented leaders tend to be most effective in situations that are moderately favorable, situations in which the leader holds only moderate power, control, and influence. Thus Fiedler's theory places the leadership emphasis on assigning the right leader to the specific situation and/or altering the situation itself, as opposed to the more popular view that individuals change their leadership style to meet the situation.

According to Lunenburg and Ornstein (1991), the major contributions of Fiedler's leadership model are as follows:

1. The contingency model was one of the first approaches to leadership to examine the situation—the people, the task, and the organization.
2. The theory implies that leadership should not be thought of as either good or bad. . . . A more realistic approach is to view an administrator's leadership style as effective in one set of circumstances but ineffective in another.
3. Leadership is a function of the interaction of leadership style and situational dimensions within the organization. (p. 142)

Other major individuals associated with the behavioral science movement included Herbert Simon, Jacob Getzels, Chris Argyris, Andrew Halpin, Rensis Likert, James March, and Henry Minsberg. Each was heavily influenced by the human element versus institutional element debate, which laid the foundation for the next important movement in the history of human resources management, the postmodern deconstructionist movement discussed in the next section.

THE POSTMODERN DECONSTRUCTIONIST MOVEMENT

Although the human relations and behavioral science movements prevalent during the 1950s, 1960s, and 1970s contributed much to our understanding of human behavior in organizational settings, new schools of thought began to emerge in the 1980s that focused on social reconstruction through innovation, change, and diversity. Throughout history there have been individuals who have advocated for major social and educational reform. Plato, Augustine, Marx, Engel, and Lenin were considered the reconstructionists of their time. During the past two decades reconstruction and change have become dominant themes that have led to what has been termed *postmoderism*, or the postmodern deconstructionist movement.

Contemporary postmodern theorists have challenged unequal power relationships as applied to class, gender, sexuality, race, and nationalism. This new breed of theorists has emphasized the importance of democracy, while denouncing the politics of exclusion. Postmodern principles have been applied to a variety of institutions and organizations, including business, government, and education. The postmodern influence can also be found in the arts, literature, philosophy, and architecture.

The major underlying assumption shared by postmodern advocates is that "human resources are the most important assets of any purposeful system . . . that decentralization, self-management, participative management practices, management by incentives, and extensive democratization of the workplace [are] conducive to effective management of human resources, and thereby to the enhancement of organizational efficiency, quality, and effectiveness" (Sudit, 1996, p. 83).

Tyson (1995) points out that the deconstruction of human resources does not mean its demise. Rather, it means that new forms of management have emerged that have reshaped the workplace. In today's workplace, knowledge and learning are integrated not only at the strategic and operational levels, but also at the transformational level. It is at the transformational level that new approaches to problem solving and decision making are being explored.

One of the major core concepts embedded in the postmodern movement is *diversity*. According to Tyson (1995), organizational transformation will occur when employees not only adapt to change, but also influence and shape change through innovation. Diversity will be depicted in the following ways:

☐ The core will be open—an external labour market. Although a certain degree of security is needed, it is more important to ensure a constant flow of fresh ideas.

☐ The core will be diverse. It is vital to obtain a variety of perspectives for innovation to occur. Therefore recruiters will actively seek out people from those already employed.

☐ The culture will be heterogeneous. Instead of having induction and socialisation processes aimed at homogenising culture, active steps will be taken to encourage diverse subcultures.

☐ Evaluation of projects will occur during their course and after their completion. Evaluative criteria will not be limited to the achievement of timetable, budget, and task objectives. Rather, the aim will be to learn from the difficulties experienced and from unexpected outcomes.

☐ Projects will be treated as a sequence of learning opportunities, and personal development plans will be developed accordingly.

☐ Development plans, reward packages, and employment contracts will be negotiated with employees individually. (Tyson, 1995, pp. 194–195)

Other examples of the postmodern movement include Quality of Work Life (QWL), quality circles, Total Quality Management (TQM), and the empowerment of employees through delegation, participatory management, and goal setting. The management approach known as *Quality of Work Life* consists of organizational strategies that emphasize productivity, motivation, and cooperation through the use of quality circles. **Quality circles** usually include a small group of employees who come together with a supervisor for the purpose of discussing issues related to quality and productivity. Giordano (1992) reminds us that QWL does not have its origin or roots in Japanese management theory, nor is it a contemporary phenomenon. The philosophy and theory of QWL date as far back as the Whitley Councils and Joint Production Committees in Britain during World War I and World War II, as well as to the Labor–Management Committees under the War Production Board in the United States during both wars. Examples of QWL can be found in numerous profit-sharing plans and human relations projects of that period. One major way that QWL of today differs from that of the past is the emphasis on developing skills that are commensurate with the needs of technical and automated work processes, such as flexibility, independent judgment, and team work (Giordano, 1992).

Another important management approach designed to achieve organizational change and make organizations effective is *Total Quality Management,* which has been defined as

> a system of management that involves all people in an organization delivering products and services that meet or exceed customer requirements. It is a preventive, proactive approach to doing business. As such, it reflects strategic leadership, common sense, data-driven approaches to problem solving and decision making, employee involvement, and sound management practice. Its basic philosophy is that the customer is the driver of the business, suppliers are joint partners, and leaders exist to ensure that the entire organization and all its people are positioned and empowered to meet competitive demand. (Carter, 1994, p. 1)

The principles of TQM have been implemented in a variety of organizations for a number of decades. Although statistical quality control measures were being used to meet the enormous mass production requirements of World War II, it was not until the late 1970s and early 1980s that U.S. companies began to consider their application beyond quality control. W. Edwards Deming (1900–1993) and Joseph Juran are credited with integrating their theories and beliefs about quality with Japanese management techniques and formulating the comprehensive management system that came to be known as Total Quality Management (Carter, 1994). Deming (1982, 1986) proposed a social system that included (1) organizational norms, role responsibilities, and sociopsychological relationship expectations; (2) status and power relationships between individual members and among groups; and (3) the extent to which the work organization is a work community (Petrick & Furr, 1995). Juran (1989, 1992) advocated a technical system that distinguished between the "big Q" (strategy, culture, and overall functioning of the organization) and the "little q" (product or process) (Druckman, Singer, & Van Cott, 1997).

A total quality leadership style differs from a more traditional style of leadership in significant ways. The type of leadership style endorsed by a total quality leader is one that is capable of generating ideas and involving individuals at all levels of the organization. According to Lawler (1996), "the ideal leader . . . is aptly described as the 'post-heroic leader,' or as the Chinese proverb says, the best leader is one who, when he is gone, they will say, we did it ourselves" (p. 41). Lawler (1996) suggested that the type of leader needed for the 21st century is one who can:

- ☐ Create the key organizational systems and processes
- ☐ Provide strategic direction for the organization
- ☐ Provide a sense of mission, vision, direction, and rationale
- ☐ Encourage leadership throughout the organization and not only at or near the top
- ☐ Recognize that flatter, more lateral organizational structures, along with a decrease in the number of traditional means of control, will require more rather than less leadership
- ☐ Encourage all employees to perceive their role as both managers and leaders

TABLE 1.1
Selected Comparison of Traditional and Total Quality Human Resource Paradigms

HR subfunctional areas	Traditional paradigm	Total quality paradigm
1. Management practices: leadership priorities	Professional specialization Individual contributions Internal–external control focus Compliance priority Operational support	Cross-functional generalist work Collective contributions Internal–external flexibility focus Customer satisfaction priority Strategic–operational involvement
2. Management practices: organizational communications– planning	Top-down communication Planning information available on a need-to-know basis Implement policy	Multidirectional communication Planning information widely shared Shape–deploy–implement policy
3. Management practices: voice and involvement	Detect and control Reactive legal grievance procedures Suggestion systems No explicit whistleblower protection Morale measurements Control through power, not principle, which breeds fear	Coordinate and build Proactive legal–ethical problem-prevention procedures Continuous improvement systems Explicit whistleblower protection Morale–ethical climate surveys Drive fear out of workplace by institutionalizing organizational ethics program development
4. Staffing and placement	Selection by manager Narrow job–task skills Promotion based on individual accomplishment Knowledge, skills, and/or abilities testing	Selection by peers Wide problem-solving skills Promotion based on group facilitation Knowledge, skills, and/or abilities and integrity testing

It is beyond the scope of this text to provide a detailed comparison of traditional human resources management and total quality human resources management. Table 1.1 presents a summary of both paradigms from a variety of human resources subfunctional areas.

Like the concept of Total Quality Management, the concept of *empowerment of employees* through delegation, participatory management, and goal setting is viewed as another example of the postmodern movement. Irwin (1995) suggested that "to empower other people is the more powerful way to go" since "everyone advances when one advances" (p. 80). In her book, *A Circle of Empowerment: Women, Education, and Leadership,* Irwin (1995) described the application of empowerment to a school system in which the administrator takes on the role of supervisor–consultant. The metaphor for empowerment that best connotes this role is that of "dance partners." "The 'dance partners' image is reinforced through the practical

HR subfunctional areas	Traditional paradigm	Total quality paradigm
5. Training and development	Develop a regulatory mind-set (enforce compliance) Job-related skills Functional departmental focus Technical skills Unit-specific skill training Short-term training Learning for individual productivity Linear career path Productivity	Develop statistical mind-set (manage variation) Organizational skills Cross-functional focus Process skills Firm- or industry-specific skill training Lifelong learning Learning for organizational effectiveness Horizontal career path Productivity and quality
6. Compensation, benefits, and job design	Competition for individual financial merit increases and benefits Job design: narrow span of control Specific job description with limited responsibility Employee expected to do job only by adhering to standard procedures Employee rewards linked with "doing the job" Cost savings shared with management	Team- or group-based rewards; financial rewards, financial and nonfinancial recognition Job design: wide span of control Autonomous, empowered work teams with wide responsibility Employee expected to accomplish results and improve procedures Employee rewards linked with "getting results for customer" Cost savings shared with all employees
7. Performance appraisal, employee and labor relations	Individual goals Supervisory review Employment-at-will Emphasize financial performance Adversarial union relations Limited, occasional measurement and feedback	Team goals Customer, peer, supervisory, and self-review Due process Emphasize quality and service Partnership union relations Extensive, incessant measurement and feedback

Source: Reprinted with permission from *Total Quality in Managing Human Resources* by J. A. Petrick and D. S. Furr. Copyright © 1995 CRC Press, Boca Raton, Florida.

principle 'giving is what makes people powerful, not taking,' which in turn produces another image, 'giving and receiving is a very powerful cycle.'" (Irwin, 1995, p. 82)

Empowerment means different things to different people and is defined by context and culture. According to McCoy (1996), "empowerment is contingent upon employee participation, employee accountability, access to information, an innovative atmosphere, and compassionate leadership" (p. 192). For a culture of empowerment to work, it will necessitate leader–managers to clearly define their expectations and outcomes and the behaviors that will achieve these outcomes. In addition, employees

TABLE 1.2

New Paradigm That Replaces Traditional Logic Principles with New Logic Principles

1. Old Logic Principle:	Organization is a secondary source of competitive advantage.
New Logic Principle:	Organization can be the ultimate competitive advantage.
2. Old Logic Principle:	Bureaucracy is the most effective source of control.
New Logic Principle:	Involvement is the most effective source of control.
3. Old Logic Principle:	Top management and technical experts should add most of the value.
New Logic Principle:	All employees must add significant value.
4. Old Logic Principle:	Hierarchical processes are the key to organizational effectiveness.
New Logic Principle:	Lateral processes are the key to organizational effectiveness.
5. Old Logic Principle:	Organizations should be designed around functions.
New Logic Principle:	Organizations should be designed around products and customers.
6. Old Logic Principle:	Effective managers are the key to organizational effectiveness.
New Logic Principle:	Effective leadership is the key to organizational effectiveness.

Source: Edward E. Lawler, "New Paradigm That Replaces Traditional Logic Principles with New Logic Principles," *From the Ground Up: Six Principles for Building the New Logic Corporation* (New York: Wiley, 1996), p. 22. Copyright © 1996 John Wiley & Sons, Inc. This material is used by permission of John Wiley & Sons, Inc.

will need help to internalize a mental vision of what it means to be an empowered employee. McCoy asserted that this transfer of power and control to the employer and employee has created a new social contract. "The old social contract provided assurances of security and care-taking in return for loyalty and proper execution of orders. This new social contract provides the opportunity for self-fulfillment in return for active "self-management." It is an entirely different paradigm." (McCoy, p. 192)

Another conceptualization of organizations and change of the postmodern movement comes from the work of Edward Lawler, founder and director of the University of Southern California's Center for Effective Organizations. In his book, *From the Ground Up* (1996), Lawler stated that many of the innovations and management practices witnessed over the past three decades have become mere transitory fads. He suggested that the changes that took place in the 1990s are dramatically different and will not be transitory or short lived. Lawler viewed these changes as transformational changes that represent a major paradigm shift that replaces traditional logic principles with new logic principles. The six new logic principles represent an integrated approach to organizing and managing and involve reward systems, structure, work design, communication, measurement, and human resources management. Table 1.2 presents Lawler's paradigm shift.

The paradigm shifts that have taken place since the beginning of the field of human resources administration are unprecedented and will continue to place ever-changing psychosocial demands on both individuals and institutions.

SUMMARY

Throughout U.S. history, education has been influenced significantly by evolving social and economic developments. Education and human resources practices have reflected the needs, demands, and pressures of America's social influences.

The scientific management movement, led primarily by Frederick Taylor, revolutionized personnel practices in business and industry and influenced educational personnel practice in the early 1900s. Workers were considered to be machines to carry out the work planned and controlled by management. Nevertheless, scientific management made many contributions to the human resources function that are found in contemporary personnel practice, including such concepts as division of labor, span of control, unity of command, standardization of tasks, and incentive pay.

Mary Parker Follett and others refuted the scientific management concepts and argued that interpersonal relationships were essential in the world of work. Follett was one of the founders of the human relations movement.

During the early part of the 20th century, the central personnel office began to emerge, both in industry and in educational practice. Such centralization increased at a rapid rate during the 1930s and 1940s.

The behavioral science movement is reflected in the work of Bernard, Herzberg, McGregor, Maslow, Fiedler, and others. Work satisfaction and human motivation became primary topics of inquiry during this period.

During the 1950s and through the 1980s, human resources administration came into its own. Although it shares the responsibility with many other functions in the school system, human resources administration has direct relationships with virtually every individual in the school system. Almost every problem and program development have implications for the human element in the organization.

The postmodern deconstructionist movement, which incorporates the period from the 1980s to the present, focuses on change, innovation, and diversity. Such changes have created new forms of management that have reshaped the workplace. Through advocates such as Deming, Juran, and Lawler, new paradigms and new ways of thinking about organizations have been formulated.

DISCUSSION QUESTIONS

1. Chapter 1 illustrates that education is closely tied to the social, political, and economic influences of its time. Discuss the various impacts of social, political, and economic events on education and human resources practices within the last 10 years.
2. Scientific management of the early 1900s had a major impact on human resources practices. Discuss its influence as reflected in various contemporary personnel practices.
3. Discuss Barnard's concept of capacity of equilibrium. What specific implications does the concept hold for human resources administrators in relation to the effectiveness and efficiency dimensions?

4. Assume that your leadership style is task motivated. You are confronted by a situation in which your relationship with the group members is good, the task is unstructured, and your leader position power is weak. What does this situation indicate to you about your chances of leading successfully in this instance? Suggest several ways that you might alter the situation to make it more favorable for your leadership style.

5. A major theme of Chapter 1 is that the postmodern deconstructionist movement emphasizes social reconstruction through innovation, change, and diversity. Discuss some examples of innovation, change, and diversity that are evident in the administration of today's schools. To what extent are these examples true paradigm shifts as opposed to transitory fads?

CASE STUDIES

1.1 Aren't You Working Too Hard, Scott?

Randall Scott was enthusiastic about his new teaching position at Union High School. It had been a difficult task completing his BS degree in mathematics while working part-time and raising two young sons. He was assigned to teach four classes of 11th-grade algebra and one class of geometry. Although first-year teachers often are excused from extra duty assignments at Union, Randall asked if he might serve as sponsor of a math club and also as an unpaid junior varsity basketball coach. These assignments were granted.

Nora Belle, district curriculum coordinator, sent a memorandum to all math teachers regarding the initiation of a curriculum committee to work on the revision of the math curriculum during the ensuing semester. After conferring with his principal, Emory Ross, Randall decided to volunteer for the committee and was named as a member.

Randall thoroughly enjoyed the math curriculum work. He took the leadership in completing two special committee projects and also chaired the textbook selection committee for 11th-grade algebra.

Randall was beginning to think this was his best year ever. His performance ratings as a teacher were excellent, and this added to his satisfaction.

At the monthly faculty meeting, Principal Ross made some brief remarks about special activities of several staff members, including the several contributions of Randall. At one point, the principal asked if anyone might be interested in working with a representative parent group on student discipline. One faculty member commented softly so that only those at his table could hear, "Let Randall Scott do it, he's got all the ideas." On the way out of the meeting, one faculty member said to Randall, "Say, Scott, aren't you working too hard?"

Questions

1. Comment on the foregoing case generally. Do you find the situation realistic?

2. What do informal groups in school settings do to "control" the work setting?

3. How do the findings of Mayo and Roethlisberger relate to this case?

1.2 Job Rotation

Union High School is one of seven high schools in the Hallmark School District. You have served as Union High School principal for 8 years, and the average time of service for the district's other principals is 8 years. Only one principal, George Schroeder, is nearing retirement.

Considerable discussion has taken place in the district relative to rotating principals in the various schools every 5 years. The school board, school superintendent, and principals tend to favor the concept. Teachers are somewhat passive about job rotation for principals, and only the general public has tended to question the implementation of such a program.

Superintendent Jones has asked you to chair the principals' group that will examine the job rotation concept in depth and recommend specific plans for its possible implementation. Such matters as the rotational timetable, selection of school assignments, articulation considerations, and communication needs are to be addressed by the principals' group.

Superintendent Jones informed you that you were selected as group chair because she and others perceive you as having good relationships with the other principals. Various assessments of your leadership behavior indicate that you are task oriented.

Questions

1. In the foregoing scenario, what can be said about the task structure relative to the group's assignment?
2. Would you expect your position power to be high or low in this situation? (Evidence suggests that your leader–member relations in this case are good.)

3. In view of the available information, what can be said about your leadership fit in this instance?
4. What might be done to change the situation so that your leadership behavior might be more effective?

1.3 Amelia, What Would You Do?

Principal Stephen Craig scheduled an appointment with his assistant principal, Amelia Wilson. "I'm getting more and more concerned about the negative attitudes of the faculty," commented Principal Craig. "I've never seen such overall apathy on the part of our teachers. I talked to Sharon Crutchfield recently. She's one of our most positive teachers, yet she inferred that faculty satisfaction in general was as low as she had ever seen it. We have to find a solution, but I'm just not sure where to begin."

"Amelia, what would you do?" Craig asked.

Questions

1. Assume the role of Assistant Principal Amelia Wilson and set forth your response to Principal Craig.
2. How might Herzberg's two-factor theory of motivation be useful in determining a solution to the situation of faculty dissatisfaction?

REFERENCES

AASA (American Association of School Administrators). (1952). *The American school superintendency* (thirteenth yearbook). Washington, DC: Author.

Barnard, C. I. (1938). *The functions of the executive.* Cambridge, MA: Harvard University Press.

Carter, C. C. (1994). *Human resources management and the total quality imperative.* New York: American Management Association.

Castetter, W. B., & Young, I. P. (2000). *The human resources function in educational administration* (7th ed.). Upper Saddle River, NJ: Prentice Hall.

Cubberly, E. P. (1916). *Public school administration.* Boston: Houghton Mifflin.

Deming, W. E. (1982). *Quality, productivity, and competitive position.* Cambridge, MA: MIT Press.

Deming, W. E. (1986). *Out of the crisis.* Cambridge, MA: MIT Press.

Druckman, D., Singer, J. E., & Van Cott, H. (Eds.). (1997). *Enhancing organizational performance.* Washington, DC: National Academy Press.

Fayol, H. (1949). *General and industrial management.* London: Sir Isaac Pitman and Sons (original work published 1916).

Fenner, M. S. (1945). *NEA history.* Washington, DC: National Education Association.

Fiedler, F. E., & Chemers, M. M. (1974). *Leadership and effective management.* Glenview, IL: Scott Foresman.

Follett, M. P. (1924). *Creative experience.* New York: Longmans, Green.

Follett, M. P. (1940). The meaning of responsibility in business management. In H. C. Metcalf & L. Urwick (Eds.), *Dynamic administration: The collected papers of Mary Parker Follett* (pp. 146–166). New York: Harper and Brothers.

Gantt, H. L. (1961). *Gantt on management.* New York: American Management Association and the American Society of Mechanical Engineers.

Gibson, R. O., & Hunt, H. C. (1965). *The school personnel administrator.* Boston: Houghton Mifflin.

Giordano, L. (1992). *Beyond Taylorism: Computerization and the new industrial relations.* New York: St. Martin's Press.

Griffin, R. W. (1987). *Management.* Boston: Houghton Mifflin.

Haimann, T., & Scott, W. G. (1970). *Management in the modern organization.* Boston: Houghton Mifflin.

Hanson, E. M. (1979). *Educational administration and organizational behavior.* Boston: Allyn and Bacon.

Herzberg, F., Manser, B., & Snyderman, B. (1959). *The motivation to work.* New York: Wiley.

Irwin, R. L. (1995). *A circle of empowerment: Women, education, and leadership.* Albany: State University of New York.

Juran, J. M. (1989). *Juran on leadership for quality.* New York: Free Press.

Juran, J. M. (1992). *Juran on quality by design.* New York: Free Press.

Kempton, J. (1995). *Human resource management and development.* London: Macmillan.

Lawler, E. E., III. (1996). *From the ground up: Six principles for building the new logic corporation.* San Francisco: Jossey-Bass.

Lewin, K., Lippitt, R., & White, R. (1939). Patterns of aggressive behavior in experimentally created "social climates." *Journal of Social Psychology, 10,* 271–299.

Lucio, W. H., & McNeil, O. (1969). *Supervision* (2nd ed.). New York: McGraw-Hill.

Lunenburg, F. C., & Ornstein, A. C. (1991). *Educational administration—concepts and practices.* Belmont, CA: Wadsworth.

Maslow, A. (1954). *Motivation and personality.* New York: Harper.

Mayo, E. (1933). *The human problems of an industrial civilization.* New York: Macmillan.

McConaughy, J. L. (1918). The worship of the yardstick. *Educational Review, 55,* 191–192.

McCoy, M. W., Gips, C. J., & Evans, M. W. (1983). *The American school personnel administrator: An analysis of characteristics and role.* Unpublished manuscript, American Association of School Personnel Administrators, Seven Hills, OH.

McCoy, T. J. (1996). *Creating an "open book" organization: Where employees think & act like business partners.* New York: American Management Association.

McGregor, D. (1960). *The human side of enterprise.* New York: McGraw-Hill.

Moore, H. E. (1966). *The administration of public school personnel.* New York: Library of Education, Center for Applied Research in Education.

Newsom, N. W. (1932). *The legal status of the county superintendents* (Bulletin No. 7). Washington, DC: U.S. Department of the Interior, Office of Education.

Petrick, J. A., & Furr, D. S. (1995). *Total quality in managing human resources.* Delray Beach, FL: St. Lucie Press.

Rebore, R. W. (2001). *Human resources administration in education: A management approach* (6th ed.). Boston: Allyn and Bacon.

Saxe, R. W. (1980). *Educational administration today: An introduction.* Berkeley, CA: McCutchan.

Stahl, O. G. (1962). *Public personnel administration* (5th ed.). New York: Harper & Row.

Sudit, E. F. (1996). *Effectiveness, quality and efficiency: A management oriented approach.* Boston: Kluwer Academic Publishers.

Taylor, F. W. (1911). *Scientific management.* New York: Harper & Row.

Tead, O., & Metcalf, H. C. (1920). *Personnel administration: Its principles and practices.* New York: McGraw-Hill.

Trist, E. (1963). *Organisational choice.* London: Tavistock.

Tyson, S. T. (Ed.). (1995). *Strategic prospects for HRM.* London: Institute of Personnel and Development.

Urwick, L., & Gulick, L. (Eds.). (1937). *Papers on the science of administration.* New York: Columbia University, Institute of Public Administration.

Van Zwoll, J. A. (1964). *School personnel administration.* New York: Appleton-Century-Crofts.

Vroom, V. H. (1964). *Work and motivation.* New York: Wiley.

Weber, M. (1947). *The theory of social and economic organization* (T. Parsons, Ed., A. M. Henderson & T. Parsons, Trans.). New York: Free Press (original work published 1910).

White, R., & Lippitt, R. (1960). *Autocracy and democracy: An experimental inquiry.* New York: Harper & Row.

2 The Nature of the Human Resources Function

Its Organization and Processes

The information in this chapter will enable you to:

■ Delineate the primary processes of the human resources function.

■ Describe the nature of the responsibilities of the central human resources unit and the characteristics of individuals in this leadership role.

■ Describe line and staff organizational structures, decentralized organizational structures, and the place of the human resources unit in each.

■ Explain the nature of competency as it relates to administrative performance and identify the major competencies required of human resources administrators.

■ Identify common problems that human resources leaders encounter in their work and the ethics and standards that apply to human resources administration.

Various contemporary issues that have a direct impact on the human resources function are discussed throughout the text. These issues and related problems have specific implications for the work of the human resources unit and school administrators throughout the school system. Some require establishing new procedures; others demand that administrators assume new responsibilities and develop additional competencies to remain effective in their role. Each issue discussed serves to underline the paramount importance of the human resources function in education—the realization that its effectiveness is essential to the achievement of school purposes.

This chapter examines the human resources function in education from several perspectives. First, how does the human resources function influence teaching and student learning? What are its primary purposes? What are the major processes that comprise the human resources function and who implements these processes in the school setting? The next section focuses on the organization and specific tasks of the central human resources unit and answers these questions: What is the work of the central human resources unit? What is its relationship with the total system?

One section examines the concept of competency as it relates to the effective performance of human resources administrators. What is the difference between the administrator who is performing effectively from a competency point of view and one who is not? Next, the position analysis and position description for the central unit human resources director are discussed. Finally, the specific nature of the problems encountered by human resources administrators and the opportunities of human resources administrators to make positive differences in the school system are discussed. In this section, the ethics and standards that guide professional practices in this field also are examined.

THE HUMAN RESOURCES FUNCTION'S IMPACT ON TEACHING AND LEARNING

As defined in Chapter 1, the guiding purpose of the human resources function is that of serving the school system in the achievement of its primary goals. Quality teaching and effective student learning certainly loom significant among school goals of every school and therefore become foundational to the purposes of the human resources function as well. As Duke and Canady (1991) comment, "We would be hard pressed to find an area of local policy making more central to good instruction than personnel" (p. 111). This underscores the fact that policies and regulations directly affect the quality of teaching and learning. "Whenever the topic of educational improvement is discussed, the importance of school personnel in such improvement becomes paramount. Educational leaders consistently have emphasized the importance of human resources in providing quality education" (Norton & Kelly, 1997, p. 93). We submit that each process of the HR function directly or indirectly influences quality teaching and student learning. "The quality of teaching depends upon the quality of the teachers, which is influenced by the policies governing teacher recruitment, selection, and remuneration. Policies related to teacher supervision and development should help teachers become and remain competent and committed" (Duke & Canady, 1991, p. 144).

Other human resources processes influence teaching quality and student learning as well. The processes of induction and orientation of teaching personnel, for instance, provide them with an enhanced opportunity for success in the classroom and directly affect teaching quality and ultimately student learning. Consider also the need for placing the teacher in an assignment that enhances his or her major strengths and personal teaching interests. Authorities are quick to underscore the fact that productivity and effectiveness are fostered when the work assignment provides opportunity for the worker's primary skills to be utilized. Such human resources processes as organizational climate can enhance or inhibit quality teaching and student learning. Evidence is clear that a healthy school climate is a major determinant of staff morale and staff motivation. Hoy and Miskel (2001) discuss the effects of various school climate types on teaching. Disengaged teacher behavior "refers to a lack of meaning and focus to professional activities. Teachers are simply putting in time and are nonproductive in group efforts or team building; they have no common orientation" (p. 193). In contrast, collegial teacher behavior is characterized by a collaborative atmosphere; teachers work well together and are supportive of their professional colleagues.

Seyfarth (1996) underscores the point that the human resources function is instrumental in determining the extent and quality of instructional support services that affect teachers' and students' efforts. Other studies (Coladarci, 1992; Taylor & Tashakori, 1994; Ebmeier, 2000) support the contention that positive teacher efficacy coupled with a commitment to goals, peer relationships, perceptions of administrative support, and a healthy organizational climate leads to a greater commitment to teaching. Administrative support in this context is behaviors on the part of school leaders that demonstrate a genuine interest in the instructional process (Ebmeier, 2000). Thus the process of organizational climate is of paramount importance to effective teaching and learning.

In the following sections of this chapter, an overview of each primary human resources process will be presented and the impact of each of these processes on quality teaching and student learning will be considered in more detail.

THE HUMAN RESOURCES PROCESSES

The processes of the human resources function and their relationships are illustrated in Figure 2.1. These 12 processes within the human resources function are shown as subsets of three major components. *Human resources utilization*, for example, is a comprehensive component that encompasses the processes of planning, recruitment, selection, induction, assignment, collective negotiations, compensation and welfare, and stability. *Human resources development* includes the processes of staff development and evaluation. *The human resources environment* component includes the processes of organizational climate and protection. Each process is interrelated in that its effectiveness depends directly or indirectly on the effectiveness of the others. Human resources planning is tied closely to recruitment, selection, assignment, compensation, and other processes. As part of planning, forecasts of human needs provide the focus for the implementation of the recruitment process, the selection of specific personnel, directions for personnel assignments, and the monetary considerations of budget and compensation. Effective human resources and the successful achievement of school goals, as illustrated in

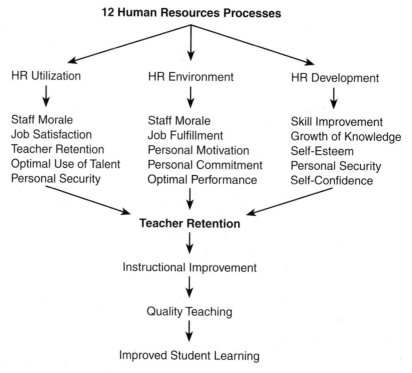

FIGURE 2.1
The Human Resources Function: Impact on Teaching and Learning

Figure 2.2, are founded on the concept of the personal competency of the system's personnel.

Each of the processes of the human resources function is described briefly in the following sections and in detail later in the text.

Processes of Human Resources Utilization

Resources Planning   *How does the school system determine its direction and priorities? What kinds of data and information are essential for the successful completion of the human resources tasks and responsibilities?*

The resources planning process serves in answering these questions. The purposes of resources planning are (1) to clarify the objectives and mission of the organization, (2) to determine in advance what the organization and its parts are to do, and (3) to determine the assets on hand and the required resources for accomplishing the desired results. Effective resources planning is essential in helping the school system to determine what it wants to be and provides a blueprint for guiding action. Such a process is essential to avoid guesswork and happenstance, to offset uncertainty, and

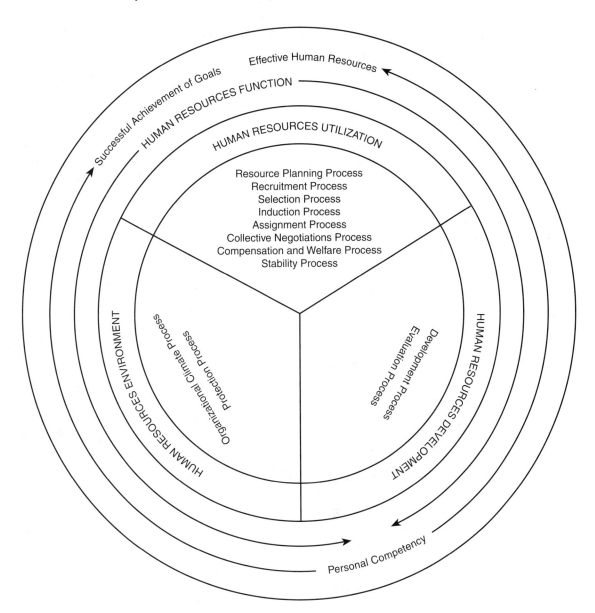

FIGURE 2.2
The Personnel Processes and Human Resources Relationships

to ensure efficient accomplishment of goals. Planning constitutes a purposeful set of activities that focuses available resources on the achievement of school goals.

Planning is not synonymous with the plan. A plan is a product of the planning process. Planning, on the other hand, is a continuous, ongoing process that is characterized by flexibility and is subject to change. Effective planning forms a foundation for decision making. It encourages responsive administration and capitalizes on employee talents by establishing goals that elicit the most effective performance from individuals in the organization. Planning is a comprehensive, continuous process that must remain flexible and responsive to changing conditions.

Activities within the human resources planning process include developing planning assumptions, determining organizational relationships and structures, completing inventories of need, making assessments of labor markets, developing forecasts of resource needs, completing projections of student populations, participating in policy development, completing position analyses and position descriptions, and evaluating the process's effectiveness. The human resources planning process is developed in detail in Chapter 4.

Recruitment of Personnel. *How can highly qualified individuals be attracted to the school system for consideration of possible employment?*

The purpose of the recruitment process is to establish a pool of qualified candidates to meet the needs of the school system. It focuses on strategies for attracting and retaining the best qualified persons for the specific positions available. The amount of recruitment necessary depends on such factors as enrollment growth and decline, staff turnover, and program design. Recruitment is not only a primary responsibility of the human resources function but, when coupled with the selection process, is considered by many practitioners as the most time-consuming responsibility. Human resources directors in one state named the recruitment process as their highest-ranked job responsibility (Norton, 1999a); 93% of the directors so responded. And 55% of the directors named recruitment, selection, and assignment as consuming the greatest amount of their time.

In the 1980s, decreasing student populations resulted in the need to implement a reduction in force (RIF) of teaching personnel; there was an excess of teachers in the majority of teaching specialties. Presently, in view of teacher shortages in most teaching areas, the recruitment of talented personnel assumes an ever-increasing role of importance. Severe teacher shortages increase the competition for quality personnel and make an effective recruitment program even more necessary. New talent sources must be identified and tapped. A recent statewide study of school superintendents (Norton, 2001b) revealed that the lack of qualified teachers was the major problem facing them.

The recruitment process begins by establishing policy guidelines during the planning process that direct such specific activities as developing recruitment resources, implementing application procedures, establishing formal interview and evaluation procedures, and designing appropriate staff involvement strategies for each of these activities. Technology has entered the recruiting process in a variety of ways. The competition for attracting quality personnel has led many school districts to develop such recruitment technology as CD-ROMs that tell about the school district and certain of its attractive features, such as its class size, teacher induction process, student clientele, and information related to parental support. Costs for the production of such material are being offset in many instances through the use of advertising; various sponsors, for example, pay to have their logos on the CD-ROM.

Although the process of recruitment is shared by the central human resources unit and personnel in other units of the system, it continues to be administered primarily by the central human resources unit. A major question facing the human resources function presently is related to the reform and restructuring issue related to school governance. With the increase of site-based management within local school districts, has the responsibility for recruitment been shifted more to local schools? Study results indicate that, although the staff selection, evaluation, development, and assignment processes are increasing as site-based responsibilities, the induction, negotiations, and recruitment processes have not followed that trend (Norton, 1999b). Chapters 8 and 13 consider the recruitment process in detail, as related to both professional and support staff personnel.

Selection of Personnel. *How does the school system determine the best person for a specific position? Does selection depend primarily on individual perceptions of an applicant's qualifications or are there "tools" that lead to staff selection on a more scientific basis?*

Selecting the right person for the right job is a basic responsibility of effective human resources administration. Many potential administrative and staff problems of a school system can be avoided through an effective selection process. In addition, effective personnel selection serves to reduce the major costs related to the retraining of inadequately prepared employees. When asked to cite their most important task, human resources administrators most often mention "the selection of personnel." Selection necessitates attention to matters other than merely filling vacancies. Although placing the right person in the right job is a primary objective, such considerations as staff load, staff balance, and staff diversity are significant. Background checks and investigations are important activities of the screening process. Fingerprinting and searches of an applicant's past for prior criminal convictions or other unethical practices are commonplace.

Selection often is carried out under complex and confusing conditions. For example, reduction in force and hiring of personnel in special areas might be necessary in the same school district. A reduction in force in spring followed by rehiring in the following summer still occurs in some school districts, although teacher shortages have curtailed this phenomenon substantially. The hiring of individuals in alternative certification programs has been necessary in shortage areas, but is nevertheless a controversial practice.

The competition for quality personnel has led to the streamlining of selection procedures. The traditional steps related to the teacher application, the interview, applicant ratings, and ultimate approval by the school board are changing. In far too many instances, a quality applicant has been lost to a district due to the time required to complete each step in the recruitment process. Thus more districts are giving hiring authority to school officials in order that they might offer a position to a potential staff member almost immediately. The teacher is hired in some instances within one or two days after the interview or perhaps on the spot. Such hires, as is the case with any newly contracted employee, ultimately are subject to the results of background checks and final school board approval.

Interviewing, legal compliance, screening, evaluation, and selection decisions are important activities of the human resources selection process. The selection process is discussed in detail in Chapters 9 and 13.

Induction of Personnel.   *How are personnel introduced into the school setting and how important are such orientation activities to the system and the individual employee?*

Induction often is given such labels as *orientation, introduction of employees, preservice programs,* or *staff development.* We define *induction* as the complex of activities designed to gain congruence between institutional objectives and employee needs. It begins with the job application and continues on an ongoing basis for as long as the employee or the organization views it as necessary. Thus the induction process assumes a comprehensive perspective, as opposed to the traditional practice in some schools of scheduling one or two days of informational sessions for employees at the outset of a school year. We view these brief, one- or two-day informational sessions as orientation activities. Induction has gained added attention and importance in view of research results. Studies have underlined the importance of planned induction activities during the early years of service, because beginning teachers and other employees need help with special problems. As emphasized by Norton (2001b), "Sensitivity to learning and addressing the needs of novice teachers may improve teacher retention, as teachers with high levels of job satisfaction are the most likely to remain in teaching" (p. 20).

Breuer (2000) reported on a study conducted by the Coca-Cola Retailing Council. The study found that employee turnover costs the typical supermarket $198,977 a year. This figure reflects a cost to the industry of $5.8 billion annually. Furthermore, the study concluded that "the first week of a new employee's experience is the most vital factor in retention" (Breuer, 2000, p. 32).

Teacher retention is discussed further in the section on the stability process later in this chapter. Induction activities are the important links between recruitment, selection, and staff development. Chapter 10 includes a comprehensive consideration of induction and its relationships with other human resources processes.

Assignment of Personnel. *How are personnel assigned so that their personal talents and interests optimally serve the system and their own self-development?*

Traditionally, assignment of personnel has centered on the match between personnel and positions, or placing the right person in the right job. Although this view remains operational in most school systems, the concept of competency modeling has gained momentum in many organizations. The structuring of tasks around the skills or competencies of employees is viewed by many authorities as the trend of the future. Effective employee assignment, of course, is instrumental in assuring the effectiveness of individuals to achieve the organization's goals. The placement of individuals in positions that best suit their individual competencies and interests remains a primary consideration of staff assignment.

Today a more comprehensive view of assignment regards it as the complex of activities related to the talents and interests of the employee and the environment in which the work takes place. Thus deployment of talent in the best interests of the system, the employee, and the student; conditions of work, including workload; effective staff supervision; staff improvement practices; organizational climate; and evaluation methods all relate to the effective utilization of personnel.

Proper assignment includes more than matching position and qualifications. Other significant factors, such as the teacher's workload, must be considered. With the exception of class size, teacher assignments have given little attention to teacher load factors. Other important factors in the teacher's workload include the number of subjects and levels taught, length of class periods, the number of class preparations required, and related cooperative or extracurricular assignments. Although teacher load is only one consideration within the assignment process, it illustrates the need for cooperative efforts among administrative personnel in the school system. Chapter 10 provides a more detailed discussion of the assignment process and other important activities related to the utilization of human resources.

Collective Bargaining. *How do employee groups and employers in school systems decide on matters of salary, working conditions, and other contractual matters? How are negotiation teams formed and how are negotiations carried out?*

The negotiations process has become the primary procedure whereby boards of education and representatives of employee groups decide such matters. In the opinion of many, no other development in education has had more impact on the human resources function than the advent of collective bargaining. Although the methods for collective bargaining differ among the various states and their actual impact varies widely, the process has penetrated virtually every human resources activity. Negotiations consume a significant part of the human resources director's time. In addition, negotiations are often named as one of the leading problems facing personnel directors.

One such problem is illustrated by news headlines such as "Teachers Union to Urge Strike Vote," an actual occurrence that took place three days before classes were scheduled to begin for 200,000 students in Philadelphia (*Arizona Republic*, September 5, 2000). Negotiators spent Labor Day at the bargaining table to resolve the union's demands for smaller classes, stronger early childhood education, a new reading program, and enhanced school security, but no progress was reported. On September 7, 2000, 3,800 teachers in Buffalo, New York, in defiance of state law, went on strike just one hour before school was to start; school for 47,000 students was affected. Mayor Anthony Masiello called the strike "an unconscionable act" that was very damaging and punitive to children and families. Matters related to wages, health care, and the outsourcing of services to serve troubled children were areas of disagreement between the teachers and the school system (*Arizona Republic*, September 8, 2000). After suspending the strike, for a period of one week, the Buffalo teachers went on strike again on September 14. It was reported on November 12, 2000, that the Buffalo school board had imposed penalties for striking teachers of four days' pay, approximately equivalent to first-year contract pay increases (*Arizona Republic*, November 12, 2000).

One of the most widespread strikes in education took place in the state of Hawaii in April 2001. Teachers and university faculty personnel led a strike that closed public schools for 180,000 children and 42,000 college students. The strike, which involved 13,000 teachers and 3,100 university professors, was believed to be the first time that the educational system of an entire state had been shut down by such an event.

These events not only underscore the difficulties that can result in the bargaining process, but the negative impacts that result on the teaching and learning for children and youth. Research studies reveal that human resources directors serve frequently as the chief spokesperson for the school board's negotiation team and are also involved in a major way in such activities as negotiation planning and proposal development, strategy sessions, and implementation of the agreement.

The matter of scope of negotiations and what is negotiable continues to change. For example, in 1991, "the Oregon Court of Appeals ruled that proposals on class size must be negotiated between a school district and a teachers' union" ("Class Size," p. 2). Under state law, the court ruled, class size is pertinent to "conditions of employment" and thus is included on the list of items to be negotiated during contract talks." The court went on to say that "substantial evidence supports the finding that the [class size] proposal significantly affects workload . . . it determines the number of parent-teacher conferences, the number of papers to be graded, and the hours spent on assistance to individual students" (p. 2). Heretofore class size was considered a matter within the jurisdiction of the governing board. Recent experiences with the use of **integrative bargaining** strategies, such as win–win and collaborative bargaining, reveal that the scope of bargaining tends to increase significantly.

For various reasons, including difficult economic times, more problem-solving approaches to collective negotiations have been implemented. Often termed **win–win bargaining**, these integrative approaches are designed to achieve agreement between the two parties and at the same time make both parties "feel good" about the agreement and one another. Variations of win–win methods include *principled bargaining, strategic bargaining, progressive bargaining,* and *collaborative bargaining.* Chapter 7 is devoted to the collective bargaining process. It examines both integrative and distributive negotiation approaches.

Compensation and Welfare of Personnel. *What factors determine the levels of compensation for professional and support personnel in the school system? What are the various kinds of compensation and benefits received by employees?*

The compensation of personnel constitutes by far the largest general fund expenditure of any school system; compensation comprises approximately 90% of most general fund budgets. The compensation and welfare process encompasses the considerations of contract salary agreements, fringe benefits, and other rewards and incentives, sometimes termed *psychic income.* The human resources unit in most school districts assumes major responsibility for administering these activities, and their impact on related personnel processes is significant. The issue of adequate compensation for personnel in education historically has been a leading concern. Its importance to the human resources function is self-evident; compensation plays a primary role in attracting highly qualified personnel to positions in education and retaining their services.

During the first half of the 1980s, there was significant activity in the area of personnel compensation. Local, state, and federal officials, concerned with educational quality, proclaimed that the status of professional staff salaries in education was unacceptable and ineffective in attracting and retaining high-quality personnel. In addition, quality performance was a major concern. As a result, new approaches to personnel compensation emerged and many were adopted by school districts. The concept of incentive pay, for example, included such pay programs as career ladders, master teacher pay, mentoring, effective schools, forgivable loans, merit school financing, and others. Legislation was enacted by the U.S. House of Representatives to provide additional financial incentives to lure top students into teaching, and many states enacted a higher level of financial support for education. In some instances, states approved special funding for scholarships in areas of teacher shortages.

In the late 1980s and early 1990s, generally due to economics, the external push for higher salaries in education waned. The average entry salaries of classroom teachers continued to fall below those of graduates in other fields who entered the world of work. Recently, the concept of competency-based compensation has emerged in business and industry. Its long-term impact on educational practices, if any, is yet to be determined. Now, in the early years of the 21st century, the push for salary increases for teachers once again is on the agendas of many state legislatures. Various tax measures to secure additional funds to support education, especially salaries, have been proposed, but not without serious opposition. National concerns such as teacher shortages and poor student performance on achievement tests have provided the impetus for much talk about increasing salaries to help to attract and retain quality personnel.

An increasing demand upon the human resources unit is that of administration of the employee benefits program. This responsibility was named ninth highest among all listings as a primary job responsibility by human resource directors in one statewide study (Norton, 1999a).

Technology has come to the rescue of human resources administrators in business and industry and to an increasing extent in education. It is now possible to bring employees directly into the world of human resources through the computer; health care enrollment, insurance coverage, and minor changes in other employee benefits can be made through on-line provisions. The Internet, World Wide Web, or private company networks can be made available to employees for HR purposes. Organizations that are using this technology for HR administration note that it frees the unit from much of the required paper work when employees sign up for benefits; it saves employees trips to the HR office. As noted by Amparano (1996), "Now employees can obtain vacation forms and medical forms. In the future, employees might be able to change 401(K) plans, obtain pension models and get the latest news on recruiting and job posting" (p. E2). Compensation and welfare are considered in Chapters 12 and 13. Chapter 13 discusses compensation for support personnel.

Stability of Personnel Services. *How does the school system maintain a viable work force over a long period of time? What conditions and programs provide stability for the school system and what conditions militate against the continuation of high-level service?*

Once the human resources function secures the personnel for the system, the responsibility for maintaining an effective work force to ensure continuous, high-level service becomes vitally important. The significance of employee stability was underscored by one company executive: "sales and profit are our number one objective, but retention is our number one priority" (Breuer, 2000, p. 29). The educational parallel to this foregoing statement might be that "teaching and learning are our number one objective, but retention is our number one priority."

Although stability encompasses a wide variety of program provisions, Castetter and Young (2000) point out that such personnel considerations include two clusters of activities: "One group is concerned with the health, safety, and mobility of continuing personnel; the second is focused on members who are voluntarily or involuntarily leaving the system" (p. 270). These clusters include teacher and staff absences, substitutes to replace them, health and safety services, personal counseling, record maintenance, separation of employees from the system, and provisions that keep the system viably staffed. Thus the process of maintaining a stable work force has gained increased attention in the last decade.

Teacher absences and scarcity of qualified substitutes are common problems in many school districts. The problems of quality and quantity continue to face the substitute teaching program in schools. The shortage of substitute teachers has resulted in changes in certification requirements in some states. For example, in the state of Arizona, the Maricopa County school superintendent announced that substitute teachers in the county no longer would be required to hold a college degree. Rather, a high school graduate who completes a 16-hour, five-day seminar at a specified university can receive an emergency teaching certificate (*Arizona Republic*, October 2, 2000). Such emergency measures underscore the severity of the teacher shortage problem nationally and tend to militate against the need for a highly qualified, fully certified teacher in all American classrooms.

An estimated 10% to 20% of the labor force utilizes mental and other health service counseling annually. It is estimated that more than 50% of the nation's school districts has implemented some form of an **employee assistance program (EAP)** to work with troubled employees. Thus personal counseling has become an essential activity of the stability process. In fact, a study in one state revealed that personal problem counseling of employees concerning family problems, grievances, personal crises, and others tied with recruitment, selection, and assignment as the job area that required the most amount of time on the part of personnel directors.

The array of activities that comprise the stability process is comprehensive and complex indeed. Technological advances have eased the burden of activities such as record keeping, which at one time was the most time-consuming activity of the human resources function. Computer technology has not only reduced the need for completing and filing most records by hand, but it also has improved immeasurably the utilization and information value of these records. Information management, an essential task within the human resources function, has been enhanced and become less burdensome, due to computer applications in personnel administration.

Outsourcing, the practice of subcontracting certain work to outside firms, also is a growing practice in human resources administration. Such personnel activities as recruiting, resource planning, accounting, and fringe benefit administration are among the responsibilites that are being assumed by agencies outside the school system's business and personnel offices. Outsourcing activities are technologically compatible in that they are generally data based and important components of the human resources information management system. Outsourcing reduces the time and effort needed by internal personnel to complete certain required work, while releasing them to focus on other personnel processes. These applications will be addressed in various chapters throughout this text.

The growing concern for employee health has led to a new emphasis on wellness programs. Also, extended programs such as child care and elder care are predicated in part on the realization that employees' concerns for their children and aging parents during working hours can serve as an inhibitor to effective work production.

A growing concern within the stability process is that of teacher retention. "[P]roficiency in identifying and selecting quality teachers is not sufficient to solve the problems of teacher recruitment and retention if working conditions in schools are such that able teachers are induced to leave" (Seyfarth, 1996, p. 2). Increasing problems related to teacher shortages have resulted in critical attention to the retention of quality personnel in education. Studies of teacher loss indicate that approximately 25% of persons entering teaching leave after their first year and that from 33⅓ to 50% leave the profession by the end of the fifth year. Such turnover is costly both monetarily and intellectually. It is estimated that it costs 25% or more of an employee's salary to replace her or him; the cost of replacing a school principal or mid-management supervisor is estimated as being much higher. By using the 25% cost figure, lose only 10% of a staff of 130 teachers making an average salary of $30,000 and the bill is $97,500, money that would be welcomed in other budget lines. Monetary costs for administrator turnover hold similar implications. A replacement hire for professionals and managers has been estimated to cost $107,970 (*Arizona Republic,* September 17, 2000).

Cost factors include administrative costs to recruit and process all candidates, interview costs, candidate travel costs, severance pay, advertising, training for new employees, relocation costs, and other "hidden costs." A conservative estimate for replacing a mid-management administrator in a typical school district (principal, central office supervisor, or other) would be $25,100. This figure is based on fees for the talent search by a contracted firm or individual and advertisement costs, $7500; related search expenses, including interviewee costs for travel and per diem, $3600; employee time spent in clerical work and participation in the selection process, $2500; loss of work due to the necessary involvement of teachers and others in the replacement activities, $3500; time spent on the induction of the new hire, $3000; and expenses related to hiring the new administrator, such as moving costs, travel expenses, and temporary housing, $5000. The foregoing cost factors do not include other expenses, such as signing bonuses, salary increases, and other fringe benefits that commonly accompany the hiring of new school officials.

But the loss of intellectual capital is perhaps even more important than monetary costs associated with employee loss. No organization can afford to lose its best personnel and continue to be optimally effective. A planned program for teacher retention is essential and this matter is discussed from several perspectives in other chapters of the text. A school district needs personnel policies that attract and retain employees, rather than drive them away. Both empirical and research evidence underscores the fact that organizations that have established stability within their work force have a competitive advantage and are more successful in achieving their stated goals.

In both business and educational organizations, employee turnover is increasing and, according to a recent report compiled by Gannett News (2001), current retention methods are failing in spite of the fact that more organizations are using monetary-related methods to retain quality personnel. In addition, more organizations also reported the use of nonmonetary methods, such as flexible hours and casual dress codes. According to a recent report by Mercer (2001), employers are expanding both monetary and nonmonetary benefits in order to retain personnel and/or to enhance recruitment and morale. For example, the percentage of employers offering work life programs, such as employee assistance programs, increased from 77% in 1998 to 84% in the year 2000. Tuition reimbursement benefits were offered by 85% of the employers in 1998; this figure increased to 90% in 2000. We submit that, although the employee retention problem in education is complex and cannot easily be resolved, changes in practices relating to the human resources function itself hold more promise for reducing employee loss than the monetary solutions mainly being implemented today.

Processes of Human Resources Development

Development of Human Resources.　*What do organizations do to motivate employees to improve personal competency? What personal growth programs tend to be most productive for the system and for the individual?*

The fact that schools will progress as their personnel are motivated to achieve personal and professional growth has direct implications for human resources administration. Clearly, effective school programs depend on the extent to which employees continue to grow and develop. Development programs that serve to foster increases in personal knowledge of subject matter and effective methods for delivering this knowledge to students serve to increase teacher confidence and, in turn, professional competence. As underscored by Zepeda and Mayers (2000), "A major tenet of supervision and staff development is change" (p. 2). Professional development activities are the primary means for helping personnel to reach their potential. As noted by Tyler in the early 1970s, "In-service education of the future will not be seen as 'shaping' teachers but rather will be viewed as aiding, supporting, and encouraging each teacher's development of teaching capabilities that he values and seeks to enhance" (1971, p. 15).

Some writers, however, have attempted to differentiate terms such as development, training, and education (Nadler, 1974). The terms *staff development, in-service training, professional growth, continuing education, self-renewal, competency-based development,* and others often are utilized interchangeably in education. Differentiation between such terms can be useful. Harris (1989) makes such a useful distinction in his definition of the term **staff development**. He notes that "one aspect of staff development is . . . referred to as 'staffing' because it involves an array of endeavors that determines who serves, where, and when" (p. 21). The other side of staff development, according to Harris, includes in-service education and advanced preparation. **In-service education** involves any planned program offered staff members for purposes of improving the personal performances of individuals in the system. **Advanced preparation** differs from in-service in that it focuses on future needs. Reassignment, promotion, and the need for new skills resulting from organizational expansion programs are examples of the focus for advanced preparation approaches.

Staff development is often a shared responsibility by several units in an educational system; however, human resources directors are involved specifically with in-service training, internship programs, student-teacher programs, mentoring, and external training support programs. The human resources development process and the responsibilities of all administrators who supervise personnel have expanded significantly. Performance assessment centers, administrator academies and cadre programs, special mentoring programs, clinical supervision, skill labs, peer-assisted leadership programs, local school district internship programs in teaching and administration, cooperative training programs between local school districts and institutions of higher education, and fifth-year teacher certification programs represent a few examples of such recent expansions.

The establishment of staff development policies, the determination of growth needs, and the implementation of special development programs are activities that concern all school administrators. Staff development and the concern for the maximization of human resources in the school system are presented in Chapter 10.

Appraisal of Personnel. *What purposes are served through personnel performance appraisal programs? Who benefits? What constitutes an effective personnel appraisal process?*

Although the instructional unit of the school system continues to assume the primary responsibility for the formal appraisal of the professional teaching staff, the human resources unit has assumed a major role in developing appraisal policy, monitoring the general process of appraisal, and maintaining the appraisal records completed by other units. Thus formal personnel appraisal is a shared responsibility, one that has assumed increasing importance in education. The level of involvement of human resources directors in appraisal activities ranges from complete responsibility to little or none at all.

Without question, the appraisal of personnel is a major concern in education. In 1996 the National Commission on Teaching and America's Future set forth a scathing report on the quality of classroom teachers and stated that an alarming number of American teachers has no business being in the classroom (Mattern, 1996). In response to the commission report, a state department official in one state recommended the testing of all prospective teachers on their professional knowledge and that, after passing such tests, teachers would be required to work for 2 years in the classroom as an apprentice, during which time they would be evaluated.

As a result of these conditions and resulting criticisms, most states have mandated programs for the purpose of certifying "qualified evaluators" in school systems. In brief, such state mandates have directed school systems to present evidence that viable personnel evaluation programs are in place and that provisions for certifying evaluators for these programs have been implemented. Yet, during the 1990s, litigation of cases in the area of personnel evaluation led the court cases under consideration in many states. Thus the quality of employee evaluation procedures holds legal implications for schools as well.

The need for improvement of appraisal policy and procedures, the continued push for personnel accountability and effective schooling, and competency-based performance concepts forecast the continued importance of the evaluation process. Chapter 11 considers this human resources process in detail.

Processes of the Human Resources Environment

Development of the organizational climate. *What do school systems do to foster a healthy working environment for employees? How can the school become a better place to work? What effect does organizational climate have on employee performance?*

The complex of personal and organizational relationships within the schools is necessarily a concern of the human resources function. **Organizational climate** is defined as the collective personality of a school or school system. It is the atmosphere that prevails in an organization and is characterized by the social and professional interactions of the people.

The concept of **organizational culture** has become a significant force in educational thought. As stated by Pai and Adler (2001), "There is no escaping the fact that education is a socio-cultural process. Hence, a critical examination of the role of culture in human life is indispensable to the understanding and control of the educative processes" (pp. 3-4). Although the concept of organizational culture differs among authorities, most agree that schools and school systems, like other organizations, develop personalities of their own. As a person has a personality, a group is said to have a **syntality** that reflects its traditions, beliefs, values, and visions. School administrators need to understand the organization's culture in order to help it to become what it can become. The school administrator must be knowledgeable about the beliefs and patterns of the organization; communication, influence, motivation, and other factors depend on such understanding.

Additionally, the administrator must have the competencies needed to assess existing climates and understand the theories and practices associated with fostering positive environments to develop harmonious and productive working relationships among employees in the system. The school leader must care about the kind of climate being created in the organization and whether the existing climate is one that encourages employees to want to remain or want to leave. The most desirable climate is one that sends a message to employees that they are valued workers and of vital importance to the achievement of the system's goals. Chapter 4 discusses culture and organizational climate as they relate to the human resources function.

Protection of Personnel.   *How are school employees protected from unfair treatment and physical harm? What are the* **liberty rights** *and* **property rights** *of school personnel?*

The human resources protection process has been receiving increasing attention because of such issues as employee rights and security. These issues have brought about major changes in school districts' policies and procedures in such matters as tenure, employee grievances, due process, academic freedom, and capricious treatment. Lessening personal employee anxiety and forecasting a more positive work climate have always been objectives of effective human resources administration. These concerns associated with personnel protection, however, have broadened in scope and are now reflected in virtually every process of the human resources function. Protection concerns include grievance procedures, transfers, dismissals, separation, liability protection, reduction in force, promotions, employee discipline, and tenure decisions.

A growing area of the protection process is that of security from bodily harm. Incidences of attacks on teachers, administrators, and other school personnel are growing problems for school districts nationally. The Aon Consulting Worldwide's Loyalty Institute has underscored the importance of employee safety and security by listing this need as one of five steps of the "performance pyramid" of workplace practices for evaluating an organizations's efforts on the commitment and employee loyalty front. As Aon stipulates, "the foundation of any good workplace is recognizing employees' need for a safe, non-threatening work environment" (Cole, 2000, p. 48). The responsibility for maintaining a safe, healthy, and secure school environment is basic to the human resources protection process. Legal considerations are discussed in Chapter 6.

These 12 major human resources processes discussed in the preceding text constitute the central focus of the human resources function in education. Each process plays a significant role in fostering a bonding between the employee and the school and promoting a collaborative relationship based on the energizing of all employees toward the accomplishment of superordinate goals. The central human resources unit, discussed in the following section, has assumed a significant leadership role in most school districts. New governance structures, exemplified by site-based management, have altered substantially some of the responsibilities of the central human resources unit. We believe that the leadership of the central human resources unit will continue as significant well into the 21st century, although the sharing of the activities related to various human resources processes will be extended; greater authority in such matters as teacher selection, assignment, evaluation, development, and organizational climate will be found at the local school level under the leadership of the school principal.

THE CENTRAL HUMAN RESOURCES UNIT

Each major human resources process relates directly or indirectly to virtually every other function in the educational enterprise, making the human resources function a shared responsibility. The responsibility for a personnel task or activity frequently is assumed in part by units other than the central human resources unit. For example, the central human resources unit often assumes responsibility for supervising such activities as position analysis and position descriptions, but the responsibility for hiring generally is shared with the instructional unit, local school administrators and staff, and other system personnel.

It was noted earlier in this chapter that new governance movements portend considerations for even greater changes in the roles and operations of the central human resources unit. And although we view the central human resources unit in school systems as the keystone to an effective personnel program, we fully support the contention that every school administrator and/or supervisor is a "director" of human resources. Neglect of the human resources processes at any level in the organization ultimately militates against the successful completion of the school system's mission. In the following section, the organization, responsibilities, and guiding ethics and standards of the human resources function are discussed.

The American Association of School Personnel Administrators (AASPA) was first established in 1959, although it evolved from the Conference of Teacher Examiners that organized in 1940 to improve the qualifications and selection of teachers for America's schools (AASPA, 1988). It can be safely estimated that there are 2,100 directors of personnel presently serving in school districts nationally. Human resources administration is a growing field. The U.S. Department of Labor (Hradsky, 2000) reported that the number of human resources positions nationally is expected to increase more rapidly than the average growth of all other occupations through the year 2005. Although *personnel director* is the most common title for the central unit's human resources administrator, less than one-half of these administrators hold that title. Other position titles for central unit administrators are *assistant superintendent for human resources, HR specialist, supervisor of personnel,* and *personnel administrative assistant,* with the title of *director of human resources* becoming increasingly popular.

A study of personnel directors in one state (Norton, 1999a) found the following:

1. Their average age was 43 years;
2. 83% were Caucasian;
3. Slightly more than one-third held the doctoral degree;
4. The mean time of service in the present position was 6.2 years; one-third had served in their present position for 3 years or less;
5. 53% was female;
6. Nearly 82% viewed their position as "increasing in importance and influence";
7. Job stress was "high" or "very high" in the role;
8. Nearly three-fourths of the directors enjoyed the role "most all of the time";
9. 18 different position titles were held by the directors;
10. Recruitment, personnel records, policy and regulation development, substitute teacher coordination, orientation of personnel, personnel planning, separation of personnel, compensation of personnel, and administration of personnel benefits were their leading responsibilities;
11. Nearly 80% served on the board's negotiating team;
12. Directors were spending 51.9 hours on the job weekly;
13. Workload and the inadequacy of resources to accomplish the job were the two leading inhibitors of their personal effectiveness. (pp. 1–38)

Organization of the Central Unit

Organizational arrangements for administering human resources vary widely. In some instances, school districts delegate various personnel responsibilities among administrators throughout the system, place the responsibilities under the jurisdiction of the superintendent and/or an assistant superintendent, perform them using an administrative team headed by a general administrative officer of the school district, or place the major human resources function within the office of a line administrator, such as an assistant superintendent, or a staff administrator, such as a personnel director or specialist.

Figure 2.3 illustrates a traditional line and staff organizational arrangement for a school district. The term **line administrator** refers to school officers in the hierarchical line of authority. A **staff administrator** is one who is not in the direct line of authority and whose position is created expressly to serve the major line functions of the organization. Thus staff positions are considered to be advisory and supportive. On a national scale, human resources administrators tend to view themselves as staff administrators, although exceptions are numerous. However, one statewide study in Arizona (Norton, 1999a) found that nearly 79% of the state's personnel directors viewed themselves as being line administrators. The solid lines in Figure 2.3 indicate authority relationships. For example, the assistant superintendent for instruction, the assistant superintendent for business affairs, and the human resources director are subordinate to and

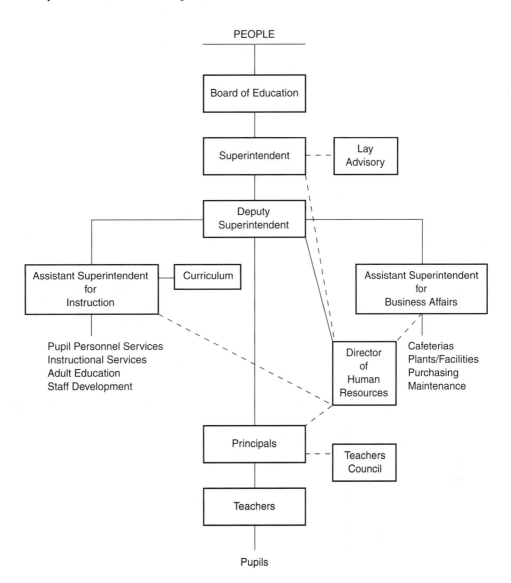

FIGURE 2.3
Line and Staff Organization for a School District

supervised by the deputy superintendent. Dashed lines indicate informal working relationships.

Organizational charts illustrate the relationships of the human resources unit within a school system. Variations in practices and arrangements make it impossible to construct an organizational plan that is applicable to all schools. Most studies reveal that practicing human resources directors hold major professional responsibilities in addition to personnel administration. Such areas of responsibility include buildings, grounds, and custodial services; business, purchasing, and payroll services; pupil personnel services; curriculum and instruction; general administration services; transportation; and federal and state grants and programs. School district size, educational philosophy, financial ability, and other such factors influence structural arrangements of the school system as well. Data are not available for determining a correlation between the size of a school district's enrollment or staff and the existence of a central human resources administrator; there is no cutoff for such a position relative to school district size. Some schools with fewer than 1000 students have a central human resources administrator; other much larger districts distribute personnel responsibilities among various units within the system.

Site-Based Governance Structures

Such developments as restructuring, site-based management, reengineering, and reform have been mentioned in previous discussions. The movement of responsibilities of many of the human resources processes to local schools is a reality in most school districts. Such developments are surrounded with much controversy; few data are available to date regarding the success of such restructuring. Reports indicate that the human resources function in the majority of school districts nationally has been decentralized in some significant ways. How do school principals view this allocation of human resources job responsibilities?

In one statewide study (Norton, 1999b), principals were asked to assess their responsibilities for all the HR processes. First, participating principals were asked to identify the human resources processes included in their job description. Of the 100 school principals in the study, 84% or more of them reported that staff selection, assignment, organizational climate, staff evaluation, staff development, and orientation were part of their job description. Similarly, the principals were asked to report the percent of responsibility that they held for 11 primary personnel processes. Over 88% indicated that staff evaluation, assignment, selection and organizational climate were their primary responsibilities, and more than 56% reported that orientation, development, and stability of staff were primary job responsibilities for them. Additionally, such personnel activities as staff counseling, handling grievances, personnel regulations, transfer requests, personnel records, and implementation of the District's Master Agreement were among those performed by the study participants.

Because the human resources function historically has been a shared responsibility among various units of the school system, it is difficult to determine the specific impact of decentralization. Because the selection process, for example, has always been a major responsibility of local schools

FIGURE 2.4
The Central Human Resources
Unit and Interrelated Units
and Agencies

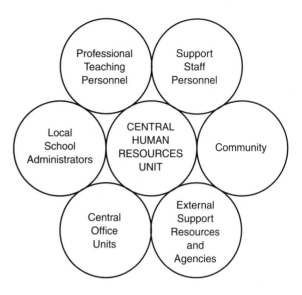

in many districts, the influence of site-based decision making on this human resources process is difficult to assess. Among the disadvantages of site-based management are differences of opinion about roles and authority, the workload increases for the local school staff, increases in purchasing costs for supplies and equipment, inequities among the various local schools, and the excessive time required to implement the process.

Figure 2.4 illustrates the interrelationship of units and resource groups within the traditional school structure to the central human resources unit. Each individual unit or group has an effect on the ability of the others to reach their objectives. The success of the human resources unit in realizing its mission also depends on the support of others. Similarly, the success of each unit or group depends in part on the effectiveness of the central unit. In this sense, the human resources unit is a part of the school district's systems management.

New organizational structures for administering the human resources function in schools are still evolving. The optimal model regarding the decentralizing of the human resources processes has yet to be established. Figure 2.5 conceptualizes one possible organizational arrangement that emphasizes decentralization of the human resources function. Similar to traditional organization, schools in the decentralized organizational arrangement still report to a deputy or assistant superintendent or the superintendent. The traditional human resources unit, however, moves to the central advisory services unit that also is responsible to the deputy or assistant superintendent

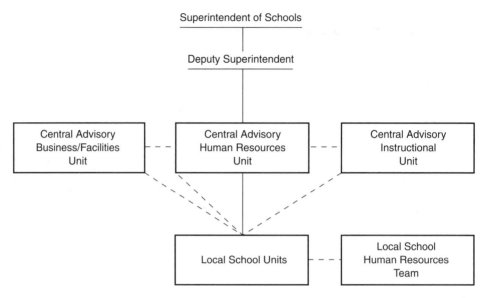

FIGURE 2.5
Decentralization of the Human Resources Unit

or the superintendent. The central advisory services unit holds a staff relationship with local schools and provides consultative services in such areas as human resources development, instructional services, and business and facility services. In such a decentralized arrangement, the central advisory unit services' personnel work cooperatively with individual schools in the determination of specific tasks that will be performed by each: the assignment of responsibility for the various kinds of decisions encountered, the identification of authority for various procedural and action approvals, and the establishment of appropriate communication channels for information dissemination.

Figure 2.6 illustrates one possible organizational arrangement for a school system with local site-based school councils or site core improvement teams. The organizational chart retains a central human resources unit, but each school has a site-based core improvement team that acts as the governing body at the local level. Each site-based core improvement team works cooperatively with several local standing committees or teams (e.g., HR utilization team, staffing team, evaluation team, policies and regulations team.) as appropriate

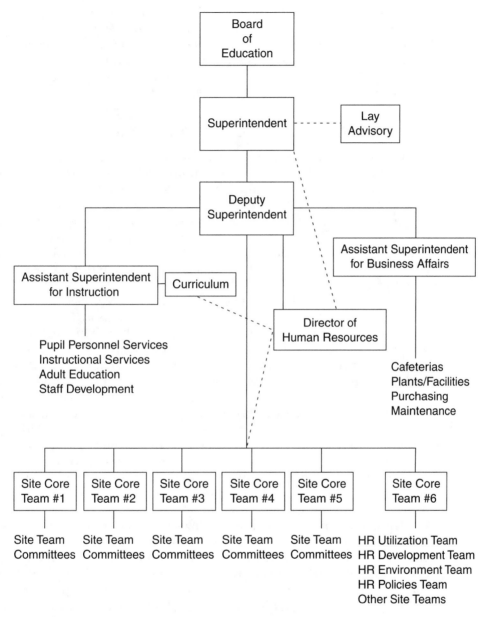

FIGURE 2.6
Site-Based Core Improvement Team: Organizational Chart

to the school situation. One member of each site-based improvement core team also serves as the liaison for each organized school team.

It must be remembered that neither decentralization nor centralization is good or bad within itself. And, as has been noted by Fayol (1984), "Everything which goes to increase the importance of the subordinate's role is decentralization; everything that serves to reduce it is centralization" (p. 74).

COMPETENCY–PERFORMANCE CONCEPTS

A **task** is a specific responsibility, obligation, or requirement associated with a professional position or function. Each human resources process discussed earlier includes numerous tasks that require specific competencies. **Competency** refers to the ability to accomplish a task at a satisfactory level of performance. To be competent is to possess sufficient skills to meet a stated purpose or to have the capacity equal to the requirements of the task. Products or behaviors that illustrate one's capacity to perform competently are known as **indicators of competency** or performance specifications.

Gibson and King (1977) state that "a primary competency is reflected in administrative action that uses *critical consciousness* for purposes of error-reduction" (p. 24). They present the model in Figure 2.7 to illustrate administrative acts. The model suggests that competent administrative behavior is viewed as the ability to analyze a specific problem or condition and relate in a purposeful way the specific behaviors or actions needed to resolve the problem or to meet the condition. Thus "behaviors in unique administrative situations are seen as logically related indicators of degree of administrative competence" (Gibson & King, 1977, p. 22). Although an intuitive administrative act might be effective or successful, it is not considered a competent action as discussed here. Unless the behavior is related consciously to situational conditions and meanings through logical analysis and human interpretations, Gibson and King would not consider the behavior to be competent.

The competent administrator realizes that a competency focus does not always ensure successful results; it is important to be able to account for gaps in intention and reality outcomes. A competency focus requires a critical examination of the total process with a conscious effort to discover errors in original assumptions and/or methods utilized. Such critical thinking supports the administrator's ability to learn from experience. Thus the administrator is able to reduce future errors and improve personal administrative performance.

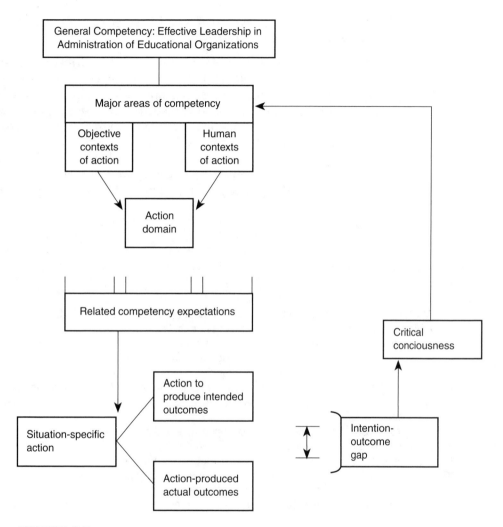

FIGURE 2.7
Conceptualization of an Approach to Competency Preparation in Educational
Administration
Source: "An Approach to Conceptualizing Competency of Performance in Educational
Administration" by R. O. Gibson and R. A. King, 1977, *Educational Administration Quarterly*,
13, p. 23. Reprinted by permission of the University Council for Educational Administration.

Tasks, Competencies, and Indicators for Human Resources Administration

Identifying the competencies that are needed by human resources administrators and the indicators of the competencies serves two primary purposes. First, identifying competencies provides insight into the nature of the role of the human resources administrator and the human resources function in education. Second, such knowledge points to the personal development required for successful performance.

It is beyond the scope of this chapter to delineate a complete statement of needed competencies in relation to all the tasks of the human resources function. Figure 2.8 presents a statement of selected competencies and indi-

---

1.1	Ability to communicate with others in the district in regard to current and future staffing needs.
1.2	Ability to evaluate data gathered on staffing needs.
1.3	Ability to identify primary sources of qualified applicants.
1.4	Ability to develop an appropriate screening process.
1.5	Ability to identify the knowledge, competencies, and abilities required for a given position.
1.6	Ability to determine the kinds of information needed by new and continuing personnel.
1.7	Ability to develop programs that enhance employee opportunities for self-improvement and advancement.
1.8	Ability to support and encourage the continuous use of self-evaluation/goal setting as a productive technique for change.
1.9	Ability to utilize effective counseling techniques with personnel.
1.10	Ability to develop and administer a program of employee compensation and benefits.
1.11	Ability to make all necessary preparations for negotiations.
1.12	Ability to develop specific records necessary to meet the needs of the human resources operation.
1.13	Ability to recognize competencies and talents of associates and utilize them effectively.
1.14	Ability to identify the unit's objectives and relate them to budget needs and limitations.
1.15	Ability to understand and interpret statutes, legal opinions, and court decisions relating to contractual relationships and employment conditions.
1.16	Ability to write viable policies and/or regulations; understand systems of codification.
1.17	Ability to assume a leadership role in developing a climate of mutual respect and trust which contributes to a high morale within the district.
1.18	Ability to articulate the human resources unit's objectives, practices, and accomplishments.

FIGURE 2.8

Selected Competencies for Administering the Central Human Resources Unit

Source: From *Competency-Based Preparation of Educational Administrators: Tasks, Competencies, and Indicators of Competencies* by M. S. Norton, 2001, Tempe: Arizona State University, College of Education, Division of Educational Leadership and Policy Studies.

cators of competency for the major tasks related to the work of the central human resources unit, although most of them apply equally well to school principals and human resources administrators in other school settings. The concept of competency-based models in the hiring, assignment, development, and compensation of managers is commonplace in business and industry. Its implementation in education is increasing as well. As stated by McLagan (1996),

> Using competencies as decision criteria isn't really new. Selection, development, assessment, and planning are always competency based. . . . Though competency models take many forms, they provide consistent criteria for job matching and human resources management decisions by managers. (pp. 63-64)

Another way of gaining insight into the nature of the work of the human resources unit is by examining the position description. Both the position analysis and position description for the position of human resources director are discussed next.

POSITION ANALYSIS AND POSITION DESCRIPTION FOR THE CENTRAL HUMAN RESOURCES ADMINISTRATOR

A *position analysis* examines in depth the nature of a specific assignment and the complex environment in which the assignment takes place. The position analysis includes such considerations as the nature of the assignment itself, the primary work required, the conditions under which the work is performed, the competencies necessary for completing the work at the required level, the physical and mental requirements of the position, the educational preparation needed to perform successfully, the kinds of internal and external contacts required, specific problems encountered in the role, and other related information (see Figure 2.9).

Good personnel practice requires that a *position analysis* be completed periodically. The position of human resources director should not be an exception. Due to the time involved in conducting a thorough position analysis, as well as the need for objectivity in its completion, outside consultants and human resource specialists often are utilized to complete this task.

The position analysis serves as the source for developing the *position description* of the human resources administrator. As noted throughout this chapter, the central unit's human resources position is not characterized by a single description. Figure 2.9 is an example of a position description for the human resources director that contains many common elements from a general perspective. Note that the position description includes basic information relative to the director's position title, contract time, general responsibilities, position qualifications, immediate supervisor, supervisory jurisdiction, and major duties.

Union High School District
Position Description

Position Title: Assistant Superintendent of Human Resources
Department/Unit: District Administration
Contract: 12 months, 23 days vacation

General Statement of Responsibilities
To plan, coordinate, and supervise the operation of the department of human resources in such a way as to enhance the morale of school district personnel, promote the overall efficiency of the school system, and maximize the educational opportunities and benefits available to the individual student.

Major Duties
1. Supervises/directs:
   a. The planning and anticipation of human resources needs of the school district;
   b. The recruitment program for certificated and classified personnel;
   c. The screening and processing of all personnel recommendations for submission to the Board of Education;
   d. Those phases of the human resources program that include:
      1) Reports,
      2) Budgeting of personnel needs,
      3) Placement on the salary schedule,
      4) Contracts,
      5) Payroll department,
      6) Employee benefits program,
      7) Certification,
      8) Unemployment compensation,
      9) The Affirmative Action Program for the District (as the officer).
2. Evaluates:
   a. All prospective teacher and administrative applicants;
   b. All prospective classified applicants;
   c. Substitute teacher applicants;
   d. All employment practices and procedures;
   e. Current human resources policies;
   f. Personnel within the division.
3. Coordinates/assists:
   a. In the selection of qualified certificated and classified candidates;
   b. In the review of requests for transfer or promotions of personnel;
   c. As an administrative representative in the Meet and Confer process;
   d. In the counseling of all personnel on matters relating to difficult or sensitive matters;

FIGURE 2.9
Position Description for Central Unit Human Resources Director

      e. In research pertaining to human resources management:
        1) Salary and benefits research,
        2) Studies of staff characteristics,
        3) Professional standards,
        4) Other pertinent projects;
      f. In the budgeting process for personnel and employee benefits programs;
      g. As a member of the District Executive Council.
4. Develops/maintains:
      a. A system for personnel records for current and former employees;
      b. An up-to-date application file of prospective candidates for all positions;
      c. Salary schedules for Administrative-Supervisory personnel, Certificated personnel, and Classified personnel;
      d. Position descriptions for all existing and all new staff positions;
      e. Human resources and procedures;
      f. Human resources for employees.
5. Demonstrates:
      a. Knowledge of current administrative procedures and practices;
      b. Ability to provide adequate and timely reports;
      c. The skills to carry through on identified needs;
      d. Written and verbal communication skills with students, staff, and community;
      e. The skills for effective interpersonal relations;
      f. Knowledge and commitment to district policies and procedures.
6. Other assignments:
      a. Special responsibilities (list);
      b. Developmental responsibilities (list).

Qualifications
1. Experience in school administration;
2. Experience in teaching;
3. Knowledge of personnel management and administration;
4. Knowledge of salary and benefit trends in education and industry;
5. Knowledge of theory and practice in discussing salaries and working conditions with various categories of employees;
6. Knowledge of problems of the classroom teacher;
7. Knowledge of office management;
8. Knowledge of school law.

Supervision Received
From the Superintendent.

Supervision Given
The employees assigned to the Human Resources Department.

FIGURE 2.9
(continued)

COMMON PROBLEMS AND SATISFACTIONS ENCOUNTERED IN HUMAN RESOURCES ADMINISTRATION AND ETHICS AND STANDARDS OF PERSONNEL ADMINISTRATION

An examination of the kinds of problems encountered by human resources administrators provides additional insights into the human resources function. The following discussion views the human resources function from three perspectives: (1) the kinds of problems and concerns encountered by human resources administrators, (2) the impact of these problems on personal attitudes, and (3) the positive nature of the human resources function and the related satisfactions in roles of personnel administration.

Kinds of Problems Encountered

A study of human resources directors in one state (Norton, 1999a) asked respondents to assess several "serious" personnel problems or conditions in relation to their own school districts. Table 2.1 indicates the specific problem and the percentage of the directors who reported the problem in their districts. The problems listed in Table 2.1 reveal a wide variety of areas in the work of the human resources administrator. A close examination of the problems indicates that more than half relate directly to the work requirements of the human resources director and the external influences on the position. For example, inadequate financing, external mandates and requirements, job pressure and stress, impact of social problems on education, and legal impacts on the personnel operation exemplify such external influences. Other problems, such as substitute teaching, teacher

TABLE 2.1

Problems Encountered by Human Resources Administrators and Their Reports of Each Problem in Their Own Districts

Problems Facing Human Resources Administrators	Percentage of Human Resources Administrators Reporting Problem
1. External mandates, requirements	63.4
2. Adequate financing	61.0
3. Substitute teaching	48.8
4. Impact of social problems on education	44.0
5. Public confidence in education	34.1
6. Personnel director's workload	29.2
7. Legal impacts on education	24.4
8. Teacher absenteeism	17.1
9. School board quality	17.1
10. Job pressure or stress in the position	17.1
11. Teacher shortage	17.1

shortage, and dismissing incompetent staff relate more specifically to teachers and other staff matters.

Impact of Problems and Concerns on Human Resources Administrators

In spite of the many and varied problems challenging human resources administrators, evidence reveals that most find the position to be one that is increasing in importance and influence, one that provides self-fulfillment and personal satisfaction, and one they consider as vital to their school district and the accomplishment of its mission. Little research attention has been given to determining the effects of personnel work on administrators. Although available data tend to be descriptive in nature, such information aids in the assessment of attitudes and conditions that surround the role. Data generated from studies on the topic reveal the following facts:

1. Human resources administrators, in general, indicate that they almost always enjoy their work. In addition, nearly all studies find that human resources administrators do find "considerable" or at least "moderate" self-fulfillment in their work.
2. Slightly more than half of the directors do not consider the position as their final occupational goal and about two-thirds of these individuals look ahead to different positions in administration.
3. Nearly all human resources administrators view their positions as being entrenched in the school system and increasing in importance and influence. Most all are of the opinion that they have "much influence" on personnel policy decisions.
4. If starting over again, nearly all human resources administrators state that they "probably would" or "certainly would" become directors again.
5. The quality of relationships between the human resources administrators and teachers, in general, is viewed by directors as "good" or "very good."

Identifying the problems and concerns of human resources administrators, as well as their contributions and challenges, illuminates the nature of the assignment as well as the personal competencies needed for successful performance in the role. In addition, the study of related problems provides insight into the increasing complexity of the human resources function in education.

The nature of human resources problems and the expectation of position responsibilities demonstrate the importance of the training and preparation required for an effective human resources administrator, the need for a better research base for the human resources function, and the need for professional guidelines that direct and support personnel programs and resources. Another means of examining the work of the human resources function is through a study of the ethics and standards on which it is founded. The following section focuses on the ethics for school administrators and on the human resources standards developed at the national level.

Ethics for School Administrators

The American Association of School Personnel Administrators (AASPA) has been instrumental in advancing personnel administration research and practice since its establishment and has set forth a statement of ethics (AASPA, 1988) to guide administrators generally. These guidelines are shown in Figure 2.10.

Another significant contribution of AASPA was the development of standards for school personnel administrators (1988) for the ethical administration of the human resources function. These standards have been updated and revised three times since 1960. The listing of selected standards in Figure 2.11 was completed in 1988 and defines and further clarifies the purposes, processes, responsibilities, and significance of the human resources function. These standards emphasize the importance of establishing a district philosophy to direct the total organization toward accomplishing its goals and objectives. Such a philosophical statement guides the school system in developing specific human resources policy and administrative regulations.

1. Makes the well-being of students the fundamental value of all decision making and actions.
2. Fulfills professional responsibilities with honesty and integrity.
3. Supports the principle of due process and protects the civil and human rights of all individuals.
4. Obeys local, state, and national laws and does not knowingly join or support organizations that advocate, directly or indirectly, the overthrow of the government.
5. Implements the governing board of education's policies and administrative rules and regulations.
6. Pursues appropriate measures to correct those laws, policies, and regulations that are not consistent with sound educational goals.
7. Avoids using positions for personal gain through political, social, religious, economic, or other influences.
8. Accepts academic degrees or professional certification only from duly accredited institutions.
9. Maintains the standards and seeks to improve the effectiveness of the profession through research and continuing professional development.
10. Honors all contracts with fulfillment or release.

FIGURE 2.10

Statement of Ethics for School Personnel Administrators

Source: From *Statement of Ethics for School Personnel Administrators* (p. 1) by the American Association of School Personnel Administrators, 1988, Virginia Beach, VA: Author. Copyright © 1988 by the AASPA. Reprinted by permission.

SUMMARY

This chapter discussed the human resources function by examining the major processes that it encompasses and their impact on teaching and learning, by viewing the organization and relationships of the central human resources unit, by considering alternatives to the centralization of the human resources function, by presenting the concept of competent performance by human resources administrators, by examining the nature of the problems and the challenges and opportunities for human resources practitioners, and by presenting the ethics and standards to guide the professional practices of human resources administration.

The human resources function is composed of several major processes, each of which is comprehensive and complex. Human resources administration was defined in terms of a planned and distinct function that serves the goals of the district through establishing an effective system of human resources and an environment that fosters high levels of accomplishment.

Human resources administration was viewed as a function with a long history, but one that is still in transition. Traditional processes and activities are encompassing new methods and professional approaches. Other new processes have been added to the responsibilities of human resources administrators, requiring new competencies for effective performance.

The central human resources unit has become a common organizational arrangement in education. Yet movements in restructuring school organization have led to more decentralization of responsibilities and further sharing of human resources activities by all units within the school system. Local school administrators are assuming an increasingly active role. The successful school administrator is aware that an effective educational program depends greatly on maintaining a high quality of human resources. In this context, human resources administration becomes the most important function of all educational functions.

Viable unit relationships, both horizontal and vertical, within the organizational structure, have paramount importance in realizing the full potential of people within the system. Basic to the success of all human resources activities are the mission of the central unit to serve all employees who contribute to the system, the need for understanding the purposes of the human resources function by all personnel, and the involvement of all administrative personnel in the achievement of the function's objectives regardless of the organizational structure. These considerations, if positively realized, will reduce the problems that human resources administrators encounter, as well as the factors inhibiting accomplishment of personnel goals. The basic significance of the human resources function is revealed in its primary concern for the human element in the system. Accomplishment of system goals is inextricably related to the accomplishment of the goals and objectives of the human resources function.

AASPA's guiding standards provide both a foundation and a direction for setting policy and guiding the work of human resources administration.

1. The basic function of the board of education is policy-making and review of the total educational program of the school district.
2. The superintendent of the school district provides the professional leadership necessary for the continuous development of the personnel program to meet the objectives of the school district.
3. The personnel administrator has a clear understanding of the goals, objectives, and processes of the school system and the role which the personnel administration function has in accomplishing those ends.
4. Written personnel policies furnish guidelines for administrative procedures relating to personnel matters.
5. The personnel department is that specific section of the administrative structure established to carry out the personnel activities of the school system.
6. Personnel operations are conducted in a manner that provides for effective and friendly employee relationships and contributes to individual motivation and morale.
7. A well-developed system of personnel accounting and research helps predict staff needs and enables the administration to make sound projections for current and future employment needs.
8. The application form requests information necessary to facilitate screening; contributes to sound decision making on recommendations for appointment; and is in conformity with local, state, and federal laws and regulations.
9. Decisions involving staff selection are based upon a carefully planned program of investigation, screening, appointment, and follow-up support.
10. Placement, assignment, and transfer of personnel is a basic administrative responsibility through which attempts are made to meet the needs of the educational program, implement affirmative action plans, provide balanced staffing, and meet the desires of individual employees.

FIGURE 2.11

Standards for Ethical Administration

Source: From *Standards for School Personnel Administration* (pp. 5–6) by the American Association of School Personnel Administrators, 1988, Virginia Beach, VA: Author. Copyright © 1988 by the AASPA. Reprinted by permission.

As implied by one of the AASPA standards, effective human resources administration is based on a strong commitment by the school board and the administrative staff to a planned and comprehensive program of developing human talent within the organization to achieve the goals cooperatively determined for the school district.

DISCUSSION QUESTIONS

1. The chapter discussion notes that effective human resources planning serves as the foundation for decision making. Consider the specific process of recruitment. Use several examples and/or illustrations to demonstrate the importance of planning as it relates to the recruitment

11. Orientation of teachers is a continuing process based upon a planned program designed to acquaint the teacher with his/her responsibilities toward the student, school, and community, and to acquaint the teacher with the resources in the school system and the community.

12. Appraisal of teaching performance is a cooperative process designed primarily to improve the quality of teaching.

13. The personnel evaluation and supervision system, while directed toward helping employees improve the quality of their performance, provides information which enables evaluators to make objective and fair decisions concerning termination, retention, or discipline when the employee's performance or conduct is marginal or clearly unsatisfactory, and rewards excellent performance.

14. In the interests of promoting high morale and leadership effectiveness, the personnel department will use its influence to assure that individuals on the professional staff are recognized for excellence and promoted on the basis of competency, performance, qualifications, fitness for the job, and probability of future growth and development regardless of age, sex, religion, and natural origin, ethnic heritage, marital status, or handicap.

15. Collective bargaining, as a personnel function, will conclude in an equitable agreement which preserves the board's responsibility to make policy and the administrator's right to manage the school district for the citizens and children and at the same time provide adequate wages, hours, and working conditions for its employees.

16. Compensation plans that place the school board in a favorable, competitive position and salary policies that encourage professional growth and personal improvement in service are essential elements of personnel administration.

17. Job descriptions and classifications include the duties to be performed, the immediate supervisor, educational preparation required, and personal qualifications needed for the position.

18. Regulations governing resignations should provide an orderly termination of service with a minimum of disruption to the school system and inconvenience to the employees.

19. The school district has written and publicized policies for the reduction of staff when needed.

FIGURE 2.11
(continued)

    process. What specific planning is required? What specific kinds of data or information are needed?

2. Examine the definitions and purposes of recruitment, selection, induction, and assignment discussed in the chapter. Illustrate specific ways in which one process is related to another. For example, how does the induction process relate to the assignment process?

3. Examine the list of specific problems encountered by human resources administrators today. Which of these problems are important ones in school districts in your area presently? Discuss these problems relative to their implications for the work performances of persons in your school district. In each case, give consideration to how these problems affect teaching and learning.

4. (*Class exercise*) Each student should list several specific problems encountered by teaching personnel today. Compare individual listings for the identification of common problems. Discuss the implications of

these common problems for the work of the human resources administrator at the central level and for building-level administrators.

5. Examine closely the position description and the selected competencies of the central unit human resources administrator. Discuss the type of preparation and experience necessary for effectiveness in such a position, as implied by the requirements of the role. What specific course work and field experiences appear essential? Then consider the school principal's role in the human resources function. What specific competencies are necessary for effectiveness in the principal's role?

6. Assume that a decision was made to decentralize the human resources function in your school system or one with which you are familiar. What kinds of administrative arrangements appear most likely? Discuss briefly these arrangements and identify the allocation of responsibility as related to human resources for implementing the human resources function.

7. Consider specifically the human resources processes of selection, stability, and organizational climate. List several ways in which each of these processes affects teaching and learning in a school setting.

■───────────   *CASE STUDIES*

2.1 Position Descriptions: Fact or Fiction?

Steven Alexander had served as director of human resources in the Union School District for 1 year. The position description for director had been written 4 years ago and listed a comprehensive set of duties and responsibilities. As was the case with other central office administrative roles, however, Steven was involved in several program activities not included in the position description. Some of the responsibilities listed in Steven's position description, and in those of other administrators, actually were being carried out by persons in other units.

In Steven's case, the position description stipulated that he was responsible for coordinating the teacher performance evaluation program for the district, yet he admitted that he spent less than 5% of his time in this area. The instructional unit in the district and local building principals were the ones who performed the evaluation activities. Steven's part was to keep a general file of evaluation reports.

Even though the school board policies did call for a position description for every position and such descriptions did exist, there was a general feeling at the administrative cabinet level that position descriptions were somewhat restraining. As was stated by the school superintendent on one occasion, "One way to inhibit individual creativity and incentive is to freeze them in a written position description."

Thus the position descriptions in the Union School District were not adhered to in a rigid fashion, and employees often were given responsibilities outside those stated in their specific position descriptions. No one was particularly concerned about this practice; in fact, it never was raised as being a major concern on the part of school employees.

Questions

1. What are the pros and cons of having position descriptions but not using them as typically intended?

2. Identify two or three specific problems that could develop from the practices described.
3. As the human resources director, Steven Alexander, what actions, if any, might you take in this situation?

2.2 Qualifications: I'd Like to Be Considered

The Columbus School District has 15,220 students and 502 teachers. Personnel responsibilities are divided between the school superintendent, who handles the secondary school personnel, and the assistant superintendent, who is responsible for personnel activities at the elementary school level. Columbus's student growth has been phenomenal during the last 5 years; student enrollment has increased from 10,400 to its current figure of 15,220 during that time period. Forecasts for growth indicate that this suburban area will continue to grow at about the same rate for at least the next 10 years.

The central administrative officials and the school board are convinced that responsibilities for the human resources function are such that some new arrangements for administering the function are necessary. Both the school superintendent and assistant superintendent agree that the responsibility for personnel needs to be placed elsewhere, especially in view of their increasing workloads over the last few years.

Tyler Scott, a retiring school board member, has expressed a personal interest in the position of personnel director for the system. He will leave the board position in June and could assume the role on a full-time basis. Scott has a B.S. degree in business management and ran a small business for more than 20 years. Although he has never served as an educator, he has served on the school board for 12 years and was board president for 3 years. All of Scott's children are graduates of the Columbus School District.

"I've done most every job a small business requires," stated Scott. "I've kept books, hired sales personnel, trained employees on-the-job, and have evaluated personal performance. If the board does decide to advertise the position, I'd hope to be a leading candidate."

Questions

1. What are the implications regarding personnel competency and position qualifications?
2. Assume that you are Columbus's school superintendent. What recommendations or actions would you set forth on this matter?
3. Consider the matter of qualifications for the central office human resources director. What minimal qualifications do you believe are needed in the position? What specific preparation is important in your opinion?

2.3 The Policy on Policy

Patrick Joseph had served in the Papillion School District as human resources director for 3 years. During that time, the school district evidenced a loss of population growth that resulted in an enrollment decrease of 1200 students. Thus the school district had to reduce its professional staff by 40 teachers in the last 3 years.

Patrick was delegated the primary responsibility for determining which teachers were to be released. In brief, Patrick examined school needs using both enrollment data and program information. Although not widely "advertised," he took the opportunity to release several teachers who were not performing at the level building principals viewed as satisfactory.

It became apparent once again that Papillion would need to RIF six teachers. Using the same general criteria for deciding who was to be given their pink slips, Patrick sent notices of release to six teachers at six different schools in the district. Within 3 days after the notices were sent, Patrick received a telephone call from Brian Scott, a social studies teacher at McClintock Junior High School.

"Why me?" asked Scott. "I've been here longer than several teachers at McClintock. Furthermore, I have been in the district longer than many teachers that I know."

"Our decision is based on need," replied Patrick. "Our policy has been to release on the basis of program need."

"I've never seen a policy relative to teacher release," responded Scott. "Is there something available in writing?"

"We've been consistent on the matter," answered Patrick, "but there is no written policy on the matter."

"I think it's unfair," said Scott. "I plan to file a complaint."

Patrick met with Superintendent Gwen Bassett the next morning and informed her of the conversation with Scott. "Don't worry about it," counseled Superintendent Bassett, "I'll have our attorney look into the matter."

Questions

1. What kinds of questions or reactions do you think the superintendent will receive from the school attorney?
2. What would be the value of a board-approved policy in this case with specific regulations outlining the procedures to be used for reduction in force?
3. Assume that you are to develop a guiding policy for the school board in this case. What specific provisions will you include?
4. What is the overall value of viable school board policies and regulations?

REFERENCES

AASPA (American Association of School Personnel Administrators). (1988). *Standards for school personnel administration.* Virginia Beach, VA: Author.

Amparano, J. (October 28, 1996). *Arizona Republic,* p. E2.

Arizona Republic (September 5, 2000). One minute news, Section A4.

Arizona Republic (September 8, 2000). Buffalo teachers defy law, strike, Section A-10.

Arizona Republic (September 17, 2000). Motivating workers for the long term, Section EC1.

Arizona Republic (October 2, 2000). District seeks parents as substitute teachers, Section B-1.

Arizona Republic (November 12, 2000). Teachers get fined for strike over pay. Section A7.

Breuer, N. L. (2000). Shelf life. *Workforce, 79*(8), 29-32.

Castetter, W. B., & Young, I.P. (2000). *The human resource function in educational administration* (7th ed.). Upper Saddle River, NJ: Prentice Hall/Merrill.

Class size must be negotiated with teachers, Oregon court rules. (April 10, 1991). *Education Week,* p. 2.

Coladarci, T. (Summer 1992). Teachers' sense of efficacy and commitment to teaching. *Journal of Experimental Education, 60*(4), 323-337.

Cole, C. L. (2000). Building loyalty. *Workforce, 79*(8), 48.

Duke, D. L., & Canady, R. L. (1991). *School policy.* New York: McGraw-Hill.

Ebmeier, H. (November 2000). How supervision works in schools: An investigation of a path model through structural equation modeling. A paper presented at the Annual Convention of the University Council for Educational Administration, Albuquerque, NM.

Fayol, H. (1984). *General and industrial management* (revised by Irwin Gray). New York: Institute of Electrical and Electronic Engineers.

Gannett News, Turnover troubles plague businesses. (May 6, 2001). *Arizona Republic,* Section D2.

Gibson, R. O., & King, R. A. (1977). An approach to conceptualizing competency of performance in educational administration. *Educational Administration Quarterly, 13*(3), 17-30.

Harris, B. M. (1989). *In-service education for staff development.* Boston: Allyn and Bacon.

Hoy, W. K., & Miskel, C. G. (2001). *Educational administration: Theory, research, practice* (6th ed.). New York: McGraw-Hill.

Hradsky, R. D. (2000). Human resources career tracks. *Careers and the MBA, 29*(2), 62.

Mattern, H. (September 13, 1996). Teachers get failing grades. *Arizona Republic,* p. A1.

McLaglan, P. (January 1996). Competency models. *Training and Development, 50*(1), 60-64.

Mercer, W. M. (2001). Employers expand benefits. *Arizona Republic,* Section EC1, July 8, 2001, from

Gannett News Service. Source: Bright Horizons Family Solutions.

Nadler, N. (May 1974). Implictions of the HRD concept. *Training and Development Journal, 28,* 23-26.

Norton, M. S. (1999a). *The school personnel administrator in Arizona.* Tempe, AZ: Arizona State University, College of Education, Division of Educational Leadership and Policy Studies.

Norton, M. S. (1999b). The work of the school principal in the area of human resources administration in Arizona. *NASSP Bulletin, 83*(603), 108-113.

Norton, M. S. (2001). *Competency-based preparation of educational administrators: Tasks, competencies, and indicators of competencies.* Tempe, AZ: Arizona State University, College of Education, Division of Educational Leadership and Policy Studies.

Norton, M. S. (2001a). *The school superintendency in Arizona: A research study.* Division Educational Leadership and Policy Studies. Tempe, AZ: Arizona State University.

Norton, M. S. (2001b). Provide school and community orientation to retain your teachers and staff. *School Public Relations, 22*(2), 16-22.

Norton, M. S., & Kelly, L. K. (1997). *Resource allocation: Managing money and people.* Larchmont, NY: Eye on Education.

Pai, Y., & Adler, S. A. (2001). *Cultural foundations of education* (6th ed.). Upper Saddle River, NJ: Prentice-Hall, Inc.

Seyfarth, J. T. (1996). *Personnel management for effective schools* (2nd ed.). Boston: Allyn and Bacon.

Taylor, D., & Tashakori, A. (1994). Predicting teachers' sense of efficacy and job satisfaction using school climate and participatory decision making. Paper presented at the Annual Meeting of the Southwest Educational Research Association, San Antonio, TX.

Tyler, R. W. (1971). In-service education of teachers: A look at the past and future. In L. J. Rubin (Ed.), *Improving in-service education: Proposals and procedures for change* (pp. 5-17). Boston: Allyn and Bacon.

Zepeda, S. J., & Mayers, R. S. (2000). *Supervision & staff development in the block.* Larchmont, NY: Eye on Education.

PART TWO

Shaping the Environment of Human Resources Administration

3 *Strategic Human Resources Planning*

The information in this chapter will enable you to:
- Define strategic and operational planning and project their use in the human resources administration strategic planning process.
- Gain an understanding of external and internal scanning as it relates to strategic planning and the human resources function.
- Gain skill in the strategies for forecasting personnel needs.
- Relate planning procedures to the human resources function, as illustrated by the process of personnel recruitment.

This chapter discusses strategic planning from the human resources administrator's perspective. The chapter begins with a discussion of the primary purposes of HR planning and their vital importance to the effectiveness of the HR function. The definition of strategic human resources planning is presented along with background developments of the concept in order to show its emergence from strategic business planning to its current level of development. Then the six characteristics of human resources planning are described, followed by a discussion of the life cycle of school organizations and an overview of a school system's professional staff mix. This discussion provides the background for a general strategic planning model that highlights the integration of human resources planning into the strategic plan of a school system.

A graphic illustration is used to show the strategic planning model. The accompanying discussion reviews the model's three main elements: environmental scanning, strategic and operational planning, and implementation.

Methods of forecasting personnel needs and technological approaches to projecting enrollments are presented in the next section of the chapter. This discussion incorporates a Markovian analysis of personnel attrition and emerging computerized systems for projecting future student enrollments. Additionally, models for forecasting student enrollments are discussed. Finally, recruitment of personnel from a strategic planning perspective is addressed in the last section of the chapter as a means of illustrating a specific application of planning in the HR function.

DEFINITION AND BACKGROUND OF STRATEGIC
HUMAN RESOURCES PLANNING

Strategy, as the term is used by organizations, is "the approach or means selected to achieve a goal" (Norton, Webb, Dlugosh, & Sybouts, 1996, p. 132). Some planners consider strategy as an objective and the specific means for achieving it. **Planning,** on the other hand, "represents an effort to antici-pate and shape the future" (Seyfarth, 1996, p. 19). And, as stated by Gómez-Mejia, Balkin, and Cardy (2001), "Human resource planning (HRP) is the process an organization uses to ensure that it has the right amount and the right kinds of people to deliver a particular level of output or services in the future" (p. 159).

The aim of planning is to focus the energies and resources of the school system on the right results. When the school system uses proper planning procedures, it encourages accountability on the part of personnel. The pri-mary intent of human resources planning is the same as that for any other type of organizational planning; to help to decide in advance what is to be done and to clarify the school system's expectations of what it envisions the total system and its parts *to be* and *to do.* In this sense, planning is the school system's way of projecting its purposes.

Human resources planning is essential because it can offset uncertainty, focus the school system's attention on important objectives, and serve as a foundation for effective operation of the school system's program. Planning serves the purposes of providing (1) a basis for agreement as to the ultimate goals and purposes of the school system, (2) a clear definition of the options and alternatives available for decision making, (3) an identification of system strengths on which an improved program can be built, and (4) a system-atized procedure for setting objectives. What, then, is **strategic planning?** Pfeiffer, Goodstein, and Nolan (1986a) provided a foundational perspective of strategic planning when they defined the term in the following way:

> Strategic planning is the process by which an organization envisions its future and develops the necessary procedures and operations to achieve that future. This vision of the future state of the organization provides both the direction in which the organization should move and the energy to begin that move. (p. 2)

Strategic planning is a dynamic process for helping a school system to shape its future. And through techniques of strategic management, school sys-tems can effectively adjust to the unpredictable demands brought on by envi-ronmental changes. Thus strategic planning is a process that was developed to guide an organization in an environment of rapid and continuous change. Organizations need strategic planning because the world changes constantly. It is foolhardy and unrealistic to assume that economic conditions, consumer needs and expectations, competition, or numerous other factors will be the same 2, 3, or 5 years from now as they are today. A strategic planning process is a systematic effort by an organization to deal with the inevitability of change and an attempt to envision its own future. The importance of this process is that it enables an organization to help shape its own future, rather than sim-ply prepare for the future (Pfeiffer et al., 1986a, p. 24).

Cook (1990) is viewed by many as the leading authority in strategic planning for schools. He noted that strategic planning involves (1) determining the organization mission, (2) understanding the environmental forces that impact the organization, and (3) determining strategies for dealing with these environmental forces in such a way that goals can be accomplished.

Therefore, any effort by a school system to respond effectively to change must include a careful analysis of information about its environment. The results of this analysis will have an important impact on the system's strategic plan and will be critical to effective human resources planning.

"Organizations tend to commit resources to counter productive or conflicting activities when organizational changes are not consistent with its strategic plan" (Kreitner & Kinicki, 1998, p. 621). Norton et al. (1996) note that although "some consider *long-range planning* to be the same as strategic planning . . . there are some key distinguishing characteristics. Long-range planning is a form of **operational planning** typically involving a time span of more than one year. . . . Strategic planning is used to set the compass heading for the institution. Long-range planning is typically of lesser import and subservient to the direction set in strategic planning" (p. 133).

As with strategic planning, **strategic human resources planning** is concerned with the effective utilization of human resources and their contributions toward the accomplishment of educational goals. "Like any good plans, strategic employment plans are built on premises—basic assumptions about the future. The purpose of *forecasting* is to develop these basic premises" (Dessler, 2000, p. 124). Thus forecasting serves to anticipate the organization's future, including its external and internal environments. Strategic human resources planning is not necessarily the making of future decisions; it is focused on current decisions and their future implications. Strategic human resources planning produces current decisions about what should be done now to realize desired outcomes in the future. Accordingly, the purpose of human resources planning is to ensure the most effective use of personnel resources to move an organization toward its mission and achieve its strategic objectives.

A strategic plan is "a long-term plan outlining actions needed to achieve planned results" (Kreitner & Kinicki, 1998, p. 621). Strategic human resources planning is based on information that justifies conclusions about existing trends, which in turn form a rationale for predicting future events. "Strategic planning, properly done . . . can be the means of moving to the future and determining what that future will provide for children and youth" (Norton et al., 1996, p. 133). And, as stated by Castetter and Young (2000), a strategic school system plan is designed to accomplish several specific ends. Among these ends are: (1) to move the system from its current state to a desired state, (2) to establish the basic system purpose, goals to be pursued, and the general means (tactical plan) by which they will be sought, and (3) to link functional goals (e.g., educational programs and services, human resources, logistics and external relations) to the goals of the strategic plan (p. 44). Strategic human resources planning is a systems function and is inextricably tied to the system's guiding strategic plan.

Through the gathering and analyzing of information, the strategic human resources planning process influences the organization's strategic plan. This information is systematically collected and necessitates (1) determining job needs, including the jobs to be performed, the abilities needed by employees to do the jobs, and the number of employees that will be needed, and (2) developing sources of supply of potential employees (Mosely, Pietri, & Megginson, 1996, p. 297).

Strategic human resources planning evolved from strategic business planning in the early 1970s. The concept of strategic business planning was an important tool for relating management decisions to organizational objectives. The process was developed to bring about an improved allocation of financial and other material resources for maximizing planned organizational outcomes. It provided ultimate accountability on the effectiveness of management decisions. The changes in net product-line profits measured in dollars gained or lost have been regarded as evidence of management's performance.

The concept served the private sector well until recent years. A number of changes and national trends have emphasized the importance of the human element in strategic business planning. Concurrently, the federal government and other agencies increasingly are involved in regulating many aspects of human resources management. Each of the several human resources processes, selection and recruitment, compensation systems, promotion policies, collective bargaining, evaluation, and others, has been affected by such external mandates. Laws, court decisions, and executive orders of the last several national administrations have made the elimination of job discrimination a national priority. Also, societal changes prompted by the emerging trends in the family structure and the shifting age distribution of the population are a few among many considerations that have focused attention on improving human resources planning. Such considerations have had a profound effect on the operations of many organizations. Moreover, the social conscience of a growing number of organizational decision makers has been raised to include such factors in the framing of strategic objectives that are characterized by a sense of social responsibility (e.g., protecting the environment). Thus data about factors of human resources have become an important part of the overall strategic human resources planning process. The educational institution is a personnel-intense industry. In most instances, school systems establish mission statements to guide their commitments of time, energy, human, and material resources. Within this context, strategic objectives are defined for the numerous subunits of the organization as a focus for operational plans. The factors that affect sound human resources planning are as important to strategic planning in education as they are in business. Strategic human resources planning must be integral to the strategic educational planning process and must possess certain characteristics to ensure its effectiveness.

Service agencies such as the public school system have a vital interest in the development of workable models of strategic human resources planning. Such models will provide school systems with the benefits of a focused program, targets for improvement, and a knowledge of the makeup and expectations of its constituencies. School systems will also have the advantage of becoming proactive, rather than reactive.

CHARACTERISTICS OF STRATEGIC HUMAN RESOURCES PLANNING

Several of a list of characteristics specific to strategic planning have direct application to the processes of planning human resources strategically. The human resources planning process should be *comprehensive*. It must include the many subunits of the organization, for example, schools, departments, and divisions. All planning is done so that changes in one unit can be anticipated from planned or observed changes elsewhere in the organization.

Human resources planning is a process that is *integrative*. All parts should interrelate to form a whole. It is not simply a collection of plans from the several subunits of the organization, but rather a single plan reflecting personnel recruitment, selection, allocation, compensation, and development for all units.

The process is *continuous* and usually conforms to the organization's planning cycle. Data are continuously updated so that decisions can be made with the highest degree of currency and accuracy.

A *multiyear planning format* is essential to the continuous process of planning and should reflect activities and developments over a period of 1 to 5 years. This plan usually becomes less specific as it projects into the latter part of the 5-year cycle. On an annual basis, the plan is updated for each successive year of the planning cycle, and a new year is added annually to maintain the 5-year planning perspective.

The many constituencies affected by the plan should have input in the formulation process. Thus the plan must be *participatory* to gain individual commitment to implementation. Involvement in the planning process is a good investment that yields important dividends in commitment.

Finally, *flexibility* must be integral to the planning process. The plan should provide for modification and change as required by changes in the school system's internal and external environments and the specific needs of its constituencies. This flexibility should also be evidenced in the plan's sensitivity to the evolutionary stage of the school system and the changes required in the professional staff mix, which is described next.

EVOLUTIONARY STAGE OF A SCHOOL ORGANIZATION

The process of strategic human resources planning is founded on premises and basic assumptions that reflect on the history of the organization and the anticipation of its future. Such a foundation helps to clarify the predictions for future human resources needs so that processes can be developed and implemented to fulfill these needs. How can such needs be derived from the consideration of a school district's life cycle?

A school system on the fringe of a major metropolitan area that is struggling with continuous enrollment increases will be at a different evolutionary stage than a well-established central city district that is trying to retain a quality program in an environment of declining enrollments. The expanding system may need leadership personnel who are flexible, innovative, and committed to program development. On the other hand, the city system may desire educational leaders who can work with communities in the closing of schools and yet maintain high-quality programs through such transitions. Thus a strategic consideration is to match personnel with the requirements dictated by the evolutionary stage of the organization.

PROFESSIONAL STAFF MIX

Baird, Meshoulam, and DeGive (1983) were among the first to portray a portfolio mix of human resources as one in which personnel with specific skills, abilities, and expertise can be moved among units of the organization to achieve the organization's strategic objectives. Specifically, procedures are established so that personnel can be transferred among units of the organization to optimize the use of their talents.

Developing the mix involves balancing the best human resources talents with program needs to achieve the strategic objectives of the school system. Similar to the example discussed earlier, several attendance areas of a school system may be growing rapidly, while several others are struggling with enrollment declines. An analysis of the professional staff mix would take into consideration the strategic objectives of both the school system and the individual schools involved to determine the optimum mix of professional staff. This analysis may suggest changes in staffing to help to achieve strategic objectives.

Special considerations are frequently given to the professional staff mix. One relates to the school districts that are under a court order to provide a particular racial blend of professional staff members in all schools. Another district may be required to balance the professional experiences of faculty members among the schools of the district. Apart from court orders, it is often worthwhile educationally to balance staff on the basis of age, ethnicity, gender, and teaching load.

Despite the need for improving the professional staff mix in a school system, the reality faced by many school organizations may mitigate against such efforts. School board policies, contract agreements, past practices, and traditions can make it difficult to optimize the professional staff composition. Although policies on transfer and assignment can be hard to modify, traditions and past practices will certainly be more difficult if not nearly impossible to change. Thus the human resources administrator must exhibit careful planning, expert leadership, and sensitivity to realize such changes.

INTEGRATING HUMAN RESOURCES
PLANNING INTO THE STRATEGIC PLAN

The professional literature is replete with models for applying techniques of strategic planning to education. The model presented in Figure 3.1 was formulated to represent a synthesis of key elements of the strategic planning

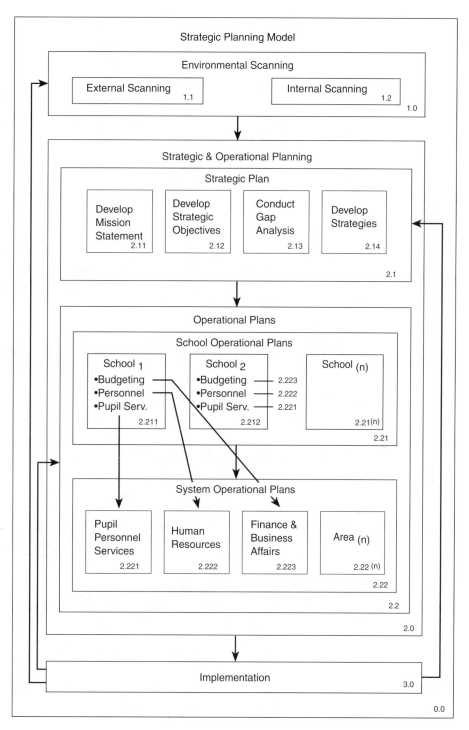

FIGURE 3.1
Strategic Planning Model

process, rather than an elaboration on the many models found in practice. Figure 3.1 graphically represents the relationship among the various elements of a general strategic planning model for a school system, with emphasis on integrated strategic human resources planning (operational planning). The major elements of the model include *1.0 Environmental Scanning*, with subelements 1.1 External Scanning and 1.2 Internal Scanning, and *2.0 Strategic and Operational Planning*, with subelements 2.1 Strategic Plan and 2.2 Operational Plans. Elements 2.1 and 2.2 in turn contain several subelements, including 2.11, 2.12, 2.13, and 2.14 and 2.21 and 2.22, respectively. The last major element of the model is *3.0 Implementation*. The following discussion will elaborate on the model presented in Figure 3.1.

Strategic human resources planning must be done within a context; this context forms a basis for establishing a school system's mission and developing its strategic and operational plans. The context is gained from **environmental scanning**. Moreover, the interpretation of the environmental scan will influence a school system's mission and all aspects of the planning process. Information gained from environmental scanning must be analyzed carefully to support the development of a comprehensive plan for administering human resources strategically (Kydd & Oppenheim, 1990). Specifically, the planning process entails the development of human resources operational plans that are consistent with the overall strategic plan (Anthony & Norton, 1991). These operational plans are dynamic because they interact with those of other organizational units. In addition, operational plans are monitored continuously and can be modified to reflect changing conditions in the school system's environment.

Environmental Scanning (1.0)

A school district's environment is viewed from two perspectives that are best illustrated by the acronym SWOT. Strengths and Weaknesses are regarded as internal environmental factors, whereas Opportunities and Threats are the key factors of the external environmental scan. Based on an interpretation of the environmental scan, assumptions can be developed to guide all planning efforts. A careful analysis of scanning information provides a school system with information that supports the development of a rationale for operating assumptions. These assumptions are used to assess the viability of the strategic plan. The assumptions relate to the external sociocultural, economic, technological, and political–legal areas and to selected factors of the internal scan, such as human and financial resources.

From a strategic perspective, a school organization must be attuned to its environment.

> Seen from a global viewpoint, the organization exists only as a part of a larger reality, supported and nurtured by the larger system on which it depends: the nation, its culture, and many interest groups, the world economy and political system, and the physical and biological planet itself. To the extent that an organization acts in ignorance of the connections that link it to other parts, and to the whole system of the global environment, it will tend to experience surprise

and shock at unanticipated events originating in the larger system. It will experience such events as deficient in meaning, and hence as a threat to its sense of reality and its own identity. (Harrison, 1983, p. 217)

Also, a description of a school system's educational environment includes many considerations that can be viewed simultaneously as constraints and opportunities. In each instance, strategic plans must be developed to minimize the negative effect of constraints and maximize the positive affect of opportunities.

Obvious environmental factors include state board policies and regulations, the state aid funding model for education and other state legislation, relationships with teacher training institutions, services of intermediate service agencies, competition from surrounding school systems that draw from the same teacher pool, the school tax digest, and federal program regulations. Other environmental factors would relate to the demographic features of the constituencies that the school system serves, including, among others, the racial and ethnic composition of the community, age distribution of residents, and socioeconomic status.

The processes of external and internal environmental scanning are continuous and fixed to the school district's planning cycle. Typically, the planning cycle is 5 years. Like the multiyear planning format, this plan is updated for each successive year of the planning cycle. A new year is added annually to maintain the 5-year strategic planning perspective. In each iteration of the planning cycle, all elements of the strategic plan are updated to reflect changing conditions, new directions, and emerging basic beliefs about the educational processes. Environmental scanning is included as an integral part of the strategic planning model, and it affects all elements of the planning process (see Figure 3.1).

External Scanning (1.1). External scanning is the monitoring, evaluating, and disseminating of information from the external environment to key people within the organization. It is a tool used to avoid strategic surprises and to ensure the long-term health of the school district. Typically, the external scan focuses on emerging trends that present *opportunities* for the school district and potential *threats* to its continued effectiveness. Central to the process of the external scan are four focal points of investigation: sociocultural, economic, technological, and political–legal. Also, Milkovich and Boudreau (1991) identified two other important scanning areas: role of government and changing demographics (e.g., age distribution of population, number of immigrants, distribution of work force by gender, and availability of workers). The scanning of these areas may be done by staff members of the school district or by external organizations such as research groups or universities.

Internal Scanning (1.2). The internal scan is usually done by the staff of the district, but it can be done by outside groups or organizations. It addresses the questions of *strengths* that support strategies and *weaknesses* in the organization that constrain strategies. Specifically, this scan investigates the structure of the organization to determine the extent to which it facilitates the implementation of the organization's developed strategies. A second area to scan is the organization's culture. An analysis of the culture determines if organizational behaviors are consistent with planned strategies (Koys, Armacost, & Charalambides, 1990). "Management must constantly be aware of culture in strategic planning. If the culture is antagonistic to a strategic change, plans should include ways to change the culture as well" (Reichrath, 1990, p. 52). To be comprehensive, the internal scan must include an analysis of the district's financial, human, and facility resources.

Every school organization has a unique culture, and the several schools of a school system often develop subcultures within the system's organization. Moreover, the system's culture is represented by the values, ideology, and goals shared by the members of the organization, including the patterns of behaviors for getting work done.

Ernest (1985) suggested an examination of certain organizational artifacts to gain insight into an organization's culture. This evidence cannot only be uncovered in an organization's policies, but also by employee greetings, dress, language, ceremonies, gossip, and jokes. He also indicated that the best understanding of culture can be found in the practices of administrators. The beliefs, values, and philosophies of top administrators influence the practices of upper- and middle-level administrators, who in turn affect the behavior of subordinates (Harris & Harris, 1982). For example, how decisions are made is an indication of culture. Some school organizations value collegiality, working together in groups, and opportunities for participatory decision making. However, others might be characterized by a number of individuals working independently within some formalized decision-making process.

The rituals of the organization can be a part of the culture and vary greatly from system to system. Some may provide public commendations for exemplary accomplishments or promotions. Others might arrange extraordinary programs of special recognition for retiring personnel (Carlson, 1991). School systems give greater or lesser emphasis to such events by publicizing their importance in both external and internal communications.

Another aspect of the culture is the control of information in the school system. Some control information very tightly; others are more open. Additionally, patterns of communication among members of the system characterize a cultural value. Some exhibit a top-down pattern of communication; top-down and bottom-up prevail in others. In a similar vein, some school systems tend to operate democratically, whereas others are more autocratic.

Many of these aspects of an organization's culture can be classified into Ernest's (1985) four-cell matrix depicting the two dimensions of people and action (see Figure 3.2). The people dimension spans the continuum of participative to nonparticipative; the action dimension ranges from reactive to proactive. School systems that respond to the external environment are classified as reactive, whereas those that attempt to affect it are proactive. Sim-

FIGURE 3.2

The Four Main Corporate
Culture Types

Source: "Corporate Cultures and
Effective Planning" by Robert C.
Ernest, March 1985, *Personnel
Administrator, 30,* p. 52. Reprinted
by permission of Sage
Publications.

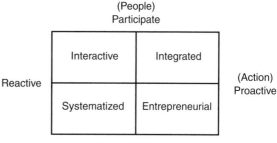

ilarly, systems that encourage interaction and communication are regarded
as high in participation.

The quadrants of Figure 3.2 identify four major cultural types. The
interactive culture provides good services and focuses on employee and community needs. The *integrated* culture has a strong people orientation, and
the system commits its energies and resources to innovative and creative activities. A *systematized* culture tends to be rule bound, with low participation of employees and other constituencies. Finally, the *entrepreneurial*
culture tends to be change oriented, with little participation by employees.

Although influenced by the system's overall culture, an individual
school often develops its own subculture. Different elements of the system's
culture can exist in a similar form at the individual school level. For example, if a school system places great value on the accomplishments of
staff members, an individual school may give great recognition to the
achievements of students. This system value is transmitted to its organizational members and is evidenced through the emphasis placed on recognizing student accomplishments.

A study of teacher perceptions offered a different perspective of the impact of organizational cultures. Page (1985) conducted an ethnographic
study of teachers' perceptions of students and a link among classrooms,
school cultures, and the social order. She stated that "teachers translate the
norms of an institutional ethos" (p. 7). Moreover, this ethos is a result of
teachers' perceptions of the environment outside the school. Her analysis
of two socioeconomically similar schools showed radically different role
perceptions and behaviors of teachers. She concluded that teachers' perceptions of students are circumscribed by the school's culture. Thus the
subculture of individual schools can be very different and can have a profound effect on several aspects of human resources management.

Strategic and Operational Planning (2.0)

Strategic and operational planning are key components of the strategic
planning process. The strategic plan is consistent with the assumptions derived from an analysis of the environment, and it forms the bases for relating all operational plans.

Strategic Plan (2.1). The four elements of the strategic plan, as illustrated in Figure 3.1, are *2.11 Develop Mission Statement*, *2.12 Develop Strategic Objectives*, *2.13 Conduct Gap Analysis*, and *2.14 Develop Strategies*. The actual strategic plan is published in a relatively brief document (usually 25 pages or less) that gives direction to all operational planning activities. Each operational plan relates to the strategic objectives and strategies in the strategic plan.

Develop Mission Statement (2.11). A critically important factor in the development of a school system's strategic plan is its educational mission. The mission statement provides direction based on a perception of the environment. Specifically, it is a reflection of the top leaders' interpretation of the educational environment. By virtue of their position, leaders influence the system's culture and can respond to their perception of the environment in ways that manifest their beliefs and values about the nature of educating young people, the task of education, and its processes. Consequently, the identified mission directly influences the major direction of a school system. For example, one system may state its primary mission as vocational education, whereas others may concentrate on basic skills, college preparation, special education, or community education.

Over a period of time, all school systems experience changing environmental factors. These environmental shifts can create a need to redefine the general mission of the school system. For example, a school system that has moved beyond the period of expansion in its life cycle may begin to see population shifts away from the central city to suburban areas with expanding pockets of non-English-speaking populations. This important environmental change should bring about an examination of the system's mission. If a new mission statement results, the system needs to make changes in its strategic plan. On the other hand, if the leaders of the school system misinterpret or ignore the changing environment and do not refocus the system's mission, obvious conflicts will invariably arise between the system and its constituencies. "Regardless of the status of the mission statement, the statement needs to be reviewed by the strategic planning council to determine if it contains vision focus, and clarity deemed appropriate in light of the strategic analysis" (Norton et al., 1996, p. 139).

Tethered to the realities of the external environment, a mission statement for a particular school system is developed. A written mission statement helps the system define its vision for the future, it provides a clear focus for the system's personnel, and it identifies a rallying point for committing the human and material resources of the district. Establishing a mission and implementing it through planned strategies permits a school system to shape the organization that it wants to become. It provides a perspective for the future of the system and a vision for the continued existence of the system. Norton and Kelly (1997) note that every administrator must have a vision. "That vision will often include expectations concerning: (1) student success, (2) the overall climate or environment of the school, (3) the processes by which decisions are made, and (4) the ways in which the administrator envisions individuals and groups interacting together" (p. 4).

Deciding what function the school system serves within its environment is the first step in deriving a mission. This function focuses on the current and emerging educational needs of the community. With a vision in mind, the question of whom it serves becomes germane. Environmental changes require a school system to reevaluate its mission statement periodically. Usually, the mission statement should be reviewed every 5 years to ensure that it meets the needs of the communities that it serves. One essential ingredient of the mission statement is an identification of the segment of the population served. No school system can be everything to everyone. Market segmentation requires a review of the actual population that the school system serves, as well as whom it might potentially serve. In addition to geographical boundaries, the school system must know the ages of the people it serves, it must know the ethnic makeup of the community, it should have a good sense of the community's financial resources, and it should fully understand the values of the people. The school system completes its mission statement by determining how it will perform its function. The "how" response in the mission statement is expressed in general terms and gives guidance to material and personnel resource allocations; for example, "the district will use the latest technologies whose effectiveness is supported by research findings and will employ the most qualified teachers who demonstrate a readiness to use the technologies."

The mission statement is carefully studied by the school system in relation to the realities of the external environment. A careful examination of the mission statement should be conducted to determine if it satisfies the following 10 criteria set forth by Pfeiffer et al. (1986b):

1. The mission statement is clear and understandable to all personnel, including rank-and-file employees.
2. The mission statement is brief enough for most people to keep in mind.
3. The mission statement clearly specifies what business the organization is in. This includes a clear statement about:
   a. "What" customer or client needs the organization is attempting to fill, not what products or services are offered;
   b. "Who" the organization's primary customers or clients are; and
   c. "How" the organization plans to go about its business, that is, what its primary technologies are.
4. The mission statement should have a primary focus on a single strategic thrust.
5. The mission statement should reflect the distinctive competence of the organization.
6. The mission statement should be broad enough to allow flexibility in implementation but not so broad as to permit a lack of focus.
7. The mission statement should serve as a template and be the means by which managers and others in the organization can make decisions.
8. The mission statement must reflect the values, beliefs, and philosophy of operations of the organization and reflect the organization's culture.
9. The mission statement should reflect attainable goals.
10. The mission statement should be worded so as to serve as an energy source and rallying point for the organization. (p. 82)

Develop Strategic Objectives (2.12).   A school system's strategic objectives should focus on critical success indicators. As the system conceptualizes its future, it must identify specific factors for measuring both success or failure in achieving that future and the progress toward its mission (Pfeiffer et al., 1986b). These indicators are translated into specific objectives that provide directions for the use of the school system's resources (time, energy, and money). Achievement of these strategic objectives demonstrates the system's success in achieving its mission.

Objectives are usually focused on outcomes and are client centered and positively stated. Moreover, the strategic objectives should be related to the indicators against which the school system's constituencies evaluate its success (e.g., improved test scores, low dropout rate, scholarships and awards, employment after graduation, and college entrance).

Leithwood, Aitken and Jantzi (2001) provide an excellent, practical tool for helping schools and school districts to determine an image that serves decision making relative to goal prioritization and needed changes to accomplish the image and improve school accountability. As stated by the authors, "*Making Schools Smarter* is a monitoring system designed to help schools and districts acquire the information they need to better realize their intentions for improvement, accountability, and school restructuring" (p. 3). In brief, a monitoring system serves to provide a description of what the school really should be along with a process to help determine what the school really is. Such tools can help schools and school districts to acquire, analyze, and interpret the information needed to achieve strategic planning and related accountability. For example, concepts and tools available in Leithwood et al. (2001) can be especially useful to school leaders in the determination of mission, objectives, and continuous program monitoring, essential components for effective planning.

Conduct Gap Analysis (2.13).   The gap analysis applies reality to the strategic planning process. It involves a review of each strategic objective by comparing the desired outcomes to current outcomes in light of internal scanning information. In other words, the analysis reveals the gap between the outcomes desired and current outcomes in relation to available human and material resources, technologies, and instructional processes. One question frequently raised is whether the objectives provide sufficient challenge to stretch the creative thinking of the organization's members during the development of strategies. A response to this question may suggest that the outcomes sought by the strategic objectives be increased to press for greater challenges or, perhaps, lowered to reflect certain realities.

Develop Strategies (2.14).   Strategies are statements about how the proposed strategic objectives will be achieved. If the objective of increasing the reading scores of middle-grade students by a specified amount in a given period of time is established, one strategy might be to evaluate the middle grade's reading curriculum; another may stipulate the creation of an intensive staff development program in reading for middle-grade teachers; and a third might create a new screening and selection program for processing applicants to teach in the middle grades. Certainly, there could be others. Strategy selection depends on the expertise of the system's strategic planners, the creativity and competencies of its staff, and the staff's interpretations of both external and internal data from environmental scans.

Strategies are the administrators most important tools for coping with change, and they provide important bases for mitigating extraneous demands on the school system. Therefore, school administrators must learn to manage strategically; that is, their day-to-day decisions must relate consistently to the strategies adopted for the system's strategic objectives, and their decisions should move the organization in the direction of its mission.

The function of human resources must be integral to the school system's strategic plan by providing direction for future developments of human resources in conjunction with the system's identified mission, strategic objectives, and strategies. And there is a consensus among planners today that human resources is a must consideration in the development of strategic objectives and/or strategies.

Human resources planning cannot stand alone; it must be part of the organization's strategic plan. The human resources operational plan is just as important as a curriculum or a financial plan and should be developed in ways that are consistent with the objectives of the system's strategic plan. Additionally, system strategic objectives and strategies provide specific direction for the development of individual school operational plans, which also reflect the need for human resource considerations.

Operational Plans (2.2). Operational plans are developed for all functional areas of the school system. These include central office departments or units as well as individual schools. To develop operational plans for the several subunits of the school system (e.g., departments, program divisions, and schools), each subunit engages in crafting plans to achieve the integrating function of the overall strategic plan.

Operational plans are specific to one or more of the established strategic objectives and strategies. The aggregate impact of all operational plans particular to the same strategic objective will contribute to achieving that objective. This concentration of effort is the appeal of strategic planning. It brings important systemwide priorities into focus through operational plans that affect in different ways the achievement of mutually agreed on objectives. For example, if some area of student achievement is a priority, then the human resources department can develop an operational plan to direct its staffing practices for improving the personnel mix serving this area of the curriculum; the staff development unit could frame operational plans to improve instructional strategies or the knowledge base of teachers in the area; the curriculum unit might map this area of the curriculum to find possible incongruencies; the administration may establish an operational plan to increase public awareness; and the finance unit may work with another unit of the school system to seek external project funding. Each of these approaches can take the form of operational plans for individual functional units of the system or represent plans of cross-functional areas. This example shows how many parts of the organization develop operational plans that target a single strategic objective, but by using several strategies.

Included in the operational plans are goals to give direction to the overall effort, objectives to establish targets or outcomes sought by the plan, procedures for implementation, policy considerations, time schedules, implementation constraints, and monitoring procedures for control and evaluation. All plans are reviewed so that a coordinated effort can be used to minimize program overlap.

School Operational Plans (2.21).   The school is the primary unit for delivering services in a school system. Each school will have its own operational plan, which reflects strategic objectives that are consistent with the system's strategic objectives. An individual school's plan will focus on the unique needs of its students and will be in harmony with its immediate environment.

As operational plans vary from school to school, people with different skills and abilities will be required to achieve the school's strategic objectives. The requirements for a professional staff mix for two elementary schools might be very different. For example, suppose that a primary component of a system's mission is basic skills and the system has the strategic objective of raising reading scores on a standardized achievement test to the national mean in 5 years. One school might identify reading as a strategic priority. Another school that has maintained a mean achievement score in reading that is well above the national norm may focus its energy and resources on another strategic priority. Accordingly, each school may require a different professional staff mix. Such considerations have important implications for staff development, recruitment, and selection. Thus these considerations should be reflected in the strategic human resources plan. In practice, the balancing of the professional staff mix has not been widely implemented, despite its importance to strategic planning. Strong school board policies that reflect the importance of professional staff mix to strategic planning may help to promote a more balanced mix in the future.

This situation can serve as another example for understanding a school's operational plan. Certainly, the strategic objective of increasing scores on basic skills tests has implications for site-based budgeting, possible curricular or organizational changes, and of course personnel. Figure 3.1 shows how these considerations become inputs into the operational plans of the system's functional areas.

System Operational Plans (2.22).   Each functional area at the system level must have an operational plan for integrating all the school unit strategies. The need for a different professional staff mix is again used for purposes of illustration. If shifts in staff are required to optimize the mix, the personnel function would incorporate in its operational plan changes that accommodate all school units at an optimal level. Similar changes in the areas of curriculum or budgeting could affect any number of functional areas.

Consequently, the specific strategies of each of these functional areas may have implications for an integrated human resources strategy. "Operational planning may be an outgrowth of a strategic planning effort. Typically once a strategic plan has been developed in which strategic goals have been specified and prioritized, operational planning teams are selected to devise a plan for reaching the identified objectives or goals" (Norton et al., 1996, p. 133).

The *human resources (2.222) operational plan* reflects an integration of the various school unit plans and the system functional plans. The model does not represent a linear flow of information; on the contrary, there is neither a beginning nor an end. It is a continuous process of integration that supports the school system's strategic plan. Each unit and functional area of the system provides input to the human resources operational plan and has a role to play in its formulation and subsequent implementation.

Norton and others (1996) identified three basic components of the strategic human resources planning process: (1) the strategic analysis, (2) clarifying the mission, and (3) strategic management. "Strategic analysis is a process in which the strategic planning council reviews all the environmental considerations they feel have a significant influence on the school system" (p. 138). The mission statement is then reviewed for the purpose of assessing its reflection of vision, focus, and clarity as determined by the results of the strategic analysis. Strategic management, the third phase of the process, focuses on the implementation of the strategic plan and making the plan operational.

The human resources operational plan should accomplish three objectives: (1) It should correlate with the strategic plan of the system. (2) It should enumerate required changes in personnel, school board personnel policies, and administrative regulations and processes so that the system's strategic objectives can be achieved. (3) It should provide a master plan for recruiting, selecting, training, promoting, compensating, and developing human resources for the system (Galosy, 1983).

Implementation (3.0)

The results of implementing operational plans provide both product and process data that become feedback to other elements of the model. This feedback gives evidence to support a need for the refinement, modification, or reformulation of other aspects of the plan. In some instances, objectives will be changed. On occasion, the mission statement will be rewritten or new strategies will be developed.

CORRELATION WITH THE SYSTEM PLAN

School systems generally have not extensively involved their human resources units in the development of strategic plans. Despite the obvious and important advantages of integrating strategic planning and human resources planning, the educational literature does not suggest that such planning is taking place. Historically, human resources administrators have not been involved in strategic decisions. Most decisions of a strategic nature have usually involved the superintendent and a small group of others, such as those responsible for finance or curriculum. If the human resources plan is to be integrated with the system's strategic plan, human resources administrators must give attention to four basic tasks (Dyer, 1984).

The first task is to discover how the school system's educational strategies are determined. Many decisions are based on formal planning procedures that are presented to the superintendent and board of education for approval. By contrast, many strategic decisions result from a response to a crisis or an ad hoc effort of a temporary task force. Thus the human resources administrator must be aware of both the formal and informal decision-making processes.

A second task is to determine how much consideration is given to human resources in the strategic planning process. Do the plans include factors of professional staffing, development, recruitment, and selection? Are appropriate data collected and correctly analyzed? Are these data used to forecast future human resources needs and the supply of personnel? Are the results of such analyses used in decision making?

The third task is to decide the amount of consideration that should be given to human resources. Although education is a personnel-intense industry, different strategies will dictate different levels of involvement. A strategic plan to close several low-enrollment schools may dictate different human resources requirements than a plan for a bond election to renovate school facilities. Both would require human resources consideration. Yet the former may be more critical when considering human resources than the latter.

The fourth task is to work toward closing the gap between the amount of consideration that should be given and that actually given to human resources in strategic educational planning. This gap can be closed by continuously giving attention to the credibility of the human resources organization. The professional staff must be regarded as competent. They must be knowledgeable about education and educational issues, as well as most other aspects of the educational processes in the school system, including curriculum design and development.

Finally, to integrate the human resources plan with the system's strategic plan, three excesses should be avoided: possessiveness, parochialism, and negativism. Possessiveness relates to those who feel that human resources issues belong to them alone. Parochialism stems from seeing everything from a personnel perspective, rather than an educational one. Negativism is indicated by an automatic negative response, rather than an attempt to formulate constructive approaches to critical personnel issues (Dyer, 1984).

INFORMATION NEEDS AND FORECASTING

Collecting and analyzing valid and current human resources information relative to the school system's strategic objectives can provide a basis for ensuring that the human resources development efforts correlate with strategic educational plans. Human resources information must be collected from the different units of the organization, compared, and reported in a form that supports strategic decisions. Specific data about compensation, professional staff mix, and performance appraisals are important factors around which data are collected.

Forecasting Personnel Needs

A forecast serves to project future events and for purposes of program planning (Krazewski & Ritzman, 1996). Personnel forecasts are needed to provide a basis of maintaining productivity levels, identifying future professional staff mix, preventing staff shortages, minimizing the costs of overstaffing, and complying with equal employment opportunity goals (Rothwell & Kazanas, 1988). Another factor includes forecasting the attrition of personnel. Attrition results from personnel who move to new positions within the organization, leave the organization for positions elsewhere, or retire. An investigation of such changes requires the human resources organization to develop expertise in forecasting.

A forecast of changes in personnel provides human resources administrators with information that can be used to guide action to achieve the strategic objectives of the system. Such changes are often studied through the use of cohort analyses, census analyses, or more complex procedures related to Markov chains. The reader is referred to the foundational work of Feuer, Niehaus, & Sheridan (1984) for a comprehensive review of current forecasting practices. The following discussion is a simple example of a Markovian analysis for forecasting personnel changes.

Table 3.1 illustrates the movement of six classifications of personnel in a school system. In this example, the hypothetical system has 1460 professional employees, including 300 primary teachers, 250 intermediate-level teachers, 230 upper-level teachers, 500 secondary teachers, 80 supervisors, and 100 administrators. These employee classifications and current employment levels are listed in columns a and b. Data in columns c through h are probability factors for each classification. The factors are based on the mean percentage of personnel changes for the past 5 years, and it is assumed that these transition probabilities remain stable over time. Column c shows a probability of 0.60 (60%) for primary teachers to remain on the job during the year, 0.15 (15%) for primary teachers to move to an intermediate-level teaching position, 0.05 (5%) to move to an upper-level teaching responsibility, 0.01 (1%) to become supervisors, and 0.19 (19%) to leave the system. In a similar manner, the intermediate-level teachers (column d) have a probability of 0.10 for moving to primary teaching, 0.70 to stay on the job, 0.10 to move to upper-level teaching, and 0.10 to leave the organization.

Projections by classifications for the following year are presented in column i. The projection for each classification is based on the sum of the products of the probability factors and their corresponding employment level for the current year. For example, a projection of the number of primary teachers available the next year is $(0.60 \times 300) + (0.10 \times 250) = 180 + 25 = 205$. Similarly, a projection of upper-level teachers is $(0.05 \times 300) + (0.10 \times 250) + (0.70 \times 230) + (0.05 \times 500) + (0.01 \times 80) = 15 + 25 + 161 + 25 + 1 = 227$. Using this

TABLE 3.1
Markovian Analysis of Personnel Attrition

Classification	Current Employment Level	Primary	Intermediate	Upper	Secondary	Supervisors	Administrators	Projection
a	b	c	d	e	f	g	h	i
Primary	300	0.60	0.10	0.10				205
Intermediate	250	0.15	0.70		0.05			243
Upper	230	0.05	0.10	0.70		0.01		227
Secondary	500			0.06	0.75			389
Supervisors	80	0.01			0.01	0.90		80
Administrators	100			0.01	0.01	0.05	0.85	96
Exit		0.19	0.10	0.13	0.18	0.04	0.15	220

procedure for the other classifications, the projection for intermediate-level teachers is 243; secondary teachers, 389; supervisors, 80; and administrators, 96.

If we wish to conduct a Markovian analysis involving more classifications of personnel, an electronic spreadsheet such as Lotus 1-2-3 would render the analysis an easy task. The use of a spreadsheet would also allow the human resources planner to ask "what if" questions through which different assumptions about attrition could be investigated.

Forecasting Student Enrollments

We cannot dispute the importance of making reliable enrollment projections, because they are related to strategic decisions about staffing, curriculum, facilities, and financing. Most projections are made from extensive data sets incorporating 10 years or more of data, which may include past school enrollments, current enrollments, parochial and private school enrollments, nonresident enrollments, children per dwelling unit, resident live births, socioeconomic indicators, shifts of population, mobility of families, in and out migration, housing starts, transfer rates, home resales, and student retention rates. Additionally, selected factors such as building patterns, types of dwellings, community patterns, transportation changes, integration, and national trends are frequently used to temper the statistical treatment of the historical data for localizing projections.

Some early forecasting methods are discussed by Strevell (1952) and include the use of data related to class projections, retention ratio projections, housing projections, and total population forecasts. About the same time, Linn's (1956) approach for making enrollment projections included school enrollment trends over a 20-year period, current enrollments, parochial and private school enrollments, nonresident enrollments, birthrate trends, residential construction, children per dwelling unit, and the number of preschool children. About two decades later, Leggett (1973) and Engelhardt (1973) asserted that accurate forecasts could be made by using birthrate trends and cohort survival ratios. Strong and Schultz (1975) demonstrated the effectiveness of a regression model that used previous years' enrollments, increases in population of children by age, students not promoted, and students entering the labor force.

The *cohort survival* method, sometimes termed the percent-of-survival method, has been a popular forecasting technique for much of the past 20 years. The cohort survival method is based on certain assumptions: that certain statistics will continue to be similar to what they have been in former years (e.g., birthrates, death rates, student migration, grade retention policy, student retention, and other population influx or outflux). Thus any major fluctuations in population growth pose problems in the ability to accurately predict enrollment data. And as noted by Seyfarth (1996), "The accuracy of any prediction diminishes as the distance from the predicted event increases. Predicting enrollments one year in advance is more accurate than predicting enrollments 5 or 10 years ahead" (p. 28). In any case, the use of

TABLE 3.2
Kindergarten Enrollment Projections

Year of Birth	No. of Births	Kindergarten Year	Enrollment	Cohort Retention Ratio
1991	3400	1996	3380	0.9941
1992	3450	1997	3401	0.9857
1993	3600	1998	3503	0.9730
1994	3701	1999	3650	0.9862
1995	3800	2000	3701	0.9739
1996	4000	2001		

any forecasting method necessitates the application of both the experience and judgment of professionals who can adjust retention ratios based on their specific knowledge of the school community. Consider the following situation: During a period of 15 years, on average, 97% of the students enrolled in kindergarten continued to the first grade the following year. And 94% of the students enrolled in first grade continued on to grade 2, on average, during the same 15-year time period. Assuming that there are 500 students in kindergarten, it can be predicted that 485 students will enroll in grade 1 next year and of 488 first-grade students, 459 will appear in grade 2 next year. Table 3.2 illustrates a cohort technique for forecasting kindergarten enrollments based on annual birthrates over a period of 6 years.

In Table 3.2, the cohort retention ratio is calculated by dividing the kindergarten enrollment by the number of births for any one year (e.g., for 1991, 3380 ÷ 3400 = 0.9941). Find the average cohort retention ratio by adding the five ratios and dividing by 5. The average cohort ratio is 0.9626. To find the enrollment projection for the year 2001, multiply the number of births 5 years previously, 4000, by the mean enrollment ratio, 0.9626. The 2001 kindergarten projected enrollment is 3850.

As enrollments began to decline in the late 1970s, "school administrators and boards of education faced a major new public relations job: explaining the cost of decline" (Neill, 1979, p. 6), and a compelling interest emerged in forecasting enrollment declines. And, as pointed out by Seyfarth (1996), "if the trend shows a decline over a five-year period, the enrollment ratio is likely to overestimate enrollments. Depending on the direction and magnitude of the trend, an adjustment of the final enrollment figure may be needed" (p. 29). Many methods of projecting student enrollments have been chronicled during the past four decades as being reliable, and each required the analysis of large data sets representing many factors with data for periods of 10 or more years. Such analyses were laborious and time consuming. Now, with the emergence of powerful microcomputers, such analyses and data management problems can be handled with ease and speed.

No statistical model can embody all important factors in projecting student enrollments. Fortunately, recent developments in formulating complex computer algorithms for forecasting student enrollments have increased the reliability of such projections through the inclusion of many more factors than was previously possible. One such software package has been developed by Ecotran Systems, Inc., of Beachwood, Ohio.

Ecotran's MAPNET system is a basic transportation package that has an enrollment projection module for forecasting population trends and future school district enrollments. The system uses advanced statistical methods and historical data to make projections by grade, school, and geographical area. The module incorporates cohort survival and advanced econometric modeling techniques and uses up to 10 years of historical data. The system has the capability of calculating future populations from birth to grade 12, as well as by ethnicity of population. Also, the projection model generated can be displayed on the school district map for further analysis.

Another system with similar capabilities is the ONPASS planning system that was developed by Educational Data Systems of San Jose, California. It is an on-line, computer-aided, student demographic system that is designed to free educational planners from the time-consuming manual procedures of analyzing alternatives in the educational decision-making process. The system is capable of making 5-year projections for the number of students attending schools of the district, percentage utilization of schools, the number of students in each grade level, the number of students in each ethnic group, and the average walk or ride distance of students from each school and from each planning area. Additionally, the system can make projections for the planning area from which students attend school, the number and demographics of students from each planning area, and the number of classrooms that will be required at each school and grade level in relation to an established minimum and maximum class size, including combination classes where necessary. All these projections are based on aging of the student population, in and out migration, new housing construction, cohort survival statistics, and entry-level enrollment projections.

EDULOG is another enrollment projection model that was developed by Education Logistics, Inc., of Missoula, Montana. Like the two previous, this system projects enrollments by grade for the system, individual schools, planning zones, racial and ethnic categories, new attendance boundaries, user-defined student attributes, and other meaningful geographically defined planning areas. The system is based on a modified cohort survival technique that separately identifies the various factors determining enrollment patterns within a district. The model is capable of making enrollment forecasts out to 15 years.

Because of the improved reliability and ease of using such forecasting systems, the work of the educational planner can be greatly facilitated through their application in making strategic decisions. Certainly, other similar systems are available, and there will be more and improved systems in the future. It is most important for all school administrators to be aware of such developments and their potential for facilitating administrative decision making.

POLICY, REGULATION, PROCESSES, AND PERSONNEL CHANGES

School policies and regulations are inextricably related to the human component in organizations. Therefore, the strategic plan of a school system will invariably require that certain school board policies and administrative regulations be changed or new ones developed so that strategic objectives can be accomplished. As a part of the strategic plan, the section of the document related to human resources should enumerate the need for these changes with specific recommendations.

For instance, the human resources plan may include the objective to raise the minimum level of certification or formal preparation for instructional personnel. This objective is to be fully implemented within a specified period of time. Also, an analysis of school board policies may suggest that there are inadequate policies and corresponding regulations for guiding the implementation of the objective. The human resources operational plan would include recommended additions or changes to policies and administrative regulations. Obviously, other functional areas, such as finance, may be affected by such changes. A school system that is experiencing serious retrenchment problems due to declining enrollments provides another example. If the school district's objective is to close a number of schools, then specific human resources objectives that relate to the reduction of professional personnel must be developed. In this regard, a human resources objective might be to establish a program to eliminate a specific number of positions within a time period consistent with the staggered closing of schools. Of course, the plan would require investigations of personnel turnover trends, age distribution of personnel, professional staff mix for the total system, and other relevant considerations, such as personnel contract agreements and legal implications. If, for example, the analysis of all important data suggests offering early retirement incentives, the plan would have to be approved by the board of education. Certain policy areas and regulations would have to be examined to provide for the plan's implementation. In addition, the plan would require the consideration of system procedures and personnel changes.

PERSONNEL RECRUITMENT

An important aspect of a human resources plan is consideration of recruiting personnel. Recruitment is a planned process by which personnel are informed of position openings and the potential characteristics and qualifications of applicants assessed. The process results in the establishment of a pool of qualified personnel who are willing to join the school system. From a strategic human resources perspective, the goal of recruiting is to identify a pool of qualified people from which to secure the services of those most qualified, who in turn would help the organization achieve its objectives. This goal sets the direction for discussing a four-element model. The elements include (1) analysis and development, (2) need, (3) a recruitment program, and (4) evaluation.

Analysis and Development

The focus of the beginning stages of the plan should center on an analysis of the system's objectives and of their implications for recruiting human resources. Such an analysis should provide a basis for developing strategic recruitment objectives. The system objective of raising the mean achievement score for students to the national mean might have as a consistent recruitment objective an increase in both the number and qualifications of persons in the pool of qualified teachers. The recruiting objective could specify seeking candidates with higher qualifications in mathematics at critical levels of need. For example, the objective might be stated as follows: "The recruitment of intermediate-level teachers of mathematics will be intensified so that the pool of qualified persons is increased by 20%, with a mean increase of 30% in formal academic training or experience." Notice that this objective provides very specific directions for the recruitment of intermediate-level teachers of mathematics. Also, the specifications of the objective will produce a measure of accountability for the personnel in charge of recruiting.

A second level of analysis relates to school board policies and administrative regulations. The previously stated objective may have implications for existing policies or regulations. Current school board policies may not provide the latitude to implement the objective. Moreover, administrative regulations may be too restrictive for out-of-state applicants and may require modifications. If a board policy prohibits out-of-state travel to recruit personnel and the pool of intermediate-level mathematics teachers graduating from state colleges is too small, the plan would have to address possible modifications to the policy statement. Of course, this assumes that the pool from other sources is also limited. Once the objective has been determined and a policy analysis conducted, need can be established.

Need

Generally, need is the gap between the number of qualified personnel required to staff a program and the number in existing positions. The assessment of need involves an analysis of information and data about several important areas. The areas include the staffing or destaffing needs of all schools and other units of the school system, the system's strategic objectives, forecast trends by classification, professional staff mix, and supply–demand studies. Supply–demand studies are often conducted by the Department of Labor, universities, and state departments of education. The Georgia Department of Education's Teacher Recruitment Office maintains data for school districts relative to teacher and administrator supply and demand.

A need analysis will provide a basis for determining the number of personnel to be recruited into each classification pool. It will help to determine where the greatest emphasis must be placed in recruitment according to classification area. It will also help to define individual roles and methods in the recruitment program.

Recruitment Program

The recruitment program identifies the involvement of specific individuals. It also identifies the most appropriate methods and the best recruitment sources for achieving the objectives of the recruitment plan.

Based on a previous analysis of school board policies, the board of education may be required to develop and adopt new recruitment policies. Policies not only provide a legal basis for the action of recruiters, but they also give specific direction about the board's commitment to the human resources recruitment process. The following examples are only a few of many policy areas that may be considered in a human resources plan:

☐ Recruitment from within or outside the system
☐ Employment of persons from other systems
☐ Travel expenses of candidates
☐ Moving expenses of candidates
☐ Involvement of building-level staff in recruiting
☐ Affirmative action

By examining this short list, it is apparent that a board of education can have a profound impact on the recruiting program of the system.

The recruitment plan can also involve others in its implementation, including the superintendent of schools, the human resources administrator and staff, other administrators, and teachers, depending on their ability to assist in meeting the objectives for the recruitment plan.

The recruitment plan should include a description of the different methods to be employed in reaching the important recruitment sources. If it is determined that several colleges in the region consistently graduate high-quality students in an area of identified need, specific plans should be established to reach this source.

Potential recruitment sources include the following:

☐ Student teachers
☐ Referrals from current employees
☐ Lateral transfers of current employees
☐ Recruitment letters to colleagues
☐ Local talent, ex-teachers
☐ Commercial agencies
☐ Media, newspapers
☐ Future Teachers of America chapters
☐ Promotions of effective personnel
☐ College and university placement offices
☐ Placement offices of professional organizations
☐ Letters to colleagues in other systems, especially in systems that are reducing their work force
☐ Advertisements in professional journals

A recent development that will help to improve the recruitment process is the use of the electronic bulletin board. A number of organizations now maintain electronic listings of positions available. Some permit those seeking positions to place short summaries of their qualifications on the bulletin board for use by potential employers. This new tool should prove to be a valuable means of bringing employer and potential employee together, especially in rural areas where recruiting tends to present special challenges to human resources administrators.

Evaluation

Finally, the plan should present an outcome or product evaluation design to consider the effects of the recruitment directed toward the strategic activities of the program. In addition, the plan should identify procedures to determine the effectiveness of the processes involved in implementing the plan.

SUMMARY

Strategic human resources planning is a process of preparing a school system for activities in the future, and its decisions related to the use of personnel must show evidence of contributing to the system's objectives. Generally, its purpose is to ensure that the human resources of the school system are employed efficiently and effectively in pursuit of identified outcomes.

The effective planning of human resources requires a system for maintaining relevant systemwide data and information. This information is used to forecast trends on which to base decision making, provide for an optimal professional staff mix, and support other functions, such as recruitment, compensation, and affirmative action.

The implementation of strategic human resources planning must be based on an analysis of the environment. It should be sensitive to the culture of the school system. In addition, the human resources objectives must be consistent with the system's mission and its strategic objectives.

The planning process should be comprehensive and include all subunits of the school system. The plans for each subunit should be integrated to form an overall plan for the total organization. The process is continuous and should conform to the planning cycle of the system, with a multiyear emphasis of 5 years. Finally, the process should be flexible and participatory to accommodate change and expert staff involvement.

DISCUSSION QUESTIONS

1. Either individually or in small discussion groups, identify two different school systems in your immediate area and describe the evolutionary stages that each school system has experienced. Share these descriptions with the class. Discuss how they are alike and how they are different. Can you predict the emerging evolutionary stage of each school system?
2. Based on the descriptions in question 1, what are some of the most important human resources needs for each system during the next 2 to 5 years? What priorities should be given to optimizing the professional staff mix? What will be the most important human resources needs in 10 to 15 years?

3. In discussion groups, make a list of cultural elements that exist in your school or school system. Discuss the differences found on each list and how the several elements affect the behaviors of personnel.

4. Methods of forecasting staff and student numbers were presented in the chapter. Without question, such activities necessitate both time and resources. Consider, however, the results of not gaining such information. What are the likely impacts on both human and monetary resources?

CASE STUDIES

3.1 Mixed Expectations

Frank Hennessy was filled with excitement as he hung up the telephone. Dr. Brad Richardson, the superintendent, had just asked him to chair the newly created planning committee for strategic planning. As the director of human resources for the Cherryhill School District, he felt that he would now be able to play an important part in shaping the future of the district. As Frank reflected on the challenges facing the committee, he felt that strategic planning would help the district to become proactive by carefully considering its primary thrust. In the past, Frank had argued to narrow the focus of the district. He felt that there were so many demands being made on the limited resources of Cherryhill that every program ended up with only limited financial or personnel support. Now he hoped that strategic planning would help the school district to narrow its focus by deciding what was important and making a serious commitment to the goals of highest priority.

The community has high expectations for the school district and has been willing to support requests for funds to improve nearly all academic programs. Parents have been very pleased with the apparent rigorous demands made of students. The district has always had a very strong college preparatory program, with 78% of its graduates entering college upon graduation, and a sizable number of the district's seniors have been successful in being admitted to some of the more prestigious colleges.

Despite the fact that the curriculum has always been geared to the college-bound students, a number of pressure groups have been successful in getting the board of education to install a vocational program that has been a drain on the district's financial resources and, according to some citizens, is "taking money away from the more important challenge of preparing students for college." On the other hand, an emerging group of young parents has been working with the coaches to get more emphasis placed on athletics. Some board policies make it difficult for students to fully participate in interscholastic competition. Recently, two star football players were not allowed to participate due to poor grades in academic courses.

The first meeting of the committee was held in a retreat setting at a country lodge, where Superintendent Richardson welcomed the committee. He also talked about the importance of the committee's work and requested their total commitment to the strategic planning process. Frank knew that the superintendent's strong statement showing a commitment to and belief in strategic planning nearly ensured a good kickoff meeting.

After the superintendent spoke, Frank led the group in a discussion of strategic planning by presenting an applied model for school district planning. This model was the one recommended by the State Department of Education in a workshop that Frank attended last year. This was followed by several group exercises that involved the members in a discussion of values related to educational issues. All the exercises focused on consensus decision making, which precipitated much more discussion and heated debate than Frank anticipated.

Later Frank administered a strategic planning readiness instrument and wrote the group's results on the chalkboard. At this point, Frank led a discussion of the results. He was surprised that the scores showed such a high degree of readiness for the team to plan strategically. This was the last activity of the day and the meeting was adjourned.

During the morning session on the next day, Frank explained environmental scanning by using the acronym SWOT. He talked about the importance of knowing both the external and internal environments of the school district. This led to a lengthy discussion of many aspects of the district's environment.

Following lunch, Frank introduced the concept of a mission statement and its relationship to strategic planning. He emphasized the importance of addressing the questions of What? Who? and How? He asked each planning team member to develop a written response to the "what" question. Frank told the committee to write their statements on the chalkboard and that they would discuss their responses after the coffee break.

As Frank scanned the statements posted, he was surprised to find statements that were very diverse. This concerned him, because he feared that a discussion of these statements would deteriorate into serious arguments. Thus he decided to ask the committee members to read only their responses, and he told them that he would make copies of these statements for the next meeting. Frank wanted to give some careful thought to how he might handle the obvious conflicts that would emerge.

Charles Winters read his statement first. He said, "Cherryhill is committed to providing programs that meet the needs of students by developing excellence in both physical and academic abilities through challenge and competition."

Jeannie Crawford followed with, "It is the purpose of Cherryhill to provide quality education with an emphasis on the basics."

Board member Fredericks followed by very forcefully stating, "Cherryhill School District is committed to providing quality educational programs that will support gainful employment of its graduates."

The Teacher-of-the-Year, Cecilia Cousins, followed with, "It is our purpose to provide

a comprehensive educational program that will satisfy the social, psychological, physical, and educational needs of our children."

Sandy Christian read, "The Cherryhill School System is committed to helping students to develop a strong self-concept and a sense of self-esteem."

Principal Joe Tensley offered, "We are committed to providing programs of quality basic education in an environment that supports trust and mutual respect."

Nelson Thomas showed his strong interest in vocational education when he read his statement. "Cherryhill School District will provide a program to support the development of job-related skills that are augmented by skills in basic education."

Terri Moore then read her statement: "Our school system commits itself to providing quality programs that support the educational development and personal interests of all citizens of the community."

Finally, Dr. Richardson stated, "We at Cherryhill commit ourselves to providing the highest quality of education for our students that is focused on student interests and academics."

Frank then thanked the group and told them that he would have the statements reproduced for the next meeting in 6 weeks. At this point he was glad that no discussion followed because he didn't want to end the meeting in controversy. As he drove home, he wondered if any of the statements really reflected what the Cherryhill community wanted. For the next several days, he was preoccupied with thoughts of what to do next.

Questions

1. What problem(s) will Frank have to deal with at the next meeting?
2. What are some symptoms of the problem(s)?
3. What are all the possible actions that Frank might take to solve the problem(s)?
4. What consequences should Frank anticipate from implementing each of the actions?
5. What action should Frank attempt?

3.2 The State Mandate

Joan Ellis, a seasoned human resources administrator, attended several workshops on strategic human resources planning that the State Department of Education offered. She tried for several years to convince the superintendent to consider strategic planning in the district, because she strongly valued the process and felt that it would greatly help her district. Also, she had reliable information from a friend at the State Department of Education suggesting that it was only a matter of time before the State Board of Education would mandate that all school districts develop annual strategic plans.

Joan knew that the superintendent did not value any type of serious planning. She frequently recalled one of the superintendent's rebuttals to her planning suggestions: "We tried that comprehensive planning once, and it was a waste of time. The governor even had a conference on it. Then we had to submit that huge report that was probably never read."

As expected, the State Board adopted a regulation that required all school districts in the state to plan strategically and submit their plans to the Department of Education for approval. When the superintendent received notification of the requirement from the State Superintendent of Public Instruction, he asked the assistant superintendent for administrative services, the assistant superintendent for business affairs, and the director of finance to write the plan. Joan was not asked to be involved.

Questions

1. Did the superintendent make a good decision?
2. What problems can be anticipated from the superintendent's decision?
3. What are the possible actions that Joan might take?
4. What consequences can be anticipated from each action?
5. What should Joan do?

3.3 Sara's New Assignment

At the last meeting of the board of education, Sara Olivia was appointed as the new assistant superintendent for human resources. The board's approval was another vote of confidence for Dr. Tyler Woods, who was appointed superintendent only 1 year ago.

Superintendent Wood's decision to recommend Sara was based on her strong background in strategic planning and previous experiences as the director of personnel in a neighboring school system. Previously, she directed the strategic planning effort of a large school system in another state.

During her first day on the job, Sara was arranging her personal belongings in a beautifully redecorated office when Dr. Woods stopped by to give her the old "Welcome aboard" greeting. After a few minutes of casual conversation, he said, "Oh, by the way, I need your help. The board is eager to support my suggestions on strategic planning for the district. They asked me to give them a set of recommended board policies that they can consider for getting this effort underway. This is going to be one of the most important things that this school system has ever done, and the community will be watching it closely. You'll have to be a key player in this effort. So, what I'd like you to do is set up whatever committees you need for developing the policies and get back to me as soon as possible."

Questions

1. What considerations should Sara give to forming the committee? Who should be involved?
2. What should be the committee agenda at the beginning of the committee's work?
3. What policy areas should be reviewed in preparation for making policy recommendations to the board?

■ ──────────────────────────

REFERENCES

Anthony, P., & Norton, A. N. (1991). Link HR to corporate strategy. *Personnel Journal, 70,* 75–82.

Baird, L., Meshoulam, I., & DeGive, G. (1983). Meshing human resources planning with strategic business planning: A model approach. *Personnel, 60*(5), 14–25.

Carlson, R. V. (1991). Culture and organizational planning. In R. V. Carlson & G. Awkerman (Eds.), *Educational planning: Concepts, strategies, and practices* (pp. 49–63). New York: Longman.

Castetter, W. B., & I. P. Young (2000). The human resource function in educational administration (7th ed.). Upper Saddle River NJ: Prentice Hall/Merrill.

Cook, W. J. (1990). *Strategic planning,* rev. ed. Arlington, VA: American Association of School Administrators.

Dessler, G. (2000). *Human resources management* (8th ed.). Upper Saddle River, NJ: Prentice Hall.

Dyer, L. (1984). Linking human resource and business strategies. *Human Resource Planning, 7*(2), 79–84.

Engelhardt, N. L. (June/July, 1973). How to estimate your future enrollment. *School Management,* pp. 38–41.

Ernest, R. C. (1985). Corporate cultures and effective planning. *Personnel Administrator, 30*(3), 49–60.

Feuer, M. J., Niehaus, R. J., & Sheridan, J. A. (1984). Human resource forecasting: A survey of practice and potential. *Human Resource Planning, 7*(2), 85–97.

Galosy, J. R. (1983). Meshing human resources planning with strategic business planning: One company's experience. *Personnel, 60*(5), 26–35.

Gómez-Mejia, L. R., Balkin, D. B., & Cardy, R. L. (2001). Managing human resources (3rd ed.). Upper Saddle River, NJ: Prentice Hall.

Harris, P. R., & Harris, D. L. (1982). Human resources management. Part 1: Charting a new course in a new organization, a new society. *Personnel, 59*(5), 11–17.

Harrison, R. (1983). Strategies for a new age. *Human Resource Management, 22,* 217–223.

Koys, R. L., Armacost, R. L., & Charalambides, L. C. (1990). Organizational resizing and human resource management. *SAM Advanced Management Journal, 55*(3), 30–36.

Krazewski, L. J., & Ritzman, L. P. (1996). *Operations management: Strategy and analysis* (4th ed.). Reading, MA: Addison–Wesley.

Kreitner, R., & Kinicki, A. (1998). *Organizational behavior* (4th ed.). Boston: McGraw-Hill.

Kydd, C. T., & Oppenheim, L. (1990). Using human resource management to enhance competitiveness: Lessons from four excellent companies. *Human Resource Management, 29,* 145–166.

Leggett, S. (January, 1973). How to forecast school enrollments accurately—and years ahead. *American School Board Journal,* pp. 25–31.

Leithwood, K., Aitken, R., & Jantzi, D. (2001). *Making schools smarter: A system for monitoring school and district progress* (2nd ed.). Thousand Oaks, CA: Corwin Press.

Linn, H. E. (1956). *School business administration.* New York: Ronald Press.

Milkovich, G. T., & Boudreau, J. W. (1991). *Human resource management.* Boston: Irwin.

Mosley, D. C., Pietri, P. H., & Megginson, L. C., (1996). *Management: Leadership in action* (5th ed.). New York: Harper/Collins.

Neill, S. B. (January–February, 1979). The demographers' message to education. *American Education,* 6–11.

Norton, M. S., & Kelly, L. K. (1997). *Resource allocation: Managing money and people.* Larchmont, NY: Eye on Education.

Norton, M. S., Webb, L. D., Dlugosh, L. L., & Sybouts, W. (1996). *The school superintendency.* Boston: Allyn and Bacon.

Page, R. N. (April, 1985). Teachers' perceptions of students: A link between classrooms, school cultures, and the social order. Paper presented at the meeting of the American Educational Research Association, Chicago.

Pfeiffer, J. W., Goodstein, L. D., & Nolan, T. M. (1986a). Applied strategic planning: A new model for organizational growth and vitality. In J. W. Pfeiffer (Ed.), *Strategic planning: Selected readings* (pp. 1–25). San Diego, CA: University Associates.

Pfeiffer, J. W., Goodstein, L. D., & Nolan, T. M. (1986b). *Applied strategic planning: A how to do it guide.* San Diego, CA: University Associates.

Reichrath, M. R. (1990). A study of strategic planning readiness in Georgia public school systems. Unpublished doctoral dissertation, Georgia State University, Atlanta.

Rothwell, W. J., & Kazanas, H. C. (1988). *Strategic human resources planning and management.* Upper Saddle River, NJ: Prentice Hall.

Seyfarth, J. T. (1996). *Personnel management for effective schools* (2nd ed.). Boston: Allyn and Bacon.

Strevell, W. H. (March, 1952). Techniques of estimating future enrollment. *School Board Journal,* pp. 35–38.

Strong, W. B., & Schultz, R. R. (1975). Models for projecting school enrollments. *Educational Evaluation and Policy Analysis, 3,* 75–81.

4 Organizational Climate and the Human Resources Function

After reading this chapter, you will be able to:

- Differentiate between organizational climate and organizational culture.
- Delineate the importance of organizational climate in the improvement of the HR function and the achievement of school goals.
- Discuss how the climate of a school or school system can be determined.
- Understand more clearly the inevitable event of conflict in school settings and how some conflict can serve to initiate positive change.
- Describe how the climate of the school system can be improved.

Human resources administration was defined previously as those processes that are planned and implemented in the organization to establish an effective system of human resources and to foster an organizational climate that enhances the accomplishment of district goals. This definition emphasizes the responsibility of the human resources function to foster an environment in which relationships among personnel, students, and others lend significant support to the work of the human resources function and the achievement of school goals. Human resources administrators throughout the school system must assume a major role in the development of a healthy school environment in which everyone works cooperatively to achieve desired ends. As stated by one authority,

> The best human resources professionals I've met over the years understand that ultimately what's important is the nature of the management–employee relationship, not the details of policies themselves. The very best policies make no difference if they aren't well integrated with all other aspects of the company's relationship with employees. (Laab, 1996, p. 60)

In this chapter, organizational climate as it relates to the work of human resources administrators in education is discussed. First, a distinction is made between organizational culture and organizational climate, and the importance of a positive climate is discussed. Next, the research related to the school characteristics associated with a healthy school climate and the assessment of climate is reviewed. This is followed by a discussion of the impact of climate on student achievement, the behavior of school staff, organizational conflict, and organizational change and innovation. In the final section the improvement of school climate is discussed, with attention given to the role of human resources administrators in this process.

ORGANIZATIONAL CULTURE
AND ORGANIZATIONAL CLIMATE

Terms such as *organizational climate, organizational culture, syntality, school atmosphere*, and *school health* are among those found in the literature to describe behavior in organizations. In some instances, these terms are considered synonymous and are used interchangeably. Deal and Peterson (1999) imply that the term *culture* evolved as a replacement for the terms *climate* and *ethos*, which were used for years to describe that special feeling held by people to describe their schools, that "powerful, pervasive, and notoriously elusive force . . . and expectations that seem to permeate everything" (p. 2).

The purposes of this chapter make it necessary to differentiate the terms **organizational culture** and **organizational climate**. More than 130 years ago, Tylor (1871) defined culture as the knowledge, beliefs, art, morals, law, customs, and other capabilities acquired by man as a member of society. Some contemporary authorities continue to define culture in terms of cultural traits. For example, Pai and Adler (2001) define culture "as that pattern of knowledge, skills, behaviors, attitudes and beliefs, as well as material artifacts produced by human society and transmitted from one generation to another" (p. 21). Rich (1992) spoke of culture from a material and nonmaterial perspective. The tools, clothing, housing, and technology used by a social group represent its material culture; its values, beliefs, norms, mores, folkways, and ideologies constitute its nonmaterial cultural dimensions. According to Cunningham and Cordeiro (2000) culture is "a continuous process of creating meaning in social and material contexts" (p. 94). And Robbins (2001) states that "organizational culture refers to a system of shared meaning held by members that distinguishes the organization from other organizations" (p. 510). We view *culture* as the set of important assumptions, beliefs, values, and attitudes that members of the school or school system share. We also endorse the view of Bullivant (1984) that culture is (1) an interdependent and patterned system of valued traditional and current public knowledge and conceptions, (2) embodied in behaviors and artifacts and transmitted to the members, and (3) used to give meaning to and cope with existing and future problems.

Organizational climate is the collective personality of a school or school system. It is the school atmosphere as characterized by the social and professional interactions within it. We sometimes speak of the collective behavior of a school as the school's personality or its **syntality**. "More specifically, climate is a relatively enduring quality of the school environment that (a) is experienced by teachers, (b) influences their behavior, and (c) is based on their collective perceptions" (Hoy & Forsyth, 1986, p. 147).

TABLE 4.1
School Culture and School Climate

School Culture	Links	School Climate
Culture is the set of important beliefs and values that members of an organization share. Culture is more normative than climate in the sense that it is a reflection of the shared values, beliefs, and underlying assumptions of school members across an array of organizational dimensions that include but go beyond interpersonal relationships.	People Interpersonal relations Collective phenomena Environmental factors Socialization Shared goals Influenced behaviors	Climate is the collective personality of a school or school system. It is the atmosphere that prevails as characterized by the social and professional interactions of people. Climate is more interpersonal in tone and substance than culture. It is manifested in the attitudes and behaviors of teachers, students, administrators, and community members. Climate is concerned with the process and style of a school's organizational life, rather than its content and substance.

For the purposes of this chapter, the terms positive climate and healthy climate are used interchangeably.

A healthy organization, according to Miles (1969), "not only survives in its environment, but continues to cope adequately over the long haul, and continuously develops and extends its surviving and coping abilities" (p. 378). The healthy organization accomplishes this end by meeting its task needs, maintenance needs, and growth and development needs. For example, a school that is meeting its task needs has a clear goal focus, communication adequacy, and what Miles termed optimal power equalization, the equitable distribution of influence among and between subordinates and superiors. Climate is a phenomenon that is influenced by both the internal and external environments of the school system. And, while climate is relatively enduring, these internal and external influences can lead to changes in the climate of the school over time.

Table 4.1 illustrates differences between school culture and school climate, as well as the characteristics that serve to link the two. As depicted in Table 4.1, school climate is characterized by the social and professional interactions of people in the school community, while school culture extends beyond the interpersonal life that takes place in the school setting.

THE IMPORTANCE OF A HEALTHY SCHOOL CLIMATE

Why is school climate such an important consideration? Why does the environmental setting within a school system require the special attention of human resources administrators? And how can school climate be instrumental in the improvement of the HR function in the school system? Several reasons can be identified.

1. Since schools, departments, and offices are staffed by people, school climate in a real sense is a human or people condition. The kind of climate in the school sets the tone for the human considerations of importance to human resources administration. An important part of the work of human resources administrators is to determine the facilitators and inhibitors of school effectiveness, those strengths and weaknesses that affect the climate of the school system. The determination of school climate is the forerunner of the determination of the strategies for school improvement generally and improvement of conditions in the workplace specifically.
2. Climate in the school sets the opportunity for growth and renewal. To remain vital and alive, human resources administrators must work to promote a school environment that fosters positive personnel development. The healthy school serves to stimulate the best efforts of people through providing meaningful work, motivating challenges, and providing continuous opportunities for learning. Through an ongoing program of people development, the school system has the ability to innovate and change as needed within a changing society.
3. Effective communication requires a climate of trust, mutual respect, and clarity of function. Such communication is inhibited in schools where distrust and poor human relations exist. Effective communication is an important component of an open, positive climate; it serves to tie the school community together. Barth (1990) speaks of collegiality in relation to a healthy school. He notes several important forms of communication and collegiality in schools: adults in schools talk about practice, talk to each other, work together in curriculum, and teach each other what they know. Craft knowledge is openly shared between and among colleagues.
4. Climate conditions the school environment for creative efforts, innovation, and change. These behaviors serve as foundations for organizational goal achievement. A positive school environment encourages innovative practices that serve the achievement of new goals. And, as has been stipulated by various authorities, rather than attempting to initiate change and then realizing subsequent failure, school leaders will find it more judicious to examine the school climate first and, if it is less than favorable, take steps to improve it before expending further energies toward program innovation.
5. Positive school climate infers positive team building in that goal development and achievement are cooperative tasks that require mutual trust and respect among faculty personnel. As emphasized by Robert Levering, cofounder of the Great Place to Work Institute in San Francisco,

> trust must be earned over time, but it can be destroyed overnight. It requires constant attention. Trust is earned by management showing a good faith—by being open, by being respectful of the individual and by being consistent . . .

professionals can play a big role in the process of building trust by encouraging more trustworthy behavior on the part of managers and by assuring that appropriate policies and practices are in place. (Laab, 1996, p. 60)

Thus school climate is important to school systems and to the human resources function because it affects all the important reasons that schools exist. Human resources leaders have an important role in determining what the school system is and what it might *become.* To have a positive influence, however, they must understand why organizational climate is important to both school effectiveness and to the effectiveness of the HR function, how it can be determined, and how to foster a positive environment within the system.

THE MEASUREMENT OF SCHOOL CLIMATE

Numerous empirical climate assessment instruments have been developed and administered in school systems in order to gain knowledge about the nature of school environments, the characteristics associated with different kinds of climate, and the impact of various leadership styles on personnel behaviors. Among the leaders in the study of organizational climate were Andrew W. Halpin and Don B. Croft, who developed the most widely used instrument for measuring climate in schools, the Organizational Climate Description Questionnaire (OCDQ) in 1962. Other scholars, such as Hoy, Tarter, and Kottkamp, completed additional research that served to improve the validity and reliability of the OCDQ for use at the elementary, middle school, and secondary levels (Hoy, Tarter, & Kottkamp, 1991). Halpin and Croft (1962) focused primarily on school climate as produced by the relationships between the school principal and the teaching staff.

The OCDQ is comprised of 64 Likert-type items to which teachers respond, thereby describing the climate of the school from their perspectives. The OCDQ yields school mean scores that are averages of the scores for all teachers' responses on eight subtests related to principal and teacher behavior. For example, two of the subtests are *disengagement* and *intimacy.* Disengagement refers to the teacher's tendency to "not be with it." This dimension describes a group that is going through the motions but is not in gear with respect to the tasks at hand. Intimacy refers to the teachers' enjoyment of friendly relationships with each other.

Using the profiles of 71 schools, Halpin and Croft (1962) developed six prototypic profiles to describe climates on a continuum from open to closed. An **open climate** is described as one in which the staff enjoys extremely high morale, works well together, enjoys friendly relations but does not engage in a high degree of socialization, and possesses the incentive to work things out and to keep the school moving. Kreitner (2001) suggested that open climates have four characteristics:

1. *Interaction with the environment.* Open systems have permeable boundaries, whereas closed systems do not. Organizations depend on the environment for survival.

2. *Synergy.* An open system adds up to more than the sum of its parts. Only when all parts are in place and working in concert can the winning edge be achieved.
3. *Dynamic equilibrium.* In open systems, dynamic equilibrium is the process of maintaining the internal balance necessary for survival by importing needed resources from the environment.
4. *Equifinality.* Open systems can achieve the same results by different means. (pp. 282–284)

In contrast to the open climate, a **closed climate** is one that is characterized by low staff morale, limited and inadequate communication, and limited socialization. In addition, closed systems are typified by impermeable boundaries and static equilibrium.

The work of Halpin and Croft and the wide use of their OCDQ in hundreds of empirical studies not only contributed significantly to the foundational concepts of school climate, but also served to motivate other researchers to study the topic from a variety of perspectives, including the characteristics associated with positive climates, the impact of climate on personnel, and the climate characteristics associated with effective schools, innovation, and change. Selected research related to these considerations is reviewed later in the chapter.

Other notable assessment instruments have been developed that address a variety of perspectives of organizational climate. Among those instruments that have been utilized over the years to determine school climate are the following:

The High School Characteristics Index (HSCI). This instrument (Stern, 1964) was developed at the Syracuse University Psychological Research Center as a standardized instrument to measure climate in schools. Students in the school respond to 300 questions relating to high school life. Thirty scales are provided on the HSCI that relate to seven factors of school climate (e.g., group life, personal dignity, and achievement standards). Such data can be invaluable in providing a school profile of existing conditions from the perspectives of the school's most important clients, the students. The school's index results can be compared with national norms for each of the 30 scales. Additional information about the HSCI is available through the Psychological Research Center, Syracuse University.

The Purdue Teacher Opinionaire (PTO). This instrument (Bentley & Rempel, 1980) is designed to provide a measure of teacher morale. The instrument includes 10 factors related to the school environment. Data collected from teaching personnel in one school result in norms that can be compared with those of the entire school system or with selected faculties in the system. Included in the 10 climate factors are teacher rapport with the principal, satisfaction with teaching, teacher load, rapport among teachers, teacher status, community support of education, and community pressures. The instrument can be useful to school administrators, school staffs, and researchers who desire an objective and practical index of teacher morale. Comparisons can be made among teachers when grouped by schools, grade levels, subject areas, and tenure status. The PTO has been empirically tested in hundreds of school settings; its reliability and validity have been thoroughly tested and retested since its first form was developed in 1961. The Purdue Research Foundation also developed the Purdue Evaluation Scale (1985), which is completed by students. The instrument provides evaluative information in six climate areas, including ability to motivate students, student–teacher communication, and fairness of the teacher. In view of recent research relative to the importance of conditions of work, including the nature of supervisor–employee relations and parental support, the PTO is of special significance. The PTO is available through the Office of Technology Commercialization at Purdue University in West Lafayette, Indiana.

The CFK Ltd. School Climate Profile. This instrument (Phi Delta Kappa, 1973) may be completed by teachers, students, and parents. It focuses on general, **program**, **process**, and **material determinants** of school climate. For example, the respondent uses a Likert-type scale in the general climate section to assess such factors as respect, trust, morale, school renewal, and caring. The instrument provides an opportunity for school personnel to compare views of teachers, students, and parents relative to several areas of school climate determinants. Additional information concerning this profile and its availability may be obtained by contacting the Phi Delta Kappa organization.

The Harrison Instrument for Diagnosing Organizational Ideology. This instrument (Harrison, 1985) differs from the previous instruments in that it helps staff personnel to compare their organization's values and their own personal values with four different cultures or ideologies. The aim is to enable participants to clarify where their organization stands on a number of important value issues and to identify differences between the organization's ideology and their own. Organizational ideologies include power orientation, role orientation, task orientation, and self-orientation. Results enable the organization to identify potential problem areas and to take steps to obviate areas of conflict. As the instrument developer noted, people deal with a bad fit between themselves and the organization in a variety of ways; some people change themselves, and some people try to change the organization. Other people respond in less positive ways by limiting their involvement in the organization or by attacking it in covert and overt ways (Harrison, 1985). The identification of potential conflict areas allows the member to share experiences in dealing with incongruous values within the organization and to deal with them in more promising ways. The instrument was developed by Roger Harrision, vice-president for Overseas Operations, Development Research Associates, Wiltshire, England, and 16 Ashton Avenue, Newton Centre, Massachusetts, 02159.

Organizational Health Inventory (OHI). This inventory (1986) is administered to teachers and uses a Likert-type scale to assess seven climate areas: institutional integrity, principal influence, consideration, initiating structure, resource support, morale, and academic emphasis. Profiles of results for each of the seven climate areas can be determined and compared with other schools in the district. The developers of the OHI believe it is a useful tool for measuring school climate since it reliably measures key dimensions of organizational health and was specifically designed, developed, and tested in the schools. Hoy, Tarter, and Kottkamp (1991) have developed OHI inventories for the secondary and elementary school levels. More information concerning these inventories may be obtained by contacting Corwin Press, Inc., Newbury Park, California, 91319.

Organizational Climate Description Questionnaire–Revised Versions (OCDQ-RE, OCDQ-RS, and the OCDQ-RM). Revisions of Halpin and Croft's OCDQ were completed by Hoy and Clover (1986), Kottkamp, Mulhern, and Hoy (1987), and Hoy, Tarter, and Kottkamp (1997). The OCDQ-RE was designed specifically for use in elementary schools, the OCDQ-RS for secondary schools, and the OCDQ-RM for middle schools.

The OCDQ-RE reveals the patterns of four climate prototypes: open, engaged, disengaged, and closed. "The distinctive features of the open climate are the cooperation and respect that exist within the faculty and between the faculty and principal. . . . The closed climate is virtually an antithesis of the open climate" (Hoy and Forsyth, 1986, p. 152). Similarly, an engaged climate, which exemplifies ineffective attempts by the principal to control faculty behavior, contrasts directly with behaviors of personnel in disengaged climates. Each of the newer OCDQ climate instruments has been tested thoroughly for validity and reliability for use at their respective school levels. The OCDQ-RS is a 34-item instrument designed to assess climate in secondary schools. It focuses on five dimensions of behavior, including the supportive and directive behaviors of teacher personnel. Two of the dimensions describe the behaviors exhibited by the principal and three center on teacher behaviors, specifically teacher relationships with students, colleagues, and supervisors. Resulting data provide descriptions of the openness and intimacy of the school climate. Intimacy refers to the level of satisfaction that teachers obtain from their friendly relationships with other teachers in the school. Since the original OCDQ was designed and tested at the elementary school level, its suitability for use at the secondary level was questioned. The OCDQ-RS "started with an attempt to create a parallel, valid, and reliable climate measure for high schools" (Hoy, Tarter, & Kottkamp, 1991, p. 48).

The OCDQ-RM, developed by Hoy and Tarter (1997), represented an effort to create a climate instrument especially designed for use in middle schools. More information about the OCDQ-RM and the OCDQ-RE is available in the publication, *Healthy Schools* (1997), Corwin Press, Inc., Thousand Oaks, California.

PEORIA SCHOOLING IMPROVEMENT PRACTICE STUDY
STUDENT SCHOOL CLIMATE SURVEY

School _____

Grade _____

DIRECTIONS:

As you read each statement please circle the number which best describes how you feel about your school. Do not circle more than one number for each statement.

Value of the number: (1) Strongly disagree; (2) Disagree; (3) Neutral; (4) Agree; (5) Strongly agree

I. SCHOOL ATMOSPHERE/MORALE

1. Our school has a friendly atmosphere.	1	2	3	4	5
2. Our school is a place where students want to be and a place where they can learn in a pleasant environment.	1	2	3	4	5
3. The students and staff take pride in our school.	1	2	3	4	5
4. School spirit and morale are high in our school.	1	2	3	4	5
5. Students and staff members in our school are usually happy.	1	2	3	4	5

II. STUDENT/STAFF RELATIONSHIPS

1. Staff members and students trust and respect one another.	1	2	3	4	5
2. Teachers in our school care about students and go out of their way to help them.	1	2	3	4	5
3. Teachers and other school personnel in our school treat students fairly and as persons.	1	2	3	4	5
4. Students and staff in our school frequently participate in activities that solve problems and improve our school.	1	2	3	4	5

FIGURE 4.1
Student School Climate Survey Instrument

In addition to those described, a number of other climate assessment instruments has been developed and tested for use in schools. Among the more widely used are the School Discipline Climate Survey: Toward a Safe Orderly Learning Environment (Grossnickle, 1993); School Climate and Context Inventory (Bobbett & French, 1992); the Tennessee School Climate Inventory (Butler & Albery, 1991); the Group Openness and Trust Scale (Bulach, 1993); and the Comprehensive Assessment of School Environments (National Association of Secondary School Principals, 1987).

In many cases, school districts have found it convenient to design their own climate survey tools. Such instruments can serve a useful purpose in gaining feedback from a variety of school stakeholders, but have the disadvantage of lacking state or national norms for comparative purposes.

5. The principal of our school is respected by students and staff members and is looked upon as an effective leader.		1	2	3	4	5
III. STUDENT BEHAVIOR/SCHOOL RULES						
1. There are relatively few discipline problems in our school.		1	2	3	4	5
2. The rules in our school are clearly defined and fair.		1	2	3	4	5
3. Most students in our school obey the school rules.		1	2	3	4	5
4. The attendance is good in our school.		1	2	3	4	5
5. Visitors in our school consider our students well-behaved and courteous.		1	2	3	4	5
IV. PEER RELATIONSHIPS						
1. The students in our school get along well with each other.		1	2	3	4	5
2. The students in our school are treated with respect regardless of race, religion, physical or mental handicaps.		1	2	3	4	5
3. Students in our school are willing to give a helping hand to other students.		1	2	3	4	5
4. There is little friction or hostility between groups of students in our school.		1	2	3	4	5
5. New students are made to feel welcome and a part of our school.		1	2	3	4	5
V. STUDENT ACHIEVEMENT/LEARNING ENVIRONMENT						
1. Student achievement is high in our school.		1	2	3	4	5
2. Students feel that our school program is meaningful.		1	2	3	4	5
3. The teachers in our school make learning enjoyable.		1	2	3	4	5
4. I like who I am and feel good about myself.		1	2	3	4	5
5. Students in our school seem to like and feel good about themselves.		1	2	3	4	5

FIGURE 4.1
(continued)

Figure 4.1 illustrates a district-designed climate assessment instrument. Such a survey can be completed by teachers and students. Results can be compared in a variety of ways, including perceptions of the school climate by students in relation to those of the faculty.

Other assessment strategies for gaining input from staff personnel are tied closely to one or more of the human resources processes and can result in findings that serve to improve current practices and ultimately lead to climate improvement. For example, although we stress the need for planned programs of teacher retention during the time of employment, valuable information can be gathered from employees who have decided to leave the system by using well-designed exit interviews. Information gained from an exit interview can help to determine why the employee is leaving and what the school system might have done to retain him or her. Questions such as the following tend to serve such purposes:

1. What did you like best about working here? What did you like least?
2. What steps would you suggest to improve the workplace in this system? What changes might you suggest?
3. To what extent were you able to realize you career goals while working here?
4. What opportunities did you have for discussing your career goals and teaching interests with others in the school system?

In view of the fact that much more of the time of human resources administrators is being spent on people management and efforts to make the school system a place where professional personnel and other workers want to be, more attention necessarily will be directed to assessments of the workplace environment and its competitive ability to attract and retain quality personnel.

RESEARCH ON SCHOOL CLIMATE

The focus on the technical aspects of work in fostering productivity, exemplified by Taylor's task system in the scientific management era, was brought into question by Follett (1924) and others. Follett contended that the central problem of any enterprise is the building and maintaining of dynamic yet harmonious human relationships. Her concepts of coordination for refocusing methods of supervisory and personnel practices to achieve organizational harmony were revolutionary. She introduced the concept of **integration** for dealing with conflict and initiated foundations for contemporary practices, such as participatory management, commitment to superordinate system goals versus personal vested interests, and integrative approaches to problem solving, including collective negotiations. Follett's work spurred many subsequent investigations that sought a better understanding of the relationship between the human element and organizational health and productivity. A number of these studies are discussed in various sections throughout this text.

Throughout the 1920s and during the next three decades, much attention was given to organizational concepts in the areas of democratic leadership, informal group influences, the school as a social system, and other organizational characteristics now studied in relation to school climate. Much contemporary thought relating to organizational climate had its beginning in the early 1960s. Since that time, numerous climate studies have been completed that center on (1) the characteristics that are found in schools with positive climates, (2) the impact of climate on student achievement, (3) the impact of climate on the behavior of personnel, and (4) the impact of school climate on school program innovation and change. Research studies related to each of these four areas are discussed in the following sections.

Characteristics of Schools with Positive Climates

Many of the studies of climate completed during the late 1970s and 1980s centered on the effective school movement. For example, Walberg (1976) investigated factors that influenced both teacher and student outcomes. Three of these factors were found to be relative to participatants' perceptions of the organizational environment: (1) tasks related to learning or productivity, (2) interpersonal relationships, and (3) organizational factors related to change. A study by Wynne (1981) examined 140 schools in the Chicago area for the purpose of differentiating effective and ineffective schools. He used the term **coherence** to describe the most common dimension of effective schools. Coherence was described as the integration of several elements in the school, such as the fact that stakeholders had a clear idea of school goals. Walberg and Genova (1982) found that the use of professional knowledge by teachers was significantly associated with such climate characteristics as equality of staff treatment, integration of staff cooperation, goal direction, and learning orientation. And Raywid's (1983) comparision of alternative public schools found that the success of alternative schools was due to their emphasis on matters related to school climate, rather than on an emphasis on curriculum and test results.

Several studies have reported a positive correlation between high expectations for students and productive school environments. Proctor (1984), after a review of the research on the relationship between teacher expectations and student achievement, maintained that organizational expectations are a critical element of a school's learning climate. Thus school climate is a key factor in the difference between effective and ineffective schools. This result was corroborated by Farrar and Flakus-Mosqueda (1986), who found that the one element all successful school improvement programs had in common was the development of a positive climate in which problems and issues could be identified and resolved. This finding is supported by Short and Greer (1997), who contend that "In the healthy organization, challenges are addressed, solutions to problems are found, and new methods and innovations are initiated. . . . Thus, a healthy organization not only has effective processes but also is likely to have a high trust culture" (p. 63). Effective people management continues to be tied closely to trust within the organization. Dobbs (2000) notes that studies consistently reveal that the commitment and retention of employees depend on their trust in and relationships with their immediate supervisors more than any other factors.

Rutherford (1985) studied perceptions of effective and less effective principals relative to five characteristics. One characteristic was the establishment and maintenance of a supportive school climate. He found that effective principals differed from the less effective in their views of school climate. For example, less effective principals were much more concerned with school maintenance related to a nonthreatening, "keep clear of problems" environment. Taylor and Tashakkori (1994) collected data from 9987 teachers and

27,994 students relative to the factors affecting climate. They found that the leadership of the school, the collegiality of the faculty, and student discipline were the major factors influencing school climate (Winter & Sweeney, 1994). Such support is exemplified in the behavior of principals that recognizes achievement, backs up teachers, encourages teachers, cares for teachers, and administers school rules fairly. Sweeney (1992) reported research results from a study of more than 600 schools nationally. The principal's effectiveness in learning environment administration, instructional leadership, and human resources management correlated highly with a positive climate. In fact, human resources management was the principal behavior most highly correlated with a positive school climate.

Buckingham (2000) reported on a study by the Gallup Organization that included more than 200,000 employees. As Buckingham states,

> From the employee's point of view, there is clear evidence that good management rests squarely on four foundations. These are:
>
> ☐ Having a manager who shows care, interest and concern of them;
> ☐ Knowing what is expected of them;
> ☐ Having a role that fits their abilities;
> ☐ Receiving positive feedback and recognition regularly for work well done. (pp. 45–46)

These research findings describe many characteristics that promote positive climates in schools and school systems. Numerous studies point to such factors as the establishment of clear school goals; high expectations for human performance; a high level of interpersonal relations and cooperative work efforts founded on trust; contacts with the culture in which the school is embedded; a supportive, caring school leader; a problem-solving capacity within the school; and the existence of high esprit within the school community. The following sections discuss the research and practices relating to organizational climate and student achievement.

The Impact of School Climate on Student Achievement

The definition of human resources used in this text emphasizes the fostering of organizational climate for the purpose of enhancing the accomplishment of school goals. Almost everyone agrees that student achievement ranks high among the goals for schools. Numerous research studies have centered on the relationship of school climate and student achievement. Borger, Lo, Oh, and Walberg (1985) reviewed 205 different studies related to effective schools. The researchers concluded that school climate was one of the constructs related to effective schools; 96% of the studies reviewed found that school climate was directly associated with student achievement.

Hopkins and Crain (1985) described efforts in a suburban high school to improve test scores through improvements in the school's climate. Climate improvements included such strategies as student participation in decision making. A 10-year high in ACT scores, improved student attendance, a significant decrease in the dropout rate, and other positive student outcomes were attributed by the school administrators to the climate changes in the school. Studies by Hoy and Appleberry (1970), Lunenburg (1983), and Deibert and Hoy (1977) support the general findings of Hopkins and Crain. For example, Lunenburg's research on students' perceptions of humanistic school climate related in a positive manner to their personal motivation, task orientation, problem solving, and attitude toward learning.

A study by Paredes and Frazer (1992) examined school climate over a 4-year period. Among the study findings were that (1) high schools with positive climates had higher student achievement and lower dropout rates, (2) student achievement was affected most directly by teacher expectations of student success and the instructional goals of teachers, and (3) school climate scores were better predictors of student dropout rates. Newman and Associates (1996) extended the foregoing findings in their report of a 5-year study related to school success and school culture. Researchers found that commitment to high student expectations, support for staff innovation and creativity, an ongoing search for new ideas, and a climate of caring and collaboration among staff were among the conditions directly related to school success.

Such factors as due process procedures for students and efforts to develop clearly written school rules and procedures, along with specific efforts to disseminate them, led to improved climates in nine schools in Kentucky and Tennessee (Bobbett & French, 1992). Bulach and Malone (1994) used three survey instruments to study the impact of the principal's leadership style on school climate and student achievement. A significant difference between leadership style and the subscale of school climate was determined.

Many local school districts have reported increases in student achievement following concerted efforts to improve the climate of the school. Anderson (1982) reported noted improvements in test scores in reading and mathematics after junior high schools in the District of Columbia adopted a specific program designed to improve the learning environment for students in the schools and in the home. Miller (1982) reported student achievement gains in one school after the implementation of climate improvement recommendations based on Wilbur Brookover's publication, *Creating Effective Schools* (1982). Similarly, Clark and McCarthy (1983) described a school improvement program in New York that had been based on Edmond's (1982) five factors that characterize high-achieving schools, one of which was the factor of an orderly school climate. For two of the three years analyzed, schools in the improvement program showed greater increases than other schools in the percentage of students reading at or above grade level, and improvement schools revealed a 6.3% increase in the number of students at or above grade level in reading, while other schools had only a 3.8% increase.

The results of the research on the relationship between climate and student achievement have been summarized by Winter and Sweeney (1994).

> For more than a decade, studies have proven that climate makes a difference in secondary school. Climate affects student achievement and behavior independent of student's intelligence or home environment. It is also reflected in the shared attitudes, beliefs, and values of the people of the school. (p. 66)

The Impact of School Climate on the Behavior of Personnel

Herzberg, Manser, and Snyderman (1959) pointed more than 40 years ago that interpersonal relationships with one's superior and the technical aspects of supervision were organizational **hygienes** associated with job dissatisfaction. In the year 2000, this contention was given major support by the Gallup Organization. Gallup interviewed 200,000 employees and concluded that the length of an employee's stay with an organization is determined by the quality of the relationship with her or his immediate supervisor. The impact of the workplace environment on employee satisfaction, commitment, and loyalty is no longer a matter of debate; virtually every study of employee attitudes and behavior reaches the same conclusion: work conditions, in the long run, loom more important to job satisfaction and worker retention than do salary and other monetary incentives. "And, the organizational climate of the school often is disrupted when high turnover occurs because the efforts to develop positive interpersonal relationships and collaborative support networks in the school system and community for the purpose of delivering effective learning environments are thwarted" (Norton, 2001, p. 16). It is clear that success in organizations today depends on a working environment that encourages input of the best ideas, regardless of the sources of these ideas, and the collaboration of workers and team efforts to implement these ideas in the most optimal ways. Such working relationships are not possible in school systems with unhealthy school climates.

Organizational climate has been found to influence staff in a variety of ways. Job satisfaction is directly related to conditions of work, which include the nature of the supervision received, administrative support, parental support, interpersonal relationships, participation in the system's decision making, and consideration of one's work and life needs. Patrick (1995) found that the principal's administrative style had much influence on the job satisfaction of teaching personnel. In related studies, researchers have found that school climate factors, such as the principal's leadership, the collegiality of the faculty, student discipline, and staff placements in school settings that provide the opportunity for them to use their personal and professional strengths and to do what they do best, were major determinants of staff job enjoyment and satisfaction.

Previously, we discussed the OCDQ-RE climate assessment instrument. Hoy and Clover (1986) developed four prototypes of climate that result in various teacher behaviors. For example, the **open climate** features cooperation and respect within the faculty and between the faculty and the school principal. Teacher behavior fosters open and professional interactions among faculty members. The open climate promotes cooperative behavior among faculty members and meaningful engagement in their work. In the **engaged climate,** teachers tend to ignore the principal's attempts to control faculty behavior. Teachers respect each other's professionalism and competence. Attention to tasks is high and the faculty is professionally responsive in spite of the principal's restrictive behaviors. In **disengaged climates,** relationship behaviors in the school are negative. Teachers are not engaged in the tasks, and teacher behaviors are exemplified by divisiveness, intolerance, and noncommitment. Teacher behaviors in **closed climates** are similar to those in disengaged situations. Task commitment is low, intimacy is low, and collegiality also is low.

Hoy and Miskel (2001) summarized the research relative to school climate and its impact on staff personnel as follows: "recent research . . . shows that open school climates are characterized by higher levels of loyalty and trust, both faculty trust in the principal and in colleagues, than closed climates" (p. 150). They stated further that research clearly indicates than open schools generate higher levels of school commitment, and the openness of the climate is related to teacher participation in decision making as well as to higher ratings of school effectiveness.

Dealing with Conflict. Webster defines *conflict* as an antagonistic state or action (as of divergent ideas, interests, or persons; opposing needs, drives, wishes or external or internal demands) (Merriam-Webster, 2001). Hoy and Miskel (2001) point out that "Administrators are faced with the classic confrontations between individual needs and organizational expectations; consequently, they spend a substantial amount of time attempting to mediate conflict" (p. 245). These authors also note that power and politics are facts of organizational life and thus conflict in organizations is inevitable. Open and closed systems were discussed earlier in this chapter; both types of systems are subject to conflict; however, open systems are much more prepared to deal with it.

Schools with unhealthy climates find it difficult to deal with conflict since personnel do not work well together; rules and regulations set the manner in which things are done, and the systems lack a needed problem-solving capacity. Thus problems are "resolved" through mandate, as opposed to an integration of ideas and alternatives; conflict often is resolved in these environments by employee turnover. In an open school climate, the right to disagree and express other points of view is not only expected but solicited. That is, the system purposely seeks input from all staff personnel through such means as suggestions systems, the use of "think tanks" for problem solving, and the use of shadow group techniques that place general staff personnel in role play exercises to examine problems faced by the system and its administrative personnel. Healthy school systems realize that any attempt to discourage disagreement will most likely result in negative outcomes, such as poor relationships and lack of confidence in the system's leadership.

In a healthy school climate, the consideration of controversial matters can be useful. Progress in terms of goal achievement and new understandings often is generated through opportunities to reflect on problems and alternative solutions. Thus the HR administrator can help to make disagreements constructive in a number of ways. One need is for the HR administrator to broaden the base of stakeholder understanding through purposeful assessment of criticism received by the school or school system. In this way, the HR administrator is in a much better position to limit unfair criticism, since assessment strategies serve to distinguish between constructive and destructive proposals.

Human resource administrators must implement viable methods for learning about the existence and specific concerns of criticism. The advantage of an open climate in this regard is that open channels of communication are most likely already in place; these channels serve as the system's nervous system, whereby school leaders are more able to discern conflict at an early stage and make an immediate, appropriate response to any attack, as well as to keep such conflict more manageable. In instances when criticism is unfair or based on irresponsible behavior, a planned strategy is necessary. The gathering of accurate information concerning the situation at hand, obtaining the participation of knowledgeable groups and individuals on the matter, and strategizing for appropriate counteraction are among the steps needed in such cases.

Public relations personnel have learned that attempts to cover up school problems or to use the tired phrase of "no comment" when working with the media and others only tend to exacerbate the problem. Thus the overall task of HR administrators is to work to maintain integrity and stakeholder confidence in a climate in which critics have the right to disagree as well as the right to use the school system's open channels of communication. Conflict and controversy can be helpful in leading to preferred solutions. Schools that maintain a communications initiative such as suggested here are much more likely to deal effectively with the inevitable conflict that they will encounter as a social institution.

School Life and Staff Commitment. The importance of gaining the commitment of staff personnel to the school system and its purposes is emphasized throughout this text. Although staff commitment is the result of various influences, research findings point out that worker loyalty is tied closely to how employees perceive that their supervisors are supporting inside and outside work life (Labbs, 1998). In fact, in a workforce commitment study by Aon Consulting (1998), it was found that the biggest driver of employee loyalty was having managers recognize the employees' need to balance work with home life. This climate conditioner differs drastically with earlier views that the worker was never to let family or home life interfere with the job. Work life matters have become of paramount importance to employees generally. It is certain that the structured work schedule for teachers and other school staff members must be reevaluated in view of the changing attitudes of today's employees toward work and life balances. New innovations in work schedules and instructional delivery in schools must be implemented. If not improved, job satisfaction will lessen and school climate will be negatively affected (see the discussion on workplace changes and flexible work schedules in Chapter 14 of this text). The implications for work life management by HR administrators include the following:

1. Studies reveal the fact that both workplace and home life support by the organization increases employee loyalty. Thus failure to give recognition to this fact will negatively affect school climate and staff commitment to the school system.

2. Schools must give full attention to work life benefits in school settings in order to attract and retain quality personnel. Recruiting, selection, and retention processes must give high priority to "advertising" how the school system is giving attention to benefits in the area of work life. Policy decisions and HR strategies must recognize the inextricable relationship between the work and personal life of staff personnel. The HR processes of recruiting, selection, and retention necessarily must place emphases on the needs of staff members, not only on the needs of the school system.

3. HR administrators must realize that giving attention to school climate and to staff commitment by recognizing work life balance is not just something they should do, but rather something they must do in order to keep the school system alive and vital.

The Impact of School Climate on Organizational Change and Innovation

Several investigators have examined the relationship between types of school climate and the rate of innovations in schools. As early as 1966, Marcum studied innovative and noninnovative schools in a five-state area. A significant difference was found between school climates of the most innovative and least innovative schools. Innovative schools were judged by school faculties as having open climates. Bennett (1969) and Christian (1972) also studied innovation in relation to school climate. Bennett found a higher positive relationship in both number and types of innovations in the more open types of climate. Christian used Halpin and Croft's OCDQ to study climate in elementary schools relative to the introduction and use of innovative educational practices. A significant positive relationship at the 0.01 level was found between openness and the rate of introduction and utilization of innovations in the school studied. The climate factors of disengagement and esprit (see Table 4.2) were most closely related to the rate of innovative utilization; the characteristics of aloofness and thrust, as related to positive principal behaviors, were most directly related to the *degree* of school innovativeness.

During the 1980s and 1990s, considerable climate research focused on school change as related to school reform. Bulach and Malone (1994) studied

TABLE 4.2
A Summary of Climate Types

Climate Type	Group's Characteristics						Leader's Characteristics			
	Disengagement	Hindrance	Esprit	Intimacy	Aloofness	Production Emphasis	Thrust	Consideration		
Open	Low	Low	High	Average	Low	Low	High	High		
Autonomous	Low	Low	Relatively high	Relatively high	High	Low	High	Average		
Controlled	Low	High	High	Low	Somewhat aloof	High	Average	Low		
Familiar	High	Low	Average	High	Low	Low	Average to high	High		
Paternal	High	Low	Low	Low	Low	High	Average	High but not authentic		
Closed	High	High	Low	Average	High	High	Low	Low		

Source: The information for this chart was abstracted from *Theory and Research in Administration* by Andrew W. Halpin. New York: The Macmillan Co., 1966, pp. 174–181.

the relationship between several school climate characteristics (e.g., group openness and group trust) and the implementation of reform efforts in Kentucky. A total of 13 schools and 292 teachers participated in the study. Researchers stated that "the results of this study lead to the conclusion that school climate is a significant factor in successfully implementing school reform" (p. 7). One interesting caution was given by the researchers: they noted the possibility that higher climate scores could have been the result of successfully implementing school reform. They were not certain which was the cause and which the effect.

Those involved in school reform have also noted the importance of climate. For example, Akin (1993) expressed the opinion that administrators who expect to be successful in school site-based management projects must first understand their school's climate and know how to change a negative climate to one that exemplifies the positive characteristics of healthy organizations. Similarly, Stevens (1990) argued that giving attention to important climate considerations is the significant forerunner of school reform. Hoy and Miskel (2001) stated that "The principal of a healthy school provides dynamic leadership—leadership that is both task oriented and relations oriented. Such behavior is supportive of teachers and yet provides directions and maintains high standards of performance" (p. 200). Yet they were cautious in suggesting that changing organizational culture, or even bringing about real change, is simplistic. And, as other researchers have noted, change is "something that emerges as an abstract, unconscious, and complex expression of needs and beliefs, it is not a maneuverable or manageable entity" (Norton, Webb, Dlugosh, & Sybouts, 1996, p. 75). Nevertheless, certain empirical truths have been discovered in relation to climate and organizational change: (1) Change in organizations is much more readily realized and effective if personnel understand what the change is all about and why it is necessary. (2) Successful implementation of change and innovation requires that attention be given to special training needs that serve to provide the necessary knowledge and skills to implement new goals and programs. (3) Strategies for recruiting, selecting, assigning, retaining, compensating, and developing personnel must focus on the changes and innovations in question.

This chapter has focused on organizational climate, and research is clear that it can be assessed and improved. The following section discusses successful programs and practices for improving school climate and the responsibilities of HR administrators in achieving this end.

IMPROVEMENT OF SCHOOL CLIMATE

The improvement of school climate is a responsibility of all school personnel. However, the school principal, as a human resources administrator, must assume a leadership role in assessing the climate and taking action for improvement based on the implications of assessment results. This contention is problematic in many ways; since the condition of school climate ties closely to the quality of the principal's leadership and ability to work with the human element, principals in some instances might be reluctant to survey staff personnel on this matter. As was seen in the previous discussion on measuring school climate, most climate instruments focus in large part on the leadership and human skills of the principal. The following section provides a review of several climate improvement efforts by school systems and other educational groups. This is followed by a discussion of operational models that can be used to improve the climate in school settings.

Program, Process, and Material Determinants of School Climate

One landmark publication in the area of school climate improvement is Phi Delta Kappa's publication, *School Climate Improvement: A Challenge to the School Administrator* (1973). Although the publication was first marketed nearly 30 years ago, its conceptual foundations remain applicable for practice in contemporary school settings. The publication, based on many of the climate concepts set forth in an earlier Charles F. Kettering Ltd. publication, sets forth school climate factors under three categories: *program*, *process*, and *material determinants*. Table 4.3 presents each of the three climate dimensions and the provisions that accompany them.

TABLE 4.3
Summary Form of the CFK Ltd. School Climate Profile
Source: Phi Delta Kappa, *School Climate Improvement: A Challenge to the School Administrator* (1973). Robert S. Fox et al. Reprinted by permission.

A.   Program Determinants
☐ Opportunities for Active Learning
☐ Individualized Performance Expectations
☐ Varied Learning Environments
☐ Flexible Curriculum and Extracurricular Activities
☐ Support and Structure Appropriate to Learner's Maturity
☐ Rules Cooperatively Determined
☐ Varied Reward Systems

B.   Process Determinants
☐ Problem Solving Ability
☐ Development of School Goals
☐ Identifying and Working with Conflicts
☐ Effective Communications
☐ Involvement in Decision Making
☐ Autonomy with Accountability
☐ Effective Teaching–Learning Strategies
☐ Ability to Plan for the Future

C.   Material Determinants
☐ Adequate Resources
☐ Supportive and Efficient Logistical System
☐ Suitability of School Plant

The CFK Ltd. School Climate Profile assessment instrument was discussed earlier in this chapter. The instrument includes each of the climate determinants set forth in Table 4.3.

Climate improvement begins with assessing the school's climate for the purposes of determining the areas targeted for improvement and a foundation for evaluating climate improvement changes resulting from specific program actions. Improvement procedures include the following action steps:

1. Human resources administrators must gain an understanding of school climate and its determinants. They must also be knowledgeable of climate assessment procedures.
2. Human resources administrators must examine their leadership role in a program of climate improvement. Such an examination centers on leadership responsibilities in assessing improvement needs, working to determine cooperative goals, determining actions strategies, implementing strategies, and monitoring progress and improvement results.
3. Human resources administrators must assume leadership in the implementation of specific climate improvement projects. For each project, assessing improvement needs, setting objectives, implementing strategies, and controlling the improvement process are required leadership actions (Phi Delta Kappa, 1973).

Thus, the route to school climate improvement depends largely on the extent to which program, process, and material determinants are being assessed, programmed, and monitored by school personnel. For example, the program determinant individualized performance expectations would be reflected in the attention given to the placement of students in appropriate learning environments scaled to their relative abilities, learning styles, and interests. Other considerations might include attention to teacher talents and interests in work assignments, the use of specially prepared teaching materials for individualizing instruction, and other program provisions that foster varied learning environments for students.

School Improvement Models and Strategies

Sweeney (1992) recommended several needs relative to the improvement of climate in schools. He suggested that the first step in the process, awareness, is often the most difficult. "People need to understand what climate is, how it affects them and others, and what can be done to improve it" (p. 71). School personnel must identify the primary beliefs and values that should guide the school and what must be done to initiate a plan of action to implement these beliefs toward the goal of climate improvement.

Wilmore (1992) suggested three keys to the development of effective school climate: (1) curriculum and instruction, (2) student affairs, and (3) parental support. She contended that curriculum should be student centered and that one of the best ways to promote positive school climate and an effective school is through a viable student affairs program. She also recognized that schools cannot be successful without a strong system of support from parents. Wilmore maintained that parental support stems largely from a sincere belief that school personnel truly care about the personal development of their child. Wilmore's contention that parental support is essential for positive school climates has been supported by other studies as well, including the 1997 study by the National Center for Educational Statistics.

A seven-step model for improving school climate was recommended by Coladarci and Donaldson (1991). These authors suggested that their process has not only resulted in improving climate, but it has promise for creating new levels of collaboration among staff members, students, and parents. Their climate improvement model is summarized as follows:

Step 1   The district determines those aspects of school climate regarded most problematic.

Step 2   School climate assessment instruments are developed for the district.

Step 3   The district distributes, administers, and returns surveys, which are then analyzed and reported in written form.

Step 4   School members meet with consultants and others to review survey results.

Step 5   School members break into small groups to pursue selected findings.

Step 6   School members generate multiple explanations for each climate condition identified in Step 5, develop a consensus approach to influencing some of the supposed causes, and construct an action plan.

Step 7   Follow-through actions are implemented to see that school members pursue the actions plans, that the effects of the plans are evaluated, and that the data and working lists of concerns are periodically revisited. (pp. 111–119)

The foregoing discussion, as well as the larger body of literature in the field, supports the following contentions relative to the improvement of school climate:

1. Schools that provide opportunities for active student learning, whereby students perceive the learning process and life of the school to be of high importance, tend to promote healthy school climates.

2. Learning environments that give due consideration to individualized performance as related to personal talents, styles, and interests tend to promote healthy school climates.

3. School programs and activities that are designed to reflect the changes in the intellectual, social, and physical development of students tend to promote healthy school climates.

4. Schools in which policies and school regulations are cooperatively developed, clearly written, and effectively disseminated tend to promote healthy school climates.

5. Schools with reward systems that place an emphasis on positive student reinforcement, rather than punishment, tend to promote healthy school climates.

6. School leaders who work purposefully to effect better systems of communication and to personalize relationships with school personnel and students tend to promote healthy school climates.
7. Schools that have developed a viable set of shared goals with expanded implications for the future tend to promote healthy school climates.
8. School leaders who give full consideration to the needs of staff and to both their work life and personal life tend to foster healthy school climates.
9. School leaders who give major attention to the general work conditions of the school, including such matters as teacher load, career goals of staff members, and to supervisor–staff relationships foster healthy school climates.

HUMAN RESOURCES RESPONSIBILITIES IN THE IMPROVEMENT OF SCHOOL CLIMATE

The concept that all school administrative personnel are human resources administrators is emphasized throughout this text. As is true with every human resources process, the organizational climate process is a shared responsibility among school leaders at all levels. Regardless of the position of the school administrator, we believe that the following primary responsibilities must be assumed. The belief is supported by the literature concerning successful programs and practices in the area of organizational climate.

1. *Development of a set of shared goals.*

   > Goals are those statements that set forth the purposes of the school system. Goals serve to clarify the aims of the school system; they provide a focus for the organization and give it a meaningful direction. Goals express what is important to the school system overall and are undergirded by the beliefs, values, traditions, and culture of the school system's community. (Norton et al., 1996, pp. 111–112)

   A primary process determinant of school climate is the development of a viable set of school goals. The significance of cooperative behavior as an important characteristic of school climate has been well established. Barnard's classic work, *The Functions of the Executive* (1938), set forth the belief that cooperation is essential for individuals in an organization. Cooperation necessitates commitment to a set of group goals and, as emphasized by Barnard, the formulation of organizational purposes and objectives is one of the three primary functions of all organizational leaders. Thus human resources administrators must assume leadership roles in developing a set of shared goals that express the school or school system's important and unique objectives. Once such goal statements are completed, a procedure for objectively examining these goals must be implemented.
2. *Self-image and high expectations.* Effective schools, ones with healthy climates, hold high expectations concerning student and personnel performance. Levels of expectation should be such as to solicit the best

performance that each teacher, student, or administrator has to offer. Viable goals provide a focus and give meaning to the people in the school. Such meaning is exemplified by the important work, personal motivations, and commitments of the school system's human element. These meanings, which are viewed as important to the system, comprise the system's self-image. A positive self-image serves as a foundational component of an open, healthy school climate. Human resources leadership must work to develop a meaningful self-image for the organization that reflects the beliefs and values of importance to its stakeholders.

3. *Opportunities for personal growth and development.* Healthy organizations understand that they will progress as people in the organization grow and develop. Schools with open, healthy climates tend to attract talented personnel who are motivated by opportunities to contribute and to be recognized for the important roles that they play in the achievement of school purposes. Human resources administrators help to develop the school system's full potential by removing obstacles that inhibit growth opportunities, by assigning personnel in positions that allow human potential to be realized, and by establishing an environment that encourages creative activity. Such an environment enables personnel in the school to be innovative, to develop different, more efficient, and more effective methods of achieving school goals and objectives. New and creative ideas must have a chance for implementation, but without the freedom to fail under controlled conditions, such ideas will not likely be tried. Human resources leaders must work to provide opportunities for staff personnel to assume the major responsibility for their own personal growth. Such opportunities are more likely to be found and practiced in school systems that encourage the use of individual strengths and in which staff personnel believe that their thoughts and creations are welcome and respected.

4. *Development of a viable set of personnel policies and regulations.* Many persons believe that a school district's personnel policies and regulations are a direct reflection of how it values its human resources. Governance policies directly influence the work and life of school employees, and human resources administrators must therefore assume a leadership role in the development of such policies. School policies and regulations affect the school climate in numerous ways. Policies are an important means of implementing the established goals that direct programs and influence interpersonal relationships. Policies serve to release human potential by providing opportunities for discretionary action on the part of the professional staff. They serve an important communication role in helping all persons to understand the school system and its purposes, and a viable set of policies and regulations releases the strength and creativity of personnel and allows them to establish a basis for intelligent decision making within the system. In Chapter 5 we suggest that human resource administrators should be given the primary authority for developing viable personnel policy for

the school district. And in Chapter 14 we emphasize the need for the HR director to be involved directly in all policy decisions of the school district. Such a responsibility provides HR leaders with an opportunity to directly influence the climate of the school that they serve.

5. *Problem-solving capacity.* Schools with healthy climates, like schools with less healthy ones, must face problems on a regular basis. A primary difference is that schools wlth positive climates have an identifiable problem-solving capacity. Climate characteristics that facilitate the availability to meet and resolve problems include open channels of communication, effective suggestion systems, a research posture, and recruitment and selection policies that encourage the hiring of a diversified staff. Human resources personnel must clearly identify ways to increase the effectiveness of communication, educate others about these channels, and facilitate their use. Effective problem solution and effective communication are inextricably related. Problem solving requires that the best ideas be heard and that they be considered on the basis of their merit as opposed to their origin. Open systems work diligently to increase the flow of ideas both vertically and horizontally within the system. Human resources leadership necessitates the development of a research posture within the school system. Problem solving often depends on the development of new knowledge. The effective human resources administrator is a consumer, facilitator, and utilizer of good research and realizes that creative solutions are often the outcome of research efforts that have objectively examined viable alternatives.

As previously emphasized, a healthy school climate is not a product but a continuous process. Organizational climate is a people phenomenon and people are the primary concern of human resources administration.

SUMMARY

The human resources function by definition holds a primary responsibility for fostering an organizational climate that enhances goal achievement. Organizational climate is of paramount importance to the operation of schools and its personnel since it affects every process of the HR function. Early work in the area of organizational climate by Halpin, Croft, and others opened the field for numerous investigations on the topic. Their OCDQ spurred hundreds of empirical studies designed to determine the type of climate in various schools and led to major studies to determine the characteristics of various climate types, the effects of climate on people behavior and student achievement, and the extent to which various types of climate influence innovation and change in organizations.

Various field studies have led to the development of frameworks that serve as models for improving climate in schools. Such models hold strong implications for leadership by the school principal. Virtually every study in the area of school climate links the type of climate to the leadership behavior of the school principal.

The improvement of school climate is viewed as the responsibility of all school personnel. Nevertheless, human resources units and administrators have specific responsibilities in the administration of organizational climate, including developing a set of shared goals, fostering a positive self-image for the school system, providing opportunities for personal growth and development, developing a viable set of personnel policies and procedures, and working to ensure a problem-solving capacity within the system.

DISCUSSION QUESTIONS

1. Give thought to the climate of the school or school system that you know most about. What climate characteristics can you identify in each situation? After noting several climate characteristics for a particular school or system, attempt to label its climate type according to Halpin and Croft's or Hoy and Tarter's prototypes discussed in this chapter.
2. Discuss the approaches that today's schools are using to change the environments. Which factors tend to foster or inhibit positive climate in educational settings? Are these factors tied closely to monetary provisions or to factors more closely related to conditions of work, such as workload and administrative support?
3. This chapter suggests strongly that school principals have much influence on the school climate in their buildings. What changes might increase this influence in the next several years? Are there changes that might serve to reduce this influence?
4. Reexamine the several characteristics of the program, process, and material determinants associated with the CFK Ltd. School Climate Profile. Which of these characteristics do you view as most important in conditioning school climate? Support your response with specific examples.

CASE STUDIES

4.1 Making the Worst of a Good Situation

Principal William McChesney was the newly selected principal for Antonio High School. He was following in the footsteps of Art Lown, who had served for 6 years. Under the leadership of Principal Lown, Antonio High School had gained a reputation as one of the best schools in the southwest region. The teaching staff at Antonio was viewed as highly creative; three on the faculty had been named teacher of the year in the state. Turnover in the high school was very low, and Principal Lown was viewed as an administrator who was highly supportive and easily approachable. Faculty and parents regretted his departure to California to head a developing program for at-risk students.

During the first week at Antonio High School, Principal McChesney sent a questionnaire to faculty members asking for their input on what improvements might be made in the school's program and activities. The feedback from the faculty revealed their creativeness; many improvement ideas were presented. One member of the staff suggested that the principal's control over curriculum be lessened and delegated largely to faculty personnel in the respective school departments. Another recommended a representative faculty advisory committee for the purpose of developing school policies and procedures in order to improve faculty involvement in participative management.

Principal McChesney did not act directly on any of the several recommendations received. At the second monthly meeting of the faculty, he commented, "I'll take your ideas under advisement. I must say, however, that I was under the impression that I was entering a school with a happier family than is apparently the case." One faculty member raised her hand to speak, but McChesney indicated that he would be following up on this matter soon. Within the next two weeks, he talked with faculty members individually about their suggestions. For the most part, he probed the matter about their apparent "unhappiness" with the present school operation. The consensus of faculty responses implied that there were really no major problems at Antonio, but that any school had some room for improvements.

Over the next several weeks, directives from McChesney's office centered on plans for focusing on performance evaluations, his desire to sit in on department meetings dealing with programs and activities within the school, and his intention to "flatten the organization" by eliminating the department heads by the end of the first semester. In addition, he sent a newly revised draft of recommended policies and procedures for the faculty's information.

By the close of the first semester, two department heads had asked to be relieved from the role, and three faculty members sent letters requesting transfers to other schools. For the first time in the school's history, Antonio students held a "sit-in" in the school cafeteria; their protest focused on the lack of opportunity for input into the decision-making process. Both student and teacher absenteeism increased significantly as well. As Principal McChesney sat in his office late one Friday afternoon, he contemplated the school situation with some bewilderment. "How did this situation change in so short a time?" he thought to himself. "What should I do now?"

Questions

1. In view of the somewhat limited information given for this case, present your thoughts as to what seems to be happening at Antonio High School?

2. At this point and time, what positive steps might be taken by Principal McChesney to reverse current climate trends? Do you believe that such a reversal is possible in this setting? Why or why not?

3. Discuss the situation in which a new school administrator moves into a school. Are there recommended procedures for entering such a new situation? Name two or more specific actions or behaviors that new administrators would be wise to consider upon moving into a new leadership position.

4.2 What's Really Important Around Here?

Virginia Royce was in her second year of teaching at College View High School. Her performance ratings for year 1 were rated "very good" in all categories. She had gained the reputation as one of the school's most promising new teachers. At the close of school on a Friday in October, Mrs. Royce went to the principal's office and asked if Mr. Henson, the principal, was available. The secretary answered in the positive and indicated that she was certain that he could visit with her.

"Come in Mrs. Royce," directed Principal Henson. "What's on your mind on this late Friday afternoon?" "Something has been troubling me for several weeks," answered Mrs. Royce. "So far this semester six football players have been absent from my English class for the last period of the day on three occasions and on two occasions they were absent for the full afternoon to play in out of town games, so they had to miss two other teachers' classes as well on those days. Pep rallies generally are held the last class period of the day before games; it all adds up to the question of what is really important around here."

Questions

1. Assume the role of Principal Henson. How might you answer Mrs. Royce?

2. Is it sufficient to respond that both subject-matter classes and extracurricular

activities are important at College View High School in your opinion? What other factors must be considered in this case?

3. Use the model for conflict resolution set forth in this chapter and apply it to this

case. Write out your action plan for each step of the model. (*Note:* Class members could be assigned roles in the case and role play the situation using the conflict model in the chapter.)

■━━━━━ ***REFERENCES***

Akin, J. (1993). The effects of site culture on school re-form. *High School Magazine, 1*(1), p. 29.

Anderson, S. L. (1982). Turning around junior highs in the District of Columbia. *Educational Leadership, 40*(3), 38–40.

Aon Consulting Worldwide Inc. (1998), America @ Work[SM], A study conducted by Aon Consulting Worldwide Inc., An HR consulting firm, Chicago, Illinois.

Barnard, C. I. (1938). *The functions of the executive.* Cambridge, MA: Harvard University Press.

Barth, R. S. (1990). *Improving schools from within.* San Francisco, CA: Jossey-Bass.

Bennett, R. E. (1969). An analysis of the relationships of organizational climate to innovations in selected schools of Pennsylvania and New York. *Dissertation Abstracts, 30*, 942A.

Bentley, R. R., & Rempel, A. M. (1985). *The Purdue teacher opinionaire.* Office of Technology Commercialization, West Lafayette, IN.

Bobbett, G. C., & French, R. L. (1992). Evaluation of climate in "good" high schools in Tennessee, Kentucky, and North Carolina. A paper presented at the annual meeting of the Southern Regional Council on Educational Administration, Atlanta, GA.

Borger, J., Lo, C., Oh, S., & Walberg, H. J. (1985). Effective schools: A quantitative synthesis of constructs. *Journal of Classroom Interaction, 20*(2), 12–17.

Brookover, W. B. (1982). *Creating effective schools: An in-service program for enhancing school learning climate and achievement.* Holmes Beach, FL: Learning Publications.

Buckingham, G. (February 2000). Same indifference. *People Management, 6*(4), 45.

Bulach, C. R. (1993). A measure of openness and trust. *People in Education, 1*(4), 382–392.

Bulach, C. R., & Malone, B. (1994). The relationship of school climate to the implementation of school reform. *ERS Spectrum, 12*(4), 3–8.

Bullivant, B. M. (1984). *Pluralism: Cultural maintenance and evolution.* Clevedon, Avon, England: Multilingual Matters.

Butler, E. D., & Albery, M. J. (1991). *Tennessee school climate inventory: A resource manual.* Memphis, TN: Memphis State University. The Center for Research in Educational Policy.

Christian, C. F. (1972). Organizational climate of elementary schools and the introduction and utilization of innovative educational practices. Unpublished doctoral dissertation, University of Nebraska, Lincoln.

Clark, T. A., & McCarthy, D. P. (1983). School improvement in New York City: the evaluation of a project. *Educational Researcher, 12*(4), 17–24.

Coladarci, T. C., & Donaldson, G. A. (1991). School climate assessment encourages collaboration. *NASSP Bulletin, 75*, 111–118.

Cunningham, W. G., & Cordeiro, P. A. (2000). *Educational administration.* Boston: Allyn and Bacon.

Deal, T. E., & Peterson, K. D. (1999). *Shaping school culture.* San Francisco: Jossey-Bass.

Deibert, J. P., & Hoy, W. K. (1977). Custodial high schools and self-actualization of students. *Educational Research Quarterly, 2*, 24–31.

Dobbs, K. (2000). Plagued by turnover? Train your managers. *Training, 37*(8), 64.

Edmonds, R. (1982). Programs of school improvements: An overview. *Educational Leadership, 40*(December), 4–11.

Farrar, E., & Flakus-Mosqueda, P. (1986). State sponsored schoolwide improvement programs: What's going on in the schools? *Phi Delta Kappan, 67*, 586–589.

Follett, M. P. (1924). *Creative experience.* New York: Longmans, Green.

Grossnickle, D. R. (1993). The school discipline climate survey: Toward a safe, orderly learning environment. *NASSP Bulletin, 77*, 60–66.

Halpin, A. W., & Croft, D. R. (1962). *The organizational climate of schools.* Contract SAE 543-8639. U.S. Office of Education, Research Project.

Harrison, R. (1985). *The 1975 handbook for group facilitation.* Newton, MA: Development Research Associates.

Herzberg, F., Manser, B., & Snyderman, B. (1959). *The motivation to work.* New York: Wiley.

Hopkins, W., & Crain, K. (1985). School climates: The key to an effective school. Paper presented at the annual meeting of the National Association of Secondary School Principals, New Orleans, LA.

Hoy, W. K., & Appleberry, J. B. (1970). Teacher relationships in "humanistic" and "custodial" elementary schools. *Journal of Experimental Education, 39*, 27–31.

Hoy, W. K., & Clover, S. I. R. (1986). Elementary school climate: A revision of the OCDQ. *Educational Administration Quarterly, 22*, 93–110.

Hoy, W. K., & Forsyth, P. B. (1986). *Effective supervision.* New York: Random House.

Hoy, W. K., & Miskel, C. G. (2001). *Educational administration: Theory, research & practice* (6th ed.). New York: McGraw-Hill.

Hoy, W. K., & Tarter, C. J. (1997). *Healthy schools: A handbook for change* (Elementary and Middle School Edition). Thousand Oaks, CA: Corwin Press.

Hoy, W. K., Tarter, C. J. & Kottkamp, R. B. (1991). *Open schools/healthy schools: Measuring organizational climate.* Newbury Park, CA: Corwin Press, Inc., A Sage Publications Company.

Kreitner, R. (2001). *Management* (8th ed.). Boston: Houghton Mifflin.

Laabs, J. J. (1996). Change. *Personnel Journal, 75*(7), 52–62.

Laabs, J. J. (November, 1998). They want more support inside and outside work. *Workforce.* Costa Mesa, CA: ACC Communications, 54–56.

Lunenburg, F. C. (1983). Pupil control ideology and self-concept as a learner. *Educational Research Quarterly, 8*, 33–39.

Marcum, R. L. (1966). Organizational climate and adoption of educational innovations. Unpublished doctoral dissertation, Utah State University, Logan.

Miles, M. B. (1969). Planned change and organizational health: Figure and ground. In F. D. Carver & T. J. Sergiovanni (Eds.), *Organizations and human behavior* (pp. 375–391). New York: McGraw-Hill.

Miller, S. K. (1982). School learning climate improvement: A case study. *Educational Leadership, 40*(3), 36–37.

National Association of Secondary School Principals (NASSP) (1987). *Comprehensive assessment of school environments.* Reston, VA: Author.

National Center for Educational Statistics (1997). *Job satisfaction among America's teachers: Effects of workplace conditions, background characteristics, and teacher compensation.* NCES 97471.

Newman, F. M., & Associates (1996). *Authentic instruction: Restructuring schools for intellectual quality.* San Francisco: Jossey-Bass.

Norton, M. S. (2001). Provide school and community orientation to retain your teachers and staff. *School Public Relations, 22*(2), 16–22.

Norton, M. S., Webb, L. D., Dlugosh, L. L., & Sybouts, W. (1996). *The school superintendency: New responsibilities, new leadership.* Boston: Allyn and Bacon.

Pai, Y., & Adler, S. A. (2001). *Cultural foundations of education* (3rd ed.). Upper Saddle River, NJ: Prentice Hall.

Paredes, V., & Frazer, L. (1992). *School climate in AISD.* Austin, TX: Independent School District, Office of Research and Evaluation.

Patrick, J. E. (1995). *Correlation between administrative styles and school climate.* ERIC, accession number ED387853.

Phi Delta Kappa (1973). *School climate improvement: A challenge to the school administrator.* Bloomington, IN: Author.

Proctor, C. P. (1984). Teacher expectations: A model for school improvement. *Elementary School Journal, 84*, 469–481.

Raywid, M. A. (1983). Schools for choice: Their current nature and prospects. *Phi Delta Kappan, 64*, 684–688.

Rich, J. M. (1992). *Foundations of education: Perspectives on American education.* Upper Saddle River, NJ: Prentice Hall/Merrill.

Robbins, S. P. (2001). *Organizational behavior* (9th ed.). Upper Saddle River, NJ: Prentice Hall.

Rutherford, W. L. (1985). School principals as effective leaders. *Phi Delta Kappan, 67*, 31–34.

Schools-in-the-middle (1993). School climate assessment encourages collaboration. *NASSP Bulletin, 75*, 111–119.

Short, P. M., & Greer, J. T. (1997). *Leadership and empowered schools: Themes from innovative efforts.* Columbus, OH: Merrill.

Stern, G. G. (1964). *High school characteristics index.* Syracuse, NY: Psychological Research Center, Syracuse University.

Stevens, M. P. (1990). School climate and staff development: Keys to school reform. *NASSP Bulletin, 74*, 66–70.

Sweeney, J. (1992). School climate: The key to excellence. *NASSP Bulletin, 76*, 69–73.

Taylor, D. L., & Tashakkori, A. (1994). Predicting teachers' sense of efficacy and job satisfaction using school climate and participatory decision making. Paper presented at the annual meeting of the Southwest Educational Research Association, San Antonio, TX.

Tylor, E. B. (1871). *Primitive culture.* London: John Murray.

Walberg, H. J. (1976). *Psychology of learning environments.* In L. S. Shulman (Ed.), Review of research in education (Vol. 4). Itasca, IL: Peacock.

Walberg, H. J., & Genova, W. J. (1982). Staff, school and workshop influences on knowledge use in educational improvement efforts. *Journal of Educational Research, 76*(2), 69–80.

Williams, R. A., & Clouse, R. W. (1991). *Humor as a management technique: Its impact on school culture and climate.* EDRS Research Report, accession number ED337866.

Wilmore, E. L. (1992). The "affective" middle level school: Keys to nurturing school climate. *Schools in the Middle, 1*(4), 31–34.

Winter, J. S., & Sweeney, J. (1994). Improving school climate: Administrators are the key. *NASSP Bulletin, 73*, 65–69.

Wynne, E. A. (1981). Looking at good schools. *Phi Delta Kappan, 62*, 377–381.

5 Policies and Regulations in the Human Resources Function

After reading this chapter, you will be able to:

- Define and identify policies, regulations, and bylaws in relation to school governance.
- Describe the benefits of a viable set of governance policies and regulations for the school district and its stakeholders.
- Implement a codification system for classifying governance policies and regulations for the human resources function.
- Identify several strategies for developing policies and regulations in a school setting.
- Identify the characteristics of effective school policies.
- Explain the compliance aspects of school policy as related to federal and state laws and rulings set forth by the courts.

THE DEVELOPMENT OF PERSONNEL POLICIES AND REGULATIONS

Many persons express the belief that a school district's personnel policies and regulations are a direct reflection of how it values its human resources. Governing board policies directly affect the work and life of the school employees and the school district's clients. One premise of this text is that schools are people; the school's human resources determine in large part the extent to which the school system will achieve its purposes. In addition, the formal **adoption of policy** by the board of education gives the professional staff the necessary support and direction for the implementation of program initiatives. For these reasons and others discussed in this chapter, the development of personnel policies and regulations is of paramount importance. In a statewide study by Norton (1999), personnel directors listed personnel policy and regulation development as their second highest rated job responsibility; only the recruitment of personnel ranked higher.

This chapter will focus on the development of policies and regulations that guide and facilitate the human resources function. Primary consideration is given to important differences between governing board policies and administrative regulations; the purposes served by a viable set of policies and regulations; the responsibilities of the school board, the human resources director, and other professional staff and laypersons in the development of policies and regulations; and ways in which personnel policies and regulations are developed. In addition, the characteristics of effective policies and regulations are discussed, and examples of policies and regulations in selected personnel areas are presented.

Goals, Policies, and Regulations

The terms goals, policies, and regulations are defined in various ways in the literature. We find it important to differentiate among these terms and to clarify others often used in relation to them.

Goals are those statements that set forth the purposes of the school system. Goals serve to clarify the aims of the school system; they provide a focus for the organization and give it a meaningful direction. Goals express what is important to the school system overall and are undergirded by the beliefs, values, traditions, and culture of the school system's community. School goals are developed through cultural sanctions embedded in the school community, through lay judgments expressed through such bodies as the district's school board, and through the professional judgments of professional and support staffs of the school district.

Governing board policies are comprehensive statements of decisions, principles, or courses of action that serve toward the achievement of stated goals for a local school system. Governing board policies answer the question of what the school system is to do; essentially, they serve as guidelines for the administration of the school district. Policies are local adaptations of stated goals; they are developed through the actions of the school board with the leadership of the professional staff.

An **administrative regulation** or **rule** is a precise statement that answers the question of how a policy is to be applied or implemented. Although administrative regulations most often are approved by the governing board, they are developed primarily through the judgments of the professional staff with representative community input and ultimately through administrative decision. For our purposes, the terms regulation, rule, and procedure are used interchangeably.

Bylaws are those procedures by which the school board governs itself. They are regulations that apply to the internal operations of the school board. Such matters as the election of board officers, voting procedures, agenda development, parliamentary procedure, and the order of business are examples of topics included in the bylaws of the governing board.

Compliance Aspects of Policy

Governing board policies, regulations, and bylaws are subject to state and national laws. A **law** is a rule recognized by the nation or state as binding on its members. Law emanates from actions by governing bodies such as the

U.S. Congress and state legislatures or from rulings by courts of law. It is not unusual for state laws and/or court actions to mandate school policy; that is, state statutes and court rulings often specify what school systems must do relative to a specific matter. Seldom is the specific law written verbatim in the school district's policy manual. Rather, a policy statement based on the requirements of the law is written as a school policy, followed by specific statute references or citations. There are exceptions to this provision. In many states, for example, policies and regulations concerning personnel dismissal are written verbatim from state statutes. This is due to the fact that dismissal cases frequently are litigated in court. As a result, school districts take all precautions to ensure that their policies and regulations are in compliance with federal and state laws. Thus it should be clearly understood that local school district policy is inextricably related to the laws of the land as determined by the U.S. Constitution, U.S. Congress, state legislatures, the courts, and other agencies and legal bodies that implement legislative acts and court rulings.

For example, local school district policy must be in compliance with federal and state legislation exemplified by such acts as Title VII of the Civil Rights Act of 1964, which prohibits discrimination in hiring, compensation, and terms and conditions of employment on the basis of race, color, religion, national origin, or sex, and the Equal Employment Opportunity Act (EEOA) of 1972, which extended race coverage stipulated in Title VII to include employees of state and local governments and educational institutions and created the EEO Commission with the authority to prohibit discrimination and file suits against organizations believed to be discriminatory (see Chapter 7).

Statutes such as The Occupational Safety and Health Act (OSHA) of 1970, which affects human resources policy by requiring schools and other organizations to comply with specific safety requirements within the working environment, and governmental agencies, such as the Department of Labor, which enforces fair labor practices such as compensation for overtime work by employees, are specific examples of how law and agency regulations affect the development and adoption of local school district policy.

The implications regarding compliance of school districts with federal and state laws are far reaching; the policies of a school district that are not in compliance with federal and state statutes or with court rulings are likely to be challenged and ultimately declared unconstitutional and can result in litigation and possible monetary penalties. The need for school leaders to be knowledgeable of the laws that apply to the administration of schools is of paramount importance; such knowledge is essential for effective policy development.

Benefits of Personnel Policies and Regulations

A viable set of personnel policies and regulations benefits the school system and the human resources function in numerous ways. First, viable policies and regulations help to establish the division of labor between the school board and the professional staff. The school board, as the legislative body of the school system, has the responsibility of adopting policies that serve to guide the school program. In this sense, the board of education controls the direction of the system through adopting policies that focus on what the school system is to do and what it wants to accomplish. The development and adoption of appropriate school policy, then, are the primary responsibilities of the school board. Viable school district policy fosters a more effective and accountable professional staff. That is, board policy serves to foster the compliance of the professional and support staff regarding the major aims of the school district; thus staff accountability becomes more attainable. Without question, policy development is the primary tool of a school board relative to district compliance and personal performance.

On the other hand, the school superintendent and the professional staff represent the executive body of school governance. A comprehensive set of well-developed policies and regulations is one of the human resources administrator's most valuable management tools. Viable school policies allow for discretionary actions by the professional staff. The implementation of board policy is administered through the development of specific regulations primarily through the leadership of the professional staff. Thus good policies and regulations help the school board to focus on its major legislative role and the professional staff to focus on its executive responsibilities. Policy provides the control that the school board must have to guide the school system and gives the professional staff the discretion it needs to operate the school program effectively.

Another benefit of school policies and regulations is that they establish the basis for intelligent decision making and help to direct decision making at proper levels within the system. Without the direction that effective policies and regulations can provide, various units in the system invariably must seek a decision from a higher-level unit before actions can be implemented. As a result, administrative effectiveness often is inhibited, and organization efficiency and initiative are lessened.

A comprehensive set of school policies and regulations is the most important source of information about the goals and objectives of the school system. As stated by Duke and Canady (1991), "We would be hard pressed to find an area of local policymaking that is more central to good instruction than personnel" (p. 111). Policy statements and accompanying regulations inform the public and the professional staff of the goals and objectives of the school system and are a foundation for effective system communication.

Viable policies and regulations help to avoid costly trial and error and to bring a sense of continuity to the organization. Board policies and regulations support the system's decision-making capability by providing a focus on what is to be accomplished and how to proceed administratively. Thus viable policies release the strength and creativity of the school administrators and other employees. Employees understand the priorities set forth by the governing board and are able to implement their professional judgment with some degree of assurance and personal security.

The importance of school policy is specifically revealed in its impact on the instructional program of the school and student learning. Not only are district policies in such areas as personnel recruitment, selection, assignment, and staff development vital to the quality of teaching and learning in the school district, but adopted policies and administrative procedures related to such matters as homework, student grading, instructional materials selection, student retention, student attendance, student discipline, early childhood programs, and other aspects of curriculum development influence the lives of teachers, students, and other stakeholders in the school community.

Finally, in view of the fact that school boards are viewed as extensions of other legislative bodies, viable policies and regulations serve an important legal function for the board and the school district. In relation to governance practices and litigation stemming from personnel lawsuits, school policies and their dissemination serve as key evidence to document school board decisions and administrative practices.

As summarized by Clemmer (1991),

> Virtually all aspects of school district operation are benefitted by the consistent administration of appropriate policies. Generally speaking, policies enable organizations to get results with people rather than through them. Cooperative policy development fosters two-way communication and induces sound working relationships. Workers in all organizations benefit from the clarification of their employer's goals and objectives. (p. 28)

Clemmer (1991) further stated that policies pay off by providing the following:

1. Greater efficiency—written policies and regulations save time and effort for board members and superintendents.
2. More unity in action—good policies presume the discretionary aspects of work as well as mutuality of interest among all school district employees.
3. Higher administrator morale—administrators are able to exercise professional judgment more effectively in behalf of established goals when they know they have support.
4. Better transitions—effective policies foster stability and continuity.
5. Permanent records—board minutes serve as the official repository of the record of board action that produces the policy manual that guides administrative behavior that directs staff that gets the job done with kids day after day after day.
6. Improved public relations—participation enhances the likelihood that decisions will be more valid and builds confidence in decision makers. (pp. 28–30)

Criteria That Identify Policies, Regulations, and Bylaws

A school policy was defined earlier as a comprehensive statement of decisions, principles, or courses of action that serve toward the achievement of stated goals. A policy is:

1. an assertion of the intent or goals of the school system;
2. related to a general area of major importance to the school system and citizenry;
3. equivalent to legislation;
4. a broad statement that allows for freedom of interpretation and execution;

5. applicable over long periods of time;
6. mainly the concern of the school board, that is, only the school board can adopt policy;
7. an action undertaken to resolve or to give direction in ameliorating a problem of importance;
8. related to the question of *what* to do.

An administrative regulation is:

1. related to a specific area or problem (it is a procedure to carry out or implement a policy);
2. mainly the concern of the professional staff (it is executive in nature);
3. a precise statement calling for specific interpretation and execution;
4. able to be altered without formal board action;
5. related to the question of *how* to do it.

A bylaw is a rule governing the school board's internal operations. It is a method by which the school board governs itself. A bylaw is:

1. a combination of parliamentary procedures and state laws that apply to school boards;
2. like any other rule in that it sets forth specific procedures, leaving little room for personal discretion;
3. a rule that applies to the internal operations of the school board only;
4. related to the question of how the school board will govern itself.

Consider the following policy statement:

The school superintendent and persons delegated by the superintendent are given the responsibility to determine the personnel needs of the school district and to recruit qualified candidates to recommend for employment to the board. The school board will employ and retain the best qualified personnel available. Concerted efforts shall be made to maintain a variation in staff relative to educational preparation, personal background, and previous experience. There shall be no discrimination against any candidate by reason of race, national origin, creed, marital status, age, or sex.

It is the responsibility of the school superintendent to certify that persons nominated for employment shall meet all qualifications established by law and by the school board for the position for which the nomination is made.

The employment of any individual is not official until the contract is signed by the candidate and approved by the governing school board.

This policy specifies *what* the board desires concerning practices for employment and sets forth what is to be done relative to employee qualifications. The policy represents a broad statement that allows the professional staff to use its judgment concerning specific recruiting and selection procedures. The policy is legislative in substance and is directly related to the question of what to do relative to the important matter of hiring school district personnel. Finally, although specific procedures regarding recruitment and selection might change, the guiding policy could remain as stated for a substantial period of time. That is, the question of what is to be accomplished

---

Personnel: Certificated
Code: 4111   Recruitment and Selection

To aid in obtaining the best available personnel for school positions, the following criteria and procedures will be utilized:

Concerted efforts will be made to maintain a variation in staff relative to educational preparation, background, and previous experience through recruiting on a broad basis. All available sources of personnel supply, including college and university career placement offices, career-information-day programs, student-teacher information, advertisements in appropriate publications, and others that serve to identify a pool of qualified personnel for position openings will be used.

Written applications, official transcripts of college work, student teaching and teaching reports and recommendations, and personal interviews provide the primary data for personnel selection. The procedures for screening and selecting personnel for teaching positions are as follows:

1. Notices of position openings in teaching will be disseminated internally through the offices of school principals and externally through selected college and university teacher placement offices.
2. The central human resources office will collect and process applications; the official application form of the school district and other application materials, as required by the human resources office, must be completed and received before an applicant can be considered for a position.
3. The central human resources office will gather all evidence for purposes of screening applicants including the application form, evidence of certification or licensure for the position in question, teacher placement records of the applicant, official college transcripts, at least three professional references from former employers and/or supervisors, and other information of importance. In addition, the district's prescreening background-check form is to be completed and returned by the applicant.
4. Preliminary interviews of applicants who are best qualified will be conducted by the central human resources office, although other representatives may participate as interviewers as the case requires.
5. Finalists for the position, as determined by the human resources office, will be scheduled for interviews with appropriate building principals and/or supervisors. The human resources office, together with the appropriate building principal and/or supervisor, will decide if the position should be offered to a specific applicant.
6. When a position is offered tentatively and accepted pending school board approval, the human resources office will send its recommendation to the school superintendent. Upon the superintendent's approval, the nomination will be made to the school board for final approval.
7. All final applicants for a position will be notified of the decision reached by the school board.

FIGURE 5.1
Procedure for Position Application

could remain unchanged even though the question of how to do it might be altered to improve current practices.

Next, consider the procedure illustrated in Figure 5.1 that sets forth steps for position application. This regulation relates specifically to the policy for personnel recruitment and selection; it is executive in nature, calling for specific procedures to be followed; it is possible to revise these procedures without having to change board policy; and it answers the question of how the selection of personnel is to be implemented.

Other examples of personnel policy and regulation statements will be examined later in this chapter. The foregoing statements emphasize the differences between policies and regulations and illustrate the various criteria that help to define them.

Topical Headings for Personnel Policies and Regulations

Policy and regulation development in human resources administration is an ongoing, continuous process. Due to the ever-changing nature of the human resources function, new policies and regulations become necessary, current ones need revision, and some become obsolete and must be deleted. The most viable topical headings for policies and regulations evolve from the vision and needs of the local school district. Because policies are comprehensive statements of decisions, principles, or courses of action that serve toward the achievement of stated goals, ideally they evolve from local school and community initiatives.

The **National Educational Policy Network of the National School Boards Association** (NEPN/NSBA) and the **Davies–Brickell codification system** (DBS) are examples of educational policy systems that have been implemented in numerous school districts nationally. Both systems provide a comprehensive classification system to guide policy development in school districts. The NEPN/NSBA, which is the most widely used classification system nationally, is based on an alpha system; letters of the alphabet are used for coding policies and regulations (i.e., each major topical heading has a letter). G is used for policies related to personnel. Thus GCBC in the system refers to section G (personnel); the third subsection, C (professional staff); the second division, B (professional staff contracts and compensation); and the third subdivision, C (professional staff supplementary pay plans and overtime).

To illustrate topical headings for policies and regulations in the area of human resources administration, section G of the NEPN/NSBA classification system is presented in Figure 5.2. Not all topical headings of the NEPN/NSBA would necessarily be included in the policy manuals of every school district, nor is the listing all-inclusive. The NEPN/NSBA does include numerous topics of importance in human resources policy development. Since policy and regulation development is a continuous process, new entries are made as needed by the local school district.

Codification of Personnel Policies and Regulations

The comprehensiveness of policies and regulations in human resources administration necessitates some method of classifying or recording them. Without such a codification system, policy manuals become disorganized

SECTION G: PERSONNEL

Section G of the NEPN/NSBA classification system contains policies, regulations, and exhibits on all school employees except for the superintendent (policies on the school chief are located in Section C, General Administration). The category is divided into three main divisions: GB has policies applying to all school employees or to general personnel matters; GC refers to instructional and administrative staff; and GD refers to support or classified staff.

GA	Personnel Goals/Priority Objectives	GBL	Staff Awards and Recognition
GAA	Evaluation of Personnel System	GC	Professional Staff
GB	General Personnel Policies	GCA	Professional Staff Positions
GBA	Open Hiring/Equal Employment Opportunity and Affirmative Action	GCAA	Instructional Staff Positions
		GCAAA	Teacher Positions
GBAA	Sexual Discrimination and Harassment	GCAAB	Guidance and Health Staff Positions
GBAB	Pay Equity	GCAAC	Resource Staff Positions
GBB	Staff Involvement in Decision Making	GCAB	Administrative Staff Positions
GBC	Staff Compensation	GCB	Professional Staff Contracts and Compensation
GBCA	Merit/Performance Pay Programs		
GBD	Communications with Staff (also BHC)	GCBA	Instructional Staff Contracts/ Compensation/Salary Schedules
GBE	Staff Rights and Responsibilities		
GBEA	Staff Ethics/Conflict of Interest	GCBAA	Merit/Performance Pay for Instructional Staff
GBEB	Staff Conduct		
GBEBA	Staff Dress Code	GCBB	Administrative Staff Contracts and Compensation/Salary Schedules
GBEBB	Staff Conduct with Students		
GBEBC	Gifts to and Solicitations by Staff		
		GCBBA	Merit/Performance Pay for Administrative Staff
GBEC	Drug-Free Workplace (also ADB)		
GBED	Tobacco-Free Workplace (also ADC)/Staff No Smoking/Smoking	GCBC	Professional Staff Supplementary Pay Plans/Overtime
		GCBD	Professional Staff Fringe Benefits
GBF	Staff Working on Federal/State Grants	GCC	Professional Staff Leaves and Absences
GBG	Staff Welfare/Protection		
GBGA	Staff Health	GCCA	Instructional Staff Leaves and Absences
GBGB	Staff Personal Security and Safety		
GBGC	Employee Assistance/Wellness Programs	GCCAA	Instructional Staff Sick Leave
		GCCAB	Instructional Staff Personal/ Emergency/Legal/Religious Leave
GBGD	Workers' Compensation		
GBH	Staff Participation in Community Activities		
		GCCAC	Instructional Staff Maternity/ Paternity/Parental Leave
GBI	Staff Participation in Political Activities		
		GCCAD	Instructional Staff Military Leave
GBJ	Personal Records and Files	GCCAE	Instructional Staff Conferences/Training/ Workshops
GBJA	Confidential Information and Disclosure of Information		
GBJB	Access to Personnel Files	GCCAF	Instructional Staff Sabbaticals
GBK	Staff Concerns/Complaints/ Grievances	GCCB	Administrative Staff Leaves and Absences

FIGURE 5.2

The NEPN/NSBA Classification System

Source: Used with permission from *The School Administrator's Guide to the NEPN/NSBA Policy Development System,* 6th ed. (Alexandria, VA: National School Boards Association, 1991). All rights reserved.

GCCBA	Administrative Staff Sick Leave	**GCIE**	Professional Staff Continuing Education
GCCBB	Administrative Staff Personal/Emergency/Legal/ Religious Leave	**GCJ**	Professional Staff Probation, Tenure, and Seniority
GCCBC	Administrative Staff Maternity/ Paternity/Parental Leave	**GCJA**	Instructional Staff Seniority
		GCJB	Administrative Staff Seniority
GCCBD	Administrative Staff Military Leave	**GCK**	Professional Staff Assignments and Transfers
GCCBE	Administrative Staff Conferences/ Training/Workshops	**GCKA**	Instructional Staff Assignments and Transfers
GCCBF	Administrative Staff Sabbaticals	**GCKB**	Administrative Staff Assignments and Transfers
GCD	Professional Staff Vacations and Holidays		
GCDA	Instructional Staff Vacations and Holidays	**GCL**	Professional Staff Schedules and Calendars
GCDB	Administrative Staff Vacations and Holidays	**GCLA**	Length of Instructional Staff Work Day
GCE	Professional Staff Recruiting	**GCLB**	Length of Administrative Staff Work Day
GCEA	Recruiting of Instructional Staff	**GCLC**	Length of Instructional Staff School Year
GCEB	Recruiting of Administrative Staff		
GCEC	Posting and Advertising of Professional Vacancies	**GCLD**	Length of Administrative Staff School Year
GCF	Professional Staff Hiring	**GCM**	Professional Staff Workload
GCFA	Hiring of Instructional Staff	**GCMA**	Professional Staff Planning Time
GCFB	Hiring of Administrative Staff	**GCMB**	Professional Staff Office Hours
GCFC	Professional Staff Certification and Credentialing Requirements	**GCMC**	Parent Conferences, Staff Meetings, and School Meetings
GCFD	Shortage of Professional Staff	**GCMD**	Instructional Staff Extra Duty
GCG	Part-Time and Substitute Professional Staff Employment	**GCME**	Administrative Staff Extra Duty
		GCMF	Class Size
GCGA	Qualifications of Substitute Staff	**GCN**	Supervision of Professional Staff
GCGB	Arrangements for Substitute Staff	**GCNA**	Supervision of Instructional Staff
GCGC	Job Sharing in Professional Staff Positions	**GCNB**	Supervision of Administrative Staff
GCH	Professional Staff Orientation and Training	**GCO**	Evaluation of Professional Staff
		GCOA	Evaluation of Instructional Staff
GCHA	Mentor Teachers	**GCOB**	Accountability of Instructional Staff
GCHB	Mentor Administrators	**GCOC**	Evaluation of Administrative Staff
GCI	Professional Staff Development	**GCOD**	Accountability of Administrative Staff
GCIA	Philosophy of Staff Development		
GCIB	Inservice Requirements for Instructional Staff	**GCP**	Professional Staff Promotions and Reclassifications
GCIC	Inservice Requirements for Administrative Staff	**GCPA**	Promotion and Reclassification of Instructional Staff
GCID	Professional Staff Training, Workshops and Conferences	**GCPB**	Promotion and Reclassification of Administrative Staff

FIGURE 5.2
(continued)

GCQ	Professional Staff Termination of Employment	**GDAA**	Fiscal Management and Office Positions
GCQA	Instructional Staff Reduction in Force	**GDAB**	Building and Grounds Management Positions
GCQB	Administrative Staff Reduction in Force	**GDAC**	Transportation and Food Management Positions
GCQC	Resignation of Instructional Staff	**GDB**	Support Staff Contracts and
GCQD	Resignation of Administrative Staff		Compensation
GCQE	Retirement of Professional Staff	**GDBA**	Support Staff Salary Schedules
GCQF	Discipline, Suspension, and Dismissal of Professional Staff	**GDBB**	Merit/Performance Pay for Support Staff
GCR	Nonschool Employment of Professional Staff	**GDBC**	Support Staff Supplementary Pay/Overtime
GCRA	Nonschool Employment of Instructional Staff	**GDBD**	Support Staff Fringe Benefits
GCRB	Nonschool Employment of Administrative Staff	**GDC**	Support Staff Leaves and Absences
GCRC	Staff Consulting Activities	**GDCA**	Support Staff Sick Leave
GCRD	Tutoring for Pay	**GDCB**	Support Staff Personal/Emergency/Legal/
GCS	Professional Research and Publishing		Religious Leave
GCT	Exchange Teaching	**GDCC**	Support Staff Maternity/Paternity/Parental
GCU	Professional Staff Membership in Professional and Union		Leave
	Organizations	**GDCD**	Support Staff Military Leave
GCV	Professional Staff Facilities	**GDCE**	Support Staff Conferences/ Visitations/Workshops
GD	Support/Classified Staff	**GDD**	Support Staff Vacations and
GDA	Support Staff Positions		Holidays

FIGURE 5.2
(continued)

and difficult to use. Two codification systems were mentioned previously, the National Education Policy Network of the National School Board Association and the Davies–Brickell System. An explanation of the NEPN/NSBA **codification system of policies and regulations** follows.

The NEPN/NSBA system uses 11 major sections (or series) in its classification system:

Sections	*Topical Headings*
Section A	Foundations and Basic Commitments
Section B	School Board Governance and Operations
Section C	General School Administration
Section D	Fiscal Management
Section E	Support Services
Section F	Facilities Planning and Development

GDE	Support Staff Recruiting	**GDLA**		Support Staff Extra Duty
GDEA	Posting and Advertising of	**GDLB**		Support Staff Meetings
	Support Staff Vacancies	**GDM**	Support Staff Career Development
GDF	Support Staff Hiring	**GDMA**		Philosophy of Support Staff
GDFA	Support Staff Qualifications and			Career Development
	Requirements	**GDMB**		Support Staff Training,
GDFB	Support Staff Selection Process			Conferences, and Workshops
GDFC	Shortage of Support Staff	**GDMC**		Support Staff Inservice
GDG	Part-Time and Substitute Support			Requirements
	Staff Employment	**GDMD**		Support Staff Continuing Education
GDGA	Qualifications of Support Staff	**GDN**	Supervision of Support Staff
	Substitutes	**GDO**	Evaluation of Support Staff
GDGB	Arrangements for Support Staff	**GDOA**		Accountability of Support Staff
	Substitutes	**GDP**	Support Staff Promotions and
GDGC	Job-Sharing in Support Staff		Reclassification
	Positions	**GDQ**	Support Staff Termination of
GDH	Support Staff Orientation and		Employment
	Training	**GDQA**		Support Staff Reduction in Force
GDI	Support Staff Probation, Tenure,	**GDQB**		Resignation of Support Staff
	and Seniority	**GDQC**		Retirement of Support Staff
GDJ	Support Staff Assignments and	**GDQD**		Discipline, Suspension, and
	Transfers			Dismissal of Support Staff
GDK	Support Staff Schedules and	**GDR**	Nonschool Employment by Support
	Calendars		Staff
GDKA	Length of Support Staff Work Day	**GDS**	Support Staff Membership in
GDKB	Length of Support Staff School Year		Professional/Union Organizations
GDL	Support Staff Workload	**GDT**	Support Staff Facilities

FIGURE 5.2
(continued)

Section G	Personnel
Section H	Negotiations
Section I	Instruction
Section J	Students
Section K	School, Community, and Home Relations
Section L	Education Agency Relations

Each major section is divided into subsections, divisions, subdivisions, items, and subitems. Section G encompasses the content area of personnel. Consider the policy entry lettered GBEC. Each letter refers to a specific topical entry. For example, the letter G indicates that the entry deals with the major section of personnel. The letter B indicates that the entry is in the second subsection, general personnel policies. The letter E notes that the entry is the fifth division under general personnel policies or staff rights and responsibilities. Finally, the letter C indicates that the entry is the third subdivision under staff rights and responsibilities or drug-free workplace. Similarly, the code GCAAB reveals that the entry is personnel (G), professional staff (C), professional staff positions (A), instructional staff positions (A), and guidance and health staff positions (B). New subsections, divisions, subdivisions, items, and subitems can be added to the policies by using appropriate letters. As a final explanation of this codification system, examine the following example. Using the NEPN/NSBA, a new subdivision, "class size," would be classified under the division "professional staff workload" as follows:

(Section)	Personnel	G
(Subsection)	Professional Staff	GC
(Division)	Professional Staff Workload	GCM
(Subdivision)	Class Size (new entry)	GCMF

The Davies–Brickell System of Classification uses a numerical code based on nine major series (e.g., 1000, Community Relations; 2000, Administration; 3000, Business and Noninstructional Operations; 4000, Personnel; etc.). The code 4151.1, for example, denotes the fourth major series, the first subseries, the fifth division, the first subdivision, and the first item. Similarly, the code 2346 denotes the second major series, the third subseries, the fourth division, and the sixth subdivision.

The use of arabic numerals for coding systems provides the advantage of easy reading and referencing. One advantage of the alpha system is that it does not limit the number of entries in any one subsection, division, subdivision, item, or subitem to nine. In a numerical system, such as 4151.9, once nine entries under any one of the classifications have been reached, some structural revision becomes necessary. For this reason, some individuals prefer the alpha system used by the NSBA. Because there are 26 letters in the alphabet, numerous divisions, subdivisions, items, and subitems can be utilized without the need to restructure. On the other hand, some persons find the use of letters for coding purposes to be less readable than numbers (e.g., 4146.2 vs. DADFB). In any case, a consistent codification system is of paramount importance. It enhances the development, readability, revision, and utilization of the school district's policy and regulation manual.

How Personnel Policies and Regulations Are Developed

Although quality varies considerably, most school districts have some form of a policy and regulation manual. Since policy development is a never-ending process, some school districts simplify completing this task by purchasing policies written by national organizations or policy consultants. Unless customized for the particular school district, such policy manuals tend to be no more than boiler-plate products that do not reflect the real climate and educational needs of the system. Therefore, it is important that human resources administrators understand fully the process of policy development and be prepared to assume a major leadership role in this activity. In 1999, 89.7% of the personnel directors in one state reported that they had the primary responsibility for personnel policy and regulation development in their school districts (Norton, 1999).

Although most school districts have a nucleus of policy already established, the need to develop an entirely new set of policies is common. Even when school districts have a "complete" policy manual, it is not unusual to have one or more sections in need of complete revision. When major revisions are necessary, the question of who is to do the work arises. One approach is to have the school board appoint the school superintendent to do the policy work. The school superintendent is generally knowledgeable about the school district and its human resources purposes and needs. On the other hand, policy development is a monumental task, and such an arrangement tends to take much time away from other work of the superintendent's office. Another approach is to set up a series of task force groups to do the policy work. Representative groups can benefit from personal involvement in policy development. Yet such an arrangement does not obviate the fact that policy development takes both time and skill. Professional staff members cannot always sacrifice the time necessary to do the work; nor are they always personally knowledgeable in the area of policy development.

Some school districts find it most expedient to use outside consultants to complete their policies. Policy consultants have special expertise for such work and are able to complete a quality product if it is founded on the district's culture and needs. Such an arrangement can be very costly, however, because the time commitments for such consulting are lengthy. We caution against the procedure of buying the policy statements from external organizations. Although such statements can result in a policy manual for the school district, unless such services are customized for the district and its goals, values, problems, needs, and situation, policies tend to be of a generic nature that betrays the real meaning and value of localized policies.

Another arrangement is to allow the central personnel unit to take the primary leadership in the development of policies and regulations in the area of human resources. The human resources director is highly knowledgeable about the personnel objectives and needs of the school district. These administrators necessarily must be fully acquainted with the legal aspects of personnel administration important to policy and regulation development.

We support the arrangement whereby the human resources director is given the primary authority to develop viable personnel policy for the school district. Such an arrangement does not set aside the fact that the school board remains as the final authority on all policy recommendations and the only body that can adopt policy officially for the school district. Such an arrangement does not suggest that policy recommendations cannot evolve from any source or that participation in policy development should not include representatives from the school system's many publics. One model for policy development that has been utilized by numerous school districts is explained in brief in the following section.

Model for Policy and Regulation Development

The human resources director might utilize the following model for completing a comprehensive study and revision of the school district's personnel policies and regulations:

Step 1   Examine various school and community documents and resources for information relative to what policies and/or decisions have already been determined. Sources of policies and regulations include school board minutes, school board manuals, teachers' manuals, board correspondence, board committee reports, staff committee reports, school publications, citizen committee reports, newspaper files, interviews with past and present members of the school board and staff, and legal documents related to the school district. Frequency of notations on certain personnel subjects may suggest the need for a definite district policy. Give special attention to specific goal statements set forth by the governing board.

Step 2   Check on established practices in the area of personnel administration. Operations of the school board and the district often reflect embedded practices that infer policy need areas. Unwritten policies often become formal statements of policy through such an analysis of practice.

Step 3   Investigate what other boards have done relative to personnel policy development. Such information is to serve as a guide to possible policy development, rather than being directly applicable to the local district in question. Such information can be useful as a sounding board in revealing local policy needs. Additionally, complete a thorough examination of state statutes related to the administration of schools and of other official documents for clues to topics that should be set forth as official school district policy.

Step 4   Consult the studies and writings of others in the area of school personnel administration. Guides and handbooks prepared by school board associations, state departments, and other organizations often are excellent sources of policy content. Once again, such information is used as a place to start, rather than as a blueprint for meeting local needs.

Step 5   Enlist the aid of all concerned. It is good practice to solicit input from citizen groups, professional and support personnel in the school district, and other stakeholders of the district. Such involvement is conducive to quality results and also to gaining the ultimate approval and effective implementation of the policies to be recommended.

Step 6   Organize study groups to examine policy needs and to recommend policy in various subsections and divisions of the personnel policy topical headings (i.e., the NEPN/NSBA section G topical headings). Include such representative personnel as teachers, support staff, patrons, administrators, and at least one school board member in the study groups. The final approval and adoption are facilitated with the sanction of at least one board member serving on the committee. Organize a steering committee of the representatives most knowledgeable of policy development and the needs and purposes of human resources administration. These committee members serve as liaisons with study subgroups in checking for consistency in the policies developed.

Step 7 Have the school superintendent and the administrative cabinet review the policy work completed. The professional staff has an ongoing role as policies are being developed in the initial stages. Thus administrator, teacher, and support staff groups can participate by completing their own review of needed policies, by providing suggestions to study groups, and by acting as sounding boards for initial study group recommendations.

Step 8 Have the school board review the policy work completed. As is the case with the administrator, teacher, and support staff groups, the school board needs to participate in the initial stages of personnel policy development in ways similar to those recommended in step 7. In addition, the school board as a whole should review the semifinal policy draft and make recommendations for revision.

Step 9 Have the draft of the policies tested for legality. The school board attorney will review the policy draft from a legal viewpoint. Legal clearance helps to build school board and district confidence and lends support to the final policy package.

Step 10 Use first and second readings of the personnel policy statements prior to official adoption by the school board. Policy is legally binding for all district personnel and in this sense is a legal contract between the school board and its personnel. Thus due consideration necessitates attention to sunshine laws and other aspects of legal procedures.

Policy development, especially in the areas of compensation and conditions of work, has become increasingly an agenda item in the negotiation process. The line between policy authority of the board of education and the scope of negotiations tends to be less and less clear. For example, a court in Washington declared the matter of class size a condition of work and therefore a matter for negotiation between the school board and the teachers' association ("Class Size," 1991). Thus, under any circumstances today, policy development can no longer be a unilateral activity of the school board and the school administration. Nevertheless, policy adoption still remains the official legislative responsibility of the governing board. The fact that such authority is being eroded in some states was discussed in Chapter 1.

CHARACTERISTICS OF EFFECTIVE POLICIES AND REGULATIONS IN HUMAN RESOURCES ADMINISTRATION

In earlier sections of this chapter, policy and regulation definitions, criteria, topical headings, codification systems, and development procedures were presented. In the following sections, consideration is given to important characteristics of effective policies, including examples of several critical policy topics facing human resources administration today. These selected policy examples are ones that every school district must consider. Duke and Canady (1991) stated that

> a good school policy is one that increases the likelihood that school goals will be achieved without adversely affecting any particular group. . . . Policies may not always please or benefit everyone, but at the very least they should not harm certain groups of young people served by the schools. (p. 7)

These writers noted further that "the key to effective schools probably has less to do with the discovery of one best policy than with ensuring that all school policies are compatible, well coordinated, and consistently followed" (p. 7).

Clemmer (1991) suggested five characteristics of effective policies:

1. *Complete.* A policy statement should tell its user what action should be taken, perhaps explaining why it should be taken and occasionally who should take it. Policies also reveal who is affected by them.
2. *Concise.* Only the barest essentials need to be included in policy statements. Policies are intended essentially to set forth the expectations one group (the board) has for the behavior of another group (district employees).
3. *Clear.* Whatever is expected of whomever should be clearly stated. A flexible policy will allow various methods of implementation but it need not be ambiguous about the desired outcome.
4. *Changeable.* Policy statements should be reasonably easy to modify in accord with changing circumstances in society or in legal codes. This capability refers not only to policy content but also to the methods of codifying and preserving collections of policies. Replacement of outdated policies in district manuals should be simple and fast.
5. *Distinctive.* Policies should always be distinguishable from regulations promulgated by the board and administrators. (p. 107)[1]

We would add *consistent* to the policy characteristics set forth by Clemmer. School policies must provide guidelines for consistently fair and equitable treatment for all employees. Although policies must provide for the use of discretionary judgments on the part of the professional staff, they must not be so stated as to permit capricious interpretations. In addition, consistency infers a compatibility between and among all district policies. The benefits of policies are negated if a specific policy can be nullified by another policy stated elsewhere in the manual. Finally, policies must be consistent with the legal requirements of the nation and state.

Attention to the language of written policies can obviate many problems of interpretation and possible conflict. Since policies and regulations are utilized by a variety of publics, they must be readable and meaningful to all concerned. Poorly written, ambiguous policies tend to confuse

---

[1]From Elwin F. Clemmer, *The School Policy Handbook: A Primer for Administrators and School Board Members.* Copyright © 1991 by Allyn & Bacon. Reprinted with permission.

rather than inform. Furthermore, since policies serve as legal extensions of the school board, precise language that is presented in a clear, straightforward manner is of paramount importance. In policy writing, the statement that "You get what you write" is a basic truth.

Consider the following personnel policy statement:

> In order to provide quality education to all students within the school district, a yearly evaluation of all certificated staff will be conducted. Evaluations should commend staff and provide avenues for staff improvement. Staff evaluations will be used to consider contract renewal.

This policy statement might appear to be clear and concise on the surface, but certain language questions must be raised. For instance:

1. Is only one performance evaluation annually permissible under this policy?
2. Is this yearly evaluation to constitute the totality of evidence for contract renewal consideration?
3. Is this evaluation to serve both formative and summative purposes?
4. How is the statement "Evaluations should commend staff and provide avenues for staff improvement" to be interpreted?
5. Are statements other than commendations permissible?
6. Does the policy suggest that the school district itself will provide the avenues for staff improvement?
7. Who will be responsible for planning and administering the evaluation program?

Appraisal of Performance

The following evaluation policy more clearly states the intentions of the school board relative to employee performance appraisals. It provides guidelines that allow for the development of specific administrative regulations and delegates the administration of the program to a specific office.

Certificated Personnel: Personnel Evaluation (GCOA)

The performance of all personnel in the Union School District will be appraised for the purposes of determining needs for individual personal/professional growth, to provide needed information for personnel compensation, and to help determine continuation of employment. Responsibility for administering appraisal programs is delegated to the superintendent of schools and those individuals designated by him or her. Appropriate performance appraisals will be administered for nontenured certificated employees that will provide sufficient evidence for the continuation of employment and will meet stipulations of law. Tenured personnel appraisals will be performed at least every third year. The school district will make every effort to disseminate to all employees the goals of the system, the position descriptions for individual roles, the standards of performance desired by the school system and the appraisal process(es) to be utilized, the criteria to be used in performance appraisals, and how appraisal results will be disseminated and discussed with them. Suggestions for improvement of performance based on appraisal results are to be part of all performance evaluations. Evaluation procedures must embody the fundamental aspects of due process, clearly articulated and properly followed. Evaluation processes are to be administered in a fair and equitable manner and with due regard for the respect and dignity of the individual.

As discussed in Chapter 6, school administrators must be aware of state laws governing performance appraisal, and appraisal procedures must embody procedural due process. Additionally, appraisal criteria must be reasonably related to job requirements, must not have adverse effects on protected groups, must avoid subjectivity of the supervisor–evaluator, and must be void of any bias related to race or gender. Chapter 11 provides a comprehensive discussion of performance appraisal and gives further consideration of viable policy in this area of human resources administration.

SELECTED EXAMPLES OF PERSONNEL POLICIES AND REGULATIONS

The purpose of this section is to discuss important guidelines for developing personnel policy and to present illustrations of policies and regulations in several selected areas of personnel practice. Specifically, the policy areas of communicable diseases, academic freedom, sexual harassment, dismissal, drug-free workplace, use of school district computer network and Internet, and voluntary transfer are considered.

Staff Health and Safety: Communicable Diseases

During the past decade in the United States, acquired immune deficiency syndrome (AIDS) accounted for significant increases in the death rate of men ages 25 to 44. And both health and school officials are increasingly fearful of the number of HIV infections in young people ages 13 to 24. At present, best estimates place the incidence of the disease between 40 and 50 million people, with approximately 5 million of these people being citizens of the United States and the majority being Africans.

Although the majority of school districts have adopted written policies for dealing with AIDS, the need to develop written policy regarding AIDS or the need to update existing policies dealing with AIDS, remains in many school districts. Many states have yet to require specific programs of health or sex education for students, and AIDS instruction has been slow in finding its way in the curriculum of many schools. According to Strouse (1990), effective AIDS policies are those that:

1. Deal specifically with AIDS.
2. Take into account all that is known about how AIDS is transmitted.
3. Voice a commitment to the AIDS-infected individual to enable him or her to remain in the school setting if at all possible.

4. Contain procedures for protecting the privacy of the infected individual, for handling the publicity surrounding a diagnosis of AIDS, and for reassuring the public through education about AIDS. (p. 87)

Hernandez and Bozeman (1990) point out that school districts that cannot answer yes to any of the following questions should review their policies.

1. Do the district's policies contain a general statement that AIDS is a handicap?
2. Do the policies require that all documents, current handbooks, and policies be audited to ensure that there is no discrimination based on AIDS?
3. Do the policies require training of all managers about AIDS, including procedures concerning medical records and examinations, employees with AIDS, systemwide approaches to employment practices, dealing with employees' refusal to work with actual or suspected AIDS-infected colleagues, and a system for answering questions about AIDS?
4. Do the policies provide a training program about AIDS for employees at all levels?
5. Do the policies require a review of pension and insurance plans to ensure that there is no discussion of or discrimination based on AIDS?
6. Do the policies provide for an ongoing public information program about AIDS?
7. Do the policies include procedures for utilizing professional expertise (internal and external) in dealing with AIDS? (pp. 22–28)

It is important that every school district have legally defensible policies for dealing with AIDS-infected students and employees that protect the rights and health of both students and employees. And the school board should develop these policies for dealing with AIDS infection prior to the time that it is diagnosed in their school population. The sample policy of the Union Unified School District shown in Figure 5.3 includes many of the previously noted criteria and characteristics of a viable personnel health policy relating to AIDS and other communicable diseases. Note that the last section of the district's policy focuses on the intentions of the school system concerning HIV–AIDS education.

Rights, Responsibilities, and Duties: Academic Freedom

Policy heading GBE of the NEPN/NSBA system centers on rights, responsibilities, and duties and specifically on professional responsibilities related to academic freedom. Academic freedom protection for teachers and the responsibility of teaching personnel for using good judgment in the classroom are included here. In one sense, academic freedom permits teachers to teach in a manner that they deem appropriate, yet the teacher must always be sensitive to the matter of indoctrination; teachers must be particularly careful about the students' freedom when teaching controversial issues and when conflicting values are present. Administrators attempting

| Union Unified School District | Topic: Staff Health and Safety |
| Governing Board Policy | District Code: GBGA |

Staff Health and Safety

Emergency Information

The Superintendent shall develop procedures to obtain and maintain emergency information for every employee.

Immunizations

The Superintendent shall develop guidelines for the immunization of employees in the event of an epidemic, in which this procedure can assist in controlling the epidemic. The Superintendent shall have the authority to require employees to be immunized except in cases where immunization would be detrimental to health or violate religious beliefs.

Health Examinations

When deemed necessary by the Superintendent, employees may be required to undergo physical and/or psychiatric examination(s), by a doctor, to determine fitness for employment or retention. The costs shall be borne by the District.

Return to Work Evaluations

The suitability for any employee returning to work from a paid or unpaid leave of absence due to illness, injury, or any other health reasons may require a written medical release, if requested by the Supervisor.

Communicable Diseases

The Governing Board recognizes that the health and safety risks and consequences associated with communicable diseases will vary depending on the specific disease an employee has and many other factors that must be assessed on a case-by-case basis. Therefore, any employee who is diagnosed as having a communicable disease shall be evaluated on an individualized basis to determine whether he/she may remain at work and, if so, the appropriate assignment for that employee. The District will also follow Department of Health Services rules and regulations.

Acquired Immune Deficiency Syndrome (AIDS)

Cases of AIDS will be evaluated on a case-by-case basis, according to current medical information at the time of evaluation. Every effort will be made to ensure there is no discrimination against employees with AIDS. The Governing Board recognizes that education about AIDS can greatly assist efforts to provide the best care and treatment for infected individuals and help to minimize the risk of transmission to others. Therefore, the District shall endeavor to provide information to students, parents, and employees about current medical knowledge concerning AIDS. In addition, all school administrators will be trained concerning AIDS and proper procedures in dealing with AIDS cases.

Adopted: February 26, 2002

FIGURE 5.3
Staff Health and Safety Policy Statement

Union School District
Sample Policy—Certificated   **Code: GBE**

Personnel Academic Freedom

This school district supports the teachers' freedom to think and to express ideas, to select appropriate instructional materials and methods of instruction, and to be free to take action within their professional domain. Such freedom carries with it the responsibility of using judgment and prudence to the end that it promotes the free exercise of intelligence and pupil learning. Through the use of good taste and professional judgment, teachers are free to conduct discussions of various issues that offer students experience in examining respective views of controversial questions.

Academic freedom must be exercised with the basic ethical responsibilities of the teaching profession and the level of student maturity in mind. These responsibilities are undergirded with a sincere concern for the welfare, growth, and development of students and the use of professional ethics and good judgment in selecting and employing materials and methods of instruction.

FIGURE 5.4
Academic Freedom Policy Statement

to implement policies related to academic freedom need to proceed with judgment and caution. An example of a policy statement concerning academic freedom is given in Figure 5.4.

Policies Relating to Staff Protection: Sexual Harassment

In 1980 the Equal Employment Opportunity Commission (EEOC) provided guidelines that define sexual harassment and clarify the responsibility of organizations concerning such activities. In brief, these guidelines defined sexual harassment as unwelcome sexual advances, requests, or demands for sexual favors and other verbal or physical conduct of a sexual nature that explicitly or implicitly are suggested as a term or condition of an individual's employment, are used as the basis for employment or academic decisions, have the purpose or result of unreasonably interfering with an individual's performance in the workplace or in a school setting, or result in a hostile or offensive work environment. Sexual harassment in the workplace is considered a form of sexual harassment under Title VII of the Civil Rights Act of 1964. Sexual harassment of students is considered sexual harassment under Title IX of the Educational Amendments of 1972.

> What this means...is that all employers—both large and small—must have a sexual harassment policy in place. They must train all employees on the policy. They must have clear procedures for reporting such behavior—including

allowing employees access to management other than their supervisor. And they must communicate policy effectively and openly. (Cole, 2000)

The human resources unit of the school district should assume leadership for establishing specific policies and regulations relating to sexual harassment involving both students and staff. At least two other responsibilities accompany this leadership role: (1) the human resources unit should lead in the development of effective education programs that focus on the nature of sexual harassment, the district's policies on harassment, and individual employees' responsibilities for eliminating sexual harassment in the school district, and (2) the human resources unit should make certain that employee assistance programs and services are available for employees who have experienced sexual harassment and need psychological counseling.

Employee training activities that include programs for educating employees about the subject of harassment and that gather information about the status of harassment within the school setting are direct responsibilities of the human resources unit and administrators in the district. Such training programs serve as a preventive measure regarding sexual harassment and can result in focusing the attention of all employees on the problem and their responsibilities in such matters. Most authorities point out that remediation of sexual harassment in the workplace is largely a matter of good management. That is, systems that are practicing good management by placing emphasis on such matters as task accomplishment, individual and unit work responsibilities, and positive work conditions, rather than matters such as personality issues will, by themselves reduce sexual harassment and discrimination (Cole, 2000). The following strategies are among those suggested by Cohan, Hergenrother, Johnson, Mandel, and Sawyer (1996) to combat sexual harassment in the schools:

- ☐ Establish a district wide sexual harassment committee that includes members of the entire school community.
- ☐ Create and disseminate a sexual harassment policy, including a grievance procedure for reporting incidences of alleged sexual harassment.
- ☐ Include in the district mission the goal to eradicate sexual harassment and promote gender equity.
- ☐ Become aware of attitudes and assumptions about sexual harassment and educate to change attitudes and behaviors.
- ☐ Identify intolerable behaviors.
- ☐ Distinguish between flirting and sexual harassment.
- ☐ Educate the school community on an ongoing basis on recognizing and responding to sexual harassment; challenge gender stereotypes.
- ☐ Educate all staff, students, and parents about the school district sexual harassment policy.
- ☐ Communicate the school district commitment to ending sexual harassment.
- ☐ Expect changes in attitudes and behaviors.
- ☐ Incorporate sexual harassment and gender equity into the entire school—classroom, hallway, playground, and school activities.
- ☐ Demonstrate appropriate behavior. (pp. 74–75)

Human Resources   **Policy 4770**

Sexual Harassment

The Lincoln Board of Education is committed to providing an environment free from unwelcome sexual advances, requests for sexual favors and other verbal or physical conduct or communication constituting sexual harassment. Sexual harassment by and of Lincoln Public Schools employees and students is prohibited.

Date of Adoption (or Last Revision):   5-12-__

Related Policies and Regulations   Regulation
                                                                                  4770.1

Legal References: Section 703 of
                                                                                  Title VII of the
                                                                                  Civil Rights Act

It shall be a violation of school district policy to harass another employee sexually, to permit the sexual harassment of an employee by an employee or a nonemployee, or to harass or permit the harassment of a student sexually. Sexual harassment may take many forms, including, but not limited to:

1. Verbal harassment or abuse including unwelcome sexually oriented communication;
2. Subtle pressure or requests for sexual activity;
3. Unnecessary touching of an individual, e.g., patting, pinching, hugging, repeated brushing against another person's body;
4. Requesting or demanding sexual favors accompanied by implied or overt threats concerning an individual's employment or student's status;
5. Requesting or demanding sexual favors accompanied by implied or overt promise of preferential treatment with regard to an individual's employment or student status; or
6. Sexual assault.

FIGURE 5.5
Sexual Harassment Policy Statement
Source: Reprinted by permission of the Lincoln, Nebraska, Public Schools.

An example of a school district sexual harassment policy statement is provided in Figure 5.5.

Employee Dismissal Policies

Dismissal has been a much-discussed topic in human resources administration. "To secure the best results in our schools, we must have able-bodied, energetic, active, industrious teachers—teachers who can control themselves under the most trying circumstances" (Bloss, 1882, p. 82). As indicated by the foregoing statement made more than 100 years ago, the significance of teacher quality historically has been recognized as critical to effective teaching and learning. Dismissal has been a matter of historical importance as well. In 1882, Bloss reported to the governor of Indiana that "the [county] superintendent may take every precaution, yet occasionally it happens that

Any person who believes he or she has been subjected to sexual harassment should follow these procedures:

1. An aggrieved person should directly inform the person engaging in sexually harassing conduct or communication that such conduct or communication is offensive and must stop.
2. If an aggrieved employee does not wish to communicate directly with the person whose conduct or communication is offensive or if direct communication with the offending person has been ineffective, the employee should contact his or her principal or supervisor or the offending person's principal or supervisor or the Title IX Officer in the Human Resources Office. If an aggrieved student does not wish to communicate directly with the person whose conduct or communication is offensive or if direct communication with the offending person has been ineffective, the student should contact any teacher or other adult in the school whom he or she trusts. That person should then contact the principal or supervisor or the Title IX Officer in the Human Resources Office.
3. An aggrieved person alleging (1) sexual harassment by anyone with supervisory authority or (2) the failure of a supervisor to take immediate action on the complaint should communicate with the Title IX Officer in the Human Resources Office or the Office of the Superintendent of Schools or follow the grievance procedure outlined in the Personnel Handbook.

Allegation of sexual harassment shall be investigated and, if substantiated, corrective or disciplinary action taken, up to and including dismissal from employment if the offender is an employee, or suspension and/or expulsion, if the offender is a student.

Date Regulation Reviewed by the Board of Education: 5-12-__
Related Policies and Regulations:
Legal Reference:

FIGURE 5.5
(continued)

one is licensed who is unworthy to exercise the functions of a teacher" (p. 84). The 1882 School Law reference, Section 36 stated:

> The county superintendent shall have the power to revoke licenses, granted by him or his predecessor, for incompetency, immorality, cruelty, or general neglect of the business of the school, and the revocation of the license of any teacher shall terminate the school which the said teacher may have been employed to teach. (Bloss, 1882, p. 84)

Tead and Metcalf in 1920 underlined the momentous effects of dismissal on the discharged worker as follows:

> So heavy a penalty as the dismissal of a workman (involving to him a serious dislocation of his life, the perils and demoralization attendant on looking for work, probably uprooting of his home and the interruption of his children's schooling, possibly many weeks of penury or semi-starvation for his family and himself) ought to be regarded as a very serious matter. (p. 245)

Today, employee dismissal continues to be a difficult and often traumatic personnel action. Norton (1999) found that personnel directors in one state viewed dismissing incompetent staff as one of the 10 leading problems facing them as administrators. And, as noted by Castetter and Young (2000), "The formidable array of constraints against severance of personnel makes development of and adherence to a systematic dismissal procedure an organizational obligation of high priority" (p. 323).

The purpose here is to emphasize the need and significance of sound board policy and regulations in this area and to present an example of such a policy. Authorities strongly recommend the need to review school board policies, local laws, and state laws pertaining to the specific dismissal charges. Keep reviewing them and your responsibilities thoroughly before any dismissal hearings are held. St. John (1983) underlined the importance of several questions for administrators to ask before a case gets to arbitration or court. Questions related to policy include the following:

1. Was the staff member adequately warned of the consequences of his or her conduct?
2. Was the school policy or procedure related to professional, efficient, or safe operations?
3. Were the rules, policies, and penalties applied evenhandedly, without discrimination, and with equal treatment?
4. Were the school and district policies and procedures communicated carefully (e.g., handbooks, bulletin boards, orientation sessions, etc.)?
5. Did the school or district use recommended disciplinary procedures and follow due process provisions as applicable? (p. 106)

Grier and Turner (1990) emphasized other necessary actions as far as policies and rules are concerned, relating to occasions when dismissal procedures must be implemented:

> Often a dismissal hearing charges a teacher with violating school system policy or school regulations. It is not enough to cite the rule or policy the teacher allegedly violated—you will need to present a copy of the rule to the hearing officer or board. And you must be prepared to establish that the teacher in question also was furnished with a copy before the infraction took place or at least was well aware of the rule or policy.
>
> Proving awareness is difficult, so it's a good idea to make sure all teachers have copies of school regulations and let them know that board policy manuals are open to them.
>
> Sometimes school officials can prove a teacher was aware of rules and policies by referring to agendas of teachers' meetings or copies of teacher handbooks. . . . The teacher contract should include a clause stating that teachers agree to abide by school system policy and their own school's regulations. (p. 21)[2]

In many states, statutes set forth both policy and regulations for dismissals. In such cases, a brief board policy statement generally is set forth, followed by the specific statute as stated in law. Policy development guidelines

Suspension and Dismissal of Certificated Staff Members
(Including Reprimand)

Suspension and Dismissal

Employees are expected to comply with the policies adopted by the Governing Board or as set forth in approved administrative regulations. Dismissal shall be in accordance with the laws of the state.

The procedures for suspension and dismissal of teachers shall be those prescribed by the State's Revised Statutes.

Legal Refs: A.R.S. 15-508; 15-521; 15-536; 15-550

Adopted: Date of Manual Adoption OC 2578
                          Tempe Elementary Schools, Tempe, Arizona

Log No. 166

Rules and Procedures for
Disciplinary Action Involving a Teacher

1. *Purpose*   These rules are prescribed pursuant to Arizona Revised Statutes, Section 15-341(A)(26) and are intended to be utilized as a disciplinary mechanism to deal with violations of statutory duties, School District regulations, Governing Board policies, and the duties of a teacher that do not constitute cause for dismissal or certificate revocation. The Governing Board reserves the right to initiate termination proceedings or to nonrenew contract for serious or multiple violations of these rules or for any incident of insubordination, unprofessional conduct, or other reasons that it determines sufficient to constitute cause for severance of the employer-employee relationship. Dismissal procedures for teachers are governed by the contract of employment, District policy, and the statutory provisions contained in A.R.S. Title 15, Article 5, Chapter 3.

2. *General Provisions*   These rules are intended to preserve the orderly and efficient administration of the school system and to serve as guidelines for the imposition of minor discipline not to exceed suspension without pay for a period of ten (10) days. Discipline may, but need not be imposed for violation of any of the following rules, that include statutory teaching duties, components of a teacher's job responsibility or any violation of Board policy, administrative rules or regulations, and any provision of the teacher or student handbooks.

   Each teacher employed by the Governing Board in this District shall:

   Statutory duties—A.R.S. 15-521.A.:

   1. Enforce the course of study for his or her assigned class or classes.
   2. Enforce the use of the adopted textbooks for his or her assigned class or classes.
   3. Enforce the rules and regulations governing the schools prescribed by the Governing Board, the Arizona Department of Education, and any other lawfully empowered authority.
   4. Hold pupils to strict account for disorderly conduct.
   5. Exercise supervision over pupils on the playgrounds and during recess if assigned to such duty.

FIGURE 5.6
Dismissal Policy Statement Based on State Statute
Source: Reprinted by permission of the Tempe, Arizona, Elementary School District.

6. Make the decision to promote or retain a pupil in grade in a common school or to pass or fail a pupil in a course in high school.
7. Present his or her certificate to the County School Superintendent before assuming charge of a school, except as provided in Arizona Revised Statutes 15-502, Subsection B.
8. Make such reports as may be reasonably required by the Superintendent of Public Instruction, County School Superintendent, Governing Board, or School Administration.

3. *Procedures*

A. *Disciplinary action alternatives*   Appropriate discipline is at the discretion of the Supervisor. The alternatives available include:
   1. Verbal warning;
   2. Verbal reprimand;
   3. Written reprimand;
   4. Suspension with pay;
   5. Suspension with pay and required remedial action, i.e., observation of other teacher, mandated in-service or educational program;
   6. Suspension without pay. A teacher may be given a suspension without pay for a period not to exceed ten (10) days;
   7. Termination. This remedy is reserved by law to the Governing Board, and procedures are described in applicable statutory provisions. The Governing Board may, if appropriate, determine that termination be imposed for serious or repeated violations of these rules. Notice of the Board's intent to dismiss and applicable procedures are not covered by these rules.

B. *Notice of discipline*
   1. An administrator, after a reasonable investigation, is authorized to impose minor discipline in any category described in Paragraph A.3 through A.6 above subject to notice, hearing, and appeal rights described below. A reasonable investigation shall include some discussion with the employee to ascertain if grounds exist to justify imposition of discipline.
   2. When it is determined that grounds exist for disciplinary action, a written notice shall be sent to the teacher. The notice shall identify:
      a. The date the infraction occurred;
      b. The rule or duty violated;
      c. A summary of the factual information supporting the recommended discipline;
      d. The nature of the disciplinary action to be imposed.

C. *Request for hearing*   A teacher who has received notice of discipline has the right to request a hearing in writing within five (5) school days after the date the teacher receives the notice. The request for a hearing shall be in writing and filed with the Personnel Office and shall contain the prior written notice of discipline.

D. *Hearing tribunal*   The hearing will be held before the Superintendent or designee.

E. *Hearing procedure*
   1. The hearing shall be scheduled within ten (10) school days after receipt of the teacher's request unless extended by mutual agreement of the parties.

FIGURE 5.6
(continued)

2. Notice of the hearing shall be served on the teacher and Supervisor by the Hearing Officer and shall contain:
   a. The time and place of the hearing.
   b. A copy or summary of the written disciplinary notice previously served on the teacher.
   c. Notice that disciplinary action will be imposed if the teacher fails to appear.
   d. A statement to advise the parties that they may present oral or written evidence relevant to the alleged violation of rules or policies.
   e. State that the hearing will be conducted informally without adhering to the rules of evidence.
   f. State that within seven (7) school days after the hearing a written decision shall be served on the parties.
   g. Advise the parties that they may, if they desire, be represented by another employee at the hearing.

3. The hearing shall be held at the time and place stated in the notice. The designated person or persons shall conduct the hearing in an informal and orderly fashion recognizing the rights of all parties. A statement should be made by the Hearing Officer as to the purpose of the hearing. Parties shall be advised if a record shall be made by tape, stenographer, or the notes of the Hearing Officer. Any party may tape the hearing for his own use, but it will not be the official record.

4. Subsequent to the hearing, the Hearing Officer shall prepare a written decision to be served on the parties within fifteen (15) calendar days.

F. *Decision*   The decision shall contain a brief summary of the hearing and a finding of whether the teacher committed a violation and if the discipline was appropriate. If it is found that the teacher committed the violation, the teacher's right to appeal the written decision to the Governing Board for review of the record shall be provided as part of the decision.

FIGURE 5.6
(continued)

usually recommend that statements from statutes not be rewritten verbatim as board policy. Rather, a policy based on the statute should be written. However, due to the sensitive nature of dismissals and the high potential for litigation in the courts, the use of specific state statutes as district policy is common. An example of a dismissal policy based strictly on a state statute is given in Figure 5.6.

It is clear that dismissal procedures and requirements will differ as the laws of the various states differ. The consideration of dismissal as it applies to tenured and nontenured personnel is discussed in more detail in Chapter 7.

Drug-free Workplace

The cost of drug and alcohol abuse to industry has been estimated to be almost $200 billion (Harvey & Bowin, 1996). Decreased productivity, increased absenteeism, increased threats to the safety of self and others, and

G. *Appeal to governing board*

1. Any appeal to the Governing Board via the Superintendent must be in writing, filed within five (5) school days after service of the hearing decision, list the issue or issues upon which review is requested, and specify the relief sought from the Governing Board.
2. All evidence the teacher wishes to have the Governing Board review shall be attached to the appeal. No new information, other than that already submitted at the hearing, will be allowed.
3. The supervisor shall be served with a copy of the appeal and have five (5) days after service to file material and information submitted at the hearing and which are deemed appropriate in support of the discipline imposed.
4. When the Superintendent receives the appeal, it shall be transmitted to the Governing Board.
5. The Governing Board has no obligation to conduct another hearing or to receive new evidence not previously presented to the Hearing Officer in a minor discipline matter.
6. The Board shall schedule an executive session to review the appeal. No additional testimony or input shall be allowed unless expressly requested by the Board.
7. Written notice of the Board's decision shall be served on the parties. The Board shall have a reasonable time, not to exceed thirty (30) school days to review the matter and render its decision.
8. Discipline shall be held in abeyance during the hearing and appeal procedures under these rules.

Cross refs: KK-R
                GBCB
                GBCC
Legal References: A.R.S. 15-341
Issued: _____

Tempe Elementary Schools
Tempe, Arizona

FIGURE 5.6
(continued)

increased loss or damage to property are among the major problems and costs associated with employee drug and alcohol abuse (Bolton, 1997). The schools have not been immune to the problems related to drug and alcohol abuse among employees. One study in education found that 90 of the 91 responding districts reported drinking and alcoholism to be the leading problem of troubled workers, and 63 of the 91 districts listed drugs or chemical dependency as a major problem area for troubled workers. Overall, drinking and alcoholism were second only to general health problems as the leading problem in the area of issues facing troubled workers (Norton, 1988).

The 1988 Federal Drug-Free Workplace Act requires federal contractors and grantees who receive more than $25,000 in federal funds to certify that they will maintain a drug-free workplace and to adopt a drug-free work environment policy, disseminate it to all employees, and notify employees that a drug-free state is a condition of employment. School districts have attempted to meet this goal by adopting alcohol and substance abuse policies, instituting drug-free awareness programs, and increasing employee assistance program services directed at drug and alcohol use and abuse. Some districts have adopted mandatory drug testing for certain safety-sensitive positions (e.g., bus drivers). Such a policy, if adopted,

> should provide for written notice to employees that testing will be conducted; explain the procedures that will be used in the testing; employ a chain of custody so that samples are not lost, switched, stolen; confirm positive tests with more sensitive tests; and ensure confidentiality of test results. (Bolton, 1997, p. 199)

School board policies and approved regulations related to drug and alcohol use have focused primarily on the elimination of alcohol or drug use on school district property, the establishment of disciplinary action in cases of the violation of alcohol and drug policies, the implementation of alcohol and drug awareness programs, procedures for alcohol and drug testing, employee assistance programs, and the establishment of employee rights, including appeal procedures. A sample policy with accompanying regulations in the area of a drug-free workplace is shown in Figure 5.7.

The courts have been somewhat consistent in rulings relative to the possession and use of alcohol and drugs by employees. As Webb, Metha, and Jordan (2000) point out, conviction for possession of illegal drugs, in and of itself, does not serve as the basis for dismissal. The primary consideration for dismissal in such cases has been the effect of the incident on students and the educational program of the school. For example, the courts might not support the dismissal of a teacher based solely on a conviction of possession of a small amount of marijuana without any evidence of unfitness of the teacher. However, they probably would uphold a dismissal based on evidence of a widely publicized conviction, combined with substantial evidence that the teacher's conduct had seriously undermined his or her fitness to teach (Fischer, Schimmel, & Kelly, 1995).

Use of District Network and Internet

Rapid advances in information technology are having major impacts on the human resources function. Although information technology has contributed positively to each major human resources process, it brings about new responsibilities for the integration of data, information, and methods of record storage and retrieval, as well as the moral and ethical considerations related to uses of electronic technology. How is information to be collected? What information is to be collected and how is it to be stored and accessed? How are personnel records to be managed and by whom? How is the security of personnel records to be safeguarded? It is not the purpose here to set forth detailed responses to these kinds of questions.

However, it is of importance to note that school districts must develop viable policies and regulations relative to the aims and regulatory provisions for dealing with information technology in general and the human resources

The governing Board recognizes that drug dependency is a major health problem and its effect has serious safety and security repercussions for both students and staff. Therefore, it is this District's intent and obligation to provide a Drug-Free workplace.

No employee shall consume or use alcohol or a drug(s) (without medical authorization) while on District property, on the job or while responsible for the supervision of students. (Drug means any dangerous drug as defined in A.R.S. § 13-34-1).

Employees shall not report to work having consumed alcohol or drug(s) (without medical authorization) when such consumption can be detected or impair their ability to perform their assigned job.

Any employee who violates this policy is subject to disciplinary action in accordance with established policies and regulations.

The Superintendent shall establish a Drug-Free Awareness Program and inform all employees regarding that program and their rights, responsibilities and privileges under the law.

Adopted: 03/05/____
LEGAL REF.   A.R.S. § 13-2911
                      13-3401 ET SEQ
                      15-341 (A) (1)
                      P.L. 100-690, Title V. Subtitle D.
                      P.L. 101-226
                      34 C.F.R. Part 86

Drug-Free Workplace

I. It is the District's intent and obligation to provide a drug-free workplace. Workplace includes:
- Any school building or District premises;
- Any property leased or used by the District for any educational or District business purposes during the time the employee is on duty;
- Any school sponsored or approved activity, event or function where students or staff members are under the jurisdiction of the District; and
- Any District-owned vehicles or District-approved vehicles used to transport staff members or students for school activities or District business.

II. The unlawful manufacture, distribution, dispensation, possession, sale or consumption of intoxicating beverages, narcotics and any other illicit drug(s) is prohibited.

III. All employees shall receive information about:
- Dangers of alcohol and drug abuse in the workplace
- Policies and regulations of the District for maintaining a drug-free workplace
- Supervisory responsibilities in administering this policy and regulations
- Alcohol and drug testing procedures
- Penalties that may be imposed for alcohol and drug abuse violations occurring in the workplace
- Alcohol and drug counseling and rehabilitation re-entry programs available to staff

IV. All employees must sign a statement indicating that they have received a copy of the current drug-free workplace policy and regulations. The signed statement will be placed in their personnel file.

Employees must, as a condition of employment, abide by the terms of this policy and report any conviction under a criminal drug statute occurring in the workplace, as defined in I. above, not

FIGURE 5.7
Drug-Free Workplace Policy
Source: Used by permission of the Creighton Elementary School District #14, Phoenix, Arizona.

later than five (5) calendar days after such conviction. Failure to report a drug conviction under this paragraph may result in disciplinary action up to and including termination.

V. Use of prescription and/or over-the-counter drugs
   A. Employees shall report to their supervisor use of prescription drugs which may impair job performance and/or affect the safety of themselves and others.
   B. Employees are expected to act responsibly with regard to use of over-the-counter drugs. It is the employee's responsibility to request reassignment or leave if use of over-the-counter drugs impairs job performance and/or affects the safety of themselves or others.

VI. Procedures when an employee appears impaired
   A. If the supervisor of an employee has probable cause that the employee's job performance has been impaired by the use of alcohol or drugs, and the Superintendent/designee concurs, the employee shall submit to alcohol/drug(s) testing.
   B. Probable cause exists where the facts and circumstances are sufficient to warrant the belief that the employee has consumed alcohol or used a drug(s) during a period of time when such consumption or use could affect job performance.
   C. If the supervisor is directed to have the employee evaluated, the supervisor or designee will contact the Office of Personnel Services to arrange for an immediate physical evaluation of the employee.

VII. Procedures for alcohol and drug testing
   A. The annually selected medical facilities shall be licensed and certified by the appropriate state or federal agency or by the College of American Pathologists. The collection facility shall comply with acceptable standards of the medical field relating to collection, storage and transportation of samples.
   B. Prior to testing, the director or supervisor shall confidentially inform the employee and provide a written affidavit of the reason(s) for testing referral. The employee shall be given an opportunity to provide an explanation of the facts and circumstances giving rise to the referral. The District may require the employee to immediately submit to testing.
   C. An employee who refuses to submit to alcohol and drug testing may be subject to termination of employment.
   D. When testing is required, the District shall assume the cost of the test provided the results are negative. The employee may elect to have a blood sample drawn and retained at the employee's expense.
   E. The employee may not be allowed to perform normal job responsibilities until test results are known.
   F. Immediately upon receipt of test results, the District shall notify the employee.
   G. If test results are negative, the sample(s) shall be destroyed.
   H. Employees with positive samples shall be informed of the right to a second testing of the reserved sample at a certified laboratory of their choice at their expense.
   I. The employee shall be informed of the right to a second testing of the reserved sample at a certified laboratory of their choice at their expense.

VIII. Appeal of test results
   The following procedures shall apply to any appeal of the test results:

   1. Any appeal of test findings shall postpone a recommendation pending outcome of the appeal.
   2. Any appeal shall be made in writing to the Superintendent/designee within two (2) working days following receipt of test results by the employee.
   3. The appeal shall specify the basis of the employee's challenge to the test findings.

FIGURE 5.7
(continued)

4. Any employee appealing the test findings shall arrange for a second testing of the sample at the employee's cost. In the event of a negative second test result, the District shall assume the cost of both tests.
5. The Superintendent/designee shall meet with the employee and their representative and the person most able to respond to the employee's challenge, to determine if there is any validity to the employee's appeal.
6. If the Superintendent/designee determines that the employee's challenge is valid, any pay withheld during suspension, between the time test results are known and the time the Superintendent/designee makes a determination, shall be reinstated.
7. If the Superintendent/designee determines that the employee's challenge to the test findings is valid, disciplinary action shall not be taken *unless* there are documented independent grounds for such action.

IX. Disciplinary sanctions and appeals

Disciplinary sanctions may include the successful completion of an appropriate rehabilitation program, suspension and/or immediate termination of employment, and referral for prosecution.

A. Employees recommended for disciplinary action shall be advised of their due process rights, including the right to a hearing before the Superintendent/designee.
B. When an employee tests positive for alcohol/drug(s), and is disciplined but not dismissed, the employee will be referred to the employee's health care provider for assessment, counseling and rehabilitation or to an Employee Assistance Program.
C. Participation in rehabilitation or treatment may be required of an employee who has violated this policy. Failure to begin or complete a treatment or rehabilitation program may subject the employee to disciplinary action, including termination.

X. Employee Assistance Program

Employees are encouraged to seek assistance if they have concerns about alcohol/drug(s) use. A staff member who requests assistance prior to the detection of a problem shall be directed to an appropriate Employee Assistance Program.

An employee who is referred to an Employee Assistance program may be placed on some category of leave until the District receives medical and/or professional Certification of the employee's ability to resume job responsibilities.

XI. Confidentiality

A. An employee with a alcohol/drug(s) problem is entitled to confidentiality. Information relating to any testing incident shall be officially communicated within the District only on a need-to-know basis. Employees who violate this provision shall be subject to disciplinary action.
B. Employee records pertaining to this regulation shall be subject to normal District procedures relating to confidential personnel records and state law. Any report of a negative test shall be destroyed after final disposition of the matter.

XII. Convictions

All convictions, when known by the District, involving employees engaged in the performance of a Grant from the United States Government shall be processed by the District as follows: Within ten (10) days of receiving any notice of conviction, the District shall notify the U.S. Department of Education of such notice. Within thirty (30) days of receiving notice of conviction, the District shall take appropriate personnel action against the employee up to and including termination.

Adopted: 03/05/____

FIGURE 5.7
(continued)

function specifically. School board policies and regulations regarding records management minimally should include a *Statement of Purpose*, guidelines for making information management decisions and improving the district's information system's effectiveness toward the goals of improved performance, increased efficiency, and improved information flow; *Integration Provisions* that focus on a plan for coordinating the district's information system with all other subunits within the system; *Personnel and Unit Assignments of Responsibility*, job responsibilities and the assignments of accountability for the information management system in the district; *Input and Retrieval Processes* that identify opportunities and set forth limitations of the system, including restrictions and ethical guidelines for users; *Funding Considerations* that include the initiation of new programs and their maintenance; *Data, Information, and Files*, with due attention to what information is to be collected and stored and how such information is to be retrieved and safeguarded.

Figure 5.8 is an example of a district's statement for use of the computer network and Internet. The statement is regulatory in nature and places emphasis on the user's responsibilities and personal ethics.

Voluntary Transfer

Human resources administration is faced with changes in personnel assignments, the placement of staff, the condition of having surpluses in some staff positions, voluntary and involuntary transfers, reduction in force (RIF), dismissals, and resignations. In each of these situations, guiding policy and administrative regulations are of primary importance. In a situation whereby a teaching vacancy occurs within a school district, direction is needed for determining just how the vacancy is to be filled and how the eligibility of current teachers within the system will be treated. Figure 5.9 sets forth an example of a partial administrative regulation dealing with voluntary transfer. The regulation includes the considerations of how vacancies will be posted and made known to current teaching staff members, the nature of the vacancy, the length of the position posting, procedures for application, communication procedures regarding follow-up contacts, interview procedures, and a related addendum that focuses on teacher exchanges.

The legal considerations relating to teacher transfers, reassignments, and demotions are documented in Chapter 6. In addition, Chapter 6 discusses the law regarding topics related to teacher personnel, including reduction in force, dismissals, suspension, discrimination, and due process. As pointed out by Clemmer (1991), "Many of today's most conscientious educational administrators and dedicated board members enter their first policy-setting assignments with little or no understanding of the impact policies have on how school districts operate" (p. xx).

This chapter has emphasized the benefits of having a viable set of school district policies and regulations in the area of human resources administration and has provided information as to how human resources administrators can assume a leadership role in their development and dissemination.

District employees have access to the district computer network and the Internet for the enhancement and support of student instruction. It is important to remember that the equipment and the software are the property of the school district.

In using the computers and the Internet, employees are agreeing to the following:

1. Since copyright laws protect software, employees will not make unauthorized copies of software on school computers by any means.
2. Employees will not give, lend, or sell copies of software to others unless the original software is clearly identified as shareware or in the public domain.
3. If an employee downloads public domain programs for personal use or non-commercially redistributes a public domain program, the employee assumes all risks regarding the determination of whether a program is in the public domain.
4. Employees are not permitted to knowingly access information that is profane, obscene, or offensive toward a group or individual based on race, gender, national origin, or religion. Furthermore, employees are prohibited from placing such information on the Internet.
5. Employees will protect the privacy of other computer users' areas by not accessing their passwords without written permission.
6. Employees will not copy, change, read, or use another person's files.
7. Employees will not attempt to gain unauthorized access to system programming or computer equipment.
8. Employees will not use computer systems to disturb or harass other computer users by sending unwanted mail or by other means.
9. Employees will not disclose their passwords and account names to anyone or attempt to ascertain or use anyone else's password and account name.
10. Employees must understand that the intended use of all computer equipment is to meet instructional objectives.
11. Employees will not use the network for financial gain or for any commercial or illegal activity.
12. Attempts to bypass security systems on computer workstations or servers, or vandalism will result in cancellation of privileges. Malicious attempts to harm or destroy data of another employee or data that reside anywhere on the School District's network or the uploading or creation of computer viruses is forbidden.
13. The School District will not be responsible for any liabilities, costs, expenses, or purchases incurred by the use of telecommunication systems such as the Internet. The employee's signed application for an email account states that the employee is agreeing to indemnify the district for any expenses, including legal ties, arising out of their use of the system in violation of the agreement.
14. The Internet is supplied for employee use on an "as is, as available" basis. The School District does not imply or expressly warrant that any information accessed will be valuable or fit for a particular purpose or that the system will operate error-free.
15. The system administrators reserve the right to refuse posting of files, and to remove files.

Any violation of any part of this agreement or any activity that school authorities deem inappropriate will be subject to disciplinary action consistent with the District's due process procedures.

FIGURE 5.8

Use of District Network and Internet

Source: Certificated Personnel Handbook (September 2000). Reprinted by permission of the Lincoln, Nebraska, Public Schools.

a. An updated list of present vacancies and known vacancies for the following school year will be posted in all school buildings, at least every two weeks starting March 15. The posting of vacancies will continue to 30 calendar days prior to the first contract day of the building with the vacancy. If all surplused teachers have not been assigned, posting shall continue past 30 days prior to the first contract day. The vacancy list shall include:

   (1) Position title
   (2) Building location
   (3) Status (i.e., permanent, temporary, part-time or itinerant
   (4) Qualifications: courses to be taught and, if elementary, the grade and subject matter emphasis

   At all times, an updated list shall be available at the Human Resources Office.

b. Posting: If posted, no vacancy shall be permanently filled within five (5) working days of the date of posting.

c. Procedures: Every employee on continuing contract shall have the right to apply for any vacancy for which he/she is certificated and endorsed by contacting the Human Resources Office within the five (5) day posting period. All certificated employees applying for a voluntary transfer shall, after contacting the Human Resources Department, be allowed to submit a letter of application and résumé to the principal or supervisor where the vacancy exists. All applicants shall receive notification within five (5) days from the principal indicating receipt of their application for the position.

   The Human Resources Department will notify all applicants, in writing, within ten (10) days of the closing date for the application when the screening process and subsequent interviewing will occur.

   Applicants selected for an interview will be notified by the Human Resources Department. Other applicants will be notified, in writing, by the Human Resources Department within ten (10) days that they have not been selected for an interview. Interviewees not selected for the position will be notified by Human Resources within ten (10) days from the time that the position has been filled.

d. Certificated employees exchange shall be defined as the exchange of assignments between two staff members in different buildings with the approval of both principals. Such exchange shall be for a one (1) year trial. At the end of one (1) year, a request for discontinuation of the exchange by any of the affected teachers or principals will be honored. An exchange extended beyond one (1) year shall become permanent.

FIGURE 5.9
Voluntary Transfer: Administrative Regulation
Source: Professional Agreement (2000–2001). Reprinted by permission of the Lincoln, Nebraska, Public Schools.

SUMMARY

Policy, by its very nature, is often surrounded by controversy. Since policy generally evolves from important issues, which are often in dispute, total consensus on specific policy is seldom the case. For this reason, some persons take the position of leaving well enough alone; after all, if one puts policy in writing, it has to be followed. Such a view overlooks the reality that all organizations are governed by policy, and educational systems are no exception. Without policies and regulations, the school district could scarcely be called a system. Policies and regulations establish orderly operations within the school district and help to define the system's functions and organizational relationships.

Most people would agree that policy is designed to provide direction and purpose for the school system. One reason policy should be studied by human resources administrators is that it has significant effects on the lives of the personnel in the system. The challenges surrounding the human resources processes of selection, assignment, evaluation, collective negotiations, compensation and welfare, protection, and others demand the direction and guidance that personnel policies and procedures can provide. As pointed out by Davies and Brickell (1988), "the whole process of policy formulation is rich with opportunities for stimulating good thinking about school goals and their relation to policies by the many persons and groups concerned with the schools" (p. iv).

This chapter has presented information that not only underscores the vital importance of policy development for the human resources function, but has also set forth the fundamentals for policy and regulation development in this area.

DISCUSSION QUESTIONS

1. You have been selected by your teacher colleagues to serve on a districtwide committee for the purpose of revising the school district's leave policy. All forms of absence from duty are concerns of the committee. Although the overriding concern is that of the development of a viable policy for all professional staff members, what are several specific provisions that you would want to have implemented as a teacher? For example, what stipulations would you see as important in the area of personal leave, sabbatical leave, and so forth?

2. Use the information provided in question 1 to set forth several specific provisions that you, as a member of the school board, would consider imperative to an effective policy on personnel leaves. Examine the differences, if any, in the stipulations arrived at in question 1 and question 2.

3. Information in the chapter indicated that the development of policies and regulations serves to clarify the division of labor between the school board and the school superintendent. Discuss this contention in more detail. Why is such a division important in school operations? Isn't there some danger that such a division will result in board–superintendent conflicts?

4. Obtain a copy of your school district's policy manual or that of another school district. Rate the following characteristics from low (1) to high (5) as they pertain to the policy manual examined: completeness, conciseness, clarity, distinctiveness, and consistency. (Review the discussion of these characteristics included in the chapter for further term clarification.)

5. Use the NEPN/NSBA system to determine each of the following topical headings. Write the topic of the series, subseries, division, subdivision, and so on, for each entry.
    a. GBEB
    b. GCAAA
    c. GCCBA
    d. GCL
    e. GDQ
6. An administrator comments, "I do all I can to keep policies strictly informal. Put them in writing and you have to carry them out. I want to keep as much freedom to act as possible." How might you reply to such a statement?

CASE STUDIES

5.1 Pay or No Play

Ce Ce Rose has taught instrumental music at East High School for 6 years. She holds a B.S. degree in music and will complete a master's degree at the end of the second term at State University.

Principal Hodson received a call from one of the school's patrons, Mrs. John Adams. Mrs. Adams, whose son is a sophomore at East, also is the mother of two daughters who both graduated from East and participated in the school's instrumental program. "Miss Rose has informed my son, Mark, that he needs special help in order to retain his place in the school band," reported Mrs. Adams. "She implied to Mark that his trumpet playing was below the standard expected for the marching band," she remarked. "Miss Rose has made herself available for special lessons at $12.50 an hour. She'll work with Mark after school on Wednesdays and on two Saturday mornings a month."

Principal Hodson was silent for a moment. If this was true, this information was new to him. "Aren't teachers supposed to give special help to students after school hours if needed?" asked Mrs. Adams. "I understand that she already is giving lessons to three other orchestra students."

"Well, many of our teachers do give help after regular classroom hours," said Principal Hodson, "and I do know that some of our teachers moonlight as tutors at night and on weekends."

"It seems to me that charging for special lessons could lead to problems," commented Mrs. Adams.

"Mrs. Adams," said Principal Hodson, "let me search for more information on this matter. I'll get back to you at the earliest possible time. I appreciate your concern and thank you for contacting me on this matter."

Questions

1. Place yourself in Principal Hodson's role. What action plan would you implement in this situation?
2. Identify three or four issues of importance in this case.
3. Assuming that the school district has no written policy concerning the issues that you identified in question 2, is a guiding policy needed to deal with such cases? Why or why not?

5.2 Teachers' Academic Freedom*

On the opening day of school in September, Keefe, a tenured part-time English teacher, who is also head of a high school English de-

---

*From "Teachers' Academic Freedom" by D. R. Davies and H. Watt, August 1970, *School Board Policies.* Copyright © 1970 by Daniel R. Davies. Reprinted by permission. Davies and Watt based this discussion on the case of *Keefe v. Geanakos et al.* (1st Cir. 1969).

partment and coordinator for grades 7 through 12, gave each member of his senior English class a copy of the prestigious *Atlantic Monthly* magazine and asked the students to read the first article that night. Keefe discussed the article with his class, especially a particular word that was used in it. He explained the word's origin and context and the reasons the author had included it (the word, admittedly highly offensive, was a vulgar term for an incestuous son). Keefe said that any student who felt the assignment personally distasteful could have an alternative one.

The next evening Keefe was called to a meeting of the school committee and asked to defend his use of the offensive word. (Parents had complained.) Following his explanation, a majority of the members of the committee asked him informally if he would agree not to use it again in the classroom. Keefe replied that he could not, in good conscience, agree. No formal action was taken at the meeting, but Keefe was suspended shortly thereafter, and school administrators proposed that he be discharged.

Claiming a violation of his civil rights, Keefe sought a temporary injunction before a federal district court forbidding any action on the part of the school board prior to a hearing on the alleged violation. The court refused to grant the injunction, and Keefe appealed to the U.S. Court of Appeals, First Circuit. His position was that, as a matter of law, his conduct did not warrant discipline and therefore there was no ground for any hearing. The position had two relevant parts:

1. His conduct was within his competence as a teacher, as a matter of academic freedom, whether the defendants (school board) approved or not.
2. He had no warning from any regulations then in force that his actions could bring about his discharge.

The school board denied Keefe's contentions, and the following statement appeared in court records:

> They [the board] accept the existence of a principle of academic freedom to teach, but state that it is limited to proper classroom materials as reasonably determined by the school com-

mittee in the light of pertinent conditions, of which they cite in particular the age of the students. Asked by the court whether a teacher has a right to say to the school committee that it is wrong if, in fact, its decision was arbitrary, counsel candidly and commendably (and correctly) responded in the affirmative. This we consider to be the present issue.

Questions

1. What do you believe about the freedom of teachers to select and use materials of instruction despite the objections of some parents?
2. Discuss your views of the position set forth by Keefe. Do the same with the statement by the school board that appeared in the court records.

5.3 Miss North's Dilemma

Miss North has served in the Jefferson school system for 19 years as an elementary teacher. Her employment record in the Jefferson schools shows that she taught at Longfellow Elementary School for 5 years, Mark Twain Elementary School for 9 years, Whitman Elementary School for 3 years, and in her present position as a grade 5 teacher at Emerson for 2 years. She has served under four different superintendents, including the present school head, Dr. Donnelly, who has been in Jefferson for 2 years. During Miss North's 2 years at Emerson, one board member called Dr. Donnelly to inquire about Miss North. The board member stated that he had received many calls about Miss North in the last two days.

"I just wanted to let you know about the calls," said the board member. "You'll most likely be receiving some yourself soon. Better be on your guard."

Dr. Donnelly reviewed the permanent file of Miss North. Evaluation reports on Miss North pointed out that it was felt that she was a strict teacher and did not have the most friendly classroom atmosphere, but most pupils performed better in her classroom than in one with more permissive surroundings.

One anecdotal notation in Miss North's file outlined a conversation between her and the assistant superintendent, Dr. Seward. Dr. Seward had telephoned Miss North to inform her that it would be necessary to transfer her from Mark Twain to Whitman. The reasons outlined for the action as recorded by Dr. Seward centered on an apparent feeling of growing parental dissatisfaction and the fact that several parents had requested that their children not be placed in her room the next year. Thus the decision was reached to move Miss North to Whitman for a new start.

The record revealed that Miss North was greatly disturbed about the transfer decision. "I don't drive an automobile," Miss North had pointed out. "How do you expect me to get back and forth to school each day? Everyone knows what it means when you're placed at Whitman," Miss North had stated, according to Dr. Seward.

Mr. Smith, principal at Whitman Elementary School, was quoted by Dr. Seward as saying, "You never know how she will react from day to day. We've gotten along as well as can be expected. She doesn't have much patience for the slow learner, but her good kids can compete with most other grade 5 pupils."

At a special board meeting later that week, a second member of the board of education mentioned the concern centering on Miss North. "Parents tell me that the pupils are afraid of her," one board member stated. "She apparently is cold toward parents. In one instance, I was told that one of her pupils had written a note on the blackboard wishing her a happy birthday. Miss North insisted that the one who wrote it on the board erase it in front of the whole class. The parent of the child indicated that her embarrassed daughter didn't

want to return to school." Another board member stated, "This must be her 30th year of teaching in Jefferson. Doesn't she retire soon?"

The matter was referred by the board to Superintendent Donnelly for immediate study. After the meeting, Dr. Donnelly conferred with Mr. Malloy, principal at Emerson. "She is a rather cold person, but I've received no official complaints from parents to date," said the principal. "However, my visit last week to her classroom revealed that some children are not responding. Her room was all business. The science lesson which I observed was well presented."

Dr. Seward apparently felt that it would be best to release Miss North. "She is starting one of her problems again. I think we've gone along with her long enough. Mr. Malloy would just as soon have her out of his building," Dr. Seward related to Dr. Donnelly. "She is a loner in my opinion. She didn't even attend the faculty social last month."

Dr. Donnelly noted that the date was March 1 and school was to close on May 27. Obviously, the board was anticipating immediate action on the part of the administration.

Questions

1. Assume the role of Dr. Donnelly, school superintendent, and discuss or write your follow-up procedures and recommendations to the school board.
2. What policy and regulation matters are significant in this case? Why?
3. Explain how a viable set of policies and regulations might have proved of special value in this case.

REFERENCES

Bloss, J. M. (1882). *Thirtieth report of the superintendent of public instruction of the state of Indiana to the governor.* Indianapolis: State of Indiana.

Bolton, J. E. (1997). *Human resources management for public and nonprofit organizations.* San Francisco: Jossey-Bass.

Castetter, W. B., & Young, P. I. (2000). The human resource function in educational administration (7th ed.). Upper Saddle River, NJ: Prentice Hall/Merrill.

Class size must be negotiated with teachers, Oregon court rules. (April 10, 1991). *Education Week,* p. 2.

Clemmer, E. F. (1991). *The school policy handbook.* Boston: Allyn and Bacon.

Cohan, A., Hergenrother, M. A., Johnson, Y. M., Mandel, L. S., & Sawyer, J. (1996). *Sexual harassment and abuse: A handbook for teachers and administrators.* Thousand Oaks, CA: Corwin Press.

Cole, J. (2000). Sexual harassment: New rules, New behavior. In Fred H. Maidment (Ed.), *Human Resources 00/01* (10th Ed.) Reprinted from *Business Horizons,* March/April, 1999. Indiana University Kelly School of Business. Guilford, CT: Dushkin/McGraw-Hill.

Davies, D. R., & Brickell, H. M. (1988). *An instructional handbook on how to develop school board policies, by-laws, and administrative regulations.* Naco, AZ: Daniel R. Davies.

Davies, D. R., & Watt, H. (August 1970). Teachers' academic freedom. *School Board Policies.* New London, CT: Croft Consulting Services.

Duke, D. L., & Canady, R. L. (1991). *School policy.* New York: McGraw-Hill.

Equal Employment Opportunity Commission. (1980). Guidelines concerning sexual harassment: Title VII legislation, 703 of the Civil Rights Act (P.L. 88-352).

Edlin, G., & McCormack Brown, K. (1997). *Essentials for health and wellness.* Sudbury, MA: Jones & Bartlett.

Fischer, L., Schimmel, D., & Kelly, C. (1999). *Teachers and the law* (5th ed.). White Plains, NY: Longman.

Grier, T. B., & Turner, M. J. (1990). Make your charges stick. *Executive Educator, 12*(2), 20-21.

Harvey, D., & Bowin, R. B. (1996). *Human resource management: An experimental approach.* Upper Saddle River, NJ: Prentice Hall.

Hernandez, D. E., & Bozeman, W. C. (1990). AIDS policies and public school employees: A review of recent court decision. *ERS Spectrum, 8*(2), 22-28.

Norton, M. S. (1999). *The personnel administrator in Arizona: A research study.* Tempe: Arizona State University, College of Education.

Rogers, J. J. (1989). Regular review will keep your AIDS policies sound and up to date. *American School Board Journal, 176*(1), 26-27.

St. John, W. (October 1983). Documenting your case for dismissal with acceptable evidence. *NASSP Bulletin,* pp. 104-106.

Strouse, J. H. (October 1990). School district AIDS policies. *Urban Education, 25*(1), 8-88.

Tead, O., & Metcalf, H. C. (1920). *Personnel administration.* New York: McGraw-Hill.

Webb, L. D., Metha, A., & Jordan, K. F. (2000). Foundations of American education (3rd ed.). Upper Saddle River, NJ: Prentice Hall/Merrill.

6 *Legal Aspects of Human Resources Administration*

Learning Objectives

After reading this chapter, you will be able to:

■ Discuss the position of the courts in regard to certification, residency, health, physical, and testing requirements of teachers and other employees.

■ Identify the basic elements of a contract.

■ Differentiate between the due process rights of tenured and nontenured teachers and dismissal and nonrenewal of contracts.

■ Distinguish between procedural and substantive due process.

■ Discuss the conditions under which a school district may be liable for the sexual harassment committed by its employee.

■ Describe the major personnel issues involved in dismissal for cause, suspension, and involuntary transfers.

■ Identify the primary grounds for legal challenges to reductions in force.

The public schools, like all other institutions in society, operate within the framework of laws generated by the federal government, the state government, and the courts (case law). The operation of the schools is also subject to a multitude of ordinances, rules, and regulations promulgated by numerous federal, state, and local agencies and government entities.

All aspects of the employment relationship have been the subject of legislative and executive pronouncements and judicial interpretation. Although school administrators are not expected to be legal experts, they should be aware of the basic legal concepts in human resources administration and know when to seek legal counsel. It is imperative that school administrators understand their rights and obligations under the law and that these are translated into everyday personnel practices in their districts (Cascio, 1998).

The purpose of this chapter is to familiarize school administrators with the basic concepts of law as they relate to employment in the public schools. Although there is some variation in the application of these legal concepts from one state or locality to another, certain topics and issues are of sufficient similarity and concern to warrant consideration. These include (1) terms and conditions of employment, (2) due process, (3) discrimination, (4) sexual harassment, and (5) adverse employment decisions. Some of these topics are also discussed in other chapters of this text; here, attention is given to the legal considerations involved in each.

TERMS AND CONDITIONS OF EMPLOYMENT

Within the framework of state and federal constitutional and statutory protection provided for school district employees, the state has plenary power to conduct and regulate public education within the state. Accordingly, the state, through its legislature, state board of education, state department of education, local school boards, and in some instances school-based councils, has promulgated the rules and regulations for the operation of schools. Among these rules and regulations are those that establish the terms and conditions of employment. These may vary considerably from state to state, but the areas most often affected by state statutory and regulatory provisions are discussed in this section and deal with certification, citizenship and residency requirements, health and physical requirements, teacher competency testing, the employment contract, and tenure.

Certification

To qualify for teaching, administrative, and many other positions in the public schools, an individual must acquire a valid certificate or license. The certification or licensure requirement is intended to ensure that the holder has met established state standards and is qualified for employment in the area for which the certificate or license is required. The courts have held that states not only have the right but the duty to ensure that school district employees meet certain minimum qualifications for employment. The certificate does not constitute a contract or a guarantee of employment; it only makes the holder eligible for employment.

Certification requirements may include a college degree with minimum credit hours in specific curricular areas, evidence of specific job experience, good moral character, a specified age, U.S. citizenship, the signing of a loyalty oath, and, more recently, a minimum score on a job-related exam. In determining whether candidates for certification meet state standards, the courts will generally interpret and enforce the standards literally and will intervene only if the denial of certification is clearly erroneous or unsupported by substantial evidence or if statutory or constitutional rights are violated (Beckham, 1983; McCarthy, Cambron-McCabe, & Thomas, 1998).

Not only is the state empowered to issue certificates, but it is also authorized to revoke or suspend certificates. Revocation or suspension of a certificate is a more severe action than dismissal, because the former forecloses employment opportunities within the state in the area of certification. As a result of their severity, the evidentiary standards and conformity to due process in suspension or revocation actions are usually more rigorous

(Beckham, 1983). The procedures to be followed in the revocation or suspension of a certificate and the grounds for the revocation or suspension are normally stipulated in statute. In a number of states a decertification charge must be job related (Valente & Valente, 2001).

A lesser penalty, nonrenewal of certification, can be imposed by the state when the individual seeking recertification fails to satisfy the requirements for recertification. In many states, teaching and administrative certificates expire every 5 to 10 years, but can be renewed if the holder meets specific requirements, which are usually related to professional growth (e.g., completion of a specified number of credits during a certain period of time or positive performance evaluations). More recently, a few states have imposed a test requirement as a precondition for recertification. The courts have upheld requirements for recertification if they are shown to be reasonably related to maintenance of standards or improved performance. If the requirement is found not to be reasonably related or the school board exceeds its authority in establishing requirements, the decertification will be overturned.

Where certification requirements exist, lack of certification can result in dismissal of the employee. For example, in a case in Texas a prospective teacher entered into a contract with a school district for a teaching position that required him to file his certificate with the personnel director no later than the issuance of the first payroll check (in this case, September 20). The prospective teacher failed the state exam that was a requirement for certification twice before the school year began, but eventually passed it and so informed the district on October 20. In the meantime the district had hired another teacher and the prospective teacher was unsuccessful in his breach of contract suit against the district (*Grand Prairie Independent School District v. Vaughn*, 1990). If a school district knowingly employs a noncertificated individual, it may be subject to nonpayment of state aid. In fact, state laws usually provide that it is unlawful for a district to pay an uncertified teacher (*Flanary v. Barrett*, 1912). If an employee knowingly provides services without a certificate, some courts have viewed this service as voluntary and, as such, not demanding of compensation (see, e.g., *Floyd County Board of Education v. Slone*, 1957; *Sorenson v. School District No. 28*, 1966).

Citizenship and Residency Requirements

The courts have upheld both citizenship and residency requirements for certification and/or as a condition of employment. With regard to U.S. citizenship, the U.S. Supreme Court has held that education is one of those government functions that is "so bound up with the operation of the state as a governmental entity as to permit the exclusion from those functions of all persons who have not become part of the process of self-government" (*Ambach v. Norwick*, 1979, pp. 73–74). Furthermore, the Court acknowledged a rational relationship between such a New York citizenship requirement and a legitimate state purpose. The Court found the requirement justified because of the critical part teachers play "in developing students' attitudes toward government and understanding the role of citizens in our society" (p. 78).

Where state statute permits, school districts may require employees to reside within the school district. Residency requirements have been upheld by the majority of state and federal courts when there is a rational basis for the requirements. For example, a residency requirement for all future district employees of the Pittsburgh school district withstood a challenge by the Pittsburgh Federation of Teachers because the court agreed that the district's stated reasons for the requirement, that employees would have an increased personal knowledge of conditions in the district, would feel a greater personal stake in the district, would pay taxes in the district, and would have reduced absenteeism and tardiness, were all rational, legitimate, and justifiable (*Pittsburgh Federation of Teachers Local 400 v. Aaron*, 1976). Similarly, the Arkansas Supreme Court held that a school district's requirement that teachers reside within district boundaries or within 10 miles of city limits did not violate equal protection, even though it did not apply to noncertificated personnel. The court determined that the policy was "rationally related to community involvement and district identity as it related to tax base in support of district tax levies, and [the] 10 mile limit was reasonable commuting distance and was not arbitrary" (*McClelland v. Paris Public Schools*, 1988, p. 908). And an Illinois court held that a state statute prohibiting residency requirements for teachers did not serve to prohibit such requirements for administrators (*Owen v. Board of Education of Kankakee School District No. 111*, 1994). It should be noted that, although school district residency requirements have been upheld in several states and at the federal level, other states have statutory provisions against school districts imposing such requirements (McCarthy, Cambron-McCabe, & Thomas, 1998).

Health and Physical Requirements

Most states and school districts have adopted health and physical requirements in an attempt to ensure that employees can meet their contractual obligations and protect the welfare of students and other employees. The courts will uphold these requirements as long as they are not arbitrary and are appropriate for the specific condition and job. And they have supported the dismissal of employees whose condition posed a threat to the well-being of students or other employees. For example, a Michigan court upheld a school district that suspended a tenured teacher for 3 years and required that before returning to work the teacher undergo physical and mental examinations at the board's expense. The court found that the board had a legitimate concern, following numerous instances of misconduct and insubordination, that the teacher might be undergoing a breakdown (*Sullivan v. River Valley Sch. Dist.*, 1998). The courts have also upheld the authority of the school district to release or reassign employees whose physical conditions (e.g., failed eyesight or hearing) have made it impossible for them to meet their contractual duties. For example, the court supported the school board against a claim of violation of the Americans with Disabilities Act when it denied tenure to a guidance counselor who suffered from depression, panic attacks, and dermatological symptoms associated with stress who had missed 41 days of work during the probationary period (*Mescall v. Marra*, 1999).

A major issue involved in the physical testing of school employees is mandatory testing of urine or blood for alcohol or drug use. Employees have challenged such tests as violating their rights of privacy and freedom from unreasonable search. In balancing the employee's rights against the government's interest, the courts have ruled that when employees occupy "safety sensitive" positions, where even a momentary lapse of attention could have serious consequences, mandatory testing for drugs and alcohol is justified without any individualized suspension (*Skinner v. Railroad Labor Executive Association*, 1989). Extending the "safety sensitive" rationale to school district employees, the mandatory, nonindividualized, suspicionless drug testing of employees in the transportation department (*English v. Talledega County Board of Education*, 1996) and custodians has been upheld (*Aubrey v. School Bd. of Lafayette Parish*, 1998). And the U. S. Supreme Court has let stand a decision of the Sixth Circuit Court with potentially far reaching consequences that allowed mandatory urinalysis of all individuals (including teachers and principals) who applied for positions or transfers in the school district (*Knox County Educ. Assn. v. Knox County Board of Educ.*, 1999). Despite the lack of evidence that drug use was a problem among existing or potential employees, the court reasoned that the in loco parentis status of educators places them on the "frontline of school security," including drug interdiction, that teachers occupy safety-sensitive positions which, combined with the special interst of the government in protecting school children, justified the policy. Also important to the court's decision was that the testing program was narrowly prescribed and not over intrusive (it was a one-time test with advance notice) and that educators participated in a "heavily regulated industry" so their expectations of privacy were diminished.

In reviewing health and physical requirements, the courts have shown increasing concern that such requirements do not violate state and federal laws protecting the rights of the handicapped. For example, Section 504 of the Rehabilitation Act of 1973, which protects "otherwise qualified" handicapped individuals from discrimination, was used as the basis for the 1987 decision of the U.S. Supreme Court in a case involving a teacher with the contagious disease tuberculosis (*Arline v. School Board of Nassau County*, 1987). The court upheld a lower-court decision that determined that the physical impairment associated with the disease justified the teacher being considered handicapped within the meaning of the Rehabilitation Act, and that discrimination based solely on the fear of contamination is discrimination against the handicapped. The lower court was instructed to determine if the teacher posed a significant risk of communicating the disease to others, which would preclude her from being "otherwise qualified," and if her condition could be reasonably accommodated by the school district. And the court said that the determination of whether a risk is significant should depend on: "(a) the nature of risk (how the risk is transmitted), (b) the duration of the risk (how long is the carrier infectious), and (c) the severity of the risk (what is the potential harm to third parties), and (d) the probabilities the disease will be transmitted and will cause varying degrees of harm" (*Arline*, 1987, p. 288). The lower court ultimately found that the teacher posed little threat of infection to others and was otherwise qualified and ordered the teacher reinstated with back pay (*Arline v. School Board of Nassau County*, 1988).

The **significant risk standard** articulated in *Arline* has been relied on by teachers with AIDS and HIV to fight alleged discrimination in employment. For example, the Ninth Circuit Court applied the significant risk standard to a case involving a teacher of hearing-impaired children and determined that medical evidence regarding the nature and transmission of AIDS did not support the conclusion that the teacher posed a significant risk of transmitting the disease to children or others through casual social contact (*Chalk v. U.S. District Court Central District of California*, 1988). A similar rationale was applied by the court in overturning a Racine, Wisconsin, school board policy that excluded from "regular school work" any staff member with AIDS or ARC (AIDS-related complex). Although the court recognized the duty of the district to protect students and staff from contagious diseases, it found fault with the policy's presumption that all employees with AIDS or ARC were inherently incapable of performing their jobs, rather than reviewing each case on a case-by-case basis (*Racine Unified School District v. LIRC Labor and Industry Review Commission*, 1991).

A major federal statute affecting health and physical requirements for school employees is the Americans with Disabilities Act of 1990, which prohibits employment discrimination against an "otherwise qualified" individual with a disability. Such a person is defined as a person who "satisfies the requisite skill, experience, education, and other job-related requirements of the position . . . and who, with or without reasonable accommodation, can perform the essential functions" of the position. This law, like Section 504, does not require that unqualified persons be hired or retained. But it does go further in prohibiting specific actions of the employer that adversely affect the employment opportunities of disabled persons (e.g., inquiry into disabilities before an offer is made, requiring a medical examination preoffer, classifying jobs or writing job descriptions on the basis of nonessential functions), as well as requiring employers to make "reasonable accommodation" for a known mental or physical disability unless the employer can demonstrate that providing such accommodation will constitute severe hardship.

Competency Testing

Beginning in the early 1980s, in response to the emphasis on educational reform and the public's concern about the quality of education and the quality of the teaching force, the number of states involved in teacher testing increased dramatically. By 1999, 44 states required some form of testing for initial certification of teachers. Commercially available tests were used by the majority of states, the most common being the National Teachers Exam

(U. S. Department of Education, 2000). In addition to testing for initial certification, a few states require testing for recertification.

The use of competency tests as either a prerequisite to initial certification or as a requirement for recertification of practicing educators has brought them under the same legal scrutiny and standards as any other employment test. The legal question is not whether tests can be used; the Civil Rights Act of 1964 specifically sanctions the use of "professionally developed" tests, as have the courts. Rather, the primary issues that continue to be litigated in regard to teacher testing involve allegations of discrimination in violation of Title VII of the Civil Rights Act of 1964 and unreasonableness in violation of the equal protection clause of the Fourteenth Amendment. In most instances where tests have been used in employment decisions, their use has disqualified disproportionately more minorities than nonminorities. In these instances the courts have disallowed the use of tests unless it can be shown that they are significantly related to "important elements of work behavior which comprise or are relevant to the job or jobs for which candidates are being evaluated" (*Albemarles Paper Company v. Moody*, 1975, p. 431).

In the lead case involving the testing of employees in education, *United States v. South Carolina* (1978), the state conducted content validation studies, pilot-tested the test (the NTE), and submitted test items to a panel of expert reviewers. Another review panel set the minimum score, which was then lowered further by the state department of education. When the test was administered, a disproportionate number of blacks, especially those educated in predominantly black institutions, fell short of the minimum score. Upon challenge, the federal district court ruled the validation procedure sufficient to support job relatedness and the test rationally related to a legitimate state purpose: ensuring that certified teachers possess the minimum level of knowledge necessary for effective teaching. The decision was upheld by the U.S. Supreme Court.

In these and other cases where the use of specific tests has been challenged, the courts have shown a concern for not only the Title VII issue of job relatedness, but also for the ultimate use being made of the test scores. The Educational Testing Service, the developers of the NTE, the most widely used test of prospective teachers, specifically recommends against the use of arbitrary cutoff scores and the use of the NTE in determining a teacher's retention or tenure. Nevertheless, some states and school districts continue this practice. For example, the state of Georgia began to use a very high score (1225) on the NTE as a qualifier for 6-year teaching certificates that entitled the teacher to higher pay. A federal district court determined that such a high score was unreasonable and that, because the state had not conducted any research to validate its use of such a score, the practice was arbitrary and in violation of the equal protection clause (*Georgia Association of Educators v. Nix*, 1976).

In several other cases the state or school district has been successful in articulating a legitimate governmental purpose for the use of test scores for salary purposes. In the South Carolina case previously discussed, the Supreme Court affirmed the use of the NTE not only for certification purposes, but also for determination of placement on a salary scale. The Fourth

Circuit also upheld a North Carolina school district's determination of salaries based on certification levels that were, in turn, based on NTE scores (*Newman v. Crews*, 1981). Although in both cases disproportionately more blacks were at lower salary levels than whites, the courts found that the practices served the legitimate state purpose of attracting and retaining the most qualified teachers and providing an incentive for teachers to improve their skills, both of which would, in turn, improve the quality of education in the district.

A similar decision was reached by the Ninth Circuit Court of Appeals in *Association of Mexican-American Education v. State of California* (2000), which involved a challenge to the use of the CBEST (California Basic Education Skills Test) as a requirement for certification for teaching and nonteaching positions (administrators, counselors, librarians) in California. The court of appeals determined that the state had established the validity of the test (e.g., that the test had a "manifest relationship to the employment in question," *Griggs v. Duke Power Co.*, 1971, p. 432) by meeting the three-pronged test established in *Albemarle* (1975): (1) a particular trait or characteristic that the test is designed to measure has been specified—here "basic skills in reading, writing, and mathematics," (2) the particular trait or characteristic is an important element of work behavior—this was established by three different validation studies, and (3) that the test is predictive or significantly correlated with the element(s) of work behavior identified—"professionally acceptable methods," including testimony from ETS (Educational Testing Service) personnel, were used to establish that the test measured the types of skills it was designed to measure. The court also ruled that the challenged cutoff score on the reading section, which had been set at the point that all the external reviewers agreed was passing, did not violate the EEOC's Guidelines, which stated that where cutoff scores are used they should "be set so as to be reasonable and consistent with normal expectations of acceptable proficiency with the workforce" [*Association of Mexican-American Educators v. State of California*, 2000, quoting 29 C. F. R. Sec. 1607.5(H)].

The most recent focus of litigation involving teacher testing is the testing of practicing educators. Teachers in several states have argued that the denial of recertification for failure to pass a state-imposed test violates state law, which states that certificates can only be rescinded "for cause" (*Connecticut Education Association v. Tirozzi*, 1989) or if the denial deprives them of their property right of a license to teach without due process of law (*Alba v. Los Angeles Unified School District*, 1983). In a Texas case, the state supreme court ruled that (1) because the teaching certificate is a license, not a contract, the constitutional prohibition against impairment of contracts is not violated; (2) due process was not violated because teachers were given the right to take the test more than once and were given the right to appeal; and (3) teacher testing is a rational means of achieving the legitimate state purpose of maintaining competent teachers in the public schools (*State of Texas v. Project Principle, Inc.*, 1987). In a separate case, a lower Texas court also found no breach of contract or violation of due process when teachers lost their certification for failure to pass the exam (*Swanson v. Houston Independent School District*, 1990). And a federal court, the Fifth Circuit Court of Appeals, in two separate cases also addressed the issue of discrimination and due process related to the Texas testing scheme and found no discrimination against teachers who were dismissed after failing the test (*Fields v. Hallsville Independent School District*, 1991; *Frazier v. Garrison I.S.D.*, 1993).

The Employment Contract

The general principles of contract law apply to the employment contract. That is, for the contract to be valid, it must contain the basic elements of (1) offer and acceptance, (2) legally competent parties, (3) consideration, (4) legal subject matter, and (5) proper form. In addition, the employment contract must meet the specific requirement of applicable state law.

Offer and acceptance. To be valid, a contract must contain an offer by one party and an acceptance by another. "For a communication to be an offer, it must create a reasonable expectation in the offeree that the offeror is willing to enter a contract on the basis of the offered terms" (Sperry, Daniel, Huefner, & Gee, 1998, p. 4). Often the form that the acceptance is to take is specified in the offer. Typically, the offer also indicates that acceptance must be made within a certain period of time of the offer of employment. Until the party to whom the offer is made accepts the offer (e.g., acceptance cannot be made by a spouse or other relative), the contract is not in force. For this reason it is good practice to require that acceptance be made in writing and within a specified period of time. And, until acceptance has been received, unsuccessful candidates should not be notified that the position has been filled.

Legally competent parties. The statutory authority to contract lies exclusively with the school board. The superintendent or other authorized employee may recommend employment, but only the school board may enter into contract. There are cases every year in which prospective employees, vendors, or contractors have relied on the presumed authority of a principal, superintendent, or other employee, only to discover that the person lacked the authority to enter into a binding contract. Moreover, a school board can enter into contract only when it is a legally constituted body. That is, contracts issued when a quorum of the board was not present or at an illegally called meeting of the board (e.g., adequate notice was not given) are not valid. In these instances the board is not considered a competent party because it lacks legal status. By the same token, a teacher or other employee who lacks the necessary certification or other requisite conditions is not considered to be a competent party for contractual purposes, nor are individuals who are mentally ill, impaired by drugs or alcohol, or under duress at the time of entering into the contract.

Consideration. Consideration is the "cause, motive, price, or impelling influence which induces a contracting party to enter into a contract" (Garner, 1999, p. 301). The consideration offered by the school district must be clear and definite. Although school boards have considerable latitude in the matter of employee compensation, they must abide by any state statutes regarding minimum salary levels, and they must abide by the terms of any negotiated contracts. In the absence of any incentive pay program, salaries must be applied uniformly to individuals or groups of individuals who have the same preparation and experience and perform the same duties.

Legal subject matter.   To be valid, a contract must pertain to legal subject matter. That is, a contract for the commission of a crime (e.g., the purchase of illegal substances or the performance of illegal services) is not enforceable. Nor can the terms of the contract circumvent state or federal requirements or statutes, common law, or public policy (Sperry et al., 1998). For example, districts cannot contract with employees to pay less than the federal minimum wage.

Proper form.   To be enforceable, the contract must be in the proper form required by law. Most states require that the employment contract be signed and in writing. In the absence of statutory specification, however, an oral agreement that contains all the legal requirements of a contract can be legally binding on both parties (McCarthy, Cambron-McCabe, & Thomas, 1998).

Terms of the contract: Duties and responsibilities.   The employee's rights and obligations of employment are derived from the employment contract. It is important, therefore, that the contract be specific in stating the terms and conditions of employment, be unambiguous, and include those rules and regulations of the school district applicable to employment conditions. Even when rules and regulations of the school board have not been specifically included, the courts have held that they, as well as all applicable state statutes, are part of the contract. However, the school board does have the responsibility to inform employees of its rules and regulations, including those in effect not only at the time of initial employment or at the time of awarding of tenure, but also on an ongoing basis as they are revised. This point is especially important, because the courts have held that, even though a teacher has tenure, each yearly contract is considered a new contract and includes whatever rules and regulations are in effect at the time of the new contract.

In most states certain terms of the contract are controlled by state law and are not subject to negotiation or the discretion of the local school district. For example, tenure and due process rights granted by state statute cannot be modified by the contract offered by a local school district. A number of state statutes require that certain terms (e.g., salary, beginning and end of contract, and duties) be detailed in the contract. In addition, the terms of the contract cannot conflict with the terms or rights of employees detailed in any collective bargaining agreement.

Although it is desirable that the contract be specific in stating the terms and conditions of employment, the courts have held that employees may be required to perform certain tasks incidental to classroom activities regardless of whether the contract specifically calls for their performance. These implied duties have included such activities as field trips; playground, study hall, bus, and cafeteria duty; supervision of extracurricular activities; and attendance at open houses. Teachers cannot, however, be required to drive a bus, perform janitorial duties, or perform duties unrelated to the school program. The courts also have found that the types of duties that may be permissibly required of school employees vary by position. That is, administrators may be expected to perform a broader range of implied duties than teachers; coaches, different implied duties than classroom teachers; and so on. The primary considerations of the courts in reviewing duty assignments is whether the duty has been expressly provided for in the contract and whether the duty in question can be considered part of normal school operations and is reasonable (Valente & Valente, 2001). If an employee refuses to perform extracurricular duties required as a condition of employment, regardless of whether the duties are specified under contract, the court may construe such refusal as an illegal strike or as insubordination justifying removal (Beckham, 1983). For example, in an Alabama case a guidance counselor was dismissed for refusing to perform his assigned rotational supervision duty before school. He maintained that counselors should be exempt from such supervision. The court upheld the dismissal (*Jones v. Alabama State Tenure Commission*, 1981).

Because of the importance of the employment contract and because it is a legally binding document, it should be prepared and periodically reviewed by the school board attorney (Greene, 1971). If the district is a party to a negotiated labor agreement, the terms of the contract must be reviewed to ensure the contract's compliance with the terms of the negotiated agreement.

Tenure

Tenure is "the status conferred upon teachers who have served a probationary period . . . which then guarantees them continual employment until retirement, subject to the requirements of good behavior, financial necessity, and in some instances, good periodic evaluations" (Sperry et al., 1998, p. 1041). Tenure is said to benefit the state by helping to create a permanent and qualified teaching force. It benefits teachers by providing them greater rights than those held by nontenured teachers. Tenure has been a fixture of American public education. However, there have been attempts in several states to do away with tenure. Given that few other workers enjoy the benefits of tenure, "it is not surprising that they begrudge their own employees a guarantee of lifetime employment" (Hess & Maranto, 2000, p. 54).

Because the tenure status (referred to in some states as "continuing" status) is created by state statute, specific provisions vary from state to state. Most statutes specify the requirements and procedures for both acquiring tenure and for dismissing a tenured teacher (dismissal of both tenured and nontenured teachers is treated in a later section). Generally, tenure can only be acquired in the area of certification. In addition, tenure is not transferable from one school district to another, even within the same state. Because tenure is created by the state, the terms of its acquisition and the requisites for dismissal cannot be altered by the local school board.

Tenure statutes normally require the successful completion of a probationary period before the awarding of tenure, usually 3 years. During the probationary period, the probationary teacher is issued a term contract valid for a fixed period of time (e.g., 1, 2, or 3 years). Renewal of the contract at the end of the term is at the discretion of the school board.

Legal issues surrounding the probationary period primarily have involved questions of what constitutes service during the probationary period and what protections are afforded probationary teachers. Most tenure statutes require "regular and continuous" teaching service during the probationary period. When teachers have spent a part of the probationary period as guidance counselors, administrators, homebound teachers, social workers, or other positions outside the classroom, questions have arisen as to their eligibility for tenure under the "regular" service requirement. Similar issues have arisen when service was as a substitute teacher, for less than full time, less than the full school year, or interrupted by a leave. In deciding each of these cases, the courts have attempted to interpret the state tenure statutes to protect the teacher's rights, while maintaining the discretion and flexibility of school officials in the administration of personnel matters. However, since the requirements of the probationary period have been strictly enforced by most courts, it is important that school administrators be aware that in asking or assigning individuals to "other" positions during the probationary period, they could in fact be jeopardizing these individuals' eligibility for tenure.

In the absence of a statute to the contrary, school boards may decide not to renew the contract of probationary teachers without giving cause or providing a hearing. However, in about half the states school districts are required to give nontenured teachers a statement of reasons for nonrenewal (Imber & Van Geel, 2000). Even successful completion of the probationary term does not entitle a probationary teacher to continued employment. In an Alabama case where a probationary teacher who had received positive evaluation each of her 3 years and had been recommended for retention was not continued, the court said that the district's adoption of an evaluation policy for nontenured and tenured teachers did not create a right of employment for nontenured teachers who received a favorable evaluation under the policy (*King v. Jefferson County Board of Education*, 1995). However, most states do require that the school board give timely notice (usually no later than April 1) that the contract will not be renewed. And in no state can the contract be broken during the term of the contract without, at a minimum, a notice of dismissal and a hearing on the causes.

In some states, tenure is automatically awarded at the end of the probationary period unless the school board notifies the teacher that he or she will not be rehired. In other states the school board is required to take some affirmative step to award tenure. When school officials fail to follow applicable state laws, the courts will attempt to balance the public policy interests of employing competent and qualified teachers against the rights of the individual. As a result, in a number of cases where the school board did not give timely notice of nonrenewal, the courts have ordered the teacher rehired, but still as a probationary teacher, until the proper evaluation and notification takes place. In an equal number of other cases where the school board failed to follow state tenure laws, the courts have said "it is the school district, not the teacher, that must bear the consequences," and the teacher has been granted tenure status (*Nixon v. Board of Cooperative Educational Services*, 1990, p. 905). However, *de minimis* (trifling, insignificant) violations of policy or state statutes have been decided in favor of school boards.

Another issue related to tenure is the positions that are eligible for tenure. A number of states do identify in statute the areas in which school personnel may acquire tenure. For example, in some states tenure can be acquired as an administrator. However, unless provided by statute, the courts have generally interpreted administrative and supervisory positions to be outside the scope of tenure. On the other hand, the courts generally recognize such non-administrative positions as guidance counselor, librarian, homebound teacher, or resource room teacher as within the scope of the tenure statutes. There has also been a question of whether teachers whose salaries are funded totally or in part by federal funds fall under teacher tenure statutes. The courts have generally held that they do unless specifically waived in the contract.

The supplementary service appointment that is most often the subject of efforts to acquire tenure is that of athletic coach. However, the courts have been almost unanimous in declaring supplementary service positions such as coaching separate from teaching and not eligible for tenure status. In many cases the courts have noted that tenure rights accrue only to employment in certified areas, and thus the lack of a certification requirement for coaching negates the tenure claim (McCarthy, Cambron-McCabe, & Thomas, 1998). In other cases, even when state certification was required, the courts have noted the extracurricular nature of coaching, the awarding of supplementary pay, and the issuance of a separate contract for the coaching assignment as distinguishing it from the teaching assignment (see, e.g., *Lagos v. Modesto City School District*, 1988).

Employees with supplementary service appointments serve at the pleasure of the board and can be dismissed from these positions at any time without any procedural or substantive due process. By the same token, these employees may resign these positions and still maintain the primary teaching contract unless the offer of the teaching contract had been made contingent on the individual performing specific supplemental duties (e.g., coaching). School administrators who consider offering contingency contracts should consult state statutes to determine the status of such contracts in their state. They should also ensure that by combining teaching and coaching positions they are not eliminating the most qualified teachers or unlawfully discriminating against female applicants.

The awarding of tenure does not guarantee permanent employment. As discussed later in this chapter, a tenured teacher may be dismissed for disciplinary reasons or as a result of declining enrollments or financial exigencies. Nor does the granting of tenure guarantee the right to teach in a particular school, grade, or subject area. Teachers may be reassigned to any position for which they are certified as long as their due process rights are not violated. In a case where a school board informed a teacher on July 5 of the board's intent to transfer her from a high school to a middle school, the court ruled that the board had violated state procedural requirements by not notifying the teacher by July 1 (*Estill v. Alabama State Tenure Commission*, 1994).

DUE PROCESS

The term *due process* is found in the Fourteenth Amendment of the U.S. Constitution, which provides that no state shall "deprive any person of life, liberty, or property without due process of law." The two aspects of due process are procedural, which guarantees fair procedures, and substantive, which protects a person's liberty or property from unfair government seizure or interference. The essence of due process is to protect against arbitrary and unreasonable action.

Procedural Due Process

Procedural due process is not an absolute right. An individual is entitled to procedural due process only if he or she can show that the government's actions denied "life, liberty, or property." Presuming that life issues are not involved in school district personnel issues, the employee must show a property or liberty interest in order to be constitutionally entitled to procedural due process. In school district employment decisions, the courts have defined a property interest to be a "legitimate entitlement" to continued employment, not merely the desire to remain employed. A legitimate entitlement to continued employment can be obtained by the granting of tenure or by an employment contract. Thus teachers or other employers who have tenure or who are operating under an employment contract are said to have a **property right** or *property interest* to that position that cannot be abridged without due process. This would mean, for instance, that a tenured teacher could not be dismissed or that a probationary teacher could not be dismissed during the contract year without being afforded due process of law.

A **liberty right** or *liberty interest* can become a factor in education employment cases if government actions create such a stigma or cause such serious damage to the employee's reputation or integrity that it forecloses future employment opportunities. That is, simply because a person is demoted or even dismissed for reasons that are made public would not be reason enough to support a violation of a liberty interest. The courts have noted that almost any reason that is given for an adverse employment decision is going to cast negatively on the affected employee. The two-part question that is asked to determine if a liberty interest has been violated is (1) did the employee actually suffer a loss of benefit, such as employment, and (2) did this happen as a result of publicly made charges by the board that resulted in the employee becoming the object of public ridicule or public scorn? (Charges made in a private meeting of the board cannot be said to hold the employee up to public scorn.) A liberty interest can also become involved if governmental actions violate the employee's constitutionally protected rights or if they infringe on the employee's fundamental rights related to marriage, family, and personal privacy.

Once it has been established that a property or liberty interest is involved and that an action requires procedural due process, the central issue becomes what process is due. In arriving at its decision, the court will look to standards of procedural due process embodied in state statutes, state agency or school board regulations, and employment contracts to determine both their propriety and the extent to which they were followed. In one case a nonprobationary cook was terminated without notice or hearing. The Supreme Court of Arkansas held that, although the board had the right to terminate the employee at any time for any reason, to do so without notice or a hearing violated the terms of the Arkansas Public School Employees Fair Hearing Act (*Gould Public School v. Dobbs*, 1999).

In determining what due process should be provided in cases not covered by statute, the courts have noted that no fixed set of procedures is applicable in all situations. Rather, the courts must decide what due process is due in light of the following guidelines:

> (1) the private interest that will be affected by the official action; (2) the risk of an erroneous deprivation of such interest through the procedures used, the probable value, if any, of additional procedural safeguards; and (3) the government's interest, including the fiscal and administrative burdens that the additional or substitute procedural requirement would entail. (*Mathews v. Eldridge, 1976*, p. 321)

Applying this standard, it would appear that, where limited interests are involved, only minimal procedures are required, whereas the deprivation of more serious interests requires a more extensive, formal process. Generally, the courts have held that an employee facing a severe loss, such as termination of employment, must be ensured the following procedural elements (McCarthy, Cambron-McCabe, & Thomas 1998):

- ☐ notification of charges
- ☐ opportunity for a hearing
- ☐ adequate time to prepare a rebuttal to the charges
- ☐ access to evidence and names of witnesses
- ☐ hearing before an impartial tribunal
- ☐ representation by legal counsel
- ☐ opportunity to present evidence and witnesses
- ☐ opportunity to cross-examine adverse witnesses
- ☐ decision based on the evidence and findings of the hearing
- ☐ transcript or record of the hearing, and
- ☐ opportunity to appeal an adverse decision. (p. 369)

Notice must not merely be given; it must be timely (on or before an established date) and in sufficient detail to enable the employee to attempt to remediate or to prepare an adequate defense (see, e.g., *McDaniel v. Princeton City Sch. Dist. Bd. Of Educ.*, 1999). Although a full evidentiary hearing conforming to all the rules of procedure and evidence is not required, the Supreme Court has ruled that, if termination of an employee with property rights is a consideration, a hearing is required prior to termination at which the employee is given oral and written notice of the charges, an explanation of the school board's evidence, and an opportunity to respond orally and in writing to the charges and evidence (*Cleveland Board of Education v. Loudermill*, 1985). The purpose of such a hearing is to determine if there are reasonable grounds to believe that the charges against the employee are true and support dismissal (Fischer, Schimmel, & Kelly, 1999). Finally, although the ability of the school board (the employer) to act as an unbiased hearing body when it is a party to the action has been frequently challenged, the Supreme Court has held that school boards are presumed to be impartial and that those challenging their actions have the burden of proving otherwise (*Hortonville District v. Hortonville Education Association*, 1976).

Substantive Due Process

Substantive due process is somewhat more difficult to ensure than procedural due process. Substantive due process is meant to protect the employee from arbitrary, unreasonable, and discriminatory governmental action, as well as vague and unclear policies and guidelines. Substantive due process is often equated with the concept of *just cause.* Substantive due process also means that school officials cannot deprive an employee of life, liberty, or property unless to do so is necessary to accomplish a legitimate state objective. In the employment context, the provision of substantive due process requires a rational balancing of the individual's right to a position or to pursue other positions against the government's interest in the improvement of the educational system (Sperry et al., 1998). The Supreme Court has not articulated precise guidelines for properly balancing these interests; rather, the guidelines are constantly being refined by the courts, and decisions are made on a case-by-case basis.

DISCRIMINATION

Discrimination on the basis of race, religion, national origin, sex, age, or handicapping condition is prohibited under both federal law and the laws of most states. Allegations of arbitrary and unreasonable actions, not overt discriminatory actions, form the basis of most discrimination suits in education. Most cases involving allegations of discrimination are brought under Title VII of the Civil Rights Act of 1964, as amended by the Civil Rights Act of 1991, or under other federal laws modeled after Title VII, such as the Age Discrimination in Employment Act of 1967, Section 504 of the Rehabilitation Act of 1973, and, more recently, the Americans with Disabilities Act of 1990. Other statutory guarantees against discrimination in employment are found in the Equal Pay Act and, to a lesser extent, Title IX of the Education Amendments of 1972, both of which prohibit sex-based discrimination. Title VII, the most used statute, prohibits employers from discriminating against employees on the basis of race, color, religion, sex, or national origin. It covers many areas of human resources administration, including recruitment, hiring, promotion, compensation, and other terms, conditions, or privileges of employment. The Equal Employment Opportunity Commission is responsible for enforcing Title VII.

Two types of discrimination claims have traditionally been brought under Title VII. The first claim, **disparate treatment,** places the burden of proof squarely on the plaintiff. The plaintiff must first demonstrate a prima facie case of discrimination. This requires that the plaintiff show that he or she was a member of a group protected by Title VII, that he or she is qualified for the position in question, and that he or she was treated less favorably than others by a particular employment practice. If the claimant can establish the foregoing facts, the employer can still rebut the claim by articulating a nondiscriminatory reason for the practice. This means that the employer must show that the challenged practice is job related and justified by a legitimate business goal. If the employer meets this burden of proof, the burden of proof shifts back to the plaintiff to show that the articulated reason is a mere pretext for intentional discriminatory intent. Intent is very difficult to prove. In 1982 the Supreme Court said discriminatory intent can only be established by demonstrating actual motive and cannot be presumed from employment data that show something less than intent (*Pullman–Standard v. Swint,* 1982).

The other type of discrimination claim that may be brought under Title VII is based on employment practices that appear facially neutral, but have a **disparate impact** on protected groups. Proof of intent is not necessary to prove discrimination based on disparate impact. According to the Supreme Court decision in *Griggs,* which was strengthened by the Civil Rights Act of 1991, if the claimant can show that an employment practice or policy results in a disparate impact on a protected class, the burden shifts to the employer to demonstrate that the challenged practice or policy is job related and is consistent with business necessity. Even if the employer does offer a business necessity for the discriminatory practice, it is still possible for the claimant to prevail by showing that the district could serve its interests by means that are not discriminatory. For example, a female applicant for a high school biology teaching position in Arizona filed a sex discrimination suit against the school district on the basis that its requirement that applicants for the teaching position also have the ability to coach varsity softball had a disparate impact on women (*Civil Rights Division of the Arizona Department of Law v. Amphitheater Unified School District No. 10,* 1983). Although the board admitted the coupling of the two positions did have a disparate impact on women, it defended the practice by maintaining that it was a business necessity. In considering this defense, the court maintained that to be successful the district must show compelling business purposes and that there were no acceptable alternative practices or policies available that would better accomplish the business purpose advanced. Because the board was unable to demonstrate that less discriminatory alternatives had been attempted when, in fact, there was substantial evidence that alternatives were available, the appellate court held for the plaintiff and remanded the case to the lower court for a determination of damages.

If an employee is successful in a discrimination complaint, the court may order a stop to the discriminatory practice and order any "such affirmative action as may be appropriate, which may include, but is not limited to reinstatement or hiring of employees, with or without pay," as well as any other "equitable relief" that the court may deem appropriate [42 U.S.C. 2000e-5(g)]. Attorney fees may also be awarded.

Sexual Harassment

Sexual harassment is considered a form of sex discrimination and as such is prohibited under Title VII of the Civil Rights Act of 1964, as well as state fair employment statutes in most states. As defined in Chapter 5, sexual harassment in the workplace occurs when unwelcome advances or requests for sexual favors are made a condition of employment **(quid pro quo harassment)** or when verbal or physical conduct is sufficiently severe or pervasive as to unreasonably interfere with an individual's work performance or creates an intimidating, hostile, or offensive work environment **(hostile environment harassment).**

Under the legal principal of agency, in cases involving quid pro quo harassment, school districts will be held liable for the sexual harassment committed by a school employee in a position of authority, such as a teacher or administrator. In cases of hostile environment harassment, the school will not be held liable for the harassment if it can prove (1) it exercised reasonable care to prevent harassment (e.g., had a sexual harassment policy in place) and acted promptly to correct any allegations of sexual harassment, and (2) the complaining employee did not take advantage of the protective or preventive safeguards provided by the employers to prevent the harm that could have otherwise been avoided (e.g., did not follow the policies dictated by the sexual harassment policy) (*Burlington Industries v. Ellerth,* 1998; *Faragher v. City of Boca Raton,* 1998). If found liable for sexual harassment, the school district may be required to pay monetary damages and attorney fees, as well as reinstate or promote the harassed employee.

ADVERSE EMPLOYMENT DECISIONS

It is almost inevitable that school administrators will become involved in adverse employment decisions. These decisions include dismissals, suspensions, involuntary transfers and reassignments, demotions, and reductions in force. Not all cases involve disciplinary actions. Decisions may result from declining enrollments or other needs of the district that require the shifting of personnel. Whenever adverse employment decisions are contemplated, it is important that the employee be assured due process in the conduct of the action. In fact, the adequacy of the due process procedures provided by school officials is one of the major issues in litigation involving adverse employment decisions (Cambron-McCabe, 1983).

Dismissal for Cause

Possibly the most undesirable task of a school administrator and/or school board is the dismissal of an employee. A dismissal may occur at any time and may be applied to tenured or nontenured employees. The impact of a dismissal on an employee's personal and professional life can be devastating. Lengthy proceedings may become costly both to the employee and the district. In controversial cases, morale and relationships among staff, administration, and the school board may be negatively affected. Nonetheless, from time to time it seems in the best interest of the school district to dismiss an employee. All states have some statutory provisions that specify the grounds for teacher dismissal. The reasons specified for dismissal vary from the very general (e.g., "good cause") to the very specific. The reasons most frequently cited in statute are immorality, incompetence, and insubordination. Other commonly cited reasons are neglect of duty, unprofessional conduct or conduct unbecoming a teacher, unfitness to teach, and the catchall phrase "other good and just cause." Although traditionally the courts have left the application and definition of each of these reasons to the discretion of the school board, the burden of proof in justifying a dismissal for cause rests with the school board and must be supported by sufficient evidence to justify the dismissal. In addition, in all cases of dismissal the school board must provide the employee all the due process to which the employee is entitled by law, policy, or negotiated agreement. If not, even though the cause may be sufficient to justify a dismissal, the dismissal most likely will not be upheld. A review of some of the most frequently cited concepts will provide some insight into those conditions or behaviors that have sustained judicial scrutiny, as well as the judicial requirements to support a charge.

Immorality. Immorality is the most cited ground for dismissal in state statutes. Nonetheless, legislatures often have been reluctant to define the term immorality or to discuss its application to specific conduct. Consequently, these tasks have been left to the judiciary. Among the definitions of immorality provided by the courts is that immorality is "such a course of conduct as offends the morals of the community and is a bad example to the youth whose ideals the teacher is supposed to foster and elevate" (*Horton v. Jefferson County-Dubois Area Vocational Technical School*, 1993, p. 183). Dismissals related to immorality generally are based on one or more of the following categories of conduct: (1) sexual conduct with students; (2) sexual conduct with nonstudents; (3) homosexuality; (4) making sexually explicit remarks or talking about sex unrelated to the curriculum; (5) distribution of sexually explicit materials to classes; (6) use of obscene, profane, or abusive language; (7) possession and use of controlled substances; (8) other criminal misconduct; and (9) dishonesty.

Whereas this listing covers a wide range of behavior, certain standards have evolved from the cases in this area and are generally applied to cases involving a dismissal for immorality. First is the *exemplar standard.* Although this concept is not as universally accepted today as in the past, the courts do recognize that "there are legitimate standards to be expected of those who teach in the public schools" (*Reitmeyer v. Unemployment Compensation Board of Review,* 1992, p. 508). A significant percentage of the public also believes that teachers should be a good role model for their students, both in and out of school (Imber, 2001). Second, while not true in all jurisdictions, the vast weight of contemporary judicial decisions in employee dismissal cases says that in order to justify a charge of dismissal there must be a nexus or link between the personal conduct of the employee and the teacher's job performance.

However, because this nexus may be said to exist in one case involving a particular conduct but not in another, school administrators cannot expect to find definitive lists of impermissible or immoral behavior in case law. For example, the dismissal of a teacher in a small, rural town in Montana for living with a fellow teacher was upheld because his cohabitation had become a matter of public discussion in the community and at the school. (In fact, he had told his class that his girlfriend had to move from his home because of complaints by persons in the community.) In the judgment of the court, this affected his teaching effectiveness and adversely affected the school and his relationship with students and other employees (*Yanzick v. School District No. 23,* 1982). On the other hand, the dismissal of a Florida teacher for living with her boyfriend was overturned by the courts. In this case the court found no evidence that her actions affected her ability to teach and that her relationship had not been commonly known until the school made the matter public (*Sherburne v. School Board of Swannee County,* 1984).

Homosexuality is another area where the circumstances of the particular case very much dictate the ruling of the courts. With the exception of the 1977 Washington Supreme Court ruling in *Gaylord v. Tacoma School District No. 10,* most courts have ruled that homosexuality per se is not grounds for dismissal (see, e.g., *Glover v. Williamsburg Local Sch. Dist. Bd. of Educ.,* 1998; the dismissal of an employee simply for being gay violated the 14th Amendment guarantee of equal protection). However, the Supreme Court has ruled that states can classify homosexual sex as criminal sodomy (*Bowers v. Hardwick,* 1986). In such states, to engage in homosexual sex *may* (not must) not only serve as the basis for criminal prosecution, but also for dismissal of a school district employee. And in cases where public sexual conduct was involved, dismissal has been upheld (*C. F. S. v. Mahan,* 1996).

Although cases involving alleged immorality must often be settled on a case-by-case basis, the courts have agreed on the factors to be considered in determining if a teacher's immoral conduct renders the teacher unfit to teach. These factors include (1) age and maturity of the teacher's students, (2) the likelihood that the teacher's conduct will have an adverse effect on students or other teachers, (3) degree or anticipated adversity, (4) proximity of the conduct, (5) extenuating or aggravating circumstances surrounding the conduct, (6) likelihood that the conduct would be repeated, (7) underlying motives, and (8) the chilling effect on the rights of teachers (*In re Thomas*, 1996, pp. 165–166).

Incompetency. The conditions or behaviors that have been most successfully sustained as constituting incompetence fall into six general categories: (1) inadequate teaching, (2) lack of knowledge of the subject matter, (3) failure to maintain classroom discipline or unreasonable discipline, (4) failure to work effectively with colleagues, supervisors, or parents, (5) physical or mental disability, and (6) willful neglect of duty. In reviewing dismissals for incompetency (referred to in some state statutes as "unprofessional conduct"), the court will presume that a teacher certificated by the state is competent unless the district can prove incompetency by the quality and quantity of its evidence. In dismissals for incompetence, the courts require that the standard against which the teacher is measured be one used for other teachers in a similar position, not the standard of the "ideal teacher," and that the dismissal be based on a pattern of behavior, not just a single incident. And, although testimony of students and parents is important, the courts pay closest attention to classroom observations by superiors (e.g., principals or curriculum supervisors) (Alexander & Alexander, 2001).

Before any action is taken to dismiss an employee for incompetency, a determination should be made as to whether the behavior in question is remediable, a notice of deficiency must be given, a program must be designed to remediate the difficulty developed, and a reasonable opportunity to correct the behavior must be provided. If remediation fails, then the teacher should be dismissed.

Insubordination. Insubordination is a "refusal to obey an order that a superior officer is authorized to give" (Garner, 1999, p. 802). Regardless of whether it is specified in state statute, insubordination is an acceptable cause for dismissal in all states. Among the meanings of insubordination that have been upheld by the courts are (1) refusal to follow established policies and procedures, (2) refusal to obey the direct and lawful orders of school administrators or school boards, (3) unwillingness to cooperate with superiors, (4) encouraging student disobedience, (5) unauthorized absence from duty, (6) inappropriate use of corporal punishment, and (7) refusal to accept a school or teaching assignment. Unlike the charge of immorality, the school district is not required to show a relationship between the alleged insubordinate conduct and the teacher's fitness to teach.

To sustain a charge of insubordination, the school district must demonstrate a persistent, willful, and deliberate violation of a lawful rule or order emanating from a school authority. While typically the courts require that there be a pattern of insubordination, a single insubordinate act, if sufficiently serious, can justify dismissal. However, if the violation involves an order that is not within the legal right of the school official or school board to issue, the dismissal for insubordination will not stand. In addition, the rule or order must be reasonable, clear, and unambiguous. Insubordination charges also may not be supported if "the teacher tried, although unsuccessfully, to comply with the rule or order . . . the teacher's motive for violating the rule was admirable . . . (or) no harm resulted from the violation" (Alexander & Alexander, 2001, p. 679). Finally, school employees cannot be dismissed for insubordination for failing to follow rules that violate their constitutional rights. For example, rules that prohibit teachers from using certain materials in the classroom may interfere with their right to academic freedom, or rules limiting what they can say or write may also violate their right to free speech under the First Amendment (Fischer et al., 1999).

Suspension

The power of the school board to suspend an employee, with or without pay, is inherent in the power to discipline employees (see, e.g., the judgment of the court in *Daily v. Bd. of Ed. of Morrill County Sch. Dist. No. 62-0063*, 1999, upholding the authority of the school board to suspend a teacher for 30 days without pay for hitting a disobedient student on the head and restraining the student by his arms). The types of conduct that can give rise to suspension are generally the same as those for dismissal, though less serious in nature, although in some cases employees may be suspended pending the outcome of a due process dismissal hearing. A few states have statutory provisions related to suspension, but more often they do not. For this reason it is more difficult to define what procedural due process must be provided. For example, in a case where an industrial arts teacher was suspended for four days without pay and then transferred after fighting with a student, the court said the teacher had a property interest in continued employment because of his tenure status, as well as a liberty interest because of the potential stigmatization resulting from a charge of child abuse, both of which warranted the granting of a due process hearing before the school board, notwithstanding the fact that during the course of the investigation into the matter he had been given the opportunity to give his version of events and notwithstanding the fact that he had been granted an administrative review by the superintendent (*Winegar v. Des Moines Independent Community School District*, 1994). One thing that does appear clear from case law is that if the suspension is longer than five days the employee should be afforded a hearing with an opportunity to respond to charges.

Involuntary Transfers, Reassignments, and Demotions

The authority to transfer and reassign is an implied power of school boards. Employees have no common law rights to a specific classroom, building, grade assignment, or position and may be transferred to any assignment for which they are qualified by certificate. Whereas the school district has the power to transfer, this power may not be exercised arbitrarily, capriciously, discriminatorily in retaliation for the legitimate exercise of a constitutionally protected right, or in violation of proper statutory or school board procedures. For example, when teachers in a Kentucky school district who supported for school board a candidate opposed by the superintendent were transferred with the sole explanation that the transfers were for "the betterment of the schools," the court determined the transfers to be punitive in nature and ordered the teachers reinstated (*Calhoun v. Cassady*, 1976).

A major legal issue in transfer and reassignment cases is whether the transfer constitutes a demotion. Depending on state statutes, a transfer or reassignment may be considered a demotion if it (1) results in a reduction in salary, (2) results in the loss of professional rank, reputation, or prestige, or (3) requires a teacher to teach a grade of subject for which he or she is not certified or has not had significant experience in the last 5 years (*Singleton v. Jackson Municipal Separate School District*, 1970). Restrictions relative to demotion are often contained in statute. Generally, such laws require proper notice, a hearing, and that the demotion be supported by substantial evidence and not be arbitrary or discriminatory. This does not mean that transfers or reassignments that are in fact demotions cannot be effected. Demotions may be lawfully accomplished for two purposes: (1) nondisciplinary reasons (e.g., reductions in force or financial exigency) and (2) discipline of the employee (Valente & Valente, 2001). Disciplinary transfers and demotions that are not arbitrary, capricious, or in violation of the employee's statutory or constitutional rights will be upheld.

The transfer or reassignment of administrators is somewhat different from that of teachers. Since administrators generally serve at the will of the board, in most states their transfer can be made arbitrarily, with no notice, reason, or hearing afforded. Principals and other administrators who have challenged transfers from larger to smaller schools, from senior high schools to junior high schools, or from one administrative position to another [e.g., transfer from assistant superintendent to principal (*Barr v. Clarendon County School Board District 2*, 1995)] or to the classroom have generally been unsuccessful. They might get a favorable judgment if (1) there has been a reduction in salary, (2) state statute provides for tenure as an administrator, (3) there are contractual provisions to the contrary, (4) state or locally mandated due process procedures were violated, or (5) there has been an abuse of discretion.

Reduction in Force

Declining enrollments, school reorganizations or consolidations, financial exigency, curriculum changes, and other reasons often result in a reduction in force (RIF) of the total number of employees needed by the district and the release of excess employees. Forty-six states have statutes that address RIF (Hartmeister & Russo, 1999). Typically, these statutes address the proper reasons, the order of release, and the order of reinstatement. Some statutes also provide detail as to the procedures to be followed and the protections afforded teachers. These same issues are often addressed in school board policies and collective bargaining agreements. Usually, these statutes, policies, and agreements require the employee be given adequate and timely notice of impending RIF and the right to an appropriate hearing (Hartmeister & Russo, 1999).

The legal challenges to reductions in force usually involve three issues: (1) whether the abolition of the position is justified, (2) whether the release of the particular individual is justified, and (3) the retention, reassignment, and call-back of employees. As a general rule, an employee has no right to a position no longer deemed necessary by the district. However, the reasons articulated by the district must be reasonable and supported by adequate justification to support the RIF decision. For example, a school business manager was terminated on the basis that the district needed to reduce the number of administrative positions. The business manager appealed, claiming religious discrimination: he was the only Catholic in a workplace where the superintendent and most of the other administrators were Mormon. In finding in his favor the court noted that (1) although the purported goal of the reorganization was to save money, it actually resulted in higher costs, (2) the person who replaced him was less qualified, but paid more, and (3) the financial condition of the district was sound and did not require any reduction in force (*White v. Blackfoot School Dist. No. 55*, 2001).

Unlike other terminations, the burden of proof for a RIF is on the plaintiff to show the stated reason to be a subterfuge for an impermissible basis (e.g., discrimination, retaliation for union activity, or the exercise of a constitutionally protected right). In the absence of evidence to the contrary, the courts presume that the board acted in good faith and with permissible motives (McCarthy, Cambron-McCabe, & Thomas, 1998). Neither does the board need to prove that it made the perfect decision in regard to a particular set of circumstances, but only that the relevant evidence supports the board's decision as being rational, not arbitrary or capricious (*Palmer v. Board of Trustees of Crook County School District No. 1*, 1990).

The RIF process may not be used as a means to circumvent state tenure laws. When an Oklahoma school board dismissed an elementary school librarian, citing declining enrollments and budgetary constraints, and then rehired nontenured teachers for positions for which the librarian was certified and had previously taught, the court ruled that the district could not "manipulate job assignments in a manner that defeats the rights of tenured teachers and circumvents the purpose and spirit of the tenure law " (*Babb v. Independent School Dist. No. I-5*, 1992). On the other hand, a Connecticut court upheld the elimination of a nurse–teacher position even though the elements of the job, clinical nursing and health education instruction, were maintained. The court ruling was based on the fact that no one employee was assigned both the clinical nursing duties and the health education (*Ballanto v. Board of Education of Stronington*, 1993).

The second issue, who should be released, involves questions of preference and has been the subject of the majority of litigation related to RIF. State statutes, school board policies, and employment contracts often specify the order of release in terms of tenure, seniority, or other criteria, as well as the procedures to be followed (notice, appeal, etc.). When preference and due process requirements are articulated, the courts will require that they be followed. When statutes, policies, or agreements are silent or ambiguous about order of release, the courts almost unanimously have accorded qualified tenured teachers priority over nontenured teachers in similar positions. Certification has been the major, but not the exclusive, criterion considered by the courts in determining the "qualifiedness" of teachers. Between tenured teachers holding similar positions or between nontenured teachers holding similar positions, seniority has been the primary, but not the exclusive, factor in determining order of release. Absolute seniority preference may be qualified by other factors, such as performance evaluations, years of teaching experience in the subject matter (see *State ex rel. Melchiori v. Board of Educ.*, 1992), affirmative action goals (see *Wygant v. Jackson Board of Education*, 1986), and collective bargaining agreements (see *Underwood v. Henry County Sch. Bd.*, 1993).

The order of reinstatement, reassignment, and recall of RIF employees should be roughly the inverse of the order of release. That is, qualified tenured teachers would be called back before qualified nontenured teachers, in the order of seniority rank within each group. The courts have been fairly unanimous in affirming that neither tenure nor seniority provides an absolute right to recall over certification or other evidence of qualifiedness. For example, a New York court held that a tenured guidance counselor whose position was abolished was not entitled to reemployment as a school social worker. While some of the duties of the two positions were similar, the positions were sufficiently dissimilar to require a separate certification, which the guidance counselor did not hold (*Brown v. Board of Education, Morrisville–Eaton Central School District*, 1995).

SUMMARY

Perhaps no other aspect of public school administration is subject to the plethora of rules, regulations, and legal mandates that govern human resources administration. Every aspect of the employment relationship has been subjected to legislative pronouncements and judicial interpretation. The courts have upheld the right of state governments and local school districts to specify terms and conditions of employment. One of these conditions, the passing of a competency test, has generated substantial controversy as the practice has spread to almost every state. Whereas the testing of teachers has been upheld by the courts, in those situations in which the tests have not been job related or test scores have been used arbitrarily or used to create unreasonable or arbitrary classifications, the courts have disallowed their use.

The major issue litigated in adverse employment decisions is the extent to which adequate due process was provided. The more severe the action and the more serious the individual interests involved, the more extensive and more formal is the due process required. The procedures to be followed in the dismissal of a tenured employee are more extensive than those required for the dismissal of a nontenured employee. However, employees who are RIFed are generally not entitled to a hearing, because the courts consider their dismissals to be impersonal, in no way impugning the teacher personally and therefore outside the scope of teacher termination statutes.

Although the specific laws related to personnel administration vary somewhat from state to state, the basic legal concepts, especially those designed to protect individual rights and ensure fairness and reasonableness, are common to all jurisdictions. A failure by the school district to adhere to these concepts leaves it vulnerable to a charge of arbitrary and capricious conduct.

DISCUSSION QUESTIONS

1. List the terms and conditions of employment that are most often affected by state statutory and regulatory provisions. For each area, discuss the basis and/or the purpose for the requirement.
2. There are two elements of due process. Define each element and discuss the protection that it affords school district employees.
3. All states have some statutory provisions regarding teacher dismissal or revocation of a certificate. What are the statutory provisions in your state? How do these compare with those most frequently cited in other states' statutes? What policies has your district adopted regarding RIFing of teachers and administrators?

■_____   **CASE STUDIES**

6.1 I Prefer Whiterock, But . . .

The Whiterock School District has had a great deal of trouble securing a permanent, certified teacher of the severely mentally disabled. The district advertised in the major educational publications in circulation in the state and attended the recruitment "round-ups" at the six institutions in the state that prepare special educators. Nonetheless, only two people applied for the position. Of the two, by far the most attractive was Mark Thompson, a graduating se-

nior at State University. His grades were excellent, as were his references. Mark had not passed the state certification exam, but was scheduled to take the exam in late May.

An invitation to interview was extended to both Mark and Susan Lewis, the other applicant. Susan interviewed on May 3 and Mark on May 16, the Monday after his graduation. Following Mark's exit meeting, James McGee, the director of human resources, and Nancy Kirch, the principal of the school at which the vacancy existed, informed Mark that they would recommend at the next school board meeting that he be offered the position. They reminded him, however, that the offer would be contingent on his passing the exam and becoming certified. Mark was excited by their announcement and assured them that he would pass the exam and would be sending them a copy of the test results and certificate as soon as they arrived. He said he wanted the position and would be looking forward to getting the board's offer. On June 3 the school board met and voted to extend an offer to Mark.

On June 6, Mark called Mr. McGee to say that he had not been able to take the exam because he had broken his foot two days before the exam while playing softball in a church-sponsored softball league. The exam would not be offered again until July 15, but Mark assured Mr. McGee that he had already made application to take the exam at that time. Mr. McGee asked Mark if he had received the board offer yet, and Mark said yes and that he would return it along with his test result. Mr. McGee told him he did not need to wait for the test results, that in fact he should notify the board of his acceptance within the next couple of weeks.

When Mr. McGee had not received the written acceptance by July 1, he called Mark and was assured by Mark that he would put it in the mail that very day. On July 6, Mark called Mr. McGee and told him that he had just received an offer from another district for $4000 more than the Whiterock offer. Mark shared that he really prefered Whiterock, but that the additional $4000 would make a big difference in his ability to pay off his student loans.

Questions

1. Balancing the district's need and Mark's actions thus far, what should Mr. McGee do? What options are there for making the Whiterock offer more competitive?
2. Is there a breach of contract if Mark accepts the second offer or if Whiterock withdraws its offer to Mark and makes one to Susan?
3. Suppose that you offer the position to Susan. Would you be honest with her regarding the circumstances that have led to the belated offer? If Susan rejects the offer, how should the district proceed?
4. Is there an issue of professional ethics that should be reported to the state certification board or state board of education?
5. Some districts send a prospective teacher an "intent to hire" letter. How binding is this type of offer on a school district? On the prospective teacher?

6.2 Lot's Wife

Phil Harris, principal of Eastwater High School, received the following anonymous note: "You should see what goes on in the coaches' showers after swim practice. Jim Murphy and Elaine Lorenzo are sinners. Fornicators and adulterers have no place in this district." Within the next two weeks several more notes arrived alleging the same thing. The last one added, "If you don't do something about this, you are as much a sinner as they are and I will see that the school board destroys you as surely as God destroyed Lot's wife for looking upon the evil of Sodom." The notes had all been delivered through school mail, so Mr. Harris assumed that the sender was someone within the school system.

Before the matter went any further, Mr. Harris felt compelled to meet with Jim and Elaine to share the essence of the letters with them. They both vehemently denied the allegations. However, they did admit that on three occasions they had both used the female coaches' showers after practice because of building repairs where the male coaches' showers are located.

Questions

1. Should Mr. Harris have confronted Jim and Elaine based on anonymous allegations? How else might he have responded? What type of investigation, if any, should take place now?
2. Based on the evidence thus far, what disciplinary action, if any, should be taken on Jim Murphy and Elaine Lorenzo?

3. If you were Jim or Elaine, how would you respond to the allegations? Would you hire an attorney? Have their rights to privacy been violated?

6.3 A Gun in Class*

On January 25, 1988, Robert T., a sixth-grade student, brought a loaded revolver into the class of Mr. Chaddock, a language arts teacher. Mr. Chaddock asked Robert to give him the gun and Robert refused. He then opened a drawer and asked Robert to put the gun in the drawer, but Robert again refused to give up the gun. Mr. Chaddock then decided to go on with class. He felt he knew Robert well enough to know that Robert would not deliberately do anything to hurt his classmates and that violence would occur only if Robert felt threatened. Toward the end of the class, the principal, who had heard that Robert had a gun, sent for him to come to her office. When she demanded that he give her the gun, Robert aimed it at her

*This case study is based on an actual court case, *Board of Education of County of Gilmer v. Chaddock*, 398 S.E.2d 120 (W. Va. 1990).

and told her to get away from him, and then he ran from the school.

At a dismissal hearing stemming from the incident, Mr. Chaddock defended his actions by stating that, because there was no school policy on handling such situations, he had to rely on his instincts. West Virginia statute states that dismissal must be reasonable based on one of the just causes listed: immorality, incompetency, cruelty, insubordination, intemperance, or willful neglect of duty, none of which are defined.

Questions

1. How should Mr. Chaddock have acted? Should Mr. Chaddock be dismissed? Under which clause could he be dismissed?
2. What about the principal? To what extent did the action taken by the principal in calling the student from the class to come to her office endanger the safety of others? What, if anything, might she be charged with? What disciplinary action, if any, should be taken in regard to her conduct?
3. Who is responsible for ensuring that the school district has a policy covering the now all too common situation of students bringing guns to school? Had someone been injured, what parties should be held responsible?

REFERENCES

Alba v. Los Angeles Unified School District, 189 Cal. Rptr. 897 (Cal. Ct. App. 1983).

Albemarle Paper Company v. Moody, 422 U.S. 405 (1975).

Alexander, K., & Alexander, M. D. (2001). *American public school law* (5th ed.). Belmont, CA: West/Thompson Learning.

Ambach v. Norwick, 441 U.S. 68 (1979).

Arline v. School Board of Nassau County, 772 F.2d 759 (11th Cir. 1985), aff'd, 480 U.S. 273 (1987).

Arline v. School Board of Nassau County, 692 F. Supp. 1286 (M.D. Fla. 1988).

Association of Mexican-American Educators v. State of California, 231 F.3d 572 (9th Cir. 2000).

Aubrey v. School Bd. of Lafayette Parish, 148 F.3de 559 (5th Cir. 1998).

Babb v. Independent School Dist. No. I-5, 829 F.2d 973 (Okl. 1992).

Ballanto v. Board of Education of Stronington, 663 A. 2d 323 (Conn. App. 1993).

Barr v. Clarendon County School Board District 2, 462 S.E.2d 316 (S.A. Ct. App. 1995).

Beckham, J. (1983). Critical elements of the employment relationship. In J. Beckham & P. A. Zirkel (Eds.), *Legal issues in public school employment* (pp. 1–21). Bloomington, IN: Phi Delta Kappa.

Bowers v. Hardwick, 478 US 186 (1986).

Brown v. Board of Education, Morrisville-Eaton Central School District, 621 N.Y.S.2d 167 (A.D. 3 Dept. 1995).

Burlington Industries v. Ellerth, No. 97-5695 S.Ct. (1998).

Calhoun v. Cassady, 534 S.W.2d 806 (Ky. 1976).

Cambron-McCabe, N. H. (1983). Procedural due process. In J. Beckham & P. A. Zirkel (Eds.), *Legal issues in public school employment* (pp. 78–97). Bloomington, IN: Phi Delta Kappa.

Cascio, W. F. (1998). *Applied psychology in personnel management* (5th ed.). Upper Saddle River, NJ: Prentice Hall.

C.F.S. v. Mahan, 934 S.W.2d 615 (Mo.Ct. App. 1996).

Chalk v. U.S. District Court Central District of California, 840 F.2d 701 (9th Cir. 1988).

Civil Rights Division of the Arizona Department of Law v. Amphitheater Unified School District No. 10, 680 P.2d 517 (Ariz. 1983).

Cleveland Board of Education v. Loudermill, 470 U.S. 532 (1985).

Connecticut Education Association v. Tirozzi, 554 A.2d 1065 (Conn. 1989).

Daily v. Bd. of Ed. of Morrill County Sch. Dist. No. 62-0063, 588 N.W.2d 813 (Neb. 1999).

English v. Talledega County Board of Education, 938 F. Supp. 775 (N.D. Ala. 1996).

Estill v. Alabama State Tenure Commission, 650 So.2d 890 (Ala. Civ. App. 1994).

Faragher v. City of Boca Raton, 524 U.S. 775 (1998).

Fields v. Hallsville Independent School District, 906 F.2d 1017 (5th Cir. 1990), *cert. denied*, 111 S.Ct. 676 (1991).

Fischer, L., Schimmel, D., & Kelly, C. (1999). *Teachers and the law* (5th ed.). New York: Longman.

Flanary v. Barrett, 143 S.W. 38 (Ky. 1912).

Floyd County Board of Education v. Slone, 307 S.W.2d 912 (Ky. 1957).

Frazier v. Garrison I.S.D., 980 F.2d 1514 (5th Cir. 1993).

Garner, B. A. (Ed.). (1999). *Black's law dictionary* (7th ed.). St. Paul, MN: West.

Gaylord v. Tacoma School District No. 10, 559 P.2d 1340 (Wash. 1077), *cert. denied*, 434 U.S. 879 (1977).

Georgia Association of Educators, Inc. v. Nix, 407 F. Supp. 1102 (N.D. Ga. 1976).

Glover v. Williamsburg Local Sch. Dist. Bd. of Educ., 20 F.Supp. 1160 (S.D. Ohio 1998).

Gould Public School v. Dobbs, 993 S.W.2d 500 (Ark. 1999).

Grand Prairie Independent School District v. Vaughn, 792 S.W.2d 944 (Tex. 1990).

Greene, J. E. (1971). *School personnel administration.* New York: Chilton.

Griggs v. Duke Power Co., 410 U.S. 924 (1971).

Hartmeister, F., & Russo, C. J. (1999). "Taxing" the system when selecting teachers for reduction-in-force. *Education Law Reporter, 130*, 989–1007.

Hess, F. M., & Maranto, R. A. (2000). Tenure's tenacious tenure in public schools. *Education Digest, 65*(5), 51–55.

Horton v. Jefferson County–Dubois Area Vocational Technical School, 630 A.2d 481 (Pa. Commw. Ct. 1993).

Hortonville District v. Hortonville Education Association, 426 U.S. 482 (1976).

*Imber, M. (2001). Morality and teacher effectiveness. *American School Board Journal, 188*(4), 64–66.

Imber, M., & van Geel, T. (2000). *Education law* (2nd ed.). Mahwah, NJ: Erlbaum.

In re Thomas, 926 S.W.2d 163 (Mo. App. 1996).

Jones v. Alabama State Tenure Commission, 408 So.2d 145 (Ala. Civ. App. 1981).

King v. Jefferson County Board of Education, 659 So.2d 686 (Ala. Civ. App. 1995).

Knox County Educ. Assn. v. Knox County Board of Educ., 158 F.3d 361 (6th Cir. 1998), *cert. denied*, 120 S.Ct. 46 (1999).

Lagos v. Modesto City School District, 843 F.2d 347 (9th Cir. 1988).

Mathews v. Eldridge, 424 U.S. 319 (1976).

McCarthy, M. M., Cambron-McCabe, N. H., & Thomas, S. B. (1998). *Public school law: Teachers' and students' rights* (4th ed.). Boston: Allyn and Bacon.

McClelland v. Paris Public Schools, 742 S.W.2d 907 (Ark. 1988).

McDaniel v. Princeton City Sch. Dist. Bd. of Educ., 72 F. Supp. 874 (S. D. Ohio 1999).

Mescall v. Marra, 49 F. Supp. 2d 365 (S.D. N.Y. 1999).

Newman v. Crews, 651 F.2d 222 (4th Cir. 1981).

Nixon v. Board of Cooperative Educational Services of Sole Supervisory District of Steuben–Allegheny Counties, 564 N.Y.S.2d 903 (App. Div. 1990).

Owen v. Board of Education of Kankakee School District No. 111, 632 N. E. 2d 1073 (Ill. App. 1994).

Palmer v. Board of Trustees of Crook County School District No. 1, 785 P.2d 1160 (Wyo. 1990).

Pittsburgh Federation of Teachers Local 400 v. Aaron, 417 F. Supp. 94 (Pa. 1976).

Pullman–Standard v. Swint, 456 U.S. 273 (1982).

Racine Unified School District v. Labor and Industry Review Commission, 476 N.W.2d 707 (Wis. App. 1991).

Reitmeyer v. Unemployment Compensation Board of Review, 602 A.2d 505 (Pa. Com-wlth. 1992).

Sherburne v. School Board of Swannee County, 455 So.2d 1057 (Fla. Dist. Ct. App. 1984).

Singleton v. Jackson Municipal Separate School District, 419 F.2d 1211 (5th Cir. 1970).

Skinner v. Railway Labor Executives Association, 489 U.S. 602 (1989).

Sorenson v. School District No. 28, 418 P.2d 1004 (Wyo. 1966).

Sperry, D. J., Daniel, P. T. K., Huefner, D. S., & Gee, E. G. (1998). *Education law and the public schools: A compendium* (2nd ed.). Norwood, MA: Cristopher–Gordon.

State of Texas v. Project Principle, Inc., 724 S.W.2d 387 (Tex. 1987).

State ex rel. Melchiori v. Board of Educ., 425 S.E.2d 251 (W. Va. 1992).

Sullivan v. River Valley Sch. Dist., 20 F. Supp. 2d 1120 (W.D. Mich. 1998).

Swanson v. Houston Independent School District, 800 S.W.2d 630 (Tex. Ct. App. 1990).

Underwood v. Henry County Sch. Bd., 427 S.E.2d 330 (1993).

United States v. South Carolina, 445 F. Supp. 1094 (D.S.C. 1977), aff'd 434 U.S. 1026 (1978).

U.S. Department of Education, National Center for Education Statistics. (2000). *Digest of education statistics 2000.* Washington, DC: The Department.

Valente, W. D., & Valente, C. M. (2001). *Law in the schools* (5th ed.). New York: Macmillan.

White v. Blackfoot School Dist. No. 55, No. 99-35820 (9th Cir. 2001).

Winegar v. Des Moines Independent Community School District, 20 F.3d 895 (8th Cir. 1994).

Wygant v. Jackson Board of Education, 106 S.Ct. 1842 (1986).

Yanzick v. School District No. 23, Lake County Montana, 641 P.2d 431 (Mont. 1982).

7 Collective Bargaining and the Human Resource Function

Working with Employee Groups

After reading this chapter, you will be able to:
- Describe the evolution of the empowerment of employee groups in education.
- Identify the responsibilities of human resources administrators in working with employee groups in the school district.
- Describe the collective bargaining process, including distributive and integrative or win–win approaches.
- Discuss the operational models for implementing the collective bargaining process.

Learning Objectives

The term *negotiations* was a repugnant word in education less than 40 years ago. In 1960, for example, an attempt by the National Education Association (NEA) to pass a resolution at its national convention in Los Angeles stating that "representative negotiations are compatible with the ethics and dignity of the teaching profession" was soundly rejected by the association's representatives (1961). The use of such terms as *collective bargaining* and *teachers' union* was slow to be accepted by a profession that viewed them as applicable only to organized labor. Yet, by 1993 more than 30 states and the District of Columbia had passed legislation approving bargaining in the public sector, and collective bargaining between boards of education and employee groups became a way of life.

This chapter examines the work of the human resources function in relation to employee groups. The discussion centers on the development of influence within employee groups in education and its impact on human resources processes. We give much attention to collective bargaining and its implications for the work of human resources administrators. The nature of the collective bargaining process, including both distributive and integrative approaches, is fully discussed. Special attention also is devoted to mediation strategies and to grievance procedures as these relate to collective bargaining.

EMPLOYEE UNIONS: DEFINITION

Webb and Webb (1920) provided an early definition of the term **union** that remains viable today. They defined a union as "a continuous association of wage earners for the purpose of maintaining or improving the conditions of their working lives" (p. 10). Over a half-century later, Lunenburg and Ornstein (2000) defined a union as "an organization of employees formed for the purpose of influencing an employer's decision concerning conditions of employment" (p. 548). In this chapter the terms *teachers' union* and *teachers' association* are used interchangeably.

Persons favoring unions in education argue that they serve several important purposes: (1) protection of teachers' rights, (2) extension of democracy in the workplace, and (3) promotion of teacher decision making and the development of better schools. Persons who oppose unions in education argue that they are (1) self-serving and devoted only to higher salaries, rather than to better education for students, (2) interested mainly in gaining more power in the governance of school programs and policy development, (3) inhibitors to needed educational reform in that they are only apologists for bad teachers, and (4) educational anachronisms and resistors to needed educational change (Nelson, Carlson, & Palonsky, 1996).

EMPLOYEE UNIONS: HISTORICAL PERSPECTIVES

By 1857 there were 15 state teachers' associations, including those in New York, Rhode Island, and Massachusetts, which had organized in 1845 (Wesley, 1957). The National Teachers Association (NTA) was organized in 1857 and in 1870 merged with the Normal Teachers Association and the National Association of School Superintendents to form the National Education Association (NEA). Twenty-seven years later, the Chicago Teachers Federation (CTF) was formed in an attempt to gain salary increases for Chicago's teachers. The CTF aggressively pressed for other teacher benefits, including a pension program and a guarantee of employment following a probationary period of service. In 1916 the CTF and several teachers' organizations from other states came together to form the American Federation of Teachers (AFT). Competition for membership between the NEA and the AFT historically has been a race to see which of the two associations could gain better salaries, working conditions, benefits, and services for the nation's teachers.

With the increase of teacher militancy during the early 1940s and into the late 1950s, the AFT placed more emphasis on the plight of teachers in America and the implementation of negotiations between boards of education and teacher groups. A major breakthrough in the NEA's position on collective negotiations came in 1960 when the United Federation of Teachers (UFT) called a strike for its members in the New York City schools. The one-day strike reportedly included from 4500 to 15,000 teachers, depending on which group's figures are utilized. As a result of the strike, the AFT

Local 2 was chosen over the NEA to represent New York City's 40,000 teachers in negotiations with the school board.

Although in 1960 the NEA-adopted resolution to recognize representative negotiations as compatible with the ethics of the teaching profession was denied, 2 years later, in 1962, the association approved its first official policy on negotiations by adopting a resolution that "insisted" on the right of teachers to negotiate with boards of education (NEA, 1962). Since that time, the NEA has placed priority on working to influence conditions of work for their membership, protecting and improving the compensation and benefits of members, demanding the use of collective bargaining in the determination of teachers' salaries and conditions of work, and expanding services in the areas of legal protection, political activities, contract grievances and arbitration, and others.

In 1999, membership in the NEA numbered 2,458,364, far surpassing the estimated 500,000 membership of the AFT. Are the NEA and AFT unions as we know them in the private sector? As pointed out by Norton and others (1996),

> (1) unions represent organizations of employees; (2) they strive to influence conditions of work for their membership; (3) they protect and enhance the economic welfare of members; (4) they demand the use of collective bargaining in determining salaries and conditions of work; (5) they lend strong support to members in matters relating to grievances and arbitration; and (6) they represent a continuous association of wage earners. (p. 275)

Both the NEA and AFT reflect each of the foregoing criteria that decribe a union. And today the NEA is the largest employee union in the United States. More important, the power of teacher and other school employee unions was named by school superintendents and professors among the top 11 challenges facing public schools (Horace Mann League, 1996). In another study, nearly 33.8% of the school superintendents reported that concerns about relations with teachers' unions were troublesome for them "very frequently," "frequently," or "somewhat frequently" (Norton, 2001). And, in the same study, "demands of the school staff" was ranked highest by school superintendents among six determinants of this administrator's workload.

CHANGES IN UNION PERSPECTIVES IN BUSINESS AND INDUSTRY

Nulty (1992) describes the decade of the 1980s as an era of turmoil and stress for collective bargaining in business and industry. He points to such new provisions in collective bargaining as lump-sum payments replacing across-the-board wage increases, negotiated wage cuts, two-tier systems in which workers doing the same job but hired at different times have different wage rates, workers forced to pay a greater portion of certain fringe benefits such as health care, contingent compensation that is based on the organization's overall performance, profit sharing, and various forms of worker ownership as evidence of this contention. As Nulty points out, all the foregoing provisions, along with the steady decline of union members in the private sector, tend to support contentions that unions and the voice of union workers have weakened in the United States. "Some observers look at the record and draw the conclusion that unions, collective bargaining, and labor relations as they have developed over the entire post-World War II period are obsolete" (p. 541). Nulty emphasizes that such conclusions are a dangerous misreading of the history of the 1980s. And many writers in the field, including the authors of this text, support Nulty's position.

There is ample evidence that many organizations in the private sector have returned to their original strategy of distributive, adversarial bargaining. For example, Overman (2000–2001) stipulates that renewed activism is being demonstrated by both union member statistics and by work stoppages; both strikes and lockouts by employers rose in 1998. There were 34 work stoppages during 1998 idling 387,000 workers; in 1997 there were 29 stoppages idling 339,000 workers. In 1998, there were employee strikes at major airlines, the General Motors Corporation, the United Automobile Workers, and the Bell Atlantic Corporation. In 1999, the Allied Pilots Association protested against American Airlines over its acquisition of another airline company (U.S Department of Labor's Bureau of Labor Statistics, 1999). And, as noted previously in Chapter 2, in the year 2000, strikes were witnessed in several school districts nationally, including the large cities of Philadelphia, Pennsylvania, and Buffalo, New York.

Distributive bargaining strategies, which will be discussed in depth later in this chapter, have always dominated bargaining methods in education, although integrative, win–win, approaches have been initiated in school districts throughout the nation. Time only will tell the extent to which school boards and school employee associations will join with the apparent trend of increased distributive bargaining, as apparently is the case in the private sector. In any case, as Savoie (1994) predicted in the mid 1990s, the trends in collective bargaining changed significantly during the second half of the last decade of the 20th century. For example, employees sought (1) both monetary and nonmonetary rewards from management and their union affiliations, (2) a workplace that values and understands diversity and provides a sense of belonging and personal worth, (3) more meaningful work and a larger part in deciding how their work will be carried out, and (4) a workplace that gives full attention to a balanced work-life for the employee and organizatonal policies that actively pursue a healthy and safe work environment. As Savoie notes, these considerations have not always been the usual subjects of traditional bargaining, but will continue as agenda items through the first decade of the 2000s. Thus, Savoie argues, partnership bargaining based on cooperative approaches best serves the realization of the foregoing purposes.

WORKING RELATIONSHIPS: THE HUMAN RESOURCES FUNCTION AND EMPLOYEE GROUPS

"School boards generally expect that the school superintendent will represent them in the area of employee relations. In this sense, the superintendent serves as the director of the school district's employee relations, although various responsibilities are delegated to other units in the school system" (Norton, Webb, Dlugosh, & Sybouts, 1996, p. 279). The four key responsibilities of the school superintendent in the area of employee relations are as follows:

1. The school superintendent must serve as the primary liaison between the school board and employee groups and between the school board and school administration on matters of employee relations.
2. The school superintendent is responsible for the development of viable employee relations policy for the school district.
3. The school superintendent is responsible for providing the instruction for school administrators and other personnel regarding the implementation of the master contract agreement and the administration of grievances related to the contract.
4. The superintendent serves as the school district's representative in matters of paramount importance concerning employee relations and school district practices in this area. (Norton et al., 1996, pp. 279–281)

For each of the listed employee relations responsibilities of the superintendent, vital support is provided by the human resources unit of the school system and other human resources administrators. For example, one study revealed that nearly 80% of the state's human resources directors served on their district's collective bargaining team and over 50% of them served as the district's chief spokesperson (Norton, 1999). Needed communication with teacher groups must be programmed so that school board members, district administrators, and employee groups are informed about the school district's goals, problems, and needs. To facilitate such communication, the human resources director should sit as a member of the superintendent's administrative cabinet. In this position the human resources director is better prepared to inform school employees of the board of education's and school administration's personnel positions and also is able to communicate the views of employees to the cabinet.

The human resources administrators of the school district must work to develop mutual support and trust between the school district's administrative staff and employees; in this sense they become advocates of the district's employees. Efforts on the part of the human resources unit to gain optimal work conditions and proper salaries for employees promote cooperation, mutual trust, and a positive image of the school district.

Under the leadership of the school superintendent, human resources personnel serve a primary role in the fair and equitable implementation of the negotiated master agreement of the school district. The school principal plays a key role in the implementation of contract provisions and agreements since he or she works most directly with personnel at the local building level.

The human resources director frequently is delegated the responsibility of representing the school district in personnel matters such as contract grievances, affirmative action, litigation of employment matters, due process, and others. Since school personnel work for the school district, and not for the employees' organization, the superintendent and the human resources administrators in the district must assume responsibility for the administration of all phases of the personnel function, including the development of a positive working relationship with school employees and employee groups.

COLLECTIVE BARGAINING: DEFINITION AND BASIC PRINCIPLES

Lieberman and Moskow (1966), early authorities in the area of *collective negotiations*, defined it as "a process whereby employees as a group and the employers make offers and counter offers in good faith on conditions of their employment relations for the purpose of reaching mutually acceptable agreement" (p. 1). The American Association of School Administrators (Redfern, 1967) defined **collective bargaining** as follows:

> the process by which school teachers, through their designated representatives, negotiate with the board of education, or its designated representative(s), with reference to salary, working conditions and other matters of interest to negotiation practices. Collective bargaining and professional negotiations sometimes are used interchangeably. (p. 112)

Professional negotiations became the official policy of the NEA at the 1962 Denver Convention. A short time later the NEA (1965) defined negotiations as follows:

> a set of procedures, written and officially adopted by the local association and the school board, which provides an orderly method for the school board and the local association to negotiate, through professional channels, on matters of mutual concern, to reach agreement on these matters and to establish educational channels for mediation and appeal in event of impasse. (p. 1)

More recent definitions of negotiations are very similar. Rebore (2001) stated that

> collective negotiations is a process by which representatives of the school district meet with representatives of the school district employees in order to make proposals and counterproposals for the purpose of mutually agreeing on salaries, fringe benefits, and working conditions covering a specific period of time. (pp. 297–298)

An additional dimension, that of serving as a method for setting the procedures to be followed in settling disputes, is part of the negotiations definition set forth by Cunningham and Cordeiro (2000). Merriam–Webster's

Collegiate Dictionary (2001) states that to negotiate "is to confer with another so as to arrive at the settlement of some matter."

For the purposes of this chapter, collective bargaining is considered to be the process whereby matters of employee relations are determined mutually by representatives of employee groups and their employer, within the limits of law or mutual agreement. Bargaining, under this definition, can occur under distributive or integrative approaches.

Regardless of the differences in phrasing of definitions, the process of collective bargaining most often is based on the following basic principles:

1. Employees have the right to form, join, and participate in the activities of organizations of their choosing for the purpose of representation on matters of employment relations.
2. An association has the right to request exclusive representation in negotiations when the majority of the employee membership so authorizes.
3. Representatives of the local association and the board of education meet to negotiate on matters relating to salaries, fringe benefits, and working conditions as set forth in cooperatively established ground rules or as set forth by law.
4. Recommendations (agreements) of the negotiation representatives, when ratified by the groups that they represent, result in the contractual agreements for the time period specified.
5. Failure to reach an agreement leads to impasse, in which case established appeal procedures are implemented to reach a settlement.

THE TWO PRIMARY BARGAINING PROCESSES

The two primary approaches to collective bargaining described in the literature are termed **distributive bargaining** and **integrative bargaining**. The collective bargaining processes exemplified by a labor–management model, which is primarily adversarial and designed to realize maximum-gain, short-term bargaining through the use of authority, power, or withdrawal of services, exemplifies *distributive bargaining* (Perry & Wilman, 1970). Distributive bargaining generally results in crisis bargaining and is the strategy most often associated with labor organizations. On the other hand, *quasi-distributive* bargaining is based on a desire to avoid a test of power.

The second major approach to bargaining, *integrative bargaining*, as described by Perry and Wilman (1970),

> is based on strong long-run mutual interests and important short-run problems . . . . A pure integrative bargaining strategy commonly leads to "problem solving" . . . problem solving has been concentrated in mature bargaining relationships in which external political and/or economic conditions force the parties to perceive a threat to their mutual survival in either continued conflict or continued reliance on short-run power as the basis for decision making. (pp. 62–65)

Quasi-integrative bargaining involves a quid pro quo, give and take process of compromise and thus has similarities to quasi-distributive strategies. However, quasi-integrative strategy places more emphasis on problem solving and is more closely associated with the *win–win approach*. Conditions that serve to determine when distributive or integrative strategies are more successful are presented in a later section.

It should be noted that both distributive bargaining and integrative bargaining have witnessed various adaptations as collective bargaining has evolved over the years. For example, terms such as **power-based bargaining** and **fractional bargaining** are associated with distributive bargaining methods. In brief, power-based bargaining refers to bargaining leverage as gauged by "the relative willingness of each side to incur the consequences of not reaching an agreement" (Loughran, 1992, p. 32). Loughran believes that the economic leverage possessed by each respective party underlies all negotiations. Closely related to this concept is that of bargaining power. As emphasized by Loughran (1992), "By and large an employer's bargaining power is determined by its ability and willingness to take and resist a strike" (p. 33). In power-based bargaining, the strike is viewed as the primary weapon that a union has to pressure management to meet its demands.

Fractional bargaining "involves the workers only as members of work groups, not as union members" (Kahn, 1979, p. 79). Fractional bargaining exists primarily because groups within the union as a whole often have different issues that each desires to negotiate on its own terms. As Kahn points out, in some instances the power of a work group within the union may be greater than that of the union as a whole, and as a result fractional bargaining allows one group to seek agreement on an issue that the union as a whole is unable to gain for them.

Integrative bargaining has assumed many different titles and varied procedures as well. Terms such as *win–win bargaining*, *partnership bargaining*, *collaborative bargaining*, *problem-solving bargaining*, *mutual-gains bargaining*, *creative bargaining*, *consensus-based bargaining*, and *interest-based bargaining* represent a few of the approaches based on integrative methods.

Win–win bargaining methods are discussed in detail later in this chapter. In brief, win–win bargaining centers on efforts to resolve mutual problems of interest to the school district as a whole. While working to arrive at creative solutions to issues being encountered by both parties, emphasis also is given to attempts to improve school board and employee relations as well.

BARGAINING BY EMPLOYEE GROUPS: HISTORICAL PERSPECTIVES

The process of collective bargaining in education has evolved over several decades. Developments that have had an impact on both the unity of employee groups and the legal pathways for negotiations in the public sector are outlined in Figure 7.1.

1806	*Philadelphia Cordwainers Case:* Employee groups were found guilty of conspiracy to raise their wages. Any such organized action was declared illegal by the courts.
1842	*Commonwealth v. Hunt:* In a decision relating to the use of group action by employees, the Supreme Court of Massachusetts ruled that labor organizations did not constitute unlawful bodies by the mere fact that they represented a combination of individuals or bodies. This decision enhanced group action by employees.
1845	First state association of teachers and school officials was established in Massachusetts.
1857	National Teachers Association (NTA) is founded.
1870	National Education Association (NEA) is founded.
1886	American Federation of Labor (AFL) is founded.
1886	Federal regulation of interstate commerce is established. Federal legislation passed to regulate interstate commerce proved to provide important support to union activity. This legislation served as the legal rationale for federal government intervention in disputes between management groups and employees on an interstate basis.
1890	*Sherman Antitrust Act:* The act expanded to find labor unions guilty of conspiracy to restrain trade by striking.
1914	*Clayton Act:* The act removed unions from application of antitrust laws. However, the United States Supreme Court did not apply antitrust laws until much later.
1926	*Railroad Labor Act:* The act represented a major step in the support of collective bargaining through legislation. Its constitutionality was reinforced four years later in a ruling by the Supreme Court.
1932	*Norris-LaGuardia Act:* The act supported the right of employees to form unions and placed restrictions on the courts concerning the issuance of injunctions to restrict labor activities. Refusal by employers to bargain with representatives of employee groups was determined to be an unfair labor practice and subject to punishment by law.
1935	*National Labor Relations Act (Wagner Act):* Congress established the right of employees to bargain with their employers on matters pertaining to wages, job-related benefits, and conditions of employment. The act concerned employees in the private sector only and excluded public employees. Most agree, however, that this act has affected employer–employee contract relations more significantly than any legislation passed to date. Even though the Wagner Act applied only to interstate commerce, it confirmed certain employee rights in the area of collective bargaining.
1938	*Educational Policies Commission:* The commission stated that the entire staff should take part in the formulation of the educational process.
1947	*Labor Management Relations Act (Taft–Hartley Act):* This act provided further expansion and clarification of employee rights in the bargaining process and added a set of unfair labor practices by unions. Although the act applied only to interstate commerce, its influence on legislation in the individual states and on bargaining in the public sector was far-reaching. Employee–employer bargaining under the Taft–Hartley Act is summarized as follows:

1. Collective bargaining is the performance of the mutual obligation of the employer and the representative of the employees to meet at reasonable times and confer in good faith with respect to wages, hours, and other terms and conditions of employment.
2. Collective bargaining also includes negotiation of an agreement or any question arising thereunder and the execution of a written contract incorporating any agreement reached if requested by either party.

FIGURE 7.1

Developments Influencing Employee Unity and Collective Negotiations

	3. Such an obligation (to bargain) does not compel either party to agree to a proposal or to require the making of a concession (Labor Management Relations Act, 1947).
1955	Merger of American Federation of Labor (AFL) and Congress of Industrial Organizations (CIO): Unionization was a powerful movement and an effective influence for bargaining in the private sector.
1959	*Labor Management Reporting and Disclosure Act (Landrum-Griffin Act):* The act established more effective controls over the operations and funds of unions. Governance practices such as voting rights, participation in union affairs, and the right to sue in case of rights' violations were covered by the act. Financial reporting procedures, open or public expense accounting, election of union officers, and "democratic practices" were also included. Teacher organizations were excluded; however, the influence of the Landrum-Griffin Act on public employee groups has been significant.
1959	Wisconsin became the first state to enact legislation pertaining to negotiations in the public sector. A state labor relations board was established to oversee the administration of the act and assist in the resolution of disputes.
1962	*American Federation of Teachers (AFT) Victory:* AFT Local No. 2 won the right to represent employees of the New York City public schools. This victory pushed the NEA to historical action at its Denver Convention in 1962.
1962	*Denver Convention of the NEA:* This convention marked the beginning of the NEA's official position on professional negotiations for teachers. Resolution 18 modified a 1961 resolution that called for the right of professional education associations "to participate in the determination of policies of common concern and other conditions for professional service" (NEA, 1961, pp. 216–217). Resolution 18, however, included the NEA's first official reference to the term *professional negotiations.* The 1962 resolution set forth such strong wording as "the NEA insists on the right of professional associations through democratically selected representatives using professional channels to participate with boards of education in determination of policies of common concern including salary and other conditions for professional service" (NEA, 1962, p. 178).
1962	*Presidential Executive Order 10988:* The executive order by President John Kennedy opened the door for bargaining for federal employees. The order had significant effects on bargaining movements in the entire public sector. E.O. 10988 provided federal workers the right to join organizations of choice, provided for the recognition of organizations for purposes of negotiations, required federal agencies to meet and confer with recognized employee organizations with respect to personnel policies and conditions of work, and established advisory arbitration of grievances in relation to agreements reached. As a result, government employee unions flourished. The order encouraged local and state government employees to take action to win negotiation rights as well.
1965–1968	*Professional negotiations agreements:* By 1965 an estimated 388 professional negotiations agreements in 35 states had been filed with the NEA. During 1967 and 1968, approximately 900,000 teachers were working under an estimated 2,200 agreements with at least some form of minimal formal acknowledgment of the existence of a teacher organization in the district (NEA, 1968). Professional negotiation legislation was passed in Oregon, Washington, Connecticut, California, and Massachusetts.
1969	*Presidential Executive Order 11491:* President Richard Nixon's order was designed to bring labor relations in closer relationship to practices in the private sector. The

FIGURE 7.1
(continued)

	order modified and expanded the earlier order by President Kennedy. E.O. 11491 established exclusive recognition in the bargaining process, required the inclusion of a grievance procedure, established the Federal Labor Relations Council to interpret the provisions of the order, and established the Federal Service Impasse Panel. The order tended to lend additional support for legislation concerning collective negotiations in the public sector, including teacher groups.
1980–1990	By 1980, 32 states had enacted collective bargaining laws that encompassed some or all categories of educational employees in the public sector. This count included those states with "permissive legislation" whereby the employing agency could enter into contract discussions with employees, but such an action was not required. Peterson, Rossmiller, and Volz (1978) cited the case of the *Norwalk Teachers Association v. Board of Education* in noting that "in the absence of a statute either authorizing or prohibiting collective bargaining by teachers the prevailing view today seems to be that teachers have that right" (p. 432). Although integrative approaches gained in popularity in education, distributive strategies remained most dominant.
1991–Present	Some movement toward the increased use of integrative, or win–win, approaches to collective bargaining was witnessed during this time period. Although distributive, quid pro quo methods remained dominant, impasse problems and negative outcomes in the area of staff and community relationships motivated some school districts to implement less adversarial bargaining procedures. Best estimates indicate that approximately 7.5% of the nation's school districts have begun to use win–win methods. Those districts using integrative bargaining typically report that the process tends to become a forum for everything that takes place in the school district; the scope of bargaining widened significantly. Thus, such topics as student discipline, curriculum, educational reform, decision-making processes, and teacher protection become agenda items. Also, negotiators who are effective in distributive bargaining situations often are found to be much less effective when integrative methods are utilized. Overall, between 1991 and 2002, collective bargaining continued as a way of life for school personnel. The scope of bargaining widened to include almost everything that happens within a school district. Although some movement toward integrative approaches was noted, distributive bargaining methods continued to dominate.

FIGURE 7.1
(continued)

The competition for membership between the NEA and AFT in the early decades of the 20th century escalated efforts to serve the welfare of teachers and resulted in the acceleration of collective bargaining activities in education. Walter (1975) described the ultimate results of the AFT and NEA competition as follows:

> While the competition was at its strongest [for membership] and under the press of that competition, the NEA became a different organization. Its teachers clearly became the dominant power, and administration affiliates became much less influential. By the end of the sixties, fewer important differences remained between AFT and NEA. (p. 16)

Negotiations in education developed rapidly following the official stand by the NEA in 1962 insisting that teachers' associations have a right to negotiate with boards of education. Bargaining procedures in the private sector generally served as the blueprint for negotiations in education. Even though the process of negotiations historically has been criticized and questioned by some as inappropriate for education, by 1965 the die had been cast, and by 1968 negotiations had become an acceptable and expected practice in the field of education (NEA, 1968).

Other developments or conditions in the period that served to foster and support negotiations in education included the following:

1. A growing discontent with compensation levels on the part of teachers, whose salaries were viewed as losing pace with professionals in other fields.
2. The increased sophistication of teacher groups and individual teachers in the actual processes of negotiations. Although teachers' expertise in collective negotiating increased, administrators and members of boards of education were reluctant to give credibility to the negotiations process and, in the 1950s and 1960s, all too often tended to ignore its impact on educational employee relations.
3. The increase of teacher strikes and threat of strikes. The NEA before 1966 avoided references to strikes in its negotiation policy. Yet, since that date, associations with NEA affiliation have been involved in numerous such actions.
4. The mere growth in the number of negotiated agreements in education had a spillover effect on nonnegotiating districts and tended to cement the process as an expected right and practice. Once initiated, withdrawal from negotiations as a process was difficult.
5. Such developments as district reorganization, which resulted in larger school districts and more adequate financial resources; the changing composition of teacher groups, especially the increase in male teachers; the teacher supply and demand, with serious shortages of teachers in the 1960s; and the increased professional development of staffs, especially in the area of advanced preparation.

By 1984 the practice of collective bargaining was common in education and encompassed both professional personnel and support staff personnel. Even in those states with no legislative provision for bargaining, the *meet and confer* concept was well established. The process of bargaining has not been restricted to teacher groups. Principals, supervisors, middle management personnel, and staff in other classifications have negotiated agreements in a growing number of school districts.

COLLECTIVE BARGAINING IN EDUCATION AND THE CENTRAL HUMAN RESOURCES UNIT

Human resources administration has been influenced by collective bargaining in two distinct ways: (1) the process of collective bargaining has affected virtually every process and activity within the human resources function, and (2) the human resources unit generally has assumed a major role in the administration of the bargaining process itself. Although collective bargaining approaches vary, the process is entrenched as a common practice in school systems today.

Human resources directors play a major role in three specific activities in the area of collective bargaining: proposal development, strategy development, and negotiations at the table. In regard to their involvement in actual negotiations, almost 80% of the personnel administrators in one state reported that they served on the school district's collective bargaining team. In the same study, 53.8% of the directors served as chief spokesperson for the school board's negotiations team (Norton, 1999). The use of the human resources director as the chief negotiator or spokesperson for the board team varies among school districts. Smaller districts tend to use the school superintendent or a member of the school board more often than larger districts, which often use a professional negotiator (from outside or inside the school district) or the human resources director as the chief negotiator. It also has become common practice for the human resources director or the director of employment relations to coordinate the entire collective bargaining process for the school board.

Because the involvement of human resources directors nationally in collective bargaining is well established, it is important to identify specific responsibilities or tasks related to negotiations in which a director must be competent. These competencies have been identified and are summarized in Figure 7.2.

1.1 Ability to understand the nature of collective negotiations and the skills involved in the process.

1.2 Ability to make all necessary preparations for negotiations by gathering information, establishing priorities, and interpreting parameters.

1.3 Ability to contribute to the resolution of a collective negotiations agreement.

1.4 Ability to prepare news releases for the media.

1.5 Ability to interpret and communicate the negotiations agreement as it relates to the personnel function and employee contractual relations.

1.6 Ability to review and recommend revision of policies, regulations, and procedures as these relate to the "newly negotiated" agreement.

1.7 Ability to interpret, communicate, and evaluate the negotiated agreement as it relates to employer–employee relationships.

1.8 Ability to evaluate the negotiated agreements as these relate to future negotiations and school district policy development.

FIGURE 7.2

Negotiations Competencies of Human Resources Directors

Source: Norton, M. S., & Farrar, R. D. (1987). *Competency-based preparations of educational administrators—Tasks, competencies and indicators of competency* (p. 109). Tempe, AZ: Arizona State University, College of Education.

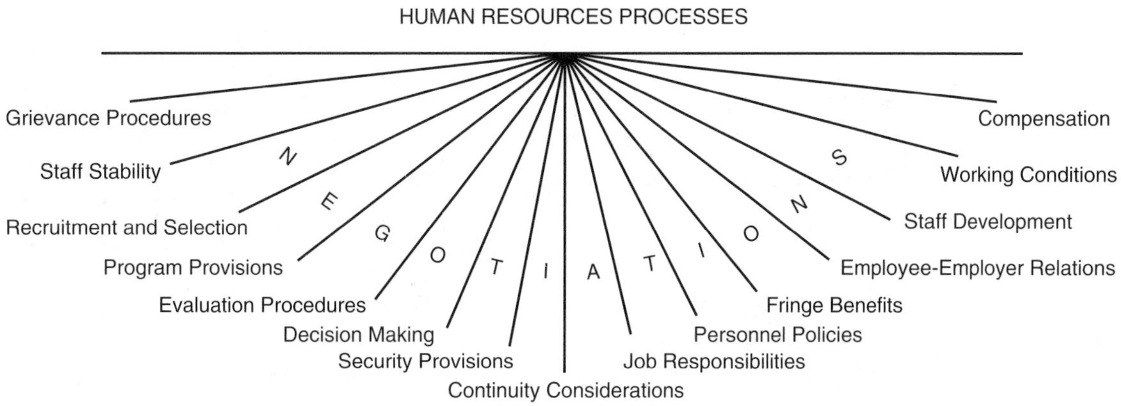

HUMAN RESOURCES PROCESSES

Grievance Procedures

Staff Stability

Recruitment and Selection

Program Provisions

Evaluation Procedures

Decision Making

Security Provisions

Continuity Considerations

Job Responsibilities

Personnel Policies

Fringe Benefits

Employee-Employer Relations

Staff Development

Working Conditions

Compensation

NEGOTIATIONS

FIGURE 7.3
Negotiating and Related Human Resources Activities

Figure 7.3 illustrates the influences and impacts of the negotiations process on the human resources function. An understanding of these relationships is essential for the effective functioning of the human resources program. For example, not only are working conditions a major negotiations consideration, but the definition of working conditions is also expanding in scope.

In the following sections, we discuss integrative bargaining and distributive bargaining in detail.

Collective Bargaining in Education

In an effort to reduce conflicts and reach more mutually satisfying solutions to problems, various integrative approaches to collective bargaining have been introduced into education. Integrative bargaining, win–win bargaining, collaborative bargaining, partnership bargaining, creative bargaining, and joint problem solving are all names for bargaining approaches designed to eliminate adversarial relationships and to serve both parties in achieving their bargaining objectives, while at the same time feeling good about the results. Of course, although each of the above-named integrative bargaining approaches is founded on win–win methods, strategies accompanying them do tend to differ. For example, *creative bargaining* features the ingenuity of the bargaining parties in searching for various alternatives to reach agreement. Thus the parties create new and different ways of approaching the manner in which negotiations is considered. Changes in contract provisions regarding the duration of contracts, percentages applied to fringe benefit payments by management, or a new focus on work benefits as opposed to salary increases are examples of creative approaches. In contrast, *partnership bargaining* strives to develop a basic understanding on the

FIGURE 7.4

PRAM Model

Source: *The Win-Win Negotiator*
(p. 84) by R. R. Reck and B. G.
Long, 1987, Kalamazoo, MI:
Spartan. Copyright © 1987 by
Spartan Publications. Reprinted
by permission.

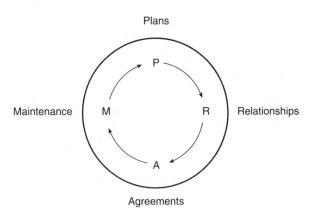

part of both parties of the economics of the organization in relation to economic conditions generally. The central focus is that of mutual cooperation that features joint programs that favor employee needs and organizational goals. However, although integrative bargaining has been in use in education for a number of years, its use has not become widespread. It is estimated that only 3,500 school districts use some form of integrative bargaining, a small percentage of all districts nationally. And in many instances when the negotiations process "gets tough," empirical evidence suggests that the bargaining parties often resort to distributive methods.

One operational model for integrative bargaining has been suggested by Reck and Long (1987). Their PRAM model for win–win negotiations is presented in Figure 7.4. The PRAM model begins with *establishing win–win plans*. In this step, parties agree on their own goals, anticipate the goals of the other party, determine probable areas of agreement, and develop win–win solutions to reconcile areas of probable disagreement. Most authorities emphasize the need for common interests and shared goals for successful integrative bargaining. Skopec and Kiely (1994) support this contention and point out that exploring the interests of both parties often consumes a considerable amount of time, but cautioned that this step is essential before attempting to develop specific proposals.

Step 2 of the model focuses on *developing win–win relationships*. Activities are planned that allow a positive personal relationship to develop; a sense of mutual trust is cultivated and the relationship is allowed to develop fully before business is discussed in earnest. Cooperation is emphasized over conflict. Building a positive relationship is essential for win–win bargaining; it provides a climate of trust in which the two parties more willingly share information and ideas. Economy (1994) used the term *agree to agree* as a primary attitude in achieving the goals of step 2. He suggested that such an attitude is most achievable when each party (1) recognizes and agrees to mutual objectives, (2) identifies and attacks key obstacles to agreement, (3) uses momentum to get through areas of disagreement, and (4) emphasizes the need for cooperative discussion. Pruitt (1981) suggested that information exchange and subsequent insight lead to win–win agreements only when a real sense of mutual trust exists, when each party believes that the other is truly concerned with its needs. Studies tend to support the contention that parties that agree to trust each other exchange more information than those that remain motivated solely by self-interest (Kimmel, Pruitt, Magenau, Konar-Goldband, & Carnevale, 1980; Pruitt, 1981; Tutzauer & Roloff, 1988).

In step 3, *the win–win agreement is formed*. The other party's goals are confirmed, areas of agreement are identified, proposals are considered for win–win solutions to the areas of agreement, and the remaining differences are jointly resolved. Skopec and Kiely (1994) suggested that proposals that evolve at this stage are likely to differ from the initial parties' statements. It is essential that proposals address the underlying interests of the two parties and that they be clearly written and easily understood. The bargaining parties meet over extended time periods to discuss and select those agreements that will be included in the contract. In some cases, subcommittees, representative of the two parties, are selected to develop specific proposals for later examination, revision, and approval of the two teams. Intensive discussion is devoted to issues on which agreement has not been reached. In some cases, a neutral facilitator is included in the discussions for the purposes of keeping discussion moving in a positive direction and pointing out areas in which the parties have similar views.

Economy (1994) recommended that often it is best to "wrap it up." He cautioned against the use of pressure to finish the bargaining; rather, each area of agreement should be emphasized and the remaining areas of disagreement downplayed. However, he noted that the "real art of negotiation is in turning disagreement into agreement" (p. 132).

Recommended procedures for resolving areas of disagreement are (1) to identify the roots of disagreement and be prepared to discuss them further; (2) to rank the areas of disagreement in their order of importance and title them as primary, secondary, or inconsequential; (3) to determine the value of each issue relative to all other issues; (4) to resolve the disagreements by the give-and-take process; to be a winner make the other party a winner too; (5) to brainstorm alternatives for resolution and find alternatives that are acceptable to both parties; and (6) to give yourself and the other party time to work through an agreement; don't be pushed into an agreement that isn't acceptable to you or your counterpart.

Step 4 of the PRAM model *addresses maintenance of the win–win agreement*. Following the agreement and ratification of the written master contract, both parties assume a responsibility for providing feedback to others concerning agreement performance, and each party works toward keeping the agreement in force. Party contracts are maintained and mutual trust is reaffirmed.

Integrative strategies such as win–win bargaining can easily result in win–lose or lose–lose negotiations when there is only the appearance of mutual goal interest, compromises, and general sincerity relative to the procedural requirements of successful win–win bargaining. In such cases, bargaining sessions tend to disintegrate as one party or the other soon recognizes that the pretense of cooperation is meant only to disguise the tactics of an adversarial mind-set (Economy, 1994). Although win–win bargaining models certainly can result in one party gaining more of its goals than the other party, when approached in good faith, neither party is denied some positive benefits from the activity (Edson, 2000).

Persons who have experienced win–win bargaining methods commonly note the following occurrences or results:

1. Integrative bargaining often results in a widening of the scope of the negotiations agenda. In some cases, the bargaining sessions become a forum for the discussion of a broad spectrum of concerns of the school district (e.g., student discipline, curriculum, educational reform, and decision making).
2. Integrative bargaining tends to change the decision-making model within the district itself. That is, integrative bargaining fosters collaboration in the decision-making process. Site-based decision making, in turn, promotes collaborative bargaining.
3. Individuals who have previously served as negotiators in distributive or traditional bargaining may not be able to serve effectively in integrative processes. Integrative strategies depend greatly on the personalities of the persons involved; the openness of the process and the attitude of power-with versus power-over necessitate somewhat different personality characteristics than are useful in distributive approaches.
4. In school districts in which win–win bargaining approaches reportedly have been successful, morale, relationships, and trust have improved, while problems have decreased. However, positive happenings appear to be closely related to the personalities involved in the specific setting, rather than to the process itself. This consideration also supports the contention that negotiators experienced in distributive procedures may not be as successful in integrative approaches.

Distributive Bargaining in Education

Quasi-distributive bargaining is based on a quid pro quo, give-and-take approach in which the utilization of power and bargaining strategy plays a major role. The general operations model for quasi-distributive bargaining, the model most frequently used in education, includes five major components.

1. Planning and preparation for collective bargaining
2. Determination and recognition of the bargaining unit
3. Determination of the composition of the bargaining team, including the chief spokesperson
4. Determination of the initial bargaining procedures and appropriate table strategies
5. Implementation of the contract agreement

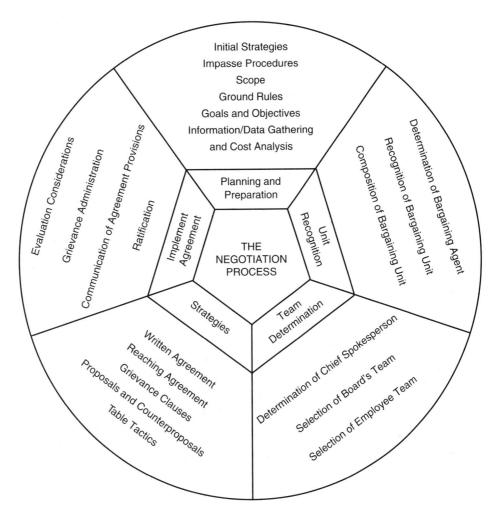

FIGURE 7.5
Negotiation Preparation Activities

Figure 7.5 illustrates the various activities related to each of these areas, which are discussed in the following sections.

PLANNING AND PREPARATION FOR COLLECTIVE NEGOTIATIONS

Authorities generally agree that the most important consideration for successful bargaining is careful planning, including the development of clear goals. Planning and preparation for collective negotiations include the following specific activities: (1) gathering the related information and data needed for decision making and cost analysis, (2) determining goals and objectives for negotiations, (3) establishing ground rules for conducting negotiations, (4) determining the scope of the negotiations, and (5) clarifying procedures in case of impasse.

Gathering Related Information for Decision Making and Cost Analysis

At the outset of the planning and preparation activities, communication with local implementors of the current contract agreement must be established. The school board bargaining team must gather and analyze all information that identifies problems related to the current agreement and the issues that most likely will, or should, be given serious attention in future bargaining sessions.

Several information sources should be utilized in preparing for bargaining, including (1) information from the school district administrative staff about its concerns and needs; (2) troublesome areas in the present contract agreement; (3) publications, reports, press releases, and public statements by the respective professional groups; (4) information concerning the agendas for bargaining and troublesome areas in bargaining in other school districts; (5) data relating to budgets and the financial plans of the school district; (6) input from the school district's various constituencies concerning attitudes and opinions on employer–employee matters; and (7) information on the results of arbitration and/or court actions under present contracts in other school districts.

Once gathered, information must be analyzed in terms of related problems and their potential significance in the bargaining process. Possible impact on the school program, employer–employee relationships, budgets, and the school district's goals must be evaluated. Cost factors must include data relative to salaries, fringe benefits, program expenditures, human resources needs, administrative expenses, and other dimensions. Such information must not only be organized and properly recorded, but also must be easily retrievable for use during the planning and preparation phases of bargaining, as well as during table negotiations. Thus some form of a negotiations "bargaining book" should be organized whereby information is organized by topic and labeled for convenient referencing and updating.

The importance of costing out contract agreements is emphasized in the following statement:

> The process of costing out the current labor agreement is one of the most important, albeit arduous, tasks that a school district entering negotiations must face. Prior to at-the-table negotiations, it is essential to examine each cost item as part of a total package and know what each item is worth to employees and how much it costs the board. This knowledge will enable management to make decisions at the table that are based on facts rather than "guesstimates." Once current anticipated costs are determined, union demands can be analyzed and costed to ensure that what is said at the bargaining table by management is accurate. (Wary, 1983, p. 1)

As stated by Rojot (1991), "It should be apparent that planning is essential to negotiations, but in practice it is very often neglected, generally with very unfortunate results . . . there is almost no doubt that a well-prepared negotiator has a definite edge over his opponents" (p. 176).

Determining Goals and Objectives for Collective Bargaining

An essential activity in planning and preparing for bargaining is the establishment of goals and objectives that serve as the foundation for all bargaining activities and provide the necessary guidelines for the entire process. The school board team must understand the bargaining objectives of the school board and the level of importance of each item to be considered.

Anticipating the requests of employee groups is another important consideration. Once identified, the board team must determine the probable level of importance to the employee group. Although this determination is difficult, clues to the importance of employee requests often are provided in such information as employee grievances during the year, the substance of conferences and journals of state and national employee groups, and the negotiation requests by school districts that already are in the process of being settled or that have been settled for the ensuing year.

Consideration of the school board's objectives and a careful anticipation of the objectives of the employee group allow the board team to be proactive, rather than merely reactive, at the table. Such knowledge is essential in determining what the team wants to accomplish in the negotiations and what strategies best serve these purposes. Attempting to gather this information during table negotiations handicaps the team and severely inhibits its ability to react intelligently to requests or to question adequately the information provided by the other party.

A team's objectives should be ranked in some manner, perhaps as primary, secondary, or tertiary priorities. Such a ranking of objectives clarifies the expectations of the team and plays an important role in determining tactics and strategies during ongoing bargaining sessions.

Establishing Ground Rules for Conducting Collective Bargaining

Ground rules consist of the statements and agreements that govern the bargaining activities. Such rules encompass the establishment of the authority of the groups' representatives, time and place of meetings, length of table sessions, procedures for handling the agenda items, use of outside consultants, use of meeting minutes, use of open or closed meetings, quorum rules, use of a spokesperson, procedural rules, use of caucuses, use of press releases, ratification procedures, impasse provisions, a time line for bargaining activities, and related guidelines.

Ground rules can be an unnecessary addendum to bargaining activities if they become dominant over primary issues of the negotiations and can inhibit later table bargaining processes if they cause major disputes. Because of the negative effects of ground rules, their use has decreased. As team members become more sophisticated in the process of bargaining and if prior relationships have established mutual trust, ground rules become less important to the process.

Nevertheless, when ground rules are used, the representative teams must agree on answers to such questions as the following:

Authority of Team Representatives

1. Can representatives sign agreements?
2. Are spokespersons serving as authoritative representatives of the respective groups?
3. When a tentative agreement is reached, will representatives work diligently within their own groups for its ratification?

Time and Place of Meetings

1. When and where will table sessions be held? During school hours? Weekends? Holidays? After school hours?
2. What will be the length of each session? Can this time be extended by mutual agreement?
3. If teams agree to meet during school hours, who pays for substitutes, if needed?

Agenda for Meetings

1. Is the agenda to be set in advance? Can new items be added? How is the agenda to be handled?
2. What if teams cannot agree on the agenda for the next meeting? Who determines the agenda?

Team Members

1. How many team members can represent a group? Must representatives be members of the school district? Can a professional negotiator from the outside be utilized?
2. What are the expected roles of team members? Will there be a chief spokesperson for each team?
3. Can parties bring in outside consultants to report or to testify? Can members of the employer and employee units attend the table sessions?
4. Can a consultant take over the spokesperson's role?

Meetings and Meeting Records

1. How are the meeting events to be recorded? Can either party use a stenographer? Can sessions be taped or videotaped? Who is to keep any records completed for the meetings?
2. Are meetings to be open or closed? If open, what kind of a group can teams bring to the meetings? Are the media to be invited? If the public is invited, what constitutes the public? Can an invited public person speak?

3. How are press releases to be handled?
4. What constitutes a quorum? Are Robert's rules or a similar procedure to be utilized?

Procedural Considerations

1. During the table discussions, can either party break at any time for a caucus?
2. What constitutes agreement on a specific item? On the total contract package?
3. How will the tentative agreement be ratified by both parties? How many days after the talks end must ratification be accomplished?
4. In case one or both parties fail to gain ratification, what are the time limits for renegotiations?
5. In case of impasse, who pays for mediation or fact finding?
6. When will an impasse be declared? What constitutes an impasse date?
7. What happens if the teams reach impasse during renegotiations? Are mediation procedures reinstated? Is arbitration to be used? Is a strike to be held if not prohibited by law?
8. In what order will issues be addressed (e.g., language issues, economic issues, and noneconomic issues)?

Even though ground rules are determined before the primary issues to be considered at the table, the answers to these questions do not necessarily come easily. It is not the intent here to discuss strategy positions appropriate for each question posed; however, it is important that both parties study the implications of various answers that might be determined.

Determining the Scope of Collective Bargaining

Although the **scope of bargaining** varies among the states and frequently is determined by statute or court decisions, in addition to salary and benefits, such matters as class size, the school calendar, jury duty, probationary period, performance evaluations, overtime pay, use of school mail, use of bulletin boards, school library hours, grading frequency, teacher aides, substitutes, security, amounts of work, voluntary payroll deductions, leaves of absence for union activities, classroom management, use of school facilities for union meetings, number of holidays, and many other conditions of work are negotiated in many states. Items considered as nonnegotiable in most states include the number of days or total hours of school, nondiscrimination, special education placement procedures, First Amendment issues, federal programs, teacher discipline if a constitutional issue, and student discipline if a constitutional issue (Thompson, Wood, & Honeyman, 1994).

State laws concerning the scope of collective bargaining vary widely. In the absence of legal guidelines, precedence is most likely to determine what is negotiable. The obvious position of representatives of employee groups is that no limits should be placed on the items that are negotiable; every matter has some influence on conditions of employment. Board of education representatives, on the other hand, argue that the public interest must be protected, and bargaining must not interfere with the board's right and responsibility to govern the school district. Consider such ground rule statements as the following: "Negotiations will encompass all educational matters of mutual concern"; "Negotiations shall encompass all matters pertaining to employment and the fulfillment of professional duties"; and "Negotiations will be determined by those matters presented to the board by the employee association." Clearly, these statements favor a broad scope for negotiations. Few matters in education, if any, would not be of some mutual concern or have some relation to employment, for example.

Preparation for collective bargaining, then, requires a careful examination of (1) existing statutes, court rulings, and legal opinions concerning the inclusions and limitations of bargaining items, (2) previously drafted preliminary statements of agreement, and (3) the role of various public groups in influencing the scope of collective bargaining and the procedures utilized for keeping such groups informed.

Clarifying Procedures in Case of Impasse

School boards and employee groups must determine well in advance of table discussions how an eventual impasse will be resolved. An impasse constitutes a difference or disagreement between the negotiating parties that has reached an unresolvable stage and brings a halt to table discussions.

Collective bargaining legislation, where enacted by the state, generally sets forth the specific means for resolving any impasse. With proper advanced planning and discussion, the parties involved are better able to design impasse procedures of a less disruptive, less traumatic nature than certain last-resort alternatives.

Procedures for resolving impasse in collective bargaining include mediation, fact finding and advisory arbitration, voluntary binding arbitration, compulsory binding arbitration, last-best-offer arbitration, and strikes. Whereas some of these procedures are similar, certain important differences can be identified. Advantages and disadvantages are associated with each procedure.

Mediation. Mediation is the most commonly used procedure for resolving impasses. An **impasse** occurs when the two parties become steadfast in their bargaining positions on one or more agenda items and a stalemate takes place. In **mediation,** a jointly appointed neutral third party serves as advisor and counselor for both parties. "The function of a mediator is to conciliate, counsel, persuade, dissuade, and assist the negotiating parties in any legitimate way so that are able to reach an agreement. The function of the mediator is not to judge, decide, or arbitrate disagreements between the two sides" (Loughran, 1992, pp. 372–373). The seeking of an agreement on the part of the two parties is the sole objective of the mediator. By conferring independently with representatives of the employer and employee groups, the mediator seeks to determine the reasons for the disagreement, the issues that surround it, and, to the extent possible, what constitutes acceptability on the part of each group. Through a process of interpretation and advisement, the mediator's objective is to bring the representatives back to the table to settle the issue at hand. Specific recommendations and alternatives most often are provided by the mediator, but are not binding on either group.

Some authorities believe that mediation is assuming a larger role in the resolution of disputes than the more traditional methods of arbitration. Through mediation, the parties involved continue to retain control of the negotiations process in that they ultimately have the opportunity to determine a solution of their own making. In fact, some states have mandated mediation before complaintants go before the courts (Payne, Kohler, Cangemi, & Fuqua, Jr., 2000). Mediation almost always keeps both parties "talking," so it serves as a major strategy for successful bargaining. Mediation research has resulted in various findings of interest relative to the effective mediator. For example, effective mediators (1) spend more time discussing possible solutions and terms of final agreements than unsuccessful mediators (Payne et al., 2000), (2) referee the interaction, clarify party views through restatement, and solicit interpersonal feedback on the part of the parties involved (Walton, 1969), (3) focus on key issues, provide ample opportunities for each party to speak, point out possible solutions, and refrain from closing an argument personally (Greatbatch & Dingwall, 1997), and (4) establish certain rules regarding the decorum of party members relative to personal attacks and other courtesies relative to participative behavior (Donohue, Allen, & Burrell, 1988). Perhaps a primary disadvantage of mediation is the extreme difficulty of the procedure itself. Because the impasse centers on complex issues and problems, mediation activities demand exemplary personal competence on the part of the mediator.

Fact-Finding and Advisory Arbitration. Fact-finding and advisory arbitration are usually considered synonymous, because almost identical procedures are generally involved in each. However, fact-finding is most often associated with impasses in table negotiations involving a future contract agreement, whereas advisory arbitration is generally associated with grievances and disputes under the present contract.

Fact-finding involves the selection of a neutral third party, who serves as an investigator in studying all the facts and circumstances that surround the impasse. As in mediation, fact-finding can proceed as a relationship between the fact finder and the parties in dispute on an independent basis; however, arrangements often are made for a hearing in which both groups of negotiators present their cases.

In either the independent or formal hearing approach, the fact finder prepares a report of the facts and recommendations for action based on the impartial findings. The representatives of each group study the findings and recommendations and respond with their acceptance or rejection. The fact finder's recommendations are advisory only.

Voluntary Binding and Compulsory Arbitration. **Voluntary binding and compulsory arbitration** are procedures for resolving disagreements through the use of a neutral third party, whose decision is mandated for both parties. In the absence of state law specifying compulsory binding arbitration, voluntary binding arbitration may be agreed on by the disputing parties. Specific procedures, including the arrangement for paying the costs of arbitration, most often are set forth in the master agreement. Empirical evidence suggests that, on average, an arbitrator spends one day in preparation and two days in "hearings." Charges for arbitrator services vary greatly; a range of $1,000 to $3,000 per day is not unusual. Most commonly, costs are equally shared between the school district and the employee association. However, a procedure whereby the school district pays if it loses the grievance case and the grievant pays if the association loses the case also is used. The third party might be an individual, a group of individuals, or a panel board (e.g., board of industrial relations). Following an in-depth study of the issue and all relative information, the arbitrator or panel renders a decision that is final and binding.

The major advantage of compulsory arbitration is its potential to avoid more disruptive events, such as a strike. The fact that compulsory arbitration places the settlement outside the jurisdiction of the bargaining parties, especially the governing board of education, is considered a disadvantage by many persons. Yet the removal of the two parties from the personally traumatic experiences of face-to-face table disputes and further professional alienation is an advantage in the minds of others.

Last-Best-Offer Arbitration. In **last-best-offer arbitration,** a neutral third party is called on to study the last best offers stated by each of the two parties in the table negotiations. Rather than reach a decision based on a "down-the-middle" compromise, the arbitrator reviews each last offer in view of the facts (e.g., salary trends, agreements settled in competitive school districts, ability to pay, and supply and demand). In the final analysis, one of the two last best offers is recommended and considered binding on both parties.

An advantage of this procedure centers on the possible results of the competitive atmosphere that it fosters. That is, because each party attempts to present a reasonable, well-intentioned best offer that might be most favorably viewed by an arbitrator, the result likely could be an agreement at the table itself. The need for arbitration is then obviated. Last-best-offer arbitration has been utilized extensively in baseball for resolving salary disputes. The primary areas of application are situations in which strikes cannot be tolerated by the public or those involving such problems as inordinate economic loss, danger to public health, or danger to personal safety.

Critics of the procedure point out that, because only one group's offer can be recommended, the other group must live with an "unfair" decision. The effects on morale due to the use of last-best-offer arbitration could be negative.

Strikes. Strikes are actions that result in stoppage of work and services rendered by an employee group. As would be expected, the National School Boards Association (NSBA) supports state legislation that makes strikes against public schools illegal and provides for mandatory penalties (National School Boards Association, 1991), whereas the NEA believes that the right to strike must be an integral part of any collective bargaining process (NEA, 1991). The American Association of School Administrators (AASA) historically has opposed strikes and has emphasized the basic responsibility of school administrators to keep the schools open during a strike, with protective measures for both students and those persons who report to work. The American Association of School Personnel Administrators (AASPA) several years ago set forth its views concerning school strikes. First, the association proposed that, if there was a strike, retroactive contract settlements should be prohibited. Second, a secret ballot of all members of the bargaining unit should be taken prior to any strike to accept or reject the school board negotiations team's last offer on the various issues. If approved, the contract is considered binding; if rejected, the alternatives of a strike or further negotiations are in order. Third, the AASPA recommended the implementation of a procedure for governing strikes, including a cooling-off period. Before any strike, a fact finder would be selected to study all issues and attempt to alleviate the dispute (American Association of School Personnel Administrators, 1978).

From the school board's point of view, planning for a possible strike must be part of the preparation for collective bargaining. Essential activities included in such preparation are the following:

1. Well in advance of table negotiations or any indication of a possible strike, a comprehensive plan must be developed to retain the services necessary to operate the schools and to resolve the strike issues as expeditiously as possible.
2. An effective means must be established for communicating important information to both internal and external groups. Alternative communication methods and means of contact must also be identified in anticipation of an interruption of the usual communication channels.
3. A central office or unit should be organized to serve as the coordination and control center for information gathering, decision making, and implementation procedures. Key personnel who will serve in the central office must be identified in advance and their roles clearly delineated.
4. Resource pools of personnel who can keep the schools open and operating should be identified. This consideration includes the identification of employees who likely would cross picket lines and others who would be employable on a temporary basis.
5. Information concerning the legality of strike activities must be gathered, studied, and distributed appropriately. Legal information concerning strike activities in the state, restrictions of law, penalties, legal implications, restraining orders, the job status of strikers, and so forth, must be clarified. Legal alternatives available for board action must be investigated.

6. Building administrators and supervisors should develop local plans for dealing with the strike situation. Responsibilities must be clarified and program alternatives that meet instructional goals should be identified. Guidelines for establishing the safety and welfare of students and other personnel must be stated and understood.

7. Local security personnel must be kept well informed of the ongoing conditions and potential problems that might occur. A straightforward approach with the media concerning developments and issues has proved to be the best policy.

8. Procedures must be determined for establishing meaningful communication with the employee group representatives. Serious efforts to keep talking in relation to the issues in dispute must be made. A well-organized, creative means for fostering ongoing internal discussions of the issues must be established in advance. Such communication must be positive and focus on a sincere attitude of resolution and possible agreement.

Teachers' groups nationally have used various means to protest salary, working conditions, and other issues. For example, besides lengthy strikes, teachers nationally have staged three-day walkouts, have had one-day "blue-outs" in which all teachers call in sick, have stacked contracts without signatures, have sponsored television commercials that portray their views of the state of education, have had work slowdowns, and have used other strategies to gain public support in order to prompt positive action from state legislators and to pressure school boards. As is basically the case with teacher strikes, the foregoing actions are designed to achieve various purposes. Their primary purpose, however, is to gain an advantage in the bargaining process by having the other party change its present position on a bargaining issue or issues.

DETERMINATION AND RECOGNITION OF THE BARGAINING UNIT

Before collective bargaining at the table can be initiated, the employee groups to be included in the bargaining unit and their official memberships must be determined. A school district consists of several different employee groups and clusters of employees within those groups. For example, teachers, librarians, nurses, counselors, and psychologists are among the professional staff personnel. Support staff personnel such as clerks, secretaries, maintenance workers, transportation staff, custodians, and food service workers represent employee groups and clusters. To which bargaining unit each of these employee groups belongs is of paramount importance for purpose of negotiations. A **bargaining unit** is a group of employees certified as the appropriate unit for collective negotiations. This unit is the one to which the negotiated contractual agreements will apply. It is not unusual for a school district to have several bargaining units, although a common practice is that one unit represents the combination of teaching and nonadministrative professional personnel. Bargaining indeed is *collective* in that various groups and clusters are being represented as one group in the process.

Procedures to determine the bargaining unit often are established by statute. In the absence of statute, the procedures for deciding which employees to include in the bargaining unit most often are determined mutually by the school board and employee groups.

Loughran (1992) points out that thousands of cases regarding the "appropriate bargaining unit" have been the subject of National Labor Relations Board and court decisions. He concludes that it is generally sufficient to conclude that the appropriate unit for bargaining purposes meets at least one of the following criteria:

1. The unit is the one certified by the National Labor Relations Board.
2. The unit is the one that the employer and union have historically recognized.
3. The unit is the one that the employer and union agree to recognize as the appropriate bargaining unit. (p. 14)

Two criteria serve important roles in determining which employees will belong to a particular unit: *community of interest* (Lieberman & Moskow, 1966) and *fragmentation* (Walter, 1975). Employees who share common employment interests and concerns, who desire to be in the same bargaining unit, and who receive similar compensation and have similar working conditions represent examples of a community of interest. It is obvious that the larger the unit, the more difficult it is to establish a community of interest. Yet small bargaining units present problems for both employees and employers. From the employees' viewpoint, very small units are far less likely to carry the bargaining strength of units with larger representation. Consider, for example, a school district with several elementary, middle, and high schools. If the schools in the district were composed of members with dissimilar interests, negotiations would be further complicated. The task for employer groups, then, is to establish bargaining units based on the community of interest principle and, at the same time, to attempt to avoid "fragmentation of their workforce into many separate bargaining units . . . since it requires the employer to bargain many times, generally over the same questions, but with different groups of employees" (Walter, 1975, p. 25).

In actual practice, unit determination is decided generally by (1) state statutes and law, (2) agreements reached by the school board and the various employee groups, (3) an external agency such as a labor relations board or other outside authority, or (4) the unilateral decision of the school board.

Bargaining Agent

The **bargaining agent** is the employee organization designated as the official representative of all employees in the bargaining unit. Two types of recognition are generally found in education: exclusive representation and multiple representation.

Exclusive representation is the certification of one particular employee organization to represent all employees in the unit. The general procedures for determining exclusive recognition include (1) the request by an employee organization to be the bargaining agent for all employees in the bargaining unit, (2) an election or other means of determining majority preference, (3) results of an election in which at least 51% vote yes, and (4) certification by the school board that the organization has exclusive bargaining rights.

One nonvoting method of determining the bargaining agent is that of recognizing the organization that, for the last 2 or 3 years, has enrolled a majority of the school employees as members.

Strahan's (1969) early descriptions of *multiple representation* are still appropriate today. It assumes one of the following forms:

1. Completely separate negotiations with each organization represented.
2. Joint negotiating committee with proportional representation based on the size of membership in the organization.
3. Joint negotiating committee with equal representation of the recognized organizations in the school.

Exclusive recognition is most widely used in education for the following reasons: (1) it is supported by both the NEA and AFT, (2) it is mandated for the public sector in many states and is the form of recognition most generally accepted when statutes do not specify what form of recognition is to be given, and (3) private business and industry serve as examples that exclusive recognition is most effective (Rebore, 2001, p. 298).

DETERMINATION OF THE COMPOSITION OF THE NEGOTIATIONS TEAM, INCLUDING THE CHIEF SPOKESPERSON

The selection of the bargaining team is a critical decision for successful negotiations. Each party must have individuals at the table who can answer the questions that will arise and who can complete the process effectively. The size of the team will vary and depends considerably on the size of the school system and the representations needed. Experience in the collective bargaining process appears to be an important criterion for team member selection. For example, experienced team members tend to spend much less time on such matters as ground rules and, as Montgomery and Benedict (1989) point out, "research reveals that a strike is more likely with new negotiators. Experienced negotiators are more able to accurately assess their opponent's position and concession curves" (p. 380). This contention ties closely to Edson's belief (2000) that the biggest mistake inexperienced negotiator's make is not listening; they often are good at talking, but lack listening skills. And, some research reveals that men and women tend to perceive conflict differently. According to the research of Pinkley (1990), men are more concerned with winning or maximizing outcomes. Women tend to be more concerned with maintaining a positive relationship with their adversary. Each of the foregoing contentions holds implications for team selection in respect to the bargaining situation at hand and the proposed bargaining strategies desired.

Mnookin (2000) points out three significant myths that surround the collective bargaining process as follows:

Myth 1. There is no relevant theory in regard to negotiations. In fact, the core idea relative to collective bargaining involves the opportunity "to expand the pie"; that is, the process has the potential to make both parties better off.

Myth 2. Negotiations can't be taught.

Myth 3. People improve their negotiation skills only through experience. In fact, negotiation skills definitely can be taught. Although people do develop habits during negotiations that sometimes serve them well, when they don't they have no idea why not. Thus persons that serve on collective bargaining teams should be well prepared to do so as evidenced by appropriate participation in related negotiations courses and workshops along with extensive reading and observation activities concerning the negotiations process.

The following criteria help to determine the selection of individuals for the bargaining team:

1. *Time.* Do the individual's schedule and responsibilities allow the time required to serve on the team?
2. *Temperament.* Does the individual have the emotional stability and personal poise necessary for serving on the team?
3. *Tenacity.* Will the individual "stay with it" and work through the complex and tenuous process?
4. *Technical know-how.* Does the individual have the necessary understanding of the process of bargaining and knowledge of the content information required in the collective negotiations?
5. *Talent.* Does the individual have the talent for participating in the art of collective bargaining?

The inclusion of school board members, the school superintendent, the human resources director, the board attorney, or an outside professional negotiator on the board of education's team will depend largely on the unique characteristics within each school district. The advantages and disadvantages in using each of these persons are summarized in Table 7.1.

Research has not determined if team size affects successful negotiations. Multiple representation usually requires larger team numbers. According to Lieberman (1969),

there is no magic in any particular figure. An appropriate number will be a compromise between several factors (i.e., smaller team facilitates ease of agreement due to factors of time and informality; need for more than one member to avoid serious mistakes and misunderstandings). (p. 30)

The size recommendations that do exist most often specify from three to five members. Some individuals view a five-member team as ideal, because

TABLE 7.1
Advantages and Disadvantages of Including Certain Individuals on the Board of Education's Negotiations Team

Position	Advantages	Disadvantages
School board member(s)	Participation can gain the confidence of the total board that their real interests are being protected; could facilitate acceptance of "final package." Participation may help the board understand the nature of the process and its complexity. Could provide a psychological advantage to the board's team. May have more time than other school district personnel who might represent the board's team.	Board members on the team are viewed as members of the board, rather than as members of the negotiating team; may tend to speak for the board instead of participating in the negotiations. May inhibit the effectiveness of the team's chief spokesperson; employee team tends to look to the board member as confirming the power of acceptance or nonacceptance. May not be skilled in the art of negotiation. Conditions surrounding the negotiations process may cause board members to lose objectivity; value of board member "as a board member" in evaluating, end product may be jeopardized; board members have to decide ultimately on ratification of the agreement.
Superintendent of schools	Most knowledgeable of the entire school system; expertise is invaluable at the negotiations table. School board generally views the superintendent as having the kinds of competence required for successful negotiations. Because of responsibilities, superintendent is in best position to view school system as a whole and to conceptualize both organizational objectives and human resource needs.	Time commitment required may interfere with other major responsibilities. Although generally accepted that superintendent represents management, involvement in negotiations can promote poor attitudes and adversary relationships with employees. Employee representatives tend to want responses of administrative authority rather than negotiation strategy responses. Membership tends to place the superintendent in untenable position—an equal at the table on one day and chief administrator of the district the next.
Human resources director	Likely to have best understanding of employee relations in school district. Normally well trained and highly skilled in negotiations and school law.	Role as an adversary at table conflicts with responsibilities of personal counselor and enhancer of positive human relationships in office.

Role	Advantages	Disadvantages
	Has key information relative to primary agenda items in negotiations. Possesses experience and knowledge of human resource needs and their importance in fulfilling mission of the school district.	Time commitments detract from other major responsibilities. Although knowledgeable of employee relations and negotiations, might be utilized much more advantageously as primary resource and consultant to negotiation team.
School board attorney	Can provide important advice and counsel relative to statutes and court decisions that relate to negotiations process. Can help develop language of the contract agreement in order to obviate unclear statements and possible problems of legal interpretations due to poor contract language. Can provide legal advice in ongoing negotiations at time of deliberations, rather than after the fact.	May not be knowledgeable of school system and its internal problems and needs. Legal expertise does not automatically translate into expertise in negotiation. May prove costly both in time and money.
Outside professional	Often can save time by understanding importance and/or unimportance of activities. Generally brings high level of expertise in negotiations to table. Allows internal personnel to concentrate on other educational matters. Has strong incentive to be highly effective in order to serve again and to build the reputation needed for expanded employment contracts.	Professional fees costly. Usually unfamiliar with school district. Does not remain to help implement contract agreement or to face possible grievances. Problems can arise concerning payment arrangements; hourly contract arrangement with outside negotiator carries certain disadvantages, whereas set fee can pose problems of performance. In lengthy negotiations that encounter impasse or work stoppage, district encounters problem of paying outside negotiator for other services or being without counsel and advice.

it is large enough to provide for representative resource personnel and meets the need for different types of individuals with various competencies, yet it is not so large as to be unwieldy. Those who suggest that team size be limited to three members stress that this number facilitates the process and enables the teams to progress under less formal conditions. In addition, members can concentrate on assigned roles as spokesperson, recorder, and observer.

The *spokesperson* is the chief negotiator for the team and serves as team captain. In a study conducted in 2001, it was reported that the school superintendent served as the chief negotiator for the board's bargaining team in 56.8% of the participating school districts in the state. A professional negotiator or other school administrator served as chief spokesperson in 9.5% and 12.2% of the reporting districts, respectively (Norton, 2001). The role of the chief negotiator is central to the success of the collective bargaining process; this individual can greatly enhance or inhibit the realization of the bargaining team's goals (Kovach & Hamilton, 1997). The focus of unity for the team, the spokesperson generally serves as the single "voice" of the team's position.

The team *observer* listens and watches for clues and behaviors communicated by members of the other party. Verbal statements and body language are monitored for clues as to priority of issues, major concerns, closing arguments, and possible closure. The *recorder* maintains written information concerning strategy and positions, as well as the facts, decisions, and events surrounding each negotiations session.

Having both teams read and approve a set of comprehensive minutes following or before each table session is not recommended. Teams can encounter many disagreements and waste valuable time in attempting to establish the accuracy of the minutes of the session. In fact, the only essential notes are the tentatively signed agreements on agenda items reached during the process of negotiations. These tentative agreements, of course, are important and must be officially recorded and signed by each team before other agenda items are considered. Tentative agreements are subject to final approval of the total contract agreement. In short, the agreement as signed by the two representative teams is the test of what the two parties said.

INITIAL BARGAINING PROCEDURES AND APPROPRIATE TABLE STRATEGIES

The decision as to whether to use a distributive approach or integrative approach to bargaining depends on the situation at hand. Schoonmaker (1989) suggested that certain conditions warrant a distributive bargaining approach, whereas a joint problem-solving approach should be emphasized when other conditions are present. For example,

Emphasize distributive bargaining when:

☐ your interests clearly conflict
☐ you are much more powerful
☐ you do not need or want a long-term, harmonious relationship

☐　you do not trust the other party
☐　the agreement is easy to implement
☐　the other party is pure bargaining

Emphasize joint problem solving when:

☐　you have common interests
☐　you are weaker or power is approximately equal
☐　you need or want a continuing, harmonious relationship
☐　you trust the other party
☐　implementing the agreement may be difficult
☐　the other party is problem solving (pp. 12–13)

The *quasi-distributive strategy* of collective bargaining is based on the desire to avoid a test of power. The "game playing" that results from quasi-distributive strategy is characterized by

1. A series of specific demands and offers on a package of bargaining issues.
2. Deferral of formal commitments until they can be supported by reference to an impending test of power.
3. Controlled, distorted private communication designed to disguise true costs and goals and permit favorable trade-offs of concessions for demands.
4. Withholding of concessions on all major issues until the last possible moment when they can be used as the final "buy-out" to avoid the impending test of power. (Perry & Wilman, 1970, p. 63)

Once quasi-distributive bargaining has been initiated and negotiation items have been submitted by the employee group, good faith bargaining requires that the board of education team respond. A first response on any one item might *be we agree, we will consider it, we cannot agree,* or *that item is not negotiable,* accompanied by appropriate reasons. From this point, experienced negotiators concentrate on listening to the other team's responses to try to uncover key issues, major concerns, and position statements.

The goal of collective bargaining is not to win a debate, but rather to reach an agreement on the proposals. The tactics that serve best are the ones that include a possible response to a proposal or a solution to differences between the two parties. A reasonable proposal or counterproposal has the potential for resolving the issue or settling the existing differences. Timing is critical. The art of bargaining requires a sense of when the best offer should be tendered and when the closing question should be posed.

Kennedy, Benson, and McMillan (1982) discuss compromise toward the goal of reaching agreement in relation to team movement and "distance between the two parties." They illustrate the distance in terms of movement and suggest that each team has a limit and "break point." The range of settlement lies between a team's most favorable position (MFP) and that break point or limit (see Figure 7.6). The final position is defined by the relative strength of the parties and their negotiating skills. If the teams' limits do not overlap, reaching agreement is highly unlikely. If the first team's range overlaps the second team's MFP, the first team holds a decided advantage in the negotiations process.

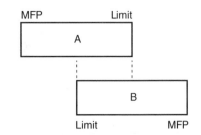

FIGURE 7.6
Range of Settlement
Source: *Managing Negotiations* by Gavin Kennedy,
John Benson, and John McMillan, 1982. Upper Saddle
River, NJ: Prentice Hall. Reprinted by permission of
the publisher.

Movement in negotiations infers flexibility; flexibility requires compromise. The Latin term quid pro quo means something for something or, in negotiation terminology, get something for something. In negotiations, each team moves closer to an agreement by giving something of value in return for receiving a desired goal. Thus both teams use the tactics involving submission of proposals and counterproposals in a give-and-take process to try to reach a tentative agreement.

Although there is no one best way to negotiate and bargaining is more art than science, empirical evidence suggests a number of guidelines for distributive bargaining that deserve consideration.

1. Always bargain from the viewpoint of the total contract amount. Never agree on economic items separately.
2. Do not submit a proposal or counterproposal and then attempt to retract it. Do not show your hand before you need to do so.
3. Be cautious about stating that your team is anxious to settle early. When this becomes known, then the "ransom" often goes higher.
4. Remember that collective bargaining is a process of compromise. Generally, it is not good in the long run to "win it all." Seasoned negotiators try to build long-term relationships that include mutual trust and respect. Any agreement must have mutuality of benefit. Do not bluff. A team must be prepared to carry out threats. Try to develop a high degree of credibility through a positive relationship.
5. In bargaining, say what you mean and mean what you say. Be certain that you write what you mean in any tentative or final agreement.
6. Do not present items for bargaining that are already within a group's jurisdiction (e.g., school board's legislative rights, administration's evaluation responsibilities, employees' academic freedom).
7. Team representatives negotiate with team representatives. The board of education, for example, should not take its case directly to the employee association.
8. Listen. A good negotiator spends the majority of time listening to the other team's responses, rationale, key issues, and major concerns. Responses such as "Tell me more," "I didn't know that," and "Why?" help the negotiator to learn more of the other team's position statements and closing arguments.

9. Use closed-ended questions to bring issues into focus. Keep dialogue going. When teams stop talking, bargaining breaks down. The sophisticated negotiator wants to reach an agreement.

10. Develop signaling techniques, such as cue cards, that serve your team (e.g., OBS, return to original bargaining statement; CQ, state the closing question). Verbal signaling, sending an intended message to the other team, is a necessary tactic as well. But be careful about body language. Hesitation in responding, for example, sends a message that you might accept the proposal.

11. Use reason rather than rhetoric to explain your stand. State your case and stay with the facts.

12. Realize that timing is a major aspect of bargaining. At the outset, very little is agreed to. In the course of bargaining, teams tell each other their priorities and what they want.

13. Use the term *we* for the team's position and never the personal *I* at the table. Team representatives do not have a position; they represent the larger group.

14. Personal poise and behavior are of major importance. Self-control is essential. Team members must be selected on the basis of their availability, temperament, tenacity, technical know-how, and talent.

IMPLEMENTATION OF THE CONTRACT AGREEMENT

The **contract, or master agreement,** is the ratified document that specifies the terms of the negotiated contract. Because the agreement is used by all parties to guide contractual employee relations, the contract language is of primary importance. Contract language represents the final product of the negotiations. It is what both parties must live with for the contract period. Carelessness in the use of words can lead to serious problems, including arbitration. The phrase "you get what you write" applies directly to the written agreement.

Consider each of the following contract statements:

Statement 1. Elementary teachers will be granted ten 30-minute breaks per week.

Statement 2. Regular teachers will be hired for summer school teaching on a first-preference basis.

Statement 3. This agreement becomes part of board policy, and board policy becomes part of the contract.

Statement 4. Employees have the right to file a grievance at any time, in case of violation of this agreement.

In statement 1, the definition of teacher needs clarification. How does the agreement apply to a half-time kindergarten teacher or to art or music specialists who come in for only 20 minutes per week in various classrooms?

Statement 2 tends to lock the school district into a summer school program. Also, how would the term first preference be applied? Is the contract agreement applicable to summer school as well? In the case of statement 3, board policy and contract agreements are two separate matters. Board policy can be changed unilaterally at any time. A contract agreement cannot be changed without mutual consent. Wording such as that in statement 3 tends to bind the board of education to no policy development without the approval of the employee group. In statement 4, a statute of limitations is needed. Such a limitation must stipulate the time period after the incident during which the grievance must be filed. With no such limitation, a grievance could be filed, withdrawn, and then refiled weeks, months, or even years later. In some cases, the language in benefits clauses in master contracts is so vague that it has resulted in losses by the school board at the arbitrator's table. Such losses can be extremely expensive for the school district (Colon, 1989).

Basic Content of the Written Agreement

Information included in the written agreement varies considerably in practice. However, most agreements include (1) a statement of recognition; (2) the nature of the agreement, its scope, time considerations, and communication channels; (3) the specific stipulations or articles of agreement; (4) mutual understandings concerning the agreement, including the responsibilities of both parties; and (5) grievance and impasse procedures.

The statement of recognition stipulates the one specific organization or arrangement for the bargaining representation of the defined employee unit. The section centered on the nature of the agreement includes the curtailment of any further negotiations until the approved agreement has elapsed and provisions for ongoing communication between the two parties. The specific agreement stipulations or articles include the agreements reached concerning compensation, employee benefits, and other conditions of employment. Included in the section concerned with mutual understandings and responsibilities are the obligations of both parties for implementation of the agreement, the responsibilities to administer professional working relationships and thus to provide high-quality education, and in some cases a statement concerning strikes. Grievance and impasse procedures are significant considerations of any written agreement as well.

Grievances

A **grievance** is a problem or complaint related to the contract agreement. It represents a violation, or purported violation, of the agreement, which must be settled through the grievance procedures set forth in the contract agreement. A grievance starts as an expression of dissatisfaction on the part of an individual or group of employees relative to the implementation or lack of implementation of a provision of the approved negotiated agreement. A significant difference exists between a general complaint by an employee on a matter of school policy and a grievance based on an alleged violation of the negotiation agreement. Whereas both kinds of employee problems are important for effective human resources practices, the grievances discussed here focus on arbitrable disagreements related specifically to the negotiated agreement. The grievance procedure is essentially a part of the ongoing collective bargaining process. Even though the written bargaining agreement should stipulate no further bargaining until the current contract expires (referred to as the *zipper clause*), the use of the grievance is one way in which the negotiations process continues. Thus designing grievance procedures that define time limitations, preliminary steps, and procedures is of crucial importance.

The grievance procedure has been described "as a means of allowing an employee to express a complaint to management without fear of reprisal and to have that complaint addressed by successively higher levels of management until an answer is provided that the grievant can or must accept" (McCollum & Norris, 1984, p. 106). In many cases, procedures for grievances are stipulated in law. The following grievance procedures are generally applicable: (1) A written grievance is filed that includes a description of the basis for the grievance; a statement of any prior informal steps taken to attempt to resolve the issue; a statement of reasons as to why the alleged actions were unfair, arbitrary, or contrary to contract provisions; and actions that the aggrieved employee believes necessary to resolve the issue. (2) The immediate supervisor prepares a written statement concerning the grounds of the grievance and recommended solutions as appropriate to the case. (3) If not resolved, the next higher level of authority (e.g., human resources director, superintendent, or other appropriate staff member) conducts a further investigation and renders a decision with a recommended solution. (4) If not resolved in the foregoing investigation, a review board or the board of education considers the case. The recommendation by the review board is considered final. If not accepted by the grievant, arbitration by a third party or litigation is a possible alternative (see Figure 7.7).

Contemporary grievance procedures tend to eliminate the board of education as a final review body. This is being done because the school board represents one of the contract parties and because this arrangement tends to place the board in the sensitive position of overruling the administration. The foregoing grievance model attempts to retain the solution of grievances within the internal jurisdiction of the school district. However, the use of advisory or binding arbitration by external individuals is also a common procedure for settling disputes. Such arbitration normally depends on existing law. In the absence of statute, arbitration procedures are subject to mutual agreement by both parties.

A grievance procedure should provide for due process and ensure that legitimate grievances and problems are heard, reviewed, and resolved. A properly designed procedure helps to place problems and complaints in the proper channels of supervisory relationships for possible solution at the most appropriate level of administration. Such procedures provide

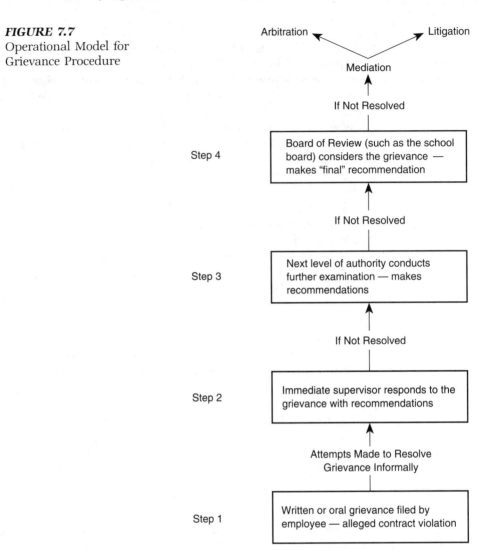

FIGURE 7.7
Operational Model for
Grievance Procedure

employees with a fair consideration of grievances without reprisal and also safeguard the rights of supervisory personnel.

IMPACT OF COLLECTIVE BARGAINING ON EDUCATION

The effects of collective bargaining on education have been the subject of much discussion and research. And, although the bargaining process is present in virtually every human resources process, the key question is its impact on employee compensation levels and conditions of work. Somewhat surprising are the findings of several research studies that collective bargaining has little or no effect on compensation levels in education, and, in fact, some studies indicate that school districts that do not negotiate have as good or better records of salary increases. Other studies, however, have disagreed with these findings. The research that attempts to isolate the effects of collective bargaining on competition levels is confounded by the difficulty of controlling for the many variables that influence the determination of salary levels. For example, the influence of bargaining districts on nonbargaining districts, sometimes termed *spillover*, is virtually impossible to measure. It should be noted that the majority of the research related to the impact of collective bargaining in education was conducted in the 1970s and early 1980s. A brief summary of the more noted impact studies follows:

1970   (Perry, C. R., & Wilman, A. W.). Their investigation of 24 school districts from New York to California found that negotiations had resulted in (1) an increase in the absolute and relative size of the total amount of resources allocated to teacher compensation within the district budget, and (2) an increase in the absolute and relative size of yearly service increments and differentials for academic training beyond the B.A. degree.

1970   (Kasper, H.). Study concluded that there is no statistically significant positive effect of teacher negotiations on salaries, once other variables such as income and urbanization are taken into account.

1973   (Hall, C. W., & Carroll, N. E.). Studied over 100 elementary school districts in Cook County, Illinois, involved in negotiations. Salary increases in the schools investigated averaged $165 per year and the study noted that teacher bargaining is associated with larger student–teacher ratios.

1974   (Balfour, G. A.). Studied New York school districts and concluded that the presence of substantive bargaining procedures, any type of union recognition, or teacher union membership had no significant positive effect on teachers' salaries or rate of change.

1975   (Moore, G. A.). Studied 181 K–12 school districts in Nebraska. Study revealed that negotiating districts paid salaries that averaged $609 higher than nonnegotiating districts.

1977   (Zuelke, D. C., & Frohreich, L. E.). Collected data from 50 randomly selected small- and medium-sized school districts in Wisconsin. Their research indicated that collective negotiations had, in most cases, a significant negative effect on teachers' salaries.

1978   (Public Service Research Council, Vienna, VA). For a 10-year period between 1969–70 and 1979–80, there were 30 states with teacher bargaining legislation. Over this period, the change in U.S. average classroom teacher salary was 89%. Of the 30 states with bargaining legislation, 15 (50%) experienced a rate of change greater than the national average. Of those states without teacher bargaining legislation, 13 (65%) experienced a rate of change greater than the national average, and 7 states (35%) were below it. The average increase in teacher salaries in the states without teacher bargaining legislation was 92.3%. For states with legislation, the average change was 87.2%. (p. 3)

1978   (Gallagher, D. G.). This study of negotiations in Illinois indicated a significant positive relationship between collective negotiations and teacher salary levels with differentials of 1.3 to 4.5% between bargaining and nonbargaining districts.

1979   (Kahn, L.). This study concluded that unions have a significant wage effect in both the short run and long run.

1979   (Marshall, A.). In a study of collective bargaining on faculty salaries in higher education, the author concluded that little, if any, difference existed between salary increases at union and nonunion institutions.

1980   (Bureau of Labor Statistics). Reported that in the most recent three years for which data were available, the major issue in 70% of all public sector strikes was "general wage changes."

1981   (Wynn, R.). Examined the rate of change in K–12 public school teachers salaries between 1960–61 and 1979–80. Study findings revealed that 52% of the states with intensive collective bargaining gained more than the national average, while 77% of the unintensive bargaining states did better than the national average.

1981   (Freeman, R. B.). Found that unionism raises the share of compensation allotted to fringe benefits, particularly vacation pay and life and accident insurance.

1984   (Eberts, R. W.). Studied 6,000 teachers and principals randomly selected from elementary schools nationally. He concluded that collective negotiations had resulted in reduction of instructional time, an increase in preparation time, an increase in experience and educational levels of teachers, and an increase in the number of teachers and administrators per student.

SUMMARY

Collective negotiations is a process whereby matters of employment relations are determined mutually by representatives of employee groups and their employer within the limits of law or mutual agreement. The development of collective bargaining in education has been influenced historically by collective bargaining in the private and public sectors.

The human resources unit in education is involved in collective bargaining in two specific ways. First, the human resources director assumes many of the responsibilities in the negotiations process itself. Second, the process of bargaining affects virtually every other facet of the human resources function. To be effective in the role, the human resources director must have a complete understanding of the tasks related to the bargaining process and possess specific personal competencies appropriate for these tasks.

The collective bargaining process includes (1) planning and preparation for collective negotiations, (2) determination and recognition of the bargaining unit, (3) determination of the negotiations team, including the chief spokesperson, (4) determination of the initial bargaining procedures and appropriate table strategies, and (5) implementation of the contract agreement.

Planning and preparation for collective bargaining include establishing goals and objectives for bargaining, establishing ground rules, determining the scope of bargaining, gathering information, analyzing costs, determining initial strategies, and clarifying impasse procedures.

The membership of the bargaining unit must be verified and the bargaining agent certified. Team representation constitutes an important matter. Available time, personal temperament, individual tenacity, technical know-how, and talent are criteria that should guide the selection of individual team members.

The tentative agreement reached by the negotiating parties must be ratified by the membership of each group. Once ratified, steps must be taken to communicate the provisions of the agreement. Grievance procedures, which have been identified in the master agreement, are implemented in case of a violation or grievance related to the contract.

Table tactics depend in large part on the bargaining strategies in place. In general, education most often has adopted the quasi-distributive strategy, in which both parties attempt to avoid a test of power and, through a procedure of proposals and counterproposals, withhold concessions on all major issues until the last possible moment. Integrative bargaining, for many reasons, has been initiated in school district bargaining and has gained increasing popularity. This approach focuses on a win–win result through problem solving.

DISCUSSION QUESTIONS

1. Ways (1979) has commented that "negotiations has been an indispensable process in free societies." What evidence supports this contention?
2. Consider the distributive bargaining strategy as compared to the integrative strategy. What evidence, if any, is available presently to suggest that the integrative approach is gaining ground in education? What factors have influenced increases or decreases in the use of the integrative strategy?
3. In the chapter it was recommended that school board representatives negotiate directly with the teachers' group representatives. That is, the school board should not take its case directly to the teachers' organization, nor

should the teachers' team take its case to the school board as a whole. Why does this recommendation make sense? What kinds of problems evolve from such actions?

4. Divide the class into appropriate triads that represent bargaining teams for the school board and for the teachers. Each team has 30 minutes to consider the following situation:

The teachers' organization bargaining team plans to request 3 personal-leave days as a negotiation item. Presently, teachers have 10 days of sick leave available per year, accumulative to 180 days. Professional leave is available with administrative approval for 3 days per year and the teacher may take 3 days for deaths in the family.

   a. During the 30-minute time period, each teacher team drafts its version of the personal-leave proposal as it will be presented at the table.

   b. Board teams are aware of the general nature of the teachers' request as presented here, but have not seen the specific proposal that ultimately will be presented. Thus, during the 30-minute time period, each school board team discusses the general proposal and considers its position relative to its provisions for compensation, approval authority, days such leave could be taken, limitation on the number of approvals, trade-offs, and so on.

   c. After the 30-minute individual team sessions, the triads meet as board and teacher teams. Each teacher team presents its proposal and the board team reacts to it. Triads take another 30 minutes to negotiate a tentative agreement on this matter.

   d. Each bargaining triad reports its results to the class as a whole.

5. Consider the rationale and strategies associated with distributive and integrative bargaining methods. Discuss why an effective negotiator in one method may not be effective in the other method?

CASE STUDIES

7.1 A Win–Win End Run

Union School District had bargained with teachers on a meet-and-confer basis for 4 years. Because no state statutes required collective bargaining between school boards and employee groups, negotiation practices varied widely throughout the state.

In the Union District, the human resources director had served as the school board's chief spokesperson for the last 4 years. Negotiations had gone well until last year, when an impasse was declared and a mediator was called in to help to resolve the matter relating to extra-duty assignments.

Budget restraints in the district were such that an override election was necessary last year to meet this year's operating expenses. The possibility of receiving a favorable vote on a second override appeared highly questionable in the eyes of the school board.

"I think we should move to a win–win, problem-solving approach in our negotiations with teachers this year," offered Merlin George, human resources director. "In view of the current economics, I can't see our past approaches to negotiations effective this year. I would be glad to serve as a resource person this year, but I recommend that someone else serve as chief spokesperson this year."

In the final analysis, the school board and superintendent agreed to George's recommendations. Thelma Morton, the school business manager, was named as negotiations team leader for the school board. Overall, teachers were receptive to the proposal for win-win bargaining.

As bargaining for the year proceeded, Thelma spent considerable time giving facts and figures relating to a tight budget and lack of needed legislative financial support. She underlined the fact that 90% of the operations budget already was directed to staff salaries and benefits. She informed the teachers' team that the voters would not stand for another override election. "Such an attempt would bring down the wrath of the community on the schools," Thelma contended.

After several weeks of conversation between the school board and teachers' bargaining teams, Thelma met with the school superintendent and Merlin George to brief them on progress to date.

"I've spelled out the budget situation for the teachers," stated Thelma. "I think it's time to present the recommendation to the teachers that it would be the best win-win strategy for all of us to forgo any salary increases for next year; only salary increments based on experience or degree credits using the present salary schedule would be provided. I think that I've got the teachers' team convinced that we're in a dire situation. Timing is good; just last week the factory workers at Specialty Supply accepted a cut in hourly pay," she noted. "Are you both agreeable to my plan?"

Questions

1. Assume the position of Merlin George in this case. How would you respond to Thelma Morton?
2. What evidence in the case justifies this situation as win-win bargaining?

3. Knowing the economic conditions prior to bargaining in this case, what approaches and recommendations for bargaining might you have suggested?

7.2 Legislative Alert!

Prior to the passing of S.B. 1008 (Negotiations for Public Employees), no state legislation had ever reached the senate floor in the area of collective bargaining. As passed, S.B. 1008 allowed boards of education to negotiate with teachers' groups on a permissive basis. That is, boards could negotiate with teachers' groups if they chose to do so. If the choice was made to negotiate, the bill stipulated that representative parties "must negotiate in good faith on topics of salary, benefits and working conditions."

Teachers' groups were active during the discussion stages of the legislation and lobbied long and hard for its approval. Because the legislation was permissive, school boards took little active part in either supporting or opposing its passage. School administrators generally were passive about the bill and had no hand in its design.

During the time that S.B. 1008 was in discussion stages, another bill, S.B. 1111, also was being considered. S.B. 1111 dealt with public employee benefits. On the day S.B. 1111 was passed, an amendment was approved on the floor. The amendment stipulated that "when the provisions of S.B. 1008 are exhausted, S.B. 1111 comes into force." In brief, the Board of Industrial Relations was authorized to intervene and to decide ongoing negotiations issues between parties.

Early in the implementation stages of S.B. 1008, one local teachers' group approached its board of education and requested to negotiate salaries for the ensuing year. The school board, using S.B. 1008's permissive provision, refused the request. As a result, the court of appeals ruled that the provisions of S.B. 1008 had been exhausted and therefore S.B. 1111 would come into effect. The matter of teachers' salaries would be determined by the Board of Industrial Relations.

The school board appealed to a higher court, claiming that its legislative responsibilities had been usurped. The higher court ruled that the Board of Industrial Relations was created by the state legislature and indeed was an authoritative extension of the legislative branch of government. Thus the decision by the Board of Industrial Relations on the matter of salaries would stand.

Questions

1. Discuss the implications of the case generally. For example, what can be learned from the case concerning involvement in legislative proposals relating to education?
2. Why is it important for administrators, teachers, and school boards to be knowledgeable about the legislative process generally and pending educational legislation specifically?

■_____

REFERENCES

American Association of School Personnel Administrators. (1978). *Trends in collective bargaining in public education.* Seven Hills, OH: Author.

Balfour, G. A. (1974). More evidence that unions do not achieve higher salaries for teachers. *Journal of Collective Negotiations in the Public Sector, 3,* 289–303.

Bureau of Labor Statistics. (1980). *Work stoppings in government,* Bulletin 2110, Washington, D.C.

Colon, R. J. (1989). Issues brought to grievance arbitration by Iowa public school teachers: January 1982 through December 1986. *Journal of Collective Negotiations in the Public Sector, 18,* 217–227.

Cunningham, W. C., & Cordeiro, P. A. (2000). *Educational administration: A problem-based approach.* Boston: Allyn and Bacon.

Diegmueller, K. (April 17, 1991). Tight budgets escalate school labor tensions. *Education Week,* p. 14.

Donohue, W. A., Allen, M., & Burrell, N. (March 1988). Mediator communicative competence. *Communication Monographs, 55,* 104–119.

Eberts, R. W. (1984). Union effects on teacher productivity. *Industrial and Labor Relations Journal, 37,* 346–358.

Economy, P. (1994). *Business negotiating basics.* Burr Ridge, IL: Irwin.

Edson, L. (April 2000). The negotiation industry. *Across the Board, 37*(4), 14–23.

Freeman, R. B. (1981). The effect of unionism on fringe benefits. *Industrial and Labor Review, 34,* 489–509.

Gallagher, D. G. (1978). De facto bargaining and teacher salary levels. *Journal of Collective Negotiations in the Public Sector, 7,* 245–254.

Greatbatch, A., & Dingwall, R. (February 1997). Argumentative talk in divorce mediation sessions. *Sociological Review, 62*(1), 151–171.

Hall, C. W., & Carroll, N. E. (1973). The effects of teachers on salaries and class size. *Industrial and Labor Relations Review, 26*(2), 2.

Horace Mann League. (March 15, 1996). Survey of 600 superintendents and professors. *Education Daily,* p. 4.

Kahn, L. (1979). Unionism and relative wages: Direct and indirect effects. *Industrial and Labor Relations Review, 32,* 520–532.

Kasper, H. (1970). The effects of collective bargaining on public school teachers' salaries. *Industrial and Labor Relations Review, 24,* 57–72.

Kennedy, G., Benson, J., & McMillan, J. (1982). *Managing negotiations.* Upper Saddle River, NJ: Prentice Hall.

Kimmel, M. J., Pruitt, D. B., Magenau, J. M., Konar-Goldband, & Carnevale, P. J. D. (1980). Effects of trust, aspiration, and gender on negotiation tactics. *Journal of Personality and Social Psychology, 38,* 9–12.

Kovach, K., & Hamilton, A. (1997). Leveling the playing field, *Business & Economic Review, 1,* October–December, 12–18.

Labor Management Relations Act of 1947 (Taft–Hartley Act). 301 (a) 61 stat. 156.29 U.S.C. 185 (a) 1964.

Lieberman, M. (1969). Forming your negotiations team. *School Management, 13*(12), 30.

Lieberman, M., & Moskow, M. H. (1966). *Collective negotiations for teachers.* Washngton, DC: Office of Professional Development and Welfare.

Loughran, C. S. (1992). *Negotiating a labor contract: A management handbook* (2nd ed.). Washington, DC: Bureau of National Affairs, Inc.

Lunenburg, F. C., & Ornstein, A. C. (2000). *Educational administration: Concepts and practices* (3rd ed.). Belmont, CA: Wadsworth.

Marshall, A. (1979). The effects of collective bargaining on faculty salaries in higher education. *Journal of Higher Education, 50,* 310.

McCollum, J. K., & Norris, D. R. (1984). Nonunion grievance machinery in southern industry. *Personnel Administrator, 29*(11), 106.

Merriam–Webster Collegiate Dictionary (10th ed.). (2001). Springfield, MA: Merriam-Webster.

Mnookin, R. H. (April 2000). Negotiation: The advanced course. ATB editor, A. J. Vogl (in a talk to Robert H. Mnookin). *Across the Board, 37*(4), 21–22.

Montgomery, E., & Benedict, M. E. (1989). The impact of bargainer experience on teacher strikes. *Industrial and Labor Relations Review, 42,* 380–392.

Moore, G. A. (1975). *Some salary effects of professional negotiations in public schools—The Nebraska experience.* University of Nebraska Studies, New Series No. 50. Lincoln: University of Nebraska.

National Education Association. (1961). *Addresses and proceedings.* Washington, DC: Author.

National Education Association. (1962). *Addresses and proceedings.* Washington, DC: Author.

National Education Association. (1965). *Guidelines for professional negotiation.* Washington, DC: Office of Professional Development and Welfare.

National Education Association. (1968). Listing of 1967–68 agreements. *Negotiations Research Digest, 1*(10), E-1 to E-29.

National Education Association. (September 1991). The 1991–1992 resolutions of the National Education Association. *NEA Today,* pp. 15–25.

National School Boards Association. (March 6, 1991). Resolutions: Proposed changes for 1991–92. *School Board News,* pp. 2–7.

Nelson, J. L., Carlson, K., & Palonsky, S. B. (1996). *Critical issues in education* (3rd ed.). New York: McGraw-Hill.

Norton, M. S. (1999). *The personnel administrator in Arizona—A research study.* Division of Educational Leadership and Policy Studies. Tempe: Arizona State University.

Norton, M. S. (2001). *The school superintendency in Arizona.* Division of Educational Leadership and Policy Studies. Tempe: Arizona State University.

Norton, M. S., Webb, L. D., Dlugosh, L. L., & Sybouts, W. (1996). *The school superintendency.* Boston: Allyn and Bacon.

Overman, S. (May 1999). Unions: New activism or old adversarial approach? *HR Focus,* New York: American Management Association, 7–8.

Payne, K., Kohler, P., Cangemi, J. P., & Fuqua, Jr., H. (2000). Communication and strategies in the mediation of disputes. *Collective Negotiations in the Public Sector, 29*(1), 29–47.

Perry, C. R., & Wilman, A. W. (1970). *The impact of negotiations in public education.* Worthington, OH: Charles A. Jones.

Pinkley, R. L. (1990). Disputant interpretations of conflict. *Journal of Applied Psychology, 75,* 117–126.

Pruitt, D. B. (1981). *Negotiation behavior.* New York: Academic Press.

Public Service Research Council. (1978). *Report on states with and without bargaining legislation.* Vienna, VA: Author.

Rebore, R. W. (2001). *Personnel administration in education: A management approach* (6th ed.). Upper Saddle River, NJ: Prentice Hall.

Reck, R. R., & Long, B. G. (1987). *Win-Win negotiator.* Kalamazoo, MI: Spartan Publications.

Redfern, G. B. (1967). *Ways and means of PN: Professional negotiations and the school administrator.* Arlington, VA: American Association of School Administrators.

Rojot, J. (1991). *Negotiation from theory to practice.* London: Macmillan Academic and Professional.

Savoie, E. J. (1994). *Rough terrain for collective bargaining: A management view.* Contemporary Collective Bargaining in the Private Sector, Paula B. Voos, Ed., Industrial Relations Research Association Series. Madison: University of Wisconsin.

Schoonmaker, A. N. (1989). *Negotiate to win.* Upper Saddle River, NJ: Prentice Hall.

Skopec, E. M., & Kiely, L. S. (1994). *Everything's negotiable . . . when you know how to play the game.* New York: AMACOM, a division of American Management Association.

Strahan, R. D. (1969). *Legal guidelines for the management of collective agreements in education.* Legal Briefs for School Administrators. Houston, TX: Gulf School Research Development Association.

Thompson, D. C., Wood, R. C., & Honeyman, D. S. (1994). *Fiscal leadership for schools: Concepts and practices.* White Plains, NY: Longman.

Tutzauer, F., & Roloff, M. E. (1988). Communication processes leading to integrative agreements. *Communication Research, 15*(4), 360–380.

U.S. Department of Labor's Bureau of Labor Statistics (1999). *Work Stoppages,* Washington, D.C.

Walter, R. L. (1975). *The teacher and collective bargaining.* Lincoln, NE: Educators Publications.

Walton, R. E. (1969). *Interpersonal peacemaking: Confrontation and third-party consultation.* Reading, MA: Addison-Wesley.

Wary, C. (1983). *Costing out the labor agreement.* Trenton, NJ: New Jersey School Boards Association.

Ways, M. (January 1979). The virtues, dangers, and limits of negotiation. *Fortune,* p. 90.

Webb, S., & Webb, B. (1920). *History of trade unionism* (p. 1). New York: Longman, Green.

Wesley, E. B. (1957). *NEA: The first hundred years.* New York: Harper.

Wynn, R. (1981). The relationship of collective bargaining and teacher salaries, 1960 to 1980. *Phi Delta Kappan,* 237–242.

Zuelke, D. C., & Frohreich, L. E. (1977). The impact of comprehensive collective negotiations on teachers' salaries: Some evidence from Wisconsin. *Journal of Collective Negotiations in the Public Sector, 6*(1), 81–88.

PART THREE

Specific Processes in the Human Resources Domain

8 *Recruitment*

After reading this chapter, you will be able to:

■ Differentiate between a job analysis and a job description.

■ List and describe the major recruitment sources and methods used by school districts.

■ Describe the major efforts being made to increase the supply of new teachers.

■ Discuss the need for and efforts to recruit for diversity.

■ Describe the impact of the fiscal resources of the district on the recruitment process.

■ Identify the major legal constraints placed on school districts in the recruitment process.

■ List the major approaches that may be used to evaluate the recruitment process.

School districts across the nation are facing an unprecedented demand for teachers and administrators at all levels. According to the American Association of Administrators, retirements will create 1000 superintendent vacancies each year for the next decade (Esparo & Rader, 2001). And more than half of the nation's 13,000 principals are expected to retire in the next 5 years (Peterson & Kelley, 2001). Even more staggering are the projections that 2.4 million teachers are needed in the next 10 years (Gursky, 2001). This demand has been created by the higher enrollments created by the Baby Boom Echo, the aging teacher population [one-quarter of all teachers nationwide are 50 or older (Recruiting New Teachers, 2000)], the high attrition rate among new teachers [50% of teachers leave the profession within 5 years (Goorian, 2000)], and competition from business and industry. Intercity and rural districts in particular are expected to be hard hit by shortages. In this near crisis situation, the recruitment of qualified individuals becomes central to the effective operation of the school district.

The recruitment system used should be one that is *effective* in terms of recruiting the best candidates, *efficient* in terms of using established, cost-effective procedures, and *fair* in terms of recruiting in a nondiscriminatory fashion (Kempton, 1995). Because recruitment decisions can be for life, the effectiveness of the recruitment program is of great importance. The costs of the recruitment program can be substantial in terms of both time and money. Yet the personnel costs associated with the recruitment activity, as well as the operational costs of the activity, are marginal compared to those associated with the orientation, training, induction, and other costs to the school district of a candidate who proves to be unsuccessful.

The recruitment process is a very visible process. It is one way those external to the district make judgments about the district. The recruitment practices of the district reflect the culture and values of the district. Everything, from the style of the advertising to whether the personnel office responds quickly and politely to all applications, says something about the district (Kempton, 1995). In this chapter the steps in the recruitment process—establishment of goals, job analysis, preparation of the description, use of internal and/or external recruitment sources, and establishment of the applicant pool—are reviewed. This is followed by a discussion of strategies to be used in the recruitment of minorities. The chapter concludes with a discussion of the fiscal and legal constraints on recruitment.

THE RECRUITMENT PROCESS

The recruitment process involves a number of steps. It begins with the establishment of goals for the recruitment program. Next is the development of the job analysis and the preparation of the job description. The district may then choose from a variety of recruitment sources to recruit internally and/or externally. The end result is a pool of qualified applicants. Finally, the recruitment process should be evaluated to determine which strategies were most effective in meeting the goals of the program.

Establishment of Goals

It is important that each year the district review and set short- and long-term goals for the recruitment process. The goals may address shortages created by the growth or reorganization of the district or the retirement, termination, or transfer of employees. In other cases, goals may address issues related to quality and the need to hire persons with advanced technological skills. Many districts may have goals related to increasing the diversity of the work force. The type of goal will be a determining factor in the decision making regarding strategies. For example, a long-term goal to increase diversity might involve a paraeducator "grow your own" program for minority teacher aides, whereas a short-term goal to increase diversity might involve targeted recruiting at traditional minority universities.

Before any action is taken to recruit for a vacant position, an assessment of need must be performed. Perhaps the position is no longer needed or the position may not be needed as it currently exists. Or perhaps someone can be laterally transferred from within the district, for example, a third-grade teacher from a school with declining enrollment transferring to the same position at a school with growing enrollment. (However, if the move constitutes a promotion for the transferee, then a selection process is required that provides equal employment opportunity to all potential applicants.) As discussed in Chapter 4, the assessment of need involves an analysis of information and data relative to the staffing or destaffing needs of all schools and other units of the school system, the system's strategic objectives, forecast trends by classification, professional staff mix, and supply–demand studies. It is important that the needs assessment not just address the here and now. A strategic view of recruitment takes a long-term view of what the district wants to look like in 5, 10, or 20 years from now by analyzing the difference between where you are and where you want to be, determining what skills will be necessary to get you there, and then recruiting for those exact skills (Canada, 2001). Use of a continually updated computer database can provide the information on vacancies, job descriptions, and personnel qualifications that is needed to determine the extent of the gap. A number of computer programs are also available to provide data (e.g., enrollment programs and retirement projections) central to projecting personnel needs.

Job Analysis

Once it has been determined that a need exists, the next appropriate step is to consider fully (or reconsider) the duties and responsibilities of the position(s) (Bolton, 1997). This task is referred to as **job analysis.** Job analysis is the process by which the knowledge, skills, abilities, and other characteristics of the position are identified, as well as the conditions under which the job functions are performed. Job analysis identifies the minimum education, certification, or licensure requirements of the job. It also describes the task and responsibilities that are considered critical functions of the job (Pynes, 1997).

If the job to be filled is a replacement for an existing or former staff member, then a considerable amount of information likely already exists about the job. If, however, the job is new, the data about the job must be obtained from scratch. Chapter 13 contains a detailed description of the methods used to obtain job analysis data. Whether for a replacement position or a new position, the job analysis should be prepared to meet the following objectives:

☐ To clarify the details of the position for which recruits are to be sought.
☐ To provide sufficient detail for the preparation of the job description.
☐ To provide a base of information from which performance appraisal criteria can be developed.
☐ To identify where the job fits into the current organizational structure and its relationship to other jobs. (Bolton, 1997, p. 36)

Figure 8.1 provides an outline for a job analysis for a professional position [adapted from Bolton's (1970) work on teacher selection], and Figure 8.2 presents a completed position analysis for a second grade teacher following this outline.

FIGURE 8.1
Position Analysis Outline

I. Strategic Nature of the Position
    A. Mission of the school system
        1. Strategic objectives of the school system
    B. Strategic objectives of the subunit
    C. Organizational structure of the subunit
    D. Expectations
        1. At the work site
        2. In relation to other system employees
        3. In relation to members of the subunit
        4. In relation to outside groups, agencies, or individuals

II. Changing Aspects of the Position
    A. At the beginning of the assignment
    B. Anticipated changes

III. Behaviors
    A. At the work site
    B. In relation to other system employees
    C. In relation to outside groups, agencies, and individuals

IV. Screening and Selection Criteria
    A. Interpersonal skills
    B. Oral communication skills
    C. Knowledge and skills base

Job Description

Job analysis provides the basis for the next step in the recruitment process, the preparation of the **job description.** The job description not only describes the position and the duties and responsibilities associated with it; it also provides information about the school and the school district in which the vacancy exists. The job description serves as an important resource for "(1) describing the job (either verbally by recruiters and interviews or in written advertisements) to potential candidates; (2) guiding newly hired employees in what they are specifically expected to do; and (3) providing a point of comparison in appraising whether the actual activities of a job incumbent align with the stated duties" (De Cenzo *&* Robbins, 1996, p. 142). Job descriptions also help to determine compensation, to provide a basis for performance reviews, and to identify the essential functions of the job to ensure compliance with the Americans with Disabilities Act (see discussion in Chapter 13). And job descriptions play an important role in career development. By providing clear expectations and responsibilities of each position, job descriptions give employees a vision of the opportunities of advancement. Job descriptions provide supervisors the information that they need to distinguish between, say, entry and intermediate level, so that they can discuss with employees what they need to do to move up, and employees can be prepared for other positions that might become available (Joinson, 2001).

I. *Strategic Nature of the Position*

   A. *Mission of the School System*

The Pine Meadows School System is committed to excellence in elementary and secondary school education. We commit ourselves to working cooperatively with parents and the community to facilitate the growth of our students intellectually, emotionally, socially, and physically, and to create an awareness of our multicultural society. To accomplish this, we will employ the best qualified professional and support personnel available, use innovative materials and technologies, exploit creative methodologies, and enlist community resources.

     1. *Strategic Objectives of School System*

The mean scores on the State Basic Skills Test (SBST) for elementary students in reading and mathematics will increase to 90% by 2005.

Computer labs will be installed in all elementary schools by 2005.

By the end of the 2005 school year, 95% of all seventh-grade students will demonstrate computer skills on a systemwide test.

   B. *Strategic Objectives of the School*

     1. The mean test scores by grade level for each reading subtest of the State Basic Skills Test will increase to 90% by 2003.

     2. The mean test scores by grade level for each mathematics subtest of the State Basic Skills Test will increase to 90% by 2003.

     3. All teachers of reading and mathematics will be able to demonstrate through classroom instruction and the presentation of lesson guides methods for technology integration into their teaching by 2003.

   C. *Organizational Structure of School*

The grade structure is K–7. Classes are self-contained and are set up heterogeneously. Students are taught material to achieve grade-level objectives. Instruction is supplemented with special remedial reading and mathematics instruction provided by specialists in each area. Leadership staff include the principal, an instructional lead teacher, and a lead teacher for student services. The school provides special classes for four categories of special education. Also, programs for gifted education and speech are provided.

   D. *Expectations*

     1. *At the Work Site*

The teacher is expected to engage in cooperative planning with other teachers by providing expertise and leadership in mathematics instruction and the integration of technology into classroom instruction in mathematics.

     2. *In Relation to Other System Employees*

The teacher is expected to work with the system's elementary school coordinator to develop methods for integrating technology into the teaching of elementary school mathematics.

     3. *In Relation to Members of the School*

The teacher is expected to work cooperatively with all members of the staff on schoolwide committees. Specifically, the teacher will be expected to guide a self-study subcommittee in mathematics that will be convened next year.

     4. *In Relation to Outside Groups, Agencies, and Individuals*

The teacher is expected to work with the PTA and be a member of professional associations at the state and national levels.

FIGURE 8.2
Position Analysis for Second-grade Teacher

II. *Changing Aspects of the Position*

   A. *At the Beginning of the Assignment*

      Most teachers will be involved in training for the educational use of the Internet and may call upon this teacher for assistance.

   B. *Anticipated Changes*
      The Writing Express Program (WEP) will be implemented in the second-year classes. The teacher will be required to participate in an in-service program during the first semester of the school year to be prepared to implement WEP at the beginning of the second semester.

III. *Behaviors*

   A. *At the Work Site*

      Flexible, cooperative, tactful, helpful, sensitive, empathetic

   B. *In Relation to Other System Employees*

      Cooperative, willing to assume extra responsibilities, high energy

   C. *In Relation to Outside Groups, Agencies, and Individuals*

      Professionalism, strong verbal facility and oral communication, enthusiasm

IV. *Screening and Selection Criteria*

   A. *Interpersonal Skills*

      Shows caring for others; open to the ideas and feelings of others; earnestly seeks candor and openness; maintains a cool and rational approach on a constant basis throughout conflict situations.

      Behavioral indicators: empathetic, caring, rational, poised, tactful, flexible, cooperative, helpful, sensitive.

   B. *Oral Communication Skills*

      Ideas are well organized and clearly presented; effective eye contact; strong voice projection and articulation; easy to understand.

      Behavioral indicators: clear enunciation, expressive, poised, self-confident, projects voice, correct grammar and usage, free of distracting mannerisms, effective nonverbal messages.

   C. *Knowledge and Skills Base*

      General knowledge of elementary curriculum and teaching with specialized knowledge in educational technology.

      Behavioral indicators: diagnostic reading skills, knowledge of effective grouping methods, computer operations and maintenance skills, including the educational use of the Internet and the World Wide Web.

FIGURE 8.2
(continued)

A job description will typically include the following:

- ☐ Job title
- ☐ Job code or job grade
- ☐ Required and desired qualifications, including education, skills, knowledge, experience, and certification or licensure requirements
- ☐ Person(s) to whom employee reports
- ☐ Person(s) supervised
- ☐ Performance responsibilities (specify those essential and those marginal)
- ☐ Evaluation (by whom and what procedure)
- ☐ Terms of employment

For many classified positions, the job description will also include the following:

- ☐ Descriptions of the physical demands of the job
- ☐ Descriptions of tools and equipment used
- ☐ Working conditions and physical environment, including any biological or physical hazards

For many positions, job descriptions may already be written. However, even if job descriptions do exist, they should be reviewed to ensure that they are still valid in terms of accurately and completely describing the job to be done and the context in which it is performed. Job descriptions should also be reviewed whenever a reorganizing, downsizing, or restructuring of the unit or department occurs. "The more accurate and current the job description, the better the chance of finding the right person for the position" (Smith, 1997/1998, p. 18). If the position is a new one, job descriptions will need to be prepared. The process for preparing job descriptions typically involves the following steps:

1. Superintendent recommends all or specified positions to be covered by written descriptions.
2. Board approves job descriptions development program.
3. Coordinator assumes overall responsibility for implementation of program.
4. Supervisors and jobholders draft job descriptions.
5. Coordinator reviews draft descriptions in terms of adequacy for meeting management goals and objectives.
6. Job description writer edits descriptions for style and format and returns clean copies to coordinator for routing to supervisors.
7. Supervisors and jobholders review descriptions for currency and accuracy.
8. Superintendent approves final descriptions.
9. Coordinator or job description writer prepares manual of approved descriptions.
10. Board receives copy of job descriptions manual for informational purposes. (National School Boards Association, 1996, p. 157)

Ultimately, a procedure should be developed to ensure that each staff member receives a copy of the job description that applies to his or her position (Lawrence & Vachon, 1997). Figure 8.3 provides a job description for the position of speech and hearing therapist.

TITLE: Speech and Hearing Therapist

QUALIFICATIONS:

1. [Certificate, license, or other legal credential required.]
2. [Degree(s) required and area of major study.]
3. [Kind and amount of prior job experience required.]
4. Such alternatives to the above qualifications as the Board may find appropriate and acceptable.

REPORTS TO:

[Person designated by the Board or the superintendent.]

JOB GOAL:

To help reduce or eliminate speech and hearing impediments that interfere with the individual student's ability to derive full benefit from the district's educational program.

PERFORMANCE RESPONSIBILITIES:

1. Serves as a resource to school staff members in the development of a balanced program for oral communication and speech improvement.
2. Provides a therapeutic program to meet individual needs of speech and hearing handicapped children.
3. Assists and guides teachers in observing, describing, and referring suspected and identified speech and language impairments.
4. Provides a thorough assessment and diagnosis of speech, voice, hearing, and language impairments.
5. Provides screening to identify speech handicapped children at regular intervals and at specified levels.
6. Assists in proper referrals of individuals to agencies and specialists in the community as appropriate.
7. Provides appropriate individualized programs of therapy to meet individual students' needs and correct existing speech or language handicaps.

FIGURE 8.3

Sample Job Description

Source: Job Description: Speech and Hearing Therapist, *The School Personnel Management System*, National School Board Association (Alexandria, VA), 1996: pp. 445–446. Reprinted with permission.

A national survey [Educational Research Service (ERS), 1994] of school districts relative to the development and use of job descriptions found that, overall, the personnel administrator is the person most often responsible for the preparation of job descriptions. The survey also found that the personnel administrator frequently has the primary responsibility of updating job descriptions and that this role was more significant in larger districts than smaller districts. In smaller districts, the superintendent had the more significant role in both preparing and updating job descriptions. Similarly, the involvement of the personnel administrator in approving job descriptions increased with school district size. In 56% of responding districts, the board of education had final authority for approving changes in job descriptions. The superintendent had final authority in 26%, and the personnel administrator in 11%.

8. Collaborates with classroom teachers and other school staff members to implement therapy by suggestions for the student's daily activities.
9. Provides information, support, and counseling to parents and families when appropriate.
10. Provides in-service education and serves as a consultant to teachers and school staff members on topics concerning speech improvement.
11. Keeps thorough ongoing records for the individual student receiving therapy or other school-provided speech services.
12. Maintains lists of referred, screened, and eligible students, as well as a directory of outside agencies, consultants, specialists, and related services.
13. Compiles case history data on those cases where additional family history, health history, early developmental history, and environmental history are deemed appropriate.
14. Assumes primary responsibility for requisitioning and maintaining needed equipment and supplies.
15. Prepares and administers the annual budget for speech therapy services.

TERMS OF EMPLOYMENT:

Ten-, eleven-, or twelve-month year. Salary and work year to be established by the Board.

EVALUATION:

Performance of this job will be evaluated in accordance with provisions of the Board's policy on Evaluation of Professional Personnel.

Approved by: _____ Date: _____

Reviewed and agreed to by: _____ Date: _____
                                         (Incumbent)

FIGURE 8.3
(continued)

According to the same survey (ERS, 1994), the positions for which job descriptions were most frequently used were principals (97%); directors, managers, coordinators, and supervisors (93%); clerical personnel (92%); superintendents (90%); and custodians and teacher aides (88%). The positions for which job descriptions were least frequently used were school nurses (72%) and bus drivers (66%). And the most frequently revised category of job description was central office administrator.

Recruiting from Existing Sources

Once the school district has determined that a position needs to be filled and has developed a job description for the position, the decision must be made about the sources and strategies to be used to generate the pool of qualified candidates necessary to provide the needed employee(s). Several factors will influence this decision. The first is whether the need is in the short term, long term, or ongoing. If the need is anticipated to be long-term and/or ongoing, in addition to recruiting from existing candidate pools, the district may engage in one or more of the activities designed to develop sources of applicants and discussed in the following section.

The second factor is the actual number of potential applicants that will need to be contacted in order to obtain an applicant pool of the desired size. That is, depending on the position, in today's competitive market, it may be necessary to reach hundreds, if not thousands, of potential applicants in order to obtain a pool of several dozen qualified applicants. Past experience should provide some guidance in determining how extensive the recruitment effort must be (Harvey & Bowin, 1996).

A third factor that will influence the choice of recruitment methods and sources is the type of job. Some sources are more effective than others for filling certain types of jobs. For example, an ad in the *APA Monitor*, a publication of the American Psychological Association, is more likely to be read by a potential school psychologist applicant than by a potential applicant for a superintendency.

A fourth factor that will affect the recruitment methods and sources used is cost. Recruitment can be a costly activity. This cost goes up as the number of advertisements placed increases, as the number and types of media used increase, as the circulation and prestige of the sources increase, as the number of recruitment trips increases, as the advertising materials become more numerous and professionally produced, as the number of mailings increases, and as the amount of internal and external staff time devoted to the effort increases.

Yet another factor influencing the decision relative to recruitment methods and sources is whether the search will be internal or external. The philosophy of some districts is that, to the extent possible, internal recruiting should be used for positions beyond entry level. **Internal recruiting** not only has the obvious saving of cost associated with external recruitment, but it also serves as an important source of employee motivation. Internal recruitment and promotion demonstrate to employees the opportunities available in the district and reduce the incentive to seek positions outside the district. Additional advantages of internal recruiting are that it is easier to evaluate the strengths and weaknesses of current employees than to evaluate other candidates based on their résumés and interviews (Warren, Gorham, & Lamont, 2000/2001). Hiring from within also reduces the time required for the new employee to become oriented to the job and rise to full productivity. And, perhaps most important, no matter how thorough and careful the recruitment and selection process may be, any external candidate is still an unknown quantity versus the internal applicant who is a proven entity (Herman, 1994).

Some of the disadvantages of internal recruiting are associated with the limiting of candidate choices. Hiring from within may also limit the introduction of new ideas and perspectives and can contribute to stagnation or complacency (Warren et al., 2000/2001). Another disadvantage of internal recruitment is that, unless it is handled very carefully, openly, and fairly, jealousies and hostilities can be engendered in those who do not receive the job (Jordan, 1997). And perhaps the biggest negative associated with hiring from within is that, although one position may become filled, the district will still be left with one unfilled position.

A variety of recruitment sources and methods are available to school districts. If the district limits itself to informal, primarily internal recruitment, beyond internal job posting to existing employees, its primary sources are previous and part-time employees and employee referrals. If recruitment is to be a more formal process of **external recruitment,** the district has available to it media advertising, employment agencies, educational institutions, computerized data banks and electronic bulletin boards, and professional organizations and unions. Although not the result of any recruitment effort, another source of applicants is unsolicited applications. Each of these sources is discussed in the following sections.

Retired Employees. Early retirees can be recruited to provide an immediate source of expert knowledge in times of staff shortage or in times of need for emergency or short-term hires. Recruiting these retirees can buy the district time to build up a pool of qualified candidates (Potter, 2001). One strategy for enticing retired teachers back is to allow them to retain their full retirement benefits: 61% of senior teachers in New York State indicated that they would be willing to return full or part time to teaching if they could retain their pension benefits (Gurskey, 2001). The Arizona legislature recently enacted legislation allowing this to happen, and neither the teacher or the employee is required to contribute to the teacher retirement system, resulting in the district not only gaining an experienced teacher, but saving money. Several other states (e.g., South Carolina, North Carolina, Missouri, Texas, and California) are passing similar legislation [Recruiting New Teachers (RNT), 2000].

Another strategy for recruiting retired employees is **job sharing.** Job sharing of teaching positions involves two teachers each working a 19-hour week to fill one teaching position (Grant, 2001). Again, this provides a savings to the district since no benefits are provided.

Previous and Part-Time Employees. Previous and part-time employees can be an important, but often overlooked, source for recruitment. In fact, former teachers reentering teaching after a break in their teaching career make up 23% of all newly hired public school teachers (U.S. Department of Education, 2000).

Part-time employees, including substitute teachers, also represent a very important recruitment source. In fact, among newly hired teachers, 28% of reentrants and 36% of all delayed entrants came from the ranks of substitute teachers (U.S. Department of Education, 2000). Part-time and substitute teachers are considered good recruitment sources for many of the same reasons as are former employees: they are known entities and have had a realistic preview of the job. However, while "encouraging experienced substitute teachers to teach full time is a good idea, some districts find that this practice adds to a growing substitute teacher shortage" (RNT, 2000, p. 20).

Employee Referrals.   Present employees are an important recruitment source for any organization. Numerous studies on recruitment have shown that employees hired as a result of a referral from a current employee typically are of higher quality and stay with the organization longer than those who come from other sources (Morehart, 2001). Other benefits of employee referrals (ER) include the facts that they

- ☐ Are among the most cost-effective methods for finding qualified candidates.
- ☐ Offer another resource for accomplishing recruitment goals.
- ☐ Help to reduce the overall cost per hire.
- ☐ Can function as team-building devices.
- ☐ Provide candidates who are "pre-screened" for cultural fit.
- ☐ Make employees at all levels feel they are part of the recruiting process by helping them to contribute to the organization and making them aware of what direction leadership is taking.
- ☐ Give current employees a first glance at career advancement opportunities.
- ☐ Provide new ER hires with a built-in network and support system on their first day on the job.
- ☐ Bring in quality candidates. Most employees won't refer those whose performance would have a negative impact on the operation. (Morehart, 2001, p. 3)

Because of the many advantages associated with hires from employee referrals, districts would be well advised to institute a formal ER program. Such a program would include instituting a reward or incentive program for hires, acknowledging the referral and expressing appreciation, informing the candidate of his or her referral and inviting an application, and publishing the results of the program in appropriate in-house publications and communications (Morehart, 2001).

While most districts encourage employee referrals, almost all districts have policies against nepotism, the hiring or giving of preferential treatment to relatives. Most often these policies bar the person(s) responsible for the hiring decision or the person who will be supervising the new employee from being a relative of the new employee. And a note of warning: by relying on employee referrals, the district must be alert to the possibility of "inbreeding" and violation of EEOC (Equal Employment Opportunity Commission) regulations. Since employees and their referrals will likely be of similar backgrounds, districts who rely heavily on employee referrals may unintentionally screen out, and thereby discriminate against, protected classes (Sherman & Bohlander, 1992).

Media Advertisements.   Advertising, in particular, classified advertising, is a major recruitment tool for most school districts and is often the only source used to fill classified vacancies. Advertising may be through radio, television, bulletins, professional journals, trade publications, newspapers, or even movie theaters. Mass media advertising has the advantage of reaching the largest possible audience. At the same time, aside from its cost, this is its principal limitation. Advertising in any of the mass media results in unpredictable responses. Selectivity may be achieved by careful consideration of where the ad is placed, which in turn is largely determined by the type of job and the labor supply. That is, although ads for unskilled or semiskilled positions could appropriately be placed in the help wanted section of the local newspaper, ads seeking persons with higher-level skills or persons in short supply would be better placed in professional journals, trade or union publications, or newspapers or journals directed toward specific audiences. In general, several factors must be considered when placing recruitment advertising:

- ☐ The number and location of potential respondents. For instance, it is likely that unskilled staff will be recruited mainly from a local pool of labor, while the recruitment of senior staff may be from a national . . . pool. This will have implications not only for the amount to be spent on advertising, but also where that advertising will be placed.
- ☐ The cost of the advertising must also be considered. It is likely (but not always the case) that the more spent on advertising, the greater the response to that advertising will be. To be efficient, recruitment advertising must aim to attract a satisfactory level and standard of response but at minimum cost.
- ☐ The frequency with which the organization wishes to advertise the position must also be considered. If daily or weekly magazines or papers are used it will be possible to advertise a position several times. If a monthly journal is selected then it is probable that the position will be advertised only once. (Bolton, 1997, p. 52)

Print Media. The primary avenues for print media advertising are newspapers of general circulation, association newspapers, trade magazines, and professional journals. Ads placed in newspapers of general circulation, including the so-called "free shoppers," have the advantage of immediacy, a large circulation, a targeted geographic market, and low cost per hire, while ads in the special audience publications, which typically attract candidates with better qualifications, may have a long lag time (Warren et al., 2000/2001). Wherever the print ad is placed, it is important to attend to certain design considerations: size, amount of white space, type and fonts, wording, and so forth. Design experts state that the "first rule of advertising is to be 'you' oriented rather than 'me' oriented. Think about what the ideal prospect is going to want from a job, and emphasize how the opening can fulfill this person's needs and wishes. Ads have more appeal when they state what the employer has to offer . . . before mentioning what the company needs" (Warren et al., 2000/2001, p. 111:1705). For example, rural and small districts have found that emphasizing the benefits of working in a small district (e.g., small class size, fewer behavioral problems, higher job satisfaction) improves their recruitment efforts (Lemke, 1995).

At a minimum, a good recruitment advertisement should include the following:

☐ The name of the school district
☐ A descriptive title of the job
☐ Some statement about the district that tells why it is a good place to work
☐ A summary of the major features of the job
☐ A clear statement of the minimum qualifications for the job
☐ Conditions of employment (length of contract, working hours, travel requirements, etc.)
☐ Some statement regarding salary, either a specific figure, a range, or a statement to the effect that "salary is commensurate with training and experience"
☐ Information about where, how, and to whom to apply
☐ An equal employment opportunity statement

When placing an ad in a newspaper and many professional journals, it is often possible (usually for an additional fee) to have the ad appear in the Internet version of the employment section of the paper or job bulletin board of the journal (Wodarz, 2001). By taking advantage of this option, districts can dramatically extend the research of the print ad at a minimal cost.

Broadcast Media.   With two exceptions, school districts do not typically advertise in the broadcast media. The two exceptions are in rural areas where newspaper coverage is poor or on radio or television stations that are aimed at minority audiences. The reasons that school districts do not use broadcast media are much the same as those for other organizations: (1) cost, (2) lack of a distinct marketplace of job seekers, and (3) the limits of the amount of information that can be communicated in the limited time frame, as well as the amount interested persons can consume or be prepared or able to take down in the same time frame (Warren et al., 2000/2001).

One segment of the broadcast media that is becoming more used by school districts is the community bulletin boards offered by cable TV companies. Most cable TV broadcasters reserve one or more channels for public service announcements. Very often a designated time slot is provided for employment opportunities. These may be presented as written text, or in some cases recruiters are able to make a personal appearance to present job opportunities. Advertising on the cable TV bulletin boards is often at a free or reduced rate.

Employment Agencies.   Sometimes it may be necessary or advantageous for the district to utilize the services of either public or private employment agencies. In addition to supplying job applicants, employment agencies often assist in the employment process by performing employment testing, evaluation, and counseling. A beneficial feature of public employment agencies is that they do the initial screening without cost to the district. In some offices this screening may include the administration of a general aptitude test designed to predict success on a broad range of jobs (Warren et al., 2000/2001).

Private agencies can be of most assistance in filling technical and professional positions. Many private agencies specialize in certain fields. Private employment agencies can differ significantly in the services that they provide. Some agencies, so-called "head hunters," will aggressively seek out and approach prospective employees. Employment agencies also differ in the fee that is charged to the applicant or the employer. The fee to a large extent depends on the perceived exclusivity of the services. Consequently, general employment agencies will typically charge a lower fee than ones specializing in the recruitment of scarce talent (Bolton, 1997). Thus, if the school district finds it necessary or desirable to use a private employment agency, care should be taken to ensure that the agency will provide the services and applicants at a cost that either the district or the prospective applicant can afford. The school district should select an employment agency that is established, receives recruiter certification through the National Association of Personnel Consultants, and provides multiple services (temporary, full-time, and management-level recruitment). Perhaps the best gauge of the caliber of the firm is to ask candidates two questions: What did the agency tell you about the school district and position? and How do you feel about your recruiter? (Falcone, 1992).

Educational Institutions. For all certified positions, as well as for some of the more advanced professional and vocational fields in the classified service (e.g., budget director, dietician, director of food services, director of transportation services, and facilities planner), it would be logical for the school district to recruit at colleges and universities. Almost all colleges and universities operate placement offices through which the school district can recruit and arrange interviews with applicants. In addition, many colleges and universities hold annual job placement days, career days, job fairs, or teacher roundups. These events provide the school district with the opportunity to meet a number of candidates in a short period of time.

Most successful school district recruiters don't wait until they need employees to contact the college or university. "Good college recruiting is labor intensive and depends on forming close relationships not only with the career placement officials . . . but also with the faculty" (Herman, 1994, p. 60). Some school districts approach recruiting student teachers much the same as others approach scouting and recruiting student athletes. That is, they encourage professors to identify their most capable students in their junior year, interview students on campus, and then invite them for an all-expense-paid visit to the district where they are given first-class treatment. For minority students, early contact is particularly important: recruiters have found that waiting until the senior year to make contact is too late (Martinez, 1996).

In planning the campus recruitment visit, it is important to work closely with the college placement office to schedule various recruitment efforts, to send ahead videos and literature describing the district and its various employment opportunities, and to involve alumni of the institution as recruiters or recruiter partners. Finally, rather than spreading your resources thin by attempting to recruit at all the colleges or universities in your region or state, a better practice is to concentrate on the schools that your best employees have come from (Herman, 1994). And, if recruiting out of state, target states and areas with a known surplus of teachers and, if increasing the diversity of the teaching pool is a goal, target predominantly minority colleges and universities. Nontargeted recruiting out of state is generally not very cost effective. The vast majority of candidates tend to stay with their geographic area. Those who are interested in moving generally have a specific area in mind (O'Laughlin, 1999) and may more effectively be attracted to the district by a well-designed Web site.

In addition, or instead of visiting numerous college recruitment officers, some districts have tried the reverse strategy and invited recruitment officers to visit them. For example, once a year the Decatur, Georgia, district invites about 30 college placement directors to visit them for two days. The directors meet with the superintendent, school board members, and teachers and administrators who are alumni of their institutions. They visit the schools and dine in the school cafeteria. The visit concludes with a visit to a major league baseball game (Grant, 2001).

For a number of classified positions, the district can recruit applicants from vocational and technical schools. The school district is also in the unique position to recruit the very best of the graduating seniors in the district. Personal references of students can be readily checked, and school records can provide some indication of on-the-job performance (Jordan, McKeown, Salmon, & Webb, 1985). Rather than letting its best graduates go elsewhere, the school district can hire them.

International Recruiting.   The shortage of teachers has led many districts to recruit foreign teachers to fill their classrooms. By offering special visas to foreigners to teach in areas of greatest need, Chicago Public Schools was able to attract math and science teachers from all over the world, including some from the best universities (Trapps, 2001). Connecticut, Philadelphia, and New York City have recruited Spanish teachers from Spain, while Houston and Los Angeles have recruited Spanish teachers in the Phillipines and Mexico. Philadelphia has also turned to India to fill jobs, mostly in math and science. Dallas has also turned to Mexico to find bilingual math and science teachers, while New York City has sought science teachers in Puerto Rico, has hired 24 Austrians via teleconference, and has even extended its recruitment efforts into Eastern Europe (RNT, 2000; "Schools seeking teachers overseas," 2001).

To recruit teachers internationally, districts have turned to a variety of sources. Working through foreign governments, recruitment agencies, and personal contracts are common approaches. Other districts have used EdJoin, an internationally based Web site where districts can advertise positions and post applications that can be submitted via the Internet (Rodda, 2000). In most states, foreign teachers are required to have classroom experience, speak English fluently, and undergo a background check to become employed ("Schools seeking teachers overseas," 2001).

Internet Recruiting. The Internet has become an essential recruitment tool. It serves as a recruitment tool in two major ways: (1) a district Web site for informing potential candidates about the district, employment opportunities in the district, and application information, including application materials, and (2) providing the district with access to national, state, and job banks for education, where jobs can be posted and candidate databases searched.

The District Web Site. Almost every school district has a Web site. However, despite their potential to reach audiences worldwide at minimal expense, many districts underutilize the Web site for recruitment. A well-designed Web site, with pages devoted to employment opportunities, provides the district with a valuable recruitment tool. Teachers, especially new teachers, no longer start their job search with classified ads but on the World Wide Web (Head, 2001). For this reason the district site should have a professional look and be easy to navigate. The following recruitment information should be included on the Web site:

☐ The district mission statement or guiding philosophy,
☐ Photographs of classrooms and special programs,
☐ Information about the region/city,
☐ Current openings,
☐ Salary ranges and benefits,
☐ The selection process,
☐ The contact person(s), including names, title, phone numbers, and e-mail and mailing addresses,
☐ Licensure information,
☐ Access to an on-line application form (or a statement as to whether the standard application forms provided at USTEACH and similar sites are accepted, and
☐ Links from career placement offices. (RNT, 2000, p. 16; Head, 2001, p. 20)

As important as what information to include on the Web site is that it be updated on a regular basis.

Job Banks and Education Employment Databases. In addition to posting jobs on its own Web site, the district can post jobs and search for candidates on an almost endless number of databases worldwide, including an estimated 21,000 teacher job applicant databases (Grant, 2001). Most sites allow the district (and the applicant) to customize the data that they import as well as the searches that they perform. Among the largest and the more established of these databases are these:

☐ American Association for Employment in Education (www.aace.org)
☐ USTEACH (www.usteach.com)
☐ CALTEACH (www.CalTeach.com)

☐ National Teacher Recruitment Clearinghouse (www.recruitingteachers.org)
☐ REAP (www.reap.net)
☐ www.K12jobs.com
☐ www.edjobsite.com

Professional Organizations and Unions. Many professional organizations and labor unions provide placement services to their members. Placement activities often are conducted in connection with the organization's state, regional, and national conferences. In addition, advertisements are carried in publications of the organization and on the associations's Web site. For certain select positions, therefore, the district may want to place an advertisement in the trade journal and/or on its Web site. For others it might be more economical for the district to send a recruiter to a conference to interview a number of applicants than to bring applicants to the district.

Labor unions, through their apprenticeship programs, are the primary source of applicants for certain types of jobs. In fact, in districts in which some or all of the classified personnel are unionized, the district must rely on the union in its recruitment efforts.

Unsolicited Applications. Almost every school district will receive numerous unsolicited applications each year. The number of unsolicited applications received depends to a large extent on economic conditions and the school district's image as an employer. Unsolicited applications provide an excellent source of stockpiled applicants (De Cenzo & Robbins, 1996). In fact, it is often believed that applicants who contact prospective employers on their own initiative may be better employees than those recruited through newspaper advertisements or college placement offices (Sherman & Bohlander, 1992). All unsolicited applications should be handled with respect and courtesy. If there is no chance of employment now or in the future, the applicant should be honestly and tactfully informed of this fact (Sherman & Bohlander, 1992). Maintaining a computerized database of unsolicited applications allows easy updating and purging of files. More important, it facilitates the matching of qualified candidates with specific positions as the need arises.

Recruitment Incentives

In an effort to attract teachers, especially in hard to fill disciplines or in certain geographic areas, a number of states and districts have turned to providing financial or other incentives. One increasingly popular strategy is offering signing or hiring bonuses. For example, Massachusetts has instituted a program offering $20,000 spread over 4 years to career changers and recent college graduates, especially those with expertise in areas such as math and science, and will also pay for them to go through concentrated summer training with the hope that the program will produce as many as 500 teachers a year (Schuerman, 2000). Examples of hiring bonuses at the district level are numerous. Most are in the $1500 to $2500 range, although there are examples like that of a small Texas district providing a $7500 hiring bonus (Texas Education Agency, 1999).

Other incentives offered to prospective employees are aimed at helping with real estate costs. For example, the state of Maryland provides low-interest loans to teachers who buy homes in "smart growth" areas, defined as urban and older suburban areas (www.ncsl.org). At the district level, Baltimore offers new teachers $5000 toward the purchase of a home in the city. Other districts have provided low-interest mortgages, subsidized housing (e.g., San Francisco), and subsidies for day care (Gurskey, 2001).

Recruiting for Diversity

Recruiting for diversity involves finding teachers, counselors, and administrators that reflect the cultural, racial, and ethnic diversity of their classrooms. The need to recruit a work force that better reflects the student population is made strikingly clear by the comparative demographics of students and educators. The minority enrollment of the public schools, which currently comprises 38% of the student population, is projected to reach 50% by the year 2020. The greatest increase has come among Hispanics: the percentage of Hispanic students has tripled over the past three decades. However, at the same time that the minority student population is growing, the percentage of minority teachers and administrators, which is already significantly disproportionate, is projected to decline from 14% in 1999 to 5% in 2010 (U.S. Department of Education, 2000). These disparities are even more acute in urban districts, which not only have difficulty attracting staff, but have high turnover rates. Unfortunately, in many school districts in this country, the only people of color that a student will see in their 12 years of school are the custodial and food service workers.

A school district can take a number of steps to enhance the success of its diversity recruitment program. To begin with, the school district recruitment policies must reflect a commitment to diversity in the work force. And this commitment must be reflected in a diverse recruitment team and administrative staff. It is also important that training programs be provided to all those involved in the recruitment and selection process to provide them with the specific skills and knowledge that will enhance their minority recruitment efforts. In addition, all recruitment practices and policies should be continually reviewed to ensure that they are not only nondiscriminatory, but also support the stated commitment to diversity. For example, an advertisement or brochure that features photographs of only Anglos, even if it also states that the district is an "Equal Opportunity Employer," delivers a powerful subliminal message that the district only pays lip service to being such an employer. "Advertisements that positively depict visible minorities attract significantly larger numbers of minority applicants than those that do not" (Herman, 1994, p. 67).

In addition to attending to these "housekeeping details," school districts can use a variety of proactive recruitment strategies to try to reach qualified minority candidates. Among the recruitment activities that districts can utilize in recruiting for diversity are the following:

☐ Advertising in print and nonprint media focused on minorities.
☐ Networking with minority professional organizations. These organizations can be found by looking in the phone book under "associations" or checking with a college or university that offers a major in the area of interest. These professional organizations offer various types of help. As already noted, many have newsletters that accept advertisements. In addition to the minority professional organizations, national professional organizations in the field of interest might also be contacted, as many have divisions devoted to minority concerns (Warren et al., 2000).
☐ Identifying and using employment agencies that specialize in minority candidates.
☐ Hiring a minority recruiter.
☐ Networking with churches and community organizations to identify and encourage individuals who might be interested in pursuing a career in teaching.
☐ Concentrating recruitment visits on schools, colleges, and universities with high minority populations.
☐ Encouraging and supporting the efforts of minority employees to recruit at their alma maters.
☐ Working with banks and other local businesses to provide low-interest loans, affordable housing, and other incentives (RNT, 2000).
☐ Expanding the geographic area of recruitment.

In addition to these strategies, the strategies described in the following section to increase the overall teaching pool can be used with a focus on minority recruitment. For example, at the high school level, special attention can be given to encouraging minority students to become involved in future-educator clubs. And college scholarships for teacher education students can be earmarked for minority students. Scholarships are particularly important to minority students, many of whom lack the financial ability to attend college.

Other efforts to encourage college students to choose teaching involve presentations to traditionally minority sororities and fraternities and at the various campus racial and ethnic centers and academic studies departments. Many students are undecided on a major when they enroll as a freshman. Many others change their majors one or more times. In fact, a National Conference of State Legislatures (NCSL) (n.d.) study found that 38% of new teachers did not decide to become a teacher until they were in college.

A proven recruitment strategy designed to attract minority teacher education students is to encourage both student teacher coordinators to place student teachers or interns in the district and teacher education students to practice teach or do their internships in the district. This way the district has the opportunity to identify the most promising future teachers and will have an edge on recruiting these teachers: research indicates that a high percentage of student teachers are interested in remaining in the district where they did their student teaching.

Building the Supply of Future Educators

With the teacher shortage, particularly the shortage of minority teachers, projected to continue into the unforeseeable future and fewer individuals choosing teaching as a career, school districts must assume a major role in developing the educational work force for the near and the long-term future. As Grant (2001), past president of the American Association of School Personnel Administrators, explains: "You can not reap what you have not sown" (p. 18). Efforts to increase the pool of qualified educators typically fall into four categories: (1) precollege recruitment, (2) college recruitment and support programs, (3) alternative certification programs, and (4) grow-your-own programs that recruit paraprofessionals and teacher aides into teaching or teachers into the principalship.

Precollege Recruitment. According to the NCSL (n.d.) study, 52% of all new teachers made the decision to become a teacher before they entered college. Therefore, human resources administrators should take the lead in encouraging their districts to sponsor such programs as Future Educators of America or some other locally devised program. The ideal would be to have a program operating in every middle and high school in the district (Grant, 2001). The purpose of such a club is to provide students with the opportunity to explore careers in education and to expose them to "meaningful experiences that allow them to understand what teaching is and the rewards of teaching so that in the future they are able to make career choices based on actual experience" (O'Laughlin, 1999, p. 32).

Future-teacher clubs or teacher cadet programs can be found in every state. Many are local affiliates of the national FTA. Others are state sponsored. One of the most successful and well-known programs designed to attract high school students to teaching is the Teacher Cadet Program (TCP) sponsored by the South Carolina Center for Teacher Recruitment. The program is designed to engage high school juniors and seniors in learning about teaching through both classroom activities and actual teaching experiences in early childhood centers, elementary and middle schools, or classes in their own schools (140 of the state's high schools participate in the TCP). The TCP is making a special effort to enlist largely minority high schools and to provide counseling and scholarship information to minority students. As a result, it has proved to be more successful than any other recruitment effort in the state in attracting top-quality minority students to teaching.

In addition to sponsoring such groups as future-teacher clubs, school districts should encourage their guidance to highlight education as a career, invite speakers from colleges of education to speak to the student body (Polansky, 1999), and take advantage of every opportunity to encourage their students to consider education as a career.

College Recruitment and Support Programs. In addition to supporting programs for middle and high school students, an increasing number of states and districts have established scholarship programs to encourage high school graduates to pursue teaching careers. For example, the state of

Georgia provides full scholarships to individuals who promise to teach in the state. And the North Carolina Teaching Fellows Program awards $6500 per year loan-forgiveness scholarships to 700 outstanding high school seniors who are interested in becoming teachers. Teaching Fellows attend teacher education programs in one of 14 state institutions that have developed academically and culturally enriched teacher education programs for Fellows. North Carolina also funds a Principal Fellows Program to attract qualified individuals into careers in educational administration. The program provides a 2-year scholarship of $20,000 per year to support full-time study leading to certification and a master's degree in educational administration. The loan is forgiven if the recipient practices full time as an administrator for 4 years within 6 years of completion of the programs.

A number of other states fund programs similar to these. A few are directed specifically to minority students. For example, the Florida Fund for Minority Teachers awards up to 1000 scholarships of $4000 each to students in 29 colleges and universities "with special consideration to community college graduates, since many minorities attend them" (Duarte, 2000, p. 23).

Alternative Certification Programs.   More than 40 states now recognize alternative routes to certification. **Alternative certification** programs are designed to attract and train midcareer persons with a baccalaureate degree in a nonteaching field for a career in teaching. An alternative certification program typically consists of an intensive summer training program followed by a year of internship or close supervision. Some alternative certification programs target returning Peace Corp volunteers or retired military personnel. The Peace Corp has sent more than 1500 of its returning volunteers into community service positions (most in teaching) in return for scholarships to earn a master's degree (Schuerman, 2000). Districts can contact the Peace Corp or Troop to Teachers (www.troops.org) for help in identifying individuals in the local area who are potential candidates for an alternative certification program. Another good source for identifying candidates is current employees. Many teachers may have a friend or relative who only needs a little encouragement to consider teaching. Every member of the professional staff should be encouraged to be on the lookout for potential candidates and refer them to the human resources office or the locally sponsored alternative certification program (O'Laughlin, 1999).

A number of districts have entered into collaborative arrangements with area institutions of higher education to produce alternative certification teachers. Such jointly developed programs provide the district with the opportunity to train teachers specifically for the needs of their district—teachers who often come from the community and are familiar with the background of their students. These teachers are also more likely to stay in the profession than other alternative certification teachers, 60% of whom leave the profession by their third year (Fenwick & Pierce, 2001). However, district involvement in an alternative certification program does place an additional burden on school district personnel, a burden that the school district must carefully consider before initiating such a program.

Grow-Your-Own Programs. Paraeducator-to-teacher, or **grow-your-own programs** have become an increasingly popular strategy for districts, especially urban districts, to address the teacher shortage, especially the shortage of teachers of color. However, many rural districts are also developing grow-your-own programs. Like urban districts, they are interested in hiring teachers who are familiar with the strengths and weaknesses of the district and the culture and background of the students.

While each grow-your-own program has its unique features, they share some basic features: (1) they require the collaboration of the school district and a college or university to recruit and select participants; (2) they offer participants a range of financial and academic support services; (3) they offer flexible course scheduling to accommodate the work schedules of participants; (4) they provide student cohort arrangements; and (5) they offer preparation programs. These preparation programs have "adopted elements of nontraditional teacher education models—field-based learning; adult degree low residency; competency-based assessment; continuing education; summer and weekend course work (distance learning); intern/mentoring; integrated learning; and links to community" (Haselkorn & Fideler, 1996, p. 49). Districts typically do not have any difficulty recruiting participants into paraeducator-to-teacher programs. Moreover, once they are trained they tend to remain in the district.

ESTABLISHMENT OF AN APPLICANT POOL

The creation of the applicant pool is the ultimate objective of the recruitment program. To establish an applicant pool of qualified persons, the human resources administrator must give careful attention to the process of handling all applications and supporting materials. This task is made easier by the use of an **electronic document management system** (EDMS). Most EDM systems provide for applications to be received via the Internet and an immediate e-mail sent acknowledging receipt of the application. Depending on the software used, the EDMS may also "send out electronic evaluation forms to the references listed, order transcripts or college placement files, electronically order copies of teaching certificates . . . [all] without human intervention" (Grant, 2001, p. 22).

Using an electronic document management system, all documents received on a candidate are electronically scanned into a computer file or converted into alphanumeric characters using intelligent character recognition, which can then be processed into the applicant's electronic portfolio. The EDMS also allows for instant retrieval of all information on any candidate. Overall, the system is far more secure than traditional paper files being transferred from one user to another. Moreover, once the information on an applicant is entered into the system it becomes permanent; therefore, when an applicant is employed it is a simple matter to change the application file to the personnel file of the new employee (O'Laughlin, 1999).

As each application is received, whether an EDMS is used or not, a letter of acknowledgment thanking the applicant for interest in the position should be sent along with a description of the selection process and information regarding persons to contact for additional information. At the same time, applicant information should be entered into the applicant database and a computer or hard copy created for the placement of transcripts, letters of reference, copies of reference checks, copies of licenses, or whatever other documentation in support of the application is required of applicants. As each required document is received or completed, the applicant database should be updated.

At this point in the recruitment process, it is also appropriate to send to each applicant a card or form asking the applicant to indicate if he or she belongs to one or more of the minority groups listed on the card or form. It should be stressed when making this request that the submission of this information is voluntary and will in no way affect the selection process. The form should be returned unsigned to the district affirmative action officer, not to the personnel office.

As the recruitment process proceeds, it is extremely important to have a well-established procedure for keeping applicants informed. A good procedure will help to maintain the interest of qualified applicants and minimize the number of inquiries received by the personnel office. A good EDMS can make this communication task an easy chore. Integrated word-processing software can be used to generate letters to applicants advising them of receipt or need of additional documents. Once all application materials have been received, dated, and filed, the screening process described in Chapter 9 can begin.

FISCAL AND LEGAL CONSTRAINTS ON RECRUITMENT

Fiscal Constraints

The fiscal condition of the school district can have a direct impact on the recruitment process. Recruitment can be an expensive process. Private employment agencies charge fees of as much as 30% of the first-year salary. The fiscal condition of the district will affect how much the district can afford to expend in terms of recruiters, recruitment trips, advertising, use of professional search firms, coverage of candidate expenses, and a number of other costs.

More important than the impact on the recruitment process, the fiscal condition of the school district can affect the ability of the school district to attract and retain personnel. High-wealth suburban districts always have a "glut" of applicants, while low-wealth urban and rural districts have the most difficulty attracting and retaining teachers and administrators (Fideler & Haselkorn, 1999). In particular, the fiscal ability of the district to offer attractive beginning teacher salaries seems to have a powerful impact on recruitment. After a review of the available evidence, Odden and Conley (1992) concluded that "beginning teacher salaries can affect both the quantity and the quality of individuals entering the teaching profession. The higher the salaries, the greater the number of able individuals encouraged to become teachers" (p. 53).

School districts must compete not only with other school districts for candidates, but also with other employers in the community. For example, the characteristics that boards and superintendents are looking for in principals are the same that business and industry are looking for in CEOs and middle-level managers. And, unfortunately, most school districts cannot compete with the financial incentives and opportunities for advancement provided in the private sector (Malone & Caddell, 2000). And, although a substantial body of research supports the proposition that most educators are in education for reasons other than money, a consistent body of research also indicates that both practicing and prospective educators are influenced by salary differentials (Han, 1994). That is, salary differentials between education and alternative occupations do influence career choice decisions (see, e.g., Rumberger, 1987; Salmon, 1988), and this is particularly true for males (Han, 1994). Thus school districts with low salaries, resulting from either a low wealth that will not support higher salaries or from a reluctance to tax themselves to provide higher salaries, will typically be less competitive in recruiting than higher-paying districts and employers.

Legal Constraints

A myriad of state and federal laws designed to prevent employment discrimination and promote equal employment opportunity (EEO) influence the recruitment process. The major federal EEO laws are summarized in Table 8.1. The recruitment practices that are most vulnerable, in terms of noncompliance with EEO principles and guidelines and possible areas of noncompliance, are as follows:

Job Descriptions. One particularly vulnerable area of job descriptions is the specification of minimum qualifications. Too frequently, arbitrary standards are used. For example, specifying "college degree" for a job that clearly does not require it creates artificial barriers that exclude otherwise capable individuals and is therefore discriminatory (Levesque, 1993). Moreover, the EEOC and the Civil Rights Division of the Department of Justice "recommend that job descriptions focus on the results or outcomes of a job function, not solely on the way it is customarily performed. This is because a person with a disability may be able to accomplish a job function, either with or without a reasonable accommodation, in a manner that is different from the way an employee who is not disabled may accomplish the same function" (Pynes, 1997, p. 77).

TABLE 8.1
Summary of Major EEO Laws Affecting Recruitment

Executive Order 11246 (as amended by 11375)	Bans discrimination on the basis of race, color, religion, sex, or national origin by federal contractors and subcontractors with at least $10,000 in contracts. Requires federal contractors and subcontractors with at least 50 employees and $50,000 in federal contracts to take affirmative action to increase the utilization of minorities and women.
Equal Pay Act of 1963	Prohibits gender discrimination in pay; requires equal pay for males and females in jobs requiring equal skills and responsibilities.
Title VII of the Civil Rights Act of 1964, as amended	Prohibits discrimination in hiring, compensation, and terms and conditions of employment on the basis of race, color, religion, national origin, or sex.
Age Discrimination in Employment Act of 1967, as amended	Prohibits discrimination in employment against persons aged 40 and over.
Equal Employment Opportunity Act of 1972	Extends race coverage of Title VII to include employees of state and local governments and educational institutions. Created the EEO Commission with authority to prohibit discrimination and file suits against organizations believed to be discriminatory.
Title IX of the Education Amendments of 1972	Prohibits discrimination on the basis of gender in programs receiving federal funds.
Section 504 of the Vocational Rehabilitation Act of 1973	Requires federal agencies and organizations receiving federal funds to take affirmative action to recruit, hire, and promote qualified disabled persons.
Vietnam Era Veterans Readjustment Assistance Act of 1974	Requires federal contractors and subcontractors to take affirmative action to hire and promote veterans and disabled veterans.
Pregnancy Discrimination Act of 1978	Provides EEO protection to pregnant workers and requires pregnancy to be treated like any other disability.
Americans With Disabilities Act of 1990	Extends the antidiscrimination provisions of Section 504 to organizations not receiving federal funds. Prohibits employment discrimination against individuals with physical or mental handicaps or the chronically ill.
Civil Rights Act of 1991	Amended Title VII and strengthened it and other civil rights laws that had been weakened by Supreme Court decisions.
Family and Medical Leave Act of 1993	Provides eligible employees of both sexes the right to take 12 weeks of unpaid leave per year in conjunction with the birth or first year of a child, the adoption or foster placement of a child, or the illness of the employee or the employee's spouse, child, or parent.

Advertisements. Ads can make no direct or indirect reference to race, religion, sex, or national origin. For instance, even ads recruiting "new graduates," "college students," "high school students," or "recent retirees" could cause problems, because they indicate an age preference. If the ad contains any job qualifications, the qualifications must be job related. "Even when a job is usually associated with one sex, the ad must indicate either male or female is acceptable" (Harvey & Bowin, 1996, p. 46).

EVALUATION OF THE RECRUITMENT PROGRAM

Since the recruitment process is both time consuming and costly, it is important that the human resources administrator evaluate the success of the recruitment process in terms of meeting both long- and short-term goals. This involves a calculation of the costs associated with each recruitment activity, as well as the total cost of the recruitment program, and a determination of what outcome criteria will be used to measure the effectiveness of the recruitment activities. Measures of effectiveness might include the number of inquiries received, the number of applications received from qualified applicants, the number of interviews granted, the number of job offers made to qualified applicants, the number of hires, and the number of minority hires.

Recruitment costs include not only the direct dollar expenditures for such things as advertising, agency fees, and travel for recruiters and candidates, but also the time spent by various school district personnel on the recruitment process. Some experts suggest that another 10% of these costs be added to total costs to account for miscellaneous costs (Dickmeyer, 2001). The personnel department will need to work with the hiring unit to ensure that accurate records are kept of costs per hire.

With the costs and outcomes attributable to each recruitment activity determined, the human resources department can then calculate and rank each recruitment activity in terms of its relative cost effectiveness and cost per hire. For example,

> calculating the cost of visiting a given campus for each hire from that campus makes it possible to compare this cost figure with that for other institutions. This simplifies decision making about which campus visits provide the greatest return. Determining the cost of a given radio advertisement for each bus driver application prompted by the advertisement makes it easy to compare the cost-effectiveness of this advertisement with others. Many such comparisons may be made. (Beebe, 1998, p. 81)

Information important to future recruitment efforts can be obtained from a review of the above data. For example, if there are many inquires about a job, but very few applications, then the content and quality of information disseminated to prospective applicants should be reviewed. If, on the other hand, many applications are reviewed, but very few applicants are suitable, then it is possible that the advertisements were inaccurately worded or inappropriately placed (Bolton, 1997).

Another source of information for the evaluation of the recruitment program is new hires. One district asked their new teachers how they came to hear about the district and why they chose that district and then used the information that they gleaned as part of their interview "pitch" in selling the district and to fine-tune their recruitment activities (Rodda, 2000).

In the long term, the success of the recruitment effort is determined not by the number of hires, but by the success of the hires. The on-the-job performance of the new hires and the degree to which they fit into the school system are the ultimate measures of the success of the recruitment process. This requires that new hires be tracked and a correlation be made of the sources and methods of recruitment and employee performance and fit.

SUMMARY

Recruitment begins with determining the need for a position, analyzing the duties and responsibilities of the position, and preparing a description of the position that can be used in the actual recruitment process. As districts undertake the recruitment process, a number of factors, including the number of potential applicants necessary to contact in order to obtain an applicant pool of the desired size, the type of job, and the recruitment budget, will influence how extensive and formal the process will become. If it appears that a pool of sufficient size can be obtained from internal recruiting, the district may limit its search activities to internal posting, recruiting previous and part-time employees, and employee referrals. If it seems necessary or desirable to engage in more extensive, external recruiting, advertisements may be placed in various media outlets, employment agencies may be used, recruitment contacts and trips may be made to educational institutions, and contacts may be made with professional organizations and unions.

Many school districts throughout the country are faced with the challenge of recruiting qualified minorities. In addition to aggressively recruiting the limited number of available minority candidates, a number of districts have attempted to build capacity. The most common capacity-building programs are the grow-your-own programs, which focus on assisting current employees to become teachers, and programs aimed at encouraging middle- and high- school students to enter teaching.

The recruitment efforts of the school district are subject to a number of fiscal and legal constraints. The fiscal condition of the district places constraints on how much the district can spend on recruitment. It also influences how competitive the district can be in the salaries paid to employees. Legal guidelines designed to prevent employee discrimination and promote equal employment opportunity also affect the recruitment process. In addition, school board policies not only provide the legal basis for the recruitment program, but also give direction for its activities.

DISCUSSION QUESTIONS

1. Interview someone in your school district or organization or an acquaintance who holds a job different from yours and write a job description for that position.
2. What are the advantages and disadvantages of a district policy promoting internal recruiting?
3. Under what circumstances should the district pay for the services of a private employment agency?
4. What strategies can a financially poor district use to make itself more competitive in its recruitment efforts?

CASE STUDIES

8.1 So You're in Charge of Minority Recruitment. Now What?

The Lebenon School District is a school district of 6300 students. The minority student population is 2% Asian American, 13% African American, and 19% Hispanic. Population projections suggest that the minority student population will increase to over 50% in the next 7 to 10 years. The Lebenon instructional staff contains no Asian Americans, 3% African Americans, and 6% Hispanics. The district has attempted to recruit minority staff by advertising in media outlets that focus on minorities and by sending recruitment materials to all the historically black colleges in the state. The results have been disappointing. Only five minority hires have been made in the last 2 years. At the same time, two minority teachers, a young married couple, moved to a neighboring district where they receive salaries of $4500 more (each) than they were making in the Lebenon district.

The superintendent has decided to put you, the assistant director of personnel, in charge of minority recruitment and has released you from other responsibilities in order to serve in this capacity. The superintendent has asked that you present her with a preliminary recruitment plan prior to the next cabinet meeting.

Questions

1. Prepare a draft of the plan for discussion with the director of personnel prior to submission to the superintendent.

8.2 Who Should Be in the Kitchen?

Arlene Kelley, the assistant food service director of the Mount St. Peters School District, retired at the end of the school year. The food services director, Neil Smith, is anxious to hire a replacement and is "bugging" the personnel director, Murray Nordin, to "get things going." He has volunteered to do some recruiting himself, saying he knows some good people who might be interested.

In the last 5 years, Mount St. Peters has closed the kitchens at its elementary schools and now serves these schools from a central kitchen. Over the same period of time, the enrollment of the district has declined by 8%, and the number of meals served at the high school has declined accordingly.

By the beginning of August, Neil is frustrated and insisting that he cannot start the new school year without an assistant director. He suggests that he be allowed to recruit as an emergency hire a cousin, Louise Smith, who currently serves as the kitchen manager at Mercy Hospital.

Questions

1. For what reasons might the personnel office have delayed the hiring of a replacement for Arlene Kelley? Is Neil justified in his frustration and insistence on the emergency hire?

2. Should Murray Nordin authorize the emergency hire? What problems are presented by the hiring of Louise Smith?

3. If the emergency hire is made, what further action should be taken by the personnel office? If the hire is not authorized, what further action should be taken? What options other than the emergency hire exist for meeting any need presented by the retirement of Arlene Kelley?

REFERENCES

Beebe, R. J. (1998). Recruiting and selecting new teachers: The recruitment budgeting cycle. *NASSP Bulletin, 82*(602), 77–82.

Bolton, D. L. (1970). *Instructor's guide for use of simulation materials for teacher selection.* Columbus, OH: University Council for Educational Administration.

Bolton, T. (1997). *Human resource management: An introduction.* Cambridge, MA: Blackwell.

Canada, B. O. (2001). A strategic view of recruitment. *School Administrator, 58*(1), 51.

De Cenzo, D. A., & Robbins, S. P. (1996). *Human resource management: Concepts and practice* (5th ed.). New York: Wiley.

Dickmeyer, W. (2001). Applicant tracking reports make data meaningful. *Workforce, 80*(2), 65–67.

Duarte, A. (2000). Wanted: 2 million teachers, especially minorities. *Education Digest, 66*(4), 18–23.

Educational Research Service (ERS). (1994). *Job descriptions in public schools* (2nd ed.). Arlington, VA: Author.

Esparo, L. J., & Radar, R. (2001). The leadership crisis. *American School Board Journal, 188*(4), 46–48.

Falcone, P. (1992). Selecting the best employment agency: It's a buyer's market. *HR Focus, 69*(8), 8.

Fenwick, L. T., & Pierce, M. C. (2001). The principal shortage: Crisis or opportunity. *Principal, 10*(10), 24–32.

Fideler, E. F., & Haselkorn, D. (1999). *Learning the ropes: Urban teacher induction programs and practices in the United States.* Belmont, MA: Recruiting New Teachers.

Goorian, B. (2000). Alternative teacher compensation. *ERIC Digest.* No. 142. Eugene: University of Oregon, ERIC Clearinghouse on Educational Management.

Grant, F. D. (2001). Fast track teacher recruitment. *School Administrator, 58*(1), 18–24.

Gurskey, D. (2001). Finding and training those 2 million teachers. *Education Digest, 66*(6), 17–22.

Han, Y. (April 1994). *The impact of teachers' salaries upon attraction and retention of individuals in teaching: Evidence from NLS-72.* Paper presented at the annual meeting of the American Educational Research Association, New Orleans, LA.

Harvey, D., & Bowin, R. B. (1996). *Human resources management: An experimental approach.* Upper Saddle River, NJ: Prentice Hall.

Haselkorn, S. J., & Fideler, E. (1996). *Breaking the glass ceiling: Paraeducator pathways to teaching.* Belmont, MA: Recruiting New Teachers.

Head, J. S. (2001). Web-based recruiting. *School Administrator, 58*(1), 20.

Herman, S. J. (1994). *Hiring right: A practical guide.* Thousand Oaks, CA: Sage.

Joinson, C. (2001). Refocusing job descriptions. *HRMagazine, 46*(1), 66–72.

Jordan, K. (1997). Play fair and square when hiring from within. *HRMagazine, 42*(1), 49–51.

Jordan, K. F., McKeown, M. P., Salmon, R. G., & Webb, L. D. (1985). *School business administration.* Beverly Hills, CA: Sage.

Kempton, J. (1995). *Human resource management and development: Current issues and themes.* New York: St. Martin's Press.

Lawrence, C. E., & Vachon, M. K. (1997). *The incompetent specialist: How to evaluate, document performance, and dismiss school staff.* Thousand Oaks, CA: Corwin Press.

Lemke, J. C. (1995). Attracting and retaining special educators in rural and small schools: Issues and solutions. *Rural Special Education Quarterly, 14*(2), 25–30.

Levesque, J. D. (1993). *Manual of personnel policies, procedures, and operations* (2nd ed.). Upper Saddle River, NJ: Prentice Hall.

Malone, B. G., & Caddell, T. A. (2000). A crisis in leadership: Where are tomorrow's principals? *Clearing House, 73,* 162–164.

Martinez, M. L. (1996). Looking for young talent? Inroads help diversify efforts. *HRMagazine, 41*(3), 73–76.

Morehart, K. K. (2001). How to create an employee referral program that *really* works. *HRFocus, 78*(1), 3–5.

National Conference of State Legislatures (NCSL). (n.d.). *State policies to improve the teacher workforce.* Denver, CO: NCSL.

National School Boards Association. (1996). *The school personnel management system.* Arlington, VA: Author.

Odden, A. R., & Conley, S. (1992). Restructuring teacher compensation systems. In A. R. Odden (Ed.), *Rethinking school finance: An agenda for the 1990s* (pp. 41–96). San Francisco: Jossey-Bass.

O'Laughlin, J. (1999). Recruiting and hiring high-quality teachers. *ERS Spectrum, 17*(4), 31–39.

Peterson, K., & Kelley, L. (2001). Transforming school leadership. *Leadership, 30*(3), 8–11.

Polansky, H. B. (1999). Combating teacher shortages: Frameworks for minority recruitment. *School Business Affairs, 65*(5), 43–44.

Potter, L. (2001). Solving the principal shortage. *Principal, 80*(4), 34–37.

Pynes, J. E. (1997). *Human resources management for public and nonprofit organizations.* San Francisco: Jossey-Bass.

Recruiting New Teachers (RNT). (2000). *A guide to today's teacher recruitment challenges.* Belmont, MA: RNT.

Rodda, C. (2000). Searching for success in teacher recruitment. *Thrust for Educational Leadership, 29*(3), 8–11.

Rumberger, R. W. (1987). The impact of salary differentials on teacher shortages and turnover: The case of mathematics and science teachers. *Economics of Education Review, 64*, 389–399.

Salmon, R. G. (1988). Teacher salaries: Progress over the decade. In K. Alexander & D. H. Monk (Eds.), *Attracting and compensating America's teachers* (pp. 249–261). Thousand Oaks, CA: Sage.

Schools seeking teachers overseas. (April 22, 2001). *Arizona Republic,* p. A17.

Schuerman, M. (2000). Scrambling for teachers. *American School Board Journal, 187*(10), 30–32.

Sherman, A. W., Jr., & Bohlander, G. W. (1992). *Managing human resources* (9th ed.). Cincinnati, OH: South-Western.

Smith, M. (1997/1998). Expanding the role of the job description to support a growing institution. *CUPA Journal, 48*(3/4), 17–25.

Texas Education Agency. (1999). *Texas teacher recruitment and retention study.* Austin: Texas Education Agency.

Trapps, T. E. (August 15, 2001). Teacher shortage expected to worsen, especially in California. *Los Angeles Times,* A22.

U. S. Department of Education, National Center for Education Statistics. (2000). *Teacher supply in the United States: Sources of newly hired teachers in public and private schools, 1987–88 to 1993–94.* Washington, DC: Author.

Warren, Gorham, & Lamont, (2000–2001). *HR series: Policies and practices* (Vol. 1). Boston: Author.

Wodarz, N. (2001). Hiring on-line. *School Business Affairs, 67*(2), 52–54.

9 *Selection*

After reading this chapter, you will be able to:

- Identify the candidate information typically being sought by the application form.
- Distinguish between the purposes of the preliminary interview and those of the employment interview.
- Identify the types of background checks that should be conducted on school employees.
- Discuss the importance of the physical setting and the psychological atmosphere to the conduct of the employment interview.
- Describe how the interviewer's interpersonal skills, listening skills, and questioning techniques influence the interview process.
- Describe the process by which employment offers are finalized in education.

The selection process represents one of the quickest ways to initiate change and improvement in a school organization. Every vacancy offers an opportunity to improve the quality and effectiveness of the organization's services. A well-planned and carefully executed screening and selection procedure can identify individuals who will potentially bring new life into the organization. A poorly planned or hasty selection can precipitate a potentially endless flow of personnel problems. The employment of the wrong person can reduce the effectiveness of instruction, jeopardize existing working relationships among staff members, and require costly remedial support. In extreme instances, a poor decision can necessitate an unpleasant termination, for both the school and the individual being dismissed. As Redeker (1989) predicted, "You hire a problem and you will have to fire a problem" (p. 6). Moreover, staffing a position with an inappropriate or ill-prepared person can cause serious professional and personal problems for the individual.

Because of the critical importance of selection decisions, screening and selection must be conducted in ways that ensure the highest probability for success. The selection process discussed in this chapter is designed to improve the reliability of selection decisions through the use of valid screening and selection criteria and processes. The process begins after the recruiting process has produced the applicant pool as discussed in Chapter 8. As discussed in this chapter, the selection process begins with the establishment of selection criteria and ends with the notification of unsuccessful candidates. The process is designed to enable administrators to choose from a pool of applicants the person or persons who best meet the selection criteria established for the position. The goal of the process is to produce, in a cost-effective manner, a highly productive work force committed to the attainment of school district goals.

ESTABLISHMENT OF SELECTION CRITERIA

The job analysis and job description described in Chapter 8 provide the basis for the articulation of the specific criteria to be used in the selection process. The selection criteria should be established before any position is advertised or application received. The selection criteria go beyond the job analysis and job description in that the selection criteria "delineate those ideal characteristics that, if possessed by an individual to the fullest extent possible would ensure the successful performance of the job" (Rebore, 2001, p. 116). The processes by which the criteria are developed vary, but the recommended practice is that it begin with current jobholders. For example, in the teacher selection process, experts suggest that

> A consensus among a system's finest teachers as to what skills and personal qualities they prize in themselves and others is the best gauge by which to look for new teachers. These consensus-based criteria (CBC) are used to focus the information-getting at each stage of the (selection) process and to evaluate the results of each step. (Smith & Knab, 1996, p. 102)

Others typically involved in the establishment of the selection criteria are the immediate supervisor and human resources personnel. Ultimately, the selection criteria will provide the basis for the rating of candidates by those reviewing application materials and conducting interviews. Figure 9.1 provides a sample of the selection criteria for an elementary teaching position.

MANAGING THE APPLICATION PROCESS

The Application Form

An application form must be completed by all applicants for a position in the district. An application form provides the school district with the means and opportunity to gather basic but important data in a cost-efficient and time-saving manner. The application form ensures consistency of information and enables the district to define precisely what is needed. According

ACADEMIC CRITERIA

1. Has appropriate college or university coursework and degree(s).
2. Has earned a grade point average in undergraduate and/or graduate courses that meets the acceptable standards of the district.
3. Demonstrates through an appropriate interview a working knowledge of the English language in verbal and written context.
4. Demonstrates an understanding and working knowledge of elementary mathematics skills that are compatible with the District's mathematics curriculum guide.
5. Demonstrates the skills necessary to teach reading in a manner compatible with the district's reading curriculum guide.
6. Has had some formal or informal training in music and has developed the skill to perform with a musical instrument.
7. Has completed courses in drama or participated in extracurricular dramatic performances, plays, or musical presentations during high school or college.

PERSONAL CRITERIA

8. Indicates a willingness to interact and communicate in a constructive fashion with district staff and community constituents.
9. Exhibits healthy, considerate, mature attitudes that would promote positive intra-staff and community relationships.
10. Dresses in a manner meeting the expectations of the school district and meets socially acceptable standards of hygiene and health care.
11. Is physically capable of actively participating with minimum proficiency in a sixth-grade outdoor experience that includes rappelling, canoeing, spelunking, and ropes course participation.
12. Expresses a willingness to abide by and implement the district's policies as prescribed by the board of education.

EXPERIENTIAL CRITERIA

13. Has relevant past teaching experience.
14. Has relevant student teaching experience.
15. Has a record of participating in extracurricular activities during high school and/or college (Extracurricular being defined as any organized school approved activity).
16. If applicant has had teaching experience, has demonstrated an interest in ongoing self-improvement by participating in professional workshops, seminars, college/university courses, or other professional programs.

FIGURE 9.1
Selection Criteria for a Sixth-grade Teaching Position
Source: Neely, S. (1993, October). *Personnel recruitment/selection/induction in small/rural schools.* Paper presented at the Rural and Small School Conference, Manhattan, KS.

to human resources experts, not even the applicant résumé provides the same benefits as the completed application form: "a résumé is really a person's own promotional piece . . . [whereas the application form] helps us get the information about a candidate that we need, to see if he or she really fits what we are looking for" (Woodward, 2000, p. 67) .

At a minimum, the application for professional positions will seek information regarding the applicant's educational background, work experience, certifications held, conviction record, and other personal data. In addition, the application form, or the instructions accompanying it, will request that the applicant submit a copy of the professional certificate, unofficial transcripts (official transcripts must be submitted if hired), test scores (if required), and letters of reference or names of references who may be contacted. The application will not be considered complete until all these are received. The application will normally conclude with a sign-off section in which the applicant (1) affirms to the truthfulness of the information given and to an understanding that falsification or misinformation may result in disqualification or dismissal and (2) gives permission for the district to verify all information and to contact references.

It is also common as part of the application process to ask applicants for professional positions to submit a written statement of their personal philosophy of education or to respond to other specific questions (e.g., the Professional Perspective section of the sample application form in Figure 9.2) that seek to determine the applicant's position on various aspects of educational theory or their response to a job-related issue or problem. For example, a district that was experiencing declining reading comprehension scores asked elementary principal candidates to respond to a writing prompt that asked them to describe the actions or steps that they would take to improve reading comprehension (Madrid, 2001). Such a writing assignment not only provides information that can be used to assess the applicant's professional values and skills, but their communication skills as well.

The application form should be made available to prospective applicants in both traditional and electronic formats. The actual design of the application is critical not only in assuring that the data most relevant to the selection decision be obtained, but that it does not violate EEOC guidelines. While all school districts have eliminated questions related to race, national origin, sex, age, religion, or disabilities from their application forms, it is not uncommon to find seemingly appropriate questions that do, in fact, violate EEOC guidelines. For example, questions that ask for the date of high school graduation and the location of the high school are indirectly collecting data on age and race or national origin (Harvey & Bowin, 1996). A list of job-related, nondiscriminatory questions and contrasting not-job-related, potentially discriminatory questions that cannot and should not be used on an application form are presented in Table 9.1. Finally, although the district may have taken great care to design its application form, if the district wants to be applicant friendly, it will accept the standard applications used by such teacher candidate databases as USTEACH.

APPLICATION FOR CERTIFICATED PERSONNEL

PERSONAL DATA

NAME _____
    (LAST)   (FIRST)   (MIDDLE)

SOCIAL SECURITY NUMBER _____

PRESENT ADDRESS _____

TELEPHONE _____

CITY_____ STATE _____

ZIP CODE _____

PERMANENT ADDRESS _____

TELEPHONE _____

CITY_____ STATE _____

ZIP CODE _____

HAVE YOU BEEN EMPLOYED BY
PARADISE VALLEY SCHOOLS BEFORE? _____

IF YES, WHEN AND WHAT LOCATION? _____

DID YOU COMPLETE YOUR STUDENT TEACHING WITH PVUSD? _____

IF SO, WHERE & WHEN? _____

HEALTH AND PHYSICAL CONDITION

CONDITION OF GENERAL HEALTH _____

DATE OF LAST COMPLETE PHYSICAL _____

DO YOU HAVE ANY PHYSICAL LIMITATIONS WHICH PRECLUDE YOU FROM PERFORMING CERTAIN KINDS OF WORK? _____

IF YES, PLEASE DESCRIBE SPECIFIC WORK LIMITATIONS? _____

_____

_____

CERTIFICATION

I AM CERTIFIED BY THE STATE OF ARIZONA TO TEACH _____

ENDORSEMENTS _____

TEACHING EXPERIENCE

(LIST FULL-TIME AND PART-TIME PROFESSIONAL EXPERIENCE, BEGINNING WITH THE MOST RECENT.
DO NOT INCLUDE STUDENT TEACHING. ATTACH ADDITIONAL SHEET IF NECESSARY.)

INSTITUTION	LOCATION OF SCHOOL CITY STATE	DATES: FROM--TO MONTH--YEAR	GRADE OR SUBJECT	ANNUAL SALARY	REASON FOR LEAVING PERSON TO CONTACT & PHONE NUMBER FOR CONFIRMATION OF EXPERIENCE

FIGURE 9.2

A Typical Application Form for Certified Personnel

Source: Paradise Valley Unified School District No. 69, Paradise Valley, AZ.

EDUCATIONAL AND PROFESSIONAL TRAINING

(PLEASE LIST ALL UNDERGRADUATE AND POST-GRADUATE CREDIT. ATTACH ADDITIONAL SHEET IF NECESSARY.)

NAMES OF COLLEGES/ UNIVERSITIES ATTENDED	LOCATION CITY -- STATE	DATES ATTENDED FROM -- TO	GRADUATION DATE	DEGREE AND/OR SEMESTER HOURS	MAJOR FIELD OF CONCENTRATION

POSITION DESIRED

HIGH SCHOOL _____   ELEMENTARY SCHOOL_____

MIDDLE SCHOOL _____   OTHER _____

PLEASE LIST SUBJECTS OR GRADE LEVELS IN ORDER OF PREFERENCE: _____

_____

WHAT EXTRA CURRICULAR ACTIVITIES ARE YOU WILLING TO SPONSOR OR COACH? _____

ARE YOU PRESENTLY UNDER CONTRACT? _____   IF YES, WHERE? _____

ARE YOU BILINGUAL? _____   WHAT LANGUAGES? _____

ARE YOU QUALIFIED TO TEACH COMPUTERS? _____   WHAT LEVELS? _____

PROFESSIONAL PERSPECTIVE

PLEASE ATTACH YOUR RESPONSES TO THE FOLLOWING QUESTIONS. MAKE SURE 1-4 ARE IN YOUR OWN HANDWRITING.

1. DESCRIBE THE CLASSROOM CONDITIONS THAT BEST FACILITATE STUDENT LEARNING. INCLUDE STRATEGIES YOU WOULD USE TO ASSURE MAXIMUM LEARNING FOR ALL STUDENTS.

2. DESCRIBE YOUR BELIEFS RELATED TO STUDENT BEHAVIOR. INDICATE WHAT YOU HOPE STUDENTS WILL HAVE LEARNED ABOUT BEHAVIOR AS A RESULT OF HAVING YOU FOR A TEACHER.

3. IN WHAT WAYS ARE YOU QUALIFIED TO ADDRESS THE ISSUE OF DIVERSITY AS A PART OF YOUR INSTRUCTIONAL PROGRAM?

4. AT THE END OF YOUR FIRST YEAR OF EMPLOYMENT IN PARADISE VALLEY, HOW WILL YOU DETERMINE WHETHER OR NOT YOU HAVE BEEN SUCCESSFUL?

5. PREPARE A LETTER WHICH COULD BE USED WHEN YOU'RE FIRST HIRED TO INTRODUCE YOURSELF TO THE PARENTS, STUDENTS AND STAFF IN YOUR SCHOOL COMMUNITY. INCLUDE YOUR BELIEFS ABOUT TEACHING AND LEARNING AND HELP US TO VISUALIZE WHAT LIFE IN YOUR CLASSROOM WILL BE LIKE.

FIGURE 9.2
(continued)

CONVICTION REPORT

Because of the tremendous responsibility Paradise Valley Unified School District has to its school children and community, the following information is needed from all applicants and employees regarding convictions*. A record on conviction does not prohibit employment; however, failure to complete this form accurately and completely can mean disqualification from consideration for employment or can be cause for consideration for dismissal if employed. Applicants and employees must report any convictions that occur subsequent to the time they initially completed this form. Questions regarding this information should be directed to the Director of Employment.

1. Name_____ Soc. Sec #_____

   Other names used/known by _____Dates of Usage _____

2. Have you ever been convicted of any offense other than a traffic violation(s)?   Yes   No

3. Have you ever been convicted of a felony?   Yes   No

4. Have you ever been convicted of a sex or drug related offense?   Yes   No

5. Have you ever been convicted of a dangerous crime against
   children as defined in A.R.S. 13.604.02?**   Yes   No

If any of the boxes above are marked "YES", fill in the information below and attach a letter of explanation.

CONVICTION INFORMATION

1. CONVICTION CHARGE	DATE OF CONVICTION		COURT OF CONVICTION
CITY	STATE	AMOUNT OF FINE	LENGTH OF JAIL TERM
REMARKS:	LENGTH AND TERMS OF PROBATION		
2. CONVICTION CHARGE	DATE OF CONVICTION		COURT OF CONVICTION
CITY	STATE	AMOUNT OF FINE	LENGTH OF JAIL TERM
REMARKS:	LENGTH AND TERMS OF PROBATION		

* CONVICTION means the final judgment on a verdict or a finding of guilty, or a plea of nolo contendere, in any state or federal court of competent jurisdiction in a criminal case, regardless of whether an appeal is pending or could be taken. Conviction does not include a final judgment which has been expunged by pardon, reversed, set aside, or otherwise rendered invalid.

** A.R.S. 13.604.01 requires applicants to give notice of any conviction for dangerous crimes against children. These crimes are defined as second degree murder, aggravated assault, sexual assault of a child, sexual conduct with a minor, sexual exploitation of a minor, child abuse, kidnapping and sexual abuse.

I authorize investigation of all the statements in this application including investigation of previous employment experiences if I am considered for employment. I certify that the above answers are true and complete and understand that falsification of facts on this application shall be considered sufficient cause for disqualification or dismissal. References and personal information which becomes a part of this record are to be regarded as confidential and will not be revealed.

Signature _____   Date _____

FIGURE 9.2
(continued)

TABLE 9.1

Avoiding Discriminatory Pre-Employment Inquiries
Some of the questions listed as potentially discriminatory may be asked legally if they relate to bona fide occupational requirements of a particular job or if there are affirmative action considerations.

Subject	Job-related, Nondiscriminatory Questions	Not Job-related, Potentially Discriminatory Questions
Name	Applicant's full name. Have you ever worked for this business or organization under a different name? Is any additional information relative to a different name necessary to check on your work record? If yes, explain.	Applicant's maiden name. Original name of applicant whose name has been changed by court order or otherwise.
Address/residence	What is your mailing address? How long a resident of this state or city? (for tax purposes)	Where did you live previously?
Sex, marital status, family	Statement of district policy regarding work assignment of employees who are related. Name and address of parent or guardian if applicant is a minor.	Questions that indicate applicant's sex, marital status, number and/or ages of children or dependents; provisions for child care, questions regarding pregnancy, child bearing, or birth control. Name or address of relative, spouse, or children of applicant. "With whom do you live?"
Race, color	None	Questions regarding applicant's complexion, color of skin, eyes, hair, etc.
Age	Statement that hiring is subject to verification that applicant meets legal age requirements. "If hired, can you show proof of age?"	Age Birth date Questions that tend to identify applicants over age 40.
National origin	Languages applicant reads, speaks, or writes, but only if relevant to the job.	Questions of nationality, lineage, ancestry, national origin, descent, or parentage of applicant, applicant's parents, or spouse. How applicant acquired the ability to read, write, or speak a foreign language.
Birthplace, citizenship	"Can you, after employment, submit verification of your legal right to work in the United States?" Statement that proof of legal right to work in the United States may be required after employment.	Requirements that applicant produce naturalization papers or alien card prior to employment. Birthplace or citizenship of applicant, applicant's parents, spouse, or other relatives. (continued)

Source: Avoiding Discriminatory Pre-Employment Inquiries, *The School Personnel Management System*, National School Boards Association (Alexandria, VA), 1996: pp. 512–514. Reprinted with permission.

TABLE 9.1
(continued)

Subject	Job-related, Nondiscriminatory Questions	Not Job-related, Potentially Discriminatory Questions
Physical condition, handicap	"Do you have any physical condition or handicap that may limit your ability to perform the job applied for? If yes, what can be done to accommodate the limitation?	Questions regarding receipt of Workers' Compensation. "Do you have any physical disabilities or handicaps?"
Physical description, photograph	Statement that photograph may be required after employment.	Questions as to applicant's height and weight. Request applicant, at his or her option, to submit a photograph.
Religion	Statement of regular days, hours or shifts to be worked.	Questions regarding applicant's religion.
Arrest, criminal record	Statement that, if recommended for employment, applicant would be required to give permission for a criminal records check.	"Have you ever been arrested?"
Dependents		"Do you have any children?" "How old are your children?" "Do you have any dependents?" "What child care arrangements have you made?"
Driver's license	May be asked about only if driving is necessary for the job.	"Do you have a valid driver's license?"
Education	Inquiry into academic, vocational, or professional education of the applicant and the schools attended.	
Emergency notification	Name and address of person to be notified in case of accident or emergency.	Name and address of nearest relative to be notified in case of emergency.
Experience	Inquiries into work experience.	
Health/pregnancy (postoffer/ pre-employment only)	Do you have any impairments— physical, mental, or medical—that would interfere with your ability to do the job for which you have applied? Are there any positions for which you should not be considered or job duties you cannot perform because of a physical or mental handicap? Inquiries into contagious or communicable diseases that may endanger others.	"Are you pregnant?" "Are you using any contraceptives?" "Are you planning to have a family?" Requirement that women be given a pelvic examination. "Do you have a disability or handicap?" "Do you use any adaptive device or aid?" "Have you ever been treated for the following diseases . . . ?"

TABLE 9.1
(continued)

Subject	Job-related, Nondiscriminatory Questions	Not Job-related, Potentially Discriminatory Questions
Height or weight		Any inquiries regarding applicant's height or weight. Postoffer/ pre-employment physical examinations are optional.
Relatives	Names of applicant's relatives already employed by the school system.	Requirement to furnish address of any relative.
Special skills	Inquiries into special skills such as typing, foreign languages, writing, operating computers, etc.	
Organizations	Inquiry into membership in professional organizations or hobby groups relevant to the job.	Inquiry into membership in specific organizations the name or character of which reveal personal information that could be used to discriminate against the applicant.

INITIAL SCREENING OF APPLICANTS

The initial screening of applicants involves the reviewing of the application forms and supporting materials to determine if the applicants meet the minimum qualifications for the job, and, if applicable, assessing the quality of the written exercise. For teaching positions, this review is typically conducted by or through the human resources department. However, in some districts the screening is performed by peer teachers or administrators. The screening process is made easier if the district has in place an applicant tracking system, as discussed next.

Applicant Tracking Systems

A complement to the electronic document management system (EDMS) discussed in Chapter 8 is the **applicant tracking system (ATS).** Applicant tracking systems provide an efficient means to process and analyze the applicant data being managed by the EDMS. The ATS allows applicants to be quickly and efficiently matched to positions. It permits the district to identify individuals within the applicant pool who meet the multiple selection criteria established for the position. "If a site administrator needs someone who can teach seventh-grade physical science, can speak Tagalog, and can coach girls' basketball, the applicant tracking system will allow that person to be identified immediately and also sorted based on rankings of 1–100" (O'Laughlin, 1999, p. 38). ATS are also used to generate many of the reports that are required of, or are of interest to, hiring officials: EEO and VETS 100 reports, cost-per-hire reports, hire by source reports, and others (Dickmeyer, 2001).

A number of different ATS software are commercially available (e.g., Sam Systems, Ivantage, and Abra Applicant). Another option, a rental option, is the use of an *application service provider* (ASP): the software remains in the provider's network and is accessed by the district through the Internet (Meade, 2000). The advantage of the ASP is that the ATS becomes instantly available, remains current, and is maintained. The major drawback is the security issues associated with having the data housed outside the district (Meade, 2000).

PRELIMINARY INTERVIEW

Following the initial screening, depending on district practice and the number of applicants remaining in the applicant pool, the selection process may move directly to an interview of the candidates identified as most qualified, or a preliminary interview may be used as an additional screening device. That is, if there are only a few applicants and the decision is made to proceed with the hiring process or if the initial screening produced only a few applicants with the necessary qualifications, all could be granted the employment interview discussed later. If, on the other hand, a number of applicants remain in the pool after the initial screening, the district may use the **preliminary interview** as an additional screening tool.

The functions of the preliminary interview are (1) to determine the correctness and completeness of the information obtained in the application file, (2) to eliminate from the applicant pool those who do not meet the profile and qualifications that the district is seeking, and (3) to provide information for the employment interview of applicants who are to be considered further (Fear, 1990; Vickers, 1996). The preliminary interview also provides the applicant with an opportunity to receive answers to questions about the position or school system.

The preliminary interview is usually conducted by human resources department personnel and may take place on campus, at job fairs, at district offices, on the telephone, or through the use of interactive video. In fact, telephone and interactive video interviews have become more common as candidates apply for positions in school districts located great distances from their present locale. Telephone interviews provide an economical way to bring the candidate and the interviewer together (Vickers, 1996; O'Laughlin, 1999). The interview is usually short and structured (typically 20 minutes), with all candidates being asked the same questions and answers recorded and scored (Smith & Knab, 1996). After the preliminary interview, only the most viable applicants remain to be evaluated.

BACKGROUND CHECKS

It has been estimated that 36% of all applicants have lied on their résumé or on a job application. In fact, 95% of college students in a research study said that they would lie to get a job and 41% said that they had already done so (Bliss, 2000). Almost every school district has had at least one experience with counterfeited transcripts, falsified licenses, or distorted work histories. Even more seriously, a number of districts have found out too late that they have in their employ persons with previous convictions for child molestation or substance abuse. And, because of their failure to conduct adequate background and criminal records checks, many of these districts have been found liable for negligent hiring. In fact, according to *Public Personnel Management*, employers lose 72% of negligent hiring suits and the average settlement is $1.6 million (Vaughn, 2001a). To protect district students and employees, it is important that the credentials, references, and employment histories of candidates be checked and that criminal background checks be conducted. In so doing, the district must maintain the proper balance between the district's need to know and the applicant's right to privacy. The district must also comply with state and federal laws and the guidelines provided by court decisions in performing background checks. In performing background checks, the district is subject to the same restrictions that are applicable to all other aspects of the selection process. That is, information is not to be solicited or used unless valid and job related.

An important consideration for the district in performing background checks is the cost of and the time required for the process. Traditionally, background checking has been a time-consuming process that could delay the selection process. In recent years, as technology has improved, as more and more public records have gone on line, it has become relatively simple to do a background check on the Internet (Siegel, 2001). Again, if the district does not have the desire or expertise to conduct the Internet background check, a number of on-line services are available to perform the research. Four of the more popular are at www.peoplewide.com, www.knox.com, www.informus.com, and www.confichek.com (Vaughn, 2001b). A major consideration in conducting background checks is who will do the checking—the human resources department, the immediate supervisor, a member of the selection committee, or an external third party. Doing background checks internally may save the district money, but many districts do not have employees with the expertise or time to perform the necessary checks and therefore use a third party to conduct the background checks. Besides providing specialized expertise, using a third party often gives applicants a greater sense of privacy, especially in regard to possible co-workers, and gives the impression that all applicants are being handled uniformly and objectively (Garvey, 2001). As discussed next, background checks are usually performed in the areas of references, credentials, and criminal background.

Reference Checks

The employment application will typically require applicants to provide the names and addresses of persons who can serve as references regarding their current and past employment. Applicants may be informed on the application form that, by supplying the names of references or letters of reference, they are agreeing that these references may be contacted, or, more typically, they may be asked to specifically sign a statement that authorizes the employer to contact current or former employers or other references for the purpose of conducting the reference check. This reference check authorization statement "typically specifies that applicants waive their rights to have access to the information provided by current or former supervisors or other references. The statement may also stipulate that applicants will not hold the individual providing the reference or the school district liable for any job related information provided or received" [National School Boards Association (NSBA), 1996, p. 516]. Although reference checking can be a time-consuming process, the more time and energy the process is given, the more accurate and useful the information gathered (Bliss, 2000).

The most commonly used methods of checking references are letters and telephone calls, with preference given to telephone calls because they save time and are more likely to produce more candid responses. At least three references should be contacted, with one being the most recent supervisor or, in the case of beginning teachers, their cooperating teacher and/or college supervisor. For experienced teachers, the person who taught next door, a parent who worked closely with the teacher, or the secretary or janitor from the previous school should not be overlooked as possible references (Slosson, 1999). The use of a standardized telephone reference check form such as that presented in Figure 9.3 helps to ensure consistency and fairness, while allowing the district to determine the areas to be addressed (NSBA, 1996). If a standardized form is not used, investigators should be supplied with a set of standard questions. Such questions might include the following:

☐ What is your name and position?
☐ How long have you been acquainted with the applicant?
☐ In what capacity did you know the applicant?
☐ What are the strengths of the individual?
☐ How would you characterize the applicant's relationship with his/her students?
☐ If we hire the applicant, in what area would you suggest that we provide additional staff development or training?
☐ Have there been any investigations concerning unprofessional conduct, incompetency, insubordination, or immorality concerning the applicant?
☐ Would you rehire this individual if given the chance? (DeMitchell, 1990, p. 10)

Confidentiality and Liability.   Present or former employers may sometimes be reluctant to share any information about a present or former employee other than factual information (e.g., dates of employment, salary, job title) because of fear of a defamation charge. In an effort to encourage employers to share information openly during reference checks, 34 states have passed laws to protect employers that provide good-faith references; some have added protections for educational institutions (Bliss, 2000). Even in the absence of such statutory protection, under the legal theory of qualified privilege, an employer has the right to share job-related

KYRENE SCHOOL DISTRICT

ADMINISTRATIVE TELEPHONE REFERENCE CHECK

Name of Candidate _____

Name of Reference _____ Title _____

Place of Business _____ Phone # _____

Reference call made by _____ Date _____

1. How long have you known (the candidate)? _____

2. In what capacity have you known (the candidate)? _____
   _____

3. What do you find to be his/her greatest strengths? _____
   _____
   _____

4. What special or unique contribution has he/she made to your school or district? _____
   _____
   _____

5. What do you believe to be his/her most important reasons for being an educator? _____
   _____
   _____

6. Please tell me about the relationships he/she establishes and maintains with:
   A. Students? _____
   B. Parents? _____
   C. Co-Workers/Staff? _____

7. What are the most common management approaches he/she uses? _____
   _____
   _____

8. How do students especially benefit from being in (candidate's) building? _____
   _____
   _____

9. On a scale of 1 to 10 (10 = highest) how would you rate his/her overall effectiveness as an
   administrator? _____ Why? _____
   _____

10. How do you believe a supervisor should work with this candidate in order to bring out the best in
    him/her? _____
    _____

11. Is there anything else you would like to add to help us understand him/her more fully? _____
    _____
    _____

Thank you for your assistance!

FIGURE 9.3

Source: Kyrene (AZ) School District.

information, even if negative, if the purpose is a legitimate business need. And the employer will be protected from defamation claims if:

☐ The statement was truthful. This is an absolute defense.
☐ The employer had a qualified privilege to make a false or defamatory statement. For this to be applicable the statement must have been made within a privileged situation—for instance, a call from a new employer or to protect your own interest.
☐ The employer can show "absence of malice" or lack of spite, intent to harm, or ill will.
☐ The employee consented to your making a reference statement. This is the strongest defense. (Bliss, 2000, p. 5)

Whatever information is obtained from reference checks, it is imperative that it not be shared with the applicant or with any other person not authorized to have access to the information.

Credentials Checks

An applicant's credentials include such items as high school or trade school diploma, college or university transcript, the teacher or administrator certificate, professional license, or a physician's verification of health. It is common practice not to require the verification of health unless the applicant is selected for the position. Transcripts and health documentation should not be accepted if presented by the applicant, but must be mailed directly to the human resources office by the school, college, university, or physician. However, because administrator and teacher certificates, as well as various other professional certificates and licenses, are issued directly to the person, they may be accepted from the applicant. Nonetheless, a check should still be made to verify that they are valid, because when a license or certificate has been suspended or revoked the actual document is not always returned to the issuing agency (Rebore, 2001).

Criminal Background Checks

The statutes of most states prohibit individuals who have been convicted of drug- or sex-related crimes from employment in the public schools. Laws are generally not as specific regarding conviction for other felonies. It is permissible to ask on the application form if the applicant has been convicted of any crime and the nature of the offense. To conduct a criminal background check to verify the accuracy of these responses is both time consuming and controversial. However, the heightened publicity given to cases of school employees involved in illegal conduct, as well as the heightened liability of school districts who have hired such persons, has led to an increase in criminal background checking. The extent of the checking will depend on state statutes and school district policy. The majority of the states have enacted statutes requiring criminal background checks of persons applying for positions in the schools. In some states, such checks are required only of prospective teachers, while in other states checks are required for administrators, custodial workers, food service personnel, coaches, substitute teachers, volunteers (other than parents), or any other individuals who have ongoing contact with students. In those states in which criminal background checks have been mandated by statute, the school district should have adopted a policy and procedures that identify the school district's role in adhering to the statute. The policy and procedures will also typically identify the state or federal agency through which the records will be obtained, who will pay the fee required, and the applicant's rights regarding receiving a copy of the report or the opportunity to explain any conviction (NSBA, 1996).

In states where criminal background checks are required, the state generally has allowed districts access to state criminal records. Under the National Child Protection Act of 1993, school districts are also given access to FBI criminal records for background checks. If the district has an electronic live-scan fingerprint machine, the candidate's fingerprints can be scanned and sent by the Internet to the FBI and the state criminal records center and a response received, possibly within seconds (Grant, 2001).

In states in which criminal background checks are not required by state law, background checks may still be conducted through state and federal law enforcement agencies or with the **Teacher Identification Clearinghouse** (TIC). The TIC is operated by the National Association of State Directors of Teacher Education and Certification and maintains records of all teachers who have been denied certification or have had their certificates suspended or revoked for moral reasons in the last 15 years. The information is provided by the certification officer of each member state and can be accessed only by states, not individual school districts. In addition to the information received from state or federal law enforcement agencies or the TIC, all states maintain registries of known sex offenders, which can also be accessed by school districts.

Dealing with Negative Information

A major challenge for human resources administrators is how to deal with any negative information that may turn up as a result of the background checks. The first thing that must be done is to ensure that the information is accurate. Unfortunately, just as there are applicants who will make false statements on their applications or résumés, there are references who will make false or misleading statements about an applicant. In some instances, persons have had their identity stolen or someone with bad credit or a criminal conviction has the same name, resulting in a negative and inaccurate report.

Information generated from the background check must comply with the Fair Credit Reporting Act (FCRA). The FCRA requires that all data based on public records (e.g., criminal charges and motor vehicle records) be accurate and up to date and that information involving civil suits and judgments be no more than 7 years old (Garvey, 2001). The FCRA also specifies the procedures that are to be followed if the information from a background check leads to a negative employment decision. Specifically, the employer must provide the employee with a copy of the negative report and the FCRA's *Statement of Consumer Rights.* Second, the employer should give the employee a "reasonable period of time" (normally considered to be 3 to 5 days) to refute the information. If the employee does not successfully respond within the designated time frame, the employer is free to take adverse action. When doing so, the employer must send the applicant a *notice of adverse action,* along with another copy of consumer rights under the FCRA; the name, address, and telephone number of the consumer reporting agency that provided the negative report; and a clear statement that the reporting agency "did not make the adverse hiring decision and is unable to provide the applicant with specific reasons why the action was taken" (Garvey, 2001, p. 103).

After all background checks are completed, the screening and selection process moves to the employment interview stage.

THE EMPLOYMENT INTERVIEW

The employment interview is the most widely used selection technique. The employment interview is a process of gathering information about an applicant relative to the predetermined selection criteria. During this process, the interviewer(s) and the applicant engage in a developmental conversation that explores the applicant's qualifications, skills, and experiences relative to the criteria. Both positive and negative aspects of the applicant's background are discussed with equal importance.

For teaching positions, the employment interview is most often conducted by the principal of the school where the candidate will teach. In many districts, team interviews are conducted. Use of interview teams not only eliminates the bias associated with a single interviewer, but helps to build cooperative relationships among faculty, between faculty and administrators, and between school personnel and parent and community representatives (Caldwell, 1993). For teaching positions, the team might consist of the principal, the chair of the department (if applicable), a teacher in the department or area, a human resource specialist, the central office administrator responsible for that curricular area, or the central office administrator responsible for that grade level. In constituting the interview team it is important that, to the extent possible, it be balanced by race, ethnicity, and gender. In still other districts, site-based decision-making teams actively participate in all phases of the selection process, including interviewing (Huling, Resta, Mandeville, & Miller, 1996). And, whether at the employment interview or as a separate interview, almost two-thirds of all teacher candidates (and virtually all finalists for administrative positions) will meet with the superintendent during this phase of the selection process (Vickers, 1996).

Whoever is involved in the interview process, it is important that they be trained in the district's selection policies and procedures and appropriate interview techniques. It is also important that they be made aware of the types of questions that are allowed and disallowed under state and federal nondiscrimination laws and the types of innocent remarks that can lead to school district liability (Clark, 1999).

The information collected through the employment interview should be viewed with the same concern for validity and objectivity as any paper-and-pencil test used in the screening processes. Every possible effort should be made to develop a structured, behavioral interview that is valid for the position to be filled. Structured, **behavioral interviews** are characterized by a set of job-related questions that seek to examine a candidate's past job behaviors, rather than to identify general traits (e.g., "the candidate is reliable" [a trait] versus "the candidate only missed one day of work in 5 years" [a behavior]) (Warren, Gorham, & Lamont, 2001). The questions used for the interview are usually ordered to support a developmental approach to the interview (e.g., chronological, career path, or professional accomplishments). The structured behavioral interview is an information-gathering process for bringing objectivity into the screening procedure. When the interview is specifically developed in relation to the selection criteria derived from the position analysis, selection decisions can be made with the assurance that the best available applicant for the position has been selected.

Planning the Interview

The first step in planning for the interview is to read carefully all materials contained in the applicant's personnel file. Next, a general first impression of the applicant is written, giving special attention to areas of strength and areas of needed development. The information is recorded on the interview planning form. Figure 9.4 illustrates one section of a completed planning form. It shows how data and information are associated with one of the predetermined selection criteria.

In recording information, the reviewer condenses information and lists only relevant phrases, comments, and data under the corresponding selection criterion. For example, as shown in Figure 9.4, if the criterion *interpersonal skills* is one of the selection criteria, each item of information found in the written materials that shows strength or needed improvement in interpersonal skills is listed below the criterion and includes a reference to its source (e.g., application form on recommendation from academic supervisor).

The individual processing a personnel file must judge the statements and other information in the file relative to the selection criteria. This is not difficult if the criteria and dimensions have been clearly defined and the reviewer is very familiar with them. One hazard for the beginning reviewer is the tendency to write evaluative statements about the applicant rather than facts from the file. For example, a letter of recommendation might include the statement, "Her single most important strength is relating effectively to the parents of handicapped children." If this statement is judged to be distinctive and related to interpersonal skills, the inexperienced reviewer might write a statement such as "She has very good interpersonal skills," rather than

Applicant: <u>Mildred Thomas</u>

Screening Dimension Number 3

On the lines provided, identify the third screening dimension that was derived from the Position Analysis. This is to be followed by a definition of the dimension. Add behaviors that would suggest evidence of strength in the dimension.

Screening Dimension:	<u>Interpersonal Skills</u>
Definition:	<u>Shows caring for others; open to the ideas and feelings of others; earnestly seeks candor and openness; maintains a cool and rational approach on a constant basis throughout a conflict situation</u>
Behaviors Suggesting Strength in Dimension:	<u>Empathetic, caring, rational, poised, tactful, flexible, cooperative, helpful, sensitive</u>

In the spaces provided, carefully review all written application information and identify each item of information that relates to the screening dimension; develop nonleading interview questions; after the interview, record responses.

Background Information: (A—application form, T—college transcript, R—reference)

Developed unit on student self-concept (A)

"Children must experience success." (A)

"On occasion, shows some impatience with other teachers." (R)

"As a general rule, she is a helpful and sensitive person. She is extremely intelligent, but can be a little abrupt with others who are having some difficulty." (R)

"Working on ability to be a better listener." (R)

Interview Questions:

Interview Responses:

FIGURE 9.4

actually quoting or paraphrasing the letter of recommendation. The evaluation of interpersonal skills is not made during the information-processing phase, but only after all written information has been recorded and combined with new or corroborating information from the behavioral interview.

After all written materials in the personnel file have been processed and pertinent information recorded, the entries under each criterion must be analyzed further. An important question must be asked about the information included under each: Is the written information for the dimension sufficient to allow an evaluation of the applicant on this factor? If yes, the dimension need not be pursued in the behavioral interview. Conversely, if more information is needed to substantiate or corroborate existing information, then relevant interview questions must be developed, questions that relate to the applicant's previous experiences. These questions are developmentally ordered and used in the behavioral interview with the applicant. The types of interview questions and the conduct of the actual interview are discussed in the following section. Notes taken during the interview are recorded in the Behavioral Interview Planning Form under the appropriate criteria.

Conducting the Interview

Essentially, the employment interview is an attempt to predict the job performance of an applicant 1 year after hiring. And, since the best predictor of what an applicant will do in the future is what he or she has done in the past, the task of the interviewer is to explore past work experiences with the applicant and record information that provides insight into strengths and areas of needed development relative to the identified criteria. The quality of information obtained has a direct relationship to the following aspects of the interview process: (1) physical setting for the interview, (2) psychological atmosphere, (3) interviewer's interpersonal skills, (4) interviewer's listening skills, (5) quality of note taking, and (6) quality of interview questions and techniques.

Physical Setting. While interactive video interviewing may be used when time, distance, or cost is a major consideration, the face-to-face interview is still the most common and preferred approach to the conduct of the employment interview. The interview should be conducted in a private location, where the environment can be psychologically supportive and free of physical distractions. Meeting these requirements will promote feelings in the candidates that they are having a conversation with an important representative of the district. The interview should not be conducted in such public locations as a hotel restaurant, lounge, lobby, or swimming pool. These places have too many distractions, do not offer privacy, and do not support a feeling of confidentiality in the applicant. The best location is a private office.

The interviewer should communicate the need for privacy to the secretary so that all telephone calls and other interruptions can be avoided. An interruption during the interview can cause the applicant to lose a line of thought at a time when important information is being communicated. In addition, it is difficult for the interviewer to show interest in the applicant and to record all relevant information if other business is being transacted simultaneously. The interviewer and applicant should not sit across a desk from each other. The desk tends to symbolize authority and may formalize the atmosphere unnecessarily. Similarly, sitting side by side on a sofa is not recommended because it creates a psychological barrier to communication (Martin, 1993). Many experienced interviewers prefer to sit at a table at a right angle to the applicant. Some have conversation areas in their offices with comfortable chairs. Finally, furnishings that cause distractions should be removed from the office (e.g., clocks that chime or fish tanks with bubblers).

Psychological Atmosphere. The psychological atmosphere must be considered with great care to promote the best conditions for the interview. For the interview to be developmental, the interviewer must minimize the applicant's stress by being friendly and accepting, genuine, open, attentive, and nonjudgmental. Stress is particularly great at the beginning of the interview, and careful efforts should be made at that time to put the applicant at ease. This atmosphere should be maintained throughout the remainder of the interview.

At the end of the interview, the applicant should feel that the experience was positive and nonthreatening. The applicant should also feel that both strengths and areas of needed development for the position were discussed with equal importance. These feelings can more readily occur when the interviewer's beliefs and assumptions about people are positive and supportive. The interviewer should end the interview by thanking the candidate for his or her willingness to be open and honest (Martin, 1993).

Interviewer's Interpersonal Skills. Another aspect of the interview process is the interviewer's interpersonal skills, or manner of dealing with people. Generally, interviewers should not try to use a set of behaviors different from those consistently employed in other settings. The interview is no place to experiment with behaviors. However, it is important for the interviewer to be aware of behaviors that can affect the quality of information gained in the interview.

Body language is one of these considerations. We all realize that our nonverbal behaviors communicate meaning to others. Likewise, the nonverbal behaviors of an interviewer can significantly affect the interview process. A frown or a smile can serve to increase or decrease the candidate's stress. An authoritative and formal manner on the part of the interviewer will tell the applicant to respond to interview questions in a formal way. On the other hand, a more relaxed manner will tend to put the applicant at ease, and the applicant will respond accordingly. When the interviewer leans toward the applicant with eye contact, it shows that the interviewer is interested and is sincerely concerned about what the applicant is saying. When the interviewer leans back and gives a periodic "ah ha" or other similar utterance to show understanding and attentiveness, the applicant will know that ample time is available to explore background experiences and qualifications for the position. Conversely, an interviewer's glance at a wristwatch, gaze out the window, or shuffling of papers may tell the applicant that the interviewer is not interested, that a negative decision has been made, or that other, more important things need to be done.

Interviewer's Listening Skills. One of the most difficult yet important interview skills to learn is listening. We not only listen to what is being said verbally, but also temper its meaning by our tone of voice, inflections, and nonverbal expressions. If the applicant responds quickly to a question, pauses before responding, or avoids responding, the interviewer must interpret whether these behaviors have important meanings. Being a good or active listener requires that the interviewer (1) avoid hearing what he or she expects to hear based on the interviewee's diction, mannerisms, dress, and the like, (2) avoid cutting off the speaker by anticipating what will be said or by asking another question, and (3) concentrate on the core of what is being said and ignore the rhetoric. It is also the interviewer's responsibility to "listen to the active spoken words of the interviewee, to direct the communication towards the final goal, and to remember key words or phrases that may need additional discussion or clarification" (Martin, 1993, p. 80).

The task of listening is difficult because the interviewer is trying to record information as it is communicated while thinking about the next question and trying to maintain eye contact with the applicant. An interviewer is obviously not listening when an applicant begins the answer to a question with, "Well, as I mentioned a few minutes ago . . . ." The interviewer must be able to listen well to be in control of the interview and accomplish its purpose. The only way that this can happen is through thorough preparation of a structured behavioral interview.

Quality of Note Taking. The recording of information obtained in the interview raises some important concerns. Many inexperienced interviewers feel that it is too difficult to record information during the interview. They say that it forces a sense of undesirable formality. Moreover, they question their ability to simultaneously take notes, maintain eye contact, and listen carefully. Although these concerns are all valid, one must not lose sight of the purpose of the interview—to obtain information about an applicant relative to predetermined dimensions or criteria. If the interviewer attempts to rely on memory alone, important information can be lost and the interview is of no value. It is difficult to conduct a 30-minute to 1-hour conversation with a person about experiences specific to him or her and remember all the significant information. In addition, applicants expect the person conducting interviews to take notes, for it signifies that what is said is important and will not be overlooked in the employment decision. It emphasizes the applicant's importance as a prospective employee of the organization. Any detriment to the interview process brought on by note taking is more than made up for by the information recorded. Many of the difficulties of taking notes can be overcome with practice. Interviewers find that they can develop their own shorthand or write down key words or phrases that can be expanded to a fuller meaning later.

Another consideration of note taking is the timing of writing notes. As a general rule, it is best to write notes at a time when it will not interfere or affect what is being said. If the applicant mentions something important, it is best for the interviewer to wait until the conversation moves to a subject where note taking is expected before the important information is recorded. For instance, an applicant may be talking about a very sensitive, job-related issue. To write a note at that moment may inhibit any further expansion on the issue. Note taking can also become a signal that whatever is being said is important, causing the applicant to direct inappropriate comments to that area.

Quality of Questions and Questioning Techniques.   Skill in developing and asking questions is the most difficult yet most important quality for the interviewer to possess. To develop appropriate interview questions, one must be aware of the many considerations that detract from objectivity or contaminate information obtained through positive or negative bias. And it is extremely important that all questions be totally job related.

To be job related, questions must be centered on previous work experiences, skills, and training in relation to the dimensions established in the position analysis. The questions presented in Table 9.1 as being inappropriate for use on the application form are equally inappropriate for use during the interview. Examples of job-related questions include the following:

- □ *Former employment:* What did you like about your former position? What did you like the least? Was your work ever criticized? Did you improve your skills and abilities? In what way? Why did you leave your last job? Why do you want to work in this school district?
- □ *Motivation to work:* Why did you select teaching as a profession? Why did you select this grade level? For noncertificated staff, why did you select this line of work? What do you hope to gain by working here? How do you keep abreast of developments in the profession?
- □ *Job stability:* What was your original career objective? How has that changed? Why did you leave your last job?
- □ *Initiative and innovation:* When you ran into a problem you could not solve, what did you do? How did you change your job? What is the most difficult problem you faced and how did you resolve it? What does it take to be a successful teacher? How did you change, create, or work within the parameters of your former employment?
- □ *Ability to work with others:* How would you supervise others if given the opportunity? How well do you believe your former supervisor did his/her job? What do you believe is the best way for a supervisor/principal to work in this job? How do you manage change? Conflict? Stress?
- □ *Self-evaluation:* If you had a formal complaint filed against you, how would you handle it? Can you identify a skill that you would like to acquire or that would be appropriate for staff development? What have you found is the best way to handle disputes with parents? Staff? What sets you apart from other candidates? (Clark, 1999, p. 3)

Two types of questions can be used in the interview. First, a direct or **closed question** can be used to obtain factual information. For example, if the applicant omitted information in the application materials, a direct question can be used to complete the record (e.g., "How many years did you teach at Cherryhill Elementary School?"). Closed questions are restrictive in nature and do not provide much opportunity for the interviewee to express opinions or give explanations.

The second type of question, the nonleading or **open-ended question,** does not suggest an obvious or preferred response. The question allows the applicant to structure an individual response. One technique of using nonleading questions involves asking two questions that are considered a polarized pair. If the interviewer wants the applicant to relate an ability to get along with the people in a previous position, the direct question "Did you get along with the people you worked with at _____?" will yield an obvious response. A polarized pair of questions might include the following two questions: "What did you like the most working with the people at _____?" would be later followed by "What did you like the least in working with these people?" Both responses may require follow-up questions to gain a greater depth of understanding.

Some words can be very threatening to the person being interviewed. In the question "What is your most serious weakness for the job?" the word "weakness" can be a threat to the applicant who may view it as a trick question. A less threatening question might be "What one area do you feel is important for you to develop professionally?" Again, follow-up questions are usually needed to explore fully the applicant's response.

Softening the impact of a question is a useful interviewing technique. When a teacher applicant is being asked about classroom management, it is sometimes helpful for the interviewer to draw on personal experiences to soften the impact of a question. "When I taught mathematics, I did many things that worked well with children. Yet most of us who have taught for a while know that certain situations or types of children give us great difficulty no matter how hard we try. Can you give me an example where you experienced this same feeling?" Usually, when this question is asked, the interviewee will give an affirmative, nonverbal nod. If this indication is not given, it might be helpful to first ask, "Have you ever had this experience?" A negative response would raise some obvious concerns about the applicant's veracity. A polarized pair of questions also can work well in pursuing this area of interest.

Avoid hypothetical questions. Frequently the interviewer of a teacher applicant will ask, "What would you do if . . . ?" A question like this will only elicit a hypothetical or "textbook response." It is far better to ask about actual experiences and accomplishments. If the applicant does not have experience, then it would be better to ask about similar situations that he or she has witnessed, rather than to ask a hypothetical question. Questions about learning situations and instruction that the applicant observed or participated in as a student would yield far better information than the reply to a hypothetical question.

One of the most widely used questions with teacher applicants is "What is your philosophy of education?" This is the kind of question that will usually yield a textbook response. If knowing the applicant's philosophy is important, evidence can be found by asking questions about previous teaching strategies, assumptions held, curriculum, and methods of evaluation. An applicant's verbal statement about philosophy may have nothing to do with the ability to teach, manage a classroom, or relate to children. Again, past teaching experiences provide the best guide to what the interviewer can expect of the applicant on the job. This is not to say that exploring the candidate's personal values or perceptions is not important. In fact, questions about their personal perceptions can tell you a lot about what they are like. For example, the answer to the question "What is the best thing that ever happened to you in education?" has quite a different meaning if the answer relates to an award the candidate won as opposed to a successful student. Other insights can be gained from the responses to such questions as "What accomplishment has made you most proud?" "Who is the nicest person you ever met?" or "What adversary do you have who respects you?" "Do you have a friend you don't admire?" "If you could be more like someone else, who would that be?" (Slosson, 1999, p. 30).

Silence is a very powerful way to ask a question without really saying it. Silence after an applicant's response to a previous question can serve as a prompt that the interviewer wants to hear more. Although this technique can be difficult to master, experience through repeated attempts will minimize the tendency to offer another question after a few seconds of deafening silence. The silence may, in fact, indicate the formulation of a thought or answer. And a hasty interruption may result in the loss of a central part of the answer (Martin, 1993). Five or six seconds may seem like 10 minutes to the interviewer, and the temptation to talk increases in intensity with each succeeding second.

Several other pitfalls that can affect the interview also should be mentioned. For example, the interviewer should not give the applicant advice. It takes valuable time and is inappropriate in the interview. On occasion, an applicant will say something with which the interviewer will greatly disagree. When this occurs, the interviewer should not argue with the applicant or attempt to "set him straight." It should be remembered that the purpose is to accumulate information about the applicant and not offer another point of view or give evaluative feedback. The best response to negative comments by the applicant is "Ah ha, I see."

Similarity attraction is another common pitfall. Research on selection suggests that even well-meaning individuals give subtle advantages to people most similar to themselves (Tallerico, 2000). If the interviewer learns that the applicant went to the same college as he or she did, this may positively skew the interviewer's interpretation of the applicant's qualifications. Other examples might include belonging to the same fraternity, sorority, or church or being involved in the same high school or college sport. A negative response can also occur if the applicant speaks very positively about a mutual acquaintance that the interviewer does not hold in high esteem. These examples have the potential of inappropriately tempering the interviewer's understanding of an applicant's qualifications for a position. Every effort should be made to guard against such biases.

In addition to these considerations, experienced interviewers also suggest the following interviewing techniques:

☐ Pace the interview and apportion interview time approximately. Don't permit the applicant to spend so much time on one area that you must rush to complete the interview in a timely fashion, thus covering other important areas incompletely.

☐ Structure the interview so that you use a variety of questioning techniques. Use open-ended questions, rather than questions that can be answered "yes" or "no."

☐ If there are statements you'd like the applicant to expand on, repeat them in another way. This is called "echoing" and is an effective information-gathering technique.

☐ Move into the structured part of the interview as soon as you have developed rapport with the candidate. She or he knows the purpose for being there and is anxious to get on with the interview.

☐ Don't interpret the questions for candidates. It is their interpretation that is important.

☐ Tape record or video the interview if possible. You will often be surprised, upon playback, that what you thought you heard and what was said are not exactly the same. Be sure you have the candidate's permission to use the tape.

☐ Follow up hunches and unusual statements. If the applicant says, "I don't get along with certain kinds of people," you will want to find out what these kinds of people are.

☐ Close the interview in a reasonable period of time. Close on a positive note, but don't lead an applicant on or promise anything you can't deliver.

☐ As soon as the interview is over, write down the facts and your impressions of the interview. (Redeker, 1989, pp. 373–374; "Conducting," 2001, p. 38).

There are innumerable lists of sample questions that can be asked during an employment interview. For example, the widely used and commercially available SRI Teacher Perceiver Inventory, which is used in interviewing teachers, contains 60 questions that are organized around 12 themes: Mission, Empathy, Rapport, Individualized Perception, Listening, Investment, Input Drive, Activation, Innovation, Gestalt (perfectionism), Objectivity, and Focus (Caldwell, 1993; Vickers, 1996). Another example, the STAR (situation, task, action, and result) structured interview for prospective teachers contains the 36 questions presented in Table 9.2.

SUMMARY EVALUATION OF CANDIDATES

When the information from both the personnel file and the interview has been recorded, the applicant can be evaluated. Usually, a scale is designed with appropriate descriptors for evaluating each selection criteria: A 5- or 7-point scale, where 1 is low and 5 or 7 is high, works well. After this

TABLE 9.2
Questions for the Structured Interview of Prospective Teachers

Teacher Relationships with Students

1. What kind of students do you like to work with? What type of students could you teach most effectively?
2. You have an assignment. A student ridicules the assignment, saying it doesn't make sense. What would you do?
3. How do you help students to experience success?
4. A student tells you that he or she is being abused at home. What steps would you follow?
5. How would you individualize instruction for students?
6. What procedures do you use to evaluate student progress besides using tests?
7. How would you challenge the slow learner and the advanced student within the same class?

Teacher Relationships with Colleagues

8. What kind of teachers do you prefer to work with? Why?
9. What activities would you like to work with in our school?
10. What quality or qualities do you have that would enhance our teaching staff?
11. What task would you find most difficult in this position? Why?
12. What are some personality characteristics you find undesirable in people?
13. Who should be responsible for discipline in a school? Why?
14. What needs and/or expectations do you have of the school administration?

Teacher Relationships with Parents

15. A parent walks into your room before the school day begins, yelling and complaining about something you don't even understand. The parent is obviously very upset. What would you do?
16. What do you feel is the most effective way to communicate with parents? Describe how you have used this/these technique(s).
17. Describe the reasons why you would contact parents.
18. What would you include in your Open House presentations to parents?
19. What role do parents play in the education of their children? How would you communicate that to them?
20. What community activities would you like to be associated with? Why?

Source: Pawlas, G. E. (1995). The structured interview: Three dozen questions to ask prospective teachers. *NASSP Bulletin, 79*, 62, 65. For more information concerning NASSP services and/or programs, call (703) 860-0200.

evaluation has been completed, a narrative summary of the evaluation is written relative to each criterion, emphasizing the applicant's strengths and areas of needed development. The written statement should be developed objectively and should include comments that reflect a synthesis of the information from the personnel file and the interview. Some interviewers include a graphic profile depicting the selection criteria on one

TABLE 9.2
(continued)

Instructional Techniques

21. Describe any school experience that you have had, particularly in student teaching (or in another teaching position), that has prepared you for a full-time position at our school.
22. How would you integrate technology into the curriculum that you would teach?
23. Describe any innovative projects that you have been involved in developing.
24. Give an example of how you have used cooperative learning in your classroom.
25. What four words would students use to describe your teaching strategies?
26. What rules do you have for your classroom?
27. Describe your teaching style and how you accommodate the different learning styles of the students in your classes.
28. What do you consider to be your strengths, and how will you use them in your teaching?

A Potpourri of Topics and Background Information

29. Why did you choose to become a teacher?
30. What are your hobbies and interests?
31. Tell about an experience that has greatly influenced you in your professional development.
32. What are your plans for continuing your professional growth?
33. Tell me about an interesting article that you have read recently in a professional journal.
34. What contributions can you make to our school?
35. What current trends in public education please you? Displease you?
36. Tell me about the three people who have most influenced your own education and educational career.

---

axis and the numerical evaluation on the other. This provides a quick view of the applicant when reviewing the summaries of several applicants for a position. The graph and the summary statement are particularly helpful if a decision is to be made several weeks after the evaluation is conducted. In the final analysis, a decision must be made to identify the one applicant profile that best fits the selection criteria.

FINAL SELECTION, OFFER, AND ACCEPTANCE

The final selection of the person to whom the position will be offered depends on the type of position and the specific procedures of the school district. Generally, the decision about teaching positions is made by the principal of the school at which the vacancy exists. The decision takes the form of a recommendation through the human resources department to the superintendent. Employment decisions for other types of professional positions are often made by high-level system administrators, also as recommendations to the superintendent. In all cases the human resources department oversees the final selection to ensure that the selection is not based on unlawful considerations. In many districts the hiring officials will be asked to indicate why other top candidates were rejected.

Because hiring practices are not uncommonly the subject of legal challenge, the human resources department should be sure to document and maintain all records relative to a particular hire.

Once the superintendent has accepted the recommendation of others, if he or she has not participated in the interview process, he or she may wish to interview the finalist(s) before making the final selection. The superintendent will almost always interview the finalists for principalships or systemwide administrator positions. The purpose of this interview is not only to confirm the candidate's qualifications, but also to determine which candidate is the best fit for the administrative team (Madrid, 2001). It is also common for the superintendent, before or after the interview, to call references, especially if they are known to the superintendent, to inquire about past performance.

After a decision has been made, it is appropriate to contact the candidate and offer him or her the position, contingent on board approval and the receipt of any required documentation. And it should be stressed that the offer is not final or legal until all required materials have been submitted and the offer has been approved by the board.

If the candidate accepts the offer, a contract is drafted for approval by the board of education. It is critical that the contract spell out as thoroughly as possible the duties and responsibilities of the position, direct and indirect compensation, and any other terms or conditions of employment or special considerations (e.g., relocation allowance). To be valid, any promises or agreements made during the selection process must be detailed in the contract. For example, if a new principal has been promised secretarial assistance in completing his or her doctoral dissertation, to be enforceable, it must be noted in the contract. Or if a teacher is to be released from a period to serve as sponsor of an extracurricular activity, this must be noted in the contract. Similarly, the terms of supplemental work assignments and compensation, such as coaching, must be contained in the contract.

It is important that the time between the selection decision and the recommendation to the superintendent and the time between the superintendent's recommendation to the board and the board's approval be kept to a minimum. Many good candidates have been lost because someone "dragged their feet," was on vacation, or failed to complete the necessary paperwork in a timely fashion. On the other side of the coin, it is also important that the candidate being offered the position respond to the offer in a timely manner so that, if the offer is rejected, an offer can be made to the candidate ranked next in order of preference. For this reason, as noted in Chapter 6, offers normally specify a deadline for notifying the district of the candidate's decision.

NOTIFICATION OF UNSUCCESSFUL CANDIDATES

Only after a position has been filled should all other candidates be notified that the position has been offered to and accepted by another. There are a couple of reasons for doing this as soon as possible after filling the vacancy. First, candidates may want to follow up on other job opportunities with other school districts as quickly as possible. A second consideration is to maintain good public relations with candidates who may want to remain in the pool of qualified persons for future consideration.

The notification is normally made by the human resources department. The notification most often takes the form of a personal letter. In addition to the formal notice, when possible or feasible, it is good public relations to make personal contact with the unsuccessful finalists. However, in no case should the unsuccessful candidates be told why they did not get the job. "Administrators are not required to provide such information, and by doing so could conceivably open themselves and their districts to unnecessary lawsuits. If pressed to give a response, any comments should first be reviewed with legal counsel (Castallo, Fletcher, Rossetti, & Sekowski, 1992, p. 104).

EVALUATION OF THE SELECTION PROCESS

The total process of screening and selection should be evaluated on a continuous basis by the human resources department in cooperation with the hiring departments. The performance appraisals of candidates employed should be compared to the screening evaluations to determine their degree of agreement. Where differences exist, a careful analysis of both evaluation procedures should be made to determine ways of improving the screening process. For example, if an applicant was employed for possessing strong organizational skills and the performance appraisal found the opposite to be true, then a careful analysis of the screening process should provide some insight into the screening problem. The involved administrators should try to learn from this experience and make the necessary changes to eliminate the recurrence of such an error.

SUMMARY

This chapter described a process to be used in the screening and selection of professional personnel. The process included establishing the criteria to be used in the selection process, the application form, the initial screening of applicants, the preliminary interview, conducting background checks, developing and conducting the employment interview, analyzing and evaluating the personnel file and behavioral interview information, writing summary profile statements, and making the selection decision. Finally, the chapter discussed the job offer and acceptance and the notification of unsuccessful candidates.

DISCUSSION QUESTIONS

1. Explain the importance of the application form to the selection process.
2. How does the information that can be gathered from the application form differ from that which can be obtained from a résumé?

3. Distinguish between the purposes of the preliminary interview and those of the employment interview.
4. Under what circumstances can background checks become an invasion of privacy?
5. What are the possible advantages and disadvantages of the involvement of site-based decision-making teams in the selection process?

CASE STUDIES

9.1 The CEO's Daughter

Sara Mobley leaned back in her chair and reflected on her first year as principal of Finley Elementary School. With a great sense of satisfaction, she thought about the progress that was made in the initial year in implementing a strategic plan for Finley. Two of the school's key strategic objectives related to reading, and Sara was pleased that the school had made great improvement in reorganizing the library media center with the hope of changing the trend in declining reading achievement scores. Sara felt that much of the credit could be attributed to Helen Monti, one of the finest library media specialists in the system. Helen was instrumental in working with the Library Media Committee to adopt new rules and regulations for library operations that were wholly supported by the entire faculty. She developed a curriculum map of the collection and established critical acquisition priorities for the basic book collection. In fact, the PTA executive council was so pleased with the apparent improvements that it approved a resolution praising the good work of Mrs. Monti and appropriated $3,000 for the acquisition of a CD-ROM system for placement in the media center. Sara thought about how lucky she was to have recruited Helen last summer.

As that thought passed through her mind, Helen appeared at Sara's door and asked to talk with her. After a short period of small talk, Helen told Sara that she would not be returning to Finley next year. Her husband was being transferred to the West Coast and they would be moving in late June. Sara expressed her deep regrets and told Helen that she could count on her for a strong recommendation when she sought employment for next year.

Within a week, Sara met with the Library Media Committee to ask for their assistance in finding a replacement for Helen. Sara told the members that it was important for the school to find a person of Helen's caliber so that the momentum of this year's efforts would not be lost. The selection of the right person for this position was not only critical to the school's program, but both the faculty and parents had high expectations for the library media program as well.

Sara and the committee worked for several weeks developing a position analysis for the media specialist. Several preliminary screening criteria were sent to the system's department of human resources, and within several weeks the director of the department sent Sara the credentials of six highly qualified candidates. The committee met to conduct a content analysis of the candidates' files in preparation for the behavioral interviews. The committee assisted Sara in preparing the interviews, and during the next three weeks all six candidates were interviewed by Sara. Also, the committee members met with each applicant to provide an orientation to the school's program and priorities, as well as get to know the applicant. When Sara completed the interviews and subsequent evaluations of the candidates, she called a meeting of the committee to present the findings and decide on the most qualified person. The committee and Sara all agreed that that person was John Ashworth. All felt that they had made an excellent choice, and Sara told the members of the committee that she would call John that afternoon.

As Sara returned to the main office, her secretary told her that Superintendent Wilks was on the phone and was anxious to speak to her. Sara picked up the telephone to greet Dr. Wilks. The superintendent expressed his pleasure with the great progress Sara was making at Finley and indicated his hopes and expectations for her long career in the system. He then mentioned that Chamber of Commerce President Fran Snell had been working to assist Henry Mallory, CEO of Albion Manufacturing Corporation, with arrangements for the firm's move of its regional headquarters to the city. Ms. Snell felt that Mr. Mallory would prove to be a strong supporter of the school system and a civic-minded member of the community. Dr. Wilks told Sara that he had assured Ms. Snell that he would do everything he could to gain Mr. Mallory's support.

The superintendent also mentioned that Ms. Snell told Mr. Mallory that she was certain that the school system could find a job for his daughter, Emily, who was graduating from an upstate college as a media specialist this spring. Dr. Wilks then asked Sara to seriously consider Emily Mallory for the media specialist position. In fact, he told Sara that he had already asked the director of human resources to hand-deliver a copy of Emily's credentials to her, and the file should be in her hands before the end of the day.

Questions

1. What problem(s) must Sara solve?
2. What are all the possible approaches that Sara can use to solve the problem(s)?
3. What are the likely consequences of using each approach?
4. Which approach is the best one to implement?
5. What outcomes can Sara expect from such action?

9.2 Inappropriate Questions

Dr. Anthony Banelli is the assistant superintendent for human resources management in the Pine Valley School District. He recently learned that Frank Honeycutt, a longtime high school principal in the system, was using interview questions related to applicants' age, family, and church membership. He also learned that Frank had been told by the superintendent on two previous occasions to avoid using such questions.

Due to a slowdown in the economy, there was a large pool of well-qualified applicants for all teaching positions in the system. Most recently, Frank received 32 applications for a vacant social science position at his school, and he interviewed 14 candidates. After one of the interviewees was recommended by Frank and hired by the board, Dr. Banelli received a telephone message from the superintendent: "Tony, I just got a call from the EEOC office about Frank Honeycutt. There are three complaints against him. I need to see you right away."

Questions

1. Should Dr. Banelli do anything prior to seeing the superintendent? If so, what should he do?
2. What should Dr. Banelli expect as an outcome of his conference with the superintendent?
3. Is it possible that Dr. Banelli may share some responsibility for the alleged complaints against Frank Honeycutt?
4. What preparations should Dr. Banelli make to remove the possibility of such interview questions being used by other administrators?

9.3 To Lead or Not to Lead?

Middle school principal Pat Kemp prides herself on her ability to interview applicants for teaching positions. She is known to use a lot of tough questions, typified by the following lead-ins: "What would you do if . . . ?" "How would you go about doing . . . ?" and "What do you believe . . . ?"

Despite her confidence in her interview skills, she has an uncomfortable and growing concern that she has not been making the best selection decisions. In fact, the last two teachers she hired are performing differently than she expected. One teacher, Cheryl Hennessy, demonstrated a lot of knowledge about classroom management in her job interview, but now she is having serious behavioral problems with children. Another newly hired teacher, Kevin Smith, articulated many innovative ideas about classroom instruction in his interview, yet parents complain that he uses worksheets as his only method of instruction. Pat recollected that Mr. Smith does spend most of his time sitting at his desk.

One afternoon Pat read an article in a personnel journal titled "The Value of Nonleading, Behavioral Focused Questions in the Employment Interview." She reflected on the content of the article and wondered how she could test such questioning techniques against her own.

Questions

1. Aside from leading questions, what other things could be causing Pat to make poor selection decisions?
2. What could Pat do to test the two approaches to interviewing teacher candidates?
3. What precautions should she make to ensure a fair test of the two approaches?

REFERENCES

Bliss, W. (2000). Avoiding "Truth or Dare" in reference. *HRFocus, 77*(5), 5–6.

Caldwell, T. G. (1993). *Hiring excellent teachers: Current interviewing theories, techniques, and practices.* Unpublished master's thesis, California State University–Long Beach.

Castallo, R. T., Fletcher, M. R., Rossetti, A. D., & Sekowski, R. W. (1992). *School personnel administration: A practitioners guide.* Boston: Allyn and Bacon.

Clark, S. G. (1999). Interviewing job applicants: Asking the right questions. *ELA Notes, 34*(8), 3–4, 6.

Conducting an unbiased job related, stress-free, and predictive interview. (2001). *School Business Affairs, 67*(1), 38–39.

DeMitchell, T. A. (1990). Negligent hiring. *Clearing House, 64*(1), 8–10.

Dickmeyer, W. (2001). Applicant tracking reports make data meaningful. *Workforce, 80*(2), 65–67.

Fear, R. A. (1990). *The evaluation interview* (4th ed.). New York: McGraw–Hill.

Garvey, C. (2001). Outsourcing background checks. *HRMagazine, 46*(3), 95–104.

Grant, F. D. (2001). Fast track teacher recruitment. *School Administrator, 58*(1), 18–24.

Harvey, D., & Bowin, R. B. (1996). *Human resources management: An experimental approach.* Upper Saddle River, NJ: Prentice Hall.

Huling, L., Resta, V., Mandeville, T., & Miller, P. (1996). Factors in the selection of secondary school principals. *NASSP Bulletin, 80,* 57–64.

Madrid, M. (2001). The right stuff. *Leadership, 30*(3), 32–34.

Martin, C. (1993). Hiring the right person: Techniques for principals. *NASSP Bulletin, 77,* 79–83.

Meade, J. (2000). Where did they go? *HRMagazine, 45*(9), 81–84.

National School Boards Association (NSBA). (1996). *The school personnel management system.* Alexandria, VA: Author.

O'Laughlin, J. (1999). Recruiting and hiring high-quality teachers. *ERS Spectrum, 17*(4), 31–39.

Rebore, R. W. (2001). *Personnel administration in education: A management approach* (6th ed.). Upper Saddle River, NJ: Prentice Hall.

Redeker, J. R. (1989). *Employee discipline: Policies and practices.* Washington, DC: Bureau of National Affairs.

Siegel, J. (June, 2001). Search me. *American Way,* 96–100.

Slosson, J. (1999). Hiring right people. *High School Magazine, 7*(2), 27–30.

Smith, M. C., & Knab, K. M. (1996). Designing and implementing teacher selection systems. *NASSP Bulletin, 80,* 101–106.

Tallerico, M. (2000). Why don't they apply? *American School Board Journal, 187*(11), 56–58.

Vaughn, S. (August 12, 2001a). Background checks are key. *Los Angeles Times,* pp. W1–2.

Vaughn, S. (August 12, 2001b). Do your homework in chosing the right person for the job. *Los Angeles Times,* p. W2.

Vickers, N. (1996). Education interviews: Convince districts you can convince their students. In American Association for Employment in Education, *AAEE Job Search Handbook for Educators* (pp. 19–20). Evanston, IL: AAEE.

Warren, Gorham, & Lamont, (1994). *HRseries: Policies and practices.* Boston, MA: Author

Woodward, N. H. (2000). The function of form. *HR Magazine, 45*(1), 67–73.

10 *Maximizing Human Resources*

After reading this chapter, you will be able to:
- Define the various concepts of human motivation.
- Explain the importance of planned induction for persons new to the school system and identify specific program provisions in this area of human resources.
- Identify the primary considerations for effective assignment of school personnel.
- Identify factors that constitute teacher load and methods for calculating the workload of teachers.
- Describe the development and implementation of effective staff development programs and activities.
- Understand strategies for dealing with controversy and conflict within the school environment.

A major responsibility of the human resources function is the **maximization of the human resources** of the school system. Earlier, human resources administration was defined as the administrative and staff processes planned and implemented for the distinct purposes of establishing an effective system of human resources and fostering an organizational climate that leads to achieving the educational goals of the school system. This definition emphasizes the purposeful utilization of people, through positive motivation, to achieve the organization's goals and employee self-fulfillment. The growing emphasis on maximizing human resources emanates from the realization that organizations progress to the extent that they are able to motivate and develop people. It is essential, therefore, that human resources administrators understand the basic concepts of human motivation as they relate to maximizing human resources. For this reason, several motivation and human behavior concepts are discussed at the outset of this chapter. Following the discussion of human motivation, the human resources processes of staff induction, staff assignment, and staff development are considered. Special attention is given to teacher workload, the troubled staff member, and other considerations that serve to maximize human potential.

THE SCHOOL AS A SOCIAL SYSTEM

Researchers note that human behavior in organizations is influenced by both institutional and personal factors. Getzels and Guba (1957) described this concept in their social systems model presented in Figure 10.1.

According to the Getzels–Guba social systems model, the actual behavior outcomes (B) within a social system are determined by the institutional role (R) and the individual's personality (P); $B = f(R \times P)$. The role represents position, office, or status within the institution (i.e., superintendent, principal, supervisor, teacher, etc.) and is defined by both role expectations and the nature of the institution. The institutional role and the unique role expectations constitute one dimension of the Getzels–Guba model. The role and role expectations of the institution are termed the *nomothetic dimension*. The individual personality and need-dispositions are termed the *idiographic dimension* (Getzels & Guba, 1957).

The Getzels–Guba social systems model is a useful framework to explain the leadership that is needed in human resources administration to maximize the human potential of a school system. According to these theorists, "The unique task of administration, at least with respect to staff relations, is just this: to integrate the demands of the institution and the demands of the members in a way that is at once organizationally productive and individually fulfilling" (1957, p. 430). The implications of the social systems model for the human resources administrator are far reaching. The administrator who considers only the institutional dimension without giving equal consideration to the individual aspects within the school system is likely to be insensitive to the environment and its elements and conditions. Such an individual not only will be indifferent to the various signals that indicate problems and needs within the school system, but also will be unable to effect possible resolutions and improvements. Both the nomothetic and idiographic dimensions must be fully considered if equilibrium within the system is to be realized. As de-

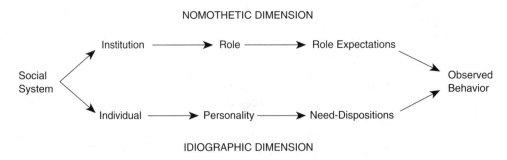

FIGURE 10.1

Social Systems and Social Behavior

Source: "Social Behavior and the Administrative Process" by J. W. Getzels and E. G. Guba, 1957, *The School Review*, 65(4), p. 429. Copyright © 1957 by The University of Chicago Press. Reprinted by permission.

fined by Barnard (1938), *equilibrium* is the organization's capacity to be productive and at the same time satisfy individual employee motives.

HUMAN MOTIVATION THEORIES

School administrators who understand human behavior will be much more effective in making positive differences in the school climate and maximizing human potential. Chapter 1 included a brief discussion of human motivation as conceptualized by Herzberg, Mausner, and Snyderman (1959) and McGregor (1960).

Numerous other human motivation theories have been set forth in the literature. Some theories center on outcome behaviors that are influenced by individuals' perceptions of past events and/or how they perceive future outcomes relative to their personal needs and beliefs. Other theories view behavior as an action that can be changed through interventions that modify an individual's responses. The terms *behavior modification*, *drive-reinforcement theory*, *operant conditioning*, and *behaviorism* all relate generally to the concept that the behavior of an individual can be altered through reinforcement of desired actions. Several leading motivation theories are considered in the following discussion.

Probably more than any other single concept in personnel literature, Maslow's hierarchy has established a direct focus on the basic needs of human beings and their importance in human behavior. According to Maslow's hierarchy, a need is a potential motivator until it is realized or satisfied. As the need is satisfied, it becomes ineffective as a motivator, and the next higher-order need becomes the motivator for the individual (Maslow, 1954/1970). Figure 10.2 illustrates Maslow's hierarchy and the five basic needs from lower to higher order.

Alderfer's (1972) *ERG theory* (existence, relatedness, and growth) relates closely to the concepts set forth by Maslow. Existence needs include, in general, Maslow's physiological and physical safety needs (Figure 10.2); relatedness needs encompass the social needs, safety needs, and esteem needs, as they relate to relations with others; and growth needs are concerned with self-actualization needs and esteem needs, as they are reflected in positive self-concepts. ERG views motivation as being present within all three levels, dependent on the extent to which various needs have been satisfied or remain unsatisfied. In this view, individuals may seek needs at higher levels even though some needs at a lower level have not been met.

Vroom's *expectancy theory* of motivation was set forth in *Work and Motivation* (1964). Vroom stated that "we view the central problem of motivation as the explanation of choices made by organisms among different voluntary responses" (p. 9). Vroom's expectancy theory incorporated three component concepts: (1) *valence*, a person's affective orientations toward particular outcomes; (2) *instrumentality*, the extent to which a person believes an object will lead to desired consequences or prevent undesired results; and (3) *expectancy*, a belief concerning the likelihood that a particular

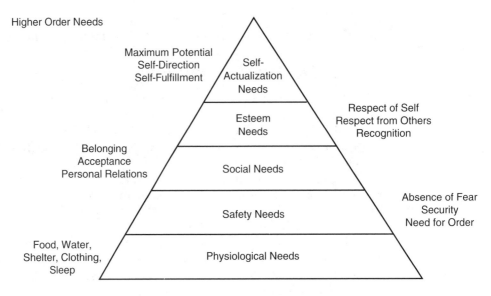

FIGURE 10.2
Maslow's Hierarchy of Basic Needs
Source: "Hierarchy of Needs" from *Motivation and Personality*, 3rd ed., by Abraham H. Maslow. Revised by Robert Frager et al. Copyright © 1954, 1987 by Harper & Row, Publishers, Inc. Copyright © by Abraham H. Maslow. Reprinted by permission of Addison-Wesley Educational Publishers, Inc.

act will be followed by a particular outcome. The expectancy theory of motivation is based on the proposition that effort, performance, and rewards are inextricably related. This concept of motivation argues that effort and performance depend on individuals' perceptions of their potential for meeting personal reward outcomes. Expectancy theory suggests that effort and performance in a particular activity (e.g., obtaining a degree or credential) depend on the individual's perception of whether that activity will increase the realization of personal goals. For example, an individual who has a certain career goal is likely to be highly motivated toward obtaining the credentials needed for the desired position and will exert the required effort and performance. In brief, expectancy theory supports the belief that employees put forth more effort and are more productive when they perceive a relationship among effort, performance, and reward.

Brayfield and Crockett (1955), among others, believed that motivation depends on the individual's pursuit of important goals. They stated that "we might expect high satisfaction and high productivity to occur together when productivity is perceived as a path to certain important goals and when these goals are achieved" (p. 416). This rather straightforward view supports the concepts of goal commitments that are important aspects of expectancy theory, theory Y, and needs theory. McGregor's theory Y places emphasis on fostering individual self-direction and full potential exceeding the mere satisfaction of personal needs. McGregor explained his theory in *The Human Side of Enterprise* in 1960. Such administrative approaches as management by objectives (MBO) are based on a path–goal theory. In *Managing by Objectives*, Raia (1974) contended that "whether or not the behavior is actually satisfying to the individual depends upon his latent motives and needs" (p. 97). Raia viewed MBO as being consistent with the path–goal theory of motivation, since MBO is based on the establishment of clearly defined work objectives, progress assessments, and a relationship between appraisal and development and compensation, as well as the element of participation in cooperative goal setting.

Theory Z organizations develop employee commitment to organizational goals and high productivity through the use of such incentives as lifetime job tenure, personal participation in decision making and problem solving by all employees, the use of team efforts to complete tasks, and a focus on the personal concerns of employees. Ouchi's (1981) theory Z has received much acclaim in business and industry and has provided an impetus for rethinking traditional approaches to management and employee relations. According to Ouchi, trust, subtlety, and intimacy exist in every theory Z organization. These components are exemplified by certain characteristics that had provided for the remarkable success of business and industry in Japan. He emphasized that positive human relations, not technology, make for increased production. The activities of participative management, consensus decision making, and reduced organizational bureaucracy promote job satisfaction and motivate the worker to make personal sacrifices that lead to extraordinary success for the organization.

B. F. Skinner's initial work, *The Behavior of Organisms* (1938), as well as his later works, advanced the proposition that an individual's behavior is modified through immediate rewards of favored responses and by no response to unfavorable behavior. Positive reinforcement, through personal reward, praise, recognition, or extended authority, is used to solidify the continuation of desired behavior. Undesirable behavior is dealt with by use of *extinction*, whereby the behavior is merely ignored. Skinner's concepts also suggest that desired responses can be learned through *shaping*. When favored responses are seldom or never demonstrated, initial rewards are given for behavior responses similar to the desired behavior. Finally, only the desired response is reinforced through appropriate rewards (Skinner, 1953, 1969).

Behavior modification suggests that providing careful feedback for positive job results to an employee would reinforce this behavior, that pay incentives or other rewards for exemplary attendance would reduce employee absence, and that rewards given an employee for reaching a desired skill level would lead to a continuation of positive personal development.

Behavior modification research provides several suggestions for administrative practice:

1. The kind of behavior desired should be determined as specifically as possible.

2. If the desired behavior is not currently present or is seldom demonstrated, shaping techniques should be utilized to bring about changes in behavior similar to the desired behavior. Similar behavior should be positively reinforced.

3. Desired behavior should be reinforced immediately. Material rewards and *psychic* or *social* rewards, such as benefits, commendations, carefully designed personal feedback, responsibility, and recognition, should be scheduled as reinforcers.

4. Results should be measured and assessed and decisions reached concerning the appropriate schedule of reinforcements needed to ensure the continuation of the desired behavior.

The discussion of motivation reemphasizes the concept stated in Chapter 2 that schools are people. Effective human resources administration requires an understanding and concern for the individual needs of personnel. In this respect, the often-heard maxim "Know your staff" assumes a more comprehensive, purposeful meaning. The maximization of human resources within the school system requires a meaningful integration of the system's goals and the employees' need-dispositions. When these considerations are brought into relatively close congruence, achievement of goals and personal fulfillment are more likely to be realized. The variables of individual behavior and the realities of human organizations often defy simple analysis. Yet the realization of the full potential of human resources requires that the concepts and theories relating to human motivation and behavior be understood, applied, and evaluated in all human resources processes.

STAFF INDUCTION

In Chapter 2 the **induction process** was defined as that comprehensive complex of activities designed to gain congruence between institutional objectives and employee needs. Induction begins with the job application, then continues through job candidacy and, on an ongoing basis, for as long as the employee or the organization views it as necessary. "The purposes of induction are to create a good first impression, relieve anxiety, set expectations, encourage socialization and team building, build identification with the employee, and prevent problems" (Starcke, 1996, p. 111). Although the entry of new employees into the school system requires special orientation considerations, the process is not limited only to new employees; nor should it be viewed only as a first-year induction activity. Rather, the induction needs of individual employees are ongoing and the induction process is continuous. Induction activities serve as important links to recruitment and selection, as well as a complement to staff assignment and development.

If effectively planned and implemented, the staff induction process serves several basic purposes:

1. Encourages individuals with qualifications congruent with district expectations to consider employment in the system.

2. Integrates effectively and efficiently new and experienced staff personnel into their respective roles in the school system.
3. Develops understanding and commitment to the stated goals and objectives of the school system.
4. Reduces and/or removes problems and conditions that tend to inhibit personal effectiveness and job satisfaction.
5. Identifies the specific talents of each employee and builds these abilities into the overall educational team.
6. Acquaints personnel with the important considerations of personal, professional, and community relationships within the school community.
7. Determines specific needs of school personnel and analyzes these needs in relation to the school system's expectations.
8. Identifies for each employee the human and physical resources that can enhance personal effectiveness.
9. Provides information and services that promote instruction and learning.

Thus induction is a purposely planned process that is based on the school system's stated goals and the roles of its human resources. The maximization of the system's human resources is the foundation and rationale for induction activities and services.

Operational Procedures for Staff Induction

The staff induction process begins with the prospective employee's first contact with the school district and continues throughout employment, as needed. Properly planned and implemented, the process involves all members of the staff, appropriate community members, and employee associations. The general administrative procedures for planning, implementing, and evaluating the induction process can be classified into four steps, as follows:

Step 1 The governing board adopts policies that commit the school system to effective induction practices and indicate what the school system desires from the process. Specific goals for the induction process are developed cooperatively by the board of education, school employee personnel, and community representatives.

Step 2 All information that would assist in identifying the induction program needs is determined. The clarification of specific position assignments and responsibilities for program implementation is completed. Individual problems and needs are identified through informal interviews or other means, such as mentoring programs.

Step 3 Previously determined plans and procedures are implemented. Individualized programs for providing special services are determined and administered.

Step 4 Information that can be utilized to evaluate the program's results is collected. Objective assessments of feedback relative to the accomplishment of program objectives and meeting individual needs are completed. These findings are used in debriefing sessions and other evaluation activities for improving future procedures.

Preemployment Activities.   Preemployment induction activities generally are provided during the period between initial contact with the school district and the time when the individual assumes a role in the school system. Upon initial contact with the school district, information is provided to a potential employee to build an understanding of the school district's nature, community makeup, and educational expectations; the general working environment; faculty–student information; and professional opportunities within the district, including compensation levels and benefits.

Preemployment induction necessitates a variety of program provisions. Face-to-face communication, use of printed materials, group sessions, audiovisual technology, and other practices are common for both gaining and disseminating information. Various strategies are employed for carrying out preemployment induction programs. The following procedures are examples of contemporary practices.

1. Over a specified time period, school district employees are surveyed as to what information and personal assistance proved most beneficial to them, as well as what communication and assistance should be added prior to employment. Results are analyzed and program activities designed to provide the most beneficial information and assistance.
2. During the initial contact with the school district, a potential employee completes a brief questionnaire to determine the kinds of information and personal assistance that might prove most helpful (e.g., employment benefits, community information, school district policy and procedures, or student evaluation procedures). Those individuals or offices assigned the responsibility for the requested information provide the information to groups and/or individual applicants.
3. Various offices and personnel gather information concerning the most frequently asked questions during preemployment, major problem areas regarding entry transition, and specific school district information of high priority. This feedback is synthesized, and appropriate induction activities are planned to provide the necessary feedback to prospective employees.
4. Every effort is made to personalize preemployment induction. Initial inquiries are expedited. To the fullest extent possible, internal personnel are assigned specific duties regarding preemployment orientation and communication. Briefing sessions are planned, one-on-one conferences are scheduled when feasible, and other special efforts are made to put the prospective employee at ease with the school system.
5. Induction teams representative of both internal and external members of the school district are established. Each team serves as the primary information resource for a specific area of the preemployment induction. In some instances, one particular resource member serves as the liaison person for one or more prospective employees.

Postemployment Induction.   Following the district's decision to hire an individual, postemployment induction must be implemented. Specific information relative to the employee's assignment, the environment in which the person will be working, professional resources available, formal staff relationships, policy and regulation resources, personal responsibilities, and provisions for personal assistance are among the induction information and activities of importance at this time. Postemployment induction focuses on facilitating an effective, efficient transition of personnel into their respective roles within the school system and community. Its primary purpose is to assist new employees in the achievement of optimal success as members of the school community. Provisions and practices that add to the induction program following employment include mentor programs, policy and regulation manuals, and personnel information handbooks.

Mentor Program.   Many school districts have a long history of providing a "helping teacher" for new personnel, but the mentor program concept presents a more comprehensive approach to induction and staff development. A **mentor** is an experienced professional who guides the personal development of a less experienced individual by serving as a role model. In a mentor program, each new employee is teamed with an experienced peer on the staff who serves as a sponsor, teacher, and advisor. Both the mentor and the new or inexperienced staff member benefit personally from this relationship. For example, the new or inexperienced staff member gains access to an experienced member of the staff for purposes of learning about the school system, its policies, and procedures. Additionally, mentoring provides help in building communication channels of importance to continued growth, allows for new knowledge relative to teaching approaches, develops a system of personal support and increased self-confidence, extends insight into district purposes, and provides a relationship with a master teacher who can serve as a role model for teaching. The mentor benefits through increased personal self-esteem and recognition as a successful teacher and contributor to the school's program. Mentoring requires keeping up-to-date on best practices in teaching and necessitates refinement and improvement of personal knowledge and skills.

Overall, the school system benefits through increases in staff knowledge about the school district, increased confidence and morale of staff members, and improved staff member effectiveness. Successful mentor programs most often are based on the special needs and interests of the new or inexperienced staff member. Mentoring, as a facilitator of professional growth in staff development, is discussed in more detail later in this chapter.

Policy and Regulation Manual.   A properly codified, comprehensive policy and regulation manual can serve as one of the primary induction resources for school personnel. Policy and regulations are of special significance to the human resources function generally, but contribute to the induction process as follows:

1. By informing school personnel as to what the school district wants to accomplish

2. By providing a common basis for understanding and a basic reference for effective communication
3. By clarifying the division of labor between the school board and professional administrative staff
4. By establishing a basis for action, effective school operations, and meaningful evaluation
5. By providing information concerning professional responsibilities and opportunities
6. By setting forth guidelines and procedures for completing specific practices and meeting personal responsibilities that meet the standards of the school system
7. By providing specific procedures for personnel in such areas as student evaluation, securing instructional resources, community participation, transfer, and professional development.

A comprehensive treatment of policy and regulation development relative to the human resources function is included in Chapter 5.

Personnel Information Handbook. The importance of the personnel information handbook in the induction process demands that its development and dissemination be given high priority by human resources administrators. The value of the personnel handbook extends beyond its contributions to the induction process; its potential for orienting both new and continuing staff is far reaching.

Although the personnel handbook often includes information related to school district policy and administrative regulations, the handbook and the policies manual are different documents. The policies manual is the governance document for the district and sets forth the legislative (policy) and executive (regulations) guidelines under which the district is to operate. The personnel handbook is designed to provide information that answers questions relative to (1) the school district's goals, services, and facilities, (2) the community and its makeup, and (3) procedures relating to securing substitute teachers, obtaining curriculum materials, completing grade reports, the school calendar, professional growth activities, insurance plans, and other information that the school district has determined to be of value to employees. A sample of one section of a personnel handbook is shown in Figure 10.3. The sample focuses on the employee assistance program in a school district.

The human resources director, school principals, teaching staff, support personnel, and other supervisory staff members need to participate in the determination of content for the handbook, the dissemination of the information, and the evaluation of the handbook's effectiveness. The development of the handbook most often is coordinated by the central human resources unit that serves as the clearinghouse for needed additions, clarifications, and changes. Such practices as using brief questionnaires to gain feedback from new personnel, various school district units, and experienced personnel are most useful in assessing the handbook's effectiveness.

Employee Assistance Program—Tempe School District No. 3 recognizes that unresolved personal problems may adversely impact the job performance of employees at all levels of responsibility. These problems may include, but are not limited to, chemical dependency, and marital, family, legal and/or financial concerns. To facilitate a timely resolution to these problems, the district provides employees and their dependents with the benefit of confidential counseling and assistance provided by the Employee Assistance Program. Employees are encouraged to take advantage of the services before any problem becomes overwhelming. Every person using the program is assured total confidentiality. For additional information call the Personnel Office, or for an appointment, call CONTACT, Inc., 820-2328.

Ref: Board Policy GCBC* and Regulation GCBC-R

FIGURE 10.3
Sample Section of a Personal Handbook
Source: From *Handbook, Certificated Personnel,* Tempe Elementary School District No. 3, 1991–1992, Tempe, AZ.

Induction for the Beginning Teacher and Other New Teaching Personnel

Special orientation programs must be provided for beginning teachers and other personnel new to the school district. Some activities that later become routine often pose considerable frustration for new personnel and detract attention from important position responsibilities. Homework regulations, required records and reports, student tardiness, parental communication, ways of securing instructional materials, and reporting student absence are common administrative problems for beginning teachers. Policies and procedures for student grading, student promotion and retention, and parental conferences are other matters significant for induction. Student discipline and governing regulations are of paramount importance as well. Induction activities must be designed to provide personnel with the necessary guidelines for action and to ensure that personal assistance and support are available to staff members. The teaching environment, teacher workload, work schedule, position assignment, and other conditions of work also influence the effective transition of personnel into the school system. These considerations are discussed later in this chapter.

Relationships with other staff members and administrators often pose problems for beginning teachers. Induction activities that establish attitudes of cooperation and team spirit are essential. The mentoring provision can be instrumental in serving this need. Position descriptions, communication channels and resources, and an explanation of personnel and office relationships are invaluable.

New personnel also need community information, such as educational support services, recreational and cultural opportunities, civic activities, demographic data, medical facilities, governance structure, and community–school support information. Faculty handbooks and planned community tours can be sources for such information.

Personal problems, such as financial need, can inhibit effectiveness on the job. During induction, information should be provided about educational credit associations within the school system or community agencies. In addition, services provided through employee assistance programs (EAP) should be explained (see Figure 10.3).

STAFF ASSIGNMENT

Staff assignment is the human resources process that maximizes human resources through the (1) deployment of talent and competency in the best interests of the total staff and student population, (2) identification of staff talent and assignment of individual employees to facilitate an effective instructional program, (3) assessment of roles, including the identification of inhibitors and facilitators, to permit optimal utilization of resources, (4) recognition of individual staff differences and implementation of leadership styles that best fulfill the potential of all personnel, (5) utilization of available research, tools, and skills to provide the best possible working conditions, and (6) examination of staff workloads that facilitate, rather than inhibit, effective work performance. This activity includes the consideration of environmental conditions that increase personal motivation, effort, and productivity: specific assignment, workload, and personal problem resolution.

Staff assignment is closely linked to other personnel processes. Selection, induction, evaluation, development, and organizational climate especially complement the activities and purposes of staff assignment. Although staff assignment clearly reaches beyond the singular consideration of proper position assignment, because of its paramount importance, position assignment will be discussed in detail.

Position Assignment

Human resources authorities agree that one of the most effective means by which human resources administrators can assist the organization to achieve its stated goals and maximize employee potential is through the determination of appropriate position assignments. Employees who are appropriately matched to their jobs exhibit higher levels of job satisfaction and performance. An appropriate and productive job match means that the required tasks of the position relate directly to the personal strengths and interests of the employee. One key for helping individuals reach their fullest potential and contribute most toward personal and organizational goals is to assign them to positions in which their knowledge and skills can best be utilized. *Gannett News Service* reported on tips provided by businessman, Peter Lowe, who underscored the importance of matching the person to the position (*Arizona Republic*, 2001) as follows:

> Match the person to the position: don't tailor the position to suit the person. One of the most common hiring mistakes takes place when you interview a

bright, talented individual you like and, even though they aren't quite right for the position, you hire them anyway. It's an understandable mistake. A good candidate in the wrong position is a bad employee. (p. D2)

Position assignment requires several essential considerations: (1) the specific nature of the position, including role expectations, necessary knowledge and skills, and conditions under which the role is performed, (2) the professional preparation, competencies, and interests of the employee, (3) the relationship of the position and the employee's characteristics and competencies, (4) the extent to which the assignment provides for the personal motivation needed by the employee and the extent to which success can be realized in the position, and (5) consideration of the forces of organizational culture and informal group structure.

Effective assignments link closely with effective recruitment and selection. While securing personnel who possess the knowledge and skills needed in the assignment, recruitment and selection must also be aimed at providing an opportunity for the employee to use the knowledge and skills that are most personally rewarding. Individuals generally have developed personal competence in a large number of task areas. Most persons also have competencies that they most enjoy using and that tend to bring both the highest level of productivity and highest level of personal satisfaction. Position assignment necessitates the careful examination of both the general qualifications of the individual and the specific competencies most rewarding to that person. When a match is found between the competencies required by the job and those most satisfying to the individual, both the school system and the employee are likely to benefit.

Information about the individual's specific qualifications for the position and his or her specific competencies is gathered through a variety of sources: placement credentials, job application forms, personal résumés, appropriately designed job questionnaires, structured interviews, examination of job references, and assessment methodology. Accurate information about job and employee competencies is necessary for proper position assignment. Proper position placement is a planned process that uses objective measurements and evaluations of position needs and individual competencies to match positions and individuals.

Owen (1984) recommended the use of a position and personal profile to enhance the scientific approach to position assignment. His technique is based on the development of a position analysis to evaluate job candidates for respective positions. As described in Chapter 8, the development of the position analysis begins with a thorough consideration of what the position is to accomplish and what primary knowledge and skills are required. Required knowledge and skill levels are quantified to the fullest extent possible and rated on a scale of 0 to 10, or some other appropriate scale. In a similar manner, all available information about the candidate is examined and rated according to the knowledge and skills required. Position and personal profile results are then plotted and evaluated to find the best fit for each candidate.

Several advantages are associated with the profile procedure. It enables the selection activities to concentrate on the requirements of the position as opposed to personality factors, provides continuity to the processes of recruitment and selection, and can be automated to facilitate analyses. In view of the importance of proper position assignment, the technique appears to have significant implications for practice in position assignments. As the process develops within the school system, more objectivity can be established in the instruments used to evaluate individual competency. Although some judgments must be subjective in the job analysis process, its potential for job placement deserves consideration. As Cavanaugh (1984) pointed out:

> When a person's abilities (intelligence, creativity, energy, maturity) are reasonably consonant with the requirements of the job, this will act as a motivating force. When the employee's abilities are significantly higher or lower than those demanded by the job, this typically constitutes a contra-motivational factor. . . . High motivational levels in employees are the result of a good job, by the right person, working for a competent supervisor, under the banner of positive company philosophy. (pp. 77–82)

An annual opportunity for teaching personnel to express interest in a change of assignments, both teaching and extracurricular, adds to the effective allocation of personal interests and talents in school systems. Figure 10.4 is an example of an assignment interest assessment questionnaire that might be used by the school principal or other human resources administrators in relation to staff deployment.

The goals, beliefs, traditions, and values of a particular school are important factors in the assignment of employees to that school. If an individual employee's personal characteristics and beliefs are significantly incongruent with the culture of the school, personnel problems most likely will develop. The leadership style of the local building administrator and the style of followership on the part of the employee also are important assessments in position assignment. The time taken to gather information concerning the matter of organizational culture, employee characteristics, and leadership–followership styles will produce positive dividends for the school district and the employee by enhancing job satisfaction and productivity.

Teacher Workload

Staff assignment requires that careful attention be given to **teacher load**. Without such consideration, inequities in the workload are certain to persist, and personnel who are most qualified to carry out an effective educational program in the school often are so overburdened that their efforts are forced to a level of mediocrity. Equity of assignment is not the only personnel consideration that undergirds the importance of teacher load. Load reductions are advisable in certain situations, including the case of individuals new to teaching. Maximization of human resources is inhibited seriously if inequitable distribution of load exists or if load is unwisely

Name of Teacher: _____

Present Position: _____ _____
                          Location   Grade Level(s)

_____
                                     Subjects Taught

Time at Present Location: _____

Teaching Assignment Change Being Requested: _____

   Grade Level Change (please explain): _____

   _____

   _____

   Subject-Area Change (please explain):
   _____

   _____

   _____

   Supervisory or Extracurricular Responsibility Change Request: _____

   _____

Comments/Clarifications: _____

_____

Principal's Recommendations: _____

_____

_____   _____
              Signature   Date

FIGURE 10.4
Assignment Questionnaire and Interest Assessment

allocated. A comprehensive examination of the teacher's workload also serves to assess what teachers actually do in meeting the responsibilities of their assignment. Human resources administrators need this information to make intelligent and defensible decisions concerning the ways in which the talents of each staff member are used. In addition, teacher load information is useful concerning the assignment of extra duties, reveals imbalances between the **teaching load** and extra-duty load of a teacher, and serves as evidence for the need for additional staff.

   The actual load of the teacher includes more factors than class size and number of classes. Other load factors to be considered are the number of subject matter preparations, the length of class periods, the nature of the subject(s) taught, the nature of the students taught, extracurricular or additional duty assignments, and, at the elementary school level, such factors as the number of grades taught. With the general exception of class size and number of classes taught, little attention has been given to these other important factors in considerations of teacher load and staff assignments. However, if staff assignment is to be considered in a more scientific and professional manner, objective measures must be used to assess these factors and must become a part of rational and justifiable decisions concerning workload assignments. The makeup of teacher load has certain commonalities that can be measured with reasonable objectivity. Two such measures are the **Douglass teacher load formula** and the **Norton–Bria formula** for elementary teacher load.

Douglass Teacher Load Formula.   As early as 1928, Douglass developed a formula to measure teaching load in high schools. Since that time the formula has been refined, validated, and tested through numerous empirical studies; it is the most carefully developed means available for measuring teacher load in grades 7 to 12. The result of the formula computation of load for each teacher is an *index of load* that may be directly compared among teachers, departments, and schools or to national norms. Several states have developed teacher load norms based on the Douglass formula for all major subject matter areas that can be utilized by individual schools to compare their school load with those of other state schools. The Douglass formula (1951) is

$$TL = SGC \left[CP - \frac{DUP}{10} + \frac{NP - 25\ CP}{100} \right] \left[\frac{PL + 50}{100} \right] + 0.6PC \left[\frac{PL + 50}{100} \right]$$

where TL = units of teaching load per week

CP = class periods spent in the classroom per week

DUP = number of class periods per week in the classroom teaching classes for which the preparation is very similar to that for some other classes

NP = number of pupils in classes per week

PC = number of periods per week in supervision of study hall, student activities, teachers' meetings, and other cooperations

PL = gross length of class period in minutes

SGC = subject grade coefficient (Appropriate SGCs for the various subjects have been calculated by Douglass; see Douglass, 1951; Jung, 1949.)

Application of the Douglass Load Formula. Determine the index of teacher load for a teacher who has the following duties:

☐ Teaches two classes of 12th-grade English with 25 and 27 students. Each class meets five times per week. The teacher has only one preparation, because one class is a duplicate. Each class period is 60 minutes.
☐ Teaches three classes of 11th-grade social studies with 30, 27, and 23 students. Each class meets five times a week. Two classes are duplicates. Each class period is 60 minutes.
☐ Spends an average of 360 minutes per week in nonteaching duties during the semester.

Determine the values for the variables:

SGC = 1.1 for 12th-grade English and for 11th-grade social studies

CP = 25 (the teacher instructs five periods each day and each period meets five times per week: $CP = 5 \times 5 = 25$)

DUP = 15 (there are three duplicate classes per day, one English and two social studies. Thus there are 15 duplicates for the five-day week: $3 \times 5 = 15$)

NP = 660 (the teacher instructs $25 + 27 + 30 + 27 + 23 = 132$ students each day for the five-day week. Thus the weekly total is 660 students: $132 \times 5 = 660$)

PL = 60 minutes

PC = 6 (the teacher's 360 minutes of cooperative duties is the equivalent of six class periods, where one class period is 60 minutes: $360 \div 60 = 6$)

Substituting into the formula,

$$TL = 1.1 \left[25 - \frac{15}{10} + \frac{660 - 625}{100} \right] \left[\frac{60 + 50}{100} \right] +$$
$$(0.6 \times 6) \left[\frac{60 + 50}{100} \right]$$
$$= 32.82 \text{ units}$$

As one gains experience using the Douglass formula, it takes only a few minutes to calculate the load of each teacher. With computerization, the time consideration is inconsequential. The computer readily can provide the administrator with subject area central tendency comparisons, school-to-school load comparisons, and, when available, school load comparisons with other states. Because the Douglass formula does not apply to the elementary school grades, other tools such as the Norton–Bria formula are used.

Norton–Bria Formula for Measuring Elementary School Teacher Load. The Norton–Bria Formula (Norton & Bria, 1992) considers the load factors of assigned hours of teaching, time spent in preparation for teaching, cooperative or extracurricular duties of a noninstructional nature, the number of students taught, and the load related to extra grades taught in a single classroom by one teacher. Unlike the Douglass formula, the following formula measures teacher load in hours of time spent per work in teaching, rather than index load units. The Norton–Bria formula is written as

$$TLH = \frac{3}{2} ATH + \frac{SL \times PH}{CM} + F \text{ or } F' \, (OG \times PH) + 0.6(CH)$$

where *TLH* = total load hours of time per week

    ATH = assigned teaching hours in the classroom per week

    PH = preparation hours (one-half the actual time for assigned hours in the classroom per week: 1/2 *ATH*)

    SL = actual number of students taught above or below the average class size for any given grade (class sizes can be altered according to local or state class size norms)

    CM = standard class mean size

    OG = other grades taught in a single classroom under the direction of one teacher (i.e., for a teacher who teaches grades 2 and 3 simultaneously in one room, *OG* = 1)

    F' = 1/16 (use for small- and medium-sized school districts)

    F" = 1/13 (use for larger school districts)

    CH = cooperative hours spent in noninstructional duties such as meetings, playground supervision, parental conferences, and other nonteaching assignments

Application of the Norton–Bria Formula.   A third-grade teacher with an enrollment of 32 in a small school district begins teaching at 8:30 A.M. and ends at 2:45 P.M. The teacher has a 30-minute lunch break and has supervision duties for a 20-minute recess in the morning and again in the afternoon. Additional duties including faculty meetings, PTA, chairing a curriculum group, advising the science club, and district-level meetings require 675 minutes weekly.

Load Calculation

    ATH = 25 hours, 25 minutes [assigned teaching hours per week are 5 days × 6 hours 15 minutes/day (8:30 A.M. to 2:45 P.M.) less 5 days × 40 minutes/day for recess and 5 days × 30 minutes/day for lunch.] *PH* = 1/2 *ATH* = 1/2 (25 hours 25 minutes) = 12 hours 43 minutes

    SL = 7 (Student load is based on the actual number of students above or below the average class size for grade 3. It is calculated as a fractional measure of the time needed for preparation. The average class size for grade 3 is 25; see below. Average class size data can be altered to reflect local norms.)

$$\frac{7 \times 12 \text{ hr } 43 \text{ min}}{25} = 3 \text{ hr } 34 \text{ min}$$

Table for Average Class Size

Grade	Students
1	24
2	25
3	25
4	27
5	28
6	28

$CM = 25$
$OG = 0$ (no extra grades taught)
$F' = 1/16$
$CH = 6$ hr 45 min (0.6×675 min/week $= 405$ min/week $= 6$ hr 45 min)

Substituting into the formula and rounding any fractional minutes to the nearest whole minute,

$TLH = 3/2$ (25 hr 25 min) $+ \dfrac{7 \times 12 \text{ hr } 43 \text{ min}}{25} + 1/16$ (0 × 12 hr 43 min) $+ 6$ hr 45 min
  $= 38$ hr 8 min $+ 3$ hr 34 min $+ 0 + 6$ hr 45 min
  $= 48$ hr 27 min/week

Consider the same teacher with the added dimension of extra grades. Assume that the teacher has 32 students in grade 3 and 16 in grade 4. The OG (other grades) factor is calculated as follows:

$$\frac{1 \times 12 \text{ hr } 43 \text{ min}}{16} = 47.7 \text{ min}$$

Add 48 min to the teacher load of 48 hr 27 min to get a *TLH* of 49 hr 15 min/week.

Tools such as the Douglass and Norton–Bria formulas have been neglected in human resources practices. In view of the time given to other utilization activities, the neglect of teacher load is indefensible. Teaching is demanding work. The workload of teachers and other personnel must be a primary consideration of any human resources program concerned with maximizing human potential.

WORKING WITH TROUBLED AND MARGINAL STAFF MEMBERS

A growing problem for human resources administrators at all levels is that of the **troubled staff member.** The interrelation between the work life and the personal life of the employee and the negative effect of problems in each is illustrated in Figure 10.5. Personal life problems contribute further to both

FIGURE 10.5
Work Life and Personal Life
Interactions

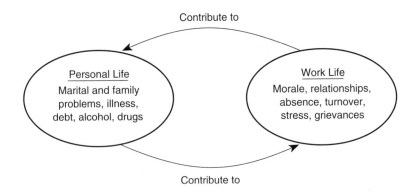

TABLE 10.1
Leading Problem Areas for
Troubled Workers in
Education
Source: "Employee Assistance
Programs—A Need in Education"
by M. S. Norton, 1988,
Contemporary Education, 60,
p. 24. Reprinted by permission.

Problem Area	Number of School Districts Reporting
Medical health	52
Problem drinking–alcoholism	50
Mental–emotional problems	47
Marital–family problems	46
Employee–supervisor relationships	29
Personal crisis	21
Financial problems	17
Drug–chemical dependency	17
Work–peer relationships	11
Others	10

job stress and the quality of job performance. Although the pattern between personal and work life is not exact, problems related to the employee's personal and work life are nonetheless interdependent and interrelated.

According to a report of the U.S. Department of Health and Human Services (1989), approximately 80% of all employees experience some degree of stress in their lives and wish to do something about it. A study of school employees in one state (Norton, 1987) revealed that job stress was the leading problem for teachers and administrators considered as troubled employees. In a national study of 91 school districts (Norton, 1988), human resources directors reported the leading problem areas for troubled workers, including teachers, administrators, and support staff, as shown in Table 10.1.

Fortunately, the number of employee assistance programs (EAP) offered by school district programs is increasing. Often these programs are administered jointly with employee organizations (National School Boards Association, 1996). EAP service arrangements include the provision of referral services to outside professionals, in-house counseling programs staffed by local district professionals, consortia that include cooperative funding for services within or outside the school districts, and the use of approved consultants who provide the necessary EAP services. As discussed in Chapter 12, many school districts provide EAP services as part of the fringe benefit program. Such personal assistance is integral to the maximization of human resources within the school district. Although the central human resources unit most often coordinates the EAP, local human resources administrators, such as the school principal, are instrumental in the program's success. Because the building principal works most closely with many troubled personnel, identification, referral, counseling, and mentoring all become part of the principal's human resources responsibilities.

Not only did the number of employee assistance programs increase during the 1990s, but the services provided by these programs also increased significantly since their initial focus on the treatment of employee alcohol problems. Doolittle (1996) noted that EAPs presently provide services for employees in all areas in which behavioral or personal problems exist. He suggested that the "next logical step is to use EAPs to integrate all organizational functions related to employee health and productivity" (p. 22). In this approach, the EAP is involved throughout the employee's referral and treatment process. That is, the EAP serves as liaison between the employee, treatment provider, and employer in the coordination of services, from identification of the problem to treatment and return to health, in the most effective way possible.

Most authorities point out the problem of referrals as related to troubled employees. Rumsey (1992) noted that the professional is in a delicate position relative to gaining the employee's trust and then creating enough distance so that the employee will accept the EAP referral without feeling unsupported. When the professional has enough information to understand the employee's problem, Rumsey recommends the following steps:

☐ Identify your concerns;
☐ Identify possible solutions;
☐ Develop strategy for the employee to look for and resolve in treatment;
☐ Match the employee with the provider(s) (case matching);
☐ Discuss providers;
☐ Explore resistance;
☐ Decide the next step; and
☐ Refer to the provider(s) (p. 42)

The following principles and personnel procedures aid the staff assignment process in serving troubled staff members and providing positive leadership in this developing area.

1. Maintain a positive viewpoint regarding troubled staff personnel. The responsibility of the human resources function is to assist and develop human potential at all levels. The personal worth and dignity of troubled employees must be protected.
2. Establish procedures for determining signs of personal problems demonstrated in the employee's behavior and effectiveness. Behavioral

signals such as irritability, lack of motivation and interest, decreased physical energy, lack of commitment, loss of concentration, and self-deprecation are clues for needed action. Decreased effectiveness is revealed in such tendencies as setting low goals, inferior or deteriorating work, avoidance of difficult tasks, and increased human error.

3. Be fully aware of the assistance resources available for troubled personnel within the school system and through external agencies. Provide the necessary leadership for gaining personal counseling services. Work to promote a positive attitude toward the use of personal assistance counseling and services. Promote the view that the use of expert help, when needed, is good judgment.

4. Use appropriate principles of effective human resources administration in working with troubled staff members. Proper position assignment, workload, and use of appropriate mentors are among the important considerations. Make certain that the employee knows about the support services available for counseling and guidance. Take special measures to establish open communication with the troubled worker. Use a sensitive approach that best fits the situation.

Marginal teachers are those individuals who are performing unsatisfactorily in one or more areas such that learning for students is inhibited. Smith (1998) points out several characteristics that serve to identify marginal teachers. The marginal teacher commonly:

- ☐ Does not teach to the curriculum in general and to the specific objectives in particular.
- ☐ Lacks enthusiasm for students and teaching.
- ☐ Has poor personal relations with students.
- ☐ Exhibits poor teaching skills.
- ☐ Has unorganized classroom and lessons.
- ☐ Does not establish expectations for student behavior and thus discipline is usually a major problem.
- ☐ Lacks knowledge of the subject matter. (p. 184)

Empirical evidence suggests that, in many cases, the marginal teacher is not fully aware that he or she is performing incompetently. One reason for this condition is the nature of performance evaluation itself. That is, the procedures utilized in the performance evaluation often are flawed, in that specific problems are not clearly identified, leaving the teacher confused relative to both improvement needs and possible remedies. In other instances, the teacher might dismiss or completely shut out stimuli that are discomforting or personally threatening. Some studies indicate that, as vague awareness of a situation becomes more clear, the individual can arrest the process so that a well-defined awareness does not occur, and perhaps at this point the threatening message is rejected or even demolished as though it never took place. Unless effective clinical procedures are implemented by a competent professional, the marginal teacher continues to perform unsatisfactorily.

In sum, five considerations are necessary in helping the marginal teacher toward improvement:

1. Implement effective performance evaluation methods that result in a clear identification of the teacher's strengths, specific needs, and problem areas.
2. Develop an improvement plan that specifies, among other things, what the teacher must do personally to improve in the problem areas and also what the school will do to help the teacher reach the improvement objectives as determined.
3. Give specific attention to those strengths that the teacher might possess in order to enhance the chances for improvement.
4. Help the teacher establish functional and supportive relations with other teachers.
5. Make certain that the school principal provides administrative support exemplified by a demonstrative attitude of caring and personal commitment to and interest in effective classroom teaching.

In regard to effective performance evaluation methods, Chapter 11 discusses in depth the determination of the purposes of performance evaluation, the evaluation plan, and standards for the development and operation of a sound evaluation system. The identification of personal strengths and needs relative to professional improvement is also discussed in relation to assessment center techniques. Assessment center methods are also discussed briefly later in this chapter.

Bridges (1990) suggests eight elements for dealing with incompetent teachers as follows:

1. Establish "excellence in teaching" as a high priority for the district.
2. Adopt and publish reasonable criteria for evaluating teachers.
3. Adopt sound procedures for determining whether teachers satisfy these criteria and apply these procedures uniformly to teachers in the district.
4. Provide unsatisfactory teachers with remediation (assistance) and a reasonable time to improve.
5. Establish and implement procedures for ensuring that principals have current competencies in the areas of supervision, evaluation, and providing assistance.
6. Provide principals with the resources needed to carry out their responsibilities.
7. Hold principals accountable for evaluating and dealing with incompetent teachers.
8. Provide incompetent teachers with a fair hearing prior to making the dismissal decision.

We would add and/or emphasize the need to make certain that the teacher clearly understands the specific problems related to teaching performance and what must be done to improve. The teacher who is not aware of problems regarding teaching performance may be completely surprised to be the target of such charges and, thus, gaining an understanding of the problem(s) is a first prerequisite for remediation.

As discussed later in this chapter, clinical supervision emphasizes systemwide instructional improvement through improved staff performance. Clinical supervision necessitates a cooperative relationship between the teacher and the supervisor.

Smith (1998) points out clearly that there are times when it is necessary to develop a comprehensive remedial plan for the marginal teacher. Although a remedial plan differs from case to case, it includes the items that are unsatisfactory according to the overall performance evaluation. Among these areas commonly included in such plans are (1) professional preparation and scholarship, (2) instructional skill, (3) classroom management, (4) handling of student discipline and attendant problems, and (5) effort toward improvement when needed. Figure 10.6 is an example of a remedial plan for area 4, handling of student discipline and attendant problems.

DEALING WITH CONFLICT AND CONTROVERSY

In Chapter 3, a closed climate was defined as one that is characterized by low staff morale, limited and inadequate communication, and limited socialization. In such a climate, one might expect that *conflict* and *controversy* among staff personnel would occur. Yet, due to the dynamics and individual differences that exist in any organization, differences of opinion and personal conflict also occur in schools with open climates. Attempts to meet the needs of the school system often conflict with the need-dispositions of individuals in the system. For example, the need to increase class size due to budgetary conditions might be contrary to the need to reduce faculty workload, or school budget priorities might differ in the minds of the administration, teachers, and various school stakeholders. Thus role, personality, priority, authority, procedural, and other types of conflict are inevitable in almost every organization.

Although conflict resolution depends on many variables, including leadership style, several considerations and/or strategies can be utilized to capitalize on controversy and conflict. An open climate, for example, expects and respects individuals' rights to disagree, and human resources administrators must recognize the right of employees to do so. Any effort to limit the right of disagreement likely will lead to other negative relationships, rather than to build organizational trust and confidence. Thus open systems seek ways to gain input from workers through the use of system surveys, think tanks, shadow groups, and other viable suggestion systems.

Controversy in an open climate can be useful. Progress in terms of goal achievement and new understandings often are generated by full reflection on existing problems, issues, and alternative solutions. School leaders, then, can make controversy constructive. Additionally, school leaders must work to broaden the base of staff and community understanding through purposeful assessment of criticism. In this way, understanding of the facts sur-

A. Your performance reflects an inability to consistently establish order and discipline in the classroom.
B. I recommend that your handling of student discipline be improved during the probationary period to reflect an ability to consistently establish order and discipline in the classroom.
C. Suggestions that will assist you in correcting the above deficiencies include:
    1. Communicate to students appropriate expectations for conduct and behavior. These would include the following:
        (a) students will arrive at class punctually
        (b) students will take their seats in a timely and orderly fashion
        (c) students will sit in their seats properly and remain in their seats unless otherwise instructed
        (d) students will be quiet and attentive when you are instructing
        (e) students will not be loud, disrespectful, or engage in rough housing
    2. Misbehavior should result in appropriate and consistent consequences. This is best accomplished through a process of progressive discipline depending on the nature of the offense. Follow the adopted school sequence for dealing with discipline:
        (a) student reprimand
        (b) conference with student
        (c) detention—give notice; maximum 30 minutes
        (d) parent contact
        (e) parent conference
        (f) referral to principal
    3. Maintain a current log on each student that you have disciplined. Each entry should state the date of misconduct, the nature of the misconduct, and action taken.

FIGURE 10.6
Remedial Plan for Handling Student Discipline and Attendant Problems
Source: R. E. Smith (1998). *Human Resources Administration.* Larchmont, NY: Eye on Education, pp. 188–89.

rounding a situation can serve to ward off unfair criticism, since it helps to distinguish between constructive and destructive proposals. Such an assessment necessitates keeping personally informed of the existence and concerns of criticisms that are expressed. Open channels of communication can serve as the school system's nervous system in that problems can be determined in their early stages; such awareness allows for further assessments and appropriate responses, as well as an opportunity to keep minor criticisms at manageable proportions. Action must be taken to counteract unfair and/or irresponsible criticism. A planned strategy for such action includes the gathering of accurate information, soliciting help on the matter from appropriate groups and individuals, and then setting forth an action plan as appropriate to the case.

The school leader's overall task in dealing with conflict and controversy is to maintain the integrity of the system and the confidence of the school system's stakeholders in an atmosphere where critics have a right both to disagree and to have access to the system's open channels of communication. Conflict and controversy can help to lead to better solutions to existing problems. A positive approach to such matters maximizes the efforts of personnel and the productivity of the school system's efforts. In short, the leader's best defense in dealing with conflict and controversy is to maintain a communications initiative with both employees and the school's public.

STAFF DEVELOPMENT

Staff development in education has many facets, as evidenced by the numerous terms in the literature that name the process. Such terms include *professional growth, in-service education, continuing education, recurrent education, on-the-job staff training, human resources development, staff improvement, renewal,* and other combinations of these terms. Although various authorities have elaborated on differences among these terms, *staff development* and *human resources development* are used interchangeably in this text.

Historically, staff development has been a reactive program. The inadequacies in the preparation of teachers before 1900 and many years thereafter required major remediation programs. As early as 1882, Bloss noted in his annual report to the governor of Indiana that "The fact that so large a portion of the teachers are inexperienced is not the only difficulty, since the statistics for the past three years show . . . the majority of teachers licensed to teach are by no means the most competent" (p. 156). In fact, the need to provide the "missing education" for the ill-prepared teachers dominated **in-service programs** in most school districts during much of the first half of the 20th century. Such motivation unfortunately continues in many schools today. As a result, participants in such programs often approach in-service with little motivation and considerable passivity.

Staff development must be proactive rather than reactive; its effectiveness depends on the extent to which it is personalized and based on positive constructs. It is not that concern for deficiencies in staff preparation or the need to update skills are not appropriate concerns of staff development; rather, remediation is not to assume the dominant role. The human resources planning process must project and predict as accurately as possible the human skills and talents necessary to meet system needs in the immediate and long-range future. Armed with this information, along with important ongoing recommendations from building-level personnel, staff development joins other personnel processes to build the human resources necessary to keep the school system alive and vital. These program activities become cooperative endeavors that account for personal interest, as well as for local building and organizational program needs. The position taken in this text is that staff development is self-development. The responsibility for personal growth must be assumed primarily by the individual.

This discussion of staff development, then, is based primarily on the following concepts:

1. Effective staff development primarily is a proactive consideration and is developmental in that its emphasis is on an ever-developing individual. It focuses on projected needs and objectives that will help the school system to remain creative and productive. Individual growth that meets these projected needs provides employees a personalized opportunity to reach higher levels of self-fulfillment and gratification. Staff development is an important investment in the school system's future.
2. Effective staff development places greater emphasis on the extension of personal strengths and creative talents than on the remediation of personal weaknesses. The major focus of growth is on what the individual can do and how this strength can be further developed and utilized.
3. Effective staff development is self-development. Growth is personal in the sense that what motivates each individual is an individual matter and in the sense that each person's self-image is instrumental in determining the incentives that will encourage personal growth. Staff development is self-development in that growth begins with a personal need, and individuals develop by taking responsibility for their own growth.

Staff development, from the foregoing perspectives, can be illustrated through the concepts of the Getzels–Guba (1957) social systems model. Each individual employee has unique need-dispositions based on personality factors. The institution has certain expectations for the purposes of the organization and what it desires from each employee. The areas of agreement between personal needs and institutional expectations for the employee constitute areas of high potential for progress. As illustrated in Figure 10.7, as each person realizes new knowledge and skills, new and broadened aspirations of development become possible. Through the use of effective motivation and a system of rewards related to improved performance, personal development becomes an ongoing, continuous process.

The major purposes of staff development can be summarized as follows:

1. To institute planned staff development programs that provide the learning necessary to enable the employee to perform at the level of competency required in current and future position assignments.
2. To provide a climate that fosters opportunity for personal self-fulfillment and institutional effectiveness, a climate that facilitates human creativity and system renewal.
3. To serve the school system's primary goals: enhancing and achieving quality teaching and learning for students.
4. To save money. It is costly to hire and then dismiss employees who do not work out. It is also costly to lose good employees because they are frustrated by the lack of opportunity for professional growth. And it is wasteful to accept barely satisfactory work as the norm (NSBA, 1996).

FIGURE 10.7
Agreement Areas for Personal
Growth

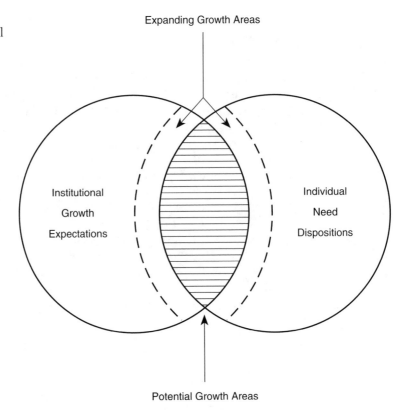

5. To establish viable and meaningful programs that enable system personnel to work cooperatively toward achieving the system's goals and their own personal goals in the areas of achievement, satisfaction, and self-fulfillment.

Operational Procedures for Staff Development

The operational procedures for the staff development process progress through five steps: (1) adopt a guiding philosophy, (2) develop goals and objectives, (3) plan programs, activities, and delivery systems and determine responsibilities, (4) schedule and deliver plans and programs, and (5) evaluate the process.

Step 1, the guiding philosophy for staff development, is adopted as official board policy. Such policy is utilized by the school district staff to determine specific procedures through which to implement the program throughout the school system. The following is an example of a board policy relative to staff development.

The board of education supports the principle of continuous personal growth and development for all personnel employed in the school district. Such development programs and activities that serve to enhance the goals and objectives of the school district and to meet the immediate and future needs of district personnel should be made available through cooperative planning and implementation by members of the school district staff.

The general responsibility for the administration of the staff development program belongs to the school superintendent, who delegates program responsibilities among the staff as appropriate and who recommends, with proper input from employees, minimal requirements for development to meet changing certification requirements, to adjust to program changes, and to gain future knowledge and the skills necessary to assure viability of human resources in the district.

This policy sets the guidelines for the administrative discretion necessary for its implementation. It emphasizes the need for development programs that relate directly to the strategic plans of the school system and its goals and objectives. Such major administrative considerations as minimal requirements, needs assessments, program activities, implementation procedures, incentives, and resources are concerns primarily of the school district personnel. Staff development is a shared responsibility, with local school personnel assuming much of the responsibility for program design and implementation. The extent to which the central human resources unit assumes major responsibility for staff development is a function of the individual school district.

Step 2 of the operational procedure includes creating goals and objectives for staff development relative to identified system and employee needs. In-service programs that focus on realistic personal needs and local school problems are likely to be more effective than others. Furthermore, programs that consider both the needs of the organization's personnel and the needs of the organization provide an important organizational balance in staff development.

Step 3 links closely with step 2. Programs, activities, and delivery systems must be planned and programmed. Both school and individual responsibilities must be determined. Ideally, school systems should have a unit or department whose prime responsibility is staff development. School district size, governance structure, and other factors, however, determine the extent to which this recommendation is possible. Sometimes the human resources unit or instructional unit serves the purpose of program coordination. In any case, the need for close cooperation and mutual sharing of program activities and responsibilities is important for program success.

Step 4 puts the plans and program options into place. The activities, experiences, and learning programs are scheduled and delivered. Staff development activities are both formal and informal. They include workshops, conferences, peer teaching, mentoring, independent study activities, assessment methodology, internships, job rotation, college courses, and other program pursuits. Selected program options are presented briefly in the next section of this chapter.

Step 5, evaluation of the staff development process, focuses on the assessments necessary to judge the extent to which the stated goals for the program are being met.

One of the most comprehensive models for the administration of staff development is the *RPTIM model* (Thompson, 1982). This model conceptualizes staff development under five stages and 38 practices. The five stages of the RPTIM model are *r*eadiness, *p*lanning, *t*raining, *i*mplementation, and *m*aintenance. Each stage focuses on several practices. For example, the readiness stage centers on the development of a positive climate before other staff development activities are attempted. Activities associated with this stage might include the collaborative writing of goals for school improvement, the establishment of goals for future program improvement, and the determination of the leadership and support needed. The 38 practices within each stage of the RPTIM model are research based, and the National Development Council and the Council of Professors of Instructional Supervision have endorsed these as practices that should serve as the basis for effective staff development in schools.

Staff Development Methods and Strategies

The comprehensiveness of the staff development process and the variety of approaches utilized to achieve its purposes have been described in numerous publications. A brief description of several approaches to staff development, including mentoring, quality circles, teacher centers, assessment centers, career development, personnel appraisal methods, task force and shadow groups, job rotation, clinical supervision, and peer-assisted leadership, is presented in this section. Others not discussed, but somewhat self-explanatory, include college and university course work, sabbaticals, exchange teaching, conferences and conventions, and professional journals and materials (NSBA, 1996).

Mentoring. The New Webster's Collegiate (1994) Dictionary defines the word *mentor* as a wise and faithful advisor or tutor. Mentoring was discussed previously as related to staff induction. Mentoring also assumes a variety of forms in staff development. As Smith (1998) points out,

> Developmental relationships such as between a mentor teacher and a protégé can be powerful stimuli for change and learning. Research indicates that mentors as well as beginning teachers find that the program enhances their classroom abilities, increases their enthusiasm for teaching, and that they experience positive results involving their teaching, professional growth, and impact on the profession. (p. 132)

Ebmeier (2000) found that school principals influence the personal efficacy of teachers by providing improvement assistance through mentoring and praise. Such factors as confidence, commitment, and satisfaction are obtained primarily by the extent to which teachers believe that the principal is interested in and is actually supportive of teaching. The interaction between the mentor and the classroom teacher, exemplified by effective mentoring techniques, is perceived as administrative support by the teacher and can lead to improved teaching and innovative practices.

Mentoring and **coaching** are terms often used synonomously, although there are differences between these two strategies. Mentoring generally refers to the art of helping to steer a subordinate or a colleague in the same field. Coaches, on the other hand, use their techniques for professionals and/or clients in a full range of backgrounds (from an interview with Antonia Allegra, career and writing coach, St. Helena, CA). For instance, a qualified coach might not only counsel professionals within their own occupational specialty, but is prepared to work with individuals in a variety of fields. Through the use of a combination of education, cheerleading and listening, the coach may help an individual client to ask and then answer such queries as the following:

☐ The challenges and problems that I am facing now?
☐ The opportunities that are available to me right now?
☐ What am I grateful for this week?
☐ What didn't I get done, but intended to do?
☐ What do I want this coaching call to accomplish?

Such broad queries inevitably lead to specifics, which the coach then discusses in relation to the person's career and special interests.

A mentor in education uses similar strategies, and although advice and guidance are offered as appropriate to the case, helping the individual teacher to think through a situation toward the goal of self-resolution of the problem or question is foremost. Thus active listening techniques serve significant purposes. It should be noted that both mentoring and coaching sessions frequently take place through distance methods by using the telephone or e-mail, for example.

Assume that a teacher is having serious problems with organizing and presenting effective teaching lessons. In this case, the mentor might initiate a session by asking the teacher to describe the planning process being used to develop each lesson. The mentor might ask, "How do you determine the objectives for each lesson and how are these objectives supported in follow-up learning activities?" During this time, the mentor serves as a listener and the teacher is the speaker. Clues relative to short-term unit objectives and their relationship to the school's instructional goals can be assessed in regard to the teacher's responses. If it is determined that the development of classroom objectives and learning experiences for students is in need of attention, the mentor can assist the teacher in the process of planning and the requirements of a well-designed daily lesson.

In some cases, depending on the situation at hand, mentors might go through any number of exercises with the teacher: working on lesson planning, role playing the actual introduction to a planned lesson, suggesting follow-up activities such as observing other teachers at work, recommending appropriate readings, or critiquing a proposed lesson plan with a follow-up classroom observation.

The emphasis in mentoring should be that of providing a positive experience for both the mentor and the teacher. Ultimately, the goal is to have the teacher seek such collaboration and become enthusiastic about the potential of self-improvement.

Empirical evidence has shown that individuals can shift from an area of weakness to one of strength, from a lack of confidence to personal self-confidence. Thus mentoring can result in changes of behavior; hesitant innovators can become more creative in their instructional approaches, and poor disciplinarians can develop into the classroom authorities that they potentially can be.

In summary, a mentor is selected to work with an individual staff member or small group of members for the purpose of personal growth. The mentor becomes the primary "coach" and counselor and (1) determines the special areas of interest and need regarding the person's personal development, (2) works with him or her to design the most viable plan for individual growth, (3) assesses the most appropriate resources for meeting growth objectives, and (4) serves as a sounding board and constructive critic in evaluating progress and commitment. The need for a nonthreatening relationship and personal confidence is foremost. Since the mentor serves as a teacher, counselor, supporter, critic, and evaluator, the term coaching often is used as a synonym for mentoring.

Quality Circles. Quality circles originated in Japan, where small groups participate actively in planning, designing, and implementing work procedures in business and industry. The use of **quality circles** for staff development in education is a technique that places the primary responsibility for personal growth on individuals linked together for the improvement of teaching and student learning. Members of a circle might include the teaching and support staff of one unit of a multiunit elementary school, the teachers within a department of mathematics in a local school, a group of primary-grade-level teachers in a local school, foreign-language teachers from several schools within a district, or others whose common work interests or personal growth objectives can be enhanced through cooperative activities. Quality circles generally are established and operated within the following guidelines:

1. The circle members focus on an area or program of instruction that is determined to be important to the school's objectives and to their personal interests. The areas of special need, sources of knowledge, and skill development are identified. Individual members or the group as a whole determine responsibilities for personal learning. At times individuals serve as resource persons for all group members. Responsibilities for teaching subject area content are determined.

2. A variety of methods and procedures is used to provide practice of the skills and knowledge required to implement the desired program or teaching methodology. The use of modeling, simulation, observation, and video techniques provides opportunities to practice in classroom and nonclassroom settings.

3. Constructive feedback is provided through a systematic procedure of self-evaluation and group review.
4. Specific provision is made for implementing the behaviors or methods desired. Mentoring, peer counseling, or coaching is structured through a system that places primary responsibility for improvement on the individual, with full support of the circle members.

Quality circles can serve several important purposes and provide numerous benefits to the system and its human resources. Primary purposes and benefits include the following:

1. The development of new knowledge and skills to enhance present and future job performance, as viewed by staff members themselves.
2. The establishment of the individual's responsibility for personal development through a process of team mentoring and individual leadership.
3. The promotion of personal motivation and work satisfaction through opportunities for achievement, relevant growth, and appropriate rewards for improved performance.
4. The improvement of personal performance and work quality to meet school goals and objectives that have been established by consensus.
5. The general improvement of staff communication, human relationships, and trust through opportunities to be a member of the local school and school district teams and to be a significant member of the decision-making process.

Teacher Centers. Another effort to place the primary responsibility for personal development on the individual teacher is through the **teacher center,** an enriched environment of resources, personal involvement, and peer communication. The teacher center concept makes the teacher an active participant in decisions and activities relating to personal growth. A teacher center need not be a permanent site or facility, but conceptually constitutes a teaching resource bank where teachers informally participate in activities that enhance their performance in the classroom. Teachers, alone or in groups with similar interests, examine instructional materials, design teaching aids, read materials related to teaching methods and strategies, develop new lesson plans, and communicate with other teachers and support personnel concerning creative ideas in an area of instructional interest. Based on the proposition that professional staff personnel are best qualified to determine the necessary training needed by their colleagues, the teacher center concept is governed primarily by teachers.

A teacher center might be a temporary site, such as a school district's reading center, that is used for a specified period of time for a specific instructional development purpose. It might be a self-contained room with a professional library, film and visual materials, a work design area for making instructional aids, and other resource banks available for examination and classroom use. In school districts that have established extensive educational facilities for teaching and learning centers, facilities for examining instructional technology of various kinds, computer facilities, curriculum resource banks, research libraries, conference and workshop rooms, instructional design facilities, media resources, and support staff personnel are available for teacher and staff use. Not all activities in a teacher center are informal. Specific workshops, designed to develop new teaching concepts and skills, are generally given high ratings by teachers.

The positive aspects of teacher centers are numerous. The concept of teachers helping teachers is supported by research. Intrinsic motivation that leads to personal development activities is one important criterion for proactive growth. One concern, however, is the possible absence of research-based development programs. Conceptual frameworks founded on tested theory, research, and empirical application are essential. If the delivery system for staff development depends exclusively on individual opinions of "effective practice," the potential exists for misdirected effort and practice.

Assessment Centers. Assessment center techniques were first adopted by the military and business and industry to select and promote administrative personnel. In education, the first use of assessment centers was also in personnel selection, the selection of school administrators. As previously noted, beginning in the 1970s the National Association of Secondary School Principals (NASSP) assumed a major leadership role in the development of assessment techniques to select school principals. Since then, assessment center methodology has proved beneficial to assess performance in teacher and administrator preparation programs and in staff development.

> In a typical assessment center, participants work through tasks designed to elicit behavior considered important for the job involved. Assessors observe the process and take notes, using specially designed observation forms . . . assessors compare observations and make a final evaluation of each candidate for that exercise. At the end of the process, the assessors develop a summary report on each candidate. (Brown, 1992, p. 35)

Such a center is not viewed as a physical location; rather, assessment activities are conducted in various settings, whenever and wherever a qualified group of assessors meets to assess the performance of an individual or group of individuals for a stated reason.

An **assessment center** is characterized by several activities:

1. Behaviors and skills, determined to be relevant to a specific job are assessed through standard methods and activities.
2. Multiple assessment techniques are utilized to gain performance data (e.g., interviews, leaderless group activities, individual task exercises, in-basket simulation, pencil-and-paper tests, personality tests, and other simulation exercises).
3. A group of assessors is used in the evaluation procedures. Such individuals are specifically trained and certified in the methods being utilized and the procedures being followed.

4. Information and individual assessor results are pooled through a process of *jurying* that leads to a final consensus of performance results.
5. If the assessment is for staff development purposes, a system of thorough feedback is provided to the person assessed.

Mentoring, in particular, appears to have considerable potential as a growth model in conjunction with assessment methodology. One major advantage of such a relational approach is its potential for personalizing the growth process by the professional involvement of a specially selected mentor who works with an individual on the strengths and needs as revealed in assessment results.

Assessment centers also can play a major role in the preparation of school administrators. The assessment center method can be used to both diagnose students' entrance and exit competencies and assess the effectiveness of the preparation program (Sirotnik & Durden, 1996; Wendel & Uerling, 1989).

Clinical supervision. Effective technical supervision significantly facilitates staff development and maximization of human resources. **Clinical supervision** emphasizes systemwide instructional improvement through improved staff performance. Assessments provide information relative to the achievement of mutually determined teaching objectives. Clinical supervision is a cyclical procedure.

Step 1 The cooperative relationship between the teacher and supervisor, which is essential to the procedure, is fostered. During this phase, they discuss the nature of clinical supervision, clarify follow-up procedures and responsibilities, specify purposes and focus on development objectives, and discuss uses of classroom observation information.

Step 2 The teacher plans an instructional unit with constructive input by the supervisor. Instructional objectives, teaching methods, instructional materials, monitoring strategies, and other teaching–learning considerations are determined. On the basis of this information, the supervisor and teacher determine the procedures relative to the actual classroom observation.

Step 3 The focus in this step is on planning the observation procedures. Information on student learning needs or problems, as well as on the physical setting, is collected.

Step 4 The supervisor makes the actual classroom observation. In this step the agreed on methods for collecting information are implemented. Following the observation, both the supervisor and the teacher examine the recorded information individually to interpret the data relative to the teaching activities that took place and the objectives of the intended lesson.

Step 5 The supervisor incorporates the data collected into the most meaningful and reportable format that the teacher can readily understand.

Step 6 The supervisor plans the postobservation conference with the teacher. The specifics to be discussed in the conference, the approach to be used, and the conference objectives are established in terms of the original planning agreements. Strengths and areas for improvement are analyzed for discussion purposes.

Step 7 The postobservation conference provides the opportunity for the teacher and supervisor to review the information collected and evaluate the results in relation to predetermined objectives. The supervisor serves as an instructor, helping the teacher to interpret the results of the classroom observation. Through a mutual discussion of actual classroom events, the teacher and supervisor focus on the kinds of changes needed in the follow-up classroom performance to achieve desired learning objectives.

Step 8 The teacher and supervisor plan the next teaching lesson and the behaviors and methods to be implemented in an effort to realize continually improved results. This final step leads to new directions in planning, the reestablishment of the relationship for the future, and the reimplementation of the steps in the clinical supervision cycle.

Career Development Planning. **Career development planning** includes such activities as personal counseling, self-concept and assessment workshops, career opportunity seminars, and close coordination of the organization's human resources processes with employee career aspirations. The work experience and the employee's personal development program are planned to facilitate the individual's career goals in relation to the organization's future human resources needs.

Personnel Appraisal Methods. The organization's appraisal process focuses primarily on gathering formative information that can direct the employee's growth and development. Rather than using summative ratings to determine job continuation, the appraisal process becomes a cooperative procedure that encompasses self-evaluation and mentoring feedback to motivate continuous employee development. A comprehensive discussion of performance appraisal is included in Chapter 11.

Task Force and Shadow Groups. Service on task force groups that focus on the creation of better, more effective methods has viable personal development potential. Representatives from community, administrator, teacher, and student groups concentrate on an educational objective through cooperative problem-solving activity.

Industry especially has benefited from the use of shadow groups, which generally involve the simulation of an activity by members of the organization. For instance, employees might assume the roles of the governing board members and conduct a board meeting using a proposed future agenda. The process helps management to anticipate problems prior to the actual board meeting and gain insight on important employee perspectives on the issues and agenda items. Employee participants and other representatives are able to gain appreciation for the agenda issues, develop a better understanding of the organization's problems, and gain new perspectives about their growth needs in relation to the goals of the organization.

Job Rotation. Industry has experienced success in the practice of moving employees and managers to various positions to enhance organizational effectiveness and employee development. Education has not generally endorsed the practice; however, the idea has received some favorable acceptance as a positive growth practice for school administrators. After a certain time period, both the individual and the organization benefit when the employee can exercise personal talents and meet new challenges in a different assignment. Additionally, experience and knowledge of the different educational units and school programs are spread to more persons in the district. Arguments against job rotation in education center primarily on its possible disrupting effect on the local school community. Authorities suggest that the practice of job rotation in the future will tie closely to personal competency. That is, the task at hand will determine required skill needs, and personnel will be assigned to such tasks accordingly.

Peer-Assisted Leadership. Using **peer-assisted leadership (PAL),** participants help other participants in the improvement of their personal skills. In 1983 the instructional management program at the Far West Laboratory in San Francisco established PAL in order to (1) help administrators develop skills that they can use to analyze their own and others' management behaviors, (2) give participants opportunities to learn how other administrators lead in their positions, (3) enable administrators to gain support from colleagues, and (4) provide a means for assisting administrators in understanding effective behavior in their specific setting. Since that time, PAL activities have proved effective with other professional staff personnel. Instruction relative to data collection through interviews, shadowing, reflective interviewing, and advanced reflective interviewing is provided. In early meetings, participants are introduced to the model of the general framework for program leadership.

PAL differs from mentoring in that peer-assisted leadership is not a mentor–protégé arrangement. Rather, peers are placed in partnerships or triads, and each participant helps others to examine and reflect on personal behaviors, skills, and activities in relation to the setting of the school environment, specific skills being implemented, and expected program outcomes.

PAL goals include helping participants to develop skills for analyzing personal behavior, enabling participants to gain support and insight from colleagues, and providing participants an opportunity to learn how others lead, teach, and create. Participants in PAL programs report that it increases awareness of their own behavior, style, and intentions. It serves as an important self-evaluation tool and leads to the learning of new strategies and personal skills.

The field of education has numerous methods and strategies for implementing staff development. Although most of the discussion in this chapter has focused on teacher development, such programs as assessment centers, peer-assisted leadership, job rotation, internships, task force groups, career development planning, and mentoring apply equally well to administrative personnel. Perhaps the underlying importance of staff development in education is reflected in the basic concept that schools will improve as people progress.

ADULTS AS LEARNERS

Because school system personnel are adult learners, staff development activities must utilize the basic principles that facilitate optimal learning and growth for them. An understanding of adults and how they learn is as vital to successful adult professional development as the knowledge of children and adolescents at the K–12 level is to their successful learning. "Knowing who is likely to participate in our programs, why adults choose to participate, and what barriers must be overcome before they can participate is knowledge that educators can put to good use in planning and delivering programs" (Merriam & Brockett, 1997, p. 129).

Research on adult learning has shown that adult learners need to experience the following:

1. To be involved in the determination of their learning activities; they must have a voice in the determination of learning goals, program content, learning experiences, and appropriate evaluations.
2. To be considered as individual learners; each adult brings a varied background of experiences and knowledge to any learning situation.
3. To see the value of the learning experiences; they need to know that the activities and experiences will be applicable to their work and to the resolution of problems in their work environment.
4. To see tangible outcomes from the learning activities and experiences; they need to receive some indication of their personal achievement toward learning goals.

Authorities in the area of adult education point to several important differences between *pedagogy*, the art or science of teaching children, and *andragogy*, the art and science of helping adults learn. Knowles and associates (1984) emphasized four underlying assumptions of andragogy that differ from those of pedagogy and their implications for adult learning.

1. *Regarding the concept of the learner.* As the individual grows and matures, his or her self-concept moves from one of dependency to one of increasing self-directedness. The psychological need to be perceived and treated as a person capable of being self-responsible holds important implications for adult learning programs. For example, situations that do not allow the individual to be self-directing tend to produce tension between that situation and the individual's self-concept.
2. *Regarding the role of the learner's experience.* As the adult engages in an ever-expanding variety of experiences, he or she is more able to relate to new

learning experiences. Adults enter into an educational activity with both a greater volume and a different quality of experience from youth. New transmittal techniques for adult learners must include an emphasis on experiential strategies that capitalize on the rich resources of experiences of the learner. Thus the use of active, participative activities such as simulation, discussion, problem solving, and team projects are favored over lectures and other more passive instructional methods.

3. *Regarding readiness to learn.* As the individual matures, readiness to learn becomes more dependent on the tasks required for the performance of his or her evolving social role. That is, adult learners are ready to learn because the roles that they are approaching or serving set forth the need. They become ready to learn when they experience a need to know or to do something in order to perform more efficiently. As Knowles pointed out, the critical implication of this assumption is the importance of timing learning experiences to coincide with the learner's developmental tasks in social roles as teachers, leaders, organizational members, and so forth.

4. *Regarding orientation to learning.* For the most part, adults do not learn for the sake of learning. They learn in order to perform a task, solve a problem, or live in a more satisfying way. Thus the immediacy of application is a critical learning motivator, and a problem-centered orientation is of primary importance. (Knowles, 1984, pp. 11–12)

These guidelines for working with adult learners underline specific questions that staff development program personnel must answer: (1) To what extent is the staff development program relevant to learner needs? (2) To what extent has the program been personalized as well as individualized; is there an opportunity for self-direction based on personal needs, problems, and interests? (3) To what extent does the program relate to the background of experience possessed by the learners? (4) To what extent does the program provide for active learning on the part of the learners? and (5) To what extent does the program provide for assessment and feedback relative to learning and behavioral change?

In brief, the facilitation of learning experiences for adults necessitates a knowledge of the social role development, problems, and needs of the individual. Thus, to be able to plan, organize, and implement effective staff development programs for adult personnel, human resources administrators must be prepared to respond in creative ways to the unique needs and interests of the individual learner. In this sense, knowledge must be personalized, not just individualized. Personalization requires that learning strategies focus on the background and experience unique to the adult learner.

SUMMARY

The maximization of human resources in the school system is a primary responsibility of the human resources function. This concern emphasizes the purposeful development and utilization of people within the organization. It also underlines the perspective set forth throughout this text that the human resources function is a primary responsibility of all personnel in the school system. An organization's progress depends on the extent to which people are positively motivated and developed.

Because the school is a social system, the behavior of individuals is influenced by the institution's expectations and the individuals' personal need-dispositions. Staff utilization serves to establish a congruence between organizational roles and personal needs toward the goal of developing behaviors that harmonize with stated organizational purposes and personal self-fulfillment. Human motivation is an important consideration of the human resources function generally and of the processes of staff orientation, staff assignment, and staff development specifically.

Each human resources process contributes uniquely to the maximization of human resources. Induction is the comprehensive complex of activities designed to gain congruence between institutional objectives and employee needs. Induction practices, when effectively implemented, enhance employee morale, development, and productivity. Mentor programs, policy and regulation manuals, personnel information handbooks, personal assistance programs, information sessions, one-on-one conferences, and socialization activities are some of the activities useful in induction programs.

Staff assignment maximizes human resources when position assignments are closely related to the employee's talents and interests. Workload and provisions for troubled staff members are other important elements of effective staff utilization. Approaches to staff development that emphasize remedial programs generally have proved ineffective. A focus on employee strengths and self-fulfillment fosters self-development from a positive perspective. Potential growth best occurs when the individual's dispositions agree with the organization's growth expectations.

The implementation of the staff development process consists of a planned sequence of procedures that begins with commitment by the board of education; continues through cooperative goal setting, program design, and delivery; and culminates in opportunities to practice the knowledge and skills gained in a wide variety of learning activities. Evaluation leads to necessary program changes and ensures continuous program improvement. In all activities, basic principles of adult learning are utilized.

Staff development methods and strategies are virtually limitless and are provided through the local school district, institutions of higher learning, and employee associations. Such developments as mentoring, quality circles, teacher centers, assessment centers, peer-assisted leadership, and clinical supervision are among the viable approaches for meeting the purposes of the staff development process.

DISCUSSION QUESTIONS

1. Examine Maslow's hierarchy of basic needs (Figure 10.2). Discuss the hierarchy of needs as related to teacher personnel generally. For example, what specific provisions and/or activities are important in meeting the safety needs of teacher personnel?
2. Consider the Getzels–Guba social systems model and the matter of institutional expectations and individual need-dispositions (Figure 10.1). Discuss several specific ideas that the school system might consider to

satisfy these dimensions. For example, what provisions can be implemented by the school system to help to meet organizational goal expectations or the employee's needs relative to self-esteem?

3. Discuss a specific school district's induction process in relation to its effectiveness. What factors tend to cause its ineffectiveness or foster its effectiveness? To what extent do the identified factors of effectiveness compare with the guiding principles for the induction process presented in this chapter?

4. Staff development was discussed as a proactive experience, rather than a reactive one. Discuss your personal staff development experiences. Have these experiences met the proactive criteria? Why or why not?

5. A high school teacher of social studies has two classes of grade 10 history with 26 and 32 students and three classes of government with 26, 31, and 33 students. The subject–grade coefficient for social studies is 1.1. Class periods are 55 minutes in length. On average during the semester, the teacher spends 11 periods per week in cooperative duties. Use the Douglass load formula to calculate this teacher's units of teacher load. (*Note:* The answer is 35.40 units.)

CASE STUDIES

10.1 A Question of Low Morale

The Union High School District is experiencing unusually high staff turnover. In addition, general morale throughout the district is low. Teacher absence has increased 20% over the last 3 years, and general faculty and support staff complaints have increased substantially as well. Apply the Herzberg two-factor theory (Chapter 2) in the role of a school principal in the Union High School District.

Questions

1. What specific practices and relationships would you examine at the outset to ameliorate the problems indicated?
2. What recommendations would you offer for obviating the problems described?

10.2 Time to Teach

As assistant director of human resources, you receive the memorandum shown in

Figure 10.8. Examine the memo and then present your ideas of follow-up in this case. Keep in mind the specific principles set forth in the chapter concerning effective in-service programs, as well as the principles of adult learning.

Questions

1. What specific problems do you determine from this scenario?
2. From the somewhat limited evidence provided, what necessary staff development practices appear to have been overlooked in this case in the past?
3. Discuss the alternatives for action at this time. As the school principal, outline a brief action plan that you would recommend in Ms. Petrov's case.

10.3 The Teacher Transfer

Melvin Schneider was in his third year of teaching at Union Elementary School when

---

MEMORANDUM

To: E. O. Herr, Assistant Director
From: Verna Petrov, Grade 3 Teacher, Union Elementary
Re: Program suggestion

I'd like to make a suggestion for you to consider in planning some of our in-service days. I know that you have run a survey of perceived needs in the district that has given you some general or overall ideas, but for some of us, surveys don't always fit our needs as individuals.
Here are a couple of things I see as needs:

1. When we test with the battery of the Columbus Test of Basic Skills, and place so much emphasis on it, teachers tend to start teaching to the test, and I'm not sure that is good.
2. I don't want to sound negative, but when I have 27 children from residents in our district in my class and then get two or more who can hardly speak English, it is becoming impossible for me to take care of the class; the few non-English-speaking students require all my time. Then, many of them will be gone again in a few weeks or months.

Please don't misunderstand me. I'm not saying we need in-service on working with these few children. I want help working with the whole class. Why not set up a training program for children with limited ability in English, and when they get up to grade level, place them in appropriate classes? It seems to me that the least restricted environment is one that would help these deserving students learn best.

Thanks!

Verna Petrov

FIGURE 10.8
Memo to Assistant Director of Human Resources

parental complaints about his relationships with students started to increase weekly. Calls from parents to Principal Thelma Morton reported that Mr. Schneider was "cold"; children were afraid of him. Then, too, others complained that he couldn't work with the slower children; he lacked the patience necessary for working with slow learners.

Principal Morton scheduled a meeting with Human Resources Director Brad Joseph and Superintendent Dorothy Rose. "I observed his classroom twice last week," offered Ms. Morton. "His teaching methods seem satisfactory, but the class atmosphere doesn't come through as a happy one. Maybe we should transfer him next year."

"Well, you know that Mr. Schneider has been in the district for 11 years now," said Mr. Joseph. "He was transferred from Whittier after his first 4 years and then again after 4 years from Whittier to Phillips."

"How do his performance evaluations look?" asked Superintendent Rose.

"As I noted earlier," replied Ms. Morton, "I've given him satisfactory ratings each of his years with me, but he doesn't come off well with parents and I have received more than the usual number of requests from the children themselves to move to Mrs. Martin's fifth-grade class."

Superintendent Rose called her secretary and asked for Mr. Schneider's personal file.

The record did confirm that he had been transferred twice during his first 8 years in the district. Remarks in the record indicated that "parental complaints" and "lack of student rapport" were the primary reasons for these transfers.

"It looks like some specific action is needed again," said Ms. Rose. "This situation cannot continue."

Questions

1. Assume that you are Superintendent Rose in this case. What specific recommendations would you offer at this time?
2. What are your assessments of the history of this case as you can best determine from the given information?
3. In view of the basic concepts of staff induction, staff assignment, and staff development, what specific steps or programs apply in this case?

10.4 A Matter of Load

"Hi, Greg, come on in," said Principal Owen, "Care for coffee?"

"Thanks," replied Greg, "What's on the agenda?"

"I want to explore the need for adding a class for beginners in band," replied Mrs. Owen. "Our one beginners' class is doing well, and the band and orchestra classes are exemplary in my opinion. The band's performance at last Friday's game made me proud to be at Union High School. However,

I'm receiving numerous requests for band instruction from both students and parents."

"What are your thoughts, specifically?" asked Greg. "As you know, my teaching load is excessive already."

Principal Owen picked up a copy of the semester's teaching schedule and commented, "Well, as you know, Greg, our typical class load is five classes per day and presently you are teaching three."

"I know," responded Greg, "but band isn't typical. Our external commitments for public performances outweigh any consideration of one or two more instructional classes. In the last month I've had to prepare the band for three Friday night performances, we've performed for two civic clubs and marched in the Chamber parade, and the orchestra has performed for the state PTA conference and our recent school assembly. Right now, I have four performance requests on my desk that need responses."

"External commitments are important to us," replied Principal Owen. "Give the additional class some further thought, and we'll visit again later. Thanks for coming in."

Questions

1. What thoughts do you have concerning Greg's workload situation? What other information or data does Principal Owen need to resolve this matter?
2. What does the case infer in general relative to problems and issues of teacher load in education?

REFERENCES

Alderfer, C. P. (1972). *Existence, relatedness, and growth: Human needs in organizational settings.* New York: Free Press.

Arizona Republic. (February 25, 2001). Workplace Browser, p. D2 (based on information compiled by Gannett News Service and tips from Peter Lowe as reported in *Success* magazine).

Barnard, C. I. (1938). *The functions of the executive.* Cambridge, MA: Harvard University Press.

Bloss, J. M. (1882). *Thirteenth report of the superintendent of public instruction of the state of Indiana to the governor.* Indianapolis: State of Indiana.

Brayfield, A. H., & Crockett, W. H. (1955). Employee attitudes and employee performance. *Psychological Bulletin, 55,* 416.

Bridges, E. M. (1990). Managing the incompetent teacher. *ERIC Clearing House on Educational Management.* Eugene, OR: Office of Educational Research and Improvement (ed.). Washington, DC.

Brown, M. (1992). Only the best. *American School Board Journal, 179*(3), 35–36.

Cavanaugh, M. E. (1984). In search of motivation. *Personnel Journal, 63*(3), 76–82.

Doolittle, T. M. (1996). Critical connections: Linking EAP with workplace health. *EAP Digest, 16*(5), 22–24.

Douglass, H. R. (1928). Measuring teacher load in the high school. *Nation's Schools, 2*(4), 22–24.

Douglass, H. R. (1951). The 1950 revision of the Douglass high school teaching load formula. *NASSP Bulletin, 35,* 13–24.

Ebmeier, H. (November 2000). How supervision works in schools: An investigation of a path model through structural equation modeling. Paper presented at the annual convention of the University Council of Educational Administration, Albuquerque, NM.

Getzels, J. W., & Guba, E. G. (1957). Social behavior and the administrative process. *School Review, 65*(4), 423–441.

Herzberg, F., Mausner, B., & Snyderman, B. (1959). *The motivation to work* (2nd ed.). New York: Wiley.

Jung, C. W. (1949). The development of a proposed revision of the Douglass formula for measuring teacher load in the secondary school. Unpublished doctoral dissertation, University of Colorado, Boulder.

Knowles, M., and Associates (1984). *Andragogy in action.* San Francisco: Jossey-Bass.

Maslow, A. H. (1970). Motivation and personality. New York: HarperCollins (original work published 1954).

McGregor, D. (1960). *The human side of enterprise.* New York: McGraw-Hill.

Merriam, S. B., & Brockett, R. G. (1997). *The profession and practice of adult education: An introduction* (1st ed.) San Francisco: Jossey-Bass.

New Webster's Collegiate Dictionary, 10th ed. (1994). Springfield, MA: Merriam Webster.

National School Boards Association. (1996). The school personnel management system. Alexandria, VA: Author.

Norton, M. S. (1987). The status of employee assistance programs in education. Unpublished manuscript, Arizona State University, Tempe.

Norton, M. S. (1988). Employee assistance programs— A need in education. *Contemporary Education, 60,* 23–26.

Norton, M. S., & Bria, R. (1992). Toward an equitable measure of elementary school teacher load. *Record in Educational Administration and Supervision, 13*(1), 62–66.

Ouchi, W. (1981). *Theory Z: How American business can meet the Japanese challenge.* Reading, MA: Addison-Wesley.

Owen, P. E. (1984). Profile analysis: Matching positions and personnel. *Supervisory Management, 29*(11), 14–20.

Peterson, L. J., Rossmiller, R. A., & Volz, M. M. (1978). *The law and public school operation* (2nd ed.). New York: Harper & Row.

Raia, A. P. (1974). *Management by objectives.* Glenview, IL: Scott, Foresman.

Rumsey, M. J. (1992). Making EAP referrals work. *EAP Digest, 12*(5), 42–43.

Sirotnik, K. A., & Durden, P. C. (1996). The validity of administrative performance assessment systems: The ADI as a case-in-point. *Educational Administration Quarterly, 32,* 539–564.

Skinner, B. F. (1938). *The behavior of organisms.* New York: Appleton-Century-Crofts.

Skinner, B. F. (1953). *Science and human behavior.* New York: Free Press.

Skinner, B. F. (1969). *Contingencies of reinforcement: A theoretical analysis.* Upper Saddle River, NJ: Prentice Hall.

Smith, R. E. (1998). *Human resources administration: A school based perspective.* Larchmont, NY: Eye on Education.

Starcke, A. M. (1996). Building a better orientation program. *HR Magazine, 41*(1), 107–114.

Thompson, S. R. (1982). A survey and analysis of Pennsylvania public school personnel perceptions of staff development practices and beliefs with a view to identifying some critical problems or needs. Unpublished doctoral dissertation, Pennsylvania State University, State College.

U.S. Department of Health and Human Services. (1989). *Health United States.* Washington, DC: Government Printing Office.

Vroom, V. H. (1964). *Work and motivation.* New York: Wiley.

Wendel, F. C., & Uerling, D. F. (1989). Assessment centers—Contributing to preparation programs for principals. *NASSP Bulletin, 73,* 74–79.

11 *Performance Evaluation*

After reading this chapter, you will be able to:

■ Match the purposes of a school district evaluation system with the primary types of evaluation.

■ Discuss the three major elements of an employee evaluation system.

■ Identify the major approach to collecting evaluation data in education.

■ Describe the technical standards that must be met by a sound evaluation system.

■ List the substantive and procedural due process standards that must be followed in the development and operation of a school district evaluation system.

Performance evaluation is important to the internal operation and effectiveness of the school system and to the public's perception of the school system. In response to the school reform movement, two-thirds of the states have passed legislation strengthening their teacher evaluation systems. Almost all states now require the evaluation of teachers, and about half have required the formal evaluation of principals. At the same time, as will be discussed in Chapter 12, many states and school districts have begun to explore compensation strategies that link compensation to employee skills and performance, as well as to student performance. As performance expectations have increased and as efforts to link performance to compensation have increased, so too has the need for every school district to have in place a sound evaluation system. High-quality performance evaluation systems are an important part of the evidence that school systems can use to demonstrate to the public that quality control is being exercised in public education (Ribas, 2000).

A sound evaluation system can be characterized as one that has (1) established performance evaluation as a school district priority, (2) determined and disseminated clearly articulated evaluation purposes, and (3) adopted an evaluation plan that has a sound methodology, that is, "provides an orderly sequence of implementation stages, and follows a natural progression from intended purposes through actual use" (Stronge, 1991, p. 78). In this chapter each of these elements is examined, followed by a discussion of the standards involved in developing and operating a sound evaluation system.

EVALUATION AS A DISTRICT PRIORITY: DISTRICT EVALUATION POLICIES

The establishment of performance appraisal as a school district priority is critical if the evaluation system is to make a meaningful contribution to the improvement of the district and individual employees. If the evaluation system does not have the strong support of the school board and the administration, evaluation will be superficial at best (Stronge, 1991). One way that the school district can demonstrate its commitment to the evaluation system is through the policies that it adopts to govern and direct the evaluation system. A strong policy statement such as that given in Figure 11.1 demonstrates the board's philosophical position regarding evaluation, the importance of evaluation to the organization, and the board's commitment to the evaluation process. Additional policies that clearly articulate the purposes and procedures to be followed in the evaluation of all employees and that emphasize administrative responsibility and accountability for the effectiveness of the system further demonstrate the importance placed on evaluation.

The active participation of all employee groups, school board members, and school patrons in the development of the policies that will guide the

---

In the Paradise Valley Unified School District the parents, Governing Board members, and staff are committed to the continued growth of the district's strong educational program designed to meet the individual needs of the student. While recognizing the integrity of the teacher's individual instructional style, an effective teacher evaluation system which focuses on the improvement of instruction is essential to this commitment.

While the primary focus of evaluation is to improve instruction, an effective system requires teachers to meet established performance expectations. Therefore, the process for teacher evaluation must clearly state performance expectations (classroom and outside the classroom), must contain criteria for measuring effective teacher performance, and must have an instrument for assessing the competencies relating to the criteria.

It is also vital that the teacher evaluation system allow for and encourage productive dialogue, appropriate commendation, and when required, specific recommendations for improvement including reference to human and material resources. The system must provide for both written and oral communications within designated time lines. The process must be continuous and constructive, taking place in an atmosphere of cooperation, mutual trust, and respect among evaluator, evaluatee, and observer.

FIGURE 11.1
School District Statement of Philosophy for a Teacher Evaluation System
Source: Paradise Valley Unified School District. (1997). *Paradise Valley Unified School District No. 69 Teacher Evaluation System.* Paradise Valley, AZ: Author.

evaluation system is critical to its success. The district should take care to ensure that policies are written in easily understandable language with clearly defined standards. Finally, to ensure the continued integrity of the process, the systematic review and revision of evaluation practices and policies should be stipulated in the district policy.

DETERMINING THE PURPOSES OF THE EVALUATION SYSTEM

Determining the purposes of the district's evaluation system before it is implemented and continuing to communicate these purposes to affected individuals is paramount to defining evaluation. Evaluation systems that lack clearly articulated purpose(s) are essentially meaningless and contribute little to the accomplishment of the district's goals (Stronge, 1991). The stated and actual purposes of evaluation meet a variety of ends. Consider, for example, the following purposes articulated by the Tolleson Elementary School District (n.d.) for the evaluation of professional staff:

- ☐ Evaluation shall determine how well the objectives held by the school are being carried out. The success of the educational program is dependent upon the quality of classroom instruction, supervision, and administration.
- ☐ Evaluation shall provide the basis for motivation and for self-improvement. Personnel must be aware of their strengths and weaknesses in order to improve.
- ☐ Evaluation shall provide the basis for in-service training and supervisory activities. Such activities can be most effective when they are based upon clear evidence of need as shown by evaluation studies.
- ☐ Evaluation shall provide the basis for administrative decisions. Such decisions may include the employment of personnel, their assignment, the granting of continuing status, promotion, demotion, or termination. (p. 2)

According to the National School Boards Association (NSBA) (1987), the purposes of teacher performance evaluation are the following:

- ☐ To ensure that students are provided high quality instruction.
- ☐ To meet statutory and contractual requirements.
- ☐ To recognize outstanding teacher performance.
- ☐ To provide opportunities for teachers to develop their professional skills.
- ☐ To provide an avenue for two-way communication about school system and individual staff member goals, objectives, and other performance-related concerns.
- ☐ To document, in a fair manner, the objective information the board and administrators need when making decisions relative to assignments, transfers, granting of tenure, promotions, or destaffing.
- ☐ To provide evidence to the community that proper care is taken to hire, develop, and retain good teachers. (p. 121)

An examination of the policy documents of a number of school systems found that the most commonly mentioned purposes for the evaluation of principals were the following:

- ☐ To promote professional growth and improvement of principals.
- ☐ To provide information for administrative decisions.

☐   To clarify and communicate role expectation.
☐   To assess the extent to which expectations are being met.
☐   To provide evidence for special recognition.
☐   To identify areas for professional development.
☐   To improve student performance. (Thomas, Holdaway, Ward, 2000, p. 225)

Other purposes of administrator evaluation, according to Peterson (2000), are to (1) reassure the practitioners of his or her valuable and competent work, (2) reassure parents, the lay public, and other audiences that good work is taking place, (3) support the teacher evaluation system, (4) recognize and disseminate good administrative practice, and (5) provide opportunities for self-improvement.

From whatever sources, the multitude of reasons for evaluating personnel relate to three broad personnel purposes: (1) staff development, (2) rewarding performance, and (3) retention, tenure, or termination. The first of these purposes is accomplished by formative evaluation and the later two by summative evaluation.

Summative evaluation is conducted at the end of an activity or period of time and is designed to assess terminal behaviors or overall performance. Summative evaluation is used to make personnel decisions regarding such matters as contract renewal, tenure, performance pay, assignment to levels of a career ladder, and termination. Summative evaluation is formal and somewhat infrequent and focuses only on the person being evaluated. The individual being evaluated is normally not as involved in the summative evaluation process as in the formative process and in many cases may only be informed of the results or decision (Sperry, Pounder, & Drew, 1992).

Unlike summative evaluation, which is a terminal activity, **formative evaluation** is an ongoing evaluation designed to provide continuous feedback to the person being evaluated for the purposes of self-improvement and professional development. Whereas summative evaluation is externally controlled and judgmental, formative evaluation is employee directed, individualized, and geared to support professional growth (Black, 2000). Unfortunately, in spite of the fact that summative and formative evaluations serve different purposes and very often involve different techniques and even personnel, too many school districts in the United States mistakenly attempt to combine the two functions, especially when conducting teacher evaluations.

ELEMENTS OF AN EFFECTIVE EVALUATION SYSTEM

Having decided the purposes of the evaluation, the school district must design an evaluation plan to achieve these purposes. The evaluation plan has three major elements, which, in effect, involve the answers to three questions: (1) What will be evaluated? (the criteria), (2) What level of performance is expected? (the standards), and (3) How will evidence be collected? (data collection).

Evaluation Criteria

The **evaluation criteria** are the job-related behaviors expected of the teacher, administrator, or other staff member (Valentine, 1992). The first place that must be looked to for guidance in determining what will be evaluated is state statutes. In the last decade, many states have enacted legislation dealing with the evaluation of public school employees. These statutes or state education department policies requiring the evaluation of school personnel vary widely as to their level of specificity. In a number of states, not only has teacher or administrator evaluation been required, but the criteria that are to be used to define effective teaching or administrative performance are also specified. A number of these states, as well as many local school districts, have adopted or adapted (1) the PRAXIS II and III from the Educational Testing Service, the teaching standards developed by the Council of Chief State School Officers' Interstate New Teachers Assessment Support Consortium (INTASC) for use in the evaluation of beginning teachers, and the Frameworks for Teaching developed by Danielson (1996) and (2) the National Board for Professional Teaching Standards for use in the evaluation of experienced teachers. Each of these provide tools for using the standards to assess teachers against various levels of performance (Odden, 2000).

Two legislative state-adopted criteria are presented in Figures 11.2 and 11.3. The criteria approved for use in evaluating teaching in Arizona are presented in Figure 11.2, and the Oklahoma criteria for evaluating effective administrator performance are presented in Figure 11.3.

In addition to compliance with state statutes, local school district evaluation plans must comply with any agreements that may exist with the teachers' and administrators' bargaining representatives (Rossow & Parkinson, 1992). Although these agreements will not normally address criteria, they typically will address the evaluation procedures and the appeal process.

Whether derived from state statute on negotiated agreement or developed by the local school district, four types of criteria may be included in the district's evaluation plan. The first type, *attribute criteria*, assumes that there are definable traits or attributes that are necessary for good performance. That is, trait criteria describe what the employee is, rather than what the employee does. Although most school districts do not rely heavily on trait criteria today, some trait criteria, such as dependability and personal appearance, are still found in many evaluation systems (Ginsberg & Berry, 1990).

A second type of criteria is concerned with *outcomes*. The rationale for this approach is that teachers and administrators should achieve certain objectives and that their performance can be meaningfully assessed by examining the extent to which these objectives have been accomplished; what teachers and administrators do does not matter if they do not get the desired results. Outcomes criteria include such things as student performance, lower dropout rates, and school climate.

A third type of criteria, *process criteria*, are typical to administrator evaluation. Processes refer to administrative activities, such as planning,

Uses Knowledge of Subject Matter
1. Demonstrates knowledge in subject area.
2. Demonstrates knowledge of curriculum development to include scope and sequence.

Displays Interpersonal Skills
1. Communicates effectively with students.
2. Promotes positive self-concepts in learners.
3. Maintains a positive and stimulating learning environment.
4. Communicates enthusiasm for learning.
5. Uses correct written and oral expression.

Plans for Instruction
1. Defines objectives and subobjectives in terms of the content to be learned and the intended behavior of the learners.
2. Assesses students' skill levels to determine the appropriate learning objectives.
3. Plans instruction to achieve selected objectives.
4. Chooses relevant academic activities to ensure appropriate student time on task.
5. Sequences learning activities to achieve specific goals and objectives.
6. Plans instruction at varying and appropriate levels of cognitive thinking.
7. Organizes instruction to meet individual differences and specific needs.
8. Organizes resources such as time, space, materials, and equipment to facilitate the achievement of goals and objectives.
9. Specifies procedures for monitoring and assessing student progress.

Provides Instruction
1. Provides instruction at students' skill levels.
2. Teaches to the learning objectives as specified in the lesson plan.
3. Teaches necessary objectives in a logical sequence.
4. Provides instruction at a variety of levels of thinking.
5. Uses strategies to maximize the amount of time students are engaged in relevant tasks.
6. Uses a variety of instructional techniques and methods related to the objectives.
7. Uses techniques to involve most of the learning time.

FIGURE 11.2
Criteria to Use in Evaluating Teaching Skills, Arizona Department of Education
Source: Arizona Department of Education, Phoenix, AZ.

budgeting, organizing, and staffing. These processes were referred to in the early part of this century as "what administrators do," and they continue to be considered in the evaluation of administrators in most school districts (MacPhail-Wilcox & Forbes, 1990).

The fourth type of criteria, and by far the most commonly used in the evaluation of teachers and administrators, is *performance-based criteria*. They "describe what effective teachers or administrators do in the course of their professional practice, the tasks that fill their days (and frequently their evenings)" (Danielson & McGreal, 2000, p. 33). Some of the criteria related to teaching will apply to all teachers in the system, whereas others will apply to teachers at certain grade levels or with certain teaching assignments. Distinc-

8. Models correct performance for students.
9. Gives clear directions and explanations related to lesson(s).
10. Assesses student learning throughout the learning process.
11. Obtains responses for each objective to check student mastery before proceeding.
12. Adjusts instruction so that students attain mastery of the objectives.
13. Provides appropriate instruction and services to exceptional students.
14. Adjusts instruction to meet individual differences and specific needs.
15. Evaluates students according to consistent objective criteria.

Uses Learning Principles in Providing Instruction
1. Communicates to students the purpose and value of learning objectives.
2. Provides sufficient teacher directed and independent practice with monitoring to ensure that students are accurate and successful.
3. Communicates the importance of the learning by holding all students accountable for learning.
4. Provides specific and appropriate feedback in a variety of ways during instruction.
5. Uses motivation techniques to enhance student learning.
6. Provides an appropriate focus for students at the beginning of learning objectives.
7. Utilizes a variety of ways to summarize learnings.

Uses Classroom Management Strategies
1. Uses effective classroom management techniques.
2. Communicates expectations for appropriate classroom behavior.
3. Demonstrates ability to work with individuals, small groups or large groups as determined by instructional objectives.
4. Manages inappropriate classroom behavior.

Displays Professionalism
1. Engages in professional development.
2. Seeks and shares professional ideas.
3. Acts in accordance with defined teacher responsibilities, both legal and professional.
4. Identifies exceptional students and refers them to appropriate specialists.
5. Uses effective strategies for parent-teacher communication, including conferences.

FIGURE 11.2
(continued)

tions are also often made between criteria that are applied to experienced teachers and criteria that are applied to inexperienced or nontenured teachers.

The use of any one of these four types of criteria is not necessarily mutually exclusive. Many districts have an evaluation system that combines more than one type (Ginsberg & Berry, 1990). What is important is that the criteria be based on recent research about teaching, learning, and leadership. This is important to ensuring the validity of the criteria. It is also important that the criteria include all the important domains of the job and not be limited to, for example, just what the teacher does in the classroom or how the superintendent interacts with the school board (Danielson & McGreal, 2000). Finally, whatever criteria are adopted must be objective, clear, unambiguous, and communicated in advance to the individuals being evaluated.

I. **Practice**
   A. **Administrator Management Indicators**
      1. Preparation: The administrator and staff develop goal statements which are the result of a needs assessment, a written analysis of student test scores and other data as well as community input.
      2. Routine: The administrator uses a minimum of instructional time for noninstructional routines thus maximizing time on task.
      3. Discipline: The administrator works with staff to develop and communicate defined standards of conduct which encourage positive and productive behavior.
      4. Learning Environment: The administrator establishes and maintains rapport with staff and students, providing a pleasant, safe and orderly climate for learning.
   B. **Instructional Leadership Indicators**
      1. The administrator works with staff in collegial and nonthreatening ways to promote and improve instruction.
      2. The administrator sets high expectations for staff.
      3. The administrator provides needed resources for staff.
      4. The administrator works with staff to establish curriculum objectives, sequence and lesson objectives.
      5. The administrator works with staff to assure that all learners are involved in the learning process.
      6. The administrator assists the staff in monitoring student progress.
      7. The administrator works with the staff to develop a program to recognize academic achievement.
      8. The administrator educates the staff to recognize and display the teaching criteria upon which evaluation is conducted.
      9. The administrator observes in the classroom the performance criteria as defined by the district.
      10. The administrator summatively evaluates staff only after classroom observations are made, performance feedback is given, growth goals are set and alternative methods are offered.

II. **Products**
   Administrator Product Indicators
      1. The administrator provides written discipline policies to which students are expected to perform.
      2. The administrator provides a written school building improvement plan that supports the district's four-year school improvement plan describing school goals, objectives and professional development activities.
      3. The administrator provides a written analysis of student test scores and other data to assure that the various student populations are benefiting from the instructional program.

FIGURE 11.3

Oklahoma Criteria for Effective Administrative Performance

Source: Oklahoma State Department of Education. (1999). *Oklahoma Criteria for Effective Teaching and Administrative Performance.* Oklahoma City: Author.

Standards

Whereas the criteria define the dimensions of performance to be evaluated, **standards for evaluation** are the indicators of performance required with respect to the criteria (Stiggens & Duke, 1988). One or more standards may be related to a specific criterion. For example, the INTASC identified 10 principles or criteria with 53 accompanying performance indicators or standards. The ultimate success of the evaluation system in assessing an employee's performance relative to a particular criterion lies not in how many standards are associated with it, but in how clear and objective the standards are and how effectively they have been communicated to the employee. Vague, subjective standards will only result later in disagreements in interpretations (NSBA, 1996).

For each standard, a rubric may be created to distinguish between levels of performance ranging from unsatisfactory to outstanding. Or they may be stated so as to require a more definitive judgment, for example, "exceeds job requirements" or "target for growth." Figure 11.4 provides an

Performance Dimension 6: Appropriateness of the lesson and pacing			
Unsatisfactory	**Needs Improvement**	**Competent**	**Accomplished**
The pacing is usually too slow, too rushed, or both, with inappropriate use of instructional time. Students waste time by avoiding work. Most activities do not reflect developmentally appropriate practices.	The pacing is inconsistent. Opportunities for student engagement are limited with inconsistently appropriate use of instructional time. Frequent off-task behaviors observed. Activities are not always developmentally appropriate.	The pacing consistently offers opportunities for active student engagement with appropriate use of instructional time. Activities always reflect developmentally appropriate practices.	All students are actively engaged in a variety of meaningful ways, with maximum use of instructional time. Activities reflect developmentally appropriate practices that challenge but do not overwhelm students. Activities consistently build on prior knowledge of students.

FIGURE 11.4

Sample Performance Standard and Rubric

Source: B.B. Howard & W.H. McColskey. (2001). Evaluating experienced teachers. *Educational Leadership*, *58*(5), 48–51. Reprinted with permission from ASCD. All rights reserved.

example of standards differentiated for four levels of performance associated with 1 (the appropriateness of a lesson and how the teacher has paced it) of the 22 performance dimensions associated with the evaluation process for experienced teachers in North Carolina.

Data Sources and Collection Procedures

Multiple sources of data should be used when making the value judgments required for the evaluation of education personnel. The use of multiple data sources is important, because no one source can address all the many and varied responsibilities of either teachers or administrators. Nor is any single data source appropriate for all employees, all purposes, or all settings (Peterson, 2000). Using multiple data sources not only gives a more complete picture of teacher or administrator practice, but it also allows districts to individualize the evaluation process. In fact, a number of districts have moved to allow teachers choice in the data to present for evaluation. For example, in Utah's Davis School District, teachers can choose among a number of data sources, including parent and student survey, student achievement data (e.g., grade-level tests, standardized tests, advanced placement exams, pre- and post-teacher-made tests), documentation of professional activity, and tests of teachers (e.g., the Graduate Record Exam or the PRAXIS series). The only requirement is the following:

> Teachers must present a certain number of data sources at each stage of their evaluation career. For example, beginning teachers must submit a minimum of four data sources per year, whereas veterans use only one to three data sources. (Peterson, Wahlquist, Bone, Thompson, & Chatterton, 2001, p. 41)

Other newly developed evaluation systems are not only using multiple sources, but are also using differential procedures, criteria, and time lines for different groups of teachers. Novice teachers receive more intensive evaluations than experienced teachers. Novice teachers also receive a formal evaluation every year, whereas a formal, summative evaluation of experienced, tenured teachers is conducted only every 2 to 4 years. In some districts that use the multiyear cycle, whether a teacher is formally evaluated in 1 to 4 years depends on their performance on the last formal evaluation (Danielson, 2001).

The data used in the evaluation process will vary not only by source, but also by the way that they are collected. For example, not only will the type of data generated from a classroom observation differ from that obtained from a survey of parents, but the classroom observation data may also vary as a result of the degree of formality of the observation, the frequency of the observation, the duration of the observation, and whether it is announced or unannounced. Ultimately, whatever process is used to collect data, it is imperative that the procedures be well defined and adhere to any state laws, employment contracts, and school board policies. It is also imperative that all evaluators receive the training necessary to competently perform the evaluation and that they adhere to all applicable laws, contracts, and policies.

A survey of evaluation practices of the nation's 100 largest school districts found that the most common teacher evaluation methods (and the percent of districts using them) were direct systematic observation of teaching (94%), informal observation of teaching (87%), teacher self-evaluation (46%), student achievement data (25%), teacher portfolio assessment (23%), peer evaluation (16%), and student ratings of teacher performance (9%) (Loup, Garland, Ellett, & Rugett, 1996). Many of these methods are also employed in the evaluation of administrators. Also common to administrator evaluation (but less common to teacher evaluation) are rating scales. A somewhat new approach, 360-degree feedback or full-circle evaluation, can be used in both the evaluation of teachers and administrators. Each of these evaluation methods is described in the following sections, along with some of the major considerations surrounding their use.

Observation. Observation is the most commonly employed methodology in the evaluation of teachers. The observation may focus on a narrow range of behaviors, or it may attempt to encompass all that is being observed. The duration of the observation may be for an entire lesson or period or for a few minutes. Observations may be spaced throughout the course of the year; in other situations it may be more desirable to conduct the observations several days in a row (Stiggens & Duke, 1988).

Observations may be classified as formal, scheduled, and structured observations or informal, unscheduled observations. According to Murphy (1987), a well-conducted formal evaluation will include the following stages:

1. a preconference in which the substantive focus and procedural conditions for the evaluation are established;
2. an observation during which the supervisor objectively describes and records activities that are occurring in the classroom;
3. a period of analysis and interpretation of the data collected during the observation;
4. a postconference during which the supervisor and the teacher review the analysis of the lesson together for the purpose of planning further efforts at instructional improvement; and
5. a postconference analysis in which the supervisor and teacher analyze the usefulness of the first four phases of the observation cycle. (p. 168)

Critical to the success of the evaluation is that the person being observed be made aware of the requirements and purpose(s) of the observation and that good communication be maintained throughout the process. It is also important that the evaluation be conducted as unobtrusively as possible and that the time and length of the observation be appropriate to ensure that the behavior observed is a representative sample. The actual classroom observation will typically be 30 to 45 minutes in length and should be audiotaped by the observer. "For most classrooms, four to six observations will provide sufficient coverage of variety in instruction. A few classes having greater variety may require an additional one to two visits. The observation should be scattered over a 30-to-60 day period" (Peterson,

2000, p. 198). Following the observation the data must be analyzed using a conceptual framework that links teacher behavior to student learning. Finally, those conducting the observations must be trained in observation skills, as well as in the purpose and methodology of the particular observation system being used, and the observation instruments themselves must be reliable and valid (Peterson, 2000).

Informal observations can often yield more important data than formal observations and are most useful for seeing specific activities (e. g., the beginning of a class, transition times, student demonstrations) or other special events (Danielson & McGreal, 2000). However, even when observations are considered informal, they should be followed by brief, written feedback on what happened during the visit. A dozen or more informal observations per class per year may be necessary to provide a complete picture of the teaching and learning that is taking place in the classroom. The time involved is worth the results. In combination with other sources of data, informal observations allow administrators or supervisors to make judgments about teacher performance with a good deal of confidence (Murphy, 1987).

Self-evaluation.   Almost all teachers and administrators engage in some form of informal self-evaluation to assess their performance. In recent years, not only have educators been encouraged to become "reflective practitioners" (Schon, 1983), but self-evaluation has also become an increasingly important component of personnel evaluation systems. The foci of the self-evaluation typically are goals, students, subject-matter content, assessment and evaluation of teaching, and teaching processes, including the affective, cognitive, and classroom management aspects (Kremer-Hayon, 1993). And, although teachers or administrators typically ask themselves what methods or strategies worked well or did not work well and why or how they might improve their own performance or that of others, for purposes of self-evaluation in a formal evaluation system, these reflections "will have maximum value when they are undertaken not just as gasps at the end of a working day, but consciously, definitely, and regularly, in a planned approach" (Withers, 1995, p. 269).

Self-evaluation can be used as part of both formative and summative evaluation (Haertel, 1993). However, because novice teachers are less skilled than experienced teachers in assessing their own practice accurately, when used, self-evaluation and self-directed growth should be provided for experienced teachers and guided self-evaluation for novice teachers (Danielson & McGreal, 2000). Self-evaluation can be accomplished by a variety of methods. Clients and colleagues may be surveyed or interviewed by the employee, or self-rating forms similar to the one in Figure 11.5 may be used. Self-evaluation may also be accomplished through the use of quantitative tools such as category systems, rating scales, and checklists (Kremer-Hayon, 1993). One popular technique for self-evaluation is videotaping a live performance, be it classroom teaching, the conducting of a faculty meeting, or conducting a parent–teacher or administrator–teacher conference. Videotaping allows those evaluated to

Name _____ School Year _____ Date _____

Directions: Your job description (performance responsibilities) is shown below. Please review each item and place a check in the appropriate column. "Area of Strength" means you believe your performance in that area is one of your strong points. "Satisfactory" means you are satisfied with your performance. If you are not satisfied with your performance, check "Target for Growth." You may also check "Target for Growth" for performance responsibilities where you also feel you are performing at a satisfactory level. Remember, this is a **SELF ASSESSMENT** and must reflect *your* judgment. We recommend you select or target at least 3 to 5 areas to become the basis for the goals you prepare for the Fall Conference with your evaluator.

Descriptor Applicable	In the left hand column check each of the descriptors which is applicable to your job responsibilities. **PERFORMANCE RESPONSIBILITY**	Area of Strength	Satisfactory	Target for Growth
	I. *Planning for Classroom Activities:* The teacher A. Consistently plans lessons and activities which incorporate the district's scope and sequence (or other approved curriculum).			
	B. Develops a plan and method for evaluating the students' work.			
	II. *Implementation of the Lesson (the teaching act):* The teacher A. Clearly communicates the objectives of the lesson (in large or small groups or, individually, or both).			
	B. Shares with the students the importance of what they are learning (in advance or by discovery, depending on the intent of the lesson).			
	C. Describes for the student how (methods, activities, etc.) the lesson is going to be taught.			
	D. Provides for discovery or acquisition of the information of the lesson.			
	E. Provides for appropriate activities and practice.			
	F. Monitors student progress.			
	G. Provides for summary of key points of the lesson.			
	H. Demonstrates command of the subject matter.			
	I. Uses effective questioning techniques.			
	J. Recognizes different learning styles and employs materials and techniques accordingly.			
	K. Makes reference to and use of other disciplines in order to expand and enrich the learning process.			

FIGURE 11.5 (continued)

Self-Evaluation Form for Teachers

Source: Paradise Valley Unified School District. (1997). *Paradise Valley Unified School District No. 69 Teacher Evaluation System.* Paradise Valley, AZ: Author.

L. Provides for enrichment of the curriculum through the use of a variety of appropriate materials and media.			

M. Other mutually identified responsibilities.
   1.
   2.
   3.			

III. Classroom and Instructional Management Responsibilities: The teacher A. Uses effective classroom and instructional management techniques.			
B. Establishes effective student-teacher and student-student relationships.			
C. Arranges the physical environment to complement the learning atmosphere.			
D. Recognizes the value of time-on-task and demonstrates overall good use of the instructional period.			
IV. Other Duties and Responsibilities: The teacher A. Maintains accurate student records.			
B. Maintains effective communication with parents.			
C. Upholds and enforces school rules, administrative regulations, and Governing Board policies.			
D. Participates in school related activities.			
E. Maintains a professional attitude in relations with other persons and programs.			
F. Keeps up-to-date in areas of specialization.			
G. Supports the goals and objectives of the district and school.			
H. Provides individual counseling and guidance to students.			

I. Other mutually identified responsibilities.
   1.
   2.
   3.			

FIGURE 11.5
(continued)

see themselves as others see them and reduces the subjectivity that is normally involved in evaluating one's own performance. Typically, a paper-and-pencil rating or observation form is completed while watching the videotape. It is also common practice for the individual evaluated to view the videotape with a supervisor, colleague, or evaluator (Haertel, 1993).

Whatever format is used, if a self-evaluation has been requested and subsequently conducted by the employee, it must be considered in the employee's overall evaluation. It cannot be ignored by the supervisor because it is perceived as being too self-serving. To ensure that self-evaluations are of maximum value and continue to improve, the supervisor should discuss the self-evaluation with the employee without placing value judgments on it, but rather focus on the basis for the employee's judgments. In areas in which there appears to be a significant difference in the employee's perception of his or her performance and the evaluator's perception, the data that led to each conclusion should be discussed in a nonconfrontational manner. In the end, the validity and reliability of self-evaluations depend on the capacity of teachers or administrators to consistently and accurately judge their own performance (Haertel, 1993).

Student Performance Data. In the 1990s a number of states and school districts instituted teacher evaluation systems based on articulated standards for teacher and administrator performance. At the same time, states were also adopting various measures focusing on improving achievement and mandating standards-based student assessment. Using achievement data as an indicator of teacher or principal effectiveness makes a great deal of sense to many people, particularly noneducators (Peterson, 2000). The logic seems simple: if teachers and administrators have a professional responsibility to enhance learning, then it is reasonable to examine their impact on learning (Stronge & Tucker, 2000). Despite the apparent logic, there are a number of concerns about the use of standardized achievement data, especially in the evaluation of teachers. The major concerns about their use include (1) achievement tests do not exist for all areas of the curriculum, (2) it is virtually impossible to determine the effect of a particular teacher on a student's test score, (3) achievement prior to the time of the teacher being evaluated accounts for 60% of the variance test scores (Peterson, 2000), (4) valid standardized assessment instruments do not effectively measure what is taught in all classes, (5) so much of what affects learning is beyond the control of the teacher, and (6) variations among students and classes taught do not allow objective comparisons among teachers.

How then can student performance data be used in the evaluation of teachers? The best answer seems to be to use classroom-based measurements of student achievement that are aligned with the curriculum. Teachers continuously measure student achievement in their classrooms. Teacher-developed classroom assessments, pre- and post-tests, and tests designed to measure the specific objectives of instruction are legitimate indicators of student performance.

In a report for the National Education Association, Stronge and Tucker (2000) examined evaluation systems in several school systems that rely on student learning as a measure of teacher effectiveness. Their examination led them to make the following recommendations for districts contemplating linking student achievement and performance:

1. Use student learning as only one component of a teacher evaluation system that is based on multiple data sources.
2. When judging teacher effectiveness, consider the context in which teaching and learning occur (e.g., class size, availability of resources and support, student characteristics, etc.).
3. Uses measures of student growth versus a fixed achievement standard or goal.
4. Compare learning gains from one point in time to another for the same students, not different groups of students.
5. Recognize that even gain scores have pitfalls that must be avoided: "In particular, a statistical artifact known as the regression effect needs to be considered. It results in a tendency for students starting with low performance levels to show larger gains than warranted. Conversely, students who start with high performance may show lower gains, or even declines, if the measure of student achievement is not adequately difficult to gauge what those high-scoring students know." (p. 56)
6. Use a time frame for teacher evaluation that allows for patterns of student learning to be documented. "Repeated measures of student learning over time enhance reliability from a statistical point of view and credibility from a decision-making perspective" (p. 56).
7. Use fair and valid measures of student learning.
8. Select student assessment measures that are most closely aligned with existing curriculum.
9. Do not narrow the curriculum and limit teaching to fit a test. (Stronge & Tucker, 2000, pp. 53–58)

Portfolios. It is not uncommon in professions other than education for members of the profession to present their credentials for assessment by other members of the profession and the public by means of a **portfolio.** For example, an artist's, architect's, or designer's portfolio is a collection of samples of the individual's best work, intended to demonstrate professional knowledge and skill (Collins, 1991). Portfolio assessment in education has been used for many years in student assessment. Only in recent years has it gained favor as an authentic approach to staff assessment. Portfolios are now used as a central component of the certification process by the National Board for Professional Teaching Standards. And, at the local level, hundreds of school districts across the country now use portfolios as a component in their teacher or administrator assessment programs.

Basically, a portfolio is a collection of information about a teacher or administrator's practice. However, it is more than an elaborate scrapbook or a collection of documents: it is a portrait of the teacher or administrator as a "professional, reflecting on his or her philosophy and practice. This portrait is fully realized through the teacher's (or administrator's) deliberate selection of artifacts and thoughtful reflections on those artifacts which provide insight into the teacher's (or administrator's) growth over time" (Painter, 2001, p. 317).

The specific structure and content of the portfolio can vary depending on how it will be used. If it is being used as part of the evaluation process, the teachers and administrators being evaluated must know the standards by which they are being assessed. And being selective about the items to be included in the portfolio does not mean constructing a biased picture, but providing a fair and generous representation. Examples of earlier work, or even the occasional flop, are worthy material for a portfolio, especially if the portfolio reveals a process of growth over time (Zubizarreta, 1994; Painter, 2001).

For the portfolio to remain manageable for both the person who constructs it and those who review it, the number of artifacts included should be kept to around a dozen. The inclusion of each entry should be supported with a written rationale that describes the artifact, justifies its inclusion in relationship to the standards, and explains what the evaluatée has learned about himself or herself and professional practice (Painter, 2001). This rationale, more than the artifact itself, tells the reviewer about the teacher's or administrator's growth (Painter, 2001). Examples of artifacts for inclusion in teacher and administrator portfolios are presented in Figure 11.6.

Performance Dimension 6: Appropriateness of the lesson and pacing			
Unsatisfactory	**Needs Improvement**	**Competent**	**Accomplished**
The pacing is usually too slow, too rushed, or both, with inappropriate use of instructional time. Students waste time by avoiding work. Most activities do not reflect developmentally appropriate practices.	The pacing is inconsistent. Opportunities for student engagement are limited with inconsistently appropriate use of instructional time. Frequent off-task behaviors observed. Activities are not always developmentally appropriate.	The pacing consistently offers opportunities for active student engagement with appropriate use of instructional time. Activities always reflect developmentally appropriate practices.	All students are actively engaged in a variety of meaningful ways, with maximum use of instructional time. Activities reflect developmentally appropriate practices that challenge but do not overwhelm students. Activities consistently build on prior knowledge of students.

FIGURE 11.6
Sample Artifacts for Teacher and Administrator Portfolio
Sources: For teacher portfolio: B. Painter. (2001). Using teaching portfolios. *Educational Leadership*, *58*(5), 31–34. Reprinted with permission from ASCD. All rights reserved. For administrator portfolio: G. Brown & B.J. Irby. (2001). *The Principal Portfolio* (2nd ed.), © 2001 by Corwin Press, Inc. Thousand Oaks, CA: Corwin Press. Reprinted by permission.

A portfolio is best presented in a zippered, three-ring binder. A more technologically sophisticated presentation is the *electronic portfolio*, which presents some or all of the portfolio on a computer disk, CD-ROM, or laser disk. Using the electronic portfolio, the evaluatee can not only scan in all written materials, but can also present visual evidence of performance, voice his or her philosophy, creatively display materials, or incorporate creative activities that best represent student achievements. The electronic portfolio also presents ease of storage and distribution and can be easily edited and updated (Riggsby, Jewell, & Justice, 1995).

Because each portfolio is unique, the evaluation of portfolios does not lend itself to the use of checklists or analytic scoring schemes. In most cases, what is involved is the exercise of professional judgment in assessing the extent to which the portfolio documents the teacher or administrator meeting preestablished criteria. This, in turn, requires "an established set of valid and reliable scoring rubrics and extensive training for the evaluators in order to assure fairness and reliability" (Danielson & McGreal, 2000, p. 94). Guidelines for reviewing artifacts included in a teaching portfolio are presented in Figure 11.7.

Peer Review.   Peer review is the process by which a formal evaluation of an employee's performance is conducted by one or more peers, usually referred to as consulting teachers; then a recommendation is made to the principal or other administrator or school board as to whether the teacher should be retained or terminated. The term *peer* means that both the person being reviewed and the reviewer have similar assignments, training, knowledge, and expertise, but are not from the same school or work site and are not socially or politically connected (Peterson, 2000). The peer review may be conducted by visitation to the classroom or workplace, by viewing a videotaped lesson, or by an examination of documentary evidence (e.g., portfolios). Peer review provides a method of including expert judgment in the evaluation process. Administrators are the ones usually charged with conducting evaluations. Yet administrators cannot be experts in all areas. Who then is more singularly qualified to judge the subject matter or the situation than one's peers? Peer review is being encouraged by both the NEA and the AFT as part of their push to give teachers a larger role in policing their own profession and in the decisions designed to improve teacher quality (Black, 2000).

Most peer review programs do not exist without an accompanying peer assistance program through which the consulting teacher serves as a mentor to help the teacher being reviewed to improve his or her knowledge and skills. In fact, the NEA–AFT proposal states that peer review is not to be implemented without a peer assistance component.

Despite their apparent success, a number of concerns have been expressed about peer review. One major concern is that in many districts that use peer review, teachers are seldom evaluated. As a result, it has had very little impact on improving the overall quality of teaching in these districts (Lieberman, 1998). Perhaps the most significant concern about the use of

Artifacts are defined as simple objects, usually a tool or ornament, showing human workmanship or modification as distinguished from a natural object. The artifacts of teaching include any instructional materials or directions employed by teachers to facilitate student learning. Types may vary from commercially prepared textbooks and learning aids, such as maps, software packages, and science kits; to teacher-improvised demonstrations, tests, and worksheets; to the use of educational technology hardware and software.

In considering educational quality, artifacts must be learner oriented and designed to meet a specific outcome or standard. Artifacts are most helpful if they are designed with built-in flexibility permitting updating or adaptation to specific ability levels and uses.

CONTENT

Quality of artifacts can be considered from the point of view of content or essential meaning. Artifacts should be valid, relevant, and current. Some considerations related to quality of content are:

1. *Information:* Is the artifact materially accurate and authoritative?
2. *Areas of Controversy:* If relevant, are alternatives clearly acknowledged?
3. *Appropriateness:* Is the content appropriate for the intended audience? Is it appropriate in detail to the level of the learner and program or lesson objectives?
4. *Relevance and Validity:* Is the content relevant to the purpose of the lesson?
5. *Motivation:* Does the artifact content stimulate interest to learn more about the subject? Does it encourage ideas for using the material?
6. *Application:* Does the artifact serve as a model for applying learning outside the classroom?

7. *Clarity:* Is the content free of regional idioms, jargon, or specialized expressions that would limit its understandability?
8. *Conciseness:* Is the artifact free of superfluous material? Does it stick to the point?

DESIGN AND CONTEXT

Design of artifacts should include characteristics that are conducive to learning. Design should proceed from an analysis of the content of the lesson or local standards or benchmarks. Appropriate artifacts are those that are linked to local standards or benchmarks. The quality of an artifact is the product of its design characteristics, its relevance to identified outcomes, and its application to content.

Objectives for Artifact Design

1. *Meaningfulness:* Does the artifact clearly support the learning outcomes? If so, is this apparent to the learners?
2. *Appropriateness:* Are the artifacts appropriate to the needs of the skill levels of the intended learners? Are time constraints considered in the artifact's design?

Design Characteristics

1. *Sequencing:* Is the artifact itself sequenced logically? Is it employed at the appropriate point in the presentation?
2. *Instructional Strategies:* Is the artifact format appropriate to the students and the teaching approach? Does the artifact's construction incorporate sound learning principles?
3. *Engagement:* Does the artifact actively engage the learner? Does it reinforce the content with appropriate practice and feedback opportunities?

(continued)

FIGURE 11.7

Guidelines for Reviewing the Artifacts of Teaching–Conducting a Document Analysis

Source: C. Danielson & T.L. McGreal. (2000). *Teacher evaluation to enhance professional practice.* Princeton, NJ: Educational Testing Service.

AESTHETIC CONSIDERATIONS

Aesthetic considerations include production and the qualities that enhance or detract from instructional effectiveness of the artifacts.

Quality of Communication

1. *Medium Selection:* Is the best medium used for meeting each specified outcome and presenting each item of content (e.g. motion pictures, videotape, textbook, teacher-prepared handout)?
2. *Economy of Time:* Is the learner's time wasted by such things as verbosity, unnecessary introduction and/or summary, or ad lib conversation without educational substance or purpose?
3. *Pace:* Is the pace appropriate to the intended audience, neither too fast nor too slow, throughout the presentation? Does the pace vary inversely with difficulty of content?

4. *Aids to Comprehension:* Are directions clearly explained? Are unfamiliar terms spelled out?

Technical Production

1. *Visual Quality:* Are subjects adequately illuminated? Do the visuals show all educationally significant details? Is composition uncluttered? Does it help the learner to recognize important content? Are essential details identified through the appropriate use of highlighting, color, tone, contrasts, position, motion, and other pointing devices? Is type size of the text legible at the anticipated maximum viewing distance?
2. *Narration:* Is the pace of the delivery appropriate for the intended audience? Can the audio component be clearly heard?
3. *Physical Quality:* Is the artifact durable, attractive, and simple? Are size and shape convenient for use?

FIGURE 11.7
(continued)

peer review is that research has shown serious problems with the validity and reliability of peer reviews, especially those involving classroom visitations. Peer review is also fairly expensive to conduct relative to other forms of evaluations. The peers conducting the classroom observations must either be released from their duties and substitutes hired to replace them or they must have their full-time contract reflect a part-time assignment as a reviewer and a part-time assignment as a teacher, department head, or whatever. In either case, the cost of the peer evaluation system can be significant. Other problems associated with peer review stem from the very collegial culture of education that pressures individuals to get along with each other, which works against judgments that might be viewed as negative or critical (McCarthy & Peterson, 1988).

In the peer review process, peer review of materials is seen as having distinct advantages over either peer visits to classrooms or peer surveys of general impressions, primarily because research has shown peer review of materials to have a high interrater reliability and, when conducted by three or more reviewers, to be basically free of bias. Peer review of materials is also logistically easier and less expensive to operate than most other types of peer evaluation. Peer reviewers do not need to leave their classrooms to participate, thereby obviating the need for substitutes or short- or long-term assignments as a reviewer (Peterson, 2000). Among the materials that might be submitted for review are curriculum outlines, sample instructional materials, video- and audiotapes, tests, student achievement data, examples of student work, grade records, lesson plans, handouts and worksheets, classroom rules and discipline procedures, and correspondence with parents.

Peer review and assistance programs have been operating in a few schools districts since the early 1980s (Danielson & McGreal, 2000). Supporters of peer review claim that "more teachers have received help and more incompetent teachers have been dismissed under peer review than under traditional methods of evaluation," citing such data as that from Columbus, Ohio, where 20% of the tenured teachers who go through intervention leave the school system and 80% of the new teachers are still on the job 5 years later, compared to only 50% in other urban districts (Hertling, 1999, p. 2). As a result of the passage of California's new Teacher Peer Review & Assistance Act, many more districts are now incorporating peer review into their teacher evaluation program.

Student and Parent Ratings. Student and parent evaluations are central to the concept of 360-degree evaluation discussed in a following section. And the popularity of this concept in the business world combined with the continued demand for greater accountability, has led the state of Alaska to request all school districts to include parental input in teacher evaluation, the state of Florida to require it, and a growing number of districts to voluntarily solicit parent or student feedback (Mathews, 2000). These states and districts believe that input from students and parents can provide valuable input to the evaluation of teachers and administrators. In fact, some would say evaluators have an "obligation to search out and invite criticism in order to become more successful," as well as an "obligation to establish and maintain a trusting relationship with their students and parents" (Brackbill, 1996, p. 50).

In developing parent (and student) surveys or in interviewing parents, care should be taken to ensure that questions are only asked about topics for which the parent can reasonably be expected to have answers. For example, parents would not have direct knowledge of whether teachers presented lessons in a manner that students could understand. However, they would know whether their children had the skills that they needed to do their homework assignments. And they would know whether they themselves can understand communications from their child's teacher and whether the teacher promptly returned their phone calls (Danielson & McGreal, 2000). Sample questions from a parent survey used in the evaluation of principals in Charlotte–Mecklenburg (North Carolina) are presented in Figure 11.8.

Unlike parents, students are in the position of observing the classroom performance of the teacher every school day. Students can be a major source of information about the accomplishment of educational goals,

I. School Discipline and School Climate
- School rules are enforced the same way for everyone at this school.
- My child is safe at this school.
- The school is neat, clean, and well maintained.
- School administrators take prompt action with discipline problems.
- This school promotes positive race relations among students.
- Violence is *not* a frequent problem at this school.

II. Communication and Parent Involvement
- The principal of this school is available to parents when needed.
- Parents are expected to participate in school activities at this school.
- Parents are warmly welcomed when they visit the school.
- Between report cards, I get adequate information about my child's progress.
- I feel free to express concerns or make suggestions to staff at this school.
- I receive enough communication to keep me informed of school activities.

III. Effective Instruction
- The class work at this school challenges my child.
- If my child needs extra help, he/she gets it at this school.
- Teachers at this school have high expectations for my child.
- My child's grades accurately reflect his/her learning.
- This school develops my child's thinking and problem-solving skills.
- My child's special interests and/or talents are developed at this school.

FIGURE 11.8
Sample Questions from Parent Survey
Source: Charlotte–Mecklenburg Schools. (1997). *Family Survey and School Assessment.*
Charlotte, NC: Author.

methods of instruction, various elements of the classroom (e. g., discipline, homework, textbooks), and relationships with the teacher (Peterson, Wahlquist, & Bone, 2000). Student evaluations have historically been criticized as being nothing more than popularity contests, grade dependent, and of little value because of the immaturity of students and their inexperience in both evaluation and distinguishing good teaching from good performing. However, the extensive body of research on student evaluation of instruction does not support any of these criticisms if the instruments and the process have been carefully developed and are valid and reliable (Aleamoni, 1999). Student assessment can provide valuable feedback to the teacher and often can be more effective in changing behavior than administrative evaluation (NSBA, 1996). Student evaluations also can direct teachers to areas in which students hold a perception different from that of the teacher. Moreover, the very process of soliciting evaluations shows students that their opinions are valued and may encourage them to become more active participants in the learning process (Herbert, 1995).

The research suggests that student evaluations can be used at all grade levels, although the level of sophistication of the judgments that they can

KINDERGARTEN AND FIRST GRADE PUPIL RATING OF THE TEACHER—FORM A

Note to Teacher: Read items to students, asking them to mark column (face) that describes how they feel about the item. Explain "teacher." Explain any terms as needed.

	Dislike or Not Agree	Neutral or Don't Know	Like or Agree
EXAMPLE:			
A. My teacher lets me choose things.	☹	😐	🙂
1. My teacher treats me fairly.	☹	😐	🙂
2. My teacher uses words I know.	☹	😐	🙂
3. My teacher makes school seem fun.	☹	😐	🙂
4. My teacher lets students tell about things in class.	☹	😐	🙂
5. My teacher shows me what to do.	☹	😐	🙂
6. My teacher helps me learn new things.	☹	😐	🙂
7. My teacher has me do lots of things.	☹	😐	🙂
8. My teacher tells me how well I'm doing.	☹	😐	🙂
9. My teacher praises me for good work.	☹	😐	🙂
10. My teacher never gets mad.	☹	😐	🙂
11. My teacher listens to me.	☹	😐	🙂
12. My teacher expects me to do my work.	☹	😐	🙂

FIGURE 11.9
Sample Elementary Pupil Survey
Source: Kyrene Elementary School District. (1986). *Certified Employee Appraisal System Teacher Guidelines* (p. D5). Kyrene, AZ: Author.

make increases as their age increases (Tuckman, 1995). This means that care must be taken to ensure that all student surveys used are age appropriate. For example, rating scales such as the one in Figure 11.9 using "smile" and "frown" faces can be used with primary grades. And, based on an item analysis of pupil surveys administered to almost 10,000 students,

	Agree		Not Sure		Disagree
I know what I'm supposed to do in class	5	4	3	2	1
Teacher shows us how to do new things	5	4	3	2	1
There is enough time to finish class work	5	4	3	2	1
This class is not too noisy or rowdy for learning	5	4	3	2	1
I learn new things I can tell you about	5	4	3	2	1
I know how well I'm doing in class	5	4	3	2	1
This is a good teacher	5	4	3	2	1
We have enough materials and supplies to learn	5	4	3	2	1
At the end of class, I understand well enough to finish the assignment	5	4	3	2	1
I know why we learn what we learn in class	5	4	3	2	1
This class is not too slow or fast to learn well	5	4	3	2	1
The rules in class help me to learn	5	4	3	2	1

FIGURE 11.10

Recommended Items for Middle and High School Student Survey

Source: K.D. Peterson, C. Wahlquist, & K. Bone. (2000). Student surveys for school teacher evaluation. *Journal of Personnel Evaluation in Education, 14*, p. 151. Reprinted with permission.

Peterson, Wahlquist, and Bone (2000) recommend the items in Figure 11.10 for use with elementary, middle, and high school students.

Parent and student surveys can provide valuable insights into a teacher or administrator's performance that are unavailable from any other sources. However, because they are based on perception, they should not be considered as completely reliable sources or evidence. "At their best, they can be used for formative feedback and to supplement other indicators of teacher performance" (Danielson & McGreal, 2000, p. 512).

Rating Scales. Rating scales are lists of items that are presumed to constitute effective performance. Items are usually grouped into categories, such as personal traits, knowledge and skills, experience, classroom behavior, and style. Rating scales typically range from 1 to 5 on a scale ranging from, for example, "below expectations" to "exceeds expectations" or "below average" to "excellent." Rating scales are popular because they are "fast, impersonal, and often give the appearance of exactness" (Cleveland, Peterson, Sharp, & Walter, 2000, p. 7). Rating scales can be used by teachers for self-evaluation purposes or by supervisors or the school board as part of the employee evaluation process. Items may be weighed and a total score obtained.

The most serious problem with the use of rating scales is that the judgment regarding any item is purely subjective and may easily be based on personal feelings rather than facts. Another serious threat to the validity of ratings scales when they are used by a supervisor is the **halo effect**, the tendency of an evaluator to form a strong general impression of the person being evaluated and then to give basically the same rating on every item on the scale (Medley, 1992). Ratings scales are not as easy to use as they appear. Terms such as "average" or "excellent" mean different things to different people. And distinguishing between relevant and irrelevant behaviors and discounting the halo effect require training and practice.

Another concern with the use of rating scales is that the scores derived from them can also be misleading. That is, "What does it mean when the superintendent gets a high score on 49 out of 50 items? Can that low score outweigh the other 49?" (Cleveland, Peterson, Sharp, & Walter, 2000, p. 17).

Notwithstanding their possible shortcomings, rating scales are used extensively by school districts throughout the nation, especially in the evaluation of supervisory personnel, including superintendents (Mathews, 2001). If the scale has been cooperatively developed, and if the criteria on the rating scale are legally and professionally defensible, and if different raters arrive at very similar ratings for the same ratee, such scales can appropriately be used for summative evaluation (MacPhail-Wilcox & Forbes, 1990).

360-Degree Feedback. Known also as team evaluation, multirater feedback, and full-circle feedback assessment (Dyer, 2001), **360-degree feedback** evaluation is in common use in business and industry. It involves the systematic solicitation of feedback from the full circle of one's supervisors, subordinates, clients, and others with whom one interacts. The rationale for 360-degree feedback is that "data gathered from multiple perspectives are more comprehensive and objective than data gathered from only one source" (Dyer, 2001, p. 35) and it "solves some of the problems associated with single-source evaluation, including lack of fairness, accuracy, credibility and usefulness to the evaluatee" (Santeusanio, 1998, p. 31). Equally important, 360-degree feedback gives teachers and administrators a full view of their performance and the opportunity to see how their perceptions of their performance compare with those of others (Santeusanio, 1998).

Typically, the evaluatee is allowed to chose the team of evaluators (except in the case of parents and students, who are selected as discussed later). The most common sources for 360-degree feedback for teachers are principals, curriculum directors, students, parents, peers, aides, support staff, and self-evaluation. Sources for principals include superintendents, assistant superintendents, peer principals, teachers, parents, site council members, students, support staff, and self-evaluation. Among the evaluators for a superintendent are school board members, members of the superintendent's cabinet, curriculum directors, principals, teachers, parents, support staff, community members, and self-evaluation. Feedback is obtained from these sources through the use of surveys or questionnaires made up of items that reflect the performance expectations of the position. Although a number of commercially available instruments can be used for data gathering, many districts have chosen to allow peer design teams to develop the survey instruments that will be used.

The School Improvement Model Center at Iowa State University has worked with a number of school districts in designing and implementing 360-degree feedback systems. They recommend that, for the evaluation of elementary teachers, all students be surveyed, that two sections of students be surveyed for a secondary school teacher, and that in surveying parents a random sample of a size that will generate a 25% response be used (Manatt, 2000). For all other categories of raters, the Center for Creative Leadership, another pioneer in the use of 360-degree feedback, suggests that a minimum of three raters be used to ensure confidentiality (Dyer, 2001).

While 360-degree feedback evaluation does offer significant advantages over most single-source assessments, which provide only one perspective, it can be time consuming and can create *survey fatigue* (i.e., a principal or even the school secretary could end up completing a survey for every teacher in the school) (Dyer, 2001). It also has been criticized by some who suggest that it may yield inflated and biased scores. However, the concerns about 360-degree evaluation, like the concerns about any of the other evaluation sources, can be mitigated by using it as one source in a multisource system.

Appraisal and Review of the Evaluation System

Once in operation, the entire evaluation system should be subjected to ongoing review by the school board, the administration, and representatives of employees to ensure that the system is fulfilling its intended purposes and that it is consistent with changes in what we know about instructional and administrative practice and student learning. As a part of this review, the performance of evaluators and the utility of the various instruments and techniques in generating the desired data should be carefully examined (NSBA, 1996). The system should also be continually monitored to verify that it is meeting the technical and legal standards described in the following section.

STANDARDS FOR THE DEVELOPMENT AND OPERATION OF A SOUND EVALUATION SYSTEM

For an evaluation system to be considered sound, it must meet certain technical and legal standards. The technical standards—validity, reliability, utility, and propriety—are primarily concerned with the accuracy of the measurements and ensuring that the evaluation system is ethical and fair to all parties. The legal standards are intended to ensure that the system meets substantive and procedural due process requirements and is free from discrimination.

Technical Standards

Validity in personnel evaluation is the extent to which the evaluation measures the performance that it is intended to measure. "Validity is perhaps the most important attribute of an assessment system" (Helm, 1995, p. 107).

The clarity of the criteria and standards, the data collection procedures, and the competence of the evaluators all affect validity (Ginsberg & Berry, 1990). Among the activities of school districts that can contribute to the validation of the district evaluation system are the following:

- ☐ Establish purpose statements.
- ☐ Analyze and present empirical data: make comparisons with alternative measures and performance assessments.
- ☐ Estimate the empirical reliability of the data.
- ☐ Establish multiple data sources, indicators, and judges.
- ☐ Establish safeguards [that] limit the use of data for purposes other than issues of performance, that ensure its safe storage, and [that] oversee the procedures to ensure [that] its provisions are carried out.
- ☐ Conduct studies on current and proposed procedures, relative costs, benefits, and improvement.
- ☐ Create archives for reviewing and checking data and as a resource for future development (Peterson, 2000).

"**Reliability** in evaluation refers to the consistency of measurements across evaluators and observations" (Ginsberg & Berry, 1990, p. 221). Evaluation is by its very nature judgmental. However, if different evaluators using the same criteria and standards to evaluate the same individual produce different results, the evaluation system is not reliable (Helm, 1995). The possibility for such subjectivity is one reason it is important to use multiple sources of data, to train evaluators in the use of the various evaluation instruments and techniques used by the school or school district, and, when possible, to use multiple evaluators.

Utility and *feasibility* relate to both reliability and validity and refer to the realistic considerations that must be addressed to ensure each. If the use of a complex evaluation process requires a great deal of training, with associated costs, before evaluators can use it reliably, the utility of the process is compromised. Likewise, even if a particular process or instrument has been judged extremely valid and reliable by measurement experts, but the time required of evaluators and/or evaluatees is excessive, or if it is opposed by the teachers and administrators, its feasibility is reduced.

The Joint Committee on Standards for Educational Evaluation (1988) developed five utility and three feasibility standards for evaluation systems in education. The utility standards state that if evaluations are to be "informative, timely, and influential," they must (1) be constructive, (2) have identified users and uses, (3) be managed and executed by credible evaluators, (4) yield reports that are clear, timely, accurate, and germane, and (5) be followed up so that users and those evaluated understand the results and take appropriate actions. The feasibility standards state that (1) evaluation procedures should produce the needed information with the minimum disruption and cost, (2) the development and monitoring of the evaluation system should involve all concerned parties, and (3) adequate time and resources must be provided to ensure the effective and efficient implementation of the evaluation plan.

Propriety standards require that evaluations be conducted ethically and with regard for staff, students, and other clients. The five propriety standards developed by the Joint Committee (1988) are as follows:

1. *Service Orientation:* Evaluations of educators should promote sound education principles, fulfillment of institutional missions, and effective performance of job responsibilities, so that the educational needs of students, community, and society are met.
2. *Formal Evaluation Guidelines:* Guidelines for personnel evaluations should be recorded and provided to employees in statements of policy, negotiated agreements, and/or personnel evaluation manuals, so that evaluations are consistent, equitable, and in accordance with pertinent laws and ethical codes.
3. *Conflict of Interest:* Conflicts of interest should be identified and dealt with openly and honestly, so that they do not compromise the evaluation process and results.
4. *Access to Personnel Evaluation Reports:* Access to reports of personnel evaluation should be limited to individuals with a legitimate need to review and use the reports, so that appropriate use of the information is assured.
5. *Interactions with Evaluatees:* The evaluation should address evaluatees in a professional, considerate, and courteous manner, so that their self-esteem, motivation, professional reputations, performance, and attitude toward personnel evaluation are enhanced or, at least, not needlessly damaged. (p. 21)

Legal Standards

The legal standards that must be followed in the development and operation of the school district evaluation system can be broadly categorized as *substantive due process standards* and *procedural due process standards.* Substantive due process standards are concerned with the objectivity of the criteria, standards, evidence, and results. Procedural due process standards are concerned with the fundamental fairness of the evaluation process. Most legal challenges to personnel evaluation are with the procedural aspects of the process (Tucker & Kindred, 1997). (See Chapter 6 for a more detailed discussion of substantive and procedural due process.) The following lists of substantive and due process standards are summarized from the discussions of Beckham (1992, 1997), Tucker and Kindred (1997), Stufflebeam and Pullin (1998), and Desander (2000).

Substantive Due Process Standards

1. The criteria on which the evaluation is based should be
   a. formalized in a written policy;
   b. consistent with state statutes, state department of education regulations, local school board policies, and collective bargaining agreements;
   c. communicated in advance to all employees;
   d. job related, validated, and observable;

     e. clear and sufficiently specific to inform a reasonable person of performance expectations;

     f. objective and attainable criteria;

     g. uniformly applied; and

     h. developed in cooperation with employees.

2. The evaluation process should yield, and decisions should be based on, evidence and documentation that is
   a. representative of the employee's job responsibilities over a period of time sufficient to identify a pattern of performance;
   b. collected from multiple sources and, when possible, multiple evaluators who have been trained to collect data in the manner specified by policy;
   c. sufficient in quantity and depth to support the evaluation conclusions and recommendations; and
   d. credible and noncontradictory.
3. Any deficiencies noted must be consistent with the job-related evaluation criteria.

Procedural Due Process Standards

1. The process should
   a. be conducted in a uniform and consistent manner by trained evaluators;
   b. follow state statutes, state department of education regulations, and school board policies and collective bargaining agreements;
   c. be communicated to all employees in advance of the process;
   d. require that the evaluation results be communicated both in writing and at a postevaluation conference;
   e. provide the opportunity for response to an unsatisfactory evaluation;
   f. provide a written statement of specific deficiencies that are related to the predetermined criteria;
   g. provide clear directions for improvements with a plan of remediation related to the identified deficiencies;
   h. provide a reasonable time to remediate; and
   i. provide the opportunity to appeal, including the right to a fair hearing.
2. The evaluation procedures must be applied in a uniform manner.
3. The evaluation process should not be used as a means of retaliating against the employee's exercise of free speech or other constitutional rights.

The courts have traditionally shown a reluctance to attempt to substitute their judgment for that of school administrators or school boards when it comes to evaluative criteria or the methods of evaluation as long as the applicable state and local evaluation procedures or the terms of negotiated agreements are followed. The main concerns of the courts seem to be to ensure that procedural requirements are followed and that the ratings were not subjectively or discriminatorily applied.

TABLE 11.1
Computer Uses in Personnel Evaluation

☐ District evaluation forms and surveys
☐ Directions for evaluation procedures (e.g., peer review)
☐ Graphics for presenting data (charts, graphs, tables)
☐ District form letters
☐ Statistical analysis routines (e.g., means, standard deviations)
☐ Bibliographies of evaluation techniques
☐ District norms on surveys
☐ Network data (e.g., teachers wishing to share information)
☐ Records of evaluation costs and time
☐ Student achievement data
☐ Individual teacher records (e.g., résumés, course lists, scores)
☐ Bibliographies in teacher evaluation
☐ Legal reviews on teacher evaluation
☐ In-service instruction on teacher evaluation

Source: Peterson, K.D. (2000). *Teacher evaluation: A comprehensive guide to new directions and practices* (p. 195). Thousand Oaks, CA: Corwin Press. Copyright © 1995 by Corwin Press. Reprinted by permission of Corwin Press, Inc.

THE USE OF COMPUTER TECHNOLOGY IN PERSONNEL EVALUATION

The growing importance of personnel evaluation in education has meant that both employees and school districts collect and use a great volume of information in the evaluation process. Computers can provide valuable assistance to employees and the district in recording, manipulating, and analyzing data throughout the process. Mention has already been made of the use of computer technology in portfolio development. Other uses of computer technology in personnel evaluation in education are detailed in Table 11.1.

SUMMARY

One of the most important and sometimes difficult jobs of the school administrator is the evaluation of personnel. Although evaluation can provide the opportunity for professional growth and school improvement, unless properly conducted it can also become a source of controversy and low morale. It is imperative that the school district demonstrate its commitment to a sound evaluation system through clearly articulated and publicized board policies and by the adoption of an evaluation system that is technically sound and ensures substantive and procedural due process. And, even though such a system may employ multiple data collection techniques and serve a number of personnel purposes, the evaluation system should not attempt to combine the summative and formative evaluation functions.

DISCUSSION QUESTIONS

1. Does your district have written job descriptions for teachers and principals? Do you feel the job descriptions accurately reflect what teachers and principals do?
2. How may a school system combine formative and summative evaluations of its professional staff without damaging morale and effectiveness?
3. How well do you feel your colleagues would be able to evaluate your performance? How well would your students be able to evaluate your performance? Name three ways that you use peer input and three ways that you use student input to improve your performance. How is this information generated?
4. If you were asked to develop a portfolio of your job-related best works, what would be the six most significant entries?

■───────────── *CASE STUDIES*

11.1 Evaluation Choice

In the Taylor School District teachers have traditionally been evaluated annually by both the principal and department chair using classroom observation procedures. During the past year, the representatives of the teachers' association met with the administration and expressed their concern that the current process was inadequate because it provided only a single source of data. Instead of the sole and uniform use of classroom observations, they recommended that each teacher be able to choose from several techniques or combination of techniques to be used for her or his annual review. Specifically, they suggested that each teacher be able to choose either portfolio assessment, client surveys, self-evaluation, or the existing classroom observation procedure as the principal method of appraisal.

Questions

1. What are the advantages and disadvantages of using differential appraisal techniques for education personnel?
2. Do you agree with the teachers' association that classroom observation provides too limited a database for appraisal? Why is classroom observation the most commonly employed assessment technique in elementary and secondary schools, whereas peer review and student evaluation of instruction are the commonly used techniques in higher education?
3. If differential performance appraisal techniques were available to you, which of those discussed in this text would you choose to be evaluated by and why?

11.2 Parent Survey

Recently, the Mayflower Elementary School District has come under great pressure from the community because of the low achievement test scores of its students. Within the context of criticism of the quality of education provided by the schools, criticism has also been directed at the quality of the instructional staff. In an effort to become more sensitive to parental concerns, Superintendent Ralph Jones decided to survey parents and guardians regarding their perceptions of the effectiveness of instructional staff. He has notified all teachers that the results of the parent survey will become the principal feature of the teacher improvement and evaluation program. The parent survey asked parents to rate their child's teacher on the extent to which the teacher met the following criteria:

1. Monitors the student's progress and provides adequate and timely feedback.
2. Introduces the goals and objectives for the lesson and how they will be obtained.
3. Creates a safe environment conducive to learning.
4. Gives clear directions for tasks.
5. Uses appropriate teaching strategies.
6. Checks regularly for comprehension and understanding.
7. Provides for active student participation.
8. Adapts the content to meet the varied needs of students.

Questions

1. Which of the listed criteria are inappropriate for inclusion on a survey of parents and guardians? Why?
2. Choose three items from the survey and reword them so that they are more appropriate and useful for evaluating the quality of instruction.
3. In addition to including surveys of parents and guardians in the annual evaluation of teachers, what other methods might the school district employ to respond to community concerns regarding the quality of instruction?

REFERENCES

Aleamoni, L. M. (1999). Student ratings myths versus research facts, from 1924 to 1998. *Journal of Evaluation in Education, 13*, 153–166.

Beckham, J. C. (November 1992). *Evaluation.* Paper presented at the annual meeting of the National Organization on Legal Problems of Education, Scottsdale, AZ.

Beckman, J. (1997). Ten judicial "commandments" for legally sound teacher evaluation. *Education Law Reporter, 117*, 435–439.

Black, S. (2000). Evaluation for growth. *American School Board Journal, 187*(4), 58–61.

Brackbill, T. E. (1996). A report card for teachers. *Principal, 75*(4), 49–51.

Cleveland, P., Peterson, G. J., Sharp, W. M., & Walter, J. K. (2000). A three state examination of school board evaluations of superintendents. *Educational Research Quarterly, 23*(3), 3–21.

Collins, A. (1991). Portfolios for biology teacher assessment. *Journal of Personnel Evaluation in Education, 5*, 147–167.

Danielson, C. (1996). *Enhancing professional practice: A framework for teaching.* Alexandria, VA: Association for Supervision and Curriculum Development.

Danielson, C. (2001). New trends in teacher evaluation. *Educational Leadership, 58*(5), 12–15.

Danielson, C., & McGreal, T. L. (2000). *Teacher evaluation to enhance professional practice.* Alexandria, VA: Association for Supervision and Curriculum Development.

Desander, M. K. (2000). Teacher evaluation and merit pay: Logical considerations, practical concerns. *Journal of Personnel Evaluation in Education, 14*, 307–317.

Dyer, K. M. (2001). The power of 360 degree feedback. *Eductional Leadership, 58*(5), 35–38.

Ginsberg, R., & Berry, B. (1990). The folklore of principal evaluation. *Journal of Personnel Evaluation in Education, 3*, 205–230.

Haertel, G. D. (1993). *A primer on teacher self-evaluation.* Livermore, CA: EREAPA Associates.

Helm, V. M. (1995). Evaluating professional support personnel: A conceptual framework. *Journal of Personnel Evaluation in Education, 9*, 105–121.

Herbert, M. (1995). Student evaluation of teachers: variables and value. *Business Education Forum, 9*(3), 15–17.

Hertling, E. (1999). Peer review of teachers. *ERIC Digest (126).* Eugene, OR: ERIC Clearinghouse on Educational Management, College of Education, University of Oregon.

Joint Committee on Standards for Educational Evaluation. (1988). *The personnel evaluation standards: How to assess systems for evaluating educators.* Newbury Park, CA: Sage.

Kremer-Hayon, L. (1993). *Teacher self-evaluation: Teachers in their own mirror.* Boston: Kluwer.

Lieberman, M. (1998). *Teachers evaluating teachers: Peer review and the new unionism.* Bowling Green, KY: Bowling Green State University.

Loup, K. S., Garland, J. S., Ellett, C. D., & Rugett, J. K. (1996). Ten years later: Findings from a replication of a study of teacher evaluation practices in our 100 largest school districts. *Journal of Personnel Evaluation in Education, 10*, 203–236.

MacPhail-Wilcox, B., & Forbes, R. (1990). *Administrator evaluation handbook.* Bloomington, IN: Phi Delta Kappa.

Manatt, R. P. (2000). Feedback at 360 degrees. *School Administrator, 57*(10), 10–11.

Mathews, J. (2000). When parents and students grade staff. *School Administrator, 57*(10), 6–9.

Mathews, J. (2001). The tenuous nature of superintendent evaluation *School Administrator, 58*(2), 6–14.

McCarthy, S. J., & Peterson, K. D. (1988). Peer review of materials in public school teacher evaluation. *Journal of Personnel Evaluation in Education, 1,* 259–267.

Medley, D. M. (1992). Teacher evaluation. In M. C. Alkin (Ed.), *Encyclopedia of educational research* (Vol. 4, pp. 1345–1352). New York: Macmillan.

Murphy, J. (1987). Teacher evaluation: A comprehensive framework for supervisors. *Journal of Personnel Evaluation in Education, 1,* 157–180.

National School Boards Association. (1987). *The school personnel management system.* Alexandria, VA: Author.

National School Boards Association. (1996). *The school personnel management system.* Alexandria, VA: Author.

Odden, A. (2000). New and better forms of teacher compensation are possible. *Phi Delta Kappan, 81,* 361–366.

Painter, B. (2001). Using teaching portfolios. *Educational Leadership, 58*(5), 31–34.

Peterson, K. D. (2000). *Teacher evaluation: A comprehensive guide to new directions and practices.* Thousand Oaks, CA: Corwin Press.

Peterson, K. D., Wahlquist, C., & Bone, K. (2000). Student surveys for school teacher evaluation. *Journal of Personnel Evaluation in Education, 14,* 135–153.

Peterson, K. D., Wahlquist, C., Bone, K., Thompson, J., & Chatterton, K. (2001). *Educational Leadership, 58*(5), 40–43.

Ribas, W. B. (2000). Ascending the ELPS to excellence in your district's teacher evaluation. *Phi Delta Kappan, 81,* 585–589.

Riggsby, D., Jewell, V., & Justice, A. (June 1995). *Electronic portfolio: Assessment, resume, or marketing tool?* Paper presented at the Summer Conference of the Association of Small Computer Users in Education, North Myrtle Beach, SC.

Rossow, L. F., & Parkinson, J. (1992). *The law of teacher evaluation.* Topeka, KS: National Organization on Legal Problems of Education.

Santeusanio, R. (1998). Improving performance with 360 degree feedback. *Educational Leadership, 55*(5), 30–32.

Schon, D. (1983). *The reflective practitioner.* New York: McGraw–Hill.

Sperry, D. J., Pounder, D. G., & Drew, C. J. (1992). Educator evaluation and the law: A case study of common statutory problems. *Education Law Quarterly, 1,* 415–429.

Stiggens, R. J., & Duke, D. L. (1988). *The case for commitment to teacher growth: Research on teacher evaluation.* Albany: State University of New York Press.

Stronge, J. H. (1991). The dynamics of effective performance evaluation systems in education: Conceptual, human relations, and technical domains. *Journal of Personnel Evaluation in Education, 5,* 77–83.

Stronge, J. H., & Tucker, P. D. (2000). *Teacher evaluation and student achievement.* Washington, DC: National Education Association.

Stufflebeam, D. L., & Pullin, D. (1998). Achieving legal viability in personal evaluation. *Journal of Personnel Evaluation in Education, 11,* 215–230.

Thomas, D. W., Holdaway, E. A., & Ward, K. L. (2000). Policies and practices involved in the evaluation of school principals. *Journal of Personnel Evaluation in Education, 14,* 215–240.

Tolleson Elementary School District. (n.d.). *Teacher evaluation handbook.* Tolleson, AZ: Author.

Tucker, P. D., & Kindred, K. P. (1997). Legal considerations in designing teacher evaluation systems. In J. H. Stronge (Ed.). *Evaluating teaching: A guide to current thinking and best practice* (pp. 59–90). Thousand Oaks, CA: Corwin Press.

Tuckman, B. W. (1995). The interpersonal teacher model. *Educational Forum, 59,* 177–185.

Valentine, J. W. (1992). *Principles and practices for effective teacher evaluation.* Boston: Allyn and Bacon.

Withers, G. (1995). Getting value from teacher self-evaluation. In A. J. Shinkfield & D. Stufflebeam (Eds.), *Teacher evaluation: Guide to effective practice* (pp. 261–271). Boston: Kluwer.

Zubizarreta, J. (1994). Teaching portfolios and the beginning teacher. *Phi Delta Kappan, 76,* 323–326.

12 *The Compensation Process*

After reading this chapter, you will be able to:

■ Identify the major determinants of school district compensation.

■ Describe the major approaches to compensating teachers and administrators.

■ Discuss the methods used by school districts to compensate teachers for extracurricular activities.

■ List the major categories of indirect compensation of school district employees.

■ Distinguish between the two major types of flexible benefit plans.

One of the most difficult processes of the human resources function is compensation administration. Compensation decisions have significant consequences for both the school district and its employees. Between 80% and 90% of the current operating budget of a typical school district is allocated to personnel salaries, wages, and benefits. Compensation affects the district's ability to attract, motivate, and retain qualified employees. Moreover, compensation of educational personnel is increasingly viewed as an integral component of efforts to reform education and increase performance.

In this chapter the compensation program is described in terms of two broad components: direct compensation (wages and salaries) and indirect compensation (employee benefits and services). The opening sections of the chapter deal with the development of school district compensation policies and the major determinants of school district salaries. The discussion of direct compensation in this chapter will focus on the compensation of certificated teachers and administrators. Direct compensation of classified personnel is discussed in Chapter 13. The discussion of direct compensation centers on the predominant approach to compensating teachers, the single salary schedule, as well as the major alternatives to this approach that reflect the broader reform initiatives in education: competency-based pay, performance-based pay, and school or group-based pay.

ESTABLISHING DISTRICT COMPENSATION GOALS AND POLICIES

Decisions about school district compensation and incentives should begin with a determination of the goals that the district wishes to achieve with the compensation program. These might include such goals as the following:

☐ Attract and retain competent teachers
☐ Improve teacher productivity
☐ Improve student performance
☐ Provide a fair and equitable compensation system
☐ Improve teacher morale and satisfaction
☐ Reward outstanding performance
☐ Reinforce accountability

Once the goals of the compensation system have been determined, the district must develop policies that are consistent with the achievement of these goals. The development of such compensation policies is central to the effective administration of the compensation program. Written compensation policies provide assurance to the community that sound procedures will be followed in employee compensation and assurance to staff that recognized policies will be followed in their compensation. Equally important, written compensation policies provide guidance to those responsible for compensation administration in the development of acceptable compensation procedures (Johns, Morphet, & Alexander, 1983). Among the guidelines that should be considered by school districts in developing and implementing compensation policies are the following:

1. All personnel in the district, certificated and noncertificated, should be included in the compensation policies.
2. The compensation system should be concerned with attracting, motivating, and retaining personnel at all levels.
3. The salary system should be equitable. This requires that each position be evaluated in terms of its relative importance to other positions, that a hierarchical arrangement be established, and that salary be awarded accordingly.
4. The compensation program should be nondiscriminatory, defensible, and legal.
5. The compensation plan should be competitive with other school districts and, as much as possible, with other public agencies and the private sector.
6. Quality of performance should be recognized. Performance appraisal and accompanying differential reward structures should provide the basis for advancement in income and overcome the limitations of the single salary schedule.
7. Indirect compensation should be a built-in feature of the compensation program. Employee benefits are normally an important component of the negotiated agreement. School districts must recognize their obligation to provide competitive and attractive indirect compensation.

8. The compensation program must be constantly monitored and reviewed to ensure its internal consistency and equity and its competitiveness with external agencies and organizations.

9. The compensation program and process should be openly derived and communicated to all employees and interested citizens. (Foster, 1960; Foulkes & Livernash, 1989; Castetter & Young, 2001)

DETERMINANTS OF COMPENSATION

A number of internal and external factors directly or indirectly determine the compensation program established by the school district, including (1) supply and demand, (2) the district's ability and willingness to pay, (3) cost of living, (4) prevailing wage rates, (5) collective bargaining, and (6) government regulations. Each must be considered as a part of a collective force that is referred to as the wage mix (Sherman & Bohlander, 1992). Each of these factors is discussed in this section.

Supply and Demand

All employee compensation, including that of school employees, is a reflection at least in part of the forces of supply and demand. The economic concept of supply and demand states that "value (compensation) is shaped by the balance or imbalance between supply, or the degree of availability of some quantity or quality, and demand, or the extent or need for some quantity or quality" (Chambers, 1996, pp. 53–54).

The *demand* for teachers is in large part determined by three market considerations: (1) the number of students to be served, (2) the number of teachers leaving through death, retirement, dismissal, and so on, and (3) pupil–teacher ratios. Demand is also influenced by nonmarket considerations. The state legislature, the state department of education, and local school boards can greatly influence both the supply and the demand for teachers and other education professionals through such actions as the establishment of certification and accreditation standards, the decision to offer certain types of programs, or the offering of retirement incentives. Because of the influence of state and local policy decisions, demand can vary greatly from one geographic location to another and from one academic discipline to another. For example, legislation in California and other states to reduce class size has created a serious demand for teachers in those states, while other areas report a surplus of teachers. And, while the demand for math, bilingual education, ESL, science, technology, and special education teachers remains high, the demand for social studies, health and physical education, and elementary teachers remains low in many areas.

The demand for teachers is expected to continue through the first decade of the 21st century as a result of the baby boom echo and immigration (Kanman, 2001). The K–12 enrollment of 52.8 million in 2000 is expected to grow to 53.5 million by 2006, the highest enrollment in the nation's history (U.S. Department of Education, 2001). This enrollment increase will add to the demand for teachers and administrators created by the record retirements discussed in Chapter 8 and the growing number of teachers, both new and experienced, who leave the profession each year. The U.S. Department of Education estimates that more than 20% of teachers leave the profession in their first 3 years, a figure that is closer to 50% in urban schools (Gursky, 2001, p. 19.). The demand for teachers is expected to reach 2.4 million in 2006, at a rate of over 200,000 per year (Fox & Certo, 1999).

The sources of *supply* of teachers are composed of four groups: (1) first time teachers, (2) delayed entrants (first-year teachers who engaged in other activities between graduating from college and entering teaching), (3) transfers from other schools, districts, or states, and (4) former teachers. In recent years the percentage of new public school teachers that were newly prepared was 29%, 17% were delayed entrants, 31% were transfers, and 23% were reentrants (Broughman & Rollefson, 2000). Projecting the supply of teachers is far more difficult than projecting the demand. Although projections of the supply of new teacher graduates are available, only about 60% of newly prepared teachers actually enter teaching (Darling-Hammond, 1999). It is also difficult to project how many former teachers currently unemployed or in other positions are considering reentering teaching or how many persons in other professions are willing to enter teaching. As discussed in Chapter 8, the increasing demand and declining supply of both teachers and administrators have made recruiting quality educators one of, if not the, most serious challenges facing school districts today.

Ability and Willingness to Pay

A fundamental determinant of school district compensation is the district's financial ability and willingness to pay (Cohn & Geske, 1990). Differences in salaries among school districts can largely be explained by variations in local fiscal capacity (assessed valuation of property per pupil or per capita income) and community willingness to tax and spend for education (effort), as King (1979) found in New York State and Kitchen (1983) found in Texas. Adkison and McKenzie (1990) discovered the same held true for administrators' salaries.

Whereas a district has little control over its tax base, unless there are statutory tax or expenditure limitations to the contrary, it does have control over the effort it makes to support education. In fact, in the process of collective bargaining, unions have often justified their demands for increases in compensation or have been awarded increases by arbitrators because the district's tax rate was substantially below that of its neighbors or below the state average.

Cost of Living

Historically, the most common method of determining salary increases has been the **cost-of-living adjustment** (COLA). Cost-of-living adjustments are based on the consumer price index (CPI), a U.S. Department of Labor index that measures the change in the costs of goods and services over time. COLAs do not reflect judgments about the economic value of persons holding positions or their performance. Rather, they reflect the sentiment that, unless personnel compensation keeps pace with the cost of living, the resulting decline in purchasing power has the same effect as a salary cut. As a result, a COLA clause is commonly included in bargaining agreements. The three most common types of COLA clauses are (1) the *escalator clause*, which provides for periodic adjustment during the contract year without additional negotiations if changes in the CPI reach or exceed a certain limit, (2) the *reopener clause*, which provides for negotiations to begin immediately or at the end of the contract year if changes in the CPI reach or exceed a certain limit, and (3) the *end-of-year clause*, found only in multiyear contracts, which automatically, without further bargaining, translate changes in the CPI into salary adjustments (Educational Resource Service, 1987).

The cost of living (COL) differs not only over time but also among states (Walden & Newmark, 1995) and school districts in a state. Costs associated with land prices, energy services, construction, consumer goods, and personnel services vary among rural, suburban, and urban areas and among geographical regions in the state. For example, intercounty cost-of-living indexes in Illinois ranged from 91.5 in rural counties to 113.8 in suburban Du-Page County (McMahon, 1994). In New York State the difference in the COL between Binghamton (99.6) and New York City (149.5) is greater than the difference in the COL between New York State and any other state (Nelson, 1994). If a school district is to maintain the purchasing power of its employees, it must consider these differences in making compensation determinations.

Prevailing Wage Rate

The second most important determinant of current wage increases is the comparability of current rates of pay with those of neighboring school districts (Beebe, 1983). It would be difficult for a school district to attract and retain competent personnel if its compensation levels were significantly below those paid by other school districts or other potential employers in the community. Data pertaining to prevailing wage rates may be obtained from state and national departments of labor, from surveys conducted by the school district human resources department, and from data supplied by employee organizations. It is common practice for employee groups to gather such data and, when supportive, to use it in collective negotiations. Although the veracity of data supplied by the union need not be automatically suspect, because of the possibility of selectivity in collection (i.e., collecting data primarily from those districts and employers known to pay higher salaries), good practice dictates that the human resources office should assume some responsibility for the systematic collection of wage and salary data. The data collected should include not only direct compensation, but also, because of its impact on the attractiveness and value of the total compensation package, indirect compensation.

Collective Bargaining

If school district employees are unionized, wages and other conditions of employment may be largely determined through the process of collective bargaining. In the negotiations process, both the union and the district will focus on those factors that support their bargaining positions (e.g., supply and demand data, ability to pay, cost of living, and prevailing wage rates). Research indicates that "bargaining is associated with positive and statistically significant salary increments for both teachers and school administrators" (Chambers, 1999, p. 271).

Government Regulations

Like many other areas of human resources administration, compensation administration has become the subject of an increasing number of laws enacted by the state and federal governments. The majority of states have statutes providing minimum salaries for teachers. In a number of states, provision is also made for minimum salaries for administrators and other personnel. In addition, numerous state and federal laws address issues related to the compensation of support personnel.

The major piece of federal legislation dealing directly with compensation is the Fair Labor Standards Act (FLSA) passed in 1938 and amended many times. The major provisions of the FLSA are concerned with minimum pay, overtime pay, child labor, and equal pay. The Equal Pay Act of 1963 has become one of the most significant amendments to the FLSA:

> No employer having employees subject to any provisions of this section shall discriminate between . . . employees on the basis of sex by paying wages to employees . . . at a rate less than the rate at which he pays wages to employees of the opposite sex . . . for equal work on jobs the performance of which requires equal skill, effort, and responsibility, and which are performed under similar working conditions. (sec. 206 [d][1])

According to the provisions of the Equal Pay Act, any difference in pay because of sex must be rationally justified and be the result of a job evaluation study. The Equal Pay Act has been the basis for numerous suits in the field of education seeking to eliminate discriminatory compensation practices.

A number of other federal laws have had a significant impact on the compensation practices of school districts. For example, the Social Security Act of 1935, the Health Maintenance Organization (HMO) Act of 1973, the Health Insurance Portability and Accountability Act of 1996, and several of the civil rights statutes are intended to protect the welfare and wages of employees. Title VII of the Civil Rights Act of 1964 and the Civil Rights Act of 1991 also protect against discrimination in compensation, as do the Equal Employment Opportunity Act of 1972, the Age Discrimination in Employment Act Amendments of 1978, the Pregnancy Discrimination Act of 1978, and the Americans with Disabilities Act of 1992. In the last quarter-century, legislatures and the courts have increasingly concerned themselves with questions of equity and discrimination in employment.

DIRECT COMPENSATION: TEACHER COMPENSATION AND INCENTIVE PLANS

The compensation of teachers has proved to be one of the most intransigent aspects of the educational system. In fact, since the 1880s there have been only three major approaches to the payment of teachers: the initial rural tradition in which teachers were primarily paid by "boarden' round" at the homes of students; the move to a grade-based schedule that accompanied the shift to larger, multigrade schools; and finally, under pressure from the growing teachers' unions, the shift to today's **single salary schedule** (Protsik, 1995). The adoption of the single salary schedule represented the culmination of a century-long struggle by teachers to overcome pay differences between elementary and secondary teachers, between men and women, and between minorities and nonminorities that characterized the profession until 1940. Teachers also saw the single salary schedule as providing objective criteria (preparation and experience) for the determination of pay that would not be subject to the whims of administrators (Firestone, 1994). The education component of the single salary schedule also provided an incentive for teachers, the majority of whom had only two years of training from a normal school, to earn a full bachelor's degree, or even a master's or doctorate (Odden, 2001).

The single salary schedule has remained popular with boards of education because it is easy to understand and administer and because it allows for a rather simple budgeting process and for projecting and awarding salaries. However, despite the historic popularity of the single salary schedule, it has fallen under serious attacks in recent years as being "not well suited to the demands of today's reform environment . . . (because it) has no element directly linked to raising student achievement, the main goal of education reform" (Odden, 2001, pp. 17–18) and as being a "straightjacket that's stifling schools, which can't reward the best teachers" (Symonds, 2001, p. 68) or be adjusted to reflect market realities (Ballou & Podgursky, 2001). As a result, as policymakers have sought ways to improve teacher quality and student achievement, there has been a growing interest in compensation schemes that link pay to performance. However, while public officials recognize that teacher salaries are a critical variable in addressing the projected teacher shortages, they are unwilling to increase teachers' salaries without some demonstration of increased teacher competence or improved student results. As a consequence, about half the states and a number of school districts have mandated or adopted policies linking compensation to teacher competencies (knowledge and skills) or student performance (see the Web site for the Center for Policy Research in Education, www.wcer.wics.edu/cpre, for information on various performance-based and knowledge-and-skills programs across the country). An additional push for performance-based pay was provided by the National Education Summit of educators, business leaders, and policymakers, which in fall 1999 made as one of its key recommendations that school districts implement pay-for-performance incentive plans.

As school districts consider the implementation of any teacher compensation plan, a primary consideration should be the extent to which the plan is likely to promote the compensation goals established by the district. In addition, before any plan is selected it is important that a thorough review of alternative plans be conducted, with particular attention given to those that have proved successful in districts most like the deciding district. The following compensation and incentive plans are those most in use or under consideration by school districts today: (1) the single salary schedule, (2) competency or knowledge and skills-based pay, (3) school or group-based performance awards, and (4) pay for performance.

Single Salary Schedule for Teachers

The single salary schedule pays equivalent salaries for equivalent preparation and experience. Assumptions underlying the single salary schedule include the following (Greene, 1971):

1. Teaching of all grade levels and subjects is of equal importance and equally difficult.
2. The more professional preparation and training the teacher has, the more effective the teacher.
3. The more experience a teacher has, the more effective the teacher.
4. Salary variations are unnecessary and undesirable motivations for teachers.
5. The single salary schedule minimizes frictions and dissatisfaction among teachers.
6. The single salary schedule is the easiest to administer.

The single salary schedule may be considered a version of knowledge-based pay in that it treats years of experience and degrees or courses taken as proxies for knowledge. The implicit assumption is that as teachers become more experienced and receive additional training they become more knowledgeable (Firestone, 1994). The single salary schedule has two basic dimensions: a horizontal dimension made up of columns generally referred to as lanes, scales, or classes, which correspond to levels of academic preparation (e.g., bachelor's degree, master's degree, master's degree plus 30 hours, doctoral degree); and a vertical dimension of rows of "steps" that correspond to the years of teaching experience. A teacher's salary schedule does not have a standard number of columns or rows, although there are usually more rows than columns so that the schedule tends to form a vertical matrix.* (See Table 12.1)

*The discussion of the single salary schedule is adapted from *Methods of scheduling salaries for teachers* (pp. 1–4, 6), Educational Research Service, 1987, Arlington, VA: Author. Copyright 1987 by the Educational Research Service. Adapted by permission.

TABLE 12.1

Glendale Unified School District 2000–2001 Teacher Salary Schedule
(Teachers with Preliminary or Clear Credentials)

STEP	CLASS I	CLASS II	CLASS III	CLASS IV	CLASS V	CLASS VI
	Bachelor's Degree	Bachelor's Degree + 14	Bachelor's Degree + 28	Bachelor's Degree + 42	Bachelor's Degree + 56 + MA or 62	Bachelor's Degree + 70 + MA
1	$ 39,463	$ 39,464	$ 39,465	$ 39,466	$ 39,467	$ 41,307
2	$ 39,464	$ 39,465	$ 39,466	$ 39,467	$ 39,904	$ 43,569
3	$ 39,465	$ 39,466	$ 39,467	$ 39,758	$ 41,960	$ 45,833
4	$ 39,466	$ 39,467	$ 39,721	$ 41,538	$ 44,043	$ 48,103
5	$ 39,467	$ 39,468	$ 41,388	$ 43,316	$ 46,130	$ 50,342
6	$ 39,468	$ 41,028	$ 43,080	$ 45,067	$ 48,213	$ 52,611
7	$ 40,748	$ 42,624	$ 44,800	$ 46,851	$ 50,298	$ 54,879
8	$ 42,259	$ 44,195	$ 46,487	$ 48,608	$ 52,352	$ 57,142
9	$ 43,804	$ 45,797	$ 48,180	$ 50,390	$ 54,176	$ 59,352
10	$ 45,313	$ 47,396	$ 49,874	$ 52,164	$ 56,520	$ 61,624
11	$ 46,824	$ 48,971	$ 51,598	$ 53,918	$ 58,601	$ 63,888
12			$ 53,286	$ 55,702	$ 60,690	$ 66,154
13					$ 60,690	$ 66,154
14					$ 60,690	$ 66,154
15					$ 60,690	$ 66,154
16					$ 60,690	$ 66,154
17					$ 60,690	$ 66,154
18					$ 63,725	$ 69,461
19					$ 63,725	$ 69,461
20					$ 63,725	$ 69,461
21					$ 63,725	$ 69,461
22					$ 66,912	$ 72,934

$100.00 per month will be paid for an earned Doctorate from a college or university accredited by a regional or national accrediting association recognized by the National Commission on Accreditation.

Source: Glendale Unified School District, Glendale, CA.

The Horizontal Dimension. There are two basic ways to establish the professional preparation scales: (1) complete or full schedules and (2) additive schedules. The complete or full schedule, the more common of the two, normally recognizes at least two academic degrees, the bachelor's and the master's, as well as intermediate lanes that recognize a specified number of college credits beyond the academic degree (e.g., B.A. + 15 hours, M.A. + 30 hours, M.A. + 60 hours). Many such schedules also have columns for educational specialist degrees and doctorates. An example of a variation of this schedule is the Philadelphia "senior career teacher" program, which provides a bonus of $5000 or more to teachers who are M.A. + 60 hours, have 10 years of teaching experience, and have dual certification (Gursky, 1992).

The additive schedule is not based on several academic degrees, but on the bachelor's degree and the number of college credit hours beyond it. Each salary scale represents a certain number of credit hours beyond the bachelor's. If an advanced degree is earned, however, a fixed amount or an amount related to a percentage of base is added beyond the salary figure represented on the schedule. The payment of the advanced degree additives creates, in effect, scales paralleling the established ones. A variation of the additive schedule establishes similar scales based on the master's degree. The major difference between the two schedules is that in the full or complete schedule all possible salaries are represented, whereas in the additive schedule salaries above those specified on the established schedule can be included.

Vertical Dimension.   The vertical steps on the salary schedule provide salary increases based on the number of years of teaching experience. An upper limit generally is placed on the number of steps, usually around 15. A common practice is to offer more steps in the higher academic preparation scales than in the lower. This provides incentive for teachers to attain additional education.

Several factors determine the initial placement of a new teacher to a specific vertical step on a scale, but the most common factor is previous teaching experience. To receive credit for any previous year's teaching, the teacher usually must have taught 75% of the school year. Most school districts place a limit on the number of years of teaching experience that will be credited toward initial placement on the salary schedule. This means that teachers who do not stay in one district for their entire careers—the typical behavior—might never reach the highest step in the salary schedule regardless of their experience (Odden & Kelley, 1997).

Other considerations in making the initial placement are credit for related experience, credit for military service, and credit for other experience. Some districts recognize related experience such as public library experience for librarians or recreational experience for physical educators. Others grant full or partial credit for military service or for experience in the Peace Corps, VISTA, or the National Teachers Corps.

Vertical advancement from one step to the next within the scale is normally automatic after a stipulated period of time, usually 1 year, although longer periods may be required for advancement to the higher steps. Teachers' groups have continued to advocate automatic advancement, but in an increasing number of districts certain restrictions are being placed on vertical advancements. These include (1) advancement at specified points contingent on additional units of academic credit or completion of in-service training programs, (2) annual advancement contingent on satisfactory performance, and (3) advancement based on merit.

To provide for teachers who have reached the maximum number of steps in a particular scale, some salary schedules also provide for supermaximum or long-term service increments beyond the highest step in the scale. Although in most instances the awarding of this increment is based solely on the attainment of a specific number of years of experience above the highest number recognized on the schedule, in some cases a performance or merit evaluation is required before the award is made.

Establishment of Salary Increments and Increases.   An increment is the difference between two points on a salary schedule and may be either horizontal or vertical. The actual dollar difference between points on scales or points on steps can be established by the following:

1. A fixed dollar amount whereby each scale or step is the same dollar amount higher than the previous one
2. A variable dollar amount between scales or steps
3. A fixed ratio schedule whereby each step in all scales is determined by applying a ratio to some base amount (index), usually the B.A. minimum, and the specific ratio at each step varies from the ratio at the previous step by a fixed value (e.g., 1.03, 1.06, or 1.09)
4. A variable ratio schedule that operates the same as a fixed ratio schedule, except that the value of the ratio from one step to the next is not fixed but varies

Both the actual dollar increments and the increases (raises) may be determined as a result of collective negotiations and may not follow any discernible pattern; however, most salary schedules are not haphazardly constructed, but reflect some methodology. The most common salary schedule changes that provide for salary increases are (1) changes in the index or ratio base, (2) changes in the index structure, (3) across-the-board changes, and (4) variable changes. If a schedule is based on the indexing method, a change in the index or ratio base (e.g., B.A. minimum) on which all other salaries are based increases all salaries by the same percentage without altering the existing index structure. Alternatively, holding the base constant while modifying the index figures by fixed index points (e.g., 1.03 increased to 1.05, 1.06 increased to 1.08, or 1.09 increased to 1.11) results in varying percentage increases at each step. Indexing is no longer the predominant method of scheduling salaries, however, so these two approaches for determining salary increases are not commonly used.

The most common method of providing salary increases is by fixed, across-the-board increases in either dollar amounts or percentages. Across-the-board dollar raises, although the more common of the two, are probably the most unfair because those at the lower end of the salary schedule receive the largest percentage increases. Those who have been with the district for a number of years or have sought additional education may feel penalized by a raise that percentage-wise is less than half that received by those at the lower levels of the schedules. Across-the-board percentage raises, on the other hand, while appearing to be a fair way of increasing salaries, especially if based on some index such as the CPI or cost-of-living index, can create another type of inequity that results from the fact that, mathematically, when using the percentage increase method, salaries at the top of the salary schedule will increase faster than those at the middle or bottom of the salary schedule. And, over time, "the difference in value relationship between the top and bottom steps is destroyed" (Plauny, 1994, p. 42). If the district does not use a percentage, it can maintain the spread between the top and bottom salary steps, as well as the value relationship between the top and bottom steps, by applying the percentage increase to a specific base salary and then applying that dollar amount to each salary (Plauny, 1994). However, this approach may be opposed by teachers' unions who view the "unfairness" created by awarding experienced teachers a lesser percentage increase than less experienced teachers as more important than the maintenance of the salary spread or the value relationship.

The variable change approach to salary allows different dollar increases to be added to different salary levels. These variable increases, however, are not randomly assigned; they reflect district policy and philosophy. For example, faced with a teaching force characterized by higher levels of experience and education, some districts have felt financially constrained to refrain from hiring persons with advanced experience or education or to decrease the percentage or dollar awards to those beyond a certain number of years of experience or education. Yet other districts have adopted just the opposite policy and reward these individuals.

Competency-Based Pay

Competency-based pay is based on the premise that the more competent employees are, the better they can perform their jobs. "Competence in this context refers to an employee's knowledge, skills, abilities, and learned behaviors" (Risher, 2000, p. 21). Competency-based pay, also referred to as skills-based pay, or knowledge and skills based pay, rewards employees with salary increases as they acquire new knowledge or skills or as they demonstrate higher-level competence at existing abilities. And, although under competency-based pay salary increases are *not* linked to performance, there is an expectation that more competent employees will perform at higher levels. There is also an implicit message to employees that it is to their advantage to develop their skills, be as good as they can be, and be paid accordingly (Risher, 2000). Teacher groups have tended to support competency-based plans because, unlike merit pay plans, which they have staunchly opposed, under competency-based pay plans, potentially all teachers can earn salary increases "because eligibility is determined by demonstrated performance to clear standards, not a mushy administrative decision" (Odden, 2000b, p. 29).

To implement a competency-based pay system the district must (1) identify the knowledge and skills associated with each position, what Risher (2000) calls the **competency profile,** (2) translate these competencies into explicit standards for teaching performance, and (3) determine ways to assess individual performance relative to the standards (Odden, 2000b). Fortunately, in the last several years, for districts considering the adoption of a knowledge and skills salary component, standards and assessment frameworks have been developed on the national level that can be useful in this process. As mentioned in Chapter 10, these frameworks include the PRAXIS series, specifically PRAXIS II and PRAXIS III, developed by the Educational Testing Service and assessments developed by the Interstate New

Teacher Assessment and Support Consortium, which are appropriate for assessing the knowledge and skills of beginning teachers. The National Board for Professional Teaching Standards (NBPTS) can be used to assess the knowledge and skills of the more experienced and presumed more competent teachers, while Danielson's (1996) Framework for Teaching covers the entire teaching career span from beginning to advanced.

Knowledge and skills can be incorporated into the salary structure in basically two ways: (1) as an *add-on* to the single salary structure or (2) by restructuring the entire salary schedule around knowledge and skills benchmarks. Most districts have chosen the add-on approach (Odden, 2001). For example, over half the states and numerous school districts across the country provide salary supplements to teachers who receive NBPTS certification (see www.nbpts.org for a complete listing). Some provide a flat dollar amount, while others incorporate increases into the existing salary schedule. For example, the state of Louisiana provides a 15% salary increase to teachers who receive board certification, while Hammond, Indiana treats board certification as the equivalent to the Ph.D. on the traditional salary schedule. Dade County (FL) adds $5000 to the state stipend, bringing the total increase to 20% of the average teacher salary (Urbanski & Erskine, 2000).

To date, only one school district has attempted to design a salary structure based almost entirely on knowledge and skills. The Cincinnati Federation of Teachers and a team of school district administrators jointly designed a new salary system to become effective in 2002–2003 that adds a school-based performance bonus to what is in essence a knowledge- and skills-based salary structure. The district adopted the Danielson Framework for Teaching for its internal teaching standards and redesigned its evaluation and professional development systems around these standards (Odden, 2000b). The evaluation system is used to place a teacher into one of four levels of performance (see Figure 12.1). Advancement from one level to another is based on assessment relative to the standards by the principal and a lead teacher. Beginning teachers must pass the apprentice level by the end of 2 years and the novice level by the end of 5 years or be terminated.

In addition to the salary increases determined by internal assessments of the benchmarks depicted in Figure 12.1, teachers can receive salary increases for acquisition of knowledge and skills determined by external assessments, such as the attainment of NBPTS certification or a master's degree. School-based performance awards of $1400 will also be made to teachers and principals in schools that reach designated school improvement goals (Odden, 2001).

Another model for a knowledge- and skills-based salary structure, a model that uses both external (e.g., PRAXIS) and internal (e.g., the Danielson Framework for Teaching) assessments, is the one depicted in Figure 12.2. Salary increases are associated with moving from one competency level to another. Districts can decide any time limits for advancement. One or more of the assessments can be used for granting full professional licensure (accompanied

Apprentice	• Salary: $30,000
	• Teachers who fail to advance to Novice within 2 years are terminated
Novice	• Salary: $32,000–$35,750
	• Must be rated 2 or better in all performance and skill categories (on a scale of 1–4)
	• Teachers who fail to advance to Career within 5 years are terminated
Career	• Salary: $38,750–$49,250
	• Must be rated 3 or better in all categories
Advanced	• Salary: $52,000–$55,000
	• Must be rated 4 in two categories
Accomplished	• Salary: $60,000–$62,000
	• Must be rated 4 in all categories

FIGURE 12.1

The Cincinnati Plan. Under Cincinnati's knowledge- and skills-based pay plan, teachers advance through five levels of professional achievement, earning salary increases based on performance.

Source: A. Odden. (2001). Defining Merit: Rewarding experience. *Education Matters*, *1*(1), 24.

FIGURE 12.2

Professional Benchmarks for a Competency-Based Teacher Salary Structure

Source: A. Odden. (2000). New and better forms of teacher compensation are possible. *Phi Delta Kappan, 81*, p. 364.

Year	Professional Benchmark
0	Graduation from college and initial licensure
1–2	PRAXIS II Content Test
1–2	PRAXIS II Test of Professional Teaching Knowledge
2–3	Danielson Basic
	PRAXIS III assessment
2–10	Danielson Proficient
	INTASC assessment
3+	Content master's
5+	Danielson Advanced
	State board certification
	Minor in second content area
	Second licensure in related field
6+	NBPTS certification
7+	Post-board-certification leadership

by a salary increase of perhaps 10%); meeting the Danielson Proficient level or the INTASC could even replace the tenure process and would bring a sizable salary increase (Odden, 2000a).

School-Based Performance Awards

The use of group-based performance awards, or collective incentive pay plans, is a compensation strategy that is gaining widespread use in business and industry. Group-based performance awards recognize that in most organizations the achievement of organizational goals is as much a result of group performance as individual performance. In industry the strategy is often used in conjunction with a plan linking salary to individual performance or, as in Cincinnati, with a competency-based pay component (Risher, 2000).

In education, group-based, or more accurately school-based performance awards (SBPA), have also gained favor among policymakers. Experts in teacher compensation also favor school-based performance rewards because it is consistent with the way works gets done in educational organizations (LaFee, 2000). Under SBPA programs, financial rewards go to schools that meet certain prescribed standards or outcomes, such as increased student achievement, lower dropout rates, or reduced absenteeism. Some programs restrict the use of the funds to school improvement projects; others allow the funds to be used for salary bonuses and/or school improvement projects. Nearly 20 states and numerous school districts have developed some version of a SBPA program (Odden, 2000a).

One such program operating in North Carolina uses the results from state-mandated tests to place schools on one of four academic achievement levels. Each school is required to design and implement annual performance standards. Regression analysis is used to remove the influence of socioeconomic and other variables and to predict performance. Rewards to faculty and staff in schools who exceed their predicted goals are $1500 per certified staff and $500 per teacher assistant; for schools that meet their expected goals, rewards are $750 per certified staff and $375 per teacher assistant (Brown, 2000). Operating on top of the North Carolina state program in the Charlotte–Mecklenburg School District is the district's Benchmark Goals Program, which also provides varying awards to certified and support staff in schools based on the attainment of predetermined school improvement goals (Kelley, Odden, Milanowski, & Heneman, 2000).

Compensation researchers at the University of Wisconsin-based Consortium for Policy Research in Education have studied a number of SBPA programs and have enumerated seven factors that must be addressed by states or districts in designing such programs:

1. The most valued outcomes of the system must be identified. In states and districts that are administering SBPA, student achievement typically constitutes 75% or more of the performance data, but other factors such as graduation or promotion rates, parent satisfaction, or student attendance may also be used.

2. Each element in the program must be measurable. Most states and districts use state tests if they exist.
3. Strategies for calculating changes in performance must be determined.
4. The measures and calculation of change for each school must be made fair by addressing such issues as the percentage of students who take the test, accommodations for students with disabilities, accounting for student mobility, dealing with students whose English proficiency is limited, and so on.
5. School systems need to determine the types and levels of awards. "Research in the private sector has found that in order to affect a worker's motivation, annual bonuses need to be at least 5 to 8 percent of salary—about $2000 for a typical teacher" (Odden, 2001, p. 20).
6. The school system must develop and provide *system enablers* that schools and teachers need in order to become fully informed about school goals and to interpret the results of students assessments. Moreover, teachers will need substantial professional development.
7. The programs must be stable and sufficiently funded: when teachers meet their performance targets, the money must be there (Odden, 2000b, p. 365).

Pay for Performance

Pay for performance systems are designed to link teacher or administrator pay to performance, usually student scores on standardized tests. As noted in Chapter 10, a number of states and districts have incorporated student performance in their teacher and/or administrator evaluation systems. Many of these have taken the next step and are experimenting with pay for performance. However, many teacher groups are concerned about pay for performance plans, as they were about merit pay systems in the past. Unions contend that standardized tests are intended to broadly assess a child's academic skills and general intellectual development, not to evaluate the teacher's abilities. Moreover, the unions point out, the scores are significantly influenced by factors outside the control of the teacher or the school, from how much time a teacher actually has with a child to the socioeconomic status and family background of the child (LaFee, 2000). Despite these concerns and others, numerous school districts have adopted some form of pay for performance.

In one of the most far-reaching (and contentious) pay for performance plans in the nation, the Colonial School District in suburban Philadelphia adopted a plan under which at least 10% but not more than 20% of teachers can receive up to $2778 in an individual award based on how their student's achievement (as measured by the Pennsylvania System of State Assessment for grades 4, 8, and 11 and Terra Nova for all other grades) compares to that of similar classes with similar children. Educators for whom appropriate grade scores are not available (e.g., librarians, physical education teachers, nurses, and guidance counselors) are evaluated based on criteria established by school district administrators in conjunction with an outside consultant (Gleason, 2000; Sultanik, 2000). Teachers are also eligible for group bonuses of up to

$2500. Groups at the elementary level are defined by grade level, at the middle school by teams, and at the high school by departments. Each group is evaluated on concrete student outcomes, such as test scores, or on outcomes agreed to in consultation with an independent educational consultant. Each group has the right to decide how the bonuses will be spent, whether as salary bonuses or for the purchase of supplies, professional development, or other things (Sultanik, 2000). Colonial's pay for performance plan was adopted over the strong objection of the teacher's union.

To address the concern's of teachers and others, Michael Allen of the Education Commission of the States suggests that states or districts considering the adoption of pay for performance plans ensure the following:

☐ A vehicle to reasonably measure student learning gains against state education standards;
☐ A method to collect and analyze data that can generate a "value-added" correlation between individual teachers and student learning gains over time;
☐ Appropriate appraisal of the data that emphasizes *patterns* of performance by students of individual teachers;
☐ An initial corrective, but not punitive, approach to deal with teachers whose students show a pattern of poor learning; and
☐ Buy-in from teachers and parents. (Gleason, 2000, pp. 82–83)

COMPENSATION FOR EXTRACURRICULAR ACTIVITIES

At one time extracurricular activities were considered normal duties that teachers had to assume as part of their work. In the 1950s, however, as teacher salaries began to lose ground in a rising economy and as many teachers sought to supplement their incomes by working second jobs, teachers' organizations became more aggressive in seeking additional compensation for time spent in extracurricular activities (Greene, 1971). Today, districts generally compensate teachers with supplemental pay for the guidance and supervision of students engaged in extracurricular activities.

The methods used by school districts in scheduling supplements for extracurricular activities vary widely. The most common approach is to provide a fixed amount unrelated to teachers' salaries. The fixed amount approach, used by 67% of districts in an ERS (Education Research Service, 1991a) study, can be a lump sum, multiple units of a specific amount, or a percentage of a fixed amount not on the teachers' salary schedule. The size of the fixed amount normally depends on some consideration of the activity involved. An example of one system used to rate activities is that of Antioch, Illinois, which is summarized in Figure 12.3. Using the rating system, each activity is given a total point score and then assigned to one of

1. *Student Contact Hours:* These are actual student contact hours and include practice time, dressing time, performance time, and travel time. (Limit of 2 1/2 hours per practice session.) 0–50 pts. 1 point/10 hours.

2. *Preparation and Planning:* This is time spent on the activity not involving the supervision of students. It would include designing formations, bookkeeping, scouting, keeping statistics, etc. 0–30 pts. 1 point/10 hours.

3. *Weekend and Holiday Involvement:* Certain activities require involvement on weekends and holidays and put an additional burden on that time as opposed to afterschool activities. 0–30 pts. 1.5 pts/Sat., Sun., or Nonschool day.

4. *Instructional and Organizational Skill:* This is a subjective category based on the preparation an individual must have to capably direct the activity and the skill necessary to instruct, organize, and conduct the activity. This category is divided into 4 sections worth a total of 25 pts as follows:

   a. Number of separate skills taught, 0–11 pts. 1 pt/skill.

   b. Success of program: 0–6 pts. Totally subjective based upon participation and holding power of the activity and reception by the public.

   c. Previous training required: 0–4 pts. 1 pt/year of participation in training at whatever level, high school, college, or teaching.

   d. Levels taught: 0–4 pts. 1 pt/level (Fr., Soph., JV, or Var.).

5. *Student–Advisor Ratio:* This is the number of student participants involved during the mid-point of the activity season. In the case of nonathletic activities that do not meet on a daily basis, only the officers are counted toward the student total. 0–20 pts. 1 pt/4 students.

6. *Equipment and Materials Management:* 0–20 pts. This determination is divided into 4 sections, 5 pts/section as follows:

   a. Budget:
   $20,000+ = 5 pts
   8,000+ = 4 pts
   5,000+ = 3 pts
   3,000+ = 2 pts
   100+ = 1 pt

(continued)

FIGURE 12.3
Antioch, Illinois, Extracurricular Pay Factors and Point System
Source: Antioch Community High School, Antioch, Illinois. Reprinted by permission.

five salary grades (each grade also has four steps) based on the total score. The five salary grades and the accompanying scores are

Grade I: 120 or more points
Grade II: 95–119 points
Grade III: 75–94 points
Grade IV: 50–74 points
Grade V: 20–49 points

b. Inventory:
   $80,000+ = 5 pts
   30,000+ = 4 pts
   5,000+ = 3 pts
   3,000+ = 2 pts
   100+ = 1 pt
c. Equipment volume (individual pieces of equipment issued)
   500+ = 5 pts
   100+ = 4 pts
   9+ = 3 pts
   5+ = 2 pts
   2+ = 1 pt
d. Handling repetitions (number of participants × pieces issued × times handled)
   500+ = 5 pts
   350+ = 4 pts
   250+ = 3 pts
   100+ = 2 pts
   25+ = 1 pt

7. *Exposure and Expectations:* This is a subjective item with points awarded by an estimate of the size of crowds and the public relations responsibility required. 0–15 pts.
   Exposure and expectations were determined by two categories:
   a. Spectator or service users per week of the season. Maximum 10 pts. 1 pt/100 users per week.
   b. Publicity contacts required. Maximum 5 pts. 1 pt/12 contacts.

8. *Travel Supervision:* This category makes provisions for the unique responsibility involved and responsibility for students while traveling in a school bus or other school vehicles above the time alone spent during the trip. 0–10 pts. 1 pt/trip.

9. *Other Adults Supervised:* This category recognizes that some positions require a supervisor of adults assigned to the activity. It does not include supervision of volunteer adults or student assistants. 0–5 pts. 1 pt/adult.

FIGURE 12.3
(continued)

Another approach to scheduling supplements for extracurricular pay is the ratio or percentage of a specific point on the teachers' salary schedule, which is used by one-third of the districts responding to the ERS (1991a) study; the supplement is related to the teachers' salary schedule by the application of a ratio or percentage of a specific point on the schedule, commonly the B.A. minimum salary. Here, again, the size of the percentage is normally determined by some consideration of the activity involved.

DIRECT COMPENSATION: ADMINISTRATOR SALARIES

Historically, principals and other school administrators had to negotiate individually for their salaries (Greene, 1971). This practice is still common in the hiring of superintendents and other top administrators. However, for most administrative positions and in most districts, salary schedules for administrators have been adopted. Three types of salary schedules for school administrators are typical: (1) ratio or index schedules related to teachers' salaries, (2) schedules based on additives to the teachers' schedules, and (3) schedules independent of teachers' schedules constructed on the basis of such variables as instructional level, scope of responsibilities, education, and experience (ERS, 1991b). In addition, as was true in regard to the determination of teachers' salaries, the push for accountability in recent years has brought an increase in attempts to link administrative pay to performance and the addition of this variable to administrative salary structures. Ultimately, the amounts that a specific district pays its administrators is generally related to three variables: (1) region of the country, (2) district enrollment, and (3) per pupil expenditure level (Williams, 2001).

Index or Ratio to Teachers' Schedule

Indexing administrative salary schedules to teachers' schedules historically was the most common practice in determining administrative schedules. In this type of schedule the administrative salary is a ratio of some point on the teachers' schedule (e.g., lowest minimum salary, highest scheduled salary, or average salary). Each administrative position may be assigned a different ratio depending on school size, school level, number of staff supervised, or other variables that reflect the relative importance and complexity of the various administrative positions.

In the last two decades there has been a growing trend away from the practice of relating administrators', particularly principals', salaries to teachers' salaries by ratio or index. According to an ERS survey of methods of scheduling principals' salaries, only 8% of school districts used a salary approach that indexed principals' salaries to the teachers' salary schedule (ERS, 1991b).

Additive to Teachers' Schedule

Also becoming less widely used according to the ERS study is the additive approach to determining administrative salaries, used by only 3% of the responding districts. Schedules that determine administrative salaries by making an addition to the teachers' schedule do so by adding either a specific dollar amount or a flat percentage to the point on the teachers' schedule at which the administrator would be classified on the basis of his or her preparation and experience. This method is more commonly used in determining salaries in lower-level administrative positions than in upper-level positions. It is not uncommon for the salary of a department chairperson or lower-level supervisor to be based on a bonus above a teacher's salary, but it would be rare to find a principal or superintendent whose salary is determined in this manner.

Administrator Schedule Independent of Teachers' Schedule

The vast majority (89% in the 1991 ERS study) of the salary schedules for administrators are established independent of teachers' salary schedules. Most salary schedules for administrators are constructed to reflect a number of factors related to the administrative function, as well as individual competence. Among the factors that may be considered in constructing a salary schedule for administrators are the following:

Instructional Level Supervised.   Most salary schedules for principals and assistant principals presume that greater responsibilities are inherent as grade levels increase. These schedules either provide a separate schedule for elementary, middle school–junior high, or senior high administrators or recognize instructional level as a factor in a single salary schedule.

Scope of Responsibility.   Obviously, administrative positions vary in responsibilities. Elements that influence the level of responsibility and consequently the points assigned each level include (1) number of adults supervised, (2) staff qualifications and experience, (3) number of students supervised, (4) number and types of special programs, (5) number and size of attendance centers, (6) size and number of budgets administered, (7) number and size of support programs (i.e., food services and transportation), and (8) student body and community characteristics.

Professional Experience.   The types of experience that are generally recognized under this factor include number of years (1) in present position, (2) in a similar administrative position, (3) of other administrative experience, (4) of teaching experience, (5) of other educational experience, and (6) of service in the school district.

Education and Professional Development.   Most administrative positions require a certain minimum academic preparation. The administrative salary schedule may be constructed to recognize levels of academic preparation above the minimum or specified professional development.

Performance.   There is growing interest in linking compensation to performance and to the attainment of organizational goals. Accordingly, advancement on the administrative salary schedule may be based on the results of performance appraisal, rather than simply on gaining additional education or experience.

Number of Contract Days.   Another important variable that affects administrative salaries is the length of the contract year. Many administrators serve beyond the normal school term. Indeed, many administrative positions are year-round positions. Because the number of contract days varies among positions, the salary schedule should reflect the longer work period.

Point-Factor Method. One approach to establishing administrative salaries that attempts to recognize the foregoing variables is the point–factor method, which is based on an evaluation of the position description for each administrative and supervisory position and the assignment of a point value to each position. In the example from Peters Township School District (McMurray, Pennsylvania) given in Figure 12.4, seven factors are used to evaluate each position on one of four levels. The average point value for each position is then calculated and a pay scale assigned commensurate with the position's total score and relationship to other positions on the organizational chart.

Definition of Factors:

Knowledge	The information gained through formal education or work experience that is essential to the performance of the job.
Supervisory Responsibility	The extent to which the job requires direct supervision of assigned staff.
Fiscal Responsibility	The extent to which the job involves direct preparation and administration of budget.
Program Responsibility	The extent to which the job involves program development and/or program implementation.
Judgment and Consequence of Errors	The degree to which the job requires independent judgment and the seriousness of the exercise of faulty judgment.
Interpersonal Skills	The range of contact in dealing with others, superiors, peers, subordinates, and the community.
Working Conditions	The total set of conditions in which the job is performed, physical environment, including weather, travel and mobility, unusual hours, expectation of constant availability, etc.

Levels of Importance and Points:

Low = 10 points	Little or no requirement or involvement in this area. Absence of requirement, absence of involvement.
Moderate = 20 points	First level of involvement. Minor degree of requirement. Some presence of difficulty.
Above Average = 30 points	Pronounced degree of involvement. Obvious requirement, presence of difficulty.
High = 40 points	Notable formal and/or legal requirement. Most pronounced level of involvement.

FIGURE 12.4

Point-Factor Method for Administrator Salaries

Source: Educational Resource Service. (1991). *Methods of scheduling salaries of principals* (4th ed.). Arlington, VA: Author. Reprinted with permission.

TABLE 12.2
Mean of Mean Salaries Paid Personnel in Selected Administrative Positions,
2000–2001

Position	Salary
Superintendents	$118,496
Deputy/Associate Superintendents	104,048
Assistant Superintendents	94,137
Administrators for:	
Finance and business	77,768
Instructional services	82,725
Public relations/information	65,505
Staff personnel services	80,969
Subject Area Supervisors	64,659
Principals	
Elementary school	59,080
Middle school	77,382
High school	83,367
Assistant Principals	
Elementary school	59,080
Middle school	63,709
High school	67,593

Source: *Salaries & Wages Paid Professional and Support Personnel in Public Schools,
2000–2001* (Table 5), Educational Research Service, 2001, Arlington, VA: Author.

Table 12.2 presents 2000–2001 salaries for a number of administrative
positions. Ultimately, each school district must decide which level and type
of administrative salary structure it can best support. If a schedule is to be
developed independent of teachers' salaries or other established bases, the
district must decide what factors to include and the weight to be given to each.

INDIRECT COMPENSATION: EMPLOYEE BENEFITS AND SERVICES

Indirect compensation, the noncash compensation of employees, has become a fundamental component of the total compensation package of
school employees and can play a major role in the ability of the district to
recruit and retain quality employees. In the past these benefits were supplemental to the paycheck and of minor value, so they were referred to as
fringe benefits. Although the term is still used, these benefits are no longer
considered fringe: fringe benefits in the United States represent 30% of total wages and salaries of all workers in state and local governments (U.S.
Department of Labor, 1996). The growth of fringe benefit programs in
school districts, as in other sectors of the economy, has been a result of
changing tax policies, which have made them more advantageous, and the
financial constraints faced by many districts, which have made the offering of fringe benefits an attractive alternative to increasing wages and

salaries. The district can purchase the benefit cheaper than the employee, and in most cases the benefit is nontaxable to the employee.

In this chapter, indirect compensation for public school personnel is discussed in terms of the following components: (1) legally required benefits, (2) health and welfare programs, (3) savings plans, (4) pay for time not worked, (5) income equivalent payments, and (6) free and reduced-cost services. In addition, one type of compensation packaging, the flexible benefit plan, is presented. Whatever benefits are provided employees, benefits communication becomes an important responsibility of the human resources administrator. This task can be facilitated by an integrated benefits portal on the district Web site that provides employees streamlined access to district-provided or voluntary benefits. This allows employees to do anything from enrollment updating, to finding out information associated with their dental insurance carrier, to applying for a car loan. Such a system not only saves the employee a lot of time, and potentially money, but it also significantly reduces the paperwork and the administrative costs of the human resources department associated with managing the benefits program (Fandray, 2000).

Legally Required Benefits

Both the federal and state governments have enacted laws to protect the welfare of employees. These laws require employers to provide certain benefits to employees whether they want to or not. These required benefits include the following:

Social Security. The Social Security Act of 1935 established the Old-Age, Survivors, Disability and Health Insurance System. The system is financed by contributions by the employee (based on a percentage of the employee's salary) and a matching contribution by the employer. Under the Social Security system, totally and permanently disabled persons may be eligible for disability payments, and retirement income is provided to workers retiring at the age of 62 or insurance benefits to those working until age 65. The actual amount the employee receives is based on the number of years worked, average earnings, and number of dependents at the time that benefits begin. The Social Security Act provides health care services (Medicare) to those 65 and older and benefits to eligible survivors of deceased workers. Only about 56% of school districts include teachers and administrators in the Social Security program (ERS, 1995a, b) because they are usually included in the state retirement system. More often, the Social Security program covers classified employees (Rebore, 2001).

Unemployment Compensation. The Social Security Act also requires states to provide unemployment compensation through state legislation that provides income payments to individuals who have become unemployed through no fault of their own. Unemployment benefits received vary from state to state and are a function of the employee's previous wage and length of service. The costs of this program are paid by the employer.

Workers' Compensation.   In addition to the protections provided by the Social Security Act, all states require almost all employers to provide employees with workers' compensation in the event of occupational injury, disability, or death. Each state has its own schedule of benefits that depend on the current and future wages of the affected employee and the type of injury sustained. Workers' compensation insurance also provides burial expenses and income benefits for widows and children.

State Retirement Programs.   All states provide retirement benefit plans for public school professional employees. The vast majority of these employees (98%) are covered by state retirement systems, whereas only about 5% are covered by local retirement systems (some individuals are in both state and local systems). Of the statewide systems, approximately 72% are teachers' systems and the remainder are operated for teachers and other public employees (ERS, 1995a, b).

State retirement systems vary regarding the service used to compute a member's retirement benefits (i.e., prior service credit, military service credit, in-state public employment other than teaching, out-of-state teaching credit, and others). They also vary on other provisions, such as vesting rights, age requirements, disability benefits (all states but Arizona and Iowa provide permanent disability benefits to members), provisions for borrowing, postretirement adjustments, work restrictions after retirement, and administration. Although administrators should be familiar with the provisions of the state or local retirement plan, they must be careful about rendering specific advice. Such advice should come only from the retirement agency.

In most states, retirement benefits are financed jointly by employee and public contributions. In a few states, however, the retirement plan is financed entirely by the state. In an attempt to increase compensation for public school employees while maintaining the present level of state aid to education, several states have passed legislation requiring local school districts to pay not only the employer's share toward retirement, but also the employee's share. This benefit has great appeal to employees, because it has a significant impact on net income without increasing gross taxable income. Consequently, in an increasing number of school districts, this provision has become a popular item for negotiations.

Health and Welfare Programs

The provision of private welfare and security programs for school employees was limited before 1960. School districts did not consider the added incentives of these benefits until they began to experience the frustrations of teacher shortages and growing competition with other districts, business, and industry (Greene, 1971). The principal private welfare and security programs provided by school districts include health and hospitalization insurance, health maintenance and preferred provider organizations, life insurance, long-term disability insurance, severance pay, tax-sheltered annuity plans, and professional liability insurance.

Health and Hospitalization Insurance. Although job-related accidents and injury are compensable under state workers' compensation laws, most illness experienced by school employees is not job related and therefore is a cause of financial strain on the employee. For this reason, various forms of health and accident insurance are provided for school employees; some are completely financed by the district and for others the costs are shared with the employee. The principal types of health and hospitalization insurance found in school district compensation programs are (1) group hospitalization, (2) medical–surgical, (3) major medical, (4) dental insurance, (5) vision care, and (6) prescription drugs.

As the data from the ERS (1995b) survey presented in Table 12.3 indicate, 97% of all responding districts provided group hospitalization insurance for teachers. Eighty-four percent of these paid the full premium for single coverage and 29% paid the full premium for family coverage. Medical–surgical insurance for teachers was provided by 95% of the responding districts and

TABLE 12.3
Benefits Available to Public School Teachers and Administrators, 1995

Type of Benefit	Percentage of Districts Providing Benefits to Teachers	Percentage of Districts Providing Benefits to Administrators
Group hospitalization insurance	96.5	97.1
Medical/surgical insurance	95.2	95.8
Major medical insurance	95.6	96.2
Dental insurance	80.9	81.4
Vision care	48.3	50.0
Prescription drugs	84.6	85.3
Group life insurance	73.3	77.5
Long-term disability insurance	38.6	44.6
Severance pay	37.0	37.7
Tax-sheltered annuity plans	76.7	76.8
Professional liability insurance	64.5	67.2
Sick leave	98.5	98.2
Personal/emergency leave	97.3	90.8
Vacation leave	N/A	72.9
Sabbatical leave	68.5	53.0
Religious leave	68.6	67.3
Tuition reimbursements	37.3	36.3
Payment of meeting and convention expenses	N/A	77.5
Payment of organizational membership dues	< 0.1	63.2
Transportation allowance	N/A	96.5
Payment of cost of physical exam	N/A	32.0

Source: Educational Research Service (ERS). (1995). *Fringe Benefits for Administrators in Public Schools, 1994–95* (Part 2) and *Fringe Benefits for Teachers in Public Schools, 1994–95* (Part 3). Arlington, VA: Author. Reprinted with permission.

major medical insurance by 96%, with 29% of districts providing full coverage for the family. A very significant increase in the last few years has also occurred in the number of districts providing dental, vision, and prescription drug insurance: 81% provided dental insurance to teachers, 48% provided vision care insurance, and 85% provided prescription drug insurance. Data relative to the provision of these benefits to administrators are also found in Table 12.3.

Managed Care: Health Maintenance Organizations, Point-of-Service Plans, and Preferred Provider Organizations. The growing cost of health care and the growing need for health care at a reasonable price have led to a dramatic increase in enrollments in **health maintenance organizations** (HMO), **point-of-service** (POS) **plans,** and **preferred provider organizations** (PPO). The Health Maintenance Organization Act of 1973 requires employers covered by the Fair Labor Standard Act to offer an HMO as an alternative to health insurance if a federally qualified HMO is available in the community. HMOs provide comprehensive health care to members for a fixed monthly fee on a prepaid services basis. PPOs and POS plans offer more choice to employees, while still providing cost-effective health care. PPOs contract with physicians and hospitals to provide services to members at discounted rates. The employee has the option of going to a physician or hospital that is not a member of the PPO (i.e., is out of the network), but must assume a larger share of the associated costs. POS plans operate similarly to PPOs, except that under a POS the employee chooses a primary care physician who coordinates in-network care. Currently, among managed care plans, PPOs have the largest enrollment (44%), followed by HMOs (28%), and POS plans (19%) ("HMO enrollment on the decline," 2001). The importance of HMOs, PPOs, and POS plans as health care providers for school district personnel has increased dramatically in recent years and is anticipated to increase as health care costs continue to rise.

Group Life Insurance. Life insurance is the oldest form of employer-sponsored employee benefit (Flippo, 1980). The group plan permits the district and the employee to benefit from lower rates. Most group life insurance plans include all employees regardless of physical condition and provide for conversion to an identical policy without physical examination if the individual leaves the district. The standard policy provides for death benefits of one to five times the employees's annual salary. Two disadvantages of group life insurance plans are that they are term insurance policies, providing coverage during a contract period only, and that they have no cash loan or paid-up value. As shown in Table 12.3, approximately 75% of the districts responding to the ERS (1995b) provided group life insurance coverage for teachers and 74% for administrators (ERS, 1995a). And 35% of districts providing group life gave teachers and 36% gave administrators the option of paying for increased coverage.

Long-Term Disability Insurance. Long-term disability insurance provides income continuation payments to employees unable to work because of health-related problems. Such insurance is a supplement to workers' compensation, which only covers occupational disabilities. Long-term disability plans may be provided in conjunction with a retirement plan or may be provided by separate coverage. Many group life insurance plans also have a total permanent-disability feature. Approximately 39% of school districts included in the ERS (1995b) survey provided long-term disability to teachers, and 45% provided this coverage to administrators (ERS, 1995b). The mean percentage of salary coverage for teachers and administrators was 64%.

Savings Plans

Tax-Sheltered Annuities. Tax-sheltered annuities (TSAs) provide a vehicle for employees to supplement their state retirement plan with additional retirement income. TSAs allow school personnel to invest part of their salaries in annuities that are not taxed as current salary. The payment to the annuity is made before any computation of taxes owed, that is, it is *tax sheltered.* Thus income tax payments are reduced at the same time that an investment is being accumulated. The annuity, or income from it, is paid to the employee upon retirement or at some future date. Income taxes are then paid on the amount received at a time when the employee's income presumably will be lower. Annuities purchased by an employee fall under Section 403 (b) of the Internal Revenue Code (IRC), and those purchased by the school district fall under Section 457 of the IRC. Because of their obvious attractiveness to employees, school districts are making an increased effort to design annuity programs that will be helpful in recruiting and retaining prospective or current employees, as well as in encouraging early retirements.

In most school districts, employees are allowed to choose a TSA from among a number of providers. Participation in TSA programs is voluntary. Currently, 30% to 35% of eligible employees in public elementary and secondary schools participate in 403(b) plans. Unfortunately, in many districts employees are given minimal education regarding basic investing concepts and the difference between the various choices (e.g., fixed annuity plans and mutual funds) in terms of such things as expenses, transfer fees, and redemption penalties. As a result, many retire with significantly less than they could have earned had the district provided them with the appropriate investing education (Hauer, 2000).

Pay for Time Not Worked

For the employee, "possibly the most desired but frequently unrecognized benefit is time off with pay" (Henderson, 1994, p. 554). The most common time off with pay provisions for public school personnel are sick leaves, personal and emergency leaves, vacation leaves, sabbatical leaves, religious leaves, family and bereavement leaves, civic and jury duty leaves, professional leaves, and military leaves. One other type of pay for time not worked, severance pay, is also offered by many districts.

Sick Leave. Virtually all school districts provide employees paid sick leave. In fact, statutory provision for sick leave has been made in most states. Included under this category are leaves for family illness and death in the immediate family. In most instances a set number of days per year is provided, with 11 being the mean number of days per year for teachers and 13 for administrators (ERS, 1995a, b). In some systems the entire allotment of sick leave is made at the beginning of the school year, whereas in others the leave is earned monthly (e.g., 1 or 1½ days per month). Districts are about evenly split between set and unlimited in terms of the maximum number of days that employees can accumulate over the length of employment. The mean of the maximum accumulation is 155 days for teachers and 167 for administrators. Application of unused sick leave toward retirement service is allowed in one-third of the districts (ERS, 1995a, b). Some districts allow a sick leave pool, which is available under specified circumstances, to employees who have exhausted their own sick leave.

Personal and Emergency Leave. School districts also recognize that employees will, from time to time, need to take leave for a variety of personal or emergency reasons. Almost all the school districts responding to the ERS survey (ERS, 1995a, b) provided personal and emergency leaves for teachers (97%) and administrators (91%). The mean number of days allowed for both teachers and administrators per year was four. In about 40% of districts, the time taken by teachers as personal or emergency leave is charged against sick leave, and in 36% of districts the same is true for administrators.

Vacation Leave. Vacation leave is normally not provided for teachers; however, most districts (73%) provide vacation leave for administrators. The mean number of days allowed is 19. Most of these districts permit accumulation of leave from year to year, with a mean of 37 days accumulation (ERS, 1995a).

Sabbatical Leave. Provisions for sabbatical leaves for teachers are found in 69% of the school districts (ERS, 1995b). Often the provision has come about as a result of collective negotiations. Professional study is the primary purpose for which sabbatical leave may be taken. The most common time periods granted, in which leave is provided, are six months (30%) and two semesters (58%).

Six years of satisfactory service is the typical prerequisite for a sabbatical leave. Most districts also require some justification in terms of the value of the proposed professional study program to the district and an assurance that the employee will either return to employment in the district for a minimum period of time, usually 2 years, or repay any salary paid during the sabbatical. The district may also have a policy limiting the number of employees who may be on sabbatical leave at the same time.

The ERS study (1995b) found that about two-thirds of the districts offering this benefit provided salary during the sabbatical. Full salary was paid by only 5% of these districts; however, a percentage of salary or some other salary provision was provided by 61%.

Sabbatical leaves for administrators are not as common as for teachers. Only 53% of the responding districts offered this benefit. When offered, the provisions for administrators were similar to those for teachers (ERS, 1995a).

Religious Leave. Leave for religious holidays not observed in the school calendar is granted by most school systems. The ERS study found slightly over two-thirds of the responding districts provided such leave, with most districts charging the leave to the teacher's or administrator's personal leave bank (ERS, 1995a, b).

Jury Duty. Although in several states teachers are exempt from jury duty, leave for jury duty is granted by the vast majority of school systems. This leave is normally considered as a separate paid leave category (ERS, 1995a, b). In most jurisdictions, any payment received for jury duty must be turned over to the school district if the employee is receiving full pay from the district. In other jurisdictions, the jury pay is simply deducted from the employee's regular salary.

Professional Leave. Professional leave was granted to teachers by 92% of the school districts in the ERS study and to administrators by 93% of the districts. Professional leave may be granted for a number of reasons, including (1) professional study, (2) attendance at professional meetings, (3) professional service, (4) research, (5) visits to other schools, and (6) educational travel.

Military Leave. Although there is no legal requirement to pay employees for military or National Guard duty (usually one or two weeks), because school districts are particularly sensitive to the public duties and responsibilities of their employees, most districts make some provision for military leave for their employees. In fact, even though the employee receives military pay while on leave, two-thirds of the districts in the ERS study considered military leave separate from personal leave and classified military leave as leave with pay (ERS, 1995a, b).

Severance Pay. Severance pay normally is a one-time payment to an individual upon severing his or her employment with the district. This severance can occur at retirement or at an earlier point in the employee's career. The size of the payment is often based in part on length of service before separation. Teachers' organizations have increasingly sought severance pay in addition to retirement benefits. When paid upon retirement, it is regarded as a bonus for long-term, loyal service and as an aid to bridging the gap between full service with pay and retirement on a reduced income (Greene, 1971). Very often severance pay is based on the number of unused sick days, with a set maximum number that will be reimbursed. Of those districts responding to the ERS survey, 37% provided severance pay for teachers (ERS, 1995b) and 36% for administrators (ERS, 1995a). Of these, in over one-half of the districts (53% for teachers and 52% for administrators) the basis for computation of the severance payment was unused sick leave (ERS, 1995a, b).

Income Equivalent Payments

Income equivalent payments have been introduced into compensation programs in response to changes in the economic situation and to tax demands. They give the employee an opportunity for an improved, more enjoyable life-style. Income equivalent payments include in-kind benefits that, if purchased by the employee, would necessitate spending after-tax dollars. Discussions of some of the more common income equivalent payments available to school district employees follow.

Professional Liability Insurance. Lawsuits alleging misfeasance, malfeasance, nonfeasance, and malpractice are increasingly being filed against school districts and their employees. Because of their involvement with children, school teachers and administrators are particularly subject to increased liability. For this reason the major professional educational organizations provide professional liability coverage as a benefit of membership or at a nominal rate. School districts also often provide such coverage under a blanket provision in the board's policy. Professional liability coverage was provided to teachers by 65% of the districts included in the ERS study and to administrators in 69% of the districts. And another 21% of districts indicated that, while they did not provide professional liability insurance for administrators, they did provide legal representation at school district expense (ERS, 1995a).

Tuition Reimbursement. Many school districts are offering tuition reimbursements. This benefit provides employees with as many educational opportunities as possible, while upgrading the knowledge and skills of the district work force. The 1995 ERS (1995b) study found that approximately 37% of responding districts offered tuition reimbursements to teachers and 36% to administrators (ERS, 1995a). In about half of these districts, however, reimbursement was limited to graduate credits only.

Payment of Meeting and Convention Expenses. Attendance at professional meetings and conventions is a means of professional renewal and development. In recognition of these benefits, many school districts reimburse some meeting and convention expenses. However, this benefit is most often provided to administrators (78%), not teachers. When such payment is provided, it almost always covers expenses associated with travel, registration, lodging, and meals (ERS, 1995a).

Payment of Organization Dues. A major function of professional organizations is educational and, as such, these organizations provide benefits both to the employee and the district. Like the payment of meeting and convention expenses, however, this benefit has been reserved almost exclusively for administrators (Table 12.3).

Transportation Allowance. School district employees who use their own vehicles while performing school district business may receive a transportation allowance or a mileage reimbursement. Normally, the only individuals affected by this benefit are administrators and supervisors. Almost all districts (97%) provide a transportation allowance to these individuals, with 86% basing the allowance on the number of miles driven (ERS, 1995a).

Free or Reduced-Cost Services

Credit Unions. Credit unions have been established by employees in many large school districts and by a cooperative arrangement of employees of several smaller districts to serve the financial needs of the employees. In some districts, if a credit union does not exist specifically for school district employees, they are eligible for membership in a credit union established by other public employees. Credit unions are operated by employees under federal and state legislation and supervision. Credit unions enable employees to make savings or loan payments through payroll deductions. This not only encourages thrift by the employee, but deposits normally earn a higher rate of interest or dividends than those paid at commercial banks or savings and loans. Loans are also made to employees at a lower interest rate than that charged by commercial enterprises. In addition, credit union members are often eligible for a variety of other benefits, ranging from no-charge purchase of travelers' checks to dealer discounts on the purchase of automobiles.

Employee Assistance Programs. In recent years, concern over employees' mental and emotional health has led to a rapid increase in **employee assistance programs** (Bray, French, Bowland, & Dunlap, 1996). Employee assistance programs (EAPs) provide "confidential evaluation, referral and outpatient counseling services for emotional and nervous disorders, marital and family distress, drug or alcohol problems, financial or legal concerns, stress related problems, and crisis intervention to employees and their families" (Martini, 1991, p. 10). EAP services may be provided internally by employees of the district or by external organizations. In many instances, employees may have access to psychological counseling through the district's health care policy or may be eligible to receive financial counseling from other sources.

District-sponsored EAPs focus on job performance and restoring employees to full productivity, not on their problems. Through self-referral or supervisor referral, employees consult with an EAP counselor who, depending on personal training, counsels with the employees or refers them to an outside agency or professional. Districts using EAPs have found them to have a positive effect on employee morale, absenteeism, and productivity.

Wellness Programs.   The health of its employees is of obvious concern to the district. Many districts require a preemployment physical. Some pay for periodic physical examinations. In addition, a number of districts have initiated **wellness programs** designed to improve the overall health of employees. Such programs include not only health education and fitness programs and the use of school fitness centers and sports facilities, but also such affirmative steps as district-sponsored smoking cessation programs, early detection programs, fitness activities, nutrition and attention to special diets, and ongoing health-related assessment. Such wellness programs pay off in terms of both increased employee health and a reduction in absenteeism and work-related injuries (Agulnick, 2001). This in turn leads to reduced health insurance premiums for the district. As a result, a few districts have followed the lead of some businesses and offer employees a waiver of the employee deductible payment or actual cash payments for reduced claims or for maintaining positive health goals (e.g., reduced cholesterol, reduced weight, reduced blood pressure).

Subsidized Food Service.   Most school districts operate a food service program that not only is nonprofit, but also is subsidized by both local and federal contributions. As a result, an adult meal purchased in the school cafeteria costs far less than a comparable meal purchased at a commercial establishment. In addition, vending machines are typically located in office areas, shops, and schools. The profits from these machines often go to some type of employee benefit or fund.

Real Estate Subsidies.   As reported in Chapter 8, in an attempt to recruit and retain qualified employees, at least one state and a growing number of school districts are using various strategies to assist present or prospective employees in securing affordable housing. This has included not only working with banks and other businesses to secure affordable housing and low-interest loans for employees, but also actually providing funds toward the purchase of a home (e.g., Baltimore) or providing subsidized housing (e.g., San Francisco).

Child Care Services.   The growing demand for child care has led many districts to add this service to their employee compensation program. Such services may be provided through a child care center operated by the district that enrolls children of both employees and students. A popular alternative is to include child care as one of the benefits in a flexible benefit plan such as those discussed in the following section.

Flexible Benefits Plans

Because each individual has different needs, no fixed compensation plan will satisfy everyone. Young married workers are interested in maternity or paternity benefits and tuition reimbursements, whereas older employees are more interested in retirement benefits. Families with two wage earners do not require duplicated benefits and services from each employer. Recognizing the differing needs and interests of employees, many school districts now offer a **flexible benefits plan,** sometimes called a cafeteria plan, that allows employees to choose, within a fixed dollar allotment and legal requirements, the combination of benefits and services that best meets their needs and life-styles. Many districts have found that the cafeteria plan allows them to provide employees with meaningful choices among an array of benefit options while controlling costs. Research has shown that employees appreciate the choice provided by flexible benefits plans (Meyer, 2000). In fact, flexible benefits plans seem to particularly fit the culture of knowledge-work organizations such as schools, which are "staffed largely by highly educated professionals who like to make decisions for themselves" (Odden & Conley, 1992, p. 79).

Before involving the employee in the selection of benefits and services, the employer must identify which benefits and services will be made available, the cost of each benefit and service, and the total permissible cost for the entire program. Benefits required by the government must be included. In one of the most common flexible benefits plan arrangements, referred to as a core-plus option plan, a common core of benefits (e.g., retirement, health, group life, disability) is offered with a menu of optional benefits from which the employee may choose. Most plans allow the employee to not only choose among optional benefits, but also among several levels of coverage for the core benefits: for example, 50% or 60% of pay for long-term disability; a $250 or a $500 deductible PPO; or $50,000, $100,000, or $200,000 life insurance.

The best way to determine which other benefits or services to offer is by an employee preference survey that requires respondents to rank their benefit choices among a number of options (Henderson, 1994). It is incumbent on the human resources office to provide adequate information and counseling about each option, both at the time that the preference survey is conducted and at the time that employee selections are made, so that employees can make informed decisions in their own best interests. Informed decision making also reduces the desire or need to change selections and the associated administrative costs. Online applications for cafeteria plans are increasingly available; they provide "a handy, easy way for employees to enroll, review plan options, make account inquiries and transactions, consult customer service, and determine the effect of specific choices on pay" (Burzawa, 2001, p. 28).

The larger the school district is, the more benefits that can be included in the flexible benefits plan. Some employee benefits specialists maintain that flexible benefits plans are most effective for school districts with 500 or more employees. This is true for the following reason:

> Since employees are free to elect whatever benefits they please, it's possible that a specific benefit would be chosen by only a small percentage of employees. And because the cost of those benefits is averaged over the number of employees likely to use them, the per person cost could be prohibitively high unless there is a large group of potential users. (Johnson, 1987, p. 30)

While almost any benefit chosen by employees could be included in the flexible benefits plan, among the more common, beyond the core, are vision coverage, accidental death and dismemberment, cancer coverage, and long-term care insurance. Other options that may be included on an after-tax basis are group homeowners and auto insurance, and, more recently, funeral and burial coverage and pet insurance (Meyer, 2000). Whatever benefits are offered, it is incumbent on human resources to ensure that they equitably address the interests of both single and married employees, older and younger employees, certificated and classified employees, and higher-salaried and lower-salaried employees.

A second type of flexible benefits plan found in school districts is the flexible spending account or a ZEBRA (zero balance reimbursement account). This type of plan takes advantage of Section 125 of the Internal Revenue Code, which allows an employee to place a portion of before-tax income into a special account, held by the employer, that can be used to pay for such allowable expenses as the employee's share of health, dental, or life insurance deductible or coinsurance payments and child or elder care. Employees must decide at the beginning of the tax year how much will be placed in the account. Then, as expenses are incurred, employees submit claims and are reimbursed.

As the example in Table 12.4 illustrates, the benefits of this plan are not only the flexibility it provides employees, but also the increased take-home pay. One drawback to the plan, at least from the employee's perspective, is that according to IRS rules all funds in the account must be used by the end of the tax year or they are forfeited. The amount forfeited, however, may still be less than what the employee would have paid in taxes. A second rule states that funds from one category cannot be used to pay expenses for another category. If, for example, near year end an employee has not used all the funds in the health care account, but has used all the funds placed in the elder care account, funds cannot be transferred from the health care account to the elder care account.

When the school district operates a flexible benefits plan, it is the responsibility of the human resources office to cost each benefit and determine the total value of benefits. It must also ensure compliance with Internal Revenue standards and establish schedules for enrollment and changes. Perhaps most important, the human resources office must assume a greater role in employee benefit counseling and in assisting employees to estimate the amounts to be placed in the flexible spending account.

TABLE 12.4
Savings with a Zero Balance
Reimbursements Account
(ZEBRA)

	Without ZEBRA	With ZEBRA
Annual salary	$30,000	$30,000
ZEBRA account contribution (for health and dental insurance and child care)		3,750
Taxable income	30,000	26,250
Federal income tax (15%)	4,500	3,937
State income tax (5%)	1,500	1,313
Social Security (7.65%)	2,295	2,008
Health and dental insurance	750	
Child care	3,000	
Net pay	$17,955	$18,992
Annual savings		$1,037

SUMMARY

The compensation of personnel is the largest item in the school district budget. Traditionally, the direct compensation of teachers has been accomplished through the use of the single salary schedule based solely on preparation and experience. However, with the renewed public interest in improved productivity, attention has focused on a number of compensation strategies designed to overcome the flatness of current compensation systems, promote the view of teaching as a career, and promote the knowledge, skills, and competencies needed by the organization. Likewise, over the last two decades school districts have increasingly abandoned fixed salary schedules for administrators and adopted schedules that are based on factors such as responsibility of position, experience, professional preparation, length of contract year, and performance.

Indirect compensation represents the fastest growing area in the compensation of employees. The growth and strength of unions have contributed to this increase, as has the realization by employers that they must provide increased benefits to remain competitive in the labor market. Flexible benefits plans are an approach to the provision of indirect compensation that has gained popularity in business and industry and is making greater inroads in education. This approach allows employees to select, within a dollar limit, the mix of benefits best meeting their individual circumstances.

Through its compensation program the district aims to attract and retain competent personnel, motivate them toward optimum and specific performance, promote skills and competencies, reinforce organizational goals and structures, and maintain control of budgetary expenditures. These goals can be accomplished only if the district and the human resources administrator, in particular, recognize and implement a compensation program that is well planned, internally fair and equitable, and externally competitive.

DISCUSSION QUESTIONS

1. Discuss the factors that directly or indirectly determine the compensation program established by a school district. How has each factor affected the compensation program in your school district or a school district with which you are familiar?
2. How do merit pay and incentive pay differ? Describe any such programs in operation in your area or state. How successful are they? If none are operating in your area or state, describe those you have read or heard about.
3. Survey three districts and compare their indirect compensation programs. Also, determine which three elements have been the most recent additions to each program.
4. Compare the advantages and disadvantages of a flexible benefits plan with those of a fixed compensation program.

CASE STUDIES

12.1 Comparable Worth

The Penzville High School Marching Band has won this year's regional band contest and has been asked to march in the Magnolia Bowl Parade on New Year's Day. Phil Smith has been the band director for 5 years and has given unlimited time and energy to transforming the band from a handful of stragglers to a full-size band and the pride of Penzville. Just before the Thanksgiving holiday, Phil asks the principal to increase his extracurricular pay for serving as band director to equal that of the head football coach. He argues that he puts in as much or more time as Doug Jones, the football coach, and that his students have been more successful. From Phil's conversation and tone, it is clear that he has given this matter a lot of thought and that he is not going to take no for an answer.

Questions

1. Does Phil Smith appear to have a legitimate comparable worth claim?
2. To what extent, if any, should student success be an issue in this case?

3. How would you respond to Phil? How would you respond to the sponsor of the debate team, who made a similar request after the team won in a national competition?

12.2 ZEBRA Plan

The Rocky Point School Board has voted to implement a ZEBRA benefits plan. A survey of employees has shown that employees' preferences are distributed among an array of possible benefits and services. To include all of them would result in high per person costs.

Questions

1. What process should be used to decide the benefits and services to be included?
2. Should specific benefits (e.g., health, medical, and dental insurance) be required in order to lower per person costs for all employees, or should employees be allowed to choose whatever they please as long as they are willing to pay the cost from their ZEBRA?
3. Is it fair for the school district to keep the funds from unexpended ZEBRAs? How should these funds be used?

12.3 Incentives or Teachers?

Plainview School District No. 12 has adopted site-based management for its 15 schools. Authority for many curricular, instructional, budgetary, and personnel matters now resides with the administrator and a school council at each school. The school council is made up of parent representatives and representatives from the school staff.

Like most communities in the state, Plainview's economy has suffered during the current recession, and the school district is not anticipating any increase in funding for next year. Because of enrollment increases, however, Digrazzi Elementary School has been allotted two additional instructional positions for next year under the funding and staffing formula.

Digrazzi serves a lower socioeconomic neighborhood and in the last few years has experienced declining test scores and a high teacher turnover rate. During the last year the staff discussed a variety of measures to tackle these problems, including incentive pay plans that would reward teachers based on improvements in student achievement.

When the Digrazzi staff learns that funding has been authorized to hire two additional teachers, a formal proposal is made to the school council to forego the hires. The proposal suggests that the money allocated for the hires be used to fund an incentive pay program that would reward teachers for increased student achievement.

Questions

1. How would you respond to the proposal if you were a member of the school council?
2. What are the possible positive and negative implications for students?
3. What is the possible impact or reaction of students and staff in the other schools in the district?
4. What alternatives to hiring two additional teachers might you propose that would improve the working conditions or welfare of the teachers at Digrazzi?

REFERENCES

Adkison, J., & McKenzie, C. M. (1990). Compensating school administrators. The impact of personal and organizational characteristics on administrator salaries. Paper presented at the annual meeting of the American Educational Research Association, Boston.

Agulnick, S. (September, 2, 2001). Wellness plans good business for companies. *Arizona Republic*, D2.

Ballou, D., & Podgursky, M. (2001). Defining merit: Let the market decide. *Education Matters, 1*(1), 16, 19, 21, 23, 25.

Beebe, R. J. (1983). Determining the competitiveness of school district salaries. *NASSP Bulletin, 67*(461), 84–92.

Bray, J. W., French, M. T., Bowland, B. J., & Dunlap, L. J. (1996). The cost of employee assistance programs (EAPs): Findings from seven case studies. *Employee Assistance Quarterly, 11*(4), 1–19.

Broughman, S. P., & Rollefson, M. R. (2000). *Teacher supply in the United States: Sources of newly hired teachers in public and private schools, 1987–1988 to 1993–94.* Washington, DC: U.S. Department of Education, National Center for Education Statistics.

Brown, F. (2000). School-based financial merit programs for academic performance. *School Business Affairs, 66*(6), 32–36.

Burzawa, S. (February 2001). Online developments in cafeteria plan administration. *Employee Benefit Plan Review,* 28–30.

Castetter, W. B., & Young, I. P. (2001). *The personnel function in educational administration* (7th ed.). New York: Macmillan.

Chambers, J. (1996). *Patterns of teacher compensation.* Washington, DC: U.S. Department of Education, National Center for Education Statistics.

Chambers, J. G. (1999). Pattern of variation in the salaries of school personnel: What goes on behind the cost of index numbers? *Journal of Education Finance, 25,* 255–280.

Cohn, E., & Geske, T. E. (1990). *The economics of education* (3rd. ed.). New York: Pergamon.

Danielson, C. (1996). *Enhancing professional practice: A framework for teaching.* Alexandria, VA: Association for Supervision and Curriculum Development.

Darling-Hammond, L. (1999). *Solving the demands of teacher supply, demand, and standards: How we* can ensure a competent, caring, and qualified teacher for every child. New York: Columbia University, National Commission on Teaching for America's Future.

Educational Research Service. (1987). *Methods of scheduling salaries for teachers.* Arlington, VA: Author.

Educational Research Service. (1991a). *Extra pay for extra duties of teachers* (5th ed.). Arlington, VA: Author.

Educational Research Service. (1991b). *Methods of scheduling salaries for principals* (4th ed.). Arlington, VA: Author.

Educational Research Service. (1995a). Fringe benefits for administrators in public schools, 1994–95. *National survey of fringe benefits in public schools* (Part 2). Arlington, VA: Author.

Educational Research Service. (1995b). Fringe benefits for teachers in public schools, 1994–95. *National survey of fringe benefits in public schools* (Part 3). Arlington, VA: Author.

Equal Pay Act of 1963 (P.L. 88-38), 29 U.S.C.A. 206.

Fandray, D. (2000). HR online: Web-based portals put employees in charge. *Workforce, 79*(10), 54–61.

Firestone, W. A. (1994). Redesigning teacher salary systems for educational reform. *American Educational Research Journal, 31,* 549–574.

Flippo, E. B. (1980). *Personnel management* (5th ed.). New York: McGraw-Hill.

Foster, C. W. (1960). *Wage and salary administration: A handbook for school business officials.* Chicago: Research Corporation of the Association of School Business Officials.

Foulkes, F. K., & Livernash, E. R. (1989). *Human resources management: Text and cases* (2nd ed.). Upper Saddle River, NJ: Prentice Hall.

Fox, J. E., & Certo, J. (1999). *Recruiting and retaining teachers: A review of the literature.* Richmond, VA: Metropolitan Educational Research Consortium.

Gleason, B. (2000). Pay for performance. *Educational Leadership, 57*(5), 82–83.

Greene, J. E. (1971). *School personnel administrator.* New York: Chilton.

Gursky, D. (April 22, 1992). Program that rewards senior teachers stirs flap in Philadelphia. *Education Week,* p. 8.

Gursky, D. (2001). Finding and training those 2 million teachers. *Education Digest, 66*(6), 17–23.

Hauer, M. (2000). Tax sheltered annuities—403(b) plans: Solving the mystery. *School Business Affairs, 66*(6), 26–27.

Henderson, R. I. (1994). *Compensation management: Rewarding performance* (5th ed.). Upper Saddle River, NJ: Prentice Hall.

HMO enrollment on the decline: PPOs, POS plans gain in membership and satisfaction ratings. (March 2001). *Employee Benefit Plan Review, 17,* 20–21.

Johns, R. L., Morphet, E. L., & Alexander, K. (1983). *The economics and financing of education.* Upper Saddle River, NJ: Prentice Hall.

Johnson, R. (1987). Flexible fringe benefit plans save you money and keep employees happy. *American School Board Journal, 174*(5), 30–31.

Kanman, J. (March 23, 2001). School enrollment equals 1970s. *Arizona Republic,* p. A 1.

Kelley, C., Odden, A., Milanowski, A., & Heneman, H. (2000). *The motivational effects of school-based performance awards.* Philadelphia: University of Pennsylvania, Graduate School of Education, Consortium for Policy Research in Education.

King, R. A. (1979). Toward a theory of wage determination for teachers: Factors which determine variation in salaries among districts. *Journal of Education Finance, 4,* 358–369.

Kitchen, W. E. (1983). The relationship between local salary enrichment, local wealth, and selected socioeconomic variables in Texas. Unpublished doctoral dissertation, Texas Tech University, Lubbock.

LaFee, S. (2000). Linking teacher pay to student scores. *School Administrator, 57*(10), 14–20.

Martini, G. R., Jr. (1991). Wellness programs: Preventive medicine to reduce health care costs. *School Business Affairs, 57*(6), 8–11.

McMahon, W. W. (1994). *Interstate cost adjustment.* Washington, DC: U.S. Department of Education, National Center for Education Statistics.

Meyer, J. J. (2000). The future of flexible benefit plans. *Employee Benefits Journal, 25*(2), 3–7.

Nelson, F. H. (1994). *An interstate cost-of-living index and state poverty thresholds.* Washington, DC: American Federation of Teachers.

Odden, A. (2001). Defining merit: Rewarding experience. *Education Matters, 1*(1), 16, 18, 20, 22, 24.

Odden, A. (2000a). New and better forms of teacher compensation are possible. *Phi Delta Kappan, 81,* 361–366.

Odden, A. (2000b). Paying teachers for performance. *School Business Affairs, 66*(6), 28–31.

Odden, A., & Conley, S. (1992). Restructuring teacher compensation systems. In A. Odden (Ed.), *Rethinking school finance: An agenda for the 1990s* (pp. 41–96). San Francisco: Jossey-Bass.

Odden, A., & Kelley, C. (1997). *Paying teachers for what they know and do: New and smarter compensation strategies.* Thousand Oaks, CA: Corwin Press.

Plauny, L. (1994). Don't get compressed: The secret to compressing salary schedules. *School Business Affairs, 60,* 43–45.

Protsik, J. (1995). *History of teacher pay and incentive problems.* Paper presented at the CPRE Conference on Teacher Compensation, Washington, DC, November 1994.

Rebore, R. W. (2001). *Personnel administration in education: A management approach* (6th ed.). Upper Saddle River, NJ: Prentice Hall.

Risher, H. (2000). Paying for employee competence. *School Administrator, 57*(10), 21–24.

Sherman, A. W., Jr., & Bohlander, G. W. (1992). *Managing human resources* (9th ed.). Cincinnati, OH: South-Western.

Sultanik, J. T. (2000). Bonus pay for teachers. *American School Board Journal, 187*(2), 34–36.

Symonds, W. C. (March 19, 2001). How to fix America's schools. *Business Week*, 66–72, 75–76.

Urbanski, A., & Erskine, R. (2000). School reform, TURN, and teacher compensation. *Phi Delta Kappan, 81*, 367–370.

U.S. Department of Education, National Center for Education Statistics. (2001). *Projections of Education Statistics to 2011*. Washington, DC: author.

U.S. Department of Labor, Bureau of Labor Statistics. (December, 1996). *Compensation and Working Conditions, 1*(3), Table 15.

Walden, M. L., & Newmark, C. M. (1995). Interstate variations in teacher salaries. *Economics of Education Review, 14*, 395–402.

Williams, A. R. (2001). Principals' salaries, 2000–2001. *Principal, 80*(5), 52–56.

13 *The Support Personnel Program*

Learning Objectives

After reading this chapter, you will be able to:

■ Identify the most common approaches to job analysis.

■ Describe the process used to establish salary schedules for classified personnel.

■ List the most common preemployment conditions for classified personnel.

■ Discuss the goals of the employee induction program.

■ Distinguish between the training approaches used in on-the-job training and off-the-job training.

■ Describe the objectives of the classified personnel appraisal system.

The major emphasis in any discussion of school human resources administration is on the certificated personnel, those individuals who are required to have some certificate of qualification from the state in order to teach, supervise, counsel, or administer. These individuals constitute the numerical majority of people in a school system, and their salaries account for about two-thirds of the school district budget, so the attention given to them seems justified. Nevertheless, a very important group of employees cannot be overlooked in any consideration of the administration of human resources in education: that group of employees known as classified, noncertificated, or support personnel. This group of employees makes up 34% of the full-time staff of the public schools and is composed of such employees as secretarial and clerical personnel, instructional and library–media aides, security officers, transportation staff, food services employees, plant operation and maintenance workers, and health and recreational staff (U.S. Department of Education, 2001). More important than simply their numbers, support staff "are assuming responsibility for more complex tasks in schools than ever before" (Zepeda, 2000, p. 42) and are vital to the successful operation of the school district and to promoting a healthy, safe, and productive school environment. The school bus driver is often the first school employee that the child sees each day. Secretaries, aides, and other support staff can make students feel significant and wanted or scorned and rejected (Welch & Daniel, 1997).

The status of classified or support personnel varies widely among the states. Some states recognize certain groups of support personnel for such purposes as tenure or retirement. State or local civil service arrangements cover all noncertificated personnel in some states. In yet other states, local school districts are given complete authority and responsibility for the establishment and administration of the support personnel system.

Whatever plan is in operation for the administration of the support personnel program, certain human resources functions and activities must be performed. Some of these functions (e.g., recruitment, selection, and employee benefits) have been discussed elsewhere in this text, primarily in regard to certified personnel. This chapter will discuss these functions as they differ from those in the certificated personnel system and will discuss other activities and problems specific to the support personnel program. The first section presents the development of a classification system, the necessary first step in establishing a classified personnel system. Other sections include salary determination, recruitment, selection, staff development, and performance appraisal.

DEVELOPMENT OF A CLASSIFICATION SYSTEM

Unlike certificated personnel, who represent a more limited range of job categories (i.e., teachers, administrators, counselors, nurses, librarians), classified personnel represent a broad spectrum of employees with varying levels of skills and responsibilities. For this reason, in all but the smallest districts, it is necessary to differentiate among positions on the basis of duties and responsibilities. This can be done only after a job analysis. Following the job analysis, positions with similar duties and responsibilities can be grouped into common classes. This classification plan, as it is called, provides the foundation for the entire personnel program. The information about positions used to develop the classification plan and the classes subsequently established provide the basis for employee recruitment, selection, assignment, and evaluation, as well as salary determination.

Job Analysis

The development of the classification system begins with **job analysis**. As noted in Chapter 8, job analysis is the process of collecting, organizing, and evaluating information relating to the responsibilities and tasks associated with the successful performance of a specific job. The data collected serve a number of human resource functions, such as recruitment, selection, and performance appraisal. "A job analysis identifies a job's activities, behaviors, tasks, performance standards, the context in which the job is performed, and the personal requirements necessary to perform a job, such as personality, interests, physical characteristics, aptitudes, and job related knowledge and skills. Each position is also analyzed in regard to its relationship to other positions in the organization" (Pynes, 1997, p. 73).

TABLE 13.1
Department of Labor Worker
Functions

Data	People	Things
0 Synthesizing	0 Mentoring	0 Setting Up
1 Coordinating	1 Negotiating	1 Precision Working
2 Analyzing	2 Instructing	2 Operating–Controlling
3 Compiling	3 Supervising	3 Driving–Operating
4 Computing	4 Diverting	4 Manipulating
5 Copying	5 Persuading	5 Tending
6 Comparing	6 Speaking–Signaling	6 Feeding–Offbearing
	7 Serving	7 Handling
	8 Taking Instruction and Helping	

The U.S. Department of Labor (1991) job analysis procedure suggests that the following four dimensions be included in a job analysis: (1) *worker functions*, what the worker does in relation to data, people, and things (see Table 13.1), (2) *work fields*, the methodologies and techniques utilized, (3) MPSMS, the *materials* being processed, the *products* being made, the *subject matter* being dealt with, and the *services* being rendered, and (4) *worker characteristics*, the worker attributes that contribute to successful job performance (education, specific vocational preparation, aptitudes, temperaments, interests, physical demands, and environmental conditions). The analysis of the physical demands and environmental conditions is particularly important in meeting the challenge of the Americans with Disabilities Act (ADA). An example of a data collection form used to make this analysis is provided in Figure 13.1.

The four most common approaches to collecting the data needed for job analysis are (1) questionnaires, (2) observation, (3) interviews, and (4) employee diaries. A *job analysis questionnaire* is designed to elicit the employee's own description and perception of the job, is usually standardized, and consists primarily of checklists or items to be rated. It seeks information relative to the type and number of tasks performed, the frequency with which the task is performed, the percentage of time spent on each task, the level of skill required, the title of the position(s) from which supervision is received and over which supervision is given, the equipment operated, the experience required, and any formal education, training, or license required. Questionnaires provide an inexpensive way to gather large amounts of data in a short period of time. However, since it is virtually impossible for any questionnaire to capture all job elements, they often suffer from inaccuracy and incompleteness. They also provide no opportunity for follow-up and clarification. And, because they are often very long, employees often delay returning or fail to return the questionnaire.

A popular worker-oriented, as opposed to job-oriented, questionnaire that lends itself to quantitative statistical input is the Position Analysis Questionnaire (PAQ) (McCormick, Jeanneret, & Mecham, 1989). The PAQ

ID No. _____

Physical Demands

Comments

Strength

Position
- Standing _____ %
- Walking _____ %
- Sitting _____ %

Weight/Force

	N	O	F	C
Lifting				
Carrying				
Pushing				
Pulling				

Controls: Hand-Arm _____ Foot-Leg _____

Strength Level: _____

- Climbing
- Balancing
- Stooping
- Kneeling
- Crouching
- Crawling
- Reaching
- Handling
- Fingering
- Feeling
- Talking
- Hearing
- Tasting/Smelling
- Near Acuity
- Far Acuity
- Depth Perception
- Accommodation
- Color Vision
- Field of Vision

Environmental Conditions

Comments

1. Exposure to Weather
2. Extreme Cold
3. Extreme Heat
4. Wet and/or Humid
5. Noise Intensity Level
6. Vibration
7. Atmospheric Conditions
8. Moving Mechanical Parts
9. Electric Shock
10. High, Exposed Places
11. Radiation
12. Explosives
13. Toxic/Caustic Chemicals
14. Other Environmental Conditions

Protective Clothing or Personal Devices _____

Analyst _____ Date _____

Field Center Reviewer _____ Date _____

Additional Reviewer _____ Title _____

FIGURE 13.1

Data Collection Form for Physical Demands and Enviromental Conditions

Source: U.S. Department of Labor. (1991). *The Revised Handbook for Analyzing Jobs.* Washington, DC: Government Printing Office.

consists of 194 job elements, which are categorized as (1) information input (where and how the employee gets the information used on the job), (2) mental processes (the reasoning, planning, decision making, and information processing involved in the job), (3) work output (the physical activities performed and the tools or devices used), (4) relationships with other persons required to perform the job, (5) job context (the physical and social environment in which the work is performed), and (6) other job characteristics. The PAQ provides quantitative data that can be computer analyzed to create a job profile. The job profile created can then be compared to standard job profiles of job families and similar jobs assigned to the appropriate job family.

A helpful practice in conducting job analysis and writing the job descriptions that follow is to store the job profile data, as well as task inventories, activities inventories, glossaries, and other data relative to job duties and responsibilities, on the computer. This information can be very helpful to the analyst, the job incumbent, and the supervisor in the development and review of completed job analyses and job descriptions to ensure that no tasks or activities have been overlooked and that they have been accurately described.

Employees may also be asked to record their work activities, time spent on them, and how performed in a *diary*. Entries are made in the diary at specified times during the work shift (e.g., every hour or half-hour) and are normally kept for a period of two to four weeks (Sherman & Bohlander, 1992). The diary method can be a useful method for analyzing positions that do not lend themselves to observation, such as many managerial or administrative positions. However, the diary method is the most intrusive method of job analysis, requiring significant time and work on the part of the incumbent (De Cenzo & Robbins, 1996) if the information is to be recorded clearly and in the level of detail needed for the analysis. The use of a lightweight tape recorder can be helpful if using this method. The employee can describe work activities as they happen, and the tape can be transcribed later by the job analyst (Henderson, 1994).

Observation of the job incumbent is conducted by a trained observer who records incumbent activities and interactions. Observation as a method of job analysis is most appropriate for jobs in which activities or behaviors are readily observable, rather than jobs involving primarily intellectual or cognitive processes (Pynes, 1997). Observation should include a representative sample of job activities. And it should be made clear to the employee being observed that the job is being assessed, not the person. Observation may be done in person by a trained, inconspicuous observer, or the observation may be videotaped and reviewed at a later date by the job analyst or by the job analyst and the employee. The latter provides the opportunity for the analyst to ask the employee questions about various aspects of the job.

One observation technique, known as Function Job Analysis (FJA), builds on the Department of Labor (DOL) methodology by adding functions to the worker functions (things, data, and people) and by including several additional scales: the *scale of worker instructions*, which identifies the levels of discretion exercised by the employee and the extent of instruction necessary for the employee to perform the job, and scales of *reasoning development*, *mathematical development*, and *language development*, which measure the extent to which these abilities are necessary for the worker to perform the job (Fine & Getkate, 1995). A functional job analysis distinguishes between the essential and marginal job functions and identifies the physical and mental characteristics necessary to perform the essential functions. Such an analysis helps both the district and the potential applicant to determine if the applicant can perform the essential job functions with or without reasonable accommodation and can be critical in ensuring ADA compliance (National School Boards Association, 1996).

The most common approach to job analysis is the *interview*. Either an individual interview, in which one or more job incumbents are interviewed extensively, or a group interview, in which a number of job incumbents are interviewed simultaneously, can be used. Because the employee acts as the observer during the interview, activities and behaviors that would often not be observed can be reported, as well as those that occur over long time periods. In addition, because of the incumbent's knowledge of the job, the analyst gains information about the job that might not otherwise be available (Cascio, 1998). Interviews also have the advantage of being flexible and therefore usable to collect different kinds of information from a range of positions. It is also the only technique that provides for the interaction of the analyst and the job incumbent. This interaction allows the interviewer to learn more about the problems, challenges, and limitations associated with the position (Harvey & Bowin, 1996). However, the danger does exist that incumbents describe what has been done, rather than what should have been done, or may inflate the importance of particular tasks. To mitigate against these distortions, more than one incumbent or a supervisor familiar with the job should be interviewed. One example of a worksheet used by interviewers to obtain information about a job is provided in Figure 13.2.

The interview itself should be conducted in private with a minimum of distraction or interruption. The interview will typically last at least 1 hour. Some suggestions for conducting a successful job analysis interview come from Henderson (1994, pp. 165–166):

1. When only a select group or small number of incumbents are to be interviewed, ask the supervisor responsible for the job to select as an interviewee the individual who knows most about the job. (The supervisor should be careful not to select a self-serving flatterer. Another danger here is that the worker singled out by the manager may feel that social interactions with the work group are jeopardized. In that case, why not let the work group make the selection?)
2. Establish immediate rapport with the interviewee, introduce yourself, know the incumbent's name, speak in easily understood language, briefly review the purpose of the interview, and explain how the selection was made and what opportunity the incumbent will have to review the final report for accuracy and validity. Do not exhibit impatience if the interviewee is nervous or ill at ease.

1. Job title _____

   Department _____

   Date of interview _____

   From what information secured _____

2. Briefly describe the primary functions of the job: _____

3. Types of duties performed (check):
   ( ) Accounting.
   ( ) Answering telephone.
   ( ) Bookkeeping.
   ( ) Calculating.
   ( ) Checking work.
   ( ) Composing letters.
   ( ) Computing.
   ( ) Confidential work.
   ( ) Contact with others.
   ( ) Decision making.
   ( ) Duplicating.
   ( ) Filing.
   ( ) Opening mail.
   ( ) Posting.
   ( ) Supervising others.
   ( ) Tabulating.
   ( ) Transcribing.
   ( ) Typing.
   ( ) Serving as receptionist.
   ( ) Report writing.
   ( ) Routing materials.
   ( ) Taking shorthand.
   ( ) Other _____

4. Description of the individual duties:

Duty	Time Spent	Description (material and information handled)

   (NOTE: This part of the form would be expanded to full page depth.)

5. Minimum educational requirements of the job. State what you think is required:
   ( ) High school diploma preferred.
   ( ) High school diploma necessary.
   ( ) Business or technical.
   ( ) College degree.
   ( ) Graduate degree.

6. On-the-job experience required for full proficiency in this position:
   ( ) Two weeks.
   ( ) One month.
   ( ) Two months.
   ( ) Three to six months.
   ( ) One year.
   ( ) More than one year.

7. Does the work of this employee's position require the use of any machines or equipment?
   ( )Yes ( )No If yes, indicate kind of machines and equipment and extent of use.
   Kind: _____
   _____
   ( ) Occasional use   ( ) Frequent use
   ( ) Continuous use

8. Does this position require working with confidential data?
   ( ) Yes ( ) No   If yes, list data by type. For example, salary data, personnel records, etc.
   _____
   _____
   _____

9. Contact with others
   ( ) Contacts with peers and supervisor within department only.

FIGURE 13.2

Job Analysis Work Sheet

Source: The Job Analysis Work Sheet, *The School Personnel Management System*, National School Boards Association (Alexandria, VA), 1996: p. 144. Reprinted with permission.

( ) Routine contacts with other departments.

( ) Contacts with other departments requiring tact and judgment.

( ) Routine contacts with public.

( ) Contacts with superintendent and/or board, presenting data that may influence important decisions.

( ) Frequent contacts involving the carrying out of programs and schedules, requiring the influencing of others to obtain the desired results.

10. Supervisory responsibilities

( ) Assigning work.

( ) Checking work.

( ) Disciplining.

( ) Establishing methods.

( ) Settling grievances.

( ) Hiring.

( ) Planning.

( ) Setting quality standards.

( ) Setting quantity standards.

( ) Routing.

( ) Scheduling.

( ) Training others.

11. To what extent are judgments and initiative required to perform this job?

( ) Job requires close immediate supervision and detailed instructions.

( ) Job requires frequent guidance with all questions referred to supervisor.

( ) Job holder follows established practice on most duties, makes some decisions, and infrequently refers questions to supervisor.

( ) Job holder plans objectives, makes many decisions, infrequently refers specific cases to supervisor.

( ) Job holder works independently under general board policies.

12. Effect of errors by job holder

( ) Of minor inconvenience or consequence to organization.

( ) Could lead to moderate waste of time and money.

( ) Could lead to considerable waste of time and money.

( ) Could be critical to the well-being of the organization.

13. Remarks _____

_____

_____

_____

Date _____

Signature of interviewer _____

FIGURE 13.2
(continued)

3. When possible, use structured outlines (or forms) to obtain job information.... It may be helpful to give the interviewee a copy of the form to be completed and explain what is meant by a responsibility and duty and how you would like to have the task information presented. In most cases, the employee will soon recognize what is desired and will provide the information by using a verb and an object and stating the effect of the action and even the work aids used.

4. If possible, confine questions to one area at a time when asking more than one question. Always focus the discussion on what the incumbent does and the processes, work aids, materials, devices, tools, machines, and so on, required in the work activities. Differentiate between what the incumbent does and what the equipment produces. If the interviewee begins to stray from the subject, summarize the data collected to that point and then return to the subject.

    Give the incumbent sufficient time to ask additional questions to stimulate thought about infrequent assignments. At this point, it may be a good idea to give the interviewee an opportunity to complain. In this manner, the interviewer may discover hidden job issues. Always close the interview on a friendly note and express appreciation for the time and the effort spent on the interview.

5. After completing the interview, verify the job data. Normally, the interviewee's immediate supervisor is the best person to ask about accuracy. The supervisor will probably be able to interpret the interviewee's comments or clarify certain hazy terms or phrases.

In practice, no one approach to job analysis will be appropriate for analyzing all jobs in the district. Accurate and sufficient data for some positions may be generated by observation. For other positions, this is not the best approach. Because no one approach is superior or applicable to the analysis of all positions, districts often use a combination approach. For example, the DOL's job analysis process combines observation and interview. Often the questionnaire, observation, and interview are used together. In fact, observation can be used well with any other approach (Henderson, 1994). It is also common to use group interviews to clarify or reach consensus on points that emerged following the survey or observation of multiple incumbents.

The actual analysis of the support positions may be performed by a qualified district personnel specialist, or it may be necessary for the district to hire a personnel consultant specializing in job analysis or job audits. Regardless of who performs the analysis or the approach employed, the importance of the fundamental task cannot be overemphasized.

It is also important that the job analyses be periodically reviewed if they and the job descriptions that emanate from them are to remain valid. Jobs do not remain stable, but change to meet current demands. In some cases technological advances have reduced once difficult jobs requiring higher levels of education to jobs that can be performed by workers with only limited formal education, but with specific technical training. Since the passage of the Civil Rights Act of 1964, numerous court decisions have emphasized a concern that job requirements be relevant and not be unrealistically high.

Over time, job activities may also shift somewhat dramatically. These shifts should be reflected in changes in job descriptions and job specifications, as well as in job training programs (Cascio, 1998).

Job Classification

After all jobs have been analyzed, jobs with similar work requirements may be grouped into a common **job class**. Typical classes involving support personnel in school districts are custodial, clerical, technical, paraprofessional, professional, and managerial (NSBA, 1996). Positions within any one class may differ in experience and skill requirements or in degree of responsibility. For example, the custodial class might include a custodian I, custodian II, and head custodian. A good classification system "provides supervisors with a convenient basis for comparing employee performance ... [and] helps administrators identify overlapping duties, unnecessary levels of supervision, unclear delegations of authority, and inefficient separation of tasks or duties" (NSBA, 1996, p. 145).

The final classification plan must be adopted by the school board. If support personnel are covered by civil service arrangements, however, the classification plan may require the approval of the civil service commission prior to presentation and adoption by the board. The preparation of job descriptions follows board adoption.

Because school districts and the jobs that they support are rapidly changing, the classification system should be reviewed every 5 to 7 years. Such a review will help identify which positions should be upgraded, downgraded, or left unchanged. Obsolete classes (e. g., keypunch operator) may be abolished, while new ones (e. g., PC network specialist) may be created (Mosley, 1998). It may also reveal any misclassifications. Unfortunately, because classification studies are both labor intensive and expensive, it is not uncommon for school districts to go years without a thorough review of the classification system (Mosley, 1998). And for misclassified or underpaid employees even 1 year is unacceptable.

Job Descriptions

As discussed in Chapter 9, job descriptions are the most immediate products of the job analysis process and provide a written, detailed outline of the duties and responsibilities of a specific job. The job description should describe the job, not the person who holds or will hold the position. Job descriptions assist human resources administrators, potential employees, and present employees in understanding existing positions and role expectations. They also enhance employees' understanding of their roles by providing a concise statement of the duties and responsibilities expected, qualifications required, and relationships expected with other employees (Jordan, McKeown, Salmon, & Webb, 1985).

The descriptions of the essential and marginal job functions and physical requirements of the job are the most important sections of the job description in terms of compliance with the Americans with Disabilities Act and the determination of whether these can be accomplished with reasonable accommodation by the district. The essential functions of the job are those that, in the district's judgment, are intrinsic to the position. In determining the essential functions, the focus should be on the desired end, rather than on the means to accomplish it. This is because a person with a disability may be able to achieve the desired outcome with or without a reasonable accommodation, but in a manner different from a nondisabled person (Pynes, 1997). In one suit that was lost by the employer, the employer had required that each employee be able to use both arms when performing a particular task. One employee could not meet this requirement because his disability caused limited mobility in one arm. However, the court found that the essential function of the job was the ability to lift and carry a particular article (which he could do), not the ability to use both arms (Greenberg & Bello, 1992).

What happens to the job descriptions after they have been prepared depends in part on the existence, if any, of any union agreements or civil service contracts. That is, in areas of high unionization, agreements may call for union agreement on initial job descriptions or any alteration of existing job descriptions (Hack, Candoli, & Ray, 1998). Ultimately, of course, it is the school board that must approve all job descriptions and classifications.

WAGE AND SALARY DETERMINATION

Once the classification plan has been established, the district is ready to develop the salary schedule for its support employees. In some cases, support personnel may be paid an hourly wage. The principles involved in the establishment and maintenance of hourly wages are the same as those involved in the establishment and maintenance of a salary schedule. The following basic rules should be followed in the development of the salary schedule.

1. School district salaries should reflect prevailing wages in the community.
2. Benchmark positions should be established for each class.
3. The salary schedule should be equitable: placement of positions on the salary schedule should reflect accepted indications of difference.
4. The salary schedule should be internally consistent.
5. All classified positions should be on the schedule.
6. The salary schedule and all adjustments to it should be public and accessible.
7. Fringe benefits should be considered.
8. Provision should be made for periodic review.

Basic to the development of the support employee salary schedule are the principles that school district salaries should be fair and competitive. A fair salary structure emphasizes unbiased decisions and justice. Competitive pay emphasizes sufficiency to attract and retain quality employees (Sibon, 1992). In the past, school districts often assumed that the value of regular employment, vacations, and fringe benefits entitled them to pay somewhat less than business and industry. For most districts this is no longer a viable assumption. The security and protection offered by unions, combined with the expanded fringe benefits programs offered by many businesses, are equal or superior to that offered by most school districts. If the district is to attract and retain qualified, competent support personnel, it must be competitive with both the private sector and other public agencies in its compensation program.

Wage and Salary Studies

The determination of the prevailing wages and salaries in the community may be accomplished in several ways. In smaller communities the human resources administrator may contact the major employers in the district and solicit wage and salary information. This may be supplemented with data from public and private employment agencies and from state and federal departments of labor. In larger communities and districts, a more formal *wage and salary study* involving the solicitation of wage and salary information from other districts, agencies, industries, and professional organizations may be conducted. Whatever data are being used for comparison should take into consideration indirect compensation (employee benefits and services), and ultimately this must be considered as a part of the total compensation program. In fact, a calculation of the cost of indirect compensation per employee should be made and shared with all employees.

It is important that classified employees be involved in the wage and salary study. Agreement must be reached as to which jobs will be compared and which districts, agencies, or industries will be contacted. Clearly, balance must be maintained between any attempts by administration to contact primarily employers known to pay lower salaries and attempts by employees to suggest only those employers known to pay higher salaries.

The most common sources of wage and salary data are mailed questionnaires, telephone interviews, and survey data compiled by others. The major concerns related to using a mail survey are designing a form suitable for mailing, the time lost waiting for responses, and the low rate of return. Internet surveys are an effective and timely alternative to mail surveys and have been used by a growing number of districts to solicit salary data. Not only can survey responses be instantly transmitted, but in some instances districts have shared salary data files. Telephone interviews can also be an effective approach if care is taken to ensure that the most appropriate person is being interviewed, if sufficient time has been allotted for the interview, and if opportunity for preparation has been provided by scheduling the telephone interview in advance (Levesque, 1993). The use of survey data compiled by others, such as that compiled by the Educational Research Service (see Table 13.2), can be useful supplements (if current), but should not be used as the only source of data. Whatever approach is used, it is also important that the

TABLE 13.2

Mean Wages and Salaries
Paid Support Personnel in the
Public Schools, 1999–2000
Source: Educational Research
Service. (ERS). (2000). *Wages and
Salaries Paid Support Personnel in
Public Schools, 1999–2000, Part 3.*
Arlington, VA: Author.

Position	Mean Annual Salary/ Hourly Wage Rate
Central Office Positions	
Secretaries	$28,405
Accounting/payroll clerks	28,498
Typists/data entry clerks	22,853
School Building Level	
Secretaries	22,630
Library clerks	16,509
Teacher Aides	
Instructional	10.00/hr
Noninstructional	9.77/hr
Custodians (not engineers)	11.35/hr
Cafeteria Workers (not supervisors)	9.02/hr
School Bus Drivers	12.48/hr

results of the salary study be made available to employees for their response and reaction before any recommendations are made to the board.

Once wage and salary data have been collected, the next step is to evaluate the results. One approach is to calculate the mean (average) for each position surveyed. Another approach is to determine the median (middle) salary or wage for each position. Yet another common approach is to calculate the average after eliminating the highest and lowest salaries or wages. The rationale behind this approach is twofold: (1) there will always be employers who pay miserably low or unnecessarily high and thus should not be included, and (2) extremes often actually reflect a noncomparability in the jobs, justifying their exclusion (Levesque, 1993).

It is generally not possible to determine the prevailing wage or salary for each position in the district. It is necessary, therefore, to identify at least one position in each class as a **benchmark position**. A benchmark position is one whose duties and responsibilities are sufficiently common that it will be found in other districts as well as in many businesses and industries. Once the prevailing wage or salary has been determined for the benchmark position, it becomes the basis for pay determinations for the other positions in the class in terms of their relationship to the benchmark position.

Establishing the Salary Schedule

Establishing the proper relationship between the benchmark position and all other positions in a class is primarily a consideration of equity and contributory worth. Among the factors to be considered are (1) education or training requirements, (2) license requirements, (3) experience requirements, (4) skills requirements, (5) number of employees supervised, (6) number and range of responsibilities assigned, and (7) decision making allowed and required. Ultimately, each position is assigned to a specific hourly, weekly, or monthly wage (the flat-rate pay approach) or, more commonly for nonexempt positions (positions subject to overtime provisions), to the pay-grade plan in which each position is assigned to a specific pay grade with a predetermined number of steps within the grade (Levesque, 1993). In the pay-grade example in Table 13.3, separate salary schedules have been created for the various classes of employees within the overall pay plan for classified employees.

The establishment of differentials between the grades and the steps in each grade is a matter of internal consistency. The benchmark position for each salary grade should be within one step (on a five-step schedule) of the average. A common salary differential between steps in a grade is 4% to 5%. The differentials between grades should also be uniform. The 4% to 5% differential is also the common differential used between grades on school district salary schedules for support personnel.

The salary schedule should also recognize length of service. This can be accomplished by adopting a schedule that has five or more steps for each grade or range. The employee advances from one step to another after predetermined periods of service.

Since exempt positions are normally paid on a flat weekly, biweekly, or monthly basis and are often paid more than nonexempt hourly employees, many districts use a separate salary schedule for salaried employees. This schedule may also be constructed with salary steps that recognize length of service or merit advancements (Levesque, 1993).

All support positions should be included on the wage or salary schedule. No position should be considered too high or too low, and no differential treatment should be given. Authority on final adoption of the salary schedule is given to the school board. The salary schedule adopted should not only be made public, as is required in most jurisdictions, but also be distributed and made easily available to employees and other interested parties.

Finally, provision should be made for periodic review of the salary schedule. Such review should consider not only data obtained from salary studies, but also data relative to the cost of living. In periods of inflation the cost of living can rise rapidly, and unless consideration is given to periodic adjustments based on some indicator of price inflation, school district employees can fall behind their counterparts in other agencies and businesses. Whereas annual review of the master salary schedule would be most desirable, it is not uncommon for salary negotiations to fix salaries for periods of 2 years or more, making formal annual review unnecessary.

RECRUITMENT

The goal of any school district support personnel recruitment program, as with any personnel recruitment program, is the identification of sufficient qualified applicants to meet the personnel needs of the district. Since the

TABLE 13.3
San Marino Unified School District 2000-01 Classified Salary Schedule: Hourly Pay

Job Title	Range	Steps 1	2	3	4	5
Clerical/Secretarial						
District Receptionist/Office Assistant	26	$11.33	$11.94	$12.56	$13.23	$13.92
Office Assistant	26	11.33	11.94	12.56	13.23	13.92
School Office Assistant	26	11.33	11.94	12.56	13.23	13.92
High School Registrar	31	12.79	13.46	14.19	14.93	15.72
Asst. Principal's Secretary	33	13.42	14.13	14.88	15.67	16.48
Department Secretary	33	13.42	14.13	14.88	15.67	16.48
Counseling Secretary	33	13.42	14.13	14.88	15.67	16.48
School Admin. Assistant	35	14.13	14.88	15.67	16.48	17.37
Administrative Assistant	35	13.42	14.13	14.88	15.67	16.48
Fiscal						
Accounting Clerk	26	11.33	11.94	12.56	13.23	13.92
ASB Accounting/Office/Assistant	29	12.22	12.86	13.55	14.27	15.03
ASB Accounting Technician/High School	32	13.10	13.81	14.53	15.28	16.10
Accounting Assistant	35	13.42	14.13	14.88	15.67	16.48
Fiscal Accounting Technician/Receivables	35	13.42	14.13	14.88	15.67	16.48
Fiscal Accounting Technician/Payables	36	14.44	15.20	16.01	16.85	17.77
Payroll Technician	37	14.85	15.61	16.44	17.32	18.24
Food Services						
Food Service Worker	16	8.78	9.23	9.73	10.27	10.80
Elementary Kitchen Manager	20	9.73	10.27	10.80	11.36	11.97
Cook/Baker	22	10.24	10.79	11.34	11.96	12.61
High School Kitchen Manager	25	11.08	11.65	12.28	12.92	13.60
Central Kitchen Manager	30	12.47	13.13	13.84	14.57	15.32
Grounds						
Grounds Maintenance Worker	31	12.79	13.46	14.19	14.93	15.72
Lead Grounds Maint. Worker	35	13.42	14.13	14.88	15.67	16.48
Athletic Facilities Maintenance Technician	38	15.20	16.02	16.87	17.77	18.70
Health						
Health Services Coordinator	33	13.42	14.13	14.88	15.67	16.48
Instructional						
Instructional Assistant 1-Classroom	24	10.76	11.33	11.94	12.56	13.23
Instructional Assistant 1-Physical Education	24	11.08	11.65	12.28	12.92	13.60
Instructional Assistant II-ELD	26	11.33	11.94	12.56	13.23	13.92
Instructional Assistant III-Special Education	27	11.58	12.20	12.84	13.53	14.25
Instructional Assistant IV-Special Education	28	11.83	12.47	13.13	13.84	14.56
Library/Instructional						
Instructional Specialist I-Library/Media	24	11.08	11.65	12.28	12.92	13.60
Instructional Specialist II-Elementary Library/Media	26	11.33	11.94	12.56	13.23	13.92
Instructional Specialist III-Middle School Lib./Media	27	11.58	12.20	12.84	13.53	14.25
Instructional Specialist V-High School Library/Media	32	13.10	13.81	14.53	15.28	16.10

TABLE 13.3
(continued)

Job Title	Range	1	2	Steps 3	4	5
Maintenance						
Skilled Maintenance Worker	38	$15.20	$16.02	$16.87	$17.77	$18.70
Building Trades Technician	40	15.98	16.81	17.70	18.64	19.63
Lead Building Trades Technician	44	17.66	18.59	19.59	20.62	21.70
Operations						
Custodian	28	11.83	12.47	13.13	13.84	14.56
Day Custodian	30	12.47	13.13	13.84	14.57	15.32
Night Lead Custodian	32	13.10	13.81	14.53	15.28	16.10
Security						
Campus Security	27	11.58	12.20	12.84	13.53	14.25
Student Services						
Attendance Technician	29	13.42	14.13	14.88	15.67	16.48
Registrar	31	12.79	13.46	14.19	14.93	15.72
Drivers						
Warehouse Worker/Delivery Driver I	29	13.42	14.13	14.88	15.67	16.48
Warehouse Worker Delivery Driver II	31	12.79	13.46	14.19	14.93	15.72

Source: San Marino Unified School District (2001). *2000–2001 Classified Salary Schedule.*

classified service requires a staff with more varied skills and background than the certificated service, their recruitment is more varied and can often be more difficult. The importance of sound recruitment policies and practices cannot be overemphasized. Not only are they critical in maintaining employee morale and faith in the board's and administration's commitment to equity and fairness, but, given the costs associated with the high turnover rate that inevitably follows poor recruitment, they are also necessary cost-saving measures.

As was true for certificated personnel, prior to the actual solicitation of applications, an announcement of vacancy must be prepared following Equal Employment Opportunity Commission guidelines. In addition, the announcement of vacancy should be as detailed as possible to allow potential applicants to determine if they are interested in the position or qualified for it. Sufficient copies of the announcement of vacancy should be prepared so that one is available to each applicant and so that some can be posted in each school or building and in other public locations in the district.

Recruitment for any support position may involve both internal and external sources. For some openings, qualified individuals, or individuals who can be made qualified, may already be employed in the district and may welcome the opportunity for transfer or promotion. Personnel records can be used to identify employees who have the qualifications for a specific vacancy. If current employees know that they will receive consideration for vacancies that are of higher salary and status, the effects will often be reflected in increased performance and morale (Jordan et al., 1985).

For some vacancies, the district may lack the capacity to "grow their own" or may find it desirable to recruit from external sources. In these instances the variety of recruiting sources described in Chapter 8 is available. The specific source(s) utilized by the district will depend on such factors as district size, district resources, the number of vacancies, and the type of position. Certain recruitment strategies, such as using private agencies, have proved to be successful in recruiting administrative or technical personnel, whereas others, such as advertisement in local newspapers, have proved more effective in recruiting for entry-level positions.

SELECTION

The selection process is essentially a series of activities designed to gain information about the job applicant that can be compared to the selection criteria and, ultimately, result in the best match of person and position. As was true in regard to the selection of certificated personnel, prior to the initiation of the selection process, selection criteria based on the job analysis and job description should be established. The actual selection process for support personnel typically includes (1) completion of an application form, (2) a preliminary interview, (3) employment tests, (4) reference and background checks, (5) an employment interview, and (6) final selection and assignment. The extent to which a particular district follows these steps depends primarily on the size of the district, the position(s) to be filled, and the policies and procedures in force in the district. The larger the district and the higher the level of the position being filled, the more comprehensive and formal the process is likely to become. Specific aspects of the selection process as they relate to support personnel are discussed in the following sections.

Application Form

Virtually every district requires all applicants for classified positions to complete an application form as a part of the hiring process. As noted in Chapter 9, application forms provide the district with an easy and systematic method of obtaining a variety of factual information about the applicant. In addition to the factual information obtained, the application form can tell a lot about prospective employees—their neatness, their accuracy, their attention to detail (Woodward, 2000). As a general rule, other than biographical data, information solicited on the application form should be limited to that pertinent to success on the job. The areas of impermissible inquiry for the application form were noted in Chapter 9.

Preliminary Interview

As noted in Chapter 9, the primary purpose of the preliminary interview is to screen out applicants who are obviously unqualified. For example, some applicants may not meet the size, legal age, or intellectual ability for the position. In addition, whereas some basic data have been obtained on the application form, most application forms do not solicit the type of detailed information relative to knowledge and experience that can be determined in an interview. Nor can the application form generate data relative to attitude and conduct. The preliminary interview also provides the applicant the opportunity to obtain answers to questions about the position and the school system. As was also noted in Chapter 9, the preliminary interview is usually conducted by personnel in the human resources department and is usually short in duration.

Employment Tests

Following the initial interview, applicants may be required to take certain tests or submit validated scores from previous tests. The extent to which tests are used and the importance given them may vary from school district to school district. Employment tests are used primarily for entry-level positions where most applicants will not have enough acquired experience to assess their performance. Employment tests allow employers to identify work-related attitudes and job skills that they cannot identify in an interview, because the type of questions that they would need to ask would be too complex (Tyler, 2000). Moreover, when properly designed and utilized, "employment tests possess the unique ability to fairly, objectively and efficiently compare and contrast job candidates' qualifications" faster and more accurately than any other screening method (Tyler, 2000, p. 76).

Tests for most support personnel positions are normally either written general intelligence and aptitude tests or skills assessment tests. The written test is often short and similar to a school achievement test for reading and math, with perhaps a few items common to those found on intelligence tests. If such tests are used, it is important that the school district recognize that test results do not guarantee subsequent performance. And, as discussed in Chapter 6, school districts must also be careful in developing and/or using employment tests to ensure that the tests are valid for the job in question and are nondiscriminatory. "Employment tests are appropriate and defensible only when there is sufficient evidence that they are job related and that success on these tests relates to the candidate's ability to perform necessary job functions" (Essex, 2000, p. 33).

The written general intelligence or aptitude test may be followed by a skills assessment. Applicants for secretarial and clerical positions may be asked to take a keyboarding test to determine speed and accuracy. A performance test for a bus driver may include starting, stopping, backing, turning, and parking the bus under specified conditions. It is important when designing any skills assessment that the test developers examine the job description and understand what the job entails so that the test will, in fact, assess what it needs to assess (Tyler, 2000).

Reference and Background Checks

After the interview and employment test, the references, previous employment, and other information provided on the application form and in the interview by those applicants still under consideration may be checked. As noted in some detail in Chapter 9, the purposes of such checks are to gain additional information about the applicant, to clarify questions or inconsistencies, and to verify the accuracy of information provided by the applicant. Figure 13.3 provides an example of a telephone reference check form used by the Kyrene, Arizona Unified School District in the screening of support staff.

Employment Interview

Whereas the purpose of the preliminary interview is to screen out unqualified or overqualified applicants, the purpose of the employment interview is to obtain further information that will assist management in choosing from among qualified candidates and to predict success on the job. Much of what was said in Chapter 9 relative to interviewing certificated staff applies to interviewing support staff. Perhaps the most important considerations are that the interview adhere to all EEOC guidelines, that the interview of each candidate be conducted using the same set of questions, and that each candidate be evaluated on the basis of the criteria enumerated on the job description.

The employment interview for support staff will normally involve the immediate supervisor for the position, an employee with the same or a similar position as the one being filled, and a human resources representative. For supervisory or administrative positions, the central office administrator responsible for that function as well as a human resources officer may be on the interview committee. For certain specialized positions, persons from business or industry may be asked to serve on the selection committee. In districts in which site-based management has delegated personnel selection to the local site, the principal or other administrator may well be on the selection committee. Depending on the position, a teacher, counselor, librarian, other education professional, parent, or community representative may also be on the committee. Regardless of who serves on the committee, it is the responsibility of the administrator in charge of the selection process to provide interviewers with the selection criteria and guidelines and strategies for conducting the interview.

Final Selection and Assignment

In most government entities, including school districts, the final selection of individuals to fill job openings must come from lists of eligible candidates who have passed all the foregoing steps in the selection process. The

Guidelines to follow:
- Speak with current or most recent supervisor if possible
- State: "We are considering candidate for _____ position."
- Remarks will be kept confidential and not available to candidate.
- Appreciate your candid honest appraisal.

Name of Candidate: _____ Date: _____

Position applying for: _____ Employer: _____

Name of Reference: _____ Title: _____ Phone: _____

Name of person acquiring this information: _____

Check of company policy prohibits release of information _____

Employed from _____ to _____ position _____

1) In general, how would you rate this person:
   - Outstanding _____   Good _____   Poor _____

2) How would you rate employee's work quality and quantity? Interpersonal skills?
   -
   -

3) What are the candidate's most outstanding qualities?
   -
   -

4) What qualities of the candidate could interfere with success in this position?
   -
   -

5) Is there anything else we should know before we hire this person?
   -
   -

6) Would you re-employ him/her?
   -
   -

7) Is there anyone else you would recommend that we contact?
   -
   -

_____   _____

Information taken by   Date

FIGURE 13.3
Support Staff Telephone Reference Check
Source: Kyrene (AZ) Unified School District.

use of eligibility lists is intended to increase the objectivity of the selection process. When a vacancy occurs, typically the names of the three individuals who ranked highest on the selection criteria are referred to the individual(s) authorized to make the final selection. Unless the requesting party can provide sufficient justification as to why none of these individuals should be selected, selection must be made from among those referred. Eligibility lists are normally declared invalid after a few months.

Before a new employee is assigned to a vacant position, consideration should be given to providing an existing employee the opportunity to make a lateral transfer to the vacancy. For example, if the vacancy is in what is considered the most desirable locale in the district, policy might provide the opportunity for an employee in what is considered a less desirable locale to transfer to the vacant position and assign the new employee to the opening created by the transfer. The opportunity for transfer is essential to staff motivation and morale. However, this consideration must be balanced against the district's interest in finding the right person for each job and in what best serves the needs of the district and its students. The human resources administrator should provide leadership in the development of policies that will govern transfers and assignments.

Preemployment Conditions

Once the final selection has been made and before the employment can be finalized, a number of preemployment conditions must be satisfied. The listing that follows is not exhaustive of all preemployment conditions placed by school districts. Nor do all districts place all these conditions on employment. However, the following list does include the most commonly found preemployment conditions.

Loyalty Oaths.   Many states require employees at the time of employment to sign an oath affirming support for both the U.S. Constitution and the state constitution. Although the practice has been challenged many times, the courts have upheld the right of school districts to have such a requirement.

Completion of Immigration and Naturalization Information.   As required by the 1986 Immigration Reform and Control Act, in order to be eligible to work, all new employees, not just aliens, must complete the appropriate U.S. Immigration and Naturalization Service (INS) form. The form asks such information as date of birth, Social Security number, address, and so forth. The school district must indicate on the form that the employee has provided the acceptable documentation for identification and eligibility to work. There are a combination of 29 documents, including birth certificates, Social Security cards, and green cards that can be used to establish identity and employment eligibility for the I-9 process (Gerbman, 2000). Unfortunately, in some areas fake documents are easy to obtain. Nonetheless, under penalty of federal law, school districts must make a good faith effort to ensure the validity of these documents. And the INS form must be completed within three business days of the hire.

Selective Service Registration. It is a requirement in some states that all new male employees born in 1960 or later show proof of Selective Service registration as a precondition to employment.

Fingerprint Checks. It has become increasingly common for states and school districts to require persons to be fingerprinted if they are to be employed in the public schools. Very often this will have been done for teachers, administrators, or others with positions requiring licenses at the time that they applied for the license. Since many applicants for support positions do not hold positions for which a professional license is required, they may not have satisfied this condition and will have to do so as a precondition of employment. The cost of the fingerprinting is normally borne by the employee. If the fingerprint check reveals convictions for certain criminal offenses or if the employee has lied about convictions on his or her application or in the interview, the employee will be terminated.

Drug Testing. As discussed in Chapter 6, testing for alcohol and drug use may be required of school employees who occupy safety sensitive positions in the schools. This designation could potentially apply to a number of classified positions and has specifically been held by the courts to apply to employees in the transportation department and to custodians.

Immunization Requirements. Most states require that prospective employees provide documentation of immunization for measles and/or rubella and mumps prior to employment.

Vehicle Driving Licenses. Persons being considered for employment for a position that requires them to drive district vehicles must have the appropriate driver's licence to operate the vehicle in question. In most states, school bus drivers are required to hold a commercial driver's licence.

Medical Examination. The preemployment medical examination is required by many school districts and, if required, should be paid for by the district. The Americans with Disabilities Act places limits on the use of medical exams in the employment process. A medical examination cannot be required before a conditional offer of employment is made, and the school district can require the examination only if it is required of all entering employees in the same job category. Examinations must be job related and consistent with business necessity (Horwitz, 1992). Applicants cannot be screened out for a position unless the medical examination determines that, even with reasonable accommodation by the school district, they cannot perform the essential functions of the job (as detailed in the job description) safely and efficiently and without posing an unduly high risk to themselves, other employees, or the public.

Any information obtained from the medical examination must be kept on a separate form and in a separate medical file; it should not be placed in personnel files. Disclosure of information about the exam is permitted only to the following persons (Horwitz, 1992):

☐ Supervisors and managers regarding necessary restrictions on the employee's work and accommodations
☐ First-aid and safety personnel, when appropriate, if the disability might require emergency treatment
☐ Government officials investigating ADA compliance (p. 7)

TRAINING AND DEVELOPMENT FOR SUPPORT PERSONNEL

In 2000, organizations in the United States with 100 or more employees spent $54 billion (not including facilities and overhead or hardware) providing formal training to their employees ("Industry Report," 2000). Unfortunately, training and development programs for support personnel in education have traditionally lagged behind not only those in other organizations, but also those provided certificated personnel in education. Only in recent years have school districts come to recognize that the term staff should include all employees, that no section of their human resources can be overlooked (Andreson & Durant, 1997). More and more districts have found that the time and expense invested in development programs for support personnel are small compared to the inefficiency, ineffectiveness, and staff turnover resulting from the lack of such programs. Research has shown that staff development can result in improved morale, an increased sense of professionalism, and higher levels of job satisfaction. As a result of the growing recognition of the importance of training and development for support staff, some states, such as Florida, have mandated staff development for support personnel and have provided earmarked funding for that purpose. And, in many school districts, staff development for support personnel is a part of contracted negotiations and included in collective bargaining agreements (Andreson & Durant, 1997).

In most school districts, development programs for support personnel are concerned with orienting employees into the district and the position and providing them with job skills. These activities are discussed under the major programs in which they fall: induction and staff development and training.

Induction

The primary goals of the induction program are to induct the new employee or newly assigned into both the social and performance-related aspects of the job (Bolton, 1997), to reduce the anxiety associated with beginning a new job, and to help the new employee feel at home and positive about having accepted the position. Initial impressions and information are important to later attitudes toward the job, co-workers, and the district. As much as 40% of the voluntary resignations in an organization occur within the first year, representing a costly recruiting expense to the school district (Harvey & Bowin, 1996). An effective orientation program can do much to reduce this turnover, as well as to ensure that employees reach their maximum efficiency as soon as possible.

In certain respects the induction needs of support personnel are greater than those of certificated personnel. Most new certificated personnel have been oriented to various aspects of schools during their teacher or administrator preparation programs. They also have some understanding of the role of the school and of education as a process. Many support personnel, on the other hand, come to the job with certain skills or training, but without a clear understanding of the role of the school and the workings of the educational system, as well as how they fit into the total picture.

Induction is most effective when approached as a cooperative activity of the human resources department and supervisors. It consists of four phases. The human resources department is normally responsible for coordinating the induction and for the first phase: the provision of information about the district and the particular school (if applicable), personnel policies, salaries and benefits, promotion opportunities, time recording and absences, holidays, grievance procedures, health and safety requirements, and other regulations. Much of this information can and should be provided in an employee handbook, which should also include an organizational chart clarifying lines of authority and communication. In presenting this information to new employees, it is best to be honest and to present a realistic preview of what can be expected in working for the district. It is important that the words used in the handbook be carefully chosen. Attempts to "sell" the district or the benefits of working for the district should not be overstated. The courts have held that statements made in the employee handbook may be binding on the employer.

The second phase of the induction program is conducted by the immediate supervisor. The supervisor introduces the new employee to other employees and describes the relationship of the new employee's position to other positions in the department, gives a tour of the department, and provides information about department rules and regulations, safety requirements, and the detailed duties and responsibilities of the job. The supervisor also provides information about such details as the location of lockers, restrooms, and lunchrooms; parking; supply procedures; hours of work; and call-in procedures. Some school districts have borrowed from industry and developed checklists of items that are to be covered by the supervisor in the initial orientation of new employees. The use of the checklist ensures that no important item is overlooked. It also compels the supervisor to pay particular attention to each new employee at a time when personal attention is most important (Sherman & Bohlander, 1992).

A third phase of the induction process is a form of on-the-job training. That is, the new employee will be assigned to a first-level supervisor or to an experienced employee, who will instruct the new employee regarding any specific skills required of the job and who will supervise the new employee for a period ranging from a few hours to a few days.

A follow-up interview several weeks after the new employee has been on the job constitutes the fourth phase of the induction program. The interview may be conducted by either the supervisor or a representative of the district human resources office. The purposes of the interview are to determine employee satisfaction with the job, answer any questions that the employee might have, review important information, and inform the employee of the perceptions of his or her performance thus far.

Staff Development and Training

As employees continue on the job, they will undoubtedly need new skills to remain effective. "Job expectations and roles change for classified employees just as they do for teachers" (Andreson & Durant, 1997, p. 19). Staff development and training for all employees is needed to meet the challenges presented by the rapid changes in technology and the pressures to improve efficiency, academic achievement, and employee performance and to restructure organized delivery systems. Yet other development and training needs are created by employee transfers or promotions, changes in district requirements or procedures, and legal and government mandates. Employee training may be used to provide information to employees about new programs, mandates, laws, or policies, as well as to provide opportunities for the acquisition of new skills.

If staff development and training programs for support staff are to be meaningful experiences, they must be seen as relevant and important to participants. Moreover, they should provide a unified thread addressing both organizational and personal learning goals and the transfer of knowledge and skills within the organization (Zepeda, 2000).

The most effective way for school districts to create meaningful staff development programs for support personnel is to engage in a systematic process such as that depicted in Figure 13.4. As seen, the model is cyclical in nature and envisions a continuous process of needs assessment, planning, implementation, and evaluation. Each of these elements is discussed next.

Needs Assessment. The specific development and training activities provided by the district should be determined by a needs assessment. Data gathering might include a review of district employment needs, changes in legal requirements, and school district records such as accident reports and grievance reports. However, the most important source of information about training needs is the target employee group itself. Staff developers should consult with representatives of the target groups, as well as the supervisors of the target groups and those to whom they provide service (e.g., principals, teachers, or other employee groups) (Welch & Daniel, 1997).

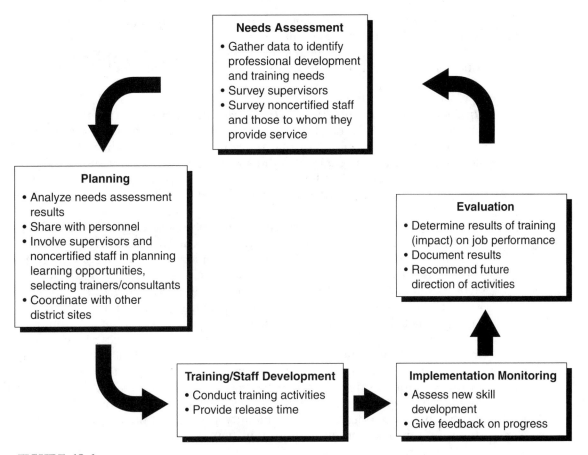

FIGURE 13.4
Steps to Develop a Professional Growth Program for Non-certified Staff
Source: S. Zepeda (2000). Needed: Professional growth opportunities for non-certificated support staff. *School Business Affairs, 66*(6), 41.

Planning. The information and data generated during the needs assessment process must be analyzed and the results shared with staff and used to determine exactly what needs and issues might be addressed by the development and training activities. Representative staff and supervisors should be involved in planning the training activities, as well as in identifying potential trainers or consultants. Many school districts outsource some or all of the development program using external consultants. Other districts rely more heavily on internal expertise. Using presenters from within the district can not only save money, but also provides the opportunity for the district to highlight the skills and talents of employees.

Planners may also want to consider entering into cooperative arrangements with other districts or regional service centers to deliver training to support personnel. School districts may also benefit from the training conducted by the state department of education (or other government agencies) and various business concerns. State departments of education commonly conduct or sponsor training workshops on topics of general interest to school districts and for the benefit of those many small districts that do not have the personnel to develop viable training programs.

Implementation: Conduct Staff Development and Training.   The formats and methods used to conduct the training activities will vary depending on the objectives of the training, the availability of qualified trainers and training materials, the size of the district, and the size of the school district's training budget. The more common approaches to staff development and training are discussed next.

On-the-Job Training.   The most commonly used training method for support personnel development programs is **on-the-job training.** On-the-job training is most appropriate when the employee is "expected to become proficient in performing certain tasks or using equipment found at their work stations" (Pynes, 1997, p. 209). In addition to being the simplest to operate, on-the-job training is the least expensive. On-the-job training is usually conducted by the supervisor or by an experienced or senior employee. This method has the advantage of providing hands-on experience under normal working conditions (Sherman & Bohlander, 1992). However, the success of the training depends in large part on the qualification of the trainers. More seniority or experience does not necessarily make a co-worker the most qualified or a good teacher. It is the responsibility of the human resources department to identify potential trainers and to provide them with instruction on how to train new employees.

Off-the-Job Training.   In addition to on-the-job training, most school districts find it necessary to provide some training to support personnel away from their normal work location. Workshops lasting one day or more for all employees within a certain department are an off-the-job training technique common to school district personnel programs. Off-the-job training not only has the advantage of avoiding disruption of the normal routine on the job site (Pynes, 1997), but it also provides for the maximum number of trainees with the minimum number of trainers and lends itself to instruction in areas in which information and instruction can be imparted by a variety of instructional methodologies, including lectures, demonstrations, video instruction, teleconferencing, or video conferencing. In addition, if properly designed, instructional activities such as case studies or simulations that maximize trainee involvement may be employed, as well as computer-based training that employs interactive video or computer-driven simulations.

Off-the-job training may be provided at a central location in the school district, in another district, or at a site selected by the state department of education or other provider. It is common for manufacturing and business concerns to provide training in the use of their materials and equipment.

School district personnel may be sent to a training facility operated by the business, or the provider may send trainers to the local school district. Companies also normally will provide materials that may be used by the district in its training efforts. Even when training related to the use of specific materials and equipment is not needed, companies often have persons available to give presentations on a variety of topics.

Scheduling. By whatever approach training is provided, it is important that it be scheduled so as to avoid conflicts with established school or district schedules. Suggestions for scheduling staff development for support staff include the following:

- ☐ extend the contract by a few days immediately before or after the school year.
- ☐ add district-wide staff development days, workdays, or both to support staff contract days.
- ☐ add "shift" hours to the school day and off staff development or training before or after school (Zepeda, 2000).

Evaluation. The evaluation of the staff development program, while important to its continued success, is often the most neglected aspect of the program (Pynes, 1997). The school district will certainly need to know if the goals of the program have been met. It may also want to know if a training program or certain parts of it were worth the investment or if one program worked better than another or was more cost-effective. To answer these questions, some form of evaluation must take place. According to Patrick (1992), evaluation of training is "any attempt to obtain information concerning the effect or value of training in order to make decisions about any aspect of the training programme, the persons that have been trained, and the organizations . . . responsible for providing that training" (p. 515).

The evaluation of training can be anything from a simple pretest and post-test to an elaborate set of experiments with trainees randomly assigned to various treatments (training) and a control group. The evaluation may focus on employees' reactions to the training activity, what employees learned, behavioral changes on the job, and the effect of the training on student learning or district goals (Geber, 1995).

Four major approaches to the evaluation of training have been identified: (1) the systems approach, which is concerned with the improvement of the training program, (2) the trainee-oriented approach, which focuses on the training effects that are valued by the trainees, (3) the cost-effective or statistical approach, which is concerned with measurement and the analysis of data in ways that support administrative decision making about training, and (4) the research approach, which is concerned with both carrying out research into training and systematically evaluating the effects of training programs (Patrick, 1992). Whether a school district uses one or all of these approaches at any time, the staff development and training program should be the subject of ongoing evaluation. And the results of the evaluation should be summarized and disseminated to participants, supervisors, and central office personnel (Welch & Daniel, 1997). Most importantly, the results of the evaluation should provide direction for future staff development and training activities.

PERFORMANCE APPRAISAL

The guidelines and principles for a successful personnel appraisal system articulated in Chapter 11 apply equally to the appraisal of support personnel. The objectives of the support personnel appraisal system also closely parallel those of the certificated personnel appraisal system. Based on an extensive review of the literature, Swan, Holmes, Brown, Short, and DeWeese (1988) identified four objectives of appraisal systems for classified personnel: (1) to inform employees of their strengths and weaknesses and share expectations for improvement, (2) to provide data for merit pay recommendations, (3) to satisfy court requirements for cases involving alleged discrimination, and (4) to serve as the basis for disciplinary action.

Swan and colleagues (1988) have developed a Generic Performance Appraisal System for Classified Employees (GPASCE) that can be adapted by most school districts to meet their individual needs. According to its developers, the purposes of the GPASCE are to (1) encourage and facilitate improvement in the performance of employees, (2) provide a documented record of the employee's job performance, (3) provide an opportunity for communication between supervisor and employee on the subjects of job requirements and work expectations, (4) specify direction for work improvement, (5) assure employees that objective criteria are used in performance appraisal, (6) demonstrate that exceptional or unsatisfactory performance will be noted, and (7) exemplify the supervisor's and school's continuing interest in performance improvement.

The sequence of actions to be followed in GPASCE are as follows (Swan et al., 1988):

1. The supervisor and employee meet at the beginning of each year and discuss the employee's job in detail, including the criteria that will be used to appraise the employee's performance on each factor on the job description and any factors unique to the position (e.g., for bus drivers, maintaining discipline on the school bus).
2. The supervisor monitors the employee's performance throughout the appraisal period to obtain firsthand knowledge for the appraisal.
3. If any concerns develop during the appraisal period, the supervisor meets with the employee to provide encouragement, assistance, and direction for improvement. If necessary or appropriate, an improvement plan may be developed and negotiated with the employee and reviewed and approved by the supervisor's superior (the reviewer).
4. Within two weeks of the end of the appraisal period, the supervisor completes the performance appraisal rating form (Figure 13.5). For any factor rated 1 or 5, the supervisor must provide narrative description. The

Employee's Soc. Sec. #	Name (Last, First, Middle)	Position Title (& Series/Grade)	
School · Rating Period From: To:	Check One: __Probationary __Mid-Year __Annual	Appraiser's Signature	Reviewer's Signature

I. Factor Appraisal System

Directions: Each employee is appraised on the common factors according to the contents of the job description (provide reference). An employee is rated on unique factors if contained in the job description. Provide narrative comments on separate page for all factors appraised as "5" or "1" and for unsatisfactory, outstanding, or postponed overall ratings.

Explanation of Appraisal Categories
5 = Exceeded requirements to exceptional degree
4 = Exceeded requirements, not to exceptional degree
3 = Met and sometimes exceeded requirements
2 = Usually met, but rarely exceeded minimum requirements
1 = Did not meet requirements
N = Irrelevant or no opportunity to observe employee's performance

A. *Common Factors—For All Employees*

	Job Description Reference	Appraised Category					
		5	4	3	2	1	N
1. *Demonstrates knowledge of job* (Includes technical, procedural, and regulatory knowledge)		|| ||	|| ||	|| ||	|| ||	|| ||	|| ||
2. *Plans, organizes, and sets priorities* (Time scheduling, orderly arrangement of procedures, and systematic planning)		|| ||	|| ||	|| ||	|| ||	|| ||	|| ||
3. *Produces expected quantity of work* (Amount of work produced/ accomplished according to goals, objectives, and activities)		|| ||	|| ||	|| ||	|| ||	|| ||	|| ||
4. *Meets schedules/timelines* (Accomplishes work on schedule/ on time)		|| ||	|| ||	|| ||	|| ||	|| ||	|| ||
5. *Communicates in written form* (Degree of completeness, clarity and conciseness, and organization of material)		|| ||	|| ||	|| ||	|| ||	|| ||	|| ||

FIGURE 13.5

Performance Appraisal Form for Classified Employees

Source: "A Generic Performance Appraisal Form for Classified Employees" by W. W. Swan, C. T. Holmes, C. L. Brown, M. L. Short, and L. DeWeese, 1988, *Journal of Personnel Evaluation in Education,* 1, pp. 297–298. Copyright © 1988 by Kluwar Academic Publishers. Adapted by permission.

	Job Description Reference	Appraised Category					
		5	4	3	2	1	N
6. *Communicates in oral form* (Appropriateness of organization of material; clarity, conciseness, impact of presentation)		|| ||	|| ||	|| ||	|| ||	|| ||	|| ||
7. *Informs/consults appropriately* (Provides information/seeks information when needed)		|| ||	|| ||	|| ||	|| ||	|| ||	|| ||
8. *Makes judgments/decisions effectively* (Sees problems, chooses, and implements solutions)		|| ||	|| ||	|| ||	|| ||	|| ||	|| ||
9. *Demonstrates positive interpersonal relationships* (Effective in working with others individually and in teams)		|| ||	|| ||	|| ||	|| ||	|| ||	|| ||
B. *Unique Factors For Employees*							
10.		|| ||	|| ||	|| ||	|| ||	|| ||	|| ||
11.		|| ||	|| ||	|| ||	|| ||	|| ||	|| ||
12.		|| ||	|| ||	|| ||	|| ||	|| ||	|| ||
13.		|| ||	|| ||	|| ||	|| ||	|| ||	|| ||
14.		|| ||	|| ||	|| ||	|| ||	|| ||	|| ||

II. *Overall Performance Rating For Employee*
_____ Unsatisfactory _____ Satisfactory _____ Superior _____ Outstanding _____ Postponed

Acknowledgement of Receipt of Appraisal (Not Concurrence): _____

Employee's Signature   Date

Narrative Comments

Factor #   Appraisal Category   Comment _____

Note:

_____

Appraiser's Signature   Date

FIGURE 13.5
(continued)

supervisor must also provide a narrative justification for any overall performance rating of outstanding or unsatisfactory. The average score across all factors is used as a guide for determining the overall rating: 5.0–4.3, outstanding; 4.2–3.4, superior; 3.3–1.9, satisfactory; 1.8–1.0, unsatisfactory.

5. The supervisor shares the completed appraisal form with the reviewer, who may provide recommendations for appropriate action for any unsatisfactory rating or provide supplementary information relative to any rating, but may not change the appraisal.
6. Within two weeks of the end of the appraisal period, the supervisor meets with the employee to share and discuss the approved appraisal with the employee. At this meeting, both the supervisor and the employee share perceptions, and the employee has the opportunity to present additional information of which the supervisor may be unaware.
7. Within one week of this meeting, the supervisor completes and signs the finalized appraisal form and submits it to the reviewer for approval.
8. Within four weeks of the end of the appraisal period, the employee receives the final performance appraisal. The employee acknowledges receipt of the appraisal by his or her signature and, if necessary and appropriate, may work with the supervisor to develop an improvement plan.
9. The final performance appraisal is filed in the employee's personnel file.
10. If the employee considers the final appraisal unfair or unreasonable, he or she may appeal directly to the reviewer for reconsideration. If reconsideration does not resolve the issue to the satisfaction of the employee, he or she may pursue the established grievance or appeal procedure of the school district.

Whatever process is used to evaluate support personnel, it is important that it be conducted on a periodic and established basis and be a cooperative venture of the staff member and the supervisor. Equally important, the evaluation effort "should be viewed as a constructive effort toward the improvement of the performance of the particular staff member and toward the betterment of the supervisory process under which that staff member operates" (Hack et al., 1998, p. 188).

SUMMARY

Because of the number and importance of support staff, it is mandatory that sound personnel policies and practices relative to support employees be in operation in all school districts. Districts need to conduct job analyses and prepare written job descriptions, after which they must develop a comprehensive classification plan. After the classification plan has been developed, the district is in a position to prepare salary schedules in which all support positions are included. Because school district funds are public monies, information related to the schedule should be made public and accessible to employees and the public. The salary schedule should be subjected to periodic review, and indirect compensation should be considered in any discussion of the compensation program.

The goal of the school district recruitment program goes beyond merely recruiting the individuals needed to fill existing vacancies. Ideally, sufficient numbers should be recruited so that the district has the opportunity to select the very best employee from a number of qualified applicants. Given the investment made in recruiting, selecting, and training employees, it is incumbent that the district have an established, systematic selection process that not only is equitable and nondiscriminatory, but also will generate the kind of data on which informed decisions can be based.

Following the lead of business and industry, in recent years school districts have placed new emphasis on the development and expansion of training and staff development programs for support personnel. There has also been an increased emphasis on the performance of education personnel, including support personnel. The performance appraisal system for classified personnel, like that for certificated personnel, should be objective and based on job-related standards, effectively communicated to employees, and subjected to an ongoing analysis of results.

DISCUSSION QUESTIONS

1. As a newly appointed human resources director, you have been asked by the superintendent to revise the salary plan for support personnel. What information will you require, and what activities must you perform to accomplish this task?
2. You are to hire a dietician, a maintenance supervisor, and a secretary. How will you design your recruitment program for these positions? What is your rationale for selecting these various recruitment methods?
3. It has come to your attention that 30% of the support employees leave the district prior to completing 1 year of service, and 60% of those who leave do so within six months. What programs might you consider implementing in order to reduce the turnover rate?
4. Describe the relationships among job descriptions, recruitment, selection, performance appraisal, and staff development.

■―――――   ## CASE STUDIES

13.1 Ruth or Roy?

The Maryvale School District has an opening for a Data Processor II. By advertising the position in the local newspapers and throughout the school system, the district has been successful in attracting 11 applicants. Of these, two candidates have emerged as having the best qualifications. The two candidates, Ruth Owens and Roy Evans, were equally ranked by the selection process. Ruth Owens was referred by Nancy Kraft, a valued and long-time employee in the same unit in which the vacancy exists. The unit is currently all female. Roy Evans, a newcomer to the community, responded to an advertisement for the opening.

Questions

1. What are the advantages of hiring Ruth? of hiring Roy?

2. What impact, if any, would hiring Roy have on the prospect of future employee referrals? What could you do to mitigate any negative effects?
3. What, if any, underlying legal issues are present in this case?

13.2 Ready to Work

Jacqueline Armstrong has been an employee of the Hartford School District for 23 years and currently is director of computing services. While driving back from a computing conference last spring, Jackie was injured in an accident that has left her permanently confined to a wheelchair. After many months of recovery, she is ready to return to work. Her office is on the second floor of the district administration office where all the computer equipment is located. The district office was formerly a high school, built in 1933, and it does not have an elevator or any wheelchair access. Architectural estimates of the cost to make the necessary renovations to the building to provide Jackie access total $163,000. The district is what would be considered a poor district and cannot make the renovations without either asking voters for a special assessment or making serious cuts in personnel and programs.

Questions

1. What legal obligations does the district have to Jackie? What moral obligations?
2. If you were the human resources director or superintendent and had the opportunity to talk to Jackie about the situation, what would you say?
3. What are the alternative solutions for the district? Which would you choose?

13.3 Harried Hank

Hank Sloane has been a bus driver for Hopeville School District No. 1 for 8 years. His on-time and safety record has consistently been one of the best in the district. Beginning in early February his supervisor, Mike Thompson, began to receive complaints that Hank was being verbally abusive to students on his bus. After a third parent complaint, Mike met with Hank to see what was going on. During the meeting, Hank denied making the alleged statements to students, but did admit that he was having marital problems and wasn't sleeping well.

Within the next 10 days two more parents called. One complained about Hank's abusive language. Another reported that Hank had pulled away from the bus stop without her son even though he had to have seen the boy, who was half a block away and yelling for the bus to stop. The boy had to walk back home a half-mile in the snow, and his mother had to cancel an important business meeting to drive him to school.

Again, Mike called Hank in, and again Hank basically denied the charges. In the case of the first complaint, Hank said that the child in question was being disruptive on the bus and needed some sharp language to settle him down. As for the second situation, Hank claimed he did not see the child.

When asked how things were going with his wife, Hank broke down and tearfully admitted that she had left him, taking his 3-year-old daughter. Mike warned Hank that his behavior must change and suggested that he seek counseling through the employee assistance program. Hank seemed reluctant to do this, saying he could handle it by himself.

Questions

1. Should Mike have required Hank to seek assistance, rather than just suggest it?
2. Should Hank be moved from driving the bus to some other position in the transportation department where he is not in contact with students, even if some retraining might be involved?
3. To what extent should the district involve itself in the emotional problems of its employees? What is Hank's responsibility to the district to solve his personal problems?

REFERENCES

Andreson, K. M., & Durant, D. (1997). Classified staff developers unite! *Journal of Staff Development, 18*(1), 18–21.

Bolton, T. (1997). *Human resources management.* Cambridge, MA: Blackwell.

Cascio, W. F. (1998). *Applied psychology in personnel management* (5th ed.). Upper Saddle River, NJ: Prentice Hall.

De Cenzo, D. A., & Robbins, S. P. (1996). *Human resources management: Concepts and practices* (5th ed.). New York: Wiley.

Essex, N. L. (2000). Fair hiring and firing. *American School Board Journal, 187*(4), 32–34.

Fine, S. A., & Getkate, M. (1995). *Benchmark tasks for job analysis: A guide for Functional Job Analysis (FJA) scales.* Mahwah, NJ: Erlbaum.

Geber, B. (September 1995). Producing deeper levels of training evaluation. *The Developer,* 7.

Gerbman, R. V. (2000). License to work. *HRMagazine, 45,* 151–155.

Greenberg, S., & Bello, R. (1992). Rewrite job descriptions: Focus on functions. *HR Focus, 69*(7), 6.

Hack, W. G., Candoli, I. C., & Ray, J. R. (1998). *School business administration: A planning approach* (6th ed.). Boston: Allyn and Bacon.

Harvey, D., & Bowin, R. B. (1996). *Human resource management: An experimental approach.* Upper Saddle River, NJ: Prentice Hall.

Henderson, R. I. (1994). *Compensation management: Rewarding performance* (6th ed.). Upper Saddle River, NJ: Prentice Hall.

Horwitz, H. A. (1992). New guidelines for medical examinations. *H R Focus, 69*(7), 7.

Industry Update: 2000. (2000). *Training, 37*(10), 36–39.

Jordan, K. F., McKeown, M. P., Salmon, R. G., & Webb, L. D. (1985). *School business administration.* Beverly Hills, CA: Sage.

Levesque, J. D. (1993). *Manual of personnel policies, procedures and operations* (2nd ed.). Upper Saddle River, NJ: Prentice Hall.

McCormick, E. J., Jeanneret, P. R., & Mecham, R.C. (1989). *Position analysis questionnaire.* Palo Alto, CA: Consulting Psychologists Press.

Mosley, S. (1998). How to survive a classification study. *Library Journal, 123*(17), 48–49.

National School Boards Association (NSBA). (1996). *The school personnel management system.* Washington, DC: Author.

Patrick, J. (1992). *Training: Research and practice.* New York: Academic Press.

Pynes, J. E. (1997). *Human resources management for public and nonprofit organizations.* San Francisco: Jossey-Bass.

Sherman, A. W., Jr., & Bohlander, G. W. (1992). *Managing human resources* (9th ed.). Cincinnati, OH: South-Western.

Sibon, R. E. (1992). *Strategic planning for human resources management.* New York: American Management Association.

Swan, W. W., Holmes, C. T., Brown, C. L., Short, M. L., & DeWeese, L. (1988). A generic performance appraisal system for classified employees. *Journal of Personnel Evaluation in Education, 1,* 293–310.

Tyler, K. (2000). Put applicants' skills to the tests. *HRMagazine, 45,* 75–80.

U.S. Department of Education, National Center for Education Statistics. (2001). *The condition of education 2000.* Washington, DC: Author.

U.S. Department of Labor. (1991). *The revised handbook for analyzing jobs.* Washington, DC: Author.

Welch, F. C., & Daniel, C. (1997). Staff development for classified staff: One school district's approach. *Journal of Staff Development, 18*(1), 12–15.

Woodward, N. H. (2000). The functions of forms. *HRMagazine, 45*(1), 67–73.

Zepeda, S. (2000). Needed: Professional growth opportunities for non-certificated support staff. *School Business Affairs, 66*(6), 37–43.

PART FOUR

Projections for the Future

14 *New Roles for the Human Resources Function*

Trending Toward 2010

After completing this chapter, you will be able to:

- Understand more clearly the current trends in the human resources function and relate them more meaningfully to future changes in the organization and administration of schools.
- Explain how the human resources function can better serve the school system in the achievement of its objectives.
- Explain the changing concepts relative to the human resources processes of recruitment, selection, assignment and others, and understand more clearly the rationale supporting these new perspectives.
- Explain how the human resources function can be instrumental in helping the school system to deal with inevitable changes in the workplace.
- Understand more fully the importance of human resources planning in view of the ever-changing nature of society and its institutions.
- Identify strategies that promote the guiding strategies of the school and school system.

People have been interested in prophesying the future for thousands of years. Some rulers used oracles such as the Oracle of Apollo at Delphi to guide important decisions that affected the life and death of the empires. Because her utterances were believed to be the words of Apollo, she greatly influenced Greek religion, economics, and politics. Today, interest in prognosticating future events is the domain of many, including mystics, fortune-tellers, economists, and demographers.

Academicians assist institutions and businesses by predicting future trends in economics, demography, politics, and society. The World Future Society, with a reported membership of 30,000, promotes the research and study of methodologies for *forecasting* and builds models of future societal scenarios. Students of business and economics study business trends and major economic cycles, historical trends in employment, and cycles of interest rates and commodity prices. Demographers investigate trends to determine future population changes, and historians study the past to provide a basis for anticipating prospective occurrences.

Any question as to whether the investment market is influenced by authoritative economic forecasts is answered by the behavior of investors following a presentation by Federal Reserve Chairman Alan Greenspan. Yet such management authorities as Peter Drucker (1974) speak disparagingly about the value of forecasting: "Strategy planning is not forecasting. It is not masterminding the future. Any attempt to do so is foolish; the future is unpredictable. We can only discredit what we are doing by attempting it" (p. 123). Drucker goes on to say, "If anyone still suffers from the delusion that man is able to forecast beyond a very short time span, let him look at the headlines in yesterday's paper, and ask which of them he could possibly have predicted a decade or so ago. . . . We must start out with the premise that forecasting is not respectable human activity and not worthwhile beyond the shortest of periods. Strategic planning is necessary precisely because we cannot forecast" (pp. 123–124). In writing this chapter the thoughts of Drucker have been kept in mind, and our focus is that of important trends in the human resources function that will significantly influence the direction of personnel activities through the first decade of the 21st century.

NEW MANDATES FOR THE HUMAN RESOURCES FUNCTION

Increases in such developments as organizational downsizing, outsourcing, decentralization, and organizational restructuring have resulted in questions in some quarters concerning the need for a central human resources unit. If indeed the local school unit is assuming an ever-increasing role in the administration of the personnel function, is a central human resources unit really necessary? We submit that the increasing importance of people in all organizations, including school systems, places the human resources function in its most exciting and relevant position to date. People have become the most important component to effectiveness in organizations, and this fact necessitates the inclusion of human resources administration in the center of policy decisions at all levels of the school system. As stated by Rana (2000), "With so many companies referring to staff as their 'greatest asset,' never before in the history of work have people been so relevant to the bottom line" (p. 16). "But the truth is, HR has never been more necessary. . . . To state it plainly: achieving organizational excellence must be the work of HR" (Ulrich, 2000, p. 22). During the next decade, the HR function will move from a support and maintenance role to a leadership role in enabling the school system and the school to meet their new demands through the realization that its ultimate success will depend primarily on the human component. And, since the new economy is based on new knowledge, creative ideas, and the need for highly competent personnel, personal development and professional growth must assume an ongoing, continuous priority on the part of the successful worker. As noted previously in Chapter 2, the number of human resources positions nationally is expected to increase more rapidly than the average growth of all other occupations through the year 2005.

This chapter answers many questions concerning the importance of the human resources function during the next decade and discusses several trends that appear significant in the changing role of personnel administration. Discussions concerning changes in the workplace setting, new attention to the employee as the key to organizational success, changing attitudes about work in the minds of workers, continuous learning and skill development needs, the new role of leadership on the part of HR administrators, organizational restructuring, the changing work force and other future considerations are included. Virtually every trend discussed has its roots already planted to some extent in business and educational practices. And, although we do not take the position of forecasting future happenings in this chapter, we do emphasize the necessity of being knowledgeable about important developments and needs within the HR function envisioning their potential impact, and strategizing ways to achieve them.

THE CHANGING ROLE OF THE HR FUNCTION

The following major changes in the role of the HR function will be witnessed during the next decade: (1) *Change from a support and maintenance function to a leadership role in the total operations of the school system* and (2) *change from the traditional focus of administering the basic processes of HR to a broader focus of people management; the employee becomes the center of attention and concern.*

Change to a Leadership Role

If the first change listed in the foregoing paragraph, that of *leadership*, is to be fully achieved, it will necessitate a new kind of leader in human resources administration. The ongoing movement that changes the HR function from one of serving only in a support and maintenance capacity to a position of leadership will require HR personnel to serve as partners in the strategic planning and implementation of key decisions of the system, not just participation in these activities. This change emanates from strong research evidence in recent years that organizational progress is inextricably tied to people—their goals, attitudes, and satisfaction concerning the workplace. This evidence is not completely new; it is more of a realization that the relationships between the worker and the workplace are paramount to the organization's ultimate success. As Losey (2000) points out, "The HR field today recognizes the dynamic relationship between strategy, people, technology and the processes that drive the organization" (p. 8).

HR strategy refers to the school system's planned partnership with the HR function in order to enhance the success of the system in meeting its challenges and achieving its goals. Losey states further that although this relationship is quite evident now, its development has been slow. Thus the HR function necessarily must be tied directly to the important work of the school system. Its leadership will be instrumental in enabling the school system to deal with its challenges and to meet its goals. Ulrich (2000) argues that, although strategy is the responsibility of the organization's executive team of which HR should be a member, "To be full fledged strategic partners with senior management, however, HR executives should impel and guide serious discussion of how the company should be organized to carry out its strategy" (p. 24). Such a new leadership role likely will require additional competencies on the part of HR administrators in education. This need will require additional time and personal motivation. Changes in the way that various HR processes are performed are part of the answer to the time question: How will the busy workload of human resources administrators permit attention to these growing work demands? Part of the answer to this question rests with technological developments that will permit entire HR processes to be automated, enabling many tasks to be completed in more efficient ways at less cost. This development will allow the personnel administrator to give necessary attention to other matters, such as HR strategy questions and the best ways to gain required knowledge and skills most effectively.

The future strategic role of the HR function has been succinctly set forth in an article by Kemske (2000) that reported the predictions of a panel of leading work force directors and consultants. Although the listing focuses more specifically on HR as related to business, each entry holds specific implications for the role of HR in education as well. The predictions regarding the strategic role of HR are as follows:*

1. Successful HR departments will focus on organizational performance.
2. HR's value will be to have the right people at the right time by recruiting leaders to join the company's mix of talent and keeping the "bench" full of enabled, competent workers.
3. The focus of the HR function will be human capital development and organizational productivity; HR may be renamed to reflect this.
4. HR will evolve from strategic business partnerships to strategic business leadership (driving change and results, not just mentoring them).
5. A key HR role in the future will be multidisciplinary consulting around individual team, business unit, and corporate performance.
6. Managers will grow to depend more on HR professionals as they realize that good people management can be the strategic advantage in the next decade.
7. Leading change will become HR's greatest contribution to the corporation.
8. More and more businesses will use HR as a strategic partner.
9. HR will have a seat at the table as part of top management and report directly to the CEO in most companies.
10. A key HR role will be managing increasingly scarce human and intellectual capital. (p. 39)

Although the HR function is presently designed to help to meet the goals of the school system, future emphases will be centered on administering the various HR processes to fit the system in a way that its work is accomplished

---

*HR 2008 by Floyd Kemske, © January 1998. Reprinted with permission of *Workforce*, Costa Mesa, California; all rights reserved. http://www.workforce.com/

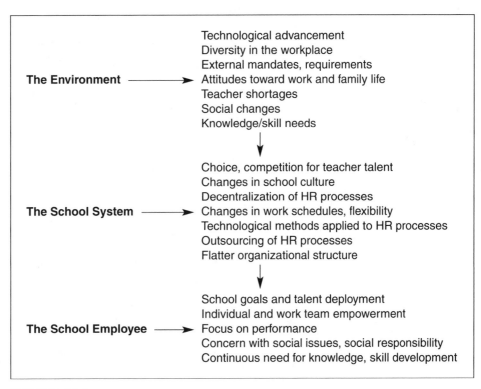

The Environment ——————▶ Technological advancement
Diversity in the workplace
External mandates, requirements
Attitudes toward work and family life
Teacher shortages
Social changes
Knowledge/skill needs

The School System ——————▶ Choice, competition for teacher talent
Changes in school culture
Decentralization of HR processes
Changes in work schedules, flexibility
Technological methods applied to HR processes
Outsourcing of HR processes
Flatter organizational structure

The School Employee ——————▶ School goals and talent deployment
Individual and work team empowerment
Focus on performance
Concern with social issues, social responsibility
Continuous need for knowledge, skill development

FIGURE 14.1
Environmental Influences and the HR Function

faster, more effectively, and at lesser cost (Kemske, 2000). Goals of the school system will remain a first consideration of the HR function; however, for any specific school strategy there will be an accompanying, integrated strategy set forth by HR administrators. Figure 14.1 illustrates influences and relationships between and among the three components of *environmental influences* on the system, *organizational changes* and structure, and the impacts on the *human element* of the system. For example, internal and external environmental influences, such as skill needs and worker shortages, relate closely to competition for employee talent and organizational culture. And competition for talent and organizational culture influence system productivity, social responsibility, and the matching of people and system objectives.

The change by the HR function to set strategies that enhance system goals will make it essential that HR administrators focus on the school system and its performance. This means that the HR administrator must gain a complete understanding of the system and and its work, including the fact that the school is truly a people business. For example, new goals set forth by the school district may necessitate a reconsideration of the recruitment and selection processes being implemented by HR administrators in order to attract and retain the type of talent needed to meet changing goals most effectively. Recommendations for changes in the compensation

FIGURE 14.2
School System Goals and
Strategies and the HR Function

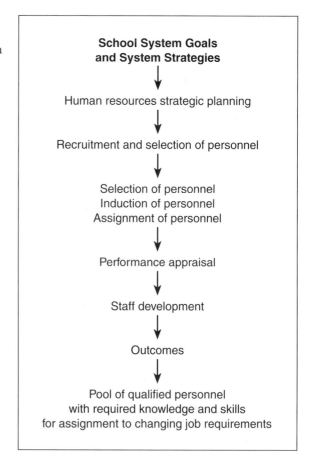

process may be necessary to support more directly the stated objectives of the school and school system. Changes in the school system's programming and student achievement objectives will demand specific attention to the kinds of in-service required to implement such programs optimally. The loss of talented personnel in the system places new accountabilities on HR administrators in the way in which recruitment, selection, assignment and induction are administered. Each strategic plan of the school system is accompanied by a related strategy in the HR function. This concept places the HR function at the center of the school system's agendas. As Hall (2000) has pointed out, human capital has become the core of organizational business. Figure 14.2 presents a conceptual model that illustrates the direct relationship of the human resources function and its processes to the overall system organization and its strategies.

The school system's goals and strategies are instrumental to the strategic planning activities of the human resources function. That is, the processes of recruitment, selection, assignment, induction, development, and others, give full consideration to the overall system's purposes. In turn, performance appraisal assumes a formative mode in that it focuses on the strengths of employees and their skill needs in relation to the accomplishment of purposes. Similarly, staff development activities serve to develop needed employee skills and to deploy employee strengths toward the end that the HR personnel assets of competent people are appropriately matched with the work needs of the system.

One must keep in mind that the HR function in education is a relatively recent development. Historically, personnel administration advanced slowly in school settings as an aftermath of World War II, which necessitated new approaches to the recruitment, induction, training, compensation, and assignment of both military personnel and citizens. Even as late as the 1960s, many relatively large school systems had not organized a central personnel unit; various personnel responsibilities were divided among administrators in the central office. As the personnel function evolved during the 1970s through the 1990s, it assumed more of an administrative role, one that performed necessary tasks such as recruiting and selecting personnel and helping to induct them into the school setting. The function, even today, is not fully integrated into the real work of the school system. In many instances the central unit human resources director does not sit with the administrative cabinet, which is generally chaired by the school superintendent. It is clear that future changes in the role of the HR function will place new demands on all HR administrators. In all too many instances, central unit HR directors have been chosen for the position without an adequate background of preparation and experience. When these individuals find themselves overwhelmed with the demands of the office, they frequently leave the role or administer the HR function by using the **golden mean decision method;** that is, they learn how other HR directors are doing it and attempt to follow their lead. Unfortunately, such a practice promotes inactive rather than proactive leadership and inhibits the concept of strategizing HR in relation to the objectives of the school system in which one is employed. In a study by Norton (1999), it was found that 42.8% of the HR directors had served in their current position for 3 years or less. Most participants in the study indicated that their previous position before becoming HR director was school principal, central office administrator, or a position in business or industry, not as an assistant director or HR director in another school district. And when asked the question concerning how well they believed that they were prepared to assume the HR director's role, nearly one-third responded "not well prepared" and 44.8% answered only "fairly well prepared" (p. 3).

The concept of leadership and the HR function will call for increased competence on the part of all HR administrators. It will require an improved preparedness for the role and a higher work quality on the part of each central and local unit in the school system. Leadership in the realm of strategic planning demands a higher level of knowledge about the work of the school, its employees, the school community, and its stakeholders.

The influences of economics and politics on social institutions such as schools must also be known. The HR director must have the knowledge and competencies required to not only meet the future demands of the school system's work, but also to deal with inevitable changes that will call for organizational restructuring and human resources development. Within the human resources unit itself, the future will demand that it possess a variety of specific competencies. These competencies include the following:

☐ Human resources competencies that encompass a variety of leadership styles to deal with a varying array of workers and work teams.

☐ A comprehensive knowledge about the school system, the local schools, and the community in which they are embedded.

☐ The ability to employ human resources thinking strategy in relation to the overall strategic plan of the school system and possession of the skills and knowledge required to apply the various HR processes to the overall objectives of the system.

☐ The competencies necessary to participate in the strategic planning of the system and deal with the ongoing changes encountered by all social systems.

☐ The capacity to apply the necessary human resources technologies to the HR strategies and be able use these resources to apply these strategies more quickly and effectively to rapidly changing conditions at less cost to the system.

Change to a Broader Focus on People Management

Less than 20 years ago, the development of policy for the reduction in force (RIF) was a high priority for school systems. With the exception of only a few specific areas of instruction (e.g., special education, mathematics, some sciences), decreases in student enrollments resulted in an oversupply of teaching personnel. Presently, the need for teachers and the lack of qualified substitute teachers are major problems facing most school districts nationally. These problems have brought about emergency approaches designed to increase the supply of teachers. Such approaches have included the reduction of certification requirements for teaching, alternative certification programs, the implementation of programs designed to encourage current teachers to remain in the profession, and other incentive program efforts for the purpose of encouraging individuals to enter the teaching profession or to return to teaching after leaving it for other career pursuits.

Projections of the need for teachers and forecasts concerning their supply are not encouraging. Although a great deal of talk has taken place in the state legislative bodies and other groups regarding the importance of promoting the attractiveness of teaching by increasing salary levels and other conditions of work, little or no significant progress has been witnessed in this regard. We submit that a major change will take place in education in this decade that results in revolutionary changes in the management of people. The following section centers on an examination of this contention and discusses both the kinds of changes that will be implemented in human resources management and the associated rationale.

Educators in the public sector are encountering increasing competition for students. The increase of new educational choices for educating children and youth today has resulted in more students attending private schools, charter schools, home schooling, and others. Not only is there a competition for students, since students represent monetary income, there is strong competition for teacher talent. For what perhaps is the first time in history, teacher personnel are in the driver's seat regarding job choices and the conditions that they require to work in any particular school and/or position. As stated by Linda Holbeche (Rana, 2000), "The challenge for HR professionals is to make their organization the place where people want to work and stay" (p. 16). And as emphasized by Tom Watson, Jr. (Mayo, 2000), former president of IBM, "all of the value of a company is in its people. If you burnt down all our plants and we just kept our people and information files, we would soon be as strong as ever. Take away our people and we might never recover" (p. 82). Watson's comment underscores the essence of the discussion here, the HR change to a broader focus of people management.

THE STRUCTURE OF THE WORKPLACE

Schools historically have been rigidly managed. Prior to the 1900s, selectmen assumed the responsibilities for personnel duties in the school. They exercised tight control over the policies of the school, the supervision of the subjects taught, and the personal habits of the teacher. In fact, teachers were expected to follow certain rules that apparently did not apply to others in the community. The concepts of the Scientific Management Era in the early 1900s spilled over into educational practices; supervisors were to determine the tasks to be done and the procedures to accomplish them. Teachers were to carry them out without question. Even in more recent times, teachers have held a poor image in the minds of many, as exemplified by compensation levels received and, in many instances, the level of respect given by their constituents.

The nature of the American worker is changing and these changes are becoming recognizable in the American teacher as well. Accompanying these behavioral changes are changes in the workplace itself. Table 14.1 presents a century of change for American workers based on data provided by the Bureau of Labor Statistics. These data reflect significant changes that have taken place in the type of jobs, the work week, life expectancy, women in the workplace and others over the last 100 years. These data hold major implications for the future work of the HR function, including the ability to work with a diverse workforce, diverse cultures, and individuals with a wide variance in their attitudes toward work and family life.

The following section discusses national demographics and the demographics of the work force in the next decade, changing structures that are

TABLE 14.1
Workplace Changes: A Century of Change for American Workers

In 1900:   ☐ Most common jobs: farm laborer, domestic servant
           ☐ Average work week: 59 hours
           ☐ Average annual salary: $375
           ☐ Unemployment rate: 5%
           ☐ Average life expectancy: 47.3 years
           ☐ Average household size: 4.7 people
           ☐ Percentage of women working outside the home: 18.3%

In 2000:   ☐ Most common jobs: office worker, sales worker
           ☐ Average work week: 43.2 hours
           ☐ Average annual salary: $23,505
           ☐ Unemployment rate: 4%
           ☐ Average life expectancy: 76.5 years
           ☐ Average household size: 2.6 people
           ☐ Percentage of women working outside the home: 63%

Source: *American Chronicle*, Bureau of Labor Statistics, U.S. Census, Federal Reserve Bank.

finding their way into the workplace, the changing attitudes of workers as related to work and their personal lives, changes in the job recruitment and selection processes, and the changes in HR administration that will be exemplied by both new recognization of school employees and their deployment within the work setting of the school system.

Comparisons of changes in the workplace in 1900 and the year 2000 are provided in Table 14.1. Note specifically the significant changes relative to the average work week, life expectancy, household size, and percentage of women working outside the home.

THE NATURE OF THE WORK FORCE IN THE NEXT DECADE

Demographic Trends

Several important demographic trends are taking place that will have a profound effect on human resources administration during the remainder of this decade. One such trend is referred to as the graying of America, which relates to the precipitant increase in the number of elderly citizens. During the last decade of the 20th century, the U.S. population of persons 65 years old and older increased from 30.984 million in 1989 to 34.882 million in the year 2000 (U.S. Bureau of the Census, 1991). Table 14.2 presents the distribution of U.S. population by age, showing the percentage of each age category for 1990 through 2080. As revealed in Table 14.2, by the year 2010, 27.8% of the nation's population will be age 45 to 64 and 14.1% will be 65 years of age or older. By the year 2050, an estimated 25% of the population will be 65 years of age or over.

TABLE 14.2
Percentage Distribution of the Population by Age, 1990 to 2080

	Age (years)								
Year	Under 5	5–13	14–17	18–24	25–34	35–44	45–64	65 and Over	85 and Over
1990	7.2	13.0	5.3	10.4	17.5	15.2	18.8	12.7	1.3
1995	6.4	13.0	5.6	9.3	15.7	16.4	20.5	13.1	1.5
2000	5.7	12.1	5.8	9.5	13.9	16.6	23.3	13.1	1.7
2005	5.4	10.9	5.6	10.0	13.2	15.0	26.7	13.2	1.8
2010	5.2	10.1	5.0	9.7	13.7	13.4	28.9	14.1	2.0
2020	4.9	9.8	4.4	8.1	13.5	13.4	27.8	18.2	2.0
2030	4.4	9.0	4.4	7.9	11.9	13.6	26.9	22.9	2.4
2040	4.3	8.5	4.1	7.7	11.9	12.3	27.3	23.9	3.7
2050	4.2	8.4	4.0	7.3	11.7	12.5	26.9	24.9	4.7
2080	4.1	8.1	3.9	7.2	11.3	12.3	26.3	26.8	5.3

Source: *Projections of Populations of the United States, by age sex and race: 1998–2080.* U.S. Bureau of the Census (G. Spenser), 1989. Washington, DC: Government Printing Office.

The aging of the American population can be better understood by considering the 45 to 64 age group and the 65 and over category. The former category increased from approximately 18.8% of the population in 1990 to approximately 23.3% in the year 2000; the 65 and over category increased from approximately 12.7% to approximately 13.1%. In addition to the decreasing number of youth in our society, life expectancy continues to increase, which adds significantly to the older age categories.

It is interesting to note that the number of children under age 5 in 1990 represented 7.2% of the U.S. population, but this is expected to decrease to 4.1% by 2080. Data indicate that 18.4 million were in the under age 5 category in 1990 and only 17.6 million in the year 2000, amounting to a 4.3% decrease in just 10 years. It is also interesting that the 1980 fertility rate was 1.84, considerably below the replacement rate of 2.1 births for every woman. This decrease produced an important drop in the 18 to 24 age category in the year 2000. Moreover, the fertility rate declined from a 1960 rate of 3.449 to a low of 1.738 in 1976. Since then it has tended upward at a very slow rate and reached the rate of 1.932 in 1988 (U.S. Census Bureau, 1991).

New census data (1999) also reveal that schools will be working with a citizenry with a higher level of education; education in America is at an all-time high and "will continue to rise for some time as younger, more educated age groups replace older, less educated ones" (*Arizona Republic*, September 15, 2000). Census data indicate that 83.4% of the American population 25 years of age and older had high school diplomas compared to 24.5% in 1940.

The distribution of the population by race is another important change. The Bureau of Census reported that African Americans, Asians, Hispanics, and other racial minorities constituted 16.8% of the U.S. population in 1970 and 18.7% in 1980. This figure jumped to 26.8% in 1992 and increased to over 30% in the year 2000. Statistics indicate that within the current decade Hispanics will become the majority population group in several states. "The U.S. census predicts that by 2050 race in America will be turned upside down. There will be more minorities and a minority of whites living in America. . . . By 2010, whites will account for only 9 percent of the world's population, compared to 17% in 1997—making them the earth's smallest ethnic minority" (Lunenburg & Ornstein, 2000, p. 289). "White students are already in the minority in the state of California. Nonwhites comprise 51.3% of California's school-age population. . . ." (Smith, 2001, p. 23). By the year 2000, the U.S. foreign-born population had grown to 28.3 million, nearly double the number just 20 years ago. Census Bureau figures estimated that 10.1% of the U.S. population in the year 2000 was foreign-born, a figure that has increased steadily since 1970 and is the highest percentage since 1930 (Armas, January 2001). These demographic trends have changed the nation to a multicultural, multiethnic society, which will necessitate more flexible human resources policies in both public and private institutions.

The successful school system and human resources function will have to deal with cultural diversity, ethnic diversity, linguistic diversity, and other such considerations, including differences in attitudes about work and its balance with one's personal life. The diverse composition of workers will require that new attention be given to the ways that human resources problems are resolved. Differences in work ethics, organizational loyalty, personal behavior, and perspectives related to professional development will have to be addressed by human resources administrators. The strategies related to human resources planning must necessarily give full attention to the differences that are inevitable with such factors as human motivation in relation to work behavior and organizational commitment. In short, HR administrators will have to become knowledgeable of diversity management and the HR diversity strategies that are needed to achieve desired results.

The Work Force

Professionals in the schools will become an ever increasingly diverse work force. Labor and demographic reports indicate that today an estimated one-third of the nation's work force is minority: African American, Latino, and other minority representatives. It is clear that the changing American work force includes a significant increase in minorities and women working side by side with white males (Lunenburg and Ornstein, 2000). It is reported that women now constitute approximately 63% of the American work force, and women with young children are entering the work force at an unprecedented rate. In the early 1950s, slightly more than 50% of male workers were married to a working wife. Today, an estimated 75% of employed male workers have working wives.

1. Collaborative cultures will be the workplace model.
2. Creative employment contracts will support more time off, flexibility in hours and work location, technological job aids, and more pay at risk with significant upside potential.
3. Company intranets will become a major tool for communication, training, and benefits administration; HR will play a leading role in developing this important tool.
4. Intelligence through knowledge transfer capability will separate the best employees from the rest.
5. Employees will have more and more choices about work arrangements, allowing them to meet their individual needs.
6. Work hours scheduling will become less important as organizations focus on performance and results.
7. Company facilities will become virtual through work-at-home, telecommuting, and outsourcing.
8. The workweek will be less structured—employees will still work 40-plus hours, but at varied times and places other than the office.
9. Legislation will lead to greater portability of health, welfare, and retirement benefits.
10. Free-lance teams of generic problem solvers will market themselves as alternatives to permanent workers or individual temps.

FIGURE 14.3
Workplace Flexibility: Predictions for 2008
Source: HR 2008 by, Floyd Kemske. Copyright January 1998. Reprinted with permission of *Workforce*, Costa Mesa, CA. All rights reserved. <http://www.workforce/com/

Projections for the nation reveal that the present population of the United States will increase by 50% to a figure of 375 million by the first half of the 21st century, and minority members, mostly Hispanics, will account for the majority of this increase.

Kemske (2000) reported the consensus of several leading work force directors relative to predictions for the year 2008 in the areas of **workplace flexibility, work and society,** and **workforce development**. Features of the area of workplace flexibility are presented in Figure 14.3.

As revealed in Figure 14.3, *flexibility in the workplace* in the future will be characterized by such features as team collaboration, flexible employee work contracts with more time off and variations in the number of hours worked, recognition of workers for special knowledge and skills, "intranet" communication techniques, more use of virtual means such as telecommunications and outsourcing of some work activities, improved health and welfare benefits, and free-lance teams and individuals that serve as alternatives to permanent workers. We submit that such trends will not only be implemented in educational settings, but will also be absolutely necessary if problems facing education are to be ameliorated or resolved. For example, there is little question that America's work force is giving more attention to changes in traditional work schedules. More fathers are taking time off work to spend at home with children. This development is due in large part to the thinking of many workers that "working to live" must take precedence over a "living to work" perspective. Thus work schedules for teachers and others in school settings will require different arrangements that include variations in daily and weekly time schedules.

Innovations in **distance education** programming, whereby both the teacher and students work outside the traditional classroom using some form of telecommunications, will permit teachers to reach many more students without reducing student achievement. Computer technology has become a way of life for most students today, and this fact will permit a much greater use of technology for instructional purposes. Thus schools will increasingly become virtual systems incorporating telecommunications, computer technology, and other distance learning approaches in the delivery of instruction to students at all levels. And even though face-to-face communication between student and teacher will be decreased, actual instructional time for students will be increased by eliminating many of the administrative tasks and classroom interruptions that have reduced instructional time in traditional classroom settings in the past. Instructional delivery necessarily will consist of a combination of face-to-face classroom teaching and distance education methods. Of course, distance learning has already been initiated in many school systems throughout the nation. Mesa, Arizona became Arizona's first school district to offer full-time distance learning for secondary schools. Some students take all their courses through the Net. The use of videostreaming, a technique that allows students to view the teacher, is one way to compensate for the lack of one-on-one teacher–student contacts (Gayle, 2000).

Outsourcing of learning programs, whereby students take advantage of local community learning settings or move to some alternative school program for a specified period of time, represents opportunities to utilize more effectively the learning resources in the local school community. Part of the resolution for teacher shortages rests in the creative use of teaching talent within the school community. Who might be in the best position to instruct students in computer programming for example? And how might community sources become part of science education for some students? Many local community sources will be tapped in this regard, and they will welcome the opportunity to become partners with the schools. Such arrangements will serve several purposes: students gain needed knowledge and skills, qualified talent within the community helps to bring relevance to the school program, and the local providers of such educational services benefit by the increased interest and competency of potential employees for their own businesses. Each of the foregoing innovations presents opportunities for gaining more flexibility in teacher work schedules. However, education will see some teaching personnel working fewer hours, some personnel working more hours, and more individuals returning or entering teaching roles for these same reasons.

Many questions arise concerning part-time and flexible work-time arrangements. Won't such work schedules tend to damage one's career? How do such work schedules affect the productivity of the organization? Does flexibility in work schedules really result in improved employee retention? And how would such flexibility work in school settings? Some insight concerning answers to these questions was provided by a study by Catalyst reported in the *Arizona Republic* (September 10, 2000). In brief, the study of part-time women employees revealed that many of the women in the study remained with their employers for many years, about half were promoted during the time that they were employed part-time, most reported that they were satisfied with the arrangement, the women believed that they could return to a full-time schedule if they so desired, and indeed half of the women in the study did return to full-time employment after their part-time work experiences.

Boomerang hiring is a term coined to describe the rehiring of former employees. The return to teaching by both former teachers and retirees is being witnessed throughout education. Although accurate figures are not available regarding the incidence of such persons returning to education, estimates are that as many as 5% of former teachers in many school districts are rehires. In a school district with 500 teachers, this 5% figure would fill 25 teaching positions in the system. Not only do boomerang personnel provide one positive response to the teacher supply problem, they also have other advantages. For example, former teachers who are rehired save both time and money in induction and professional development costs. And, as noted by Link in an article by Strother Clarke (2001), "Often, the employee who comes back has a different perspective and a more positive attitude. They become our best spokesmen in cheering the troops and recruiting new workers" (p. D2).

Other trends related to work and society will affect the profession of education as well as other enterprises (see Figure 14.3). Several changes related to work and societal attitudes were alluded to in the foregoing discussion on workplace flexibility. Attitudes that demand a more acceptable balance between work life and social life influence both workplace flexibility and societal attitudes. One example is that of the "work to live" view discussed previously. Although the United States ranks first as the country putting in the most hours on the job, according to a study by the United Nations-based International Labor Organization (MacIntyre, 2000), a survey by Management Recruiters International found that the majority of executives believe that the traditional 9-to-5 workday in America will disappear in the next decade. Many American workers already have given up the traditional workday schedule for various reasons. "Americans today are also increasingly trying to balance their family life with their workplace responsibilities" (*Arizona Republic*, September 3, 2000, p. EC1). There is substantive evidence that such provisions as flexible work scheduling have become an ongoing practice in most companies today. For example, the Society for Human Resources Management reported that in

1997 about 48% of the companies surveyed had flexible scheduling as one of their personnel benefits. In 2001, this figure jumped to nearly 60% (*Arizona Republic*, April 29, 2001, Section D, p. 7).

Although some persons contend that education is different and therefore flexible scheduling wouldn't work in this field, the facts are that this practice has already found its way into educational practices. Education will have to alter work schedules for its employees in order to attract and retain qualified personnel. Other trends that are becoming part of the culture in educational systems and will increase during the present decade are increases in community activities and greater involvement in social issues. Issues and problems of society are inextricably related to education, and society will look ever pressingly to educational leaders to help to resolve these problems. If schools find themselves unwilling or unable to serve in this manner, society will look to other sources for such solutions (e.g., other educational agencies, government agencies, and advocacy groups). Thus "community involvement and social responsibility will become part of an organization's business vision" (Kemske, 2000, p. 38).

Each of the foregoing trends hold implications for workplace development. Changes in strategic planning, flexibility in work schedules and changes in work life attitudes will require new, creative approaches to professional development. Rather than the traditional approaches that have programmed in-service training periodically to improve knowledge and skills, future workplace development will require professional growth and personal development on an ongoing, continuous basis. Emphasis in professional development in schools will focus more on enabling teachers and teacher teams to resolve problems and make instructional decisions more quickly at their level of operation. Such developments will permit a much greater use of talent within the school and a more efficient response to the needs and concerns of school clientele. Technological change and other societal, economic, and political influences on education will place new challenges on schools that require individual and team adaptability in the work environment. Thus school system organization will witness changes in the manner in which administrative personnel serve the system and its employees.

For example, administrators will assume a partnership relationship with instructional teams, channels of command will be de-emphasized, and flatter organizational structures will become more common. Decision making becomes less operative from the top-down approach in such organizations; rather, achievement depends more on solicitation of existing knowledge and competency related to the situation at hand and the coordination of these talents toward the goal of optimal problem resolution. As pointed out by most authorities, such an arrangement depends to a large extent on a committed work force and, therefore, human resources administrators will assume an ever-increasing role in facilitating this end through a growing emphasis on staff management and development.

TRENDS IN STAFF MANAGEMENT
AND STAFF DEVELOPMENT:
IMPLICATIONS FOR THE HR FUNCTION

Losey (2000) has set the foundational tone for the future management role of the HR administrator.

> While maintaining the special body of HR knowledge, professionals in human resources management must also be generalists who understand economics, politics, social and cultural trends, technological innovations, changing work values, skill shortages, government mandates in labor laws, diversity management, health care management, privacy concerns, international trends, and a myriad of other issues. For HR professionals, the challenge of today's business environment is to understand and manage the important interaction of technology, work flow, organizational strategies and, most important, people (p. 17).

Losey's contention points directly to the fact that human resources administration in education not only will continue to deal with an ever-growing HR practices agenda, but must address specifically the concerns of the changing work force employee, including the matter of job satisfaction and employee retention.

The importance of teacher retention was addressed in some detail in Chapter 2. Earlier studies by Herzberg, Manser, and Snyderman (1959), Robinson and Galpin (1986), Taylor and Tashakkori (1994), and others consistently found that employee satisfaction is tied to many factors other than money. And more recent research not only supports this contention, but has also given new support to the importance of administrative leadership in the morale of workers and their length of stay in an organization. For example, a recent Gallup Organization poll of 2 million workers employed in 700 different companies concluded that commitment to an organization is directly related to the quality of the relationship of the employee with the immediate supervisor. Dissatisfaction with "how the employee is being supervised" is the primary reason that workers leave organizations. Results of another recent study emphasize the fact that organizational climate and conditions of work influence in a much greater way than money matters the determination of worker job satisfaction; the more favorable the conditions, the higher the satisfaction scores of workers (National Center for Educational Statistics, 1997). This study found that work conditions such as administrative leadership and support, school climate, teacher autonomy in the classroom, student behavior, and parental support are more directly associated with the job satisfaction of workers than salary and benefits. Implications for the future work of human resources administrators are many; such processes as organizational climate, induction, assignment, development, and stability necessarily will receive new emphases during this decade. A major difference, however, will be that the worker's interests, both immediate and long range, will be viewed as of paramount importance in the administration of these processes.

Improvement of HR quality will necessitate improvement in the consistency and timeliness of the delivery of the HR processes. The needs of the school's clientele and meeting the demands of changes described in this chapter will require HR administrators to be much more aware of best practice, as demonstrated by action research activities and the monitoring of program results. Such perspectives will require school leaders to be less concerned with routine administrative tasks and more involved in the strategic operations of the school and school system relative to (1) the alignment of HR practices with those of the total organization, (2) the improvement of communication among and between all employees on matters that depend on the knowledge and collaboration of workers in different units, and (3) the status of worker assignments and attitudes in the workplace, such as employee workload and supervisor relationships with employees that are enhancing or inhibiting the effectiveness of goal achievement. Workload, for example, was listed among the top 10 serious problems facing personnel directors in a study by Norton (1999). And various studies of teacher workload have revealed that workload indexes of teachers in any one school can vary significantly; the highest load indexes of a teacher may be two to three times greater than the teacher with the lowest load index in the same school setting.

Furthermore, teachers new to the school setting often, but not always, are found to be carrying the heaviest teacher loads. Thus the status of worker assignment and attitudes applies to management concerns as discussed here. And since more effort will be expected of all HR administrators at all levels in the educational system, a more highly qualified HR administrator will be required to meet the new demands as we approach the second half of this decade.

SUMMARY

This final text chapter has focused on trends that are viewed as most certain to influence the human resources function throughout the present decade. Although some consideration was devoted to the impacts of such factors as economics and politics, the trends discussed here have related more directly to future trends in the role of the human resources function itself. Human resources within organizations were viewed as the most important consideration relative to the continued viability and ultimate success of the school system. A leadership role, rather than the more traditional role of support and maintenance, was emphasized as being necessary if the HR function is to become an integral partner in the key strategies of the system as a whole.

Changes in the demographics of society will continue to become more diversified. The growth of minority populations will necessitate new considerations in the area of people management and the administration of the workplace. Teacher shortages, teacher retention, and the achievement of school objectives will necessitate major changes in the approaches to the employee recruitment, selection, induction, assignment, and development processes. Only time will tell the extent to which activities within these processes will be performed using technological programs. However, there is little question that technology applications will serve to complete HR work faster, more efficiently, and at less cost to the school district. As a result, additional time will be made available for the HR administrator to focus on strategizing human resources processes more directly with the educational strategies of the total system.

Some quarters see the demise of the centralized HR function in school systems, since decentralization practices tend to place HR responsibilities at the local level. Our view is that the HR function will continue to be the most important function in the school system, but changes in its perspective from an administrative role to a leadership role will have to be realized. When this leadership role comes to fruition in school systems, both the centralized HR function, local school HR administration, and the overall school system will be more effective and more successful.

DISCUSSION QUESTIONS

1. Consider the social trends in a school and community with which you are familiar. Describe several ways in which these trends appear to be influencing educational practices in the school and school system. Make special note of new and or changing policies in the area of human resources management that appear to be the result of the social trends identified.
2. To what extent do you believe that the talents and interests of teachers and administrators could be more fully utilized in their professional roles? What might be done to identify worker talents in a better way?
3. Consider the practice of work flexibility in education. Set forth several practices for implementing flexible work schedules for teachers that would be realistic considerations in schools with which you are familiar. What are the inhibiting factors facing such practices in schools today?
4. First, list two or three specific strategies that a school system might develop in its strategic plan. For each system strategy, list and briefly describe an HR strategy that would serve to enhance the accomplishment of the system's strategy.

CASE STUDIES

14.1 Something's Missing

The College View School District is a suburban system adjacent to a large metropolitan area. Its minority student enrollment is 25% compared to the metropolitan district, which enrolls 65% minority students. The student enrollment in the College View School District has declined over the past 3 years due primarily to various educational alternatives that have developed within or near the district. The school enrollment of 7433 dropped to 6229 during a 3-year period. The word that the district is on the decline has resulted in several personnel problems as well. For example, the human resources office has reported a significant drop in the number of applicants for teaching positions in the district. Teacher retention rates also have dropped significantly.

Superintendent Gomez sent the following memorandum to Pat Scott, director of the system's human resources department:

To: Pat Scott
From: Supt. Gomez
Re: Attendance at the next Administrative Cabinet meeting, Oct. 8
Pat: Please mark your calendar for October 8 to join the Administrative Cabinet at its biweekly meeting. The school board has expressed concern regarding the district's enrollment losses and problems in attracting teachers to our district. Please be prepared to present your thoughts on this matter with any recommendations that you view as possible "resolutions" to these matters.

Questions

1. Assume the role of Pat Scott, director of human resources. What information do you view as important in the consideration of this matter and in the preparation of your meeting with the Administrative Cabinet?
2. On the basis of the limited information given in the case regarding the district and its policies, what recommendations might you view as appropriate in this case at this time?
3. What implications for the human resources function and its processes are apparent in this case?

14.2 Going, Going, Gone!

Gwen Ryon taught in the Whittier Middle School for 9 years and in the school district for a total of 13 years. For each of the 13 years of service, Gwen's performance received a rating of "exemplary." She served in the capacity of mentor teacher for 10 or more teachers new to the system over the years and served for a period of 6 years as instructional resource leader for Whittier, but resigned from that role 2 years ago in order to spend more time, as she put it, "smelling the roses."

In March of the school year, Gwen sent a letter of her intention to resign from her teach-

ing position at the close of the school year. Her letter was brief, expressing her thanks for the wonderful years spent at Whittier and noting that she wanted to do "other things," including spending more time with her two young grandchildren. Apparently, education and the Whittier Middle School had lost one of its outstanding teachers.

Questions

1. Assume the position of principal of the Whittier school. What thoughts do you have about this matter and the loss of Mrs. Ryon?
2. Assume also that the district personnel policy requires an exit interview with each employee leaving the district. Who should be involved in an exit interview with Mrs. Ryon? What questions seem most appropriate to ask Mrs. Ryon in this case? As principal, what steps might you take with other school officials in this case, even before any formal communication with Gwen?
3. What incentives might possibly be appropriate in this situation for the purpose of retaining Mrs. Ryon's services in some fashion? Do you consider the allocation of incentives to retain quality personnel to be fair and equitable? What personnel problems could develop?

Inbasket 14.1

HELP Is on the Way

Questions for Inbasket 14.1

1. Assume the role of principal Henson. What actions will you take before responding to Mr. Rodriquez? As school principal, what are the implications of this situation for your work as personnel administrator of the Whittier Middle School?
2. Now place yourself in the role of Tyler Woods, director of personnel for the school district. How would the strategies of the school district influence your recommendations on this matter?

HELP

HISPANIC EDUCATIONAL LEADERSHIP PROGRAM

May, 2002

Pat Henson, Principal
Wymore Elementary School
Wymore, Lafayette

Dear Mr. Henson:

As you are aware, nearly 40% of the students at Wymore Elementary School are Hispanic and, reportedly, only 15% of the teachers are Hispanic. The Hispanic Educational Leadership Program (HELP) has two goals for the ensuing year, as follows:

(1) increase the percentage of Hispanic faculty in the school district proportionally to that of the Hispanic student enrollment, and

(2) increase the program of bilingual education to accommodate all students in the school.

At this time, HELP requests your support in achieving these important goals. May we hear from you at this time regarding your thoughts and your action plan for the Wymore Elementary School relative to the above-stated goals?

Sincerely,

Raul Rodriquez, Chairman
HELP

cc: Emanuel Evans, Supt.
    Tyler Woods, Director of Personnel

Inbasket 14.1

REFERENCES

Arizona Republic (September 3, 2000). 9-to-5 work to fade out, survey finds, Section EC1, Gannett News Service.

Arizona Republic. (September 10, 2000). Part-time needn't damage career, Margaret Steen, News, Section D5, San Jose Mercury News.

Arizona Republic. (September 15, 2000). Educated Americans at record levels, Section A6, Associated Press Release.

Arizona Republic. (April 29, 2001). An added benefit for workers: flexibility. Section D7, Matt Murray, *Wall Street Journal.*

Armas, G. C. (January 2, 2001). U.S. foreign-born grow to 28.3 mil. *Arizona Republic*, p. A-1.

Bureau of the Census, G. Spenser, 1989. Washington, D.C.

Drucker, P. E. (1974). *Management, tasks, responsibilities, practices.* New York: Harper & Row.

Gayle, J. S. (September 12, 2000). More students choosing school from a distance. *Arizona Republic*, Section Tempe, p. 1.

Hall, P. (2000). Feel the width. *People Management, Viewpoint*, 6(1), p. 23.

Herzberg, F., Manser, B., Snyderman, B. (1959). *The motivation to work.* New York: Wiley.

Kemske, F. (2000). *HR 2000. Human Resources 00/01* (10th ed.). Guilford, CT: Dushkin/McGraw-Hill. Reprinted from an article in *Workforce*, January 1998.

Losey, M. (2000). *HR comes of age. Human Resources 00/01* (10th ed.). Guilford, CT: Dushkin/McGraw-Hill. Reprinted from an article in *HR Magazine*, 50th Anniversary Edition (1998).

Lunenburg, F. C., & Ornstein, A. C. (2000). *Educational Administration: Concepts and Practices* (3rd ed.). Belmont, CA: Wadsworth.

MacIntyre, J. (November 2000). *Facts of life. Spirit.* Fort Worth, TX: AA Publishing.

Mayo, A. (2000). Memory bankers. *Human Resources 00/01* (10th edition). Guilford, CT: Dushkin/McGraw-Hill. Reprinted from an article in *People Management*, January 1998.

National Center for Educational Statistics. (1997). *Job satisfaction among America's teachers: Effects of workplace conditions, background, characteristics and teacher compensation.* NCES 97471.

Norton, M. S. (1999). *The personnel administrator in Arizona: A research study.* Tempe: Arizona State University.

Rana, E. (January 2000). Enter the people dimension. *People Management*, 6(1), 16–17.

Robinson, D. C., & Galpin, T. (July 1986). In for a change. *HR magazine*, 47(7), 90–93.

Smith, R. E. (2001). *Human resources administration: A school-based perspective* (2nd ed.). Larchmont, NY: Eye on Education.

Strother Clarke, S. G. (January 2, 2001). *Arizona Republic*, p. D2.

Taylor, D. L., & Tashakkorri, A. (1994). Predicting teachers' sense of efficacy and job satisfaction using school climate and participatory decision making. Paper presented at the annual meeting of the Southwest Research Association, San Antonio, Texas.

Ulrich, D. (2000). A new mandate for human resources. *Human Resources 00/01* (10th ed.). Guilford, CT: Dushkin/McGraw-Hill. Reprinted from an article in *Harvard Business Review*, January/February 1998.

Glossary

Administrative regulation. A precise statement that answers the question of how a policy is to be applied or implemented.

Adoption of policy. The official legislative responsibility of the governing board.

Advanced preparation. A focus on future needs for new skills resulting from organizational expansion and innovative programming.

Alternative certification. State provisions for awarding a teaching license to persons with a baccalaureate in a teaching field who have not completed a traditional teacher education program.

Applicant tracking system. A computer-based system designed to process and analyze applicant data.

Assessment center. A center in which various activities and exercises are conducted to assess the administrative performance and skill levels in such areas as organizational ability, judgment, leadership, and human relations.

Bargaining agent. The employee organization designated as the official representative of all employees in the bargaining unit.

Bargaining unit. A group of employees certified as the appropriate unit for collective negotiations.

Behavioral interview. An employment interview characterized by a set of job-related questions that seeks to examine a candidates's past job behaviors.

Benchmark position. A position whose duties and responsibilities are sufficiently common to be found in most organizations and thus serves as a basis for making comparisons.

Boomerang hiring. The rehiring of former employees.

Bylaw. A rule or procedure by which the school board governs itself.

Career development planning. Activities such as personal counseling, self-concept and assessment workshops, career opportunity seminars, and close coordination of the system's human resources processes with employee career aspirations.

Clinical supervision. Methods of supervision that focus on instructional improvement through improved staff performance. It features a cooperative relationship between the teacher and supervisor.

Closed climate. A school climate that is characterized by low staff morale, limited and inadequate communication, and limited socialization.

Closed question. Question that seeks specific responses without providing the opportunity for opinion, explanation, or elaboration.

Coaching. A term often used synonymously with mentoring. Mentoring generally refers to the art of helping to steer a subordinate or a colleague in the same field. Coaches use their techniques for professionals and/or clients in a full range of backgrounds.

Codification system of policies and regulations. A method of classifying or recording policies and regulations; a code for identifying specific sections, subsections, divisions, subdivisions, items, and subitems of a particular policy or regulation.

Coherence. The most common dimensions of effective schools, such as the fact that stakeholders have a clear idea of school goals or the expectation that every student is to perform at a maximum level.

Cohort survival method. A method of forecasting future school enrollments; it is based on certain assumptions, such as the stability of birthrates, death rates, student migration, population mobility, and others.

Collective bargaining. The process whereby matters of employee relations are determined mutually by representatives of employee groups and their employer within the limits of law or mutual agreement.

Competency. The ability to accomplish a task at a satisfactory level of performance.

Competency-based pay. An approach to compensation of employees that rewards employees for the acquisition of new knowledge and skills or the demonstration of greater competency in existing abilities.

Competency profile. A delineation of the knowledge and skills associated with a position.

Contingency leadership theory. A theory of leadership that contends that the most effective leadership style in a specific situation is contingent on the nature of the task to be performed, the power position of the leader in the situation, and the relationship between the leader and the individuals involved.

Contract or master agreement. The ratified document that specifies the terms of the negotiated contract.

Cost-of-living adjustment. Increases made to salary schedules based on increases in the consumer price index (a measure of the costs of goods and services).

Davies–Brickell codification system. A coding method devised for classifying policies and administrative regulations based on arabic numbering.

Disengaged climate. A school climate characterized by negative relationships and the fact that teachers are not engaged in the important tasks of the school.

Disparate impact. Discrimination that occurs when a facially neutral employment practice has an unequal impact on a member of a group protected under Title VII.

Disparate treatment. Discrimination that occurs when a qualified employee who is a member of a group protected under Title VII is treated less favorably than others by a particular employment practice.

Distance education. A wide variety of instructional delivery methods that takes place outside the traditional classroom setting by generally, but not always, using some form of telecommunications.

Distributive bargaining. A bargaining process exemplified by a labor–management model of power-based, quid pro quo strategies. Considered to be adversarial in nature and designed to realize maximum gain through the use of authority, power, or withdrawal of services.

Douglass teacher load formula. A comprehensive formula for measuring teacher load in high schools; produces an index of load that can be compared to system, state, and national load norms.

Electronic document management system. A software system that provides for the storage, retrieval, and manipulation of the various documents received and generated in the personnel recruitment and selection process.

Employee assistance program. A program established by an employer to provide confidential psychological, financial, and legal services to employees.

Engaged climate. A school climate characterized by the fact that teachers ignore the principal's attempts to control their behavior, attention to tasks is high, and the faculty is professionally responsive in spite of the principal's restrictive behaviors.

Environmental scanning. An examination of the school's internal and external environments that identifies the system's strengths and weakness and its opportunities and threats. Scanning information supports the development of a rationale for operating assumptions.

External recruitment. Recruitment of personnel from outside the organization using such recruitment techniques as media advertising, employment agencies, educational institutions, computerized data banks and electronic bulletin boards, and professional organizations and unions.

Evaluation criteria. The job-related behaviors expected of the person being evaluated, which serve as the basis for what will be evaluated.

Fact finding. Synonymous with advisory arbitration. However, it is most often associated with impasses in table negotiations involving a future contract agreement.

Flexible benefits plan. A benefit plan in which employees select benefits and services within a fixed dollar allotment.

Formative evaluation. Ongoing evaluation that is designed to provide continuous feedback to the person being evaluated for the purposes of self-improvement and professional development.

Fractional bargaining. A process that involves the workers only as members of work groups, rather than as members of a union. It allows one work group to seek an agreement based on an issue that the union as a whole is unable to gain for them.

Goals. Statements that set forth the purposes of the school system.

Golden mean decision method. The practice of learning how other administrators have implemented a certain practice and then following their lead.

Governing board policies. The comprehensive statements of decisions, principles, or courses of action that serve toward the achievement of stated goals for a local school system.

Grievance. A problem or complaint related to the contract or master agreement. It represents an alleged violation of the agreement.

Ground rules. Statements and agreements that govern the bargaining activities of two negotiation parties.

Grow-your-own program. A strategy for increasing the pool of qualified teachers and administrators. It involves a collaborative arrangement between a college or university and a local school district to provide the necessary coursework to a cohort of employees under a flexible scheduling arrangement, with the district providing some level of financial or other support to participants.

Halo effect. The tendency of an evaluator using a rating scale to form a strong general impression of the evalutee and then give basically the same rating to every item on the scale.

Hawthorne effect. The observation that showing interest or attention to workers can have a more positive effect on worker efficiency and work production than the physical conditions of the job or workplace.

Health maintenance organization. An approach to health care management whereby comprehensive health care is provided to members for a fixed monthly fee on a prepaid services basis.

Hostile environment harassment. Sexual harassment that occurs when verbal or physical conduct in the workplace is sufficiently severe to create an intimidating, hostile, or offensive environment.

HR strategy. The school system's planned partnership with the HR function in order to enhance the success of the system in meeting its challenges and achieving its goals.

Human resources administration. Processes that are planned and implemented in the organization to establish an effective system of human resources and to foster an organizational climate that enhances the accomplishment of effective teaching, student learning, and other primary educational goals.

Hygienes. Term used by Frederick Herzberg in his conceptualization of his Theory Y. Hygienes are those factors found to be related to job dissatisfaction, such as poor supervisory relationships and other unhealthy conditions of work.

Impasse. A situation in which two parties become steadfast in their bargaining positions on one or more agenda items and a stalemate takes place.

Indicators of competency. Products or behaviors that illustrate one's capacity to perform effectively; a performance specification.

Indirect compensation. The noncash compensation of employees, which includes both legally required benefits (e.g., Social Security, unemployment compensation, retirement), health and welfare programs, pay for time not worked, and free and reduced-cost services.

Induction. The process designed to introduce a new or newly assigned employee into the social and performance-related aspects of the job.

Induction process. The complex of activities designed to gain congruence between institutional objectives and employee needs.

In-service education. Any planned program offered staff members for purposes of improving the personal performances of individuals in the system.

Integration. A concept set forth by Mary Parker Follett that focuses on problem solution and conflict resolution through gaining commitment to superordinate system goals versus personal vested interests.

Integrative bargaining. A process that centers on efforts to resolve mutual problems of interest to the school district as a whole. Emphasis also is given to attempts to improve school board and employee relations.

Internal recruitment. Recruiting of current and previous part-time employees within the organization and through employee referrals.

Job analysis. The process by which knowledge, skills, abilities, and other characteristics are identified with conditions under which job functions are performed.

Job class. A group of jobs with similar work requirements.

Job description. A formal description of a job, which includes the job title, code, required and desired qualifications, person(s) supervised, person(s) to whom the employee reports, and the terms of employment.

Job sharing. Two or more employees each working part-time to fill one position.

Last-best-offer arbitration. An arbitration procedure whereby a neutral third party is called on to study the last best offers stated by each of the two parties in the table negotiations. Each last offer is studied, and one of the two is recommended and considered binding on the two parties.

Law. A rule recognized by the nation or state as binding on its members.

Liberty right. The right to a fundamental constitutional liberty (speech, press, etc.)

Liberty rights. Employee rights as related to due process, academic freedom, and freedom from capricious treatment.

Line administrator. School officers in the hierarchical line of authority.

Marginal teacher. An individual who is performing unsatisfactorily in one or more areas so that learning for students is inhibited.

Maximization of the human resources. The purposeful utilization of people, through positive motivation, to achieve the organization's goals and employee self-fulfillment.

Mediation. A situation in which a third party serves as an advisor and counselor for both parties in an attempt to keep the bargaining process in place during an impasse.

Mentor. An experienced professional who guides the personal development of a less experienced individual by serving as a role model; a wise and faithful advisor or tutor.

Motivators. According to Frederick Herzberg, those job-related factors that are associated with job satisfaction.

National Educational Policy Network of the National School Boards Association. A coding method devised for classifying policies and administrative regulations based on an alpha system.

Norton–Bria formula. A calculation that considers the load factors of assigned hours of teaching, time spent in preparation for teaching, cooperative assignments, number of students taught, and the load related to extra grades taught in a single classroom. Measures teacher load in hours of time spent per week, rather than index load units.

On-the-job staff training. Instruction regarding the knowledge and skills provided in the work setting, typically by a supervisor or experienced employee.

Open climate. A school climate in which the staff enjoys extremely high morale, works well together, enjoys friendly relations, but does not engage in a high degree of socialization; possesses the incentive to work things out and to keep the school moving.

Open-ended question. A nonleading question that is not designed or intended to elicit an obvious or preferred response.

Operational planning. Plans that are specific to one or more of the established strategic objectives and strategies as established through the strategic planning process. The human resources operational plan reflects an integration of the various school unit plans and the system's functional plans.

Organizational climate. The collective personality of a school or school system; the atmosphere that prevails in an organization that is characterized by the social and professional interactions of the people.

Organizational culture. The set of important beliefs, values, and assumptions that members of the school or school system share.

Outsourcing. The contracting of certain school services and/or programs to other educational or noneducational agencies. Outsourcing of learning programs includes the practice of allowing students to take advantage of local community learning settings or move to some alternative school program for a specified period of time.

Peer-assisted leadership. The basic concept of participants helping other participants in the improvement of their personal skills.

Planning. An effort to anticipate and shape the future; its aim is to focus the energies and resources of the school system on the right results.

Point of service plan. A health care plan by which members choose a primary care physician who coordinates their health care within a network of physicians and hospitals who contract with the plan to provide services at a discounted rate. Members who go outside the network pay a higher percentage of the cost of services.

Portfolio. A collection of artifacts related to an individual's professional practice selected to reflect growth over time.

Power-based bargaining. A term that refers to bargaining leverage as gauged by the relative willingness of each side to incur the consequences of not reaching an agreement.

Preferred provider organization. A health care plan by which members choose their health care providers, but pay a lower percentage of the cost of services if they use a provider who has contracted with the plan to pay services at a discounted rate (in-network).

Preliminary interview. An interview to determine the correctness and completeness of the information provided on the application, to eliminate candidates who do not meet the qualifications that the district is seeking, and to provide information for the employment interview.

Procedural due process. The process by which individuals are provided fair and equitable procedures in employment practices.

Program, process, and material determinants. School climate factors set forth by the Charles Kettering Foundation. A program factor, for example, is the opportunities provided for active student learning.

Property right. The right to specific real or personal property, tangible and intangible (e.g., the right to continued employment).

Quality circles. Related to a technique that places the primary responsibility for personal growth on individuals linked together for the improvement of teaching and student learning.

Quid pro quo harassment. Sexual harassment that conditions employment or terms of employment on the granting of sexual favors.

Reliability. The consistency of measurements across evaluators and observations.

Scope of bargaining. Those items considered as negotiable by statute, law, or mutual agreement.

Significant risk standard. Standard applied by the courts in reviewing cases involving alleged discrimination against employees with contagious diseases; to support a change in employment status or locale, the employee must pose a significant risk of transmitting the disease.

Similarity attraction. The attraction to those who are most similar to oneself: a pitfall to be avoided in employee selection.

Single salary schedule. A salary schedule designed to include all teachers in a district and based on equivalent pay for persons with equivalent education and experience.

Staff administrator. A school administrator who is not in the direct line of authority and whose position is created expressly to serve the major line functions of the organization.

Staff assignment. The human resources process that maximizes human resources through such administrative actions as deploying talent and competency in the best interests of the total staff and student population.

Staff development. The process of providing ongoing opportunities for employees to improve their knowledge and skills.

Standards for evaluation. The indicators of performance required with respect to the evaluation criteria.

Strategic human resources planning. A procedure concerned with the effective utilization of human resources and their contributions toward the accomplishment of educational goals.

Strategic planning. A document that gives direction to all operational planning activities for the school system.

Strategy. The approach or means selected by organizations to achieve a goal.

Substantive due process. Guidelines and procedures designed to ensure the objectivity and equity of standards, evidence, actions, and results.

Summative evaluation. Evaluation that is conducted at the end of an activity or period that is designed to assess terminal behaviors or overall performance.

Syntality. As an individual has a personality, an organization is said to have a syntality that reflects its group personality.

Systems theory. A theory that views the organization as being composed of two interrelated and interdependent parts, the social (individual) and the technical domains, which must be balanced for the organization to function most effectively.

360-Degree feedback. The systematic solicitation of feedback from the full circle of an employee's supervisors, subordinates, clients, and others with whom the employee interacts.

Task. A specific responsibility, obligation, or requirement associated with a professional position or function.

Teacher centers. An enriched environment of resources, personal involvement, and peer communication in which the teacher participates for purposes of professional growth.

Teacher Identification Clearinghouse. National database of all teachers who have been denied certification or have had their certificates suspended or revoked for moral reasons.

Teacher institute. A 19th-century teacher training activity, typically conducted by the county superintendent, to provide teachers with the latest techniques of professional practice.

Teacher load. The comprehensive workload of a teacher that includes such components as class size, number of classes taught, subjects taught, cooperative assignments, class preparations, and others.

Teaching load. The workload related exclusively to teaching; it excludes cooperative assignments.

Theory X. According to Douglas McGregor, the scientific management view of the worker as having no ambition, initiative, or intelligence and as being opposed to change.

Theory Y. According to Douglas McGregor, a view that sees the worker as a self-directed individual concerned with more than the satisfaction of personal need.

Troubled staff member. A staff member whose personal or behavior problem(s) negatively affect his or her professional performance. Most often the troubled worker has lower performance evaluations, has a higher rate of absenteeism, and files more grievances than other staff personnel.

Union. A continuous association of wage earners for the purpose of maintaining or improving the conditions of their working lives.

Validity. The extent to which an assessment instrument or system measures the performance that it is intended to measure.

Voluntary binding and compulsory arbitration. Procedures for resolving disagreements through the use of a neutral third party whose decision is mandated for both parties.

Wellness program. A program designed to improve the overall health of employees, which may include health and fitness programs, use of school fitness and sports facilities, and health-related assessments.

Win-win bargaining. Integrative approaches of collective bargaining designed to achieve agreement between the two parties and at the same time make both parties feel good about the agreement and one another.

Work and society. A workplace that permits employees to engage in personal life interests and family responsibilities. The involvement of organizations in community life and the implementation of services to meet social needs.

Workforce development. New considerations of human resources development that focus on professional and personal growth on an ongoing, continuous basis.

Workplace flexibility. Employee work contracts that allow for flexible schedules with more time off and variations in the number of hours worked. Also includes the considerations of telecommunications and the outsourcing of some work activities.

Author Index

Subject Index